LOST PURITAN

Also by PAUL MARIANI

BIOGRAPHY

William Carlos Williams: A New World Naked (1981)
Dream Song: The Life of John Berryman (1990)

POETRY

Timing Devices (1979)
Crossing Cocytus (1982)
Prime Mover (1985)
Salvage Operations: New & Selected Poems (1990)

CRITICISM

A Commentary on the Complete Poems of Gerard Manley Hopkins (1970)
William Carlos Williams: The Poet and His Critics (1975)
A Usable Past: Essays on Modern and Contemporary Poetry (1984)

LOST PURITAN

A Life of
Robert Lowell

PAUL MARIANI

W·W·NORTON & COMPANY
New York   London

The text of this book is composed in Galliard
with the display set in Galliard
Composition and manufacturing by The Haddon Craftsmen, Inc.
Book design by Jacques Chazaud

Library of Congress Cataloging-in-Publication Data

Mariani, Paul.
Lost puritan : a life of Robert Lowell / Paul Mariani.
p.   cm.
Includes index.
1. Lowell, Robert, 1917-1977—Biography.   2. Poets, American—20th
century—Biography.   I. Title.
PS3523.089Z74   1994
811'.52—dc20   93-48018
[B]

ISBN 0-393-03661-8

W. W. Norton & Company, Inc., 500 Fifth Avenue, New York, N.Y. 10110
W. W. Norton & Company Ltd., 10 Coptic Street, London WC1A 1PU

1 2 3 4 5 6 7 8 9 0

For Ed Callahan, 1939–1992

We are poor passing facts,
warned by that to give
each figure in the photograph
his living name.

Contents

PART III

PART IV

Illustrations follows pages 96, 224, and 320.

Preface

In the fall of 1963 while I was at Colgate, studying for my English Master's, one of my professors suggested I might want to look at something written *after* Emerson, Coleridge, and Hopkins. Since I was a practicing Catholic, and so rather an anomaly on campus, he thought I might read the poems of Robert Lowell, especially something called "Quaker Graveyard in Nantucket." I can still remember standing in the stacks of the library one dreary rainy afternoon soon afterwards and, as I read that poem, feeling as if the top of my head were coming off.

By then, Lowell himself had long since left his Catholicism behind and had gone on to write the more secular and Flaubertian *Life Studies*. In less than a year he would publish *For the Union Dead*. Only once, at New York's Guggenheim Museum, in the fall of 1964, when he introduced Randall Jarrell, who that evening was there to read the poems of Elizabeth Bishop, did I ever catch a glimpse of Lowell: too-tall, marmoreal, imposing, silent, dark-suited. I remember shaking Jarrell's hand in the reception line afterwards, and wishing I might somehow shake Lowell's as well. I was twenty-five then, and star-struck by the poet I had belatedly "discovered."

For the rest of his relatively short life I followed Lowell's career, teaching his poetry at the University of Massachusetts from the late 1960s on, reading each new book as it appeared, sometimes vigorously, too frequently stymied. Often

I thought of making the two-hour drive into Cambridge to sit in on his classes at Harvard, of speaking to him of some line, some image. I remember too reading of his death in September 1977, as another semester was getting under way, remember that moment with stunned disbelief. He was just sixty, and—compared to Yeats, Stevens, Frost, Eliot, and Williams—he should have been entering hearty middle age, though he did manage to outlive many others of his tragic generation: Roethke, Schwartz, Jarrell, Berryman, Sexton, and Plath. In this regard, and aware that both his parents had died in their early sixties, he preferred to measure his life's span against Shakespeare, dead at fifty-two, rather than against Thomas Hardy, who lived to almost ninety.

With Lowell's death, the United States lost the last of its influential public poets, poets in the tradition of Emerson, Frost, and Eliot. One is aware that such a statement—made now in the closing years of the twentieth century—is open to revisionist qualifications. Nevertheless, it remains true that no poet since has received the kind of sustained national attention and interest Lowell received, in part perhaps because he *was* a Lowell. Too much has changed in the national makeup in the last thirty years, and for better or worse something like the balkanization of interests has replaced what used to be called the Great Tradition. Many voices, each with its own diverse interest, seem to have created a swirling vortex of concatenations, with no single voice to which anything like a majority can turn.

Perhaps this question of who speaks for America is the wrong question to pose, or this is the wrong way to phrase the question. Still, the desire to bring order out of the swirling aphasic river of daily events and the language which accompanies those events remains strong in us. For a while, until the close of that watershed year, 1968, Lowell seemed intent on speaking for his time. Then, exhausted and disappointed by national events as well as by personal, he turned to England and inward to the problems of divorce and alienation and the illusory bubble of eros, before settling finally on elegy and heartbreak and an extended meditation on the weight of time and history, particularly—as he had earlier—on the weight of his native *New* England, and to the particular landscapes which had shaped him for better and worse. If anyone, Lowell is *the* poet-historian of our time, aware like Nathaniel Hawthorne and Henry Adams of our history judging us even as we undertake to judge it.

By dint of sheer honesty and enormous labor, Lowell manages to give us back part of the terrifying truth about ourselves. Like Jonathan Edwards and Hawthorne and Melville, he shows us something of the luminous darkness within us: our destructive self-interest, our racial fears and self-delusions, our murderous innocence. As a young man, he acted with the fervor of the true believer, the recent convert and conscientious objector, insisting on going to jail for his beliefs when he could just as easily have avoided that humiliation. He spoke out against Roosevelt's policy of unconditional surrender and later against Johnson's and Nixon's miscarriage of the Viet Nam War. And always he avoided the easy rhetoric one hears in time of war, shunning too the false language which covers so much talk about race and gender, that he might grapple with the underlying illnesses that are still tearing the country apart. He was a serious student of history and of human psychology, and he worked those interests against the sea of events which were incessantly and too swiftly shaping his own life.

But there is more to Lowell than this. If he could fend one off with his imposing stature and intelligence, so that one found oneself thrown offguard by the way he approached you, boyishly embracing you even as his keen mind sized you up, he was also a delightful raconteur with a startlingly original way of expressing himself. He had the true self-effacement of the self-possessed aristocrat, taking you into his confidence, yet capable in his early manic phases of breaking one friend on another. Many who knew him can attest to his air of intense self-preoccupation, only to watch him reenter a conversation with a judgment so right and true that it startled. Enough witnesses have remarked that he could act callously and irresponsibly, especially when he was ill, but it is equally true that he was contrite once reason returned. Moreover, the record shows that he commanded loyalty, even awe, from those he knew, and that he also made many lifelong friendships.

For the past twenty years I have thought often of writing a life of Lowell. First there was Hopkins, then Williams. Then—after spending several years working on Lowell—I turned instead to John Berryman and his *Dream Songs*, then turned again to Lowell. I am glad I have, because, difficult as Lowell's life was in many ways, it also turned out to be not only extraordinary but exemplary, filled with unexpected turns and happy surprises each step of the way.

In truth, it has been a joy to write this book, for my admiration for Lowell and his work only increased as I entered more deeply into his life. The unpublished letters in particular have been a delight, for everywhere they are filled with the insights and aperçus of someone devoted to the play of language, someone who had the uncanny ability to record the history of ourselves. And of course there is the poetry, from the early "Quaker Graveyard in Nantucket" and "Colloquy in Black Rock" and the brilliant suite of poems which comprise *Life Studies,* through the powerful public poems written during the Viet Nam War, to the poems of middle-age eros and the final elegies to his friends and to his own disrupted life which one finds so heartbreaking. Several critics have noted—and Lowell has been blessed with some excellent critics—that Lowell's reputation since his death has suffered a decline. If he was flawed, which of us is not? And though it was certainly not my original intention, I see now that I have written this book to help in some small measure to set the record straight, to give Lowell, as he gave others, a semblance of his proper name.

Acknowledgments

In writing a critical biography of someone of Lowell's stature one cannot but be aware of the enormous debts owed to many. Some of these debts go back twenty years, and if I have forgotten any kindness it is simply by oversight. First of all, this book owes a debt to Lowell's original biographer, Ian Hamilton, who went through the record and interviewed so many of those closest to Lowell to give us a broadly informative, and highly readable life of the poet. And while my own biography differs in emphasis from his, particularly in giving Lowell more of his own words and in recognizing Lowell as a major poet at every step of his development, Hamilton's life was the text with which and against which I have worked for the past dozen years.

Time too has thrown up sources unavailable to Hamilton, including Lowell's extensive correspondence with Elizabeth Bishop. But there are other materials as well: Lowell's letters to George Santayana, Carley Dawson, Mary McCarthy, Adrienne Rich, and a treasury of anecdotes which have appeared over the years. Then there have been several important studies of Bishop, including Brett Millier's biography, *Elizabeth Bishop: Life and the Memory of It*. Add to these the publication of Randall Jarrell's *Letters*, edited by his wife, Mary Jarrell, and William Pritchard's *Randall Jarrell: A Literary Life*, as well as the veritable explosion of interest in Jean Stafford, including three recent biographies, the best perhaps being Ann Hulbert's *The Interior Castle: The Art and*

Life of Jean Stafford. I have also been able to read Stafford's extensive correspondence with Peter Taylor, William Mott, and James Robert Hightower, especially as it concerns Stafford's stormy, idiosyncratic, and tragic relationship with Lowell. Lowell scholarship has also been enriched by Helen Vendler's essays, reviews, and memoir, by Philip Booth's and Daniel Hoffman's memoirs of Lowell's years in Castine, by Steven Gould Axelrod and Helen Diese's 1986 volume, *Robert Lowell: Essays on the Poetry*—especially for me the essays by Axelrod and Albert Gelpi—and most recently by Richard Tillinghast's efforts to restore Lowell's literary reputation.

I particularly want to thank the following: William Alfred, Blair Clark, Robert Dana, Kate Berryman Donahue, Brian Dyson, Richard Eberhart, Valerie Eliot, Penelope Laurens Fitzgerald, Robert Giroux, Elizabeth Hardwick, Richard Harteis, Seamus Heaney, Edward Hirsch, Daniel Hoffman, Donald Junkins, Donald Justice, James Laughlin, Philip Levine, Allen Mandelbaum, Gail Mazur, William Meredith, Robert Pack, Frank Parker, Lesley Parker, J. F. Powers, Wyatt Prunty, Adrienne Rich, Selden Rodman, Lloyd Schwartz, Kathy Shorr, Robert Siegel, Mark Strand, Stephen Tapscott, Helen H. Tate, Peter Taylor, Richard Tillinghast, Michael Waters, Richard Wilbur, and Michael Wrezin. A special word of thanks as well to two quarterlies and their editors for the hospitality they have shown in publishing sections of both my Berryman and Lowell biographies: Peter Stitt at *Gettysburg Review* and Hilda Raz at *Prairie Schooner*. As Executor of the Lowell estate, Frank Bidart gave me help at critical stages along the way, and I owe him a special word of thanks. His devotion toward Lowell became more and more palpable to me, especially as the story of Lowell's later years unfolded.

Also the following libraries and their librarians: Cathy Henderson, Research Librarian, the Harry Ransom Humanities Research Center, University of Texas, Austin, Texas; Rodney Dennis, Curator, and staff, the Houghton Library, Harvard University, Cambridge, Massachusetts; the Henry W. and Albert A. Berg Collection, New York Public Library; Astor, Lenox, and Tilden Foundations, New York, New York; Special Collections, Columbia University Library; Philip Cronenwett, Special Collections, Dartmouth College Library, Dartmouth, New Hampshire; Jami Peele, The Greenslade Special Collections, Olin and Chalmers Libraries, Kenyon College, Gambier, Ohio; Special Collections, Firestone Library, Princeton University, Princeton, New Jersey; Manuscripts Department, The Lilly Library, Indiana University, Bloomington, Indiana; J. Fraser Cocks, III, Special Collections, University of Oregon Library, Eugene, Oregon; Alan K. Lathrop, Manuscripts Division, University of Minnesota Libraries; Diane Murphy, St. Mark's School Library, St. Mark's School, Southborough, Massachusetts; Special Collections, The Newberry Library, Chicago, Illinois; Lori N. Curtis, McFarlin Library, University of Tulsa, Tulsa,

Oklahoma; Eva Mosely, The Arthur and Elizabeth Schlesinger Library on the History of Women in America, Radcliffe College, Cambridge, Massachusetts; Leslie Morris, Marianne Moore Papers, The Rosenbach Museum & Library, Philadelphia, Pennsylvania; Michael Sims, The Jean and Alexander Heard Library, Vanderbilt University Library, Nashville, Tennessee; Lisa Brower and Nancy MacKechnie, Vassar College Library Special Collections, Poughkeepsie, New York; Kevin Ray, Washington University Library Special Collections, St. Louis, Missouri; Patricia Willis, Collection of American Literature, Beinecke Library, Yale University, New Haven, Connecticut. And, again, a special word of thanks to the research librarians at the University of Massachusetts, Amherst, for answering literally hundreds of my queries—in person or over the telephone—over the past quarter century.

I owe too a word of special thanks to the following administrators at the University of Massachusetts, Amherst, who helped make the writing of this book possible: former Chancellor Joseph Duffey, Vice Chancellor for Graduate Affairs Samuel F. Conti, former Dean Murray Schwartz, former Chair Robert Bagg, and my present Dean, Lee Edwards, and Chair, Vincent DiMarco. For secretarial assistance: Fran Hamilton and Wendy Matys. For their careful reading of all or parts of this manuscript: Edward Hirsch, Philip Levine, Allen Mandelbaum, Wyatt Prunty, Richard Tillinghast. A special note of thanks too to my agent, John Brockman, my editor, Ed Barber, for believing in this book and making it possible, and to Amy Loyd and Ann Adelman for their diligence and attention to detail. Thanks too to my students, who have given me far more than I could ever give them in return: that polyphony of voices and insights which has never ceased to dazzle and amaze.

And finally, thanks to my wife Eileen, and my sons, who have been there day after day, night after night, as I hauled the thousands of scattered bits and bytes of information across the dining-room rug and up the stairs to pace the floor and sit transfixed before a blue computer screen, trying with my own breath to breathe life into this figment, this ghost, this man named Robert Lowell.

LOST PURITAN

Prologue

I wanted an art as disciplined
and dark as Calvin in his Institutes. . . .

"The Ark," *Notebook*

Who am I?, he thinks, as the fog begins to give way to the solidity of the white wall he has been staring at. The Thorazined fixture sits on the bed and stares, struggling to swim up out of the leaden murk which has been choking him. It is a mid-morning in early July 1954, and he has already spent three weeks on the locked ward of New York Hospital's Payne Whitney Clinic. He is bespectacled, myopic, six-one, stoop-shouldered, dark-haired, and, in spite of the ravages his illness has cost him, still has more than the vestiges of those Hollywood good looks, as a friend once called them. And though he looks vulnerable when he moves, he maintains the raw power of a linebacker. Within him too the complex assets and drawbacks of the Boston brahmin. He knows he is slightly out of date, that the vortex of imaginative energies with which he has until now been identified—meaning Boston and New England—has already swerved south to the metropolis of postwar New York.[1]

But now he is beginning to find himself once more. At thirty-seven, though still childless, he has been married twice, both times to writers. For the past five years he has been diagnosed as manic-depressive. It is his fourth illness in as many years for which he has had to be sent for extended stays to a hospital: three times for mania, once for acute depression. Ironically, this is the same man who has already been recognized by the critics as the country's leading younger poet, having—at twenty-nine—already won his first Pulitzer.

At the moment he is trying desperately to recover from an attack of "pathological enthusiasm," characterized—as usual—by violence and the violent attempt to start over, remake himself, get the picture of who he is clearer in his fractured mind. To do this he has already abandoned his latest "girl" and is trying hard to swim back to his wife, Elizabeth Hardwick. Once more the "girl" is someone younger than himself, who does not know just how ill her lover is. There is too the problem of the language. The girl's name is Giovanna Madonia. She is Sicilian, a former student of his, married, with very little English. Four months before, when his mind began speeding out of control, he inundated her with letters, pressing her to marry him and start life over again. Thinking him in the hospital for a rest, she has written to say that she is still waiting for him. For his purposes Giovanna is someone unformed, someone he feels he can educate and make over into his own version of Eve, someone he thinks of as the very antithesis of his overbearing mother.

That his mother is now dead, that her death is what has in fact initiated this latest attack, he does not yet see, though in the weeks and months of therapy which have already begun, and in the hundreds of hours he will spend struggling to get fragments of his life down onto paper if he can only make them sit still long enough, this leviathan will have to face up to the damage he has left in his wake. He will also have to face up to the damage done to him. His name is Robert Trail Spence Lowell IV, a scion of the old Lowell family, whose origins in the New World go back to their English beginnings. To those who know him he is Cal.

The name has stuck like a burr for twenty years, ever since his high school days at St. Mark's. He has not been given it out of affection. He knows too well that as a boy he was feared and hated for his bullying, filthy habits, sullen ways. The strongest boy in his form, in fights he is terrible and unforgiving. In the way these things happen among fifteen- and sixteen-year-olds at private schools, the name derives in part from Caliban, in part from Caligula, perhaps in some small part from Calvin. Caliban: Shakespeare's mooncalf in *The Tempest,* something bestial and unclean, not quite human, something to make sport of, something to fear. In time he will reject these associations in favor of those of his other namesake, Caligula, a military brat (not unlike himself), emperor of the Roman Empire at its height, a creature—like those other fascinations of his, Alexander the Great, Napoleon, Hitler—in love with enormous power, by turns brilliant and insane. Like Cal himself, the sharp edges of the name foisted on him at sixteen will in time rub soft, like a face on an old gold coin.

The episode that has landed him in Payne Whitney can be dated back to his mother's death that winter. In early February 1954, barely a week after taking up his duties as Elliston Professor of Literature at the University of Cincinnati,

Cal receives a cable from Italy telling him that his mother has suffered a stroke and is in the hospital in the resort town of Rapallo, Ezra Pound's old haunt. Cal sets off for his mother's bedside, flying a circuitous route from Cincinnati to Boston, then New York, London, and Paris, on the way stopping in the suburb of Neuilly to see his old friend Blair Clark, now a CBS correspondent based in Paris.

Instead of flying on to Milan at once, Cal spends the night, drinking and talking nonstop with Blair, who has seen the telltale signs before and knows from the heady, brilliant monologue and the darting eyes behind thick glasses that Cal is speeding up again. The following afternoon Cal flies on to Milan. Landing in heavy rain, he takes a tram across town to the Stazione Centrale, and from there catches a train south to Rapallo. By the time he reaches his mother, it is just past midnight. Tears streaming down her face, the Italian nurse tries to explain through a torrent of half-familiar syllables that Signore Lowell is too late, too late, that his mother passed away an hour before. *E morta.* It is February 14th, Valentine's Day.

It is no accident that Cal should have passed by the old Navy Yard in Boston en route to Logan Airport on his way to see his mother. He knows too well what the Yard means, for it was the scene of his father's fall from whatever dignity his Navy commission had to offer him, and the beginning of twenty years of steadily downward-spiralling blank obscurity ending in death. Now, as he passes the acetylene-flickering hellish shadows of the Yard, Lowell can feel his first world coming to its end.

Off to one side in the distance he can make out the red light atop the Hancock Life Insurance Building flashing storm warnings, and—as he passes the Yard—he thinks of the men there working with blowtorches "on the blistered gray of old battleships" in what was once his father's "old hunting ground." He thinks too of the ancestral cemetery of the Winslows and Starks up in Dunbarton, New Hampshire, high in the White Mountains, where as a boy he raked leaves, sprucing up the family plot with his Grandfather Winslow. He knows that now, in midwinter, the graves are buried under ice, and thinks of his father lying there, dead these four years, waiting with open arms for the bride about to join him. He remembers the frozen brook, "the pruned fir trunks, the iron spear fence . . . the memorial slates" all "turning blacker." It is as if his father, the one Lowell among some twenty-five Starks and Winslows, needed his wife to validate his pale presence among these ice-fiery New England bones.

When Cal tries to understand what has happened to him, his first instinct is to write in the one idiom he has mastered, a sort of symbolist/millenialist mode fitted together like steel plate from those early masters of his: Milton, Hart Crane, T. S. Eliot, Gerard Manley Hopkins:

In Boston the Hancock Life Insurance Building's beacon flared
Foul weather, Father, as far as the Charlestown Naval Yard.
And almost warmed . . .

But now he leaves off, dissatisfied, for he knows he has exhausted this way of speaking. For even though it has yielded him three books of poetry and a Pulitzer, it has become for him a shouting into the void. He has still not found the new voice he has been searching for these past three years, and it will be another three before he does.

For the rest of his life he will recall the solidities of his mother's face in death, the bruise "the size of an earlobe" over her right eye, the tears running down the nurse's face and then his own, as the nurse rambles on "in a patois that even the Italians would have had difficulty understanding" about the hemorrhage to his mother's brain. Afterwards he will travel by train to Genoa to purchase a black-and-gold baroque casket suitable enough, he will smile to himself, for burying Napoleon—Mother's hero—at Les Invalides. He will see her body wrapped in cellophane, not unlike a loaf of Genoese *panetone*. In the end they will even manage to get Mother's—and his—name on the coffin wrong: Lowell levelled to *Lovel*.

He will travel to Milan to meet Blair, where they will hear Elizabeth Schwarzkopf sing in *Figaro* at La Scala. Cal's real reason for being here will be to arrange a tryst with Giovanna, and he will employ Blair to keep the husband occupied while he and his girl go off to plan their fairytale existence together. It will be a fitting if grotesque climax to Cal's fevered sense of things. Suddenly, he will tell Giovanna, he has been "orphaned into a new & heady self-determination . . . a new life," even as his eyes dart wildly and his speech becomes ever more ebullient and witty.

On the train ride down from Milan to meet the U.S.S. *Constitution* in Genoa, he will assail Blair for two hours with detailed accounts of the Nuremberg Trials, having pored over the complete twenty-volume transcript three years before. In his exuberance he will keep coming back to the figure of Hitler, for Cal the supreme over-reacher. Then he will begin the nine days' ship journey to New York, accompanied by Clark as far as Cannes, the rest of the way by the body of his mother. He will remember the Genoese shoreline in late February already "breaking into fiery flower," remember too the "crazy Piedmontese" skipping across the prow of the *Constitution* "in a parti-colored sea sled" while his mother's body shone "in her bridal tinfoil" waiting to join her husband.[2] In a blinding sheet of euphoria, everything is about to unravel. "Uncle, honey," he will tell his wife once he is back in Cincinnati, "it's all over."[3]

Hard grainy photographs in an old album, all that seems left of his past. The image of his mother in her wedding dress, looking like "a tall white stone bride" holding a blunt knife with which to cut the "hard enamelled wedding cake." Another of Sainte-Chapelle on an island in the Seine, "built to house a thorn." And he thinks of the hospital where he is now being watched, it too built on an island between two rivers, built to house the thorn embedded in his brain.[4]

The unvarying routine of Payne Whitney: breakfast, the making of one's bed, televised baseball, televised news. Shadowy images of Eisenhower and Nixon. A walk around the courtyard in mottled sunshine, "two by two . . . round and round," trying to make conversation, the women aloof, "distant, thorny, horny, absentminded, ineptly polite, vacantly rude." The dusty dreariness of New York all about him and the great iron gate at the hospital entrance like something out of Dante's hell, twenty feet high, impossible to climb over, separating the inmates "from the city and the living." Out on the East River, Hart Crane's river, he can hear the constant mew of seagulls and glimpse the orange tugboats churning hard against the black current.

In the shower next morning, "purifying" himself, he will sing a medieval hymn to the tune of "Yankee Doodle" and "the *mmm-mmm* of the padlocked Papageno." Then he will remember being abruptly transferred to another floor,

> where the patients were deprived of their belts, pajama cords, and shoestrings. We were not allowed to carry matches, and had to request the attendants to light our cigarettes. For holding up my trousers, I invented an inefficient, stringless method which I considered picturesque and called Malayan. Each morning before breakfast, I lay naked to the waist in my knotted Malayan pajamas and received the first of my round-the-clock injections of chloropromazene: left shoulder, right shoulder, right buttock, left buttock. My blood became like melted lead. . . . I wallowed through badminton doubles, as though I were a diver in the full billowings of his equipment on the bottom of the sea. I sat gaping through Scrabble games, unable to form the simplest word; I had to be prompted by a nurse, and even then couldn't make any sense of the words the nurse had formed for me.

He will remember returning to his bedroom and winding the window open to its maximum six inches to watch the patients walking about in pairs below, then for no reason letting his glasses fall out the window, effectively blinding himself:

How freely they glittered through the air for almost a minute! They shattered on the stones. . . . I blundered about, nearly blind from myopia. . . . I felt the cool air brushing directly on my eyeballs. And I was reborn each time I saw my blurred, now unspectacled, now unprofessorial face in the mirror. Yet all this time I would catch myself asking whining questions. "Why don't I die, die?" I quizzed my face of suicide in the mirror, but the body's warm, unawed breath befogged the face with a dilatory inertia. I said, "My dreams at night are so intoxicating to me that I am willing to put on the nothingness of sleep. My dreams in the morning are so intoxicating to me that I am willing to go on living. . . ." Waking, I suspected that my whole soul and its thousand spiritual fibers . . . had been bruised with a rubber hose. In the presence of persons, I was ajar. But in my dreams I was like one of Michelangelo's burly ideal statues that can be rolled downhill without injury.[5]

For dreams in this scenario one is tempted, as Lowell seems to have intended, to substitute the poem. A friend would remember his deep and constant need to reinterpret experience through the lens of language, as if, until he had translated what had happened to him into words, phrases, sentences, the experience itself remained inchoate, without significance.[6] Everyone, certainly every writer, has felt this way from time to time, but with Lowell it seems to have been a constant, rendering him incapable of action until he could wrestle into some order the oceanic alinguistic chaos threatening to engulf him.

"I am writing my autobiography literally to 'pass the time,' " Lowell closed one fragment of his autobiography, which he thought of ending with the summer of 1934, just before—he noted—he had "found" himself. In the fall of '34 he would have been seventeen, just entering his fifth year at St. Mark's, about to write his first poem. He was writing now, twenty years later, severely damaged but recovering, because he hoped the words would supply him "with swaddling clothes, with a sort of immense bandage of grace and ambergris for my hurt nerves."[7]

Historians "learn by writing, rather than by reading." The words are Lord Acton's, and they seem to have acted for Cal as a kind of revelation, though by then he must have known that that is how all writers learn their craft. And because he was never fully able to uncover the original hurt embedded in his psyche, Lowell would spend the rest of his life desperately searching for a way of making sense of what was happening to him, beginning grandly with prophecy and myth, and ending, after more than forty years of it, with the more humble fragments of the quotidian.

PART I

1

Unwanted

1917–1934

Toward the end of his life, Robert Lowell would finally confess the unthinkable, thus providing for his autobiography its twisted mainspring. Looking back to his college years, he would remember Merrill Moore, his psychiatrist (and perhaps his mother's lover), telling him he'd been unwanted from the start. Did Moore know how those words would continue to sting, long after Moore and Lowell's parents were gone? To be an only child, and *still* to be unwanted?[1]

In another sense, he must have felt his mother's alienation from early childhood, even before she confided to him how surprised and disappointed she'd been to find herself not only pregnant, but separated from her father and from Boston, living with her weak Navy husband's mother and grandmother on Godforsaken Staten Island while her husband had somehow managed to get posted to Guantanamo. In the winter of 1917, on the eve of America's entrance into the Great War, Charlotte would take long walks by herself along the edge of the roiling North Atlantic, staring into the bleak reaches of her future, as she repeated over and over to herself like some Cumaean Sybil, "I wish I could die. I wish I could die."[2]

Charlotte: a Boston Winslow, in the direct line of the *Mayflower* Winslows. A woman who all her life lacked some "self-assurance for wide human experience," as her son would sum it up, this woman who "needed to feel liked, admired, surrounded by the approved and familiar. Her haughtiness and chilliness," he insisted, seemed to derive from some deep "apprehension." She had an older brother, Devereux—named for the North Carolina Devereuxs on their mother's side—and a younger sister, Sarah. Their father was Arthur Winslow, a six-foot self-made millionaire who had gone as a youth to Stuttgart, Germany, instead of to Boston Latin for his schooling and had learned to graft northern German manners onto an already formidable puritan character. Back home, he went west to Colorado as a mining engineer to rip his fortune from the mountains, marry Mary Devereux of Raleigh, North Carolina, and return east to the attenuated, hardly-passionate world of Beacon Hill to raise his three children.

Winslows had been active in the affairs of the Massachusetts Bay Colony from its beginnings. One, Edward Winslow (1595–1655), signed a peace treaty with the Massasoits and the Wampanoags, then built the first blockhouse for the defense of the fledgling community of intruders at Marshfield, Massachusetts. In 1633 he was elected governor of Plimouth Plantation, then again in 1636, and again in 1644. His son, also named Edward, earned his reputation as an Indian killer. In 1621, a year after the original Winslow's arrival, John Winslow, Edward's brother, arrived on the *Fortune*. Eventually he too became governor of Plimouth, not once but twice. During the American Revolution the Winslows would support the Crown, so that they too suffered the general displacement of American Tories in the years following the war. In the early nineteenth century, the family prudently allied themselves through marriage with the Starks of Dunbarton, New Hampshire, one of whose ancestors had been a general under Washington, and the Tory allegiance became a thing of the past.[3]

For its part, the Lowell pedigree in the New World dated back almost as far as the Winslows. These were Somerset Lowles, linked to the Spences—Scots from the Orkney Islands—and they came in 1639, early enough to make the list of Massachusetts' first families. First came Percival Lowle (the name would take on its modern spelling with Percival's son), who settled forty miles north of Boston on the Atlantic seaboard at Newbury. Robert Lowell himself had a marvelous New England patrician manner of underplaying his pedigree. "I never knew I was a Lowell till I was twenty," he once remarked. Of the two poets in his family, James Russell and Amy, he dismissed the first as "a poet pedestalled for oblivion," the second as "big and a scandal" among the family, as if one were to have Mae West for a cousin.

Lowell's great-grandfather—James Russell Lowell's older brother—had been headmaster of St. Mark's boarding school in the countryside west of Boston, and had left behind him "a memory of scholarly aloofness." In 1874, this first of the Robert Trail Spence Lowells published "an ironic Trollopian *roman à clef* about the school" called *Anthony Brade, a Story of a School.* There were even a mixed assortment of rich Lowells, though none as rich as Cal's "classmates' grandfathers in New York." His line of Lowells, in fact, was rather like being "the Duke of Something's sixth cousins," and hardly stood any more, its "last eminence" having been Amy's brother, A. Lawrence Lowell, "president of Harvard for millenia, a grand *fin de siècle* president, a species long dead in America."[4]

Cal's father, the third Robert Traill Spence Lowell, had never known his own father, who had died at twenty-seven, when Cal's father was five months old, and so had been brought up in a world of women—an unassuming mother and grandmother—until at fourteen he'd left home for Annapolis. The first RTSL had been an Episcopalian priest, following the religious observance of his mother rather than the Unitarian line of the earlier Lowells, and in his time had ministered in parishes ranging from Bermuda to Newfoundland. Besides novels, he wrote endless didactic narrative poems, one of which, "The Relief of Lucknow," a stirring account of the Scots defenders of Fort Lucknow in India against the Sikhs, could be found in American schoolbooks as late as World War I.

This Lowell was the younger brother of Charles Russell, who would give two sons to the Union cause, one of them Colonel Charles Russell Lowell— "Beau Sabreur." Already fatally hit in the chest in the hellish fighting around the Wilderness in the fall of 1864, Colonel Lowell had had himself strapped to his horse so that he could lead a final cavalry charge against the Confederate lines. Two years earlier this same Lowell had married the sister of Colonel Robert Shaw, who would lead the Black Massachusetts 54th in the fatal assault on Battery Wagner, part of the network of forts protecting Charleston Harbor. When the smoke cleared, Shaw's bullet-riddled body would be tossed into a common pit along with his soldiers. Of all his Lowell ancestors, Cal used to say, the one he would most have liked to have known was Beau Sabreur.

But Arthur Winslow, author of a book on the Winslow connection, was not one to be awed by the Lowells, nor by the thought of his Charlotte marrying into the line of Lowells from which Robert Traill Spence Lowell III, a young Navy lieutenant, had devolved. After all, Bob was definitely *not* one of your robust Captains-of-Industry Lowells, having descended through the much thinner line of Unitarian and Episcopalian ministers and poetasters. Stern, unyielding, inordinately proud, Winslow was adored and feared by Charlotte, as later her only child would also learn to adore and fear him. Frank Parker, who knew Cal from the time both of them were thirteen, would remember Winslow as "a dreadful, self-centered old tyrant." It was the grandfather, then, and not the father, who would become the dominant male force, absent or present, in the Lowell household.[5]

From the beginning Winslow made his presence known to any young man who might come snooping around to see his Charlotte at their fashionable home at 18 Chestnut Street, just off Beacon Street. The imposing house had its own Louis Seize room and two exterior brownstone pillars modelled after those fronting the Egyptian Temple of Kings at Memphis. Moreover, it lay in the shadow of the State House. Among his prestigious neighbors, Winslow could count Edwin Booth, Julia Ward Howe, the Harvard historian Francis Parkman, the neo-Gothic architect Ralph Adams Cram, Supreme Court Justice Oliver Wendell Holmes, and another Lowell—Percival—the celebrated Boston astronomer, who discovered a ninth planet floating in the emptiness of space, his initials—PL—nestled there in the planet's first two letters.

In the winter of 1916, Charlotte's primary suitor became Bob Lowell. Charlotte's best friend, Kitty Bowles, had just become engaged to Bob's cousin, Alfred Putnam Lowell, which was how Bob came to meet Charlotte. Charlotte's friends dismissively accepted this young naval officer in his collarless white uniform as a mixture of the compliant, the dull, the oafish. For her part, Charlotte saw her beau as someone she could easily manage. And one young Winslow woman summed Bob up as a man "without a mean bone, an original bone, a funny bone in his body," adding that if Bob were hers, she would have had him lobotomized and his brainpan stuffed "with green peppers."[6]

When Bob began courting Charlotte, she was already twenty-six, and Bob two years her senior. It was a point of honor with Arthur Winslow not to be introduced to his daughter's suitors, in order—ostensibly—to allow her a free hand in her own social affairs. At the same time he also insisted on sitting behind a painted screen in his Louis Seize room, reading the papers and smoking, while Charlotte sat a few feet away conversing with her suitors. At twenty, Bob had graduated Annapolis with the class of '07. He was an engineer, a sliderule man, a wizard in math and the nascent science of radio, and had gone on to do advanced work in radio at Harvard and MIT. "By the time he graduated from Annapolis," Cal would write, his father "had reached, perhaps, his final mental possibilities." Lowell tersely summed him up as a "matter-of-fact man of science" with "an unspoiled faith in the superior efficiency of northern nations,"[7] a bumbling, smiling mumbler, who handled the black on black family Hudson the way he handled his sliderule: with unvarying, monotonous efficiency.

Though hardly a warrior, Bob had sailed round the world as part of Theodore Roosevelt's gunboat diplomacy. As the "old man" on a U.S. gunboat, Bob had, at the age of twenty, patrolled the upper Yangtze during China's Civil War. Afterwards, during the Nicaraguan revolution, he'd patrolled the waters off the Gulf of Papayo as part of the U.S. presence there. Later he

would be stationed in California and at Guantanamo and—for two-year intervals—at three East Coast naval shipyards: Philadelphia, Boston, Washington,
before returning again to Boston. Long after his mother had persuaded his
father to resign from the Navy in 1927, Cal would recall the casualties from his
father's class at Annapolis: two drowned in a foundered launch off Hampton
Roads, another killed by the Moros, and the 1918 influenza epidemic, which
took off more of Bob's classmates than all the skirmishes and accidents combined. There were also, of course, the class's success stories, from which Bob's
name would be notably missing: "Chips" Carpenter, whose destroyer, the
Fanning, had forced a German sub to rise to the surface and surrender during
World War I, and the three Navy pilots who were the first to cross the Atlantic
by seaplane.

After a brief courtship in the winter and spring of 1916, Charlotte and Bob
were married. For their honeymoon they travelled by Pullman to visit the
Grand Canyon. Twenty years later, Charlotte would confess with a frankness
which amazed her son when he at last read her diary after her death, that she
had married simply "because she thought it was time to. She was not at all in
love with the man, nor did she really admire him, but he seemed the best that
was offered. She rather enjoyed his admiration, and thought she might improve
him, and would be free herself, and away from the constant family frictions and
quarrels, which she thought degrading."[8]

In the summer of 1916 Bob was posted to the Jamestown Naval Station,
outside Newport, Rhode Island. For months at a time, while Bob was away at
sea, Charlotte found consolation in the society offered by the post's proximity
to Newport. Then, in the fall, with his wife three months' pregnant, Bob
found himself transferred once again, this time to Guantanamo Bay in Cuba,
and Charlotte went to live with Bob's mother and Grandmother Myers on
Staten Island. When she could no longer take her isolation or the platitudes of
her in-laws, Charlotte returned to her father's house on Chestnut Street, where
she could once more breathe the iron in the air and prepare for her baby's
arrival.

It was here, then, on March 1, 1917, that Charlotte and Bob's only child,
Robert Traill Spence Lowell IV, was born. Taking his cue from the opening
lines of *The Education of Henry Adams,* Lowell would remember with a mixture of diffidence, pride, and irony that he too, like that other New Englander,
Henry Adams, had been "born under the shadow of the Dome of the Boston
State House, and under Pisces, the Fish." Like Adams preoccupied with the
sense of history pressing upon him from all sides, Lowell would note that his
birth had coincided with America's entry into World War I, where she would
"play her part in the downfall of five empires."

By the summer of 1917, Charlotte and Bob had moved to a house on nearby Brimmer Street, still in the shadow of Beacon Hill. Nearly forty years later, Lowell would write "Antebellum Boston," a prose reminiscence meant to help him in his recovery from his most serious breakdown to date.[9] It is a highly self-conscious reconstruction of a period long past, written to aid him to better understand who he was. In terms of the minor *Prelude* in which he saw his life's work defining itself, Lowell understood that the interior and private world of his childhood, especially with both his parents gone, would be lost to history unless he himself recreated it.

Blue, he would write: the color of the sea, the color of the Navy, the color of manhood. Blue . . . and then the absence of blue. But the absence of the mother as well, "that . . . transfigured Sunday-best version of my nurse," filled in by the various young women who would become his mother surrogates. Like Katherine, his eighteen-year-old Irish Catholic nurse. When, at the age of two, Bobby discovered he would have to take second place even to the silver figure dangling from the crucifix on Katherine's glass rosary, he contrived to make it disappear. An early theft, a young child's way of forcing attention from his mother, a way of paying her back for the love he sensed even then had been withheld. "I was questioned," he would write with wry and pained amusement, remembering how he had smiled "in the perplexing way my father smiled and smiled and smiled," even as he denied he knew anything about the missing crucifix:

> A day or so later the rosary was found, hidden under the corner of the rug, where it had slipped by mistake according to the decision taken by the household. However, it was noted that the Christus was missing, and also, with embarrassment, that the chain of the rosary had been chewed. I returned to my denying smile, but later Mother saw me pushing strips of paper down the register. "You will burn up the house," she said. But two days later she again saw me pushing a whole handful of paper strips down the register. "You are setting the furnace on fire," she said. I smiled and smiled, to her intense displeasure. "Yes, I know," I said. "That's where Jesus is."[10]

The family's first exodus from Boston came in the fall of 1919, when Commander Lowell was assigned to the Philadelphia Navy Yard. Charlotte, of course, hated anywhere that wasn't Boston. But Cal would remember with wonder the long train ride south into "a bigger, warmer Boston," and a pleasant-enough apartment on a street of "indistinguishable houses" off Rittenhouse Square, which gave onto a "clammy, snowless, sooty, sunless prospect." For him, moving was an adventure, like setting off for Europe. His enthusiasm, however, was dampened by his mother's dramatic and exaggerated calmness, her harrowing wit and "child gaiety," which could not hide from him the mix of rage and panic seething just below the surface. The new apartment she soon dubbed "The Black Hole of Calcutta." Lowell would remember sitting in a room alone, holding his knees against his chest, and rocking back and forth, back and forth, for hours on end.[11]

He would remember too how his parents handled the onslaught of the flu. His father came down with it first, and, with a show of self-sacrifice, moved his bed into the hall to keep Charlotte from contracting the disease. "In his quiet, smiling, feverish banishment," Lowell would recall, his father had

> meant to be an ideal husband whose demands were infinitesimal. But, neverthe-less, with every move we stumbled gracelessly upon the unselfish invalid. The strain brought about by his effort to make himself heroically nonexistent was extreme; all was hushed, vexed, and ajar. . . . After a day of such exposure and boldness, Father was cured. His object, however, was defeated, because Mother caught flu and was sick for a week. She lay in warmth and splendor in her bedroom, supported by hot-water bottles, gardenias, doctors, and trays with pink napkins on them. In her self-indulgent illness, nothing was set at odds in the household; instead, everything was more smooth than ever, as if music were playing and we were all living in a floating palace.[12]

Then it was Bobby's turn to be ill. For three glorious weeks he was cared for by his mother. "She made sickness something of a pleasure and a privilege and surrounded it with good sense, humor, and ease," his illness giving her com-plete control over him, which after all was what she wanted. By stages he would come to understand this about her, and would refuse her insofar as possible the consolation of his illness. This unwillingness to get sick would become, he saw, "an assertion" of his will against hers.[13]

In the winter of 1920 Bob Lowell, then at sea, sent his son "a grim, gray wooden model of a German U-boat" with a spring that, triggered, broke apart to show that war meant business. Bobby would remember his mother disem-bowelling the boat's spring and returning the shell to him, "a miserable, weightless, warped wreck of its former war-like self." He would remember his father home from sea in his dress uniform, telling him that the little U-boat "was skippered by a six-foot blond boy from Stuttgart . . . who was drowned whenever the spring was snapped."[14] From Stuttgart, exactly like Bob's over-bearing father-in-law who had made his life hell, and whom he could afford to attack only obliquely, as Bobby would also learn to do.

Another theft Lowell would recall suggests a lifelong pattern, more and more openly and aggressively sexual in nature, as he himself came to recognize. It involved a "Quakerish" Philadelphia woman named Martha Bent, who genuinely seemed to bring out an earnestness and energy in the otherwise cowed and compliant Bob Lowell. In time, sensing a rival, Charlotte came to dismiss Martha as "dreary and a flirt." Bobby, taking all of this in—like Agrippina in the house of Nero, her son *and* her enemy (as he himself would note)[15]—saw in Martha someone to be both "wooed and rejected." Whatever his mother rebuked or condemned, he came to understand, became "a possible ally" of his own.

This time the theft involved the small, cracked ivory elephant dangling from the chain around Martha's neck. This became for him a symbol of Martha herself, "the heart that Martha wore on her sleeve," and he wanted it as a sign that she loved him, as well as for its "small, heavy, precious, useless" self, the qualifiers obliquely and poignantly defining Lowell's assessment of his child self. Somehow, he would remember, he came into possession of the elephant, taking it to bed with him and tasting it as he had tasted the glass rosary he'd stolen earlier from Katherine, then sucking on it as if it were "rock candy," until at last he swallowed it. "Doctors came," he would remember, and "Mother kept saying with Gargantuan suavity, 'Bobby has swallowed an elephant.' Then it was unmentionably ascertained that the ivory elephant had come out in my chamber pot. I was told it was broken into three pieces so that I couldn't see it again. And that was the sly, stupid end of a little trinket cherished by a foolish woman and by me."[16]

In the summer of 1921, Bob Lowell was reassigned to the Charlestown Navy Yard, and the family spent the next two years at 44 West Cedar Street in Boston. Thirty-five years later, Lowell would remember little more than the restored brick front, the big brass eagle knocker standing out in bas-relief against a dark green door, remember too the sloped backyard and the tall elms framing the basin of the Charles River. Summers were spent at Grandfather's "shaggy summer place" fourteen miles from the fashionable summer watering spot of Mattapoisett in southeastern Massachusetts. Winslow had named the retreat "Chardesa," an anagram for his children, Charlotte, Devereux, and Sarah, though the family name for the "cottage" became "Rock."

Rock, that "little one street and one filling station country village near a group of lakes some forty miles south of Boston." Rock was Cal's retreat, his "Carcassonne," a two hundred-acre farm his grandfather had bought and furnished after his own tastes with Adirondack furniture and guns and a duck blind for hunting when the flocks went over in the fall. Old farmers still worked his grandfather's fields, including one in his nineties who'd fought in the Civil War. The rough house with its snapshots of Stuttgart and Colorado, its Edwardian cuckoo clock, its Rocky Mountain chaise lounge, all of it a shadow portrait of his grandfather: "manly, comfortable, overbearing, disproportioned."[17]

Lowell's poem, "My Last Afternoon with Uncle Devereux Winslow" is set in the summer of '22, six months before Devereux Winslow, thirty, married and the father of two, finally succumbed to the dreaded Hodgkin's. "No one," Lowell, who was five at the time, would ironically recall, "had died there in my lifetime." The poem creates a literal still life of a world—the Boston of Henry Adams and of self-made men like Arthur Winslow—whose power was already passing. Like Elizabeth Bishop's "In the Waiting Room," Lowell's poem is about a child's initiation into the reality of death, as young Lowell, dressed up by his mother in his "formal pearl gray shorts" like something out of "Rogers Peet's boy's store," rebels against her yet again by picking away at the anchor on his navy blouse as he sits between a pile of lime on one side of him and a pile of earth on the other, one hand on each, blending the black and the white into a uniform gray, even as Uncle Devereux and his world, come winter, would "blend to the one color."

That fall, Bobby began kindergarten at the Brimmer School on Brimmer Street, just off Beacon Hill. If the lower grades allowed a few boys, the upper grades were exclusively the girls' domain, so that, when he returned to the school two years later, young Lowell would seem surrounded by Amazons not unlike his mother. But his kindergarten year at least was happy. Here he learned Bible stories, "illustrated and edifying, of Samuel and King David, also how to play soccer, and the game of the good deed, making some one smile once a day."

In the summer of '23, however, Bob Lowell was transferred again, this time to Washington. Again, Charlotte grieved the loss of Boston and the move to a climate whose summers she likened to "a herd of tepid elephants sinking in seedy mud." Still, Winslow cousins lived in Washington and across the Potomac in northern Virginia, including the middle-aged woman who would eventually replace Charlotte in Cal's affection: his Cousin Harriet. Because Charlotte hated the move, she made life miserable for those around her. Bobby was sent to the Potomac School and remembered the time mainly as an outsider's enforced stay in which he sulked his way through first and second grade.

Then, in the summer of 1925, Bob Lowell was made second-in-command at the Charlestown Naval Shipyard and the family moved back once more to Boston. Because of Commander Lowell's new position and responsibilities, he was expected by his commanding officer, Admiral de Stahl, to live on base in quarters provided for him and his family. Charlotte, however, had other plans. Back once more from the provinces, she had no intention of living in military housing and insisted on her husband buying a house and settling in. What they found was a nineteenth-century brick rowhouse at 91 Revere Street, fifty yards up from Louisburg Square, "the trembling edge of respectability" and "worryingly close to Boston's Italian North End."

The house was furnished in part by a legacy of oversized furniture and paintings of Lowell ancestors left to Bob by his cousin Cassie Myers. But all was not well, and, finding themselves surrounded by "lace-curtain" Irish Democrats who'd made money in construction or politics, Charlotte and Bob pined for the day when a "non-grafting, lowtaxing Republican" mayor would once again govern Boston. Lowell would remember Sundays filled with "a glacial purity and sacrifice," or with the standard reading fare of do-it-yourself books on topics such as "carving roasts, tennis, chess, bridge, the Cup Defender races." On those occasions when he and his mother attended Trinity Episcopal, Bob, who considered churchgoing "undignified for a naval man," stayed behind to putter around the house.[18]

Each night Commander Lowell donned his dress uniform and took the trolley down to the Navy base, where he slept in the quarters Admiral de Stahl had insisted his second-in-command occupy. The situation was bound to create a strain on the Lowells, and soon Charlotte began hinting, then insisting, that Bob resign his naval commission. Often at night young Lowell awoke "with rapture to the rhythm of my parents arguing, arguing one another to exhaustion." Lowell's exquisite memoir, "91 Revere Street," recalls that first Christmas in the new house, when his father had to change from tuxedo into uniform, bid his wife and in-laws goodnight, and return to his base. That proved too much for Charlotte, who immediately phoned the admiral. "Sir," she told him, "you have compelled my husband to leave me on Christmas Eve!" Then she turned to her son. "Oh Bobby," she told him, "it's such a comfort to have a man in the house." And Bobby: "I am not a man. I am a boy."[19]

With a certain *schadenfreude* Lowell would recall his father's naval world, especially as it intersected with the world of 91 Revere Street, in the figure of his father's old roommate from Annapolis and later shipmate: the rough-mouthed, cigar-smoking Commander Billy ("Battleship Bilge") Harkness, from Louisville, Kentucky. Neither Prohibition nor naval duty could keep Commander Billy from getting drunk the Sundays he spent with the Lowells. "Bilge," Lowell would remember his father saying, in his best old-boy Navy manner, even as he was negotiating with Lever Brothers for a civilian position on the eve of resigning from the Navy, "I want you to meet my first coupon from the bond of matrimony." And Bilge: "So this is the range finder you are raising for future wars." And then Bobby would have to "salute, stand at attention, stand at ease." Then too, forebodingly, there were Billy Harkness's tirades against the lady poet in the family, Amy Lowell, who had recently died: a "cigar-chawing, guffawing, senseless and meterless, multimillionheiress, heavyweight mascot on a floating fortress." Lowell would remember the adults all agreeing to equate her free verse with freethinking, holding up instead Frost's dictum that writing such stuff was "like playing tennis without a net."

But already an era was coming to an end and with it the old camaraderie. Soon Commander Lowell would leave what Harkness called "that impotent field nigger's job of second-in-command at the defunct Boston Yard" to become a salesman for Lever Brothers, while Harkness himself would rise to vice-admiral and legendary status in the coming war. What must have particularly stung, though, was Harkness's observation one Sunday evening, as Commander Bob prepared to return to his bachelor quarters at the Yard, that he knew *now* "why Young Bob" was "an only child."[20]

In his son's eyes, all that had kept Bob from being completely emasculated by his wife was the companionship he had with the U.S. Navy. And now Charlotte, even with the best intentions in the world, was bent on putting an end to that. It was imperative that the family never leave Boston again, and—as the time for the next transfer approached—she kept pressing him to resign, until at last he did. "In his forties," after he finally retired, Lowell would recall, "Father's soul went underground." As if that were not enough, Charlotte insisted that Bob sign over the house to her, threatening to move back with her father with Bobby if he refused. In due course, Bob acceded to that demand as well. In the spring of 1927, after his resignation and his new job with Lever Brothers—a job that paid twice what he'd made in the Navy—the family moved to 170 Marlborough Street, a fashionable residence only a few streets down from the Boston Gardens. One seventy was a four-story town house with bay windows, a skylight, a small front yard, a wrought-iron fence, and a small courtyard giving them some privacy from their neighbors. The address was clearly respectable.

In the fall of 1925 Bobby returned to the Brimmer School for two more years. "I was distracted in my studies," he would recall, "assented to whatever I was told, picked my nose whenever no one was watching, and worried our third-grade teacher by organizing creepy little gangs of boys at recess." His teacher, Miss Manice, in charge of the four lower grades, put an end to the "snake-dance" script Lowell had learned at the Potomac School and insisted instead that he learn to print in childlike, sometimes illegible block letters, a way of writing he kept for the rest of his life, alleviated—mercifully if belatedly—only by his learning to type.[21]

Third grade at the Brimmer School proved more demanding than had kindergarten. By then, Bobby's unhappiness and general sullenness had metamorphosed into qualities which, with his growing size and physical strength, he himself would come to describe as "thick-witted, narcissistic, thuggish." Worse, since grades four through twelve at Brimmer were all-girl, Bobby felt not only dominated by his mother at home but now by the bigger girls at school who made their power felt. He would remember the migraines, the suffocating asthma, the growing myopic vision. He even began wishing he could *be* an older girl, since "to be a boy at Brimmer was to be small, denied and weak."[22]

To compensate for this state of affairs, Bobby became a bully. In the nearby Public Gardens, he played often among the bronze reliefs of Union soldiers, or the swan boats on the lake, or around the captured World War I German tank, its interior stuffed with old newspapers. He would remember the all-but-incomprehensible soapbox orators arguing back and forth the merits of the Sacco-Vanzetti case, remember too that his illustrious cousin, A. Lawrence Lowell, president of Harvard, had been part of the three-man panel brought in to judge the fairness of the state's case against those "two Anarchist Dagos," as that same cousin was reported to have called them. It was here, too, against the pedestal of the statue of George Washington, that Bobby bloodied first the nose of Bulldog Binney and then the nose of Dopey Dan Parker. He would remember pelting his fellow third graders with wet fertilizer, until even the unflappable Officer Lever became for once an avenging angel, expelling Cal from the Public Gardens.

To console himself, Cal spent long hours in his attic playing with the tin French soldiers he'd been collecting since his time in Philadelphia. Like his mother, though even more powerless than his father, he fantasized about power and the idea of the Superman, becoming especially enamored with the figure of Napoleon. He kept an entire shelf of books in his bedroom devoted to the Corsican, and memorized the names and dates of over two hundred French generals. He also created an imaginary creature named "Arms of the Law" to keep him company and amuse his friends. "Arms" was part bear, part Irish cop, part proper Bostonian. Like Dr. Frankenstein, Bobby gave his creation a voice, an airy habitat, a life of his own until at last Arms became a veritable figure of authority assuming Bobby's uncanny physical strength, though at other times, left to himself, Arms was content to be an old sleeper, a family pet who liked to tag along with Bobby, taking rides on Sunday afternoons around the Fenway in Bob Lowell's massive black Hudson.

In the spring of 1927, ten-year-old Bobby went with his father to look over a number of suburban day schools in and around Boston to find a stopgap until Bobby was ready to attend St. Mark's in Southborough—his great-grandfather's and his father's alma mater. Together they visited Dexter, Country Day, and Rivers Country Day, before settling on the last. Lowell would remember his father hobnobbing with janitors and junior faculty, without ever getting around to interviewing the schools' headmasters, much to the disgust of Charlotte. The Rivers School he remembered primarily for the pride it took in being an open-air facility, which turned out to mean merely unheated. It was one of those rugged individualist's private schools popular in the twenties "where scholarship was low, health . . . high, [and] manners . . . hearty."[23]

Here Bobby spent his next three years, learning to play marbles (which he loved) and baseball (which he did not), while he continued to amass more and more tin models of Napoleonic infantry and cavalry. He caught frogs and turtles and put them in stone urns and fed them until they turned belly-up. In his poem "First Love," he would remember his confused, sexual awakening for "Leon Straus, sixthgrade fullback, his reindeer shirt," two years older and two inches shorter, remember the first casting of his "saffron sperm" before he learned, at fourteen and fifteen, to look to young girls lying on their backs in the strewn hay of old buttermilk-sweet barns, "breasts stacked like hawk-nests," in those early Depression summers along the Maine coast.[24]

By the time he was eleven, Bobby had already become the school tough at Rivers, willing at the least provocation to smash all comers. Once he broke his arm in a fight, though that did not stop him from attacking his enemies on the playground, pushing through a barrage of flying pears with only a garbage can lid for a shield and a couple of small children as allies. Bleeding and battered, he returned victorious to his mother, who smiled on her Bobby and christened him her "old soldier." He preferred intense, one-on-one friendships, and at Brimmer took only one other boy into his confidence, Werner Ash, a boy very much like himself. For a time the two allies terrified their classmates and lifted small objects from the local merchants.

Then, in September 1930, at thirteen, Bobby entered St. Mark's as a second former. Before he left home, he made out a will, turning over all his savings to his parents. Touched, his mother bought a toaster with the money. After all, tuition and expenses at St. Mark's did come to $2,000 a year, which was indeed a "sacrifice," as she often reminded her son. When Bobby entered St. Mark's, the school had been in existence for sixty-five years and, under Dr. William Greenough Thayer—who had just retired after serving as headmaster for the past thirty-six years—had risen into prominence as one of the country's better private schools. The new headmaster had been handpicked by Thayer himself. His name was Francis ("Torch") Parkman, a liberal historian from Harvard and a relative of the great historian, Francis Parkman. He was tall, and—though still only in his early thirties, his red hair (which had earned him his nickname) was already thinning and turning gray. He was shy, diffident, and earnest, and he would serve as headmaster throughout Cal's five years at St. Mark's and then another seven beyond that.

Like Groton, Kent, and Exeter, St. Mark's was modelled on the British public schools and was staffed mostly by Episcopal clergy and a devoted group of dedicated bachelors. The campus buildings of red brick and red stone, set among tall elms and maples, were modelled on Oxford and Cambridge's cloistral quadrangles. The school's emblem was the St. Mark's lion, its motto, AGE QUOD AGIS: "Whatever you do, do well." The aim of the school was to inculcate an easy, agreeable superiority among its nearly two hundred young men, all white (blacks would not be admitted until the mid-1960s), and nearly all from affluent New England, New York, and New Jersey families. By comparison with most of the families represented by the student body, the Lowells' means were at best modest.

Reading Mary McCarthy's *The Group* more than thirty years later, Cal remembered the "curious clubby monosexual, but seething with tentacles world of St. Mark's. How close the eye was for changes and vicissitudes of character! I think the whole form's popularity chart could have been made from one to thirty-seven, and each week two or three digits would have to be changed. Of course we were four or five years younger [than Mary McCarthy's group at Vassar], straight Republicans, and hardly aware of any countercurrents, and expecting to move ahead on our advantages along the shining grooves of business." True to the American dream, many of the "most brilliant and promising" students in Lowell's class would eventually wind up selling real estate.[25]

Two weeks after his parents had deposited him at St. Mark's, Lowell wrote his grandfather to tell him what a day at the school was like. Each morning he rose at 7:00 A.M. and was out of his dorm (he was in Thayer) and in the dining hall by 7:30. From 8:30 until 12:30, except for a fifteen-minute recess, he was in class, taking Latin, French, English, Math, and History. With his penchant for the Napoleonic Wars and his fascination with the powerful, history was not only his favorite subject but his best. At one o'clock everyone had "launch," followed by a rest and then football from 3:00 to 4:30 P.M. From 5:00 until 6:30 there was study hall, then dinner, then chapel, followed by another hour of study. At 8:45 it was "lights out." Wednesday and Saturday afternoons were free to do with whatever one liked. On Saturday afternoons, when there was no football game, the boys were free to walk into the nearby village.

The loneliness in the letter to his grandfather is palpable. He missed Granpa and he missed Granpa's Scottish Airedale, Cinder. "Yesterday," he added in his letter, "I met a Scotie [sic] named Cinderella who says the following to his cousin Cinder. He would not let me see what he wrote but he promised to tell how wonderfully I am doing in my study." And, to Cinder, he added a drawing of a bone, accompanied by his characteristically misspelled block letters: "Hay cindar you flea biten ront . . . don't you wish you had this Grrr snap."[26] Three weeks later he wrote again, pleading with his grandfather to "PLEASE COME UP this Sunday." He talked about the latest football news—a scrimmage between the varsity team and one of the Harvard dorms which had ended in a tie. He promised to tell him a lot more when he came up.[27]

Two weeks later, another letter, after his grandfather had visited, hoping Granpa would "kill a lot of birds" on his hunting trip up to Dunbarton. He drew a stick figure of a dead bird, and added—what was nothing less than an heroic stretch of the imagination—that he was "doing pretty well in my studies this weak [sic]."[28] A week before Thanksgiving he wrote again, thanking his grandfather for sketching the various birds he'd bagged, which Bobby identified as a woodcock, a male and female partridge, and a pheasant. He slipped in that, though he'd been dead last in the second form in October, he promised to do better. The varsity, he added, had lost that week to Groton.[29]

"St. Mark's last football game with Groton lost on the ice-crust," Lowell's poem, "Bobby Delano," written thirty-five years later, remembers, recalling too the hazing, the bullying, the being sent on interminable errands by the sixth formers who turned the terrorizing of second formers into a fine art:

> *the sunlight gilding the golden polo coats*
> *of boys with country seats on the upper Upper Hudson.*
> *Why does that stale light stay? . . .*
> *first day being sent on errands by an oldboy,*
> *Bobby Delano, cousin of Franklin Delano Roosevelt—*
> *deported soused off the Presidential yacht*
> *baritoning* You're the cream in my coffee . . .
> *his football, hockey, baseball letter at 15;*
> *at 15 expelled. He dug my ass with a compass,*
> *forced me to say "My mother is a whore."*
> *My freshman year, he shot himself in Rio,*
> *odious, unknowable, inspired as Ajax.*[30]

There were others, some of them bullies like Cal himself, like Billy Butler of Dedham, Massachusetts, who chased him around the common room until he caught Bobby "under the stone hood of the chateau-sized fire-place," telling him that God did *not* speak only to the Cabots and the Lowells. When Bobby asked his father about this, his father explained that really what God spoke was Yiddish, then added, to Bobby's surprise: "You Bostonians want everyone, even God and Calvin Coolidge, to be cold fish and close as clams."[31]

Bobby had been the name his parents and grandparents had called him by for thirteen years now. But his classmates, with their boys' genius for renaming, soon came up with another, and one that would stick. For it was now that Bobby became Cal—signifying not only Caliban but for good measure the mad emperor, Caligula. In renaming Cal, the intention, naturally, had been to hurt, but Lowell came to actually like the name, especially as the Caliban elements receded and the Caligula elements with their mix of Faustian madness and degenerate aristocracy bubbled more and more to the surface.

Cal's first three years at St. Mark's—up through the Fourth Form—were as undistinguished as his letters home suggest. But in the fall of 1933, when he was sixteen, he singled out two classmates from the rest of his form with whom he would make lifelong friendships. These were Frank Parker, of Cambridge, the grandson of the former headmaster, and Blair Clark, of Princeton. Both would remember Cal's matted hair, his mutterings, the clothes he wore unchanged for days at a time, the untied shoelaces. They would remember too his sudden, intense rages . . . and his fists. Blair would remember Cal chasing him around a room and wrestling him to the ground because he refused to stop smoking after Cal had told him to. And Frank would remember getting into a wrestling match with him once, calling out "Uncle" to no avail as Cal, oblivious to his cries, seemed intent on tearing Frank's head off.

In Lowell's last book, the sixty-year-old smiling public man would look back at his time at St. Mark's with a mixture of wry humor and painful self-knowledge. In "St. Mark's, 1933," he recalled meals in the dark Tudor dining hall, with its portraits of various headmasters and its stained-glass windows, each bearing the college seal of one of the Ivy League schools the boys would be expected to attend. Each of the six forms sat at its own table, "six boys to a side," a faculty member at one end. Cal would remember Mr. Prendie—J. Augustus Prendiville—known among the boys as "the Woodchuck," woodworking instructor at the school for thirty years and ten into his reign when Lowell caught him in this poem, already "dead to the world, off picking daisies." Because of Cal's manic strength, which only increased with time, the others tended more and more to leave him alone, except as they might, wolf-packlike, rouse each other to torment him:

> Mid-meal, they began
> to pull me apart.
> "Why is he always grubbing in his nose?"
> "Because his nose is always snotty."
> "He likes to wipe his thumb in it."
> "Cal's a creep of the first water."
> "He had a hard-on for his first shower."
> "He only presses his trousers once a term."
> "Every other term." "No term."
> Over the years I've lost
> the surprise and sparkle of that slang
> our abuse made perfect.

How then to get revenge? "All term I had singled out classmates," he would recall,

and made them listen to and remember
the imperfections of their friends.
I broke one on the other—
but who could break them,
they were so many,
rich, smooth and loved?

Rich, smooth, and loved. The very things Cal knew he himself lacked. What he did have was an intense desire to survive beyond the way he saw his father surviving. His father, each year as the Depression deepened, descending deeper into an unending spiral as he went from job to lesser job, until, still smiling, he saw his brokerage consulting firm reduced to a single customer: himself. And then, in his early fifties, the first of the strokes which would finally kill him.

That would not be Cal's way. Like Caligula he would plot, cajole, turn one boy on another. If he could not make them like him, then like his mother he would make them acknowledge and fear him. He was fifteen when his classmates finally made him cry in public. But, he would look back, "Perhaps they had reason," knowing how even now, after nearly half a century, in spite of his genius for friendship, there was something about him, something in his "callous unconscious," that could still drive him to "torture my closest friend." That honor would devolve on a wife, two ex-wives, and at least three friends, but probably on no one more heavily than Frank Parker.[32]

Since sports was a central part of the school's philosophy, everyone participated, no matter how badly. So each fall Cal went out for football, first as guard, later as tackle; in the spring he played baseball (badly) before switching to crew. He wrestled and played ice hockey, played them lumberingly, myopically, but with force, often smashing into his own teammates. On the football field he joined forces with Smelly Ben Pitman at Center and the other tackle, Everett of Colorado, to dominate the midfield. By sheer determination, at six feet, 165 pounds, he worked his way up to varsity by his senior year, despite the fact that the other tackles outweighed him by 30 pounds. In every scrimmage he could be found on the bottom, "as if defying the combined might of both teams to crush him under." The novelist John Marquand, a younger contemporary of Lowell's at St. Mark's, would recall his and Lowell's old football coach, Roland "Tom" Sawyer, telling him that, while Marquand had a reputation like Cal for "always fighting the world," Cal had been "stronger and a whole lot wilder," ready to take on anyone and everyone. Which was why they'd called him Caligula in the first place.

But in the fall of '33 Cal began reorganizing his powers along intellectual and creative lines. He teamed up less with his football cronies than with Parker and Clark, who found it astonishing to watch his new focus, even as he quickly became their acknowledged leader. "We were never subversive of the order at St. Mark's," Clark would later explain, "however contemptuous we were of it." What was formed now was "a priestly thing," with Cal as priest and Parker and Clark his two "rather laggard acolytes." From time to time the two might chafe under Cal's scrutiny and orders, but he knew what was right for his two lieutenants and—for their own good—bullied them into submission. Parker's desk was next to Cal's, and while Cal read history, Parker read poetry. But soon Cal, who up to that time had shown no interest in poetry, also became interested in what Parker was reading.[33]

Parker would recall Cal and himself on their way to chapel or to meals, stopping to admire the large Meissonier reproductions of Napoleon. One time, up in the school attic, they found a discarded mountain of books and spent hours searching through them for engravings of Napoleon and pictures by Gustave Doré. Parker also turned Cal on to Elie Faure's 1927 art textbook, *Spirit of Forms,* and soon dynamic form had become the key to understanding both painting and then, by extension, poetry. Cal spent hours tracing the outline of Leonardo da Vinci's *Last Supper* onto a sheet of paper, searching for the lines of dynamic symmetry which he believed held every successful painting in tension. He also read Charles Eliot Norton's commentary on the *Divine Comedy,* and took quite seriously Norton's insistence that it was the individual and not God who put the self in Hell. Here too will was the key. Will decided an individual's fate. If that was so, Cal reasoned, it was up to each person to decide what one would be. All that was necessary was the will and the determination to do the required work and one could succeed at anything one set one's mind to. Had not his long study of Napoleon taught him just that?[34]

By the summer of 1934, the seventeen-year-old Cal was ready at last to *be* something of his own, something not of his mother's making. But what? He did not feel called to be a painter or a musician or even a poet, and he had no wish to be either a statesman or a soldier. The engine was primed; all that was needed was to find something that would adequately engage his fierce and intense energies. Then, in August, he decided to become a counselor at Brantwood Camp in Peterborough, New Hampshire. Brantwood was run by St. Mark's for underprivileged boys from the Boston area, and staffed by upper-form boys. Cal would use this time to test his new theory of self-development by becoming, improbably, a counselor for two weeks. Naturally, he insisted that Parker join him. Counseling meant watching over a group of eight boys, cleaning up after them, accompanying them on both an overnight and a three-day hike. Parker would remember the experiment vividly:

> Moody, solitary, antisocial, Cal nonetheless wanted to prove that he could be a
> good counselor. Community life, songs, hikes, competition for the cleanest hut,

best record for knot-tying and campfire-building—to all these tasks Cal brought an unnatural fervor. We were each assigned a hut with about eight boys. In Cal's were "Mohawks," in mine "Massasoits." . . . In the evenings we would gather in the head counselor's hut to discuss the day's problems with our boys. The senior counselors—relaxed and smoking—were often disconcerted by Cal, who took these sessions with a seriousness that tolerated no frivolous humor. . . . Cal forced himself to sing or tell stories at the evening campfires. He cleaned his hut himself, threw himself into the contests and games, and although he cared nothing for competition, he was extremely put out if his hut was not the first— for that meant to him he had not *done the work*.[35]

At last, after the final hike, when the boys had gone to bed for the night, Cal and Parker sat around the campfire, "talking out the soul-lit night," as Cal would phrase it in a late poem he wrote for Parker,

> *and listened to the annual*
> *unsuffering voice of the tree frogs,*
> *green, aimless and wakened:*
> *"I want to write." "I want to paint."*[36]

Cal was ready now to set his course. Lying on his back under the August stars, his mood expanded into one of wonder and exaltation. He would throw his body into the game and win his letter in football to show he could do it. Coincidentally, St. Mark's would win every game that fall and trounce even its archrival, Groton, 33–6. More importantly, Parker recalled, Cal "would be a writer, he said (meaning prose). He would work at it, as he had worked at Brantwood, and he would be great." That fall the two roomed together for their last year at St. Mark's, and Cal wrote his first poem. At seventeen he had begun to find himself at last.[37]

2

Apprenticeship

1934–1937

One of the teachers the new headmaster brought to St. Mark's was Richard Ghormley Eberhart, twenty-nine and already an acknowledged poet who had studied at Cambridge with the Experiment group that included I. A. Richards and William Empson. In the fall of 1934, when he returned to St. Mark's for his last year, Cal learned that Parker had been talking with "Cousin Ghormley" about poetry. Infuriated, he roughed Parker up and told him to stay away from Eberhart. Poetry, Parker had to understand, was too important to waste on such dilettantes. But when Parker countered that Eberhart seemed to be the real thing, Cal read some of his poems and was so taken by "The Groundhog" that he changed his mind.

Miracle of miracles: St. Mark's actually had a poet in its midst and soon Cal had arranged to make him his senior adviser. Within weeks of the start of the semester, Eberhart was helping to shape the Gang of Three's literary self-awareness by reading their work and providing them with lists of books. That October, Cal quietly dropped off a manuscript of thirty poems on Eberhart's desk while he was out of the room. It was, Eberhart would later recall, "the first fruits of Cal's labor," and though "it showed the young poet heavily influenced by Latin models," there were "true strokes of imagination" everywhere.[1]

But this was Eberhart's later view, arrived at after Cal had gained international fame. His earlier view of the boy was far different. Though Eberhart expected the deference due him by his years and his position as teacher and poet, Cal was reluctant to give either him or anyone any more respect than absolutely necessary. Several years after Cal left St. Mark's, Eberhart drew on him for the protagonist of his play, *The Mad Musician*. The hero there is a tormented schoolboy poet. In this heavyhanded drama, the boy is defined by the schoolmaster, the school psychiatrist, and a professional psychiatrist as someone possessed, something who eats toenails and rarely bathes, a surly loner, a Caliban.

Worse, part of this harsh portrait derived from Eberhart's professional contact with Cal's psychiatrist, someone handpicked for her son by Mrs. Lowell herself: Merrill Moore, a Harvard specialist, a poet who wrote at least one sonnet every day, a fringe member of the Nashville-based Fugitives. Mrs. Lowell, herself a patient of Moore's, was by this time convinced she was being driven to distraction by her son's rebellious behavior, since Cal—unlike his beaten father—had learned to stand up to her nagging. There was, therefore, something very wrong with the boy, which only a psychiatrist could treat. Blair Clark, who met Moore about this time, never recovered from his low opinion of him. Once, he would recall, Moore had tried to recruit him as a patient as well, on the grounds that when Moore asked him what he planned to do after he graduated (Clark was a Harvard sophomore at the time), Clark told him he had no idea. Moore put this down as a sure sign of illness, and told Clark to make an appointment to see him, something Clark refused to do. Cal—thanks to his mother—was not so fortunate.[2]

In his senior year, besides playing varsity football, Cal became associate editor of *Vindex*, the literary magazine of St. Mark's. He wrote several essays for the journal, including pieces on Velázquez, Dante, the *Iliad*, and—in the midst of Japan's occupation of China—an ambitious piece justifying war when waged to preserve civilization. Now it was crafty Ulysses who became Cal's model: that man "of hardship and war," who radiated "life, energy and enthusiasm." War united mankind, the young political Darwinist argued, and greatness came through cooperation. In the thick of the fray, even cowards and thieves might earn self-respect and honor. It followed, then, that "the most progressive and advanced peoples should have the most territory, the largest population . . . the greatest wealth." So with the conflict between Japan and China. Let the most advanced civilization win, for what was "a little temporary confusion" for the "invaluable lessons and infinite progress" that would follow? He might have been talking about Alexander the Great, Napoleon, or Hitler, or about the way he felt he had to manage Parker and Clark.[3]

Cal was no easier on himself, and worked hard at disciplining body and spirit by following the Way of Self-Abnegation. He worked doggedly at an epic about the heroism of the Crusaders and, finally, just before he graduated, published his first poem in the June 1935 number of *Vindex*. Tame even for a slot in a school magazine, it was called "Madonna":

> *Celestial were her robes;*
> *Her hands were made divine;*
> *But the Virgin's face was silvery bright*
> *Like the holy light! Which from God's throne*
> *Is said to shine.*

Whatever else the poem was about, it managed to present an image of the Good Mother who "will not mar the quietness," but instead calmly announces to the world the news of her son's advent. On several levels, then, the poem seems to have been Cal's announcement, in spite of the opposition he felt from his real parents, that he was about to arrive as a poet.

In the late spring of 1935, shortly before graduation, Cal wrote his grandfather in a voice mixed with confidence and apprehension: "I have had five very pleasant years at school and I will be extremely sorry [to] leave," for after the heady freedom of the Sixth Form, come fall and Harvard, he would once again be the new boy on the block. Still, he thought he had found himself. Unhappy about his parents' choice of Harvard for him, he was at that point willing to keep a stiff upper lip and hoped to find the experience there "profitable as well."[4]

In time Cal's estimate of St. Mark's would sour, and he would come to excoriate the education he had received there. In his graduation speech at Kenyon in 1940, he would be at pains to point out that at prep schools like St. Mark's only literature of all the arts was taught, and that without distinction. There was virtually nothing by way of art history or painting or music appreciation and the study of modern languages was at best "dilatory." A student never really learned to speak another language, and if he read the classics, read them "without taste." True, Lowell had been taught Latin and Greek better than those subjects were taught at most other prep schools, "but even at that with incomparably less discipline than in the last century." Even English was "studied without enthusiasm or perception," so that "after six uncomfortable years the student, still bordering on illiteracy," graduated with "no notion of literature's urgency and value."[5] But such an evaluation could come only with hindsight, and only after studying the classics under the tutelage of no less a master than John Crowe Ransom.

In two essays for *Vindex*, Cal, taking his cue from *Paradise Lost*, had discussed the uses and misuses of power. In his reading of the *Iliad*, he reiterated what he'd earlier told Frank Parker, that the "accomplishments of man are unlimited . . . that when he places all the strength of his mind and his body to the task, a new almost divine power takes possession of him." The thing, of course, was to use power correctly.[6] In the second essay—an explication of an allegorical drawing of St. Simeon Stylites by Parker—he spoke of what happened when effort was directed toward the wrong end. All the work in the world, he insisted, even if propelled by the greatest intelligence in the world, "if applied to the advancement of evil or petty ends," would be to no avail. There were many kinds of false knowledge, but only the saint was "elevated high above everyone else by comprehension of the true light." And yet, he already understood, thinking not only of St. Simeon but of Melville's Ishmael perched in his crow's nest high above everyone else, and feeling for the moment quite superior, it was after all only a step and a fall "from the sublime to the ridiculous."[7]

At the end of June Cal embarked on an intense program of self-improvement when he and Parker took the ferry out to Nantucket to spend two months in a small, isolated cottage next to the Coast Guard Station at Madaket. The place had a bedroom and a small living room, which served as a second bedroom, and a kitchen. Cal imposed a reading program on them both, as well as monastic rules of conduct. He even insisted on a strict diet: each morning a natural grain food called *Bekus Puddy* (Breakfast Pudding), which Cal ordered through the mail and served with raw honey. Most evenings they fried up eels, bought from a local fisherman "named Captain Coffin, who had a crazy daughter, Millie, who'd slept with half the Coast Guard." It was to be a summer of nothing less than *mens sana in corpore sano*.[8]

Two weeks into the regime Cal wrote Eberhart a telling letter about his progress. He and Parker had spent the time since their arrival studying the Bible, "especially the book of Job," and he was now convinced that parts of the Bible ranked "with Homer and Shakespeare and that for vigor and force the Hebraic poetry [was] unequalled." Even more importantly, he'd been reading Wordsworth—*The Prelude*—and Amy Lowell's life of Keats, looking for what they could show him of "the young poet forming into a genius, their energy, their rapid growth and above all their neverending determination to succeed." Since graduation, he explained, he'd "come to realise more and more the spiritual side of being a poet . . . the actuality of living the life, of breathing the same air as Shakespeare . . . and of coordinating all this with the actualities of the world." He was actually "beginning to *feel*" now what before he'd "merely thought in a more or less impassioned or academic sense."[9]

By mid-August he'd written twenty poems, including "Jonah" in twenty-two wooden Spenserian stanzas. "Jonah" was a retelling of the story of the unwilling prophet imprisoned in a sea monster for three days before being freed to witness to God's power and mercy. It was in fact Lowell's first extended attempt at what would nine years later become the explosive and prophetic "Quaker Graveyard in Nantucket." Every few days he managed another poem: an elegy for Archie Smith, killed in a car crash, the first of his classmates to die; another called "Easter"; another on "Art" ("O art, I am a beggar at thy shrine"), and, on August 30, when he and Parker took the ferry back to the mainland, a Keatsian sonnet "On Leaving Nantucket."[10]

But something else was happening that summer, something harder to define: a growing sense that his writing was a gift from God. In their rustic cabin on the edge of the North Atlantic, his and Parker's monastic aims had "narrowed down to an expression of God which I feel as an infinite and ever-present power, always working objectively on man for what is good." His sense of God, he confided to Eberhart, was that "he always forgives, suffers what we suffer, and . . . seeks only to serve, and never punishes." God was a force, then, striving to perfect man. Personifying this universal force was not "so foolish as it sounds," for man was "the highest thing we know of and what can be greater than the highest virtues in man infinitely expanded?" In short, he ended, the Nantucket experiment had been about understanding God and growing in love with one's art and with "those who were great in it."[11]

In September 1935 Cal entered Harvard. By then his desire to educate himself had hardened into a state of near rebellion against his parents. He was at Harvard, he knew, only because *they* wanted him there, and *they* were paying the bills. In retaliation, he refused to take anything but English courses, which included several unexceptional writing classes and a course on Chaucer by the renowned Fred Robinson, "the best teacher I ever had," Lowell would say long after, a man whose simple and direct method of teaching he himself would come to emulate. "All he did," he would explain, "was read aloud from his own edition of Chaucer, giving his agreeable interpretations, explaining words explained in his own edition."[12]

By then, Cal had worked out both Parker's and Clark's futures for them. Each would dedicate his life to the arts: Parker as a painter (largely on the grounds of Parker's high school line drawings), Clark as a musician (on the grounds that he'd been in the choir) or—when Clark vehemently insisted that he could barely carry a tune—a philosopher. Cal himself would be a poet. As a result, Parker left Harvard midway through his first year for California to pursue his career as a painter. For his part, Clark attended Yale until a serious illness caused him to withdraw, the following year entering Harvard with the class of 1940. Afterwards he would go on to newspaper journalism and—in the 1950s—television reportage with CBS.

Meanwhile Cal continued to devote every spare moment to his poetry. On

September 2, just back from Nantucket, he wrote a poem about a sailor, drowned while trying to save a girl whose body had been washed up on the beach. Two weeks later it was a poem addressed to Milton, his central poetic influence. By the end of the month he'd also written something in Spenserian stanzas called "The Knight," followed by an apocalyptic piece called "The End of the World," and another about the hidden God:

> *Is it the whispering voice of Christ?*
> *Is it a glimpse of the cross?*
> *Blood dripping on wood*
> *The cross grim and realistic*
> *Bleading [sic] behind blankets of smoke.*[13]

Before leaving for Nantucket in June, Cal had visited his grandfather, already ill with cancer, at his summer retreat at Rock. Now, at Harvard that fall, in what he hoped would sound something like Wordsworthian tranquility in their blank verse cadences, Cal recalled that visit with deep affection:

> *I was tired and sat in the shade, my head rested*
> *Against my palm and pine needles creased my bare*
> *Elbows. A man, almost motionless, leaned on*
> *A rake, gossiping with another, just as*
> *He had always done, or so it seemed. A cow*
> *Dozed in the hot shade. . . .*

The poems continued over the winter and into the spring of 1936, many of them baroque in their syntax and imagery, as in these lines from something called "After the Lady's Letter of Refusal":

> *Imagination phantasies enscreened*
> *Upon his retina and tension swirled*
> *Filters of sensibility and mists*
> *Of personality around the man*
> *Abandoned, inward whelming self on self.*

He tried everything: blank verse, heroic couplets, sonnets, free verse, imitations of Spenser, Milton, Keats, Wordsworth, William Carlos Williams. He even tried a world-weariness derived from Eliot, Laforgue, and surrealism, anything to locate his own voice:

> *It amuses me*
> *to acquaint myself with setters of rafters,*

and to gossip with them on giraffes,
private museums and mongolian vases.

At nineteen he was even ready to give a Dadaesque millenarian explanation for
the decline of the West, blaming it on everything from the rise of Hitler and
Freudian psychoanalysis to the spread of African-American culture:

Herr Hitler dressed in spatted leather greaves. . . .
Hitler, Napoleon, Wordsworth and Freud
You fruited us with alloyed fruit; our age
Drops nude beneath your savage light, negroid
In sex and drive, here soiled her sacred gauge.[14]

Among the entire faculty at Harvard, however, he could find no poet equal
to Eberhart to work with. But when Robert Frost came to Harvard as that
year's Charles Eliot Norton lecturer, Lowell went to see him. To impress Frost
with his industry, Lowell showed him the epic on the Crusades he'd been
diligently working on for the past year, hacked and garbled from his reading of
Joseph Michaud's nineteenth-century *History of the Crusades.* Looking it over,
Frost merely remarked that the poem *did* seem to go on a bit. Then, from
memory, he recited William Collins's "How Sleep the Brave" as a model of the
sort of conciseness Cal would do well to emulate. In spite of Frost's patronizing dismissal toward the young poet, the meeting managed to mark the beginning of a long friendship between the two.

By May 1936, at the end of his freshman year, Cal had added Blair Clark's
younger brother, Bill, and Harry Brown, Harvard's most promising young
poet, to his select group.[15] It was then that Parker introduced Cal to his
cousin, a twenty-four-year-old Bostonian named Anne Tuckerman Dick. Anne
was five years older than Cal, independent-minded, attractive, and had already
published in *Hound & Horn,* which was in itself enough to make Cal look up
from his books to notice.

In Boston, Anne was considered to be too vehement and driven, and
Charles Francis III, scion of the Adams family, is reported to have told her that
none of *his* people would marry her because she'd been to a psychiatrist.[16] Not
that any of that mattered to Cal. What he did put down against her was her
being a woman, for there was always the danger that sexual contact would
enervate the group's high, monastic purposes. When Anne asked him if he
liked dances, he told her he didn't know, since he'd never been to one. In turn,
when he showed her one of his recent poems, a Williamesque piece called
"Fishing: the Siesta" (she would later describe it as a poem "about sitting in a
rowboat waiting for a bite"), Anne found the work pathetic. One did not

speak to high priests like that, and Cal told Parker his cousin simply wouldn't do. Who was this kid, Anne wondered, "some new kind of meatball?"

But Cal was struck by something in Anne and decided to give her another chance. One evening he took her out to dinner in Cambridge with the group. There was an easy, humorous, intelligent flow to the conversation, she remembered, including a long give-and-take on the fortunes of the English Royal Family, and she found herself feeling happier than she ever had. A week later Cal went to visit her at her grandmother's place at Appleton Farms near Ipswich and, as they walked around the garden, Cal asked if he might become "one of her suitors." They walked on, as in a dream, Anne would remember, and then, on the landing by the water's edge, Cal kissed her. It was not something Cal enjoyed doing, Anne realized, and not something he'd had much experience with, which was too bad, she thought, "because kissing was all I was interested in."

For Cal, the kiss amounted to an engagement, and he offered her his grandfather's watch as a sign of their secret pact. Engaged, Anne thought. What did she know except that he could talk about the kings and queens of England?[17] For Cal's part, now that Anne was about to become part of his life, it was time to assume responsibility for her education as he had educated the others. Each night, accompanied by either Parker or Clark, he went to Anne's house on Pinckney Street in Boston to stage a communal reading from the masters—Milton, Donne, or Shakespeare—as well as enjoy dinner at Mr. Dick's expense, even as he ignored his host's presence at the table.

Not that Cal's relations with his own parents were much better, for that whole first year Cal was at Harvard they could feel rebellion crackling in every fiber of their son's body. In fact, at the end of his first year, Cal told his parents he had no intention of returning to Harvard. But now his engagement to Anne had changed all that, for he knew he would need a degree if he was to support a wife. He left it to Anne to tell his parents of his change of heart. "Bobby has decided to go back to college," she wrote Mrs. Lowell in late June. By then Bobby had returned to Nantucket and the cottage out at the Madaket Coast Guard Station for a second summer. "We are happy about this final decision as I am sure you are," she wrote, obviously unsure of how exactly the news would be greeted. She and Cal were ready to announce their engagement, which seemed "best considering all things—unless for some reason you do not wish it."[18] So the Lowells would be left to fume over the engagement of their nineteen-year-old son while Cal, with Blair in tow this time, began his second summer of self-edification off on his island. For a time it looked as if a complete break with his parents was at hand.

That summer Cal gave himself over to an intensive study of Milton, assigning Clark and Parker seventy-five Elizabethan and Jacobean plays each to read by late August. Parker wisely chose to stay on the mainland that July and August, though he had to promise to visit Nantucket periodically. For her part, Anne was instructed to do an in-depth reading of *Troilus and Cressida* and other Shakespearean plays and to mail Cal her comments, which he then returned with tart annotations. Once, when Blair decided to smoke in the cabin, Cal forbade him, and when Blair persisted, beat him up. Blair, who had suffered from a bout of childhood polio, was no match for Cal. This was the same Cal, Blair would recall sixty years later, who eventually wound up smoking four packs of Kools or Trues a day.[19]

"I have written two fairly long poems and a mass of scrap work," Cal wrote Parker a week after settling in at Madaket. In truth, the reality of what had transpired between him and Anne was only now beginning to sink in, yet he felt honor-bound to see his new commitment through:

> I don't know how much Anne has told you, but we are engaged. Reality and time crawl on us fast before we know it. 2 months ago marriage, working for a living etc. seemed far away at least 3 or 4 years in the future and now the curtain appears to have fallen almost overnight. I love her and know her as deeply and as much as anyone could in a few weeks, but must admit that she has not yet the same reality to me as you have.

If the engagement complicated matters, he suggested, it must not deter any of them from the life he'd chosen for them. It was still necessary to "live and fight thru life together always working toward realizing our ideals." Nor must any of them ever "sink into school teaching" as Cousin Ghormley and their other masters at St. Mark's had done, nor were they ever to break from their commitment to one another. Moreover, they had to continue to "throw aside all convention that we cannot believe in." This had to continue to be their campaign.[20]

The regimen with Clark was pretty much what it had been with Parker the year before. *Bekus Puddy* and fried eels for sustenance, and the once-a-week seven-mile trek across the moor into Nantucket to buy supplies. Otherwise, they stayed at the cottage reading. There were also seminars in life "experiences," necessary to every artist, Cal believed. That summer, for example, he insisted all three of them experience drunkenness. This was done by mixing rum with a batch of hot cocoa and swilling it down. In twenty minutes Blair was stumbling about blind drunk and vomiting. The experiment was dubbed a success.[21]

Another life experience occurred over the Fourth of July weekend, when Cal returned to the mainland to visit Anne at Appleton Farms for her twenty-fifth birthday. Many years later she would remember that night, when her fiancé came to her room and told her he wanted to make love to her. He also told her that his entire lovemaking experience to date had consisted of two early visits to a whorehouse. He could tell her what the whores had done, and she could try and do the same thing. For the first and only time in their relationship, fumblingly, they tried. From that point on, the relationship sputtered out.[22]

In early August, he heard from his mother about his engagement. "Neither Daddy nor I wish in any way to force you into our way of life or behavior," she told him. After all he was nineteen now and "practically a man." But, she warned him, if he insisted on going his own way, he would also have to become "self-supporting." They would help him only when they approved of what he did, she ended, otherwise not.[23] A few days later Cal answered by postcard with a little ditty:

> *We wish you joy*
> *We wish you health*
> *But would destroy*
> *You for your pelf* [24]

"Apart from necessity (which incidentally is not very pressing)," he wrote again, "the honor of earning one's own living is a small thing when set against the honor of writing lasting literature." He was also aware that worthwhile writing paid little, "especially at first."[25] In any event, money or not, he meant to continue the career he'd set for himself. When he returned home at the end of August, he took Anne to meet his parents. If he meant to catch them by surprise, he certainly succeeded beyond his wildest dreams. For there stood Mr. Lowell smiling his inane smile, while Mrs. Lowell's face instantly metamorphosed into an impenetrable mask. The ensuing silence said what each was feeling.

At the close of his second Nantucket summer, Cal had sent Eberhart a progress report. He'd spent most of the summer "wrestling with technique" and meant now to try his hand at "satire and prose."[26] Years later Lowell would sum up the poems he'd written during his first year at Harvard as "blusteringly Miltonic," "grand," "ungrammatical," and with a certain "timeless, hackneyed quality" about them.[27] But now, in the fall of '36, as he began his second year at Harvard, he fared better under the tutelage of James Laughlin, just back from Europe and studying with Ezra Pound. Laughlin had returned to Harvard to finish his degree and to get under way with his new publishing venture, New Directions, which in time would do much to alter the American literary landscape.

"Our only strong and avant-garde man was James Laughlin," Lowell would recall twenty-five years later. "He was much taller and older than we were. He

knew Henry Miller, and exotic young American poetesses in Paris, spent summers at Rapallo with Ezra Pound. . . . He knew the great, and he himself wrote
deliberately flat and anecdotal poems. We were sarcastic about them, but they
made us feel secretly that we didn't know what was up in poetry." Laughlin's
practice, Lowell learned, was "based on the practice of W. C. Williams, a poet
and pediatrician then in his early fifties living in Rutherford, New Jersey."[28]
For a while, in fact, Laughlin was able to turn Lowell's attention away from
Shakespeare, Spenser, and Milton toward Pound and Williams. What came of
the experiment was a new directness and self-confidence in Cal's poems, as
hymns to the Sublime and the potency of Art gave way to the more modest aim
of accuracy of observation and more natural speech rhythms. In a discarded
draft of a poem written twenty years later, Lowell would acknowledge Laughlin's help, remembering how Laughlin had treated the tired Crusades epic
which Frost had already dismissed:

> *"This won't set the Thames on fire,"*
> *J. Laughlin said, when I was a Harvard sophomore*
> *And brought him my pro-Arab epic:*
> *"The night was whitely late and June was passed*
> *In Palestine, when de Bouillon sailed through haze."*[29]

Just before Christmas 1936, the Lowells at last decided to act on behalf
of their son. Mr. Lowell wrote Anne Dick's mother that he and Mrs. Lowell
did not feel they could "co-operate in an engagement which would not be
for Bobby's good at present."[30] Then Mrs. Lowell wrote Anne herself that
Bobby could not "possibly marry with our consent until he is at 21 and self-
supporting." She asked her to postpone the engagement for another year,
adding that Anne could meanwhile consider herself engaged to her son if she
wished to. In the meantime she hoped Anne would give Bobby "an inspiration
to work for."[31] Then, two days before Christmas, Anne's father received a call
from Bob Lowell's lawyer cousin, Alfred Lowell. Could Mr. Dick meet them at
the Gourmet Club "on a matter of vital importance?"

At that meeting, Bob mumblingly explained that Anne had acted rather
immodestly by visiting his son in his rooms at Harvard without a chaperone. As
if that was not enough, that evening, evidently at Mrs. Lowell's urging, Bob
followed up with a letter addressed to Evans Dick. "In continuation of our
conversation this evening," he wrote, "I wish to ask that you and Mrs. Dick
not allow Ann [sic] to go to Bobby's rooms at college without proper chaper-
onage. We know that she has been there once, and rather think that she is in
the habit of doing so. Such behavior is contrary to all college rules, and most
improper for a girl of good repute." If the letter was meant to wound, it
certainly succeeded.[32]

Two days after Christmas, Evans Dick wrote with admirable restraint that he did not believe there had been any impropriety in Anne's seeing Cal. "Cal and Anne both tell me this," he explained, "and I believe them." He wondered whether there were not "some person trying to make a situation already bad enough—even worse."[33] The following morning Anne showed Cal the letter his father had written her father. "I can still crackle that slight note in my hand," Lowell would remember thirty years later:

> *I see your pink father—you, the outraged daughter.*
> *That morning nursing my dark, quiet fire*
> *on the empty steps of the Harvard Fieldhouse in*
> *vacation . . . saying the start of* Lycidas *to myself*
> *fevering my mind and cooling my hot nerves—*[34]

Cal told Anne to drive him to 170 Marlborough and, while she waited in the station wagon, he went in to confront his father. His father was in the living room, his mother upstairs. There were angry words and then Cal hit his father so hard he knocked him down. It would take the son a lifetime to say what happened that day, concealing the trauma when he first came to write of this act of rebellion under the guise of the Battle of Bunker Hill and the struggle for colonial independence from the Crown, then in terms of Cain's murder of Abel, then of Satan's rebellion against his Creator. But the fact would remain: he had dared to lift his hand against his father. And nothing, no matter how many times he tried to deal with the reality in his poetry, could ever scar over that wound:

> *I knocked my father down. He sat on the carpet—*
> *my mother calling from the top of the carpeted stairs,*
> *their glass door locking behind me, no cover; you*
> *idling in the station wagon, no retreat.*

Eventually there would be a reconciliation of sorts between father and son. The father would forgive the son, but it was the forgiveness itself which would rankle the son so much. Things would change, "the *Anschluss,* the ten or twenty million war-dead," landscapes would alter, year in and year out "old Helios turning the houseplants to blondes,"[35] the "blood of our spirit" in time drying "in veins of brickdust." What would *not* change was the guilt sticking like a burr long after Cal's father was gone, long after Cal himself became a father, even after he was older than his own father had been when he'd hit him. "Christ lost," he would write, "our only king without a sword, / turning the word *forgiveness* to a sword."[36] "I struck my father," he would write when he was past fifty, knowing that what was done was done, and beyond time's redemption. "Later my apology / hardly scratched the surface of his invisible / coronary . . . never to be effaced."[37]

The morning after the incident Frank Parker went out to 170 Marlborough Street, where he found Mrs. Lowell "raging like a tiger." "If you had a German shepherd," she spat out, "taking care of it and getting the best food and care and so on, and then it bit you, wouldn't you shoot it? Or wouldn't you want it shut out?" Parker was appalled. "That's what she said to me. Anger, fear. . . . Mr. Lowell was nowhere to be seen. He was nursing his jaw."[38] For weeks she swore to make good on her promise. Not only was Cal barred from the house, but Merrill Moore was called in to see about having Cal committed for psychiatric observation. It took two and a half months before Moore could persuade Cal to apologize to his father. For his part, Cal had been sorry almost as soon as he'd realized what he'd done, though the reason he'd done it was because his father had called the woman he intended to marry little better than a whore.

It was time, then, for Cal to get away from Boston. He was halfway through the second semester of his sophomore year at Harvard and unhappier there than ever. That winter he kept in touch with his parents, who refused to see him, through his grandparents and his Aunt Sarah, and it was not until mid-March that he was at last admitted "back in the family." On the 24th he wrote his Aunt Sarah—stiffly and too formally—to thank her "for being so kind to both Anne and myself during this awkward 'interregnum.' " In reconciling, he believed his father had acted reasonably, and he could see better now that there had been misunderstanding on all sides.

Still, he could have cut the chill at 170 Marlborough with a knife. His father was "leaning over backwards too much, more than he can enjoy," he saw, and it was impossible to have an easy conversation with either of his parents. He had been back home only once since the fight, and had yet to speak to his mother. Times had to be made for meetings with either of them. "All this is inevitable after a wide rupture," he knew, for no one knew how to talk with the others.[39] "A small amount of experience has taught me to be less intolerant," he told his grandmother, "less headstrong."[40] But beneath the formal exterior each kept, Cal was desperate to reach his parents, to somehow begin to talk to them as people.

Still, he was as determined as ever not to be deterred from his literary vocation. That March he also tried out for the *Harvard Advocate*'s literary board, telling his grandmother that he believed he had "every chance of making it." If he did, she would "have the doubtful pleasure" of seeing him in print.[41] But the *Advocate* was not nearly as friendly as the *Vindex* had been, and when he showed up at its offices to learn if he had been accepted, he was told to tack down a carpet in the main office to see how he responded to orders. Then, when he'd finished, he was told not to come back again. It was time not just to leave Boston, then, but Harvard as well.

Which was also how Merrill Moore saw matters. His plan was to get Cal away from his parents and—incidentally—Anne Dick, while allowing Cal to both pursue his poetry and a more amenable education. Moore considered his Nashville connections. Allen Tate and John Crowe Ransom, old literary friends, were there. And Moore's mother was there to help keep an eye on Moore's young charge. As luck would have it, Ford Madox Ford, friend of Joseph Conrad, of Pound, of Williams, of Hemingway, author of some eighty works—poems, essays, travel books, memoirs, children's books, and a brace of novels which included the famed Tietjens war tetralogy and *The Good Soldier*—was just then in Cambridge, giving lectures and readings. The great man, ailing as he was, had been in the States for the past five months, intent on earning enough simply for his young wife, Janice Biala, and himself to live on.

In a few days he would be on his way south to Tennessee to stay with the Tates, before heading later that summer to Michigan and Olivet College, where the Tates had been instrumental in getting him a residence-in-writing for the coming academic year. "The only man I have known in some twenty years of literary experience who was at once a great novelist and a great teacher . . . was the late Ford Madox Ford," Tate would acknowledge several years after Ford's death. "His influence was immense, even upon writers who did not know him, even upon other writers, today, who have not read him. For it was through him more than any other man writing in English in our time that the great tradition of the novel came down to us."[42] When the twenty-year-old Lowell met Ford, Ford was sixty-three, a lumbering mastodon of a man, puffing and wheezing with every step he took, and just two years away from death. "He was out of cash," Lowell would recall thirty years later, "out of fashion, and half out of inspiration, a half-German, half-English exile in love with the French, and able to sell his books only in the United States."[43] But he was still on his feet, with great generous schemes for literature, and he was still writing.

It was decided to have a cocktail party in Ford's honor at the Dicks' house, where Cal felt freer to have such a gathering than at his own home. Cal summoned Parker and Clark to round up as many of the local poets as they could who were to make themselves available to their distinguished guest. But things did not go well. When Clark tried to draw Ford into a conversation, Ford explained that he spoke only French. And when Ford began praising the breakthrough work of Gaudier-Brzeska, so important to both Ford and Pound, Parker breezily dismissed him as "admirable but trivial."[44] By compari-

son with Clark and Parker, Ford found Cal "the most intelligent person" he'd
yet met in Boston, though Cal believed that was more Ford's "low opinion of
Boston than his high opinion of me."[45] As a result of the meeting, and with
Moore's prompting, Ford wrote to tell Harvard's President A. Lawrence Lowell that Cal did after all seem to warrant a leave of absence for the sort of
apprenticeship Moore had in mind. A few days later Cal and Moore were on a
train, heading south to Nashville.

   From a hotel room in Pittsburgh, Cal wrote Anne, her reeducation still
uppermost in his mind. Moore was planning to take her on as a patient, if she
was amenable, and in the meantime get her invited to several literary parties.
She might even be hearing from Frost in a few days with an invitation to
dinner. Meanwhile, he was reading the Fugitives, whom he would be meeting
in a few days. Tate especially was "very topnotch, a painstaking technician [sic]
and an ardent advocate of Ezra Pound." There were three things he needed to
do now, though he doubted Moore was in sympathy with any of them. First,
he wanted—as Laughlin had done—to somehow reach Pound. He also
wanted to keep to his schedule for becoming a poet. And he wanted Anne to
begin preparing for their marriage.[46]

   In mid-April, shortly after reaching Nashville, Lowell drove out to Clarkes-
ville and Benfolly, the Tates' country house, forty miles northwest of Nashville.
He was dressed in a crumpled white suit, and his head was "full of Miltonic,
vaguely piratical ambitions," he would recall with delicious irony twenty years
later. "My only anchor was a suitcase, heavy with bad poetry. . . . I was
brought to earth by my bumper mashing the Tates' frail agrarian mailbox
post." "A schoolboy's loaded .22 rifle hung under the Confederate flag over
the fireplace," he would remember, and a reproduced sketch of Leonardo's
Virgin of the Rocks over against "an engraving of Stonewall Jackson." Crackling symbols each of these, recalling Tate's strongly southern biases, his romantic depiction of the Old South (a decade earlier he had written one biography
of Jackson, and another of Jefferson Davis, as well as his famed "Ode to the
Confederate Dead"), the Da Vinci reflecting Tate's proto-Catholic sensibilities, the loaded rifle signalling his readiness to take offense.[47]

   Ford and Biala were already with the Tates: thirty-eight-year-old Allen Tate,
and his Kentucky-born wife, Caroline Gordon, forty-two, author of three
novels and finishing up her fourth, *The Garden of Adonis,* all set in the South.
Somehow Cal had thought the Tates would simply open their house to the
future of American poetry; but an incredulous, amused Tate explained that
there was no more room in the house, unless, of course, the young man was
willing to pitch a tent out on the lawn. Misreading the irony in the invitation,
Cal took him at his word, drove into town, bought himself a Sears, Roebuck
olive green umbrella tent, and proceeded to pitch camp out on the Tates' front

lawn for the next three months. From there, visited from time to time by cows leaning up against his tent, Cal proceeded to turn out poems in both free and formal verse forms, meanwhile driving into Nashville to attend Ransom's classes at Vanderbilt.

The day Cal arrived at Benfolly, the Tates had been outside admiring two blossoming lemon lillies, Caroline Gordon would remember. The first view they had of him was his climbing out of his car and urinating on their lawn. He was from Massachusetts and had heard Ford lecture in Boston, Caroline Gordon would recall, "and as he wasn't getting on well at Harvard decided to come South to learn further about writing. I think Ford really rescued him from a bad situation. His family decided he was crazy because he wants to be a poet and [wanted to have him placed] in a psychopathic sanatarium." In time they would see that, while he did seem to have "a queer eye on him," at Benfolly he'd been "very well behaved and affable." But, she added, "imagine a Lowell (yes, the poor boy's mother is a Cabot)—imagine one coming all the way from Boston to sit at Southern feet!"[48]

"The Lowell boy turned up twice, and we like him but feel that he is potentially a nuisance," Tate wrote his friend Andrew Lytle on May 19. "His family decided that anybody who wanted to be a writer was insane; so they tried to have him judged crazy and committed to an asylum. Merrill [Moore] evidently put on his bedside manner and got their consent for him to come to Tennessee, which doubtless in the Lowell mind is not unlike a madhouse."[49] But Cal only needed the chance to show how serious he was about writing, and soon the Tates were ready to take him under their wing.

By 1937 Tate was already known for his work with the *Fugitive* magazine, which he'd edited with Ransom, his former professor at Vanderbilt, and Robert Penn Warren, who had been his roommate there. But it was Tate's growing international reputation which had drawn Lowell south. Ten years earlier, Tate and Gordon had lived in Greenwich Village, where they'd been friends with Hart Crane, followed by two years in Paris and London, where they'd come to know T. S. Eliot. "All the English classics, and some of the Greek and Latins, were at Tate's elbow," Lowell would write. Tate "maneuvered through them," slaughtering "whole Chicago droves of slipshod Untermeyer anthology experimentalists. He felt that all the culture and tradition of the East, the South, and Europe stood behind Eliot, Emily Dickinson, Yeats, and Rimbaud. I found myself despising the rootless appetites of middle-class meliorism." Working now with him and Ransom, Cal came quickly to define himself in heightened relief as something "Northern, disembodied, a Platonist, a Puritan, an abolitionist."[50]

As it turned out, the southern experiment was about to regroup further north, in the foothills of Gambier, Ohio. Even as Cal was preparing to take classes at Vanderbilt, John Crowe Ransom, who had been negotiating that spring with Vanderbilt for a raise and better working conditions, had told the administration that Kenyon College was interested in his resettling there. For complex reasons, and after some foot dragging on the part of Vanderbilt, Ransom found himself with no choice but to leave. Tate, along with a number of Ransom's students at Vanderbilt, was dismayed and outraged at the way the university had mismanaged things, and in late May Tate published an open letter. "It is now common knowledge," he addressed the university, "that Mr. John Crowe Ransom is about to leave Vanderbilt to join the faculty of a college in Ohio. I know nothing of the reasons that may prompt Mr. Ransom to go, after twenty-five years at his Alma Mater, to another institution. If he goes, it will be a calamity from which Vanderbilt will not soon recover." But one of the many ironies of the new situation, he pointed out, was that the "Lowell family of Boston and Harvard University," which had just sent "one of its sons to Nashville to study poetry with Mr. Ransom," would be seeing that son follow Ransom north to Ohio.[51]

In the six weeks he'd been away from home, Cal heard nothing from his parents. Finally, on May 24, he wrote his mother. "I suppose," he began, "someone is to break the silence and write first." He wanted her to know that his two visits home before leaving Boston had been "less strained and more sympathetic" than any he'd had in over a year. Here in Tennessee he'd seen some people, "done some reading and angled about for next year." In other words, he'd done pretty much what he would have done had he stayed on at Harvard. The big difference had been Ford and Ransom and the Tates—"a great relief," really, "making acceptance and comprehension of many things hitherto out of reach simple." He was driving up to Kenyon with Ransom in two days, where Ransom was about to accept a position as head of the English Department. Ransom had already asked him to join him there. "The conditions," Cal added, giddy with the prospect, "would be almost ideal."[52]

A week later he wrote his father that he would not, after all, take his final exams at Harvard. "I am pursuing a course of action," he explained, "justifiable in itself." Before he'd left for Tennessee, he'd told him as much, reminding him again that he did not want a Harvard degree. Far from wasting his time that term, he'd actually made more progress "than in any other period of double the length." Moreover, the two conferences he planned to attend that summer—the first in Michigan, the second in Colorado—would be no "picnic, but represent work similar to college." He could not see, therefore, that he had either shirked his responsibilities or been "evasive" in his conduct. "I may have been rash or wrong," he was willing to admit, but he'd done the best he could and hidden nothing.

Which was more than he could say for his father, who continued to be agreeable on the surface (smiling and smiling and smiling) while seething underneath. In truth he'd hoped for something more when he'd apologized that March: a breakthrough, a better understanding between father and son. But in the nearly two months he'd been in Nashville he'd yet to receive a single communication from him which was either "serious or affectionate." All "initiative for our personal relations" (and he meant his mother as well) had been thrown on his shoulders.[53] Then he wrote his grandmother asking after Granpa, suffering now from cancer. And how was the new dog getting on with old Cinder, he asked, as if Cinder were still the closest link he had with his family.[54]

But there were strains too at Benfolly. By June, the atmosphere there, with the Tates and Ford in such close proximity, had become "Olympian and somehow crackling."[55] There were just too many chickens and dogs and flies and geniuses there for anyone's comfort, and then there was that young man out in his tent writing. When the well went dry from overuse, Ford had an old bathtub sunk into a nearby dried-up pond in the hopes of collecting dew. The experiment failed. Water and showers were rationed. "Consorting with the Tates is like living with intellectual desperadoes in the Saragoza [sic] sea," Ford wrote a friend on the 11th, the lack of potable water still evidently on his mind.[56] And Biala, to a friend ten days later: "It's awful here. In every room in the house there's a typewriter and at every typewriter there sits a genius. Each genius is wilted and says that he or she can do no more but the typewritten sheets keep on mounting."[57] Tate was busy writing his novel *The Fathers,* Gordon *The Garden of Adonis,* Ford *The March of Literature from Confucius' Day to Our Own.* And Cal, under Tate's tutelage, was in the process of shifting from the influence of Williams and Pound over to Tate, writing "grimly unromantic poems—organized hard and classical."[58]

Even Cal's political views began changing in Nashville. "The South of course should have seceded," he wrote Eberhart that June. "It would have been better for the North." As for American communism, that was just a "ruse" to "maintain the New York supremacy." And though all the poems he'd so far written at Benfolly had been rejected by both Tate and Ransom, it didn't matter, because—like Flaubert—he was in "no hurry for recognition." He had no doubt that in the end he would produce something of value. At the moment he was "not on speaking terms with Mr. Ford, the explanation given being that he is afraid I will write memoirs 30 or 40 years from now in which I will describe him as an over-stout, gouty old gentleman deluded by the poetry of Christina Rossetti and potentialities of the ideogram." Thinking back on that summer years later, Cal had to admit that Ford hadn't much liked "the idea of a young man seeing him lounging around unshaven, with a fat bulging stomach and all his buttons undone."[59]

Ford's instincts, as usual, were exactly right, for Lowell had already written one poem in his journal with the title, "A Month of Meals with Ford Madox Ford," which contained these lines:

> *I crouched at board next to the grumpy man*
> *And scarcely dared look upon his span*
> *Of sleepful, swollen flesh, rolling in line . . .*
> *[He] had immortalized himself in one*
> *Clear-written book, deathless in style and tone. . . .*[60]

The "deathless" book Lowell was referring to was *The Good Soldier*. But when, fifteen years later, he composed his elegy for Ford, it was nothing Ford need have been ashamed of. In its own way, it was as superb a tribute as Williams Carlos Williams's written shortly after Ford's death "To Ford Madox Ford in Heaven." "Provence," Williams's poem would read:

> *the fat assed Ford will never*
> > *again strain the chairs of your cafés*
> *pull and pare for his dish your sacred garlic,*
> > *grunt and sweat and lick*
> *his lips. Gross as the world he has left to*
> > *us he has become*
> *a part of that of which you were the known*
> > *part, Provence, he loved so well.*[61]

"Ah Ford!", Lowell would write, addressing the old ghost,

> *Was it war, the sport of kings, that your* Good Soldier,
> *the best French novel in the language, taught*
> *those Georgian Whig magnificoes at Oxford,*
> *at Oxford decimated at the Somme? . . .*
> *Ford, five times black-balled for promotion,*
> *then mustard-gassed voiceless some seven miles*
> *behind the lines at Nancy or Belleau Wood. . . .*
> *But master, mammoth mumbler, tell me why*
> *the bales of your left-over novels buy*
> *less than a bandage for your gouty foot.*
> *Wheel-horse, O unforgetting elephant,*
> *I hear you huffing at your old Brevoort,*
> *Timon and Falstaff, while you heap the board*
> *for publishers. Fiction! I'm selling short*

your lies that made the great your equals. Ford,
you were a kind man and you died in want.[62]

On June 22, Parker, Blair Clark, his brother Bill, the poet Harry Brown, and Cal's fiancée, Anne Dick—"half of social Boston," as Harry Brown put it in a letter to a friend[63]—arrived by car in Nashville to spend two weeks with Cal, who in turn invited them (unasked) to stay at the home of Merrill Moore's mother through the Fourth of July. Cal himself stayed at the home of Milton Starr, a friend of Merrill Moore's, who ran a chain of "Negro movie houses" and had been given power of attorney over Cal while he was at Benfolly.[64]

From the start it was clear that Cal was no longer interested in Anne, and that for him, at least, the engagement had already fizzled out. On July 5, back in his tent at Benfolly, Cal wrote his mother that his muse was his only mistress now. Never before in his life had he "worked so hard or reaped such favorable results as in the past three months." Writing was his life, and if he failed at that he would "certainly fail in anything else."[65] Looking out from his tent at the pasture land about him, he may well have recalled the closing lines from *Lycidas,* the poem which had quieted his raging blood that morning six months before when he'd taken Anne with him to confront his father:

At last he rose, and twitched his mantle blue:
Tomorrow to fresh woods, and pastures new.

3

Jean

1937–1940

The first new pasture was the Michigan Writers' Conference at Olivet College. On July 15, 1937, Cal squeezed into the Tates' car along with "fat-assed" Ford and Biala to begin the long drive up to the conference which would begin on the 18th. But after a day with Tate's erratic driving, compounded by the overstrained car and the stifling heat, Ford and Biala insisted on taking the train the rest of the way, and the Tates drove on with Lowell in tow. The lecturers at the conference would prove uneven, Cal would write his mother, with Ford, Tate, and Katherine Anne Porter the best, "all of whom I think would be numbered among the score of living writers worth reading." In the meantime, he'd been encouraged—as many of the young at such conferences are—to "keep on as I have been doing and that someday I will be a really good poet, and good poets are rare." He'd been particularly impressed by Ford's saying that the writer served a sacred function in society, a notion which chimed well with his own sense of what he was about.[1]

On July 29, while the Tates set off with Porter to tour Washington D.C. and Virginia, Cal left with Ford and Biala by train for the Colorado Writers' Conference in Boulder, where the stars would be John Peale Bishop, Sherwood Anderson, Evelyn Scott, Howard Mumford Jones, Ransom, and of course Ford. As he had at Benfolly, Cal pitched his tent once again, this time behind the house of Edward Davison, the conference director. But when Davison caught him defecating in his yard, he ordered Cal to find other accommodations. That first Saturday night Cal tried crashing a party at the Davisons and Natalie Davison had to tell him bluntly she did not like his manners. Cal left, but the following morning churchgoers were treated to the sight of a young man urinating on the Davisons' lawn.

On August 3, Ford, who was finding it difficult to breathe the rarefied air at Boulder, mumbled into the microphone for ninety minutes on the literary life, going on about his long collaboration with one Jozef Korzeniowski, forgetting to mention that the man he was speaking of was better known as Joseph Conrad. Before Ford was half through his talk, most of the 650 people in the audience had walked out. "I watched an audience of three thousand walk out on him," Lowell would recall years later, exponentially expanding the number of those present that day, "as [Ford] exquisitely, ludicrously and inaudibly imitated the elaborate periphrastic style of Henry James."[2]

In spite of Ford's disastrous reading, however, he bore no grudge toward those who had walked out on him and, when the time came, generously volunteered to prepare the conference's farewell dinner: Soup de Poissons au Cocktail, Chevreuil de Prés Salés, Sauce Poivrade, Salade de Saison, and Syllabube la Syrène. For Lowell, it was the best meal he ever remembered having: "the wines were balanced, and every course came as it should, and the venison came and we ended with syllabub and you felt in Paradise at the end. We never realized that the venison was mutton that Ford had cooked."[3]

But by far the most important event for Cal during the eleven-day conference was meeting a very attractive young woman in Heidelberg braids named Jean Stafford. Stafford, who had just turned twenty-two, had graduated from Boulder the year before, the daughter of a popular writer of western yarns who went by the name Jack Wonder a.k.a. Ben Delight. She had just returned from a postgraduate year in Heidelberg, Paris, and London. Like Lowell, she was still unpublished, but her fiction showed promise, and she was soon to make good on that promise. Both, in fact, would be awarded honorable mentions for their work at the conference. As the conference's receptionist, Jean did her work so adroitly that Ransom would remember her as "the sanest and most charming and at the same time most promising girl" he'd seen during his stay.[4] It was not long before Cal had also noticed Jean and, before he left on August 10, the two had made some sort of arrangement to keep in touch. For his part, Cal may even have thought they had come to a special understanding. If he did, he did not yet understand Jean Stafford.

By mid-August, Cal was back in Olivet, where for the next month he served as Ford's personal secretary ("conscripted" was the word he used), each morning taking down at Ford's dictation whole sections of his *March of Litera-*

ture and typing them up each afternoon, supplying new words for those he'd had to guess at.[5] When a rumor—perhaps started by Jean—reached Olivet that Cal was planning to be on the boat when the Fords returned to Europe, Natalie Davison wrote Ford that if she were in his boots, and that boy "succeeded in his little plan, I am sure I would push him off the rail before we reached Cherbourg."[6] For his part, Cal was more than happy to serve as Ford's secretary, especially since, as he wrote his mother, Ford was "a very great master of English prose" and the training therefore "very valuable."

As for the Flat Irons and the Rockies and the whole Far West, he had not much cared for it. There were no seasons here such as he'd known in New England, no "familiar touches of scenery," and many of the young western writers he'd met at Boulder were themselves eager to come east. Who, after all, wanted to be "harrassed by foolish problems such as whether mountains and extending skies" were "legitimate subjects for poetry"? Michigan, though different from Boulder, was equally "non-descript," and where the country wasn't "flat it might be anywhere, part of New Hampshire perhaps, only the fields are greener, the roads are better and fewer." He'd worked hard that summer, but it had all been worth it, thanks to Dr. Moore "for his initial decisions which made it all possible."[7]

Moore, however, was still not finished doing what he could for his young charge. Knowing how eager Cal was to make contact with Pound, especially after what Cal had heard from Jim Laughlin the previous spring, Moore wrote Pound in September to explain that, while young Lowell was as yet "undiscovered" here in America, he was already under the tutelage of Ransom. Without realizing how much Pound detested the Lowell name, Moore went on to say that Cal was a cousin of Amy Lowell's with "the same type of poetic ability that she had only his is more definite, more modern and more tensely knit." Moore explained that he himself was "in the happy relationship of mentor in some capacity" to young Lowell and had even encouraged him to read the *Cantos*. With the letter he enclosed a copy of his own sonnets.[8] Pound shot back tartly, dismissing Lowell (and by extension Moore) as the "hooey," which prompted Moore to respond this time that young Lowell was "no hooey" and that it would be good for the boy to meet Pound when he got to Europe, if, that is, there still *was* a Europe for him to go to.[9]

"I often doubt if I would have survived without you," Lowell would tell John Crowe Ransom in 1961. "I was so abristle and untamed, nor would any discipline less inspired and kind than yours have held me."[10] And, again, after Ransom's death in 1974: "The kind of poet I am was largely determined by the fact that I grew up in the heyday of the New Criticism. . . . It is hard for me (now) to imagine a poet not interested in the classics."[11] For it was Ransom who would undertake Cal's education in the classics, beginning in the fall of

1937 at Kenyon. "When Lowell came to Kenyon," Ransom would recall, "he was at least as familiar with the range of English verse as is the ordinary man at the University with a year or two of graduate studies behind him. (He could distinguish a dozen lesser poets of the eighteenth-century school of Pope, and easily from one another; as I could not.) Therefore he studied Latin, and after three years graduated with highest honors" in the classics. Putting the best face on things, Ransom recalled Cal's high "animal spirits" and his "spontaneous" personality, which Ransom—like others—had once found "a little bit over-powering."[12]

When Ransom said this in 1961, he was wondering aloud if Lowell had not by then become America's Virgil, "celebrating our public griefs." But in 1937, he was writing Tate that, while Cal was a good fellow who kept busy "sawing wood and getting out to all his college engagements," he did everything with a rather un-Jarrellian "businesslike but surly manner."[13] As he had at St. Mark's, Cal continued to play football, though still rather badly, bulldozing his way through the line or moving crablike sideways, once again plowing into his own teammates. Recalling that time, Lowell was no easier on himself. He remembered having a brand-new Brooks Brothers suit hanging in his closet—gift of his mother—which he almost never wore, preferring instead to go about as a "loud-humoured, dirty and frayed" young man, needing "to be encouraged to comb my hair, tie my shoe-laces and say goodbye when leaving a house."[14]

When Cal arrived on campus on September 14, he was given a second-floor room of the Ransoms' on-campus house to share with Randall Jarrell, who had also followed Ransom up from Vanderbilt. The twenty-three-year-old Jarrell was at that point completing his M.A. in English while he gained experience teaching and proctoring. Three years Cal's senior, Jarrell was the first person of his own generation Cal genuinely held in awe. First of all there was Randall's "preternatural" brightness and quicksilver wit. But there was also his southern *sprezzatura:* the way he played tennis, the teacher girlfriend he had in town, his willingness to say whatever was on his mind, his criticism even of Ransom, his conceit, his intransigence, even his primness. Peter Taylor, Cal's roommate for their last two years at Kenyon, recalled that "Randall never in his life used a four-letter word" and "couldn't stand a joke about sex." And once, as Jarrell was skiing downhill, Ransom had heard him sigh, "I feel just like an angel."[15]

Jarrell, who would serve as a U.S. Army navigational instructor during the war, already had an expert's knowledge of military aircraft, and Cal would remember "sitting with him in 1938 on the hill of Kenyon College and listening to him analyze in cool technical detail the various rather minute ways in which the latest British planes were superior to their German equivalents. He then jokingly sketched out how a bombing raid might be made against the college."[16] Naturally the jocks found Randall hard to take, especially since he spared no one his critical comments, until only Taylor and Cal were willing to stick by him. Cost what it might, Cal was determined to learn whatever he could from this strange, luminous presence.

In truth, Lowell had found a home for himself at Kenyon. "Dr. Moore writes me that you are considering coming down here," he wrote his mother in mid-October. "Don't do it. I am just getting a grip on things and have absolutely no spare time. There would be nothing for you to do and Mr. Ransom looks out for me better than you could wish, getting me to take exercise and even making my bed for me one night."[17] He was taking Latin, Greek, two English courses—one in the novel, the other in Pope and Dry-den—and a course in Aesthetics, in which he was studying treatises on the Sublime by Longinus, Burke, Kant, Hegel, Schopenhauer, Shaftesbury, Rus-kin, Reynolds, A. C. Bradley, and George Santayana. No longer was he merely taking courses as he had at Harvard. This time round he meant to get an education.

On November 9 he wrote Frank Parker, who was then studying art in New York. Now that "Arcadia" was "in full bloom," he complained, Jarrell, that "happy shepherd, having forsaken his rustic tennis rackets, pursues the nymphs." At best a mere "epicene in a state of pre-puberty," Randall had found "a girl who comes for him in a grey car. She teaches French and perhaps as Katherine the daughter of the mad king of France [in *Henry V*], she teaches him to say: 'la plus belle de la monde'." As for his own studies, Cal was coming to see—thanks to the hard classicism of Ransom—that Virgil was a "much better writer than Shakespeare." In fact, if "simplicity and urbanity" were the touchstones, how "gilded" Shakespeare's vocabulary seemed compared to either Milton or Chaucer. So many of Shakespeare's so-called profundities, he'd decided, turned out on close inspection to be "merely inexactitudes of phrasing."[18] Ransom and Jarrell "had each separately spent the preceding summer studying Shakespeare's *Sonnets,* and had emerged with unorthodox and widely differing theories," Lowell would recall thirty years later.

> Roughly, Ransom thought that Shakespeare was continually going off the rails into illogical incoherence. Jarrell believed that no one, not even William Empson, had done justice to the rich, significant ambiguity of Shakespeare's intelligence and images. I can see and hear Ransom and Jarrell now, seated on one sofa, as though on one love seat, the sacred texts open on their laps, one fifty, the other just out of college, and each expounding to the other's deaf ears his own inspired and irreconcilable interpretation.[19]

Of all the letters he'd written from Kenyon, Cal complained to Parker, only Cousin Ghormley had written back, and then only to say that he didn't have time to write and was sending instead one of his poems for Lowell to comment on. On November 12, Cal did just that, calling Eberhart's "generalities" mere "commonplaces," and warning his former master that if he was going to write poems that would outlast the age, he would have to learn to condense.[20] Lowell's tone sent Eberhart into a fury, and a few days later he answered from his superior vantage that only the immature had ambitions to "outlast the age." Wise types (like himself, he added) aimed simply at getting "through life without pain." The trouble with Cal was that he'd been spoiled by Tate's good opinion of him, when in truth he would probably "peter out" instead, as so many young poets did, by the time he was twenty-five. Not of course that Cal had anything to worry about, for he could always "relapse into the soft arms" of his Harvard background, though his name would probably get him down before it set him up.[21]

"If you mention my relapsing into the soft arms of a Harvard background," Lowell shot back, "I'll ask you about becoming a celibate in a fancy boarding school." He'd had too little praise from anyone to allow him to become spoiled, nor did he have any intentions of petering out. As if that were not enough, he underlined several words in Eberhart's letter which he'd found undecipherable. "Please reproduce them in the established alphabet," he added.[22] That retort quieted things down between the two for several months. When the correspondence did resume again, the relationship had shifted to a more equable plane. By now it was clear to both men that Cal had grown beyond the easy advice of his former tutor.

That fall Jean had begun teaching composition at Stephens Junior College in Columbia, Missouri, where her stipend was room, board, and a hundred dollars a month. Even as she fielded letters from Cal, she was writing intimate love letters to her old confidant, James Robert Hightower, then beginning graduate work in Chinese studies at Harvard. Jean had met Hightower two years before, and they'd spent enough time together in Europe the previous year (though they were not yet lovers) that they had come by then, Hightower believed, to some sort of understanding. At Boulder, however, Jean had said nothing to Cal about Hightower, and neither suitor would learn of the other's existence for another year.

Meanwhile, Jean had also made enough of an impression on a third party, Bill Mock, a fellow instructor at Stephens College, that he would propose marriage before the fall semester was out. But Mock was just a good guy, Jean wrote Hightower at the end of September, someone with money and a car, who drank good whiskey and hung around with a bunch of drunken cigarette salesmen. He was also "fat and short and black and has a mustache and athlete's foot. He bounces."[23] As for the young women she was forced to teach, she found them all "loathsome little bitches who are homesick and have rumps like a kitchen stove."[24] The truth was they intimidated her. At Christmas, she drove up to Chicago to stay with Mock's wealthy family and attend the Modern Language Association Convention, anxious to make contact with Ransom once again. Hightower had been against her going with Mock, but she was too protean and determined to let his protests deter her.

On New Year's Day, 1938, Ransom wrote Tate to praise Jean, whom he'd just seen in Chicago, and to bring Tate up to date on Lowell, "a fine boy, very definitely with great literary possibilities." He did not know whether Lowell would end up as a critic or a poet, but he was "making fast progress in both lines."[25] But the truth was that Lowell's poems were still far too stiff, pretentious, and artificial, and increasingly weighted with classical allusions, a dense, sometimes impenetrable, Latinate vocabulary, and a tortuous syntax which it would take him years to smooth out. "Each poem was more difficult than the one before," Lowell would recall, "and had more ambiguities. Ransom . . . was impressed, but didn't want to publish them," so "forbidding and clotted" did he find them.[26]

In the late thirties, there were two literary magazines at Kenyon: first, the prestigious *Kenyon Review,* founded in 1938 by Ransom and edited by him, its aim being to fill the gap left by the demise of T. S. Eliot's *The Criterion.* In his three years at Kenyon, Lowell would publish only two poems in the *Review,* both in the December 1938 issue. Ransom erred on the side of charity in taking even these two, and it would be another five years before Lowell saw any of his work published again. The other magazine was the undergraduate journal, *Hika,* which printed some of Lowell's criticism. His review of Ransom's *The World's Body* in the October 1938 issue gives a sense of the sort of thing he was capable of producing at twenty-one.

The best contemporary poetry, he offered there (having by then rejected Williams's Objectivist poetics), took its cue from Baudelaire, Eliot, and especially Tate, and was "characterized by its strenuous, alexandrian complexity." The poetry of the "common and quotidian," poetry like Williams's, in fact, was "beneath the grace of art." Imagism's value lay in rendering the physical world. At its best it was "filled with [the poet's] submerged intentions." But Metaphysical poetry made "the miraculous explicit." In religious and aesthetic terms, the Incarnation of Christ—the Word made flesh—underwrote the felt presence of a physical world in a Metaphysical poem, something Lowell's Calvinist bent had made it difficult to appreciate. The real value of Metaphysical poetry—poetry like Donne's, Herbert's, and Vaughan's—lay in its symbolic weight, in other words, in its ability to preserve "the richness of particulars" like flies in an amber jelly, in order to "make explicit the most supernatural reality, God." It was emblems Lowell was after now, symbolic poetry and *not* photographic realism. Tate's poetics had for the time being won out over Williams's.

By February 1938, it was clear that Arthur Winslow's cancer had spread and that he would not last much longer. On the 8th, Cal wrote his mother from Kenyon that he did not think he would see his grandfather alive again.[27] But in mid-April, with his grandfather still hanging on, Cal drove home to see the man who had so shaped him and his mother. A mere shadow of his former robust self, Winslow was now in a private hospital room at Phillips House at Massachusetts General Hospital. Cal had raced home from college with Frank Parker, in the process smashing Parker's brand-new car into the rear of a lineman's truck.[28] He would remember his grandfather looking up at him and scrutinizing the pimples on his chin, before asking his grandson disgustedly why he had so many "bruises" on his face. It was the last time Cal saw his grandfather alive.[29]

That August, he read six poems at Mount Holyoke College for the annual Glascock competition. Then, in September, he returned to Kenyon, moving this time into "old" Douglass House, a wood Victorian structure with Gothic windows and gingerbread in the center of campus. The Kenyon fraternities looked on the Douglass House crowd as something of an "isolation block" on campus, home of eggheads and longhairs. Randall, as the house's chaperone, was responsible for the eleven residents there, each of whom identified himself as a budding writer and a "Ransom man."[30] Besides Cal and Taylor, there were John Thompson, Robie Macauley, and David McDowell, all of whom would remain Cal's friends long after he'd left Kenyon, and all of whom would go on to become successful writers and editors.

They were also mild iconoclasts who broke with the school's traditions whenever they could. One Kenyon tradition was staying on in the great hall after Sunday lunch to sing college songs. On one occasion, Cal and Taylor both made a point of leaving before the singalong was finished and were booed roundly on their way out. The two of them walked the country roads for miles together, Taylor would recall in his short story, "1939," and read Auden and Yvor Winters and Wyndham Lewis and Joyce and Christopher Dawson and James's *The Wings of the Dove* and Delmore Schwartz's *In Dreams Begin Responsibilities.* Indeed, it was a glorious time.

But Cal was still Cal, his personal habits unchanged since St. Mark's. His bed was still his desk and workshop, surrounded by veritable compost heaps made up of dirty socks, books, letters from family and friends in Boston, half-eaten sandwiches, muddy football boots. He still insisted on having things his way. Often, whether Taylor wanted it or not, Cal read to him far into the night. But once, when Cal wanted lights out and Taylor demurred, Cal stood over him like a grizzly and with one yank ripped the wires out of the lamp while sparks shot into the darkness. Often, in fact, Cal became "Arms of the Law", his Doppelgänger bear, grabbing his friends in bone-crushing hugs and arresting and scolding them. There would be the transforming, schizophrenic, high nasal voice, half policeman, half Bostonian, and then those huge, playful and menacing paws.

For fifteen months, preoccupied with his studies, Cal pursued Jean by post. She finished out her year at Stephens College, spent the summer writing in Colorado, and then, in the fall of 1938, went to the University of Iowa to teach and write. She was there only six weeks, however, when she found herself so tired and bored that she finally decided to leave and join Hightower in Cambridge. "I have wanted to be your wife and not much more," she had written him in early October, trying to sound as if she meant it. "I have wanted to bear a child for you. . . . I have wanted to be consumed in your body." Now at last they would be together.[31] A month later, on the night of November 4, having so far managed to avoid intimate entanglements with Mock or Hightower or Lowell, she left Iowa without telling anyone, her destination Cambridge. Because her itinerary would take her through Cleveland, she wired Lowell at Kenyon, asking him to meet her there.

Many years later, long after he'd lost sight of Jean, Bill Mock, then a law enforcement officer in Florida, would remember "the intensity of [Cal's] adoration" from the letters Jean had received from him when she was still at Stephens College and which she had shared with Mock. Cal's ardor and intensity, he would recall, were "obvious and amused us both."[32] And while Jean shared some of the literary gossip she heard from Cal with Hightower, she kept the fact of Cal's affections to herself. The one person she did take into her confidence was the novelist Evelyn Scott, whom she'd met at Boulder, a woman who had already had her share of love affairs, including one with Thomas Merton's father and another with William Carlos Williams. "Yes, that Lowell struck me as a proper ass," Scott wrote Jean, apparently agreeing with Stafford's own assessment of Lowell. Nor did Scott care at all for Lowell's daddys, the Fugitives. "All that Tate-Ransom crowd has to revive the 'mysteries,' in their worst meaning, in order that Tate-Ransom may be sure of dictatorial officiation at the altar." That young Lowell was clearly one of theirs.[33]

When Jean left Iowa, she simply boarded a Greyhound bus in the middle of the night and headed for Chicago. From there she took another bus bound for New York, with a stopover in Cleveland. On the afternoon of the 6th, Cal was there to meet her. They spent the evening together talking and, when he asked her to marry him, she told him yes, if he bought her another drink. Then, as quickly as she had come, she was gone. After staying briefly in New York, she went on to Boston, where Hightower met her and took her to his apartment in Cambridge. There, according to Hightower, after years of circling each other, they made love once, before Jean confessed to him that she was frigid. And, though she continued to stay on at his apartment, the affair itself was over. It was from Hightower's that she wrote Cal, saying she had decided to go down to Virginia for a visit. In the meantime, she gave him a New York address where he might write her.

Twelve days later Cal and Taylor, off for the Thanksgiving holidays, borrowed a friend's car and drove to New York, where Cal planned to find Jean. On the 20th, after driving for two days, they reached New York. But when Cal knocked on the door of the apartment whose address Jean had given him, he was met by yet another college friend of Jean's, Robert Berueffy, who, not willing to tangle with the grizzly looming in his doorway, gave him James Hightower's address. Immediately Cal sent the following Western Union Telegram to Jean: "ARRIVING TOMORROW MORNING TELEGRAPHIC RESTRAINT FORBIDS OBJURGATION. CAL." It was a message which Hightower would translate long after as saying: "I would tell you what kind of doublecrossing bitch you are, if I weren't writing a telegram."[34] The following morning—the day before Thanksgiving—Cal was in Cambridge. Frightened by his sudden and impetuous arrival, Jean said nothing about Hightower. When she left the apartment to see Cal, she left a note behind for Hightower. It read: "Darling, he called again so I left without doing anything to the house. I'll be back as soon as possible. I am *scared*."[35]

When Cal left Boston that Sunday with Taylor to return to Kenyon (this time by train), both men were miserable. Taylor's date had also fizzled, and now the two sat across from each other on the long trip back, one tormenting the other. Soon words led to shoving and pushing, until the conductor intervened and stared them both into submission.[36] That same Sunday, just after Cal had left, Jean wrote Mock a long letter explaining what had happened. During the summer, she said, Cal had written, asking her

to come up to Kenyon sometime and he wd. pay the fare, etc. so when I left [for Boston], I figured he was probably good for a couple of drinks in . . . Cleveland, O. so I wired him and said meet me and he did and we drank a good deal of beer and he said he was in love with me and wd. I marry him and to avoid argument I said sure, honey, drink your beer and get me another one. Well, I left him without giving him an address and promptly forgot about him. But my conscience started bothering me and I wrote him from N.Y. saying that I was off to Virginia but if he wanted to write me, send the letter to Berueffy's address. I got up here [to Cambridge] and a couple of days later, H[ightower] came trooping over with a telegram from Lowell saying he was arriving in N.Y. on such and such a day and one from Ber[euffy] saying, My God, what'll I do, I had to give him Hightower's address. Then Hightower got a series of long distance telephone calls, and he said I was living at 111 Queensbury Street, which is a real address and fortunately a very large apt. house. So Lowell said well I will be in Cambridge at this telephone number and you tell her to call me here. So I called him the next day and he came over and I had to go up to Bedford with him for lunch and he kept saying if I didn't marry him he wd. just run the car off the road, etc. so I said he cd. go to hell . . . and he got savage and I got scared, so I said well I will see you once more but only in the company of other people. . . . So he let me go but he went down to 111 Q. St. and waited five hours that night to see if I got in and I never did.

Worse, Blair Clark, whom she met while Cal was in Cambridge, told her that Cal "wanted me more than anything else in his life and that I wd. never be free of him, that he will continue to track me down as long as I live, a very unpleasant thought. It makes me perfectly sick because he is an uncouth, neurotic, psychopathic murderer-poet."[37]

Meanwhile, armed with two hundred pages of a novel and a letter of introduction from Howard Mumford Jones, whom she'd met at Boulder, Jean went to the offices of the Atlantic Monthly Press in Boston to negotiate an advance. In December she moved into an apartment at 2 Monument Street in Concord, just off the small green in the town center. Here, she hoped, she could hide from Lowell. "I will probably be again hounded by Cal (Caliban) Lowell who is the worst monster I know," she wrote Mock on the 6th. "He is laboring under the illusion that I am leading him a Romantic Chase and that in the end he will carry me home as a bride."[38]

Two weeks later Cal was back in Boston for Christmas. With his usual persistence, it took him only hours to find Jean. On the evening of the 21st, he took his father's big blue Packard—without permission—and drove Jean to the Crawford House, a nightclub in downtown Boston. Both of them drank a good deal, and, late that night, as Cal drove through west Cambridge back out to Concord, he took a wrong turn at a fork off Alewife Parkway, entered a dead-end lane, and, without slowing down, ran head-on into a brick wall. Later, trying to explain, he would tell Parker that he'd simply looked up and there was the wall and Jean's head smashed against the windshield. It was like a horrible nightmare and all he had wanted to do after the accident was go home and forget that anything had happened.[39]

But in the instant of that impact, Stafford's life was changed forever. When her face hit the windshield, her nose was completely crushed and her skull badly fractured. There are no surviving police records, but someone called for a taxi to get an hysterical, bloodied Stafford over to Mount Auburn Hospital. The taxi driver remembered that Lowell was drunk and that in the confusion had tried to leave the scene of the accident. In Cambridge District Court Lowell was fined $50 for operating a motor vehicle while intoxicated, and another $25 for operating to endanger. In addition, his license was revoked. In spite of which, Cal refused to take any blame for the accident. It was something that had happened, Cal told Parker, and that was all.

But it was Stafford who would spend the next month in the hospital recuperating. Throughout the spring and early summer of 1939, she suffered through five operations, which attempted to reconstruct her face. Most of the work was on her nose, which consisted of a submucous resection to remove the pulverized gristle and bone. A life mask which had been made of her beautiful face while she was still a student at Colorado had to be used to help in the reconstruction of her facial bones. "My teeth can't be fixed," she wrote bitterly to Bill Mock in mid-January, "and oh god I look so hideous and if I want my old nose back I have to have a complete plastic with two bones completely removed and others grafted in and everyone says oh don't be silly that nose is good enough which is true but it isn't *my* nose."[40]

The new nose would be squarer than the other and mostly she would breathe through her mouth from then on. Her crushed right cheekbone would remain noticeable, and her eyes would take on the appearance of a perpetual welling up. In her powerful story "The Interior Castle," written in 1946, she would remember being strapped to the table, the physician over her:

> A murmur, anguine and slowly perceived, reached her, and after the words had been spoken, she recalled them as though they were echoed: "Careful, careful, I'm near the brain." Instantly she became an animal and though her attempt to escape was abortive, she jerked her head, and as she did so felt the pain flare.
>
> "Relax!" cried the surgeon angrily.
>
> Now she heard the busy scissors clipping the cartilage like rough old toenails. That place where her thoughts originated was buried shallowly and the points crept around the bones, through the tunnels to her brain.[41]

Without any money beyond her small book advance, Jean had no choice but to sue the Lowells. The irony was that, on the advice of the Lowells' lawyers, Cal, still bent on marrying her, was told not to see her until after the case was settled, which meant late summer at the very least. This may explain why Cal visited Jean only once at Mount Auburn Hospital before returning to Kenyon in January, when he once more proposed marriage by letter. For their part the Lowells hardly knew of the existence of Jean, since Cal knew what they would think of a girl from Colorado—and a writer!—whose mother ran a boarding-house for students and whose father was a writer of pulp westerns.

After Jean was released from the hospital in late January, Mrs. Lowell invited her over for lunch to meet Jean for herself. Clearly she considered Jean a hick, and several times asked Jean to remind her of where it was exactly Jean was from. For her part, Jean thought Mrs. Lowell ran 170 Marlborough "like a battleship, donning white gloves to go over the furniture to be sure maids were doing a good job."[42] Mrs. Lowell had served spinach, pork, cornbread, and "an emetic steam pudding with a blob of whipped cream on top" which had nearly made her "faunch," she reported back to Mock. And, since Jean was still too skittery to get behind the wheel of a car, Mrs. Lowell had driven her home. That turned out to be "the most ghastly experience" she'd ever had, for Mrs. Lowell drove as badly as her son, and had taken her home over icy streets in the same car Cal had driven the night of the accident. Not only did Mrs. Lowell have "very little brain," she was also "a match maker, very embarrassing in a neurotic woman, and an advocate of psychoanalysis and I suspect that she is herself being analyzed—it's quite a Boston fashion," Jean had gathered.[43]

On March 20, Jean went down to New York for ten days. There she visited Ford and Biala in their Manhattan apartment, "dimlit, cluttered with teacups and easels and a beautiful black cat with a fierce disposition." She'd proceeded to get "a little drunk," she confessed to Mock—she seemed to be getting drunk more and more now and had somehow picked up a Wall Street bond salesman the night before and got drunk with him too—but the Fords "seemed amused . . . and most sympathetic that I should now be the victim of the Back Bay Grizzly." Biala had warned her she thought Cal capable of murder, and pitied any girl that boy fell in love with. Cal was due back in Boston for spring break in a week and Jean was uneasy. The only solution was "to go hide again," she added, "and for that I have neither the energy nor the inclination."[44]

But Jean was being disingenuous here, for in fact she was darkly attracted to Lowell's persistent attentions and the hypnotic way he had of insisting on doing things his way. Moreover, by that point he'd convinced himself that he and Jean were already engaged. Now he meant to convince her that he was serious by acting seriously. When she did see him again, she was stunned to find him "completely metamorphosized." He'd invited her—"politely"—to tea at his grandmother's on Otis Place, and then escorted her to the opening of a production of *Hamlet,* Cal in a tux and Jean in a friend's second-hand evening dress. Together they'd sat "in the 4th row among old Boston so that I felt as decadent as if I had lived all my life on Beacon Street."

Cal also introduced her to Richard Eberhart, still teaching at St. Mark's, who proceeded to see Jean after Cal returned to Kenyon. On one occasion he drove her up to Marblehead and fed her "a very large lobster that nearly made me faunch and brought me his book," which she was to read while she was in the hospital recovering from yet another operation.[45] But within a month, she'd had enough of Cousin Ghormley. "I am haunted by a full grown chimpanzee named R. Eberhart who is about the worst thing in Mass," she wrote Mock at the end of May. "He regards himself as a minor Auden . . . and bores me unutterably."

In fact, she'd just heard Auden read at Harvard and thought him "the ugliest pansy you ever clapped eyes on." Ezra Pound, back in the United States for the first time in nearly twenty years, had also read at Harvard and she'd gone to hear him as well:

> I heard him read three unpublished cantos and honestly they aren't poetry and they aren't history and Hightower [himself a specialist in Chinese language and culture] who was with me agreed, in fact he had an encounter with P[ound] in the Chink library the day before and he says that P. is not only a fake but he is also not very intelligent and he cannot speak without using at least four of those A....o-S...n words in every sentence, such as speaking of universities, "I went to one of these s-filled p-pots with their f-ing bastard academic pimps" and so forth.[46]

Shortly before Cal returned to Boston for the summer, he contacted Blair at Harvard and told him to bring Jean down to Baltimore. Cal would be waiting at the train station, along with his Kenyon classics professor, Frederick Santee. Santee, it turned out, had connections with the medical staff at Johns Hopkins, and had decided, from listening to Cal, that Jean had not received proper treatment in Boston and should be operated on at Johns Hopkins. Jean went with Blair to Baltimore, but once they were in the station, she became frightened and begged Blair not to let Cal and Santee take her to the hospital. Blair told her that of course they couldn't take her if she didn't want to go, so that, right there, she decided to return to Boston.

There was a scene but no fight, Blair would remember, and Cal finally gave in. Santee, who was apparently not all that stable himself—to Blair he was that "Crazy Santee"—told Cal that it was obvious that his friend was in love with his fiancée. He could tell, Santee insisted, because he'd noticed the way Blair walked in Jean's presence. But Blair walked as he did because of a childhood bout with polio. At first Cal accepted what Santee had said and wrote Jean about his new suspicions. The letter nearly caused a break between them, Blair would recall, but eventually Cal realized he'd been wrong and apologized to Jean and Blair both.[47]

With Jean's court case scheduled for July, the Lowells decided it would be better to spend the summer of '39 in Europe, away from Boston. On the eve of their departure, after another scene between Bob and his son—this one generated by Bob's praising his son, Cal thought, too fulsomely, Bob turned Cal over to Merrill Moore's care with power of attorney. "I resent your father's putting me in the role of holding the purse strings," an irritated Moore wrote Cal on July 11. "I would not want this position and had he not surreptitiously done it on the eve of his departure to Europe I would have refused." Cal's father, he added, was really the "problem child no. 1" here. Moreover, Bob was squandering the family's money in bad investments and "heading for serious financial trouble." Perhaps Cal and his mother could still do something "to prevent further dissipation of his property."[48]

But as far as Cal was concerned, the problem was out of his hands. Besides, he did not intend to give anyone—including Moore—any more control over him than was absolutely necessary. Nor did he much like the new intimacy he detected between his mother and this psychiatrist thirteen years her junior, no matter how much Moore had interceded for him in the past. On the other hand, Cal had by now learned not to create difficulties where they could be avoided. He would stay at the Harvard Faculty Club for the summer and take a course in physics needed to graduate from Kenyon. He also meant to see as much of Jean as he could, quietly, without jeopardizing the trial. In late June, in fact, he had written Moore that, while his family was "still a trifle difficult," he hoped with Moore's help and his own "diplomacy and good will" to see the summer go by amicably.

He also offered Moore a progress report covering the last year, avoiding the matter of the accident. It had gone so well, he thought, that he was confident "that given anything like an even break, I shall in the future achieve things of considerable value. By an even break I mean chiefly to be able to act without the autocratic guidance of friends and parents." Perhaps Moore would get the hint. Cal also hoped his career as a poet would be "exceptional rather than queer," and to that end was learning to conform at least outwardly, "dressing inconspicuously and neatly, living by a stable economy, flaunting convention by penetration rather than by eccentricity." He knew what was essential to poetry—"beauty, passion and comprehension"—and that looking the part of the poet had little to do with the genuine article.[49]

At the same time Moore was writing to Bob Lowell to tell him that he'd seen Ransom in Boston and had been assured that Cal *was* planning to return to Kenyon and that Jean would not be welcomed there.[50] One of the places the Lowells planned to visit was Zurich, where Moore had secured an appointment for Mrs. Lowell to meet with Carl Jung to discuss her son's case. That summer, Lowell would write many years later, Jung reportedly told his mother, "If your son is as you have described him, / he is an incurable schizophrenic." In time this information would, like everything else, be passed on to Cal to deal with as he could.[51]

In mid-July, Cal wrote his father in Europe that there were those in Boston who believed the Lowells, in deciding to fight the case against Jean and leave the legalities to be worked out by their lawyers, had "behaved shabbily." And though their opinion was not his concern, he could not "feel the action of my family has in all cases been ethicily [sic] ideal." He was not angry with them, merely telling them what was on his mind, "as a suggestion for a better understanding, an understanding which seemed to be making such strides this winter." The letter, Charlotte noted, made her husband "see red."[52]

Cal also made Dr. Moore see red at least once that summer. On July 19, Cal and Blair had lunch with him. "I . . . continued to make suggestions about interesting and constructive things to do," Moore wrote Charlotte the following day. "When [Cal] is in a friendly attitude he accepts suggestions readily and easily." But at lunch he and Blair had made pointed attacks on the medical profession. "I realize Cal is coming up for trial," he reasoned, and so he was willing this time to attribute Cal's hostile feelings toward him to "latent guilt reactions."[53] A week later the case was before the judge. Jean's lawyer, "Stitch" Evarts, was from an old Boston family and, because he hated the Lowells, pursued a vigorous prosecution. Cal's lawyer was a Mr. Pochross, whom Jean stereotyped as "very fat and excessively greasy," with a "Bronx accent."[54] As instructed, Jean and Cal refrained from speaking to each other in court. Jean had sued for $25,000. She was awarded $4,200.

But the Lowells' insurance company appealed and a second trial had to be set for November. Meanwhile, during July and August, Jean rented a room in a rundown hotel in Nahant, ten miles north of Boston, where she and Cal could see each other away from Boston. At the beginning of September, she turned in a draft of her novel, *The Autumn Festival,* to her editor at Atlantic Monthly, and then left by train with Cal—Cal to return to Kenyon for his last year, and Jean to visit her sister at her 300-acre ranch in Hayden, Colorado. Over the radio that morning they learned that Germany had just invaded Poland. Ironically, the war itself would keep the novel she'd just turned in, pro-German and set in Heidelberg, from ever seeing publication.

The initial trial had been "intensely unpleasant," Cal wrote his father afterward. He thanked him for paying the $300 tuition for the upcoming term, at the same time refusing to pay Pochross's $250 fee, since he had never wanted him in the first place. Since, in fact, all of their misunderstandings had been over money, Cal asked his father if he would finally turn his trust fund over to him. After all, he was nearly twenty-two, and the trust would yield him "about $500 twice a year," which—though he did not say this—would give him the means to get married. He still meant to marry Jean, he assured his father, though just when was uncertain. Nor did he want his father feigning enthusiasm for Jean. He asked only that he "let things happen as they will."[55]

In November, Jean returned east to Boston for the new trial, stopping off first at Kenyon to see Cal. "She was a real knockout," John Thompson would recall. "We were callow youths. She thought she was a callow youth, but not compared to us. Here she was with her white gloves. She was much more sophisticated than any of us, including Cal, except possibly Peter [Taylor], who was a Memphis society boy. She'd been in Germany, and she knew a lot more about contemporary writing than we did."[56] Taylor for his part would remember Jean's long stride and big steps and the way she sprinkled her speech with German and French quotations and made allusions to Proust. As a fiction writer himself, he was fascinated by the way she kept turning her own past into fiction. He also remembered Jean going to see Cal at Douglass House, off limits to women, and Cal trying awkwardly to neck with her.[57]

This time Jean moved into an apartment in Cambridge with two other women: Bunny Cole and Anne White. At the second trial, she had to settle for $4,000, $200 less than she'd been awarded four months' earlier. In the meantime, she took a job working for the Basic English Institute in Cambridge, and through her work came to meet I. A. Richards and William Empson. True, Hightower was only five blocks away, but by now his role had changed to that of confidant. When Anne White met Cal that Christmas, she thought he looked like "Heathcliff [as] played by Boris Karloff." He was still very uneasy around women, and used to simply stand in the hallway of the apartment saying nothing until Jean was ready to go. But his awkwardness did not stop him from asking Jean once again to marry him, and this time, when she said yes, she meant it.[58]

"You said it would happen," she wrote Hightower a week before Christmas. "You said it in your letter and I did not believe it." In the beginning she had hated Cal, she admitted, but she'd become fascinated by the way he could dominate her, and she'd always felt the need to be dominated by a strong man. If Hightower had scars from their long, tortuous relationship, she wrote, then so did she. To his surprise, when he finally met Cal, Hightower actually liked the man. Cal had stability; someday he would have money; and he really did seem to have the makings of a major writer. Hightower could see that Cal was, after all, the genuine article.[59]

When Cal left for Kenyon on January 4, 1940, Jean stayed behind in Cambridge. She was nervous, once again uncertain about her engagement, and irked that Hightower was now having an affair with her roommate, Bunny Cole. Didn't he understand that she relied on him? It was at this point, finally, that she told him what had been troubling her for the past four years: that she'd had an affair sometime during her eight months in Europe and had there contracted gonorrhea. It was that, she said, truthfully or not, which had made her frigid: her fear of transmitting the disease to Hightower, and now to Cal.[60] By March, as the time for the marriage grew closer, she tried to win Hightower back, before she realized that both she and Hightower had now made their beds and would "have to lie in them."[61] When she saw Cal during spring break, there was a quarrel, tempers flared, and she apparently went to Hightower, asking him to go away with her. But the following morning she did another aboutface. It was all her fault, this terrible waffling, she admitted. "I should never . . . [have] articulated possibilities." At last even she understood, she told herself, that she "really and truly" was in love with Cal. The letter was sent a week before her marriage.[62]

Altogether innocent of Jean's relationship with Hightower, Cal's major preoccupation during his last term at Kenyon was far more academic: getting into graduate school and winning the state contest of the Ohio Inter-Collegiate Oratory Association. The previous fall he had once again tested his theory that he could do whatever he set out to do. To graduate from Kenyon, every student had to pass tests in both swimming and oratory. Everyone in Douglass House dreaded public speaking and so, for mutual support, they'd taken the same public-speaking class together. Peter Taylor, who was in that class with Cal, remembered him as the worst of a bad lot, so nervous he kept "rubbing his bottom against the blackboard" the whole time he spoke.[63] Finally, Cal decided he would master the art, and by semester's end had done just that, winning the right to give the valedictory address at graduation.

In February he wrote Cousin A. Lawrence Lowell, president at Harvard, about the possibility of a fellowship for the fall. The letter was stilted, overblown, too hugely earnest. He appeared to be "embarked on the turbid waters of poetry and scholarship," he began, and found he had to keep "spiritually . . . and brilliantly alive, for poetry is, as the moral Milton conceded in practice and precept, a sensuous, passionate, brutal thing." Actually, he had to admit, he'd added the final qualifier because he was "modern and angry and puritanical." His qualifications for a scholarship, he explained, were his "wide reading in English and an ability to read poetry extremely closely," together with an understanding of the classics which would enable him in a few years to emulate Pound by reading "fluently not only Greek and Latin but all Romance languages."[64] After first contacting Merrill Moore (this at Charlotte's suggestion), Cousin Lowell wrote Cal that the time for a fellowship was not yet propitious, and that because of Cal's differences with his parents, it would be better for him not to return to Boston just yet.[65]

A week later, Moore wrote Cal directly. There was too much unhappiness at

170 Marlborough for Cal to consider returning home just now. Cal's father was still "deeply antagonistic" to his plans to marry Jean, and that antagonism had "boomeranged" on Mrs. Lowell and him. Moreover, being back home would only waste Cal's creative energies.[66] Moore's letter had the tone of an aggrieved suitor, almost as if he had succeeded in neutralizing one Lowell and was anxious to keep another out of the way. For in truth, Bob Lowell, dimwitted as he may have been, did seem more amenable to his son's plans than Moore seemed to allow. "I want to help you in every way that I can," he had written Cal in the spring of 1937, when Cal had left for Vanderbilt.[67] And in December 1938 he'd sent Eberhart a copy of the *Kenyon Review* with his son's poems in it. What he *was* against were his son's precipitous plans to marry before he was ready to support a wife.

By the time he returned to Boston in late March 1940, Cal had made up his mind to get married at once. On the 27th there was a quarrel with Jean which was quickly resolved, then, on the 29th, Cal and Jean went down to Princeton to talk to the Tates about their plans. The following day they checked into the Biltmore Hotel in New York. So far, Jean had said nothing to her parents, and Cal, knowing how set against the marriage his own parents were, had decided against inviting them. That night he and Jean had dinner with Blair, Robert Frost ("we talked about farms," Jean quipped to Hightower), and several old friends of Jean's from her college days. "It was a hideous meal of irritations, recriminations and unspeakable fatigue," and the whole affair had quickly degenerated into "a very frightening business."[68]

On Sunday, March 31, Cal and Jean moved to the Hotel Albert in the Village. That night each visited their own friends, but by the time Jean returned to the hotel she was very drunk. "Cal got back unfortunately before I did and was furious," she wrote Hightower, "and justly and unjustly [so] and oh God, Ma, I'm insane." Then Cal had slammed the door and left. Well, there was a bottle of rum in the room and she would sit up with it till four in the morning. "Say a novena for me," she added.[69] What lay between Jean and Hightower would have to remain a secret now forever. She had finally told Cal not about her German lover, though that may have been on her mind, but instead that she really did not know German as she'd pretended, "and he was absolutely stopped in his tracks & revolted. What wd he do if he knew me?"[70]

On Tuesday, April 2, at five in the afternoon, Cal and Jean were married at the Episcopal church of St. Mark's-in-the-Bowery. Allen Tate, "looking very like a banker" in his blue suit, gave Jean away, and Blair Clark served as Cal's best man.[71] There were few guests and there would not be much of a reception afterwards. Just before the wedding, Jean wrote a postcard to Hightower: "It is 4:10. At 5 it will be over." She was, she wrote, both terrified and happy. At five minutes past six, having by then been led trembling to the altar, she scribbled a final P.S. on the card: "It's done."[72]

4

Catholics

1940–1943

The morning after the wedding the Lowells boarded a train out of Grand Central bound for Cleveland, where Cal took the bus back to Kenyon and Jean continued on to Chicago. Waiting in the Chicago terminal for the train that would take her on to Colorado and her sister's ranch in Hayden, Jean wrote Hightower another of her progress reports: "I am beginning to see what comfort there is in being married. [Cal] will, I think, make me an honest woman. I am curiously agonized at his tenderness for you." How typical of her "peculiar genius for the uncomfortable," she noted, that her honeymoon should take place "on a train and in Cleveland. . . . Poor Cal! What a life he will have with me." Well, at least they were both writers, and, if neither she nor Cal had much in the way of role models in their parents for setting up a marriage, thank God they could hold up "the superb marriage of the Tates."[1]

Cal's parents took the news of their son's wedding hard. Charlotte was sure the precipitousness of the wedding—during spring break, and with her son about to graduate—would make it look like a forced marriage, and A. Lawrence Lowell wrote Cal to remind him that by marrying in this way he had seriously compromised his academic future. Rumors thick and fast out of Boston began reaching Jean and Cal both. "Gossip . . . is said about me in [Boston's] Chilton Club and so forth," Jean wrote Hightower on April 23, "initiated by Mrs. Lowell and turned into neat phrases by Merrill Moore before she publishes them in the club as well as in letters."[2]

Tate, who had already taken it on himself to serve as Cal's surrogate father, once again took matters into his own hands. He wrote Charlotte first. He'd known Cal for three years now, he reminded her, and in that time had come not only to love and respect him but to hold "the highest opinion of his literary capacity." When he'd first met Cal, what he'd seen was "a badly adjusted boy," but already he'd witnessed rapid progress. There was also Cal's brilliant record at Kenyon. All Cal needed now was to get on with his work. Tate had watched artists and poets up close for twenty years now—Hart Crane among them—and Cal was like them all "in his single-mindedness, his powers of concentration, and the clear vision of what he wants to do." He asked both parents to help their son, for without that a literary career would be impossible. There'd been a lot of loose talk about Cal's behavior, but "as a detached observer," Tate could assure them that Cal was as sane as he was, "and that the attentions of a psychiatrist are what he least needs."[3]

Then Tate turned his guns on Merrill Moore. "Robert Lowell's marriage has been very much in my mind," he wrote Moore that same day, "and because I know that you are interested in him I want to give you my point of view. . . . I gather from Robert that you consider him your patient; and I wish to say that he is not, and never will be again." Cal was "as sane as any boy" he'd ever seen, knew what he had to do and was determined to do it. It was Tate's job, then, to help him do it by protecting him from outside interference. True, Cal had "made a mess of Harvard" and couldn't get along with his family, and "had he stayed in Cambridge he might well have been insane in a short time." But all he really needed was to be left alone, and anyone who meddled with him now did so at his own peril. "I understand that you will be at Kenyon early in May," Tate closed, throwing down the gauntlet. He too planned to be there.[4]

Five days later Cal wrote his parents. All sorts of rumors out of Boston had reached him by then, so that he might just "as well be sitting in Dr. Moore's office or dining at the Chilton Club." He wanted to make it clear that he had *not* sacrificed a fellowship to Harvard because he had not been offered one, nor had his marriage been forced. Nor was he flattered by the remark that his parents still didn't know where he was heading. He was heading exactly where he'd been heading for the past six years. Exasperated, he reminded them that one could "hardly be ostracized for taking the intellect and aristocracy and family tradition seriously."[5]

Jean's parents responded to the belated news of the marriage somewhat differently, accepting it with a sort of "tepid tolerance," Jean wrote Hightower, quoting—or parodying—her mother's letter that they'd been "rather surprised, but it's O.K. Yesterday I invested in a new corset." Jean had been married three weeks now, and separated from Cal for nearly the same period, yet she felt experienced enough to tell Hightower what marriage was all about. "Even with respect, with awe of a superior mind and a shining talent," there was still the claustrophobia. Nor was there anything very remarkable about sex, which one might observe "in swine and high-school girls."[6]

In effect, she was banished from Kenyon those last two months while Cal finished up his degree. Worse, Cal was so busy with papers and exams that he failed to answer Jean's letters, so that she had to write Peter Taylor instead, telling him that she wanted to see Cal the minute he was through. Worse, Hightower was also "contemptibly marrying," so that she was completely alone "in any extramarital sense." In the meantime, she spent her days and nights out in the middle of Colorado reading the *Encyclopaedia Britannica* on Swedenborg, Astrology, and Cantharides, all the while wishing she were in Cleveland.[7]

Commencement at Kenyon was June 9. At the beginning of the month, Hightower married Bunny Cole, and the two of them headed west by train for California to sail for China, where Hightower planned to continue his Chinese studies. While the Hightowers were spending the night of June 6 in Omaha, Hightower was summoned by Jean. She had to see him at once, she insisted, to tell him a secret. What she told him, apparently, was that she had turned out to be frigid with Cal and did not think she could actually live with him. Hightower was still the one, she told him, and she asked him to leave his new wife and take her with him to China. Hightower calmed her down, then put her back on the train bound for Chicago and Cleveland.

"I graduated summa cum laude, phi beta kappa, highest honors in classics, first man in my class and valedictorian," Cal would write his mother shortly after graduation.[8] It was a way of reminding her that he'd kept his promise to do what he'd set out to do. As valedictorian, Lowell, with Jean present, proceeded to attack the hollow privilege of American private schools like his own St. Mark's, seeing in them Boston's fall from the eminence it had earned under figures like Jonathan Edwards, Hawthorne, Emerson, Thoreau, Parkman, and the line extending from John to Henry Adams. No longer could Boston claim to be the Athens of the New World. Yes, the New England aristocracy still had its wealth and other "special advantages," but it was merely an empty shell of its former glory, and could no longer claim to possess a "superior way of life." For any aristocracy to flourish, he went on, it had to continue to aspire after the best. There was a millenarian cast to his words, as if Oswald Spengler's prophecy of the decline of the West and Yeats's bleak vision in "The Second Coming" had finally come to pass. For even as he spoke, France was being overrun by Hitler's stormtroopers and the lights of civilization and tolerance were being extinguished all over Europe. What was the German Blitzkrieg, after all, but the destruction of a faded European aristocracy by the new Goths, as the world continued on its mindless cycle of "retrogression, advance and repetition."[9]

By late May, Cal learned that Ransom's plans to keep him and Jean on at Kenyon had fallen through, the administration having decided that Cal was too young yet to take on college classroom responsibilities. Ransom's next move was to use his connections with Cleanth Brooks and Robert Penn Warren at Louisiana State University to get Lowell a junior fellowship and Jean a typing job at the *Southern Review*. Months earlier, in fact, Ransom had written Brooks that there was "a strong man" at Kenyon, "the last of the Lowells bearing the name, due to give a good account of himself before he is done." If he was still "a bit slow and thorough," he nevertheless had "enormous critical sense."[10] Something was quickly found, and Stafford would later joke that Cal had wired her: "HAVE JOB. COME AT ONCE," only to learn that the job was for her.

The requirements for the junior fellowship were modest enough. Cal would take two courses each semester and receive a stipend of $30 a month. So, right after graduation, he and Jean left Kenyon with Taylor and travelled south to Taylor's home in Memphis. As the train pulled into Memphis, passing through the freightyard and the city's slums, Cal, himself in need of a haircut and a decent pair of shoes, waved his hand in the general direction of the slums and told Taylor that all of that would have to go. The Lowells spent a week as guests of Taylor's family before heading south by train to Baton Rouge, arriving there on the first day of summer. "The torch-pipes wasting waste gas all night," Lowell would recall thirty-five years later,

> *O Baton Rouge, your measureless student prospects,*
> *rats as long as my forearm regrouping toward*
> *the sewage cleansing on the open canals—*
> *the moisture mossing in the green seminar room*
> *where we catnapped,*
> *while Robert Penn Warren talked three hours*
> *on Machiavelli . . . the tyrannicide*
> *of princes, Cesare Borgia, Huey Long,*
> *citing fifty English and Italian sources—*
> *our dog-eat-dog days in isolationist America,*
> *devouring Stalin's unmeasured retreats,*
> *as if we had a conscience to be impartial.*[11]

On the evening of their arrival, Katherine Anne Porter invited them to her home for a mint julep and a taste of southern hospitality. Baton Rouge was "hot and steamy," Jean wrote Taylor, and the three-room apartment at 1106 Chimes Street, which the Warrens had just vacated, crawling with calf-sized cockroaches.[12] For his part, Cal reported to his mother that the people in Baton Rouge were "affable," the architecture "parvenue," the graduate work "tough but useful."[13] To his grandmother, he wrote that Baton Rouge was "inland, windless, waterless, suburban," a nexus of "iron pipes blazing with crude oil, palm-beachy trees and Huey Long's two million dollar sky-scraper capitol."[14] The campus itself, Huey Long's darling, was made up of immense twentieth-century fake-Mexican dormitories, a relief after the gray, Gothic-heavy architecture of Kenyon.[15]

Settled, they reported to the offices of the *Southern Review*. Cleanth Brooks, Penn Warren, and Albert Erskine, Jean wrote Hightower, ignoring what had happened between them in Omaha two weeks earlier, ran the magazine with a kind of editorial arrogance. "Letters from contributors are received with shrieks of laughter, mss. are sneered at, rejection slips go out furiously." At the moment Cal was working there too—rather ineptly, she noted—upset by the quality of writing he was finding in the submissions.[16] The magazine was then in its fifth year, already the leading quarterly of its kind in America, and it was preparing for a major offensive in the New Critics' campaign to convert the academic world to their kind of criticism: the close critical analysis of Modernist texts. To the north, Ransom was simultaneously preparing a symposium for the *Kenyon Review* on "Literature and the Professors." Both were scheduled for the fall.

Brooks and Erskine were easy enough to work for, Jean found, but the office itself was "a hogsty with an accumulation of years of manuscripts."[17] Years later she could still recall "the scorched smell" of the storeroom and how, "after going in to fetch paper or an early issue" of the magazine, she'd felt as if she "were groping up out of deep anaesthesia."[18] LSU itself was turning out to be just another university, all the talk centered on "language requirements for the Ph.D," the "deficiencies of the Freshman English curriculum," and the "necessity of subordinating historical scholarship to criticism" or the other way round, what matter, and Cal was already wishing they'd gone to China with the Hightowers. For six hours their first Saturday night there she and Cal had had to sit in Cleanth Brooks's home, with "food on our laps in a brightly lighted and much too small room . . . hearing those three things" from "delightful, charming, amusing" but academic people.

Then there were the college boys living all around them, "the genuine kind" that wore "funny clothes and at stated intervals hang pins on sorority girls." Cal, who would be taking classes with these boys in the fall, thought he was witnessing a new species, so different were they from Jarrell and Taylor. As for Jean, reduced to taking night classes to learn shorthand for her job, her life seemed to be becoming "annually more fogged" and her "retrogression" steadier. In a week she would turn twenty-five. At twenty-six, she wondered, what would she be? A telephone operator, or a receptionist in a city laundry?[19]

By August the furniture and sputum cups had arrived, and Cal could write Robie Macauley that he liked watching Jean fix up their apartment, puzzling where to put the "23 chairs and 22 imitation Navajo carpets" his relatives had sent them, until the apartment had been transformed from starkness to opulence.[20] It was all new to Cal, this world, he told his grandmother, including "a coeducational summerschool and a negro woman, named Loyola, who arrives at six-thirty every other day to give us a grand house-cleaning." There was, of course, the larger world beyond, and he was aware that it was only a matter of time before America was drawn into the war already raging in Europe and the Far East. When that war finally reached America, he told her, the draft would level everyone, and no one would have "good, unclouded prospects." But he was not, he reassured her, in school simply to mark time. He knew *exactly* what his vocation in life was. If war came and they wanted him, he would go. If they did not, he would continue "in this peaceful and sedentary occupation of university work."[21]

Besides fixing up the apartment and working full time, Jean also looked after visitors—I. A. Richards and Randall Jarrell were two—and prepared (as her mother had before her) to take in boarders. These were Peter Taylor, whom Cal and Jean had persuaded to undertake graduate work at LSU, and Taylor's girlfriend. The woman, who became Jean's assistant at the magazine, was—in Jean's eyes—"a great gauche lummox . . . from Memphis," and Taylor, though "considerably more attractive," someone in want of a brain.[22] But of course Taylor had a brain, and wit, and southern charm, and an affinity soon blossomed between Taylor and Stafford that often left Taylor's girl and Cal, who was still tongue-tied and ponderous when it came to social discourse, feeling excluded. Prose writers might be less elevated than poets, Stafford quipped, but they also had more fun. Since neither Peter nor Cal seemed to be able even to boil water, each noon Jean walked home from her job to make lunch for them, often finding them still in their pajamas. "Except for meals and two games of chess after dinner," she complained, her husband did "nothing but read." She was sure he was going to "die soon and die blind."[23]

At one party at the Warrens that fall, Cal, Jean, and Taylor all got drunk. "I'd never had that much to drink in my life," Taylor would recall, and when Cleanth Brooks drove them back home, they were still trying to carry on "a conversation . . . about Donne and Herbert and all of that" when Jean suddenly "opened her purse, said, 'Well, I think John Donne—' and proceeded to throw up in her purse." When they reached the apartment, Taylor, going to thank Brooks for the ride, also threw up over the trunk of the car. Then, as

Brooks drove away, Taylor got his jacket off and began running after him, trying to wipe the mess off. When he finally walked back into the apartment, Jean was "in the bathroom, washing dollar bills."[24]

Jean's take on the evening was different. "Peter and I got incredibly drunk," she would remember, "& exchanged words over the extent of Peter's love for me & the peril of it so that Cal, who spent the evening talking with Mr. Brooks about belief, did not speak to Peter for 1 week thereafter."[25] There were other English Department parties as well, at all of which, as was the custom in those days, everyone drank too much. But there were also day trips with friends out to the cemetery at St. Francisville to see the Spanish moss on the live oaks, or rides on the ferry back and forth across the Mississippi, listening to boogie-woogie tunes on the ferry jukebox. Once, when Cal insisted on talking about how much Anne Dick reminded him of Bette Davis, Jean told him that if he mentioned her name one more time she promised to do him violence.

But every time she looked into a mirror, it was Jean who was reminded of Cal's violence. In a letter to Hightower at Halloween, she mentioned in passing that she was once again "in the hands of a nose surgeon."[26] Three weeks before, Blair and Parker—en route by car to visit Mexico—had stopped by to see them. Then they'd all piled into Parker's car and driven down to New Orleans for a night on the town. After dinner and drinks, they stayed the night at a local hotel. But in the early hours of the morning, while Blair was watching Frank whirl his pajamas around and around the overhead fan he'd tied them to, Jean came down in her nightgown, sat on the bed, and began to tell them how awful Cal was. There'd been a fight and Jean had walked out. After a while, Cal came down and ordered her back to their room, where the argument continued until Cal suddenly lashed out and broke Jean's nose for a second time.

When she came downstairs again, blood was streaming down her face and onto her nightgown. Sickened, Blair raced her to the hospital. When Parker later asked him if he really did do it, Cal had said, "oh yes, he sort of didn't know what he was doing yet he sort of did. He felt the nose go under his fist." Whatever had caused him to lash out like that, perhaps jealousy, perhaps being upset over her drinking, he seemed to show no compunction. He would not be cowed as his father had been. Instead, as he had that night in Cambridge, he simply disassociated himself from what had happened.[27]

Afterwards, when Jean had trouble breathing through her nose, Cal would tell her she breathed too much. No wonder that by November she was near despair. "My life has become subordinate to all other lives to which I am related," she wrote Hightower, until it was now merely "a monstrous pattern of struggle against rules and frustration so that my desire for anarchy has never been so passionate and the possibility of it . . . never . . . so remote." No day passed without anger; no night "with any articulated hope for the next day."

Since coming here, she had not had "one experience of joy or one hour of solitude."[28] Her job, the house, and a husband who did nothing but read had left her with no time for her own creativity. Worse, she didn't even care any more. By then, rum-based Cuba Libres had become her one companion.

By the time fall classes began, Cal had discovered a plethora of critical methodologies operating at the university, including, besides the New Criticism, "the aesthetic approach," "metaphysical poetry," and "drama in the lyric." The students were "weak and worthy," but "Brooksandwarren" excellent. He was especially taken with Red Warren, with the result that he had begun reading English theology, which was providing him with a critical vocabulary of his own, one that employed—he told Tate—such theoretical terms as "heresy," "diabolic," and "frivolous gnosticism." His new critical terminology, he joked, was enough to "worry the solemn and liberal English majors." Among the texts: Etienne Gilson's *Philosophy of Thomas Aquinas* and *The Spirit of Medieval Philosophical Experience* (the key text he read that year at LSU), Cardinal Newman, Jacques Maritain, E. I. Watkin ("the best English philosopher, a bit off the Thomist line"), Pascal, and Hopkins. He also struck up a friendship with Patrick Quinn, a Catholic student studying philosophy.[29]

Brooks soon saw in Lowell a brilliant reader of Milton and a serious critic in the making. For a while, in fact, Lowell seriously considered editing George Herbert's poetry for LSU press. Moreover, for two hours each afternoon over a period of several months, Cal and Warren read Dante in the original to each other in Warren's office. That fall Cal also took Warren's seminar in Sixteenth-Century Literature. He "was always a naif of one kind or another," Warren would say of Lowell. A "calculated" naif, who had "charm and . . . great intelligence" and who "read widely." He was also "wonderfully good company," though Warren couldn't help noting something unstable there as well.[30]

Late that fall Warren asked Father Maurice Schexnayder, college chaplain for the Catholic students on campus, to talk to his class on the Reformation. Father Schexnayder, forty-three, Pennsylvania Dutch, tall, gaunt, and austere, so impressed Cal that day that he followed him out into the hall afterwards and asked for instruction in Catholicism. Forty years later, in her short story/ memoir "An Influx of Poets," Jean would describe a thinly disguised version of Cal: "Half a year after we were married, [Cal], immersed in the rhythms of Gerard Manley Hopkins the poet, was explosively ignited by Gerard Manley Hopkins the Jesuit and, as my mother would have said, he was off on a tear."[31] By sheer dint of will, Cal had already transformed himself into a scholar, a classicist, a Fugitive manqué, a critic, a poet. Perhaps—like his beloved Hopkins—he was ready now to become a saint.

"Cal is becoming a Catholic," a bemused, ironic Stafford wrote Hightower on February 10, 1941. "A real one with all the trimmings, all the fish on Friday and the observance of fasts and confessions and grace before meals and prayers before bed." As an undergraduate she too had been attracted to Catholicism and had taken instruction from a priest. Then, through what she called her own "indolence," she had fallen away soon after being received into the Church. Now she stood off, watching the changes in her husband, wondering at, even admiring, his tenacity. At the same time she was appalled "to hear him talk piously and to see in him none of the common Christian virtues [such] as pity and kindness but only . . . fire-breathing righteousness." She was "tired of his moods and disapproval and complaints." Tired too of his bullying and cajoling. Since coming to Baton Rouge Cal had written almost no poetry. Now he told Jean that it was no longer important whether or not he became a writer. If he could not write devotional poetry—the poetry of Dante, Milton, Herbert, and Hopkins, the poetry of Eliot—then he would write nothing.[32] The descendant of Puritan and Unitarian and Episcopalian clergy, the descendant of Jonathan Edwards, the man who had once told Taylor that Catholicism was the religion of Irish servant girls, was about to become a Catholic himself.

At the same time, however, Jean was becoming increasingly ill: fever, continual coughing, chest pains that kept her in bed—on the doctor's and Cal's orders—for a month. The doctors diagnosed tuberculosis, due in part to the lush rankness of Baton Rouge. For, lovely as Louisiana was, she wrote Hightower in March, it was also "lethal, teeming with serpents, disease, spiders, tainted meat." In truth she was relieved to have this respite, for it gave her a chance to begin writing the novel which would become *Boston Adventure*. It also gave her a chance to think about what was happening to her and Cal now that he was fired with the zeal of the convert.

"I have some new opinions of life," she told Hightower. She knew she'd been drifting for years now and needed "some higher authority" to guide her. What she could not yet do was accept Catholicism as the "agent" of that guidance, especially when she felt Cal was forcing his solution on her. At the same time she knew he was "doing the sound thing by going into the Church and going the whole way." Perhaps she would "come around in time," for she saw "no other institution as rewarding." As for Hightower's own brand of orderly anarchy, that seemed as worthless to her as her own chaotic variety.[33]

On March 29, 1941, Lowell was received into the Church. Father Schexnayder baptized him in Christ the King Chapel on the LSU campus, Patrick Quinn standing as sponsor. Jean was there, and Taylor, and a handful of other students, Quinn would remember. "It was the full ceremony and vows were taken," so that all seemed "forbidding, oppressive," and overwhelming in view of the "magnitude of the promises" Cal was making. Then, afterwards, Cal went into the confessional with Father Schexnayder and stayed there for the next half hour while the others waited awkwardly outside.[34] A week later, concerned that his marriage might be sacramentally invalid, Lowell insisted on Jean and he being remarried by Father Schexnayder.

Jean went along with Cal's new passion, Taylor would recall, for the most part keeping a lighthearted view of it all, though she did have her "serious moments about it."[35] Cal, on the other hand, was totally serious about his conversion, and that meant Mass at six-thirty each morning, grace before and after meals, benediction in the evening, two rosaries a day. In April he spent a week in retreat at a nearby Jesuit church. Years later, Jean would let slip in an interview that, while they'd had glorious sex before they'd married, she and Cal never slept together again after they were remarried in the Church.[36]

By mid-April she was coughing up blood and thoroughly miserable with her life in Baton Rouge. To make matters worse, Taylor was by then back in Memphis. Cal himself was away more and more now, off visiting friends, which left Jean alone to work in the vaporous offices of the *Southern Review* with a "goddamn dunghill-minded, vain, ignorant, stupid, asinine, awkward . . . bitch" of an assistant.[37] It was time for her to clear out and breathe in once again the clear mountain air of Colorado. "It's got to be you and me," she wrote Hightower, drunk. "Make plans. Send yours by clipper." She had money and Cal was sure to be drafted soon. "Get rid of your encumbrance"— she meant Mrs. Hightower—"because oh dear God I cannot live this way without your help."[38] That was on April 17. Two days later she was on her way to her sister's ranch in Hayden for an extended rest cure.

By late June, recovered from what had turned out to be a bout of pneumonia rather than tuberculosis, Jean was back in Baton Rouge with Cal. By then they both knew Jean's condition would not allow them to remain in Louisiana. They toyed with the idea of Cal's returning to Harvard, until he himself decided against it. It was imperative that he find a Catholic community, he explained, and Harvard was hardly the place. "I couldn't begin to tell you, convincingly, the extent to which [Cal] will go for a conviction," Jean wrote Hightower that August. Once again she was so distraught she thought she was "cracking up completely, which," she added, "I have done several times anyway with nearly disastrous results." Cal was now reading nothing but religious books—and only those with the imprimatur—and would see only those movies approved by the Censor. Each Saturday he went to confession, and talked of "*nothing* but the existence of God." For the past two weeks he'd been after her every day to make a retreat, until she was ready to do another "Iowa City disappearing act."

The truth was that she and Cal differed vastly over the idea of the Church.

Hers was an image of "grand dignity, superb intellectual exercise . . . a composite of ritual and philosophy in which God, the saints and the angels" remained "absolutely timeless." No wonder she was put off by the "provincial, pious, embarrassing" way in which Catholics actually practiced their faith. Like the biblical Ruth, she confessed to Hightower, she would always stand outside, "in alien corn."[39] Thirty years later, Cal would remember Jean as she'd been then, their

> *days of the great books, scraping and Roman mass—*
> *your confessions had such a vocabulary*
> *you were congratulated by the priests.*
> *I pretended my impatience was concision.*[40]

They decided on New York. With the help of Father Schexnayder, Cal found a job working for the Catholic publishing house of Sheed & Ward, at 63 Fifth Avenue on the edge of Greenwich Village. Two weeks before the Lowells left for New York, Randall Jarrell, who had just married Mackie Langham in Nashville, brought his bride to Baton Rouge to see Cal and meet Jean. For her part, Jean dismissed Jarrell as "the queerest looking thing" she'd ever seen.[41]

By summer, after a fallow half year, Cal had begun writing poems again, poems of a devotional, or at least millennialist, cast. One of these was "The Protestant Dead in Boston," which showed the influence of both Hart Crane and Milton in a diction heavy, polysyllabic, latinate, epical, punning, and allusive, as if the rhythms were dragging chains behind them. Yet, in spite of his conversion, Cal sounded less like the Catholic Hopkins and rather more like the Puritan Cotton Mather. The result was a parody of Tate's style at its most unremittingly baroque. Lowell was still only part way to realizing "The Quaker Graveyard in Nantucket," the poem these lines seemed struggling to become:

> *Boston cemetery is the world—here in the heyday,*
> *the spirit hawked elections, and the decemvirate*
> *of Morals, Ten Commandments, fostered*
> *the perfection of a faction, regimented a mortal*
> *yard of provincial, enterprising, prolific*
> *Protestants. These dissenters, now the servants*
> *of the earth, were fatally chosen and beatified:*
> *secured from temporal torrents, the ocean's*
> *masterless surges, the contagion of human*
> *contact, their lives were as single as their skeletons. . . .*[42]

He kept busy with a long satire on England, though clearly satire was not where his strength lay. He also wrote one poem that spring which John Berry-

man would learn about years later from Jean, and which became for Berryman
a comic touchstone about Cal's penchant for continually revising his poems.
Cal had begun the work by celebrating Jean's confirmation into the Church
("Jean, / Strong soldier, kneels and takes the bishop's dub") and had ended
by revising it into a poem entitled, "Nonsense Verses to a Whore."[43]

On September 1, 1941, the Lowells left for New York by train, first stop-
ping off in Memphis to see Taylor, who'd been drafted into the Army that
June. All of Cal's friends, in fact, were in the armed services now, including
Blair and Frank. Since seeing Lowell and Jean ten months before, Blair had
worked for the *St. Louis Despatch* until being called up in February. In May he
too had married, and was still living with his family in Princeton when the
Lowells came through. Parker, on the other hand, had gone directly from
Mexico back home and then on to Canada. In June 1940 he was in Paris
driving an ambulance when the German Panzer divisions moved on the city
and he'd been lucky to get out of the country. Both he and his father were
eager to fight the Germans and, unwilling to wait for the United States to enter
the war, had joined up, Frank with the Canadian Black Watch, his father
with the British Naval Reserve, doing destroyer duty in the Western Approaches. In the summer of 1941, while Commander Bob moldered at home,
Frank's father had been killed when a German torpedo struck the deck of his
destroyer. Now, in the late summer of that year, Frank was in England preparing for the surprise invasion of Dieppe.[44]

When Cal and Jean reached Greenwich Village, they booked into the Hotel
Albert on University Place and 10th for a week, then moved to 63 West 11th
Street, a short distance from Sheed & Ward. The publishing house had been
founded in London in 1927 and specialized in Catholic writers from the
medieval philosophers to Dorothy Day and Fulton J. Sheen. Lowell's main
responsibilities were to write jacket blurbs and copy-edit manuscripts, including Frank Sheed's translation of Augustine's *Confessions*. Jean would remember working on that translation

> 12 hour days, from dark and wintry seven until seven in the small, English-cool
> bare and cluttered office in that old house with its broad, commanding marble
> stairway, our smudged windows overlooking 5th Ave. as it peters out below 14th
> St. . . . My typewriter was tall and stiff and [Frank] Sheed, forever in overshoes
> and sometimes in a dinner jacket in which he had slept in the back office,
> translated indefatigably and excellently and with so little evident delight that
> everything about him—including his faith—came to me to seem learned rather
> than experienced.[45]

Cal liked his colleagues at Sheed & Ward, but, as Jean told Hightower, he
quickly found them "less Catholic and less intellectual" than himself. Cal really

Arthur Winslow, Lowell's maternal grandfather. "It seemed spontaneous and proper," Lowell would acknowledge in *Life Studies*, "for Mr. MacDonald, the farmer,/ Karl, the chauffeur, and even my Grandmother/ to say, 'Your Father.' They meant my Grandfather." [*Harry Ransom Humanities Research Center, University of Texas*]

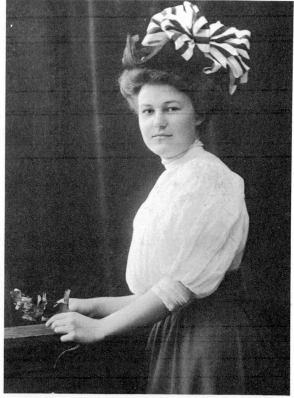

Charlotte Devereux Winslow in 1907, age eighteen. She throve, she thought, under the iron hand of her father, and measured all men by him. [*Harry Ransom Humanities Research Center, University of Texas*]

Robert Traill Spence Lowell, Sr., in the uniform of a naval officer; Charlotte Lowell; and Robert Traill Spence Lowell, Jr., in Navy blouse and shorts. 1920. [*Harry Ransom Humanities Research Center, University of Texas*]

Robert Lowell at five, 1922. [*Harry Ransom Humanities Research Center, University of Texas*]

Robert Lowell at about sixteen, 1933. [*Harry Ransom Humanities Research Center, University of Texas*]

Frank Parker and Robert Lowell, both seventeen, as upper-form counselors at Brantwood Camp in Peterborough, New Hampshire, August 1934. "Moody, solitary, antisocial, Cal nonetheless wanted to prove" that he could do anything he set out to do, including being "a good counselor," Parker would recall forty-five years later. Cal took his job "with a seriousness that tolerated no frivolous humor, and was extremely put out if his hut [the Mohawks] was not the first—for that meant to him he had not *done the work.*" [*Courtesy of Frank Parker*]

Robert Lowell *(top row, far left)*, substitute tackle on St. Mark's varsity football squad, late November 1934. At seventeen he weighs 160 and is a shade over six feet. By sheer will he played four games against boys 30 pounds heavier to earn his varsity letter. Frank Parker, at five eight and 135 pounds, played halfback from the sidelines. Blair Clark opted to become the squad's manager. Somehow, St. Mark's went undefeated against all six opponents that season. Halfback Jimmy Fearon, 185 pounds, the team's captain, holds a football with the final score against their arch rival, Groton. [*Harry Ransom Humanities Research Center, University of Texas*]

"A brackish reach of shoal off Madaket," Lowell would begin "The Quaker Graveyard in Nantucket," thinking back to his Nantucket summers in 1935 and 1936. Blair Clark snapped this picture of Parker and Lowell out back of their monastic shack next to the Coast Guard Station at Madaket on Nantucket in the summer of '36. Here Lowell pondered Milton while insisting that he and his friends—*mens sana in corpore sano*—survive on a diet of natural grain *Bekus Puddy,* raw honey, and fried eels. [*Courtesy of Frank Parker*]

Caroline Gordon, Janice Biala, Ford Madox Ford, and Allen Tate on the Tates' lawn at Benfolly, Clarksville, Tennessee, in June 1937, at the time when the twenty-year-old Lowell pitched his Sears, Roebuck tent there. When this photograph was snapped, Lowell was "not on speaking terms with Mr. Ford," because, as Lowell told his mother, "he is afraid I will write memoirs 30 or 40 years from now in which I will describe him as an over-stout, gouty old gentleman deluded by the poetry of Christina Rossetti and potentialities of the ideogram." Ford needn't have worried, however, for when Lowell came to write his elegy for the "master, mammoth mumbler" twenty years later, he ended by addressing him simply as "a kind man" who had "died in want." [*Division of Rare and Manuscript Collections, Cornell University Library*]

Robert Lowell, Jean Stafford, and Peter Taylor in New Orleans, 1940. When Hardwick sent him this picture among others in a scrapbook in the spring of 1973, Lowell thanked her for the "artfully arranged pages, sequences, like my long poems, full of profundity for me if no one else. Way back, I have . . . Peter and me and Jean in New Orleans, looking hung over, except unbelievably for Jean." [*Harry Ransom Humanities Research Center, University of Texas*]

Frank Parker and his cousin, Anne Dick, Lowell's first fiancée, in Boston, 1941. "I don't know how much Anne has told you," the nineteen-year-old Lowell wrote Parker from Nantucket that summer of 1936, "but we are engaged. . . . I love her and know her as deeply and as much as anyone could in a few weeks, but must admit that she has not yet the same reality to me as you have." [*Courtesy of Frank Parker*]

Damariscotta Mills, Maine, July 1946. Lowell, twenty-nine, holding one of the three kittens from Oranges' litter which Delmore Schwartz sent Jean Stafford for her birthday. Half of John Berryman, thirty-one, is visible to the left. When the Lowells closed up the house that September, their marriage in shambles, Cal rowed out into Damariscotta Lake and—according to Jean—dropped the kittens in a gunnysack over the side of the boat. [*University of Minnesota*]

FACING PAGE: Allen Tate, Marcella Winslow, a friend of Tate's, and Robert Lowell in Monteagle, Tennessee, 1943. From June 1942 to early July 1943, Lowell, Stafford, Caroline Gordon, and Allen Tate worked on their various poems and novels. It was here that Stafford wrote much of *Boston Adventure* and Lowell the poems that would make up his first book, *Land of Unlikeness*. [*Harry Ransom Humanities Research Center, University of Texas*]

Jean, thirty, in her Heidelberg braids and Cal in a lumberjack shirt at Damariscotta Mills, August 1946. The strain of their imminent breakup is caught in this overexposed snapshot, probably taken by Gertrude Buckman, Delmore Schwartz's ex-wife. "The clever quicksilver, the heartless fey, the no-woman, the bedeviller," Stafford would remember her thirty years later, after Lowell himself was gone, the memory of that loss still raw and vivid. [*Courtesy, Houghton Library*]

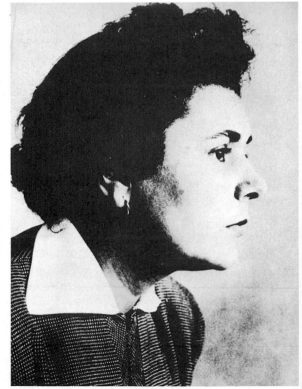

Elizabeth Bishop in 1946, as she looked when Lowell and she first met at Randall Jarrell's apartment, Bishop "tall, long, brown-haired, shy but full of ideas and anecdote as now," Lowell wrote in 1973, he still "largely invisible" even to himself, both "swimming in our young age, with the water coming down on us, and we were gulping." Asking her to marry him, he finally told her in the summer of '57, just before writing "Skunk Hour," was "the one towering change, the other life that might have been." [*Photograph by Joseph Breitenbach, Special Collections, Vassar College Libraries*]

was "a catch," she added, hoping they realized who they'd hired, "for he edits mercilessly and from the looks of their proofs, they have lacked just that." Jean herself was working "part time" as Frank Sheed's secretary. And while Sheed got along well with Jean, his relations with Cal remained problematic. First of all, he didn't care for Cal's devotional verse. And then there was Sheed's new business manager, who thought Cal some "veritable messiah, . . . destined to lead us all out of the paths of sin and war," which sentiments gave Sheed the creeps. Cal himself found the messianic notion rather splendid.[46]

Lowell, still fired by his conversion, worked twice as hard as he needed to: late into the night, as well as on Saturdays, when the office was closed. For a time he took typing lessons at the WPA night school four nights a week. Their first Sunday in New York he and Jean had gone to Mass "at a queer dirty little St. Anne church," and Jean had been appalled to find a sign on the altar rail near the relic which read: "Please use towel before and after kissing the relic," for the towel itself was filthy. In fact, she complained to Taylor, all New York seemed filthy. Moreover, Cal, anxious to live a life of poverty, had hoped to move into the filthiest apartment he could find, where, the landlord had assured them, "the walls were disinfected twice a week. He probably should have added that the Morgue came twice a week, too, to collect the murdered babies, it was that nasty."[47]

Much better was the apartment she herself had found on 11th Street in what she called a "respectable" neighborhood. It helped too when Cal learned that their new landlord and his wife were Catholic intellectuals and refugees from Germany, the landlord having served time in prison on "grounds of high treason" against the Nazi government.[48] In mid-September it was down to Princeton to see Tate and meet R. P. Blackmur, both of whom had been there for the past two years teaching creative writing in an experimental program funded by the Carnegie Foundation. Blackmur, Jean had noticed, had the peculiar habit of talking to no one when he spoke, the only interesting comment he'd made all evening being that one could buy the complete works of Henry James unbound for seven dollars.

Since Jean was working only part time, Cal insisted she also do Catholic volunteer work. Soon she found herself walking downtown to the dilapidated offices of Dorothy Day's *Catholic Worker* on Mott Street in the Bowery. It was frightening, she told Taylor, having to walk alone "through the kind of slums you do not believe exist when you see them in the movies, in an atmosphere that was nearly asphyxiating. The Worker office was full of the kind of camaraderie which frightens me to death and I was immediately put at a long table between a Negro and a Chinese to fold papers, a tiring and filthy job. The second time it was about the same except that Mott St. seemed even more depressing and that time I typed." When she told Cal how run down the place was, he became so excited he decided they should move there at once. It took a priest friend, at Jean's prompting, to tell Cal that his work should be "intellectual." After that, he no longer insisted that Jean work in the Bowery. From now on she could work "in a friendship house in Harlem under a Baroness de something."[49] So insistent was Cal on living simply that it would take another seven months before they could splurge on a second-hand record player and a single album—the Haydn Harpsichord Concerto in D Major—and four prints, all chosen by Cal: a Fra Angelico *Annunciation,* a St. Francis, a St. Thomas More, and a St. Jerome.

When the Japanese attacked Pearl Harbor on December 7, 1941, the Lowells were living in New York, Cal immersed in Catholic apologetics, Jean working and writing *Boston Adventure.* Three months later, Cal tried to enlist in the Navy and was rejected because of his myopia. That winter Eberhart sent him his verse play based on Cal as a malfunctioning student at St. Mark's. Hurt and angered by the unflattering portrait, Cal managed to take the high road. When he wrote Cousin Ghormley, he quoted Eliot's line from "Burnt Norton" that human kind could not "bear very much reality," the "reality" being not so much Eberhart's attack on him as the way in which Eberhart had "substantiated"—in the language of the Scholastics which Lowell had adopted—Cal's flaws by reference to the type of the dirty, introspective, nail-biting student his former teacher had drawn. Speaking for himself, Cal welcomed "any criticism, public or private, direct or artistic," which might help him better see himself. But he did object to the fact that the play would "rather fruitlessly wound" his parents. Reduce anyone to a stereotypic pattern of "manners, mannerisms or recorded acts," Cal added, and the satirist won every time.[50]

In late April, Jarrell flew into town, staying with the Lowells in New York and making two "lightning-paced trips," one to Princeton and the other to Cape Cod to see Edmund Wilson. Randall, Jean noted, had turned out to be "a rather exhausting joy to see."[51] On the 30th, she and Cal went down to Princeton to hear Randall deliver his first public lecture. It was called "Levels and Opposites," part of a series of talks on "Structure in Poetry." Waiting in Pennsylvania Station for the train down to Princeton, they ran into Philip Rahv, editor of *Partisan Review,* and his wife, Natalie. Thirty years later, Cal would recall that first meeting, when he'd seen the Rahvs emerge out of "the black brown smelly barrenness" of the station. Somehow they became "instant friends," though on the trip down the Lowells had been "too shy" and the Rahvs "too laconic" for much conversation to pass between them. They were, Cal would remember, "the first non-Catholic intellectuals" he'd met since coming to New York.

Cal would also remember Randall's lecture, bristling as it did with quotations from Kenneth Burke, Arnold Toynbee, and Marx. It was lumpily abstract, hard to follow and fifteen minutes too long. It was fireworks, so much so that Randall would often pause and look smilingly at his audience. He assumed our sympathy against wittily disguised opponents. Sometimes he would chuckle. As he stepped from the platform, intoxicated—he didn't drink—Allen [Tate] came up, took his arm, and said, "Randall, the contents of your piece are wonderful, but take it from an old hand, your delivery is appalling."[52]

Afterwards, Cal and Jean went to the Tate's home where Jean signed a contract for *Boston Adventure,* Caroline Gordon turning the signing into a small ritual by placing a lighted candle on either side of the paper. Robert Giroux, as editor with Harcourt, Brace, brought the contract for Jean to sign. It called for a $500 advance: $250 on signing, $250 on delivery. At last she had a real contract, she told some friends, and "not the twaddle" she'd "had with the *Atlantic Monthly.*"[53]

At the end of June the Lowells joined the Tates in Monteagle, Tennessee, a sort of turn-of-the-century Chatauqua five miles north of Sewanee. For the next year the four of them would live simply and write, Tate working on the sonnets for *Winter Sea,* Gordon on a novel, Jean on *Boston Adventure,* and Cal first on a biography of Jonathan Edwards and then—when that refused to ignite—on the poems that would make up his first book: *Land of Unlikeness.* Cal, whose poetry had mostly lain fallow for the past several years, hoped to recapture the spirit of that first, crucial southern summer five years before. He also worked with Tate on an anthology of English lyric poetry, spending weeks and weeks reading the sixteenth- and seventeenth-century English poets, whose verse forms Tate would use in several of the poems he was writing, including "Ode to Our Young Pro-Consuls of the Air." During a shortlived spurt of inspiration late that summer, Lowell wrote an "Ode to the New England Seamen," borrowing from the poets he was reading a wire-tight six-line rhymed stanza (abccab). Part of the poem memorialized General MacArthur and the outnumbered and trapped American defenders on Bataan:

> *And while McArthur courts*
> *Immeasurable blessings*
> > *From fox-hole of Bataan,*
> > *And bluff Japan*
> *Handsomely snorts:*
> *Add Homa to your greetings.*

During the summer of 1942, Peter Taylor was stationed at Fort Oglethorpe, just over the line in Georgia, and he managed to get up to Monteagle to see

Cal and Jean that July. Cal he found as Catholic as ever. Several times a week the carless Lowells took a bus to the nearest Catholic church in Winchester, a dozen miles away. Because they had to fast until after communion, Jean packed a breakfast for them while they waited for the bus back to Monteagle. One Sunday morning, as they were getting ready to go into Winchester, Jean told Cal about a dream she'd had in which she'd been reading the missal of a saint inexplicably named St. Rook, a "deep old Jew." Outraged at what he took to be Jean's flippancy, Cal ordered her to read the Gospel for the day.[54] Another time Cal diagnosed a depression Jean was experiencing as a "dark night of the soul," and told her to read St. John of the Cross. Instead, she read "The Interior Castle" of St. Teresa of Avila, St. John's close friend, and—to her surprise—found she had actually gained much of sustenance from Teresa's writings.[55]

Then, in August, Jean developed bronchial problems once again and had to be taken to a specialist in Nashville, who advised Cal that she was very ill and would have to be admitted to the hospital at once. Cal stayed in Nashville to be near her, but, since they'd expected to return home the same night, he had only the suit he was wearing, over which he proceeded to spill ice cream his second day there, so that by the time Jean was released five days later, Cal looked a mess. The infection, he insisted, was due to Jean's nonstop smoking, and he kept badgering her until she reminded him that the real problem was her crumpled nose and they both damn well knew who'd broken that.[56]

That first night in Nashville Cal had gone to a party with several friends he'd met through the Tates. Considering how the war was going, they warned him, it was just a matter of weeks before he was drafted. As soon as he could, therefore, he went into Winchester to enroll in Army Officers Training School, but again he was rejected because of his eyesight. That same month Frank Parker landed on the beaches of Dieppe with the British-Canadian forces. Half of the 2,500 men involved in the attack were killed outright and the rest taken prisoner, Parker among them. He would spend the rest of the war doing forced labor in a beet factory and as a farmhand in Germany. But immediately after his capture he was chained to a wall, where he spent his days dreaming of Cal as Commander in Chief of Allied forces coming to set him free.[57]

In November, Jean took the bus into Chattanooga to spend an afternoon with Peter Taylor, who came up from Fort Oglethorpe to meet her there. They had a terrific time rehashing the old days, except that Jean became so drunk that the owner of the restaurant had to ask Taylor to escort her out. Taylor stared at him. How could the man be so insensitive? Couldn't he *see* that his sister was crippled? With that the abashed owner retreated. Jean was still drunk when the bus dropped her off at Monteagle. When he saw the condition his wife was in, Cal forbade her to drink any more. He also forbade her reading the newspapers or any novels "except Dostoevsky, Proust, James and Tolstoy." In making these "prohibitions," a contrite Jean wrote Taylor afterwards, Cal was "quite justified if tyrannical," and she was not complaining, for she knew better than anyone what "a prize jackass" she was when she drank.[58] Cal in fact screened everything, including the food. Once, when Jean made him soup on a Friday, he suspected the presence of meat stock and proceeded to dump the whole pot into the sink.

Most of that fall Cal was occupied with reading up on the life of Jonathan Edwards as he prepared to undertake a biography of his Puritan ancestor. But that November, reading through Randall's first book of poems, *Blood for a Stranger,* he finally dropped the idea of a biography and began again to write poems. Jean had seen too many of these "fits and starts" over the last several years to think Cal's new spurt of inspiration would last very long, but this time it did.[59] On December 8, the Feast of the Immaculate Conception, Lowell wrote a poem invoking Christ's mother, his lines despairing at how little the human blood lust had changed in six millennia, as the newspaper and radio coverage of the war in Europe and Asia revealed each day. Again he employed an intricate metrical rhyme scheme. The new poem not only showed the influence of the Marian Hopkins but of Tate as well:

> *Bring me tonight no axe to grind*
> *On wheels of the Utopian mind:*
> > *Six thousand years*
> *Cain's blood has drummed into my ears,*
> *Shall I wring plums from Plato's bush*
> *While Burma's and Bizerta's dead*
> > *Must puff and push*
> > *Blood into bread?*
>
> *Oh, if soldiers mind you well*
> *They shall find you are their belle*
> > *And belly too:*
> *Christ's bread and beauty came by you,*
> *Celestial Hoyden, when Our Lord*
> *Gave up the weary Ghost and died,*
> > *You shook a sword*
> > *From his torn side.*[60]

In another poem, "The Crucifix," he attacked Roosevelt—"the nation's head-piece"—for plunging America into what he read as a reckless war. The language here is both apocalyptic and oracular, and recalls not only Wilfred

Owen's *"Dulce et Decorum Est"* but also the New World prophet calling up the terrible cost of a nation arming itself with the dragon's steel scales— Sherman tanks and B-17s and armored half-tracks—while the corpse of Jesus, who had turned the other cheek, lay naked:

> *now the dragon's*
> *Litter buckles on steel-scales and puffs*
> *Derision like confetti from ten thousand*
> *Scrap-heaps, munition pools and bee-hive camps:*
> *"Pleasant and gracious it is to die for America."*[61]

In the 1930s, Lowell would later sum up, there seemed to be three kinds of poetry possible for him to write. There was "a rather watered-down imitation of 19th century poetry," a popular poetry that had gone completely dead. There was also the leftist poetry of the *New Masses* variety, pro-Marxist and "usually quite pro-Russian." And finally there was the group to which he himself belonged: a hard, classical poetry derived from Yeats and Eliot in England, and Ransom and Tate in the States. "A rather strange position was built up," Lowell would explain, where "poetry was considered a form of knowledge, at least as valid as scientific knowledge" and where "the whole man would be represented in the poem." A poetry of classical form combined with felt experience was what mattered, so that now the Romantics became the enemy. Nor did poetry have anything to do with causes. It did not try "to persuade people to do anything better or to make the world better." Rather, it provided a catharsis, a purging by pity and terror. It was a way of looking at poetry only intelligible in the 1930s, he would come to see, and served as a counter against "being swept" into any cause other than poetry.[62]

Time passed: guests, picnics, literary discussions, fishing expeditions. After-noons and evenings were spent playing three-handed bridge or Russian Bank with Zov—the Lowells' name for Tate—who played both games wretchedly. Pantherina, the Tates' large black cat, had a litter of kittens. In January 1943, A. Lawrence Lowell of Harvard died. And even at this distance Mrs. Lowell— or Charlotte Hideous, as Jean had taken to calling her—continued to grate on her. "She would have a person think she was down to her last hundred thou-sand from the letters she writes us," Jean complained to Taylor. True, the woman had helped them out with money, but it was hard to keep hearing about how hard up Charlotte claimed to be.[63] There were also the little annoy-ances at Monteagle which bothered her: Cal's making jokes about her large feet, a condition he called Megaposity; the "tuneless singing" of Caroline and her teenage daughter, Nancy; the thin beaverboard partition which separated the Lowells' bedroom from the girl's.[64]

Nor did Jean much like being treated as a child by the Tates, so that things were bound to come to a head as they finally did that winter, when Jean lost her temper and lashed out against the imperious Gordon. The argument was so disconcerting to Jean—it was the first time in her life she'd ever burst out like that at anyone but Cal or her family—that she was left "completely bewildered" and suffered "a violent attack of vertigo."[65] To amuse himself, perhaps to surround himself with a protective layer, Cal gave Bear names to Jean (she became "Eanbeaner") and to everyone else in the Tate household, and made a recording of his alter ego, "Arms of the Law." "The Tates, when we first knew them," Jean would later recall, "were delightful company, they were wise critics, they were helpful, they seemed fond of us. I remembered the anguish of the year in Tennessee and I was struck in a heap to think of how Caroline had always said she thought of us as her children, because we *were* children, we have been everyone's children."[66]

But by early 1943, things began looking up for both Cal and Jean. In February, Jean sent off a 250,000-word draft of *Boston Adventure* to Harcourt, Brace (in mid-March it would be sent back to weed out some of the Proustianisms, but with the manuscript also came a check for $250, the rest of the advance, sealing the book's acceptance). And Cal, after four years of seeing nothing published, suddenly had eleven poems accepted: four by Philip Rahv for inclusion in the *Partisan Review* ("Song of the Boston Nativity," "Christmas Eve in Time of War," "Salem," and "Concord"), two by Oscar Williams for his anthology of American poetry, then four more by the *Sewanee Review* ("On the Eve of the Feast of the Immaculate Conception, 1942," "In Memory of Arthur Winslow," "Leviathan," and "Dea Roma") and finally "Satan's Confession," which Ransom accepted for the *Kenyon Review*.

By March, Cal had written sixteen new poems, nearly all of them anti-war, apocalyptic, and prophetic in the style of Jeremiah and the Old Testament prophets, all of them as allusive as Milton and the Counter-Reformation poets. And all of them, he explained to his mother, "cries for us to recover our ancient freedom and dignity, to be Christians and build a Christian society." The title of his book, *Land of Unlikeness,* had been inspired, he explained, by a hymn of Blake's.[67] Like Blake before him, he had turned the values of contemporary civilization on their head, the angry young prophet intent on restoring a divinely ordained order to things:

> *I shall not cease from mental fight*
> *Nor shall my sword sleep in my hand*

Till we have built Jerusalem
In England's green and pleasant land.

By mid-March 1943, Tate had convinced Cal to send the new poems to Harry Duncan and Katherine Frazier at the Cummington Press in western Massachusetts. This was a small hand-setting press and one of the few still printing poetry under wartime paper restrictions. Even William Carlos Williams, unable to convince James Laughlin at New Directions to publish his new collection, *The Wedge,* would soon turn to the Cummington Press as his last chance, where the book would be printed in an edition of under 400. Duncan wrote Lowell at once. He would print 250 copies, if Lowell would send enough poems to make up a book and *if* Tate promised to provide an introduction. Publication would be set for September. Both men agreed, and Lowell sent Duncan six new poems, all of them written during the last two weeks of March.

In June, Taylor married Eleanor Ross at Monteagle. Lowell was best man, Jean maid of honor, and Tate gave the bride away. Then, on July 4, the Lowells returned to New York, stopping first at Fort Oglethorpe to say goodbye to the Taylors. There, on the afternoon of the 5th, the Lowells found the train station jammed with soldiers on three-day passes. Cal had to struggle on, weighed down with two bags and his "wretched Fra Angelico" *Annunciation,* while Jean searched frantically for two seats, which they found "granitehard." The trip up to Virginia in the July heat proved a torture and Washington a "perfect bedlam," so that they were hours late by the time they reached the Clarks in Princeton.[68] There Cal stayed to visit, while Jean went on alone to Saratoga Springs. Though she was suffering once more from pneumonia, she insisted on going on to the writers' colony at Yaddo for July and August to finish her revisions on *Boston Adventure.*

But Yaddo turned out to be worth the purgatorial passage north, for Jean found that the place surpassed even "the Biltmore for luxury." The "Mansion" itself was "full of Florentine thrones and three-cornered Spanish chairs and tremendous gold plush sofas," she wrote Taylor two days later, the grounds "vast and perfectly beautiful" and full of "innumerable lakes and pools and gardens and woodland walks."[69] Even the food was superb. Among those there that summer with her were Carson McCullers, Langston Hughes, Margaret Walker, Agnes Smedley, Katherine Anne Porter, and the woman in charge: Elizabeth Ames, who Jean found "a truly angelic woman."

Slow to mix with the other guests, Jean made one friend only at Yaddo that summer: a six-foot Irish girl named Kappo Phelan who wrote theater criticism for the Catholic weekly, *Commonweal,* and who reminded her of a female Cal. "Kappo and I do not like the people here," she wrote Taylor. "They are not nice people for the most part." She especially did not like the black writer Margaret Walker, whom she found a bore: "She does not know whether to be a poet or a professional Negro and . . . is so cantankerous about the south." Most of the writers at Yaddo, in fact, were "half-baked communists." There'd also been an incident at a bar in Saratoga Springs over whether or not Walker should be admitted—trouble which could have been avoided, Jean believed, by Walker's simply walking in and ordering a drink, as Langston Hughes had already done.

Agnes Smedley, who wore "the strangest clothes I have ever seen," and who sported a masculine haircut and talked a blue streak, she distrusted most of all.[70] Married to Cal, Jean had drifted even more to the right than was usual for her, and soon she was coming under attack by the others at Yaddo both for her Catholicism and for what were perceived as her racial prejudices. On top of which her illness—was it, she wondered tubercular or streptococchic in nature?—continued to dog her, so that after two weeks at Yaddo she'd lost thirteen pounds, and by August was sure she was on the verge of a "nervous crack-up."[71]

Cal, meanwhile, had taken an apartment in the Village at 12 Gansevoort Street, where he continued working on his poems. In mid-July he wrote Taylor, telling him what he thought postwar America would look like. The family, he emphasized, would still be "the primary social unit," but he was afraid America was slipping into a totalitarian state, and that there would be "another and worse war" (he meant with Russia) after the present one was concluded. Such an apocalyptic scenario might take years, might take forever, he knew. In the meantime, and at its worst, life was still "pretty wonderful," though having escaped the worst ravages of the war so far, he knew he had no right to talk. In truth, all he really cared about anyway was "writing and trying to be a halfway decent Christian." As for politics, it was, finally, nothing more than "a spider's web of unreality."[72]

Since by then Cal had been examined and rejected for the draft at least twice, he wrote his mother reassuring her that he was sure to be rejected again if he were called up. Not that he was very practical about filling out the various questionnaires sent him by the Army. In March, for example, Jean was appalled when she read what Cal had answered for one such questionnaire: that he had one dependent under eighteen living with him, "and another one not living with him but deriving it's whole support from him." That he had graduated from a trade school, that his surname was Robert, "and that he could read 'forig' languages." She corrected that one before mailing it.[73] Then, on August 6, he was called up again. He was to report to his local induction center in lower Manhattan on September 8.

But sometime during the first week of September Lowell had a change of heart. In his notebook, under the title "The Red Sea," he wrote that "for over two years" he had had "every intention and expectation of serving in our armed forces." He'd already volunteered for both the Navy and the Army, only to be "rejected for physical disabilities."[74] and stood every chance of being rejected once more. But this time, he decided, he would *not* fight, so opposed was he to Roosevelt's insistence on unconditional surrender of the enemy, as well as to Roosevelt's and Churchill's *de facto* policy of bombing civilian populations.

Twenty-five years later, in an interview with the Trinidadian novelist V. S. Naipaul, Lowell would try to set the record straight as to why he had refused to fight. "I was a Roman Catholic at the time, and we had a very complicated idea of what was called 'the unjust war.' This policy of bombing German cities seemed to be clearly unjust. So I refused to go to the army and was sent to jail."[75] No doubt too his long talks over the past several years with Tate on the devastation of the southern states caused by Grant's policy of "unconditional surrender" also figured into the equation, since even three quarters of a century after Appomatox the South had yet to recover from the long-term economic effects of war. Moreover, Lowell hated both Stalin and Communist Russia, and felt that unconditional surrender would leave China and Europe at the mercy of "a totalitarian tyranny committed to world revolution and total global domination through propaganda and violence."[76]

On September 7, Lowell drafted a "Declaration of Personal Responsibility" and sent a copy to Roosevelt, with a copy to Matthias F. Correa, Federal District Attorney in New York. "Dear Mr. President," he began,

> I very much regret that I must refuse the opportunity you offer me in your communication of August 6, 1943, for service in the Armed Forces. . . . You will understand how painful such a decision is for an American whose family traditions, like your own, have always found their fulfillment in maintaining, through responsible participation in both the civil and military services, our country's freedom and honor.

When Pearl Harbor had been attacked, he went on, he believed his country had been "in intense peril and, come what might, unprecedented sacrifices were necessary for our national survival." Twice already he'd volunteered for service. Nor had he been much disturbed even by news of atrocities by American soldiers, since such "savagery was unavoidable" against "diabolic adversaries." Now, however, Germany and Japan were being "rolled back on all fronts and the crisis of war" was past. The deciding factor for him had been his realization that in June the war had taken a terrible moral turn for the worse with the Allied bombing of civilian populations, with casualties already reaching staggering proportions. In mid-August alone, 200,000 non-combatants had been killed in the razing of Hamburg. These, Lowell had come to realize, were not isolated incidents but rather a policy endorsed by Roosevelt. This, "in a world still nominally Christian," was *news*.

Since, therefore, America was no longer fighting merely a defensive war, he could not see that it fit any longer under the Church's definition of a just war. And if the United States was no longer fighting a just war, he could not in conscience bring himself to fight in that war. The United States was after all still a democracy in which each citizen was "called upon to make voluntary and responsible decisions on issues which concern the national welfare." But now his country was carrying on a war with means which differed in no way from what Russia, that "most unscrupulous and powerful of totalitarian dictators," was pursuing. To serve in the armed forces at this point, therefore, would mean "a betrayal" of the principles on which his country had been founded. He and Jean mailed 110 copies of his Declaration to family, friends, and the newspapers.[77]

"Please believe that I have taken the only course that was honorable for me," he wrote his mother that same day. "I cannot ask you to support or even in any way concern yourself with my ideas. I do ask for your love, above all for Jean whose part in this is much the hardest." He asked her not to be "too alarmed" about what would happen to him, for he believed the penalty would be "within just limits."[78] And to his southern-born grandmother, who had grown up there in the aftermath of the Civil War, he wrote: "You know more about American history than I do and can certainly judge whether our recent actions in this war are justifiable. I think only a Southerner can realize the horrors of a merciless conquest."[79]

Over the next few days news of Lowell's refusal to serve made the New York and Boston papers. Asked by a reporter for the *Boston Post* for a comment, Mrs. Lowell explained that her son had called her from New York at midnight on the 7th to say he'd notified the D.A. of his refusal to appear before the Draft Board. The problem, she explained, was her son's "poetic temperament, which had caused him to protest against the bombing, and"—getting the name of the city only symbolically right—"especially of Rome." If Bobby had just gone down there for his exam, she added, "he would have again been turned down for poor eyesight."

Now it became a waiting game between Lowell and the authorities. He knew that conscientious objectors were being handed three-year sentences. He was even given a month to reconsider his position. But in mid-September, knowing his decision was firm, he moved Jean into an apartment at 315 East 17th Street. Then, on Monday morning, October 11, he was arraigned in the downtown District Court in Manhattan and the story made the front page of the *New York Times*. When he appeared before Judge Samuel Mandelbaum, Lowell explained that he was not technically a conscientious objector, though his conscience had been "revolted at the bombing of whole cities." Judge Mandelbaum begged him to reconsider. After all, he was from a "distinguished family," and this action was bound to mar his "family traditions." But when Lowell refused to change his mind, he was given the legal minimum sentence of a year and a day, the extra day making him in the eyes of the law a felon.

That same day he wrote his grandmother once more. "I don't [know] what to say to you," he told her, "except that I love you and am sorry to have caused you so much worry." He had talked "at great length" to his confessor in New York and had written Father Schexnayder in Baton Rouge. They were "both very shrewd and experienced men," he explained and—more important— "very good men," and both had told him to follow his "conscience and trust God." He had prayed, hoping to persuade himself that he was mistaken, but in the end he had not changed his mind. He would have to go to jail, though there was good reason to hope that he would shortly be transferred "to the medical corps or to an objectors' camp."[80]

On the morning of October 13, after a month in which he'd been treated, as he wrote Taylor, "with almost alarming courtesy,"[81] Lowell was arraigned before the Southern District Court of New York and heard his sentence read out. He would be sent to the Federal Correctional Center in Danbury, Connecticut. Until he could be moved to Danbury, however, he would be sent to the federal house of detention on West Street near the Hudson. Jean did not learn of Cal's arrest until she returned to the apartment late in the afternoon to find it empty. "It's unnecessary," she wrote the Taylors, "to tell you that he behaved like a gentleman and as a result was treated like a gentleman by everybody but the reporters who failed, however, to get him to pose for a picture." Two friends—one of them a Princeton chaplain—had gone with her to the courthouse. Everyone had been unfailingly kind. There were no hardened criminals at Danbury, she was assured, only COs and first offenders.[82]

When she saw Cal for the first time the following day in the forbidding nineteenth-century brick structure in the Village, a "great slab of plate glass was between us and we had to talk over the telephone." Regulations were strict, and prisoners "allowed only two visits a month and those only from his mother and father and me." He would be able to write only seven people, five of them relatives. He had named Peter and Blair as the other two. Cal's Cousin Harriet Winslow—his parents' age—had come up from Washington to help out and had been "incredibly nice" to both of them. But when Jean told her that Cal had finally been sentenced and was now in jail, Winslow that she was, she'd replied by saying, "Oh, how boring!"[83]

At West Street Jail, Cal was put in a cell next to Louis Lepke of Murder Incorporated. Another CO, like Cal awaiting transfer, would recall Lepke asking Cal, "I'm in for killing. What are you in for?" And Cal: "Oh, I'm in for refusing to kill."[84] Twenty-five years later a bemused Lowell would remark that Czar Lepke looked rather like the eminent New York art critic Clement Greenberg.[85] And in the late 1950s, long after he'd renounced his Catholicism, he would write one of his most poignant and disturbing poems, a nightmarish shadow portrait of himself in the figure of the lobotomized killer in the next cell, with his "two toy American / flags tied together with a ribbon of Easter palm." By then the flag and the Easter palm would be reduced to mocking symbols of Church and State, reminders of what he'd once been willing to go to prison for. He would remember watching the back of the T-shirted figure in the next cell, drifting

> *in a sheepish calm,*
> *where no agonizing reappraisal*
> *jarred his concentration on the electric chair—*
> *hanging like an oasis in his air*
> *of lost connections. . . .*[86]

On Friday morning, October 22, after spending ten days at the West Street jail, Cal was suddenly taken from his cell, handcuffed between two short Puerto Rican draft dodgers, and shoved into the back of a police car. Then, with two sheriffs up front, the five of them drove up the Hudson River Parkway, through Tarrytown, and up onto the Merritt Parkway to Danbury. Lowell would remember a "sand-red sow / grubbing acorns by a cinder pile," remember too the woodchucks sunning themselves near the parkway, the photo of a child sticking from the trouser cuff of one of the other prisoners, and the sheriff in the passenger seat up front, half facing Lowell in case he or one of the others moved too quickly and he had to bring his club down on them fast.[87]

5.

Lord Weary's Castle

1943–1946

With Cal in prison in Danbury, Jean would have to rely on the hundred a month coming in from his trust fund to live on. Half of that would go for rent (actually, a generous allowance for a New York apartment rental in 1943), ten for Cal, ten for her own medical expenses. That left thirty for food, cigarettes, the electric bill. Of course Mrs. Lowell was ready, if not with money, at least with some free advice. In missives hurled from Boston, she told her Colorado daughter-in-law that if she'd only known how Bobby had felt *before* he'd sent that declaration, all of this trouble could have been avoided. She also blamed the Tates for their influence on her son, in particular for persuading him to give up his steady job at Sheed & Ward, and for helping him become too involved in all this "emotional excitement of poetry." She was glad that dear Jean was going to try to support herself while Bobby was in prison, and hoped she would see "in the present situation an opportunity for courage, self-development, and integrity of purpose." Less forgivably, she forged one of Bobby's checks and kept the money for herself.[1]

But that was not the worst of it. In mid-November, Tate, who had in effect counselled Cal in the principles for which he'd gone to jail, wrote Jean that he was "greatly distressed" he could not feel more sympathy for Cal, for in his eyes Cal was simply trying to escape his social responsibilities. He was also sorry to learn that Cal had blamed Caroline for Jean's physical collapse that summer at Yaddo, when it was clear to him that it was Cal who was to blame. And now here he was, refusing to serve in the armed forces. The boy would never really suffer, Tate knew, unless of course his mother got him in her clutches again. In fact, he'd just had a letter from that woman that "for stupidity, insensitivity, and ill-breeding" had no peer. Then, having sounded off, he offered Jean $200 to help her over the next few months.[2]

Jean was allowed to see Cal for the first time on Saturday afternoon, November 20, five weeks after being sent to Danbury. "He looks very well and has gained weight and is in pretty good spirits," she wrote the Taylors afterwards. "He is the most attractive and lovable man I know. . . . I cannot tell you how glad I am that I am married to him and how sick down to my bones it makes me feel that he isn't in this room and won't be for ages." She'd returned to the city the night before and had gone to a cocktail party at the Rahvs. It was late, everyone had been drinking, and she knew she should have gone home instead and "spent the evening looking at . . . snapshots of Cal."

By the time she arrived at the Rahvs, in fact, everyone there had heard about Cal. "The greatest snobs in the world are bright New York literary Jews and the name Lowell works like a love-philtre," she told the Taylors, and before long total strangers were coming up to her and asking her how her husband was. Soon Sidney Hook, social critic and philosopher, was baiting her. "Your husband is a heretic," he carefully explained to her. "He cannot be a conscientious objector and a Catholic for he is going against the dictates of the Pope." Of course that was nonsense, Jean knew, and besides, it was "an unnice thing to be told by a logical positivist that your husband is a heretic." There had also been a "little set-to over Saint Augustine," but there she'd felt on steadier ground because she'd worked closely on the *Confessions* when Frank Sheed had translated them eighteen months before.

The drinking continued afterwards at the apartment of one of the *Partisan Review* editors. By then most of the men had told her Cal was either a fool or hysterical to go to jail for an abstract principle. Hook's wife kept after her about the Catholic notion of a just war. Then the topic changed to the Spanish Civil War. Jean answered that she knew only the papal encyclicals. "But," she added, there must be "something to be said for Franco." Then, suddenly, she broke down and wept. Here was her husband, in jail for his beliefs, and she was tired and—like everyone else—a little drunk, and now she felt trapped. Mrs. Hook offered her a handkerchief, while "everyone else sort of turned away in horror." Literary people in New York were "such cutthroats, such ambitious and bourgeois frights." And yet she also knew she needed them.[3]

She saw Cal a second time two weeks later. It proved to be a less depressing visit than the first, for by then Cal was busy reading Proust and had received permission from the prison authorities to proofread galleys for *Land of Unlikeness.* In fact, she noticed, he actually seemed to be thriving and gaining weight.[4] Three years later, Jean would tell Eileen Berryman that being crazy had made prison easier for Cal. In the meantime she continued working on the revisions of *Boston Adventure,* as well as doing research at Bellevue Hospital on paupers' burials. In December, Hightower returned from China on the *Gripsholm* as part of a prisoner exchange, and he and his wife stayed with Jean at her apartment. She began drinking heavily again, then abruptly stopping, then drinking even more heavily. Allen Tate blew into town for his Christmas drunk and had her and Mary McCarthy up to his hotel room for a dinner party with his old drinking buddy, Joe Horrell.

During the time Cal was in prison, Jean also saw something of one of the *Partisan Review* editors, Delmore Schwartz, enough in fact that Lowell would later come to believe they'd had an affair during the time he was in prison. On the other hand, it would be Frank Parker's belief that Delmore, who was forever contriving byzantine schemes among his friends, had merely wanted Lowell to *think* there'd been an affair between the two of them. But who can chart the wellsprings of eros? The Jean whom Parker and Clark both knew, they insist, did not see her male friends as sex objects.[5] And Cal, who kept mostly silent about such matters, would later quip that Jean was so bashful all the years he'd known her that she always dressed and undressed in the closet. And when, thirty years later, Delmore's biographer asked Cal how he knew Jean had had an affair with Delmore, Cal merely shrugged and told him, "you could tell by the way Delmore lit Jean's cigarette."[6]

Two weeks before Christmas, Jean shared a taxi from the Danbury train station to the prison with two "flashylooking articles," one of whom held a baby. "They were so opulent in their fur coats and highheeled shoes, so redolent of Chanel No. 5" that she felt a pang of envy that *their* husbands "had left them well provided for while they were off being castigated for their ideals." It took her a while to realize that the husbands of these two were not COs at all, one being "a big-time bootlegger," the other "an OPA violator who had sold nylon stockings for $15 a pair." On the train back to the city, she sat with "a beautiful society girl who, having married a low-born Armenian (now a C.O.) was cast out by her family." The woman was educated, had studied philosophy at Barnard, and it had been "a joy to have so profound a companion" to talk with—until the woman gave away her literary ignorance by advising Jean to send Cal a copy of one of the best novels she'd ever read: Lloyd C. Douglas's *The Robe.*[7]

Danbury Correctional Center was a minimum security installation for first offenders and COs, and here Cal had far more freedom to write and receive letters than he'd had at West Street. Nor was the manual labor particularly onerous. Ten years later he would recall this period, when he'd "belonged to a gang that walked outside the prison gates each morning, and worked on building a barn. The work was mild: the workers were slow and absent-minded. There were long pauses, and we would sit around barrels filled with burning coke and roast wheat-seeds." Israel, the black foreman, and some of the other prisoners were members of a Harlem-based group called the Israelites, who believed they were the chosen people and appeared to know everything about "herbs and nature."[8] Twenty years later, in the poem "The Mouth of the Hudson," Israel would appear again, this time as a shadow portrait for Lowell himself, staring out at the Hudson as if it were a river of time drifting by without meaning, without hope. But in an unpublished draft of the poem, Lowell would name the genesis of the troubling image: a January morning in 1944, Israel circling

> *his forefinger around the horizon,*
> *beautiful country, beautiful Connecticut,*
> *and us, shivering as we roasted wheat seeds by a coke barrel,*
> *under guard, and a few flimsy houses, saying:*
> *"Only man is miserable!"*

That comment, Lowell would later remark, came to sum up his morals and aesthetics.[9]

With his penchant for sloppy dress and ill-fitting denims and workshirts, Cal looked like any other prisoner. But he was still very much a loner. When Jim Peck, the fellow CO who had been with Cal at the West Street jail, tried to get him involved in a strike protesting the segregation of black and white prisoners, Cal showed little interest. Later, when Peck attacked him for his cousin, Lawrence Lowell's, part in the conviction of Sacco and Vanzetti fifteen years before, Cal refused to be drawn in. Cal seemed interested in one thing only: organizing a Catholic community with strict monastic rules. Not surprisingly, he had no takers. But in time, when the others—many with their own extreme agendas—saw that Cal was not a fraud, they took him in.[10]

By mid-February, Jean was beside herself with worry over Cal's sanity. "Prison has been dreadful for him," she wrote Taylor just before he was shipped out to England. Cal had become "so fanatical, so insanely illogical that our conversations and his letters could be written into a case history of religious mania." Desperate, she had gone to see Father Gardiner, the editor of the Jesuit weekly, *America,* and a "sound man with sensibilities," for advice. To her relief, Father Gardiner, who had already met Lowell several times and had read an article he had sent the magazine, confirmed Jean's conviction that Cal was indeed being "more Catholic than the church."

She reread Cal's letters from Kenyon "to try to find in them the seeds of this protesting idealism," but the letters only made her sicker because Cal was "nothing like the person he was then." Worse still were his plans for the future, from which he would not be hindered: to be, as Frank Sheed in his youth had been, "a sort of soapbox preacher with . . . the Catholic Evidence Guilds which operate in city parks, etc, preach and answer the baiting questions of the hecklers." When she'd asked him how the two of them would live, Cal had told her to read the Gospels to see that they were not to worry, for God would provide. He had no intention of being a wage slave, he told her, and meant to take time to serve the Church. It would take him three years, she figured, before he fully "recovered from the pleasurable monasticism of the penitentiary."[11]

On March 15, 1944, having served five months of his sentence, Cal was released and turned over to his parole officer, "a tiny old nun" at St. Vincent's Hospital in Bridgeport. Until October, when his sentence would be over, his job would be to mop floors in the Army cadet nurses' dormitory, beginning at 7:00 A.M. each morning. That meant he would have to get up six days a week at five-fifteen to get to work on time. For this he received a weekly salary of fifteen dollars. He told Jean he felt like the Tates' daughter's valet, and spoke "distastefully of the 'pink things' hung out to dry" by the nurses in his work vicinity. Still, St. Vincent's was a vast improvement over Danbury, which had become rather "like living in the City of Tomorrow."[12] Still, the work hadn't been all that bad, he told Ransom, and had even had about it "a harsh somehow moral monotony," rather like the swimming and running he'd done to keep in shape back at Kenyon.[13]

For the first two weeks after his release, he lived in "a wretched hovel with a horrid buggy bed, a bathroom which he shared with half a dozen defense workers and which smelled like a train, all supervised by a garrulous and ill-tempered landlady with bright yellow hair and the conviction that Cal was a draft-dodger."[14] Then, in April, Jean found an apartment for them both in Black Rock, a working-class neighborhood of mostly Hungarian immigrants several blocks from Long Island Sound. The address itself—68 Ocean Avenue, Harbor View—promised vistas. But in truth what they moved into was a "large, shapeless, yellow stone" building, the rear view of which faced onto an inlet which at low tide became "a black and stinking mud-flat."[15] Worse still was the huge town dump close by. Soon Cal was blaming Jean for having chosen rooms in the middle of a marsh. From the front steps of the apartment one could make out the spires of two local Catholic churches: St. Peter's and St. Stephen's. The apartment itself was owned by a Catholic priest who'd bought it for next to nothing from a rumrunner who had used it as a cover during Prohibition.

"We have a large room with a bay window and a fireplace, and a smaller room and a bath," Jean wrote Eleanor Taylor. Unfortunately, the harbor view only brought "tears to Cal's eyes. He had expected the ocean from the address and when he saw the pitiful little drop of water visible from our windows, he behaved as if he had been deliberately cheated." Still, on clear days, they *could* see the Sound "far far off and we have the illusion, at least, of being in the country." For this illusion, "and for cleanliness and a bath of our own we pay $15 a week, just exactly what Cal makes." Bridgeport itself had turned out to be "even more dreadful" than her "wildest nightmares," and made her feel "as impermanently settled as the blackbirds in the scraggly tree outside my window."[16]

In June, Cal and Jean went down to New York for another *Partisan Review* cocktail party. "It was Cal's first public appearance since Danbury," Jean wrote Eleanor Taylor, "and I've never seen him in such good spirits. Sidney Hook was there, quite drunk and very affable, greeting me as 'Ah, my enemy.' " Tate too was there, very drunk, and once again behaving badly. He monopolized Marianne Moore, who was dressed in her "old lady grey," so that the Lowells did not even get to meet her. Cal, in fact, was so "horrified" to see his mentor in such bad shape that he refused to talk to him. The following day the Lowells went to a Russian church and heard the Mass of St. John Chrysostom sung in Russian in a tiny chapel amid thick clouds of incense. Then it was lunch with Tate and E. E. Cummings, followed by "a long, long hour on the terrace of the [Hotel] Brevoort drinking Tom Collins's" and having a lengthy, dreadfully desultory conversation with the hungover Tate.[17]

That summer Jean worked over the galleys of her novel while Cal continued to revise the poems in *Land of Unlikeness,* worried that "the imagination and technique" of the work he was about to publish had already become crude. He and Jean made two weekend retreats to the Trappist monastery in Portsmouth, Rhode Island, attending all the services, including Vespers, Benediction, Compline. The chapel, they noticed, had a real della Robbia and a Van der Weyden Madonna, and they'd even been served at table "by monks with white aprons over their habits."[18] An idyllic setting for a monastery, far different from the monastery at Monte Cassino obliterated by American bombers that past February with great loss of life, a tragedy Lowell would recall in "The Benedictines," where "steel feathers whistle down and bomb / Monte Cassino Abbey, where they pray."[19] After their second visit to Portsmouth in late June, as they waited in Providence for the train that would take them back to Bridgeport, they watched a huge troop train filled with POWs, most of them Germans, the first fruits of the invasion of Normandy. Jean was shocked to see how much the prisoners looked like American boys in strange uniforms.[20]

Since leaving Monteagle, Cal had done almost no writing, except to revise a poem for *Partisan Review* and to continue working on the long Miltonic satire on Britain he'd begun years before. But here in Black Rock, after working all day mopping floors at the hospital in Bridgeport, he began writing again, gorgeous poems like "Colloquy in Black Rock" (originally titled "Pentecost"), "The Dead in Europe," and "The Quaker Graveyard in Nantucket." He was "working with the same intensity he did in that great period of fertility in Monteagle," Jean told Peter Taylor at the end of July, which left her, resting from the prodigious effort of *Boston Adventure,* feeling completely worthless.[21]

"Colloquy in Black Rock" was "the only poem that came to me Wordsworthian-wise—walking," Lowell would tell Babette Deutsch years later. "I hadn't written a line for a year, and had just come home one evening from mopping floors as a conscientious objector. I was strolling about and staring at the low-tide litter and wishing. That the War were over, and that the [transformative] event in the last stanza would lift me out of my pails of dirty water. Then the lyrical outline came."[22] One feels in the percussive jackhammer jabbing into the Sound, the "nigger-brass percussions," and the erratic pulse of the speaker speaking to his own pounding heart something of Lowell's own physical and mental pain, his isolation, his manic enthusiasm, his interior agony, his hunger for Christ's great mercy to transform the world of Black Rock, for Christ the kingfisher to dive in pentecostal fire on the poet.

It is a poem of pain and exultation which threatens to explode beyond its formal restraints at any moment.[23] And yet the tension of the lines is held in check by the fastidiousness of the form: an iambic line with sprung feet, three six-line stanzas (abcabc) alternating with two four-line stanzas (abab, with the same heavy and terrible rhymes repeated: *death, Mud, blood, death. Death, Mud, blood, death*). In time everything—*everything*—wears down to death, the poet understands. Black Rock reduced to the oil-stained "mud-flat detritus" of Black Mud; St. Stephen, proto-martyr, witnessing to the transfiguring possibility of human life, stoned to death; the poet ground down by the system for witnessing to his beliefs. Each of these tensions is caught in the mesh of the lines. Everywhere too there are echoes of Eliot's *Four Quartets,* not least in the figure of the pervasive dust and in the kingfisher itself. And of course Hopkins is there in the peculiar pitch of Lowell's visionary stance. Only Hart Crane of all the American moderns comes close to this Dionysian frenzy, which can still be heard breaking the silence half a century later:

> *Here the jack-hammer jabs into the ocean;*
> *My heart, you race and stagger and demand*

More blood-gangs for your nigger-brass percussions,
Till I, the stunned machine of your devotion,
Clanging upon this cymbal of a hand,
Am rattled screw and footloose. All discussions

End in the mud-flat detritus of death.
My heart, beat faster, faster. In Black Mud
Hungarian workmen give their blood
For the martyre Stephen, who was stoned to death.

Black Mud, a name to conjure with: O mud
For watermelons gutted to the crust,
Mud for the mole-tide harbor, mud for mouse,
Mud for the armored Diesel fishing tubs that thud
A year and a day to wind and tide; the dust
Is on this skipping heart that shakes my house,

House of our Savior who was hanged till death.
My heart, beat faster, faster. In Black Mud
Stephen the martyre was broken down to blood:
Our ransom is the rubble of his death.

Christ walks on the black water. In Black Mud
Darts the kingfisher. On Corpus Christi, heart,
Over the drum-beat of St. Stephen's choir
I hear him, Stupor Mundi, *and the mud*
Flies from his hunching wings and beak—my heart,
The blue kingfisher dives on you in fire.

Then came the first of Cal's seizures. At the communion rail early on the morning of July 9, he had "a terrifying seizure of some sort," Jean told Taylor, "and I thought he was going to faint." When he got back to the apartment, he "doctored himself with brandy" (in itself unusual for him, since he hardly ever drank any more), until color came back to his face and he seemed to return to normal.[24] But at month's end he was still ill. "Last week I was given three days off," he confided to Tate on the 31st. "My blood-pressure is a *little* low and I am a *little* anaemic." But instead of resting, he had spent "the whole time, day and night, writing," and was now sending Tate seven poems in a style "more lyrical and lucid" than anything he'd done before.[25] Since Tate had also been reading the *Four Quartets* again, Cal thought he might pick up some of the echoes of Eliot in the new poems. Two were revisions and two more had been pillaged from the long satirical poem on England which he'd worked on now for the past five years, but which he'd finally let go of when Ransom rejected it as too big and oppressive to publish. By then even Lowell had realized there was something inhuman about the poem. He'd also heavily revised his sonnets and written two new poems, "The Dead in Italy" (later changed to "The Dead in Europe") and "Colloquy in Black Rock," both of which Tate would publish that October in the *Sewanee Review.*

That summer Lowell also read several articles on Hopkins which Ransom had sent him for the Hopkins centenary issue. He liked them, he said, but more would be needed if Hopkins was to "get the same expert treatment" Yeats and Hardy had already received in the *Kenyon Review.*[26] In August, he sent Ransom an essay of his own called "Hopkins' Sanctity," though he feared it might be "both pretentious and slight."[27] In fact it was neither, and reveals what Lowell hoped for from his own religious poetry, as he struggled to imitate Hopkins's life in his own. He stressed Hopkins's "inebriating exuberance" (a shadow of his own mania), an exuberance which Lowell noted had been held in check by Hopkins's "strict fastidiousness" in his religious life. Hopkins had led "a soldier's life," he wrote, not unlike the North American Jesuit martyrs, a life "close to the physical Incarnation." And though Hopkins had died young, his life "short and broken," he had somehow managed to win through. The truly amazing thing about the poet/priest, the thing he wished for himself, really, was the realization that Hopkins had led a life that seemed in retrospect to have made "continuous substantial progress toward perfection."

By contrast, Lowell argued, the beliefs and practices of most modern poets excluded the very notion of the possibility of perfection, and to shut that out was to shut out the possibility of true greatness in poetry. Actually, he pointed out, many poems written in the past two centuries centered on the theme of human perfection: "An Essay on Man," *The Prelude,* "Ode on a Grecian Urn," Yeats's "Among School Children," *The Waste Land.* But placed against "The Wreck of the Deutschland" or Hopkins's late sonnets, even these poems seemed "abstract and superficial." True, Hopkins had his technical faults, Lowell conceded. Yet even so, he had managed to write religious lyrics "unsurpassed by anything written in the great ages of religion." His real place was with Dante, Villon, Ben Jonson, Donne, Herbert, Milton.[28] Surely that was the same place to which Lowell too aspired.

In September, when money from the sale of *Boston Adventure* began coming in, Jean went down to New York to close up the East 17th Street apartment, then returned to close up the Black Rock apartment. On the 20th, she and Cal moved to "the Barn," their new rented home in Westport, deep in the Connecticut countryside. It had, she told Hightower, "nine acres, five bedrooms, four bathrooms, two kittens and the handsomest pig-sty in Fairfield County." But in the week leading up to the move, she found herself doing everything, Cal having managed "every blessed time . . . to be inaccessible both at the packing and the unpacking." In fact, he was already "becoming a Tory" on the money that was beginning to come in from *her* novel.[29]

For by then it was clear that *Boston Adventure* was going to be a huge financial success. "Very odd people like Howard Mumford Jones and Dorothy Parker are enthusiastic about it," Cal wrote Ransom on the 6th. "We are very excited and appalled."[30] To begin with, Jean received $2,300 from Harcourt, Brace, $1,800 more than her contract called for, to help cover a first printing of 22,000. By April 1945 the book had gone into a fifth printing. In the first seven months, 400,000 copies were sold. The Book League, with its 200,000 readers, featured the novel, which brought her another $6,000. By June 1945, she'd earned $21,000. Part of the book's success was its old-fashioned style and plot, at the heart of which was the class issue—a shadow of Stafford's own reception by the Lowells, the western hick in Boston brahmin society. That she dedicated the novel to Frank Parker suggested her own ambivalence toward Cal's role as a CO, for by then all of Cal's closest friends, like her brother, were in the armed services.

September 1944 saw not only the publication of Jean's novel, but the publication as well of all 250 copies of Lowell's thin first book of poems. "In my father's openly biased view," Frank Sheed's son, Wilfred Sheed, would recall, "Jean made a great mistake in becoming a success before her husband did. . . . *Boston Adventure* was a best seller, while Lowell was still fighting his way up through the coteries . . . I can imagine he made Jean pay for this a bit." An image in point: Stafford drinking champagne in the offices of *Mademoiselle*, where she was being feted with a fellow honoree, Lauren Bacall, while Cal was recognized more often as a draft dodger than as a poet.

Yet, for all its miniscule size, *Land of Unlikeness* received a surprising number of reviews, due to the ability of the New Critical network to get the word out. Tate's short Introduction certainly helped by placing Lowell squarely among Formalists like himself. "T. S. Eliot's recent prediction that we should soon see a return to formal and even intricate metres and stanzas was coming true, before he made it, in the verse of Robert Lowell," Tate wrote. It was, after all, only a first book, the two strains in Lowell's work as yet imperfectly aligned. On the one hand, there was the "Christian symbolism," more willed than felt along the pulse, pointing "to the disappearance of . . . Christian experience from the modern world," and standing here for "the poet's own effort to recover it." On the other hand, there were already in these poems signs of a poetry of a more personal experience. Whatever one felt about these poems, Tate summed up, there was "at least a memory of the spiritual dignity of man, now sacrificed to mere secularization and a craving for mechanical order."[31]

There were decent reviews in *Poetry, Accent,* and *Partisan Review,* plus a rather sharp notice by Blackmur in the *Kenyon Review,* who remarked that there was "not a loving metre in the book," and that the Boston strain in Lowell was at sharp odds with the Catholic, the struggle producing "not a tension but a gritting."[32] But the best review was Randall Jarrell's in *Partisan Review,* all the more surprising because Jarrell's hope was not so much for these poems as for those Lowell would someday write: "In a day when poets aspire to be irresistible forces," he noted, Lowell had become "an immovable object," a rock in the stream that would have to be reckoned with. "Some of the best poems of the next years," he concluded, "ought to be written by him."[33]

On October 15, Lowell's sentence would be officially completed. In late September he was notified by the government that he would have to secure a job "essential" to the war effort by that date or face being sent back to prison. Cal seemed merely to shrug the warning off with a "so be it," but the news so alarmed Jean that she went down to New York to look for a job "which would not interfere with his principles." Finally, she found something for Cal "working with delinquent boys," one of whom proceeded to steal Lowell's watch, then "drank a bottle of Lysol but didn't die, all of them were under 15 and were in for murder, arson, grand larceny, etc."[34] On a second trip down to New York to be sure Cal really had the job, she slipped while getting into a taxi and twisted her ankle so badly she had to be put on crutches.

When Cal came home that evening, he was carrying a letter from Jean's father with the news that her brother, Dick, had been killed in action in France. On September 18, the same week her novel was published, Dick had died in an ambulance accident after first being wounded as his unit advanced with Patton's Third Army. Jean had last seen her brother in New York that July, just before he'd sailed for Europe. "I am so glad, in this terrible thing, to be a Catholic," she wrote her sister. "You must believe, as we have all got to believe, that he is just somewhere else."[35] Late in the month, dressed in a modest navy blue suit and coat, Jean travelled by train to visit her family in Portland, Oregon. Each morning she attended Mass; each evening she walked to the local Piggly-Wiggly for several bottles of wine. With this loss, she saw, her parents had suddenly grown old and broken, and she returned to Westport as soon as she felt she decently could, only to find Cal had turned the house into a disaster.

In November, because of his poor eyesight, Cal was at last classified as "limited service," the equivalent of 4-F, and would have to serve only "in the case of a great catastrophe like the bombing of New York."[36] He would not have to go back to prison, or even have to serve as a non-combatant in the medical corps. Financially secure for the first time in her life, Jean quickly settled down to the blessings of domesticity in Westport. "I have developed into so ardent a cook," she wrote a friend that fall, "that if I weren't honor-bound to write, I should spend all my time making the most complicated soups and stews, the sort that require a bag of every known herb together with calves' feet and twenty-four hours of steady vigil."[37]

At Thanksgiving she and Cal went up to Boston to visit with Cal's parents, whom Cal was at last becoming "very fond of." He also had an ulcer on his throat removed, a condition, Jean noted wryly, called proudflesh. Thanksgiving Day they visited Grandmother Winslow in the hospital. Though she was very weak, she managed to tell her grandson that nothing could have given her greater pleasure than seeing him again. The following day she slipped quietly away.

Eager for company beyond what the taciturn, brooding Cal or she herself could offer each other, Jean invited friends to share the house at Westport. Albert Erskine, former editor of the *Southern Review,* and his new wife, Peggy, visited and then moved in, while others came for shorter or longer visits: the Cleanth Brookses, the novelist Marguerite Young, and Gertrude Buckman, who had worked with Jean in New York and who was now divorced from Delmore Schwartz. Jean even made plans for an old-fashioned Victorian Christmas, the kind she could only dream about when she was growing up. Cal managed to cut a tree without hurting himself, and Jean's sister shipped them a fourteen-pound turkey from Colorado. Again, they invited a large number of guests, and again the drinks flowed freely, both factors contributing to the disastrous outcome of the holiday.

"Christmas was grim," she wrote a friend afterwards, "our guests were unharmonious and made no effort to adapt themselves to one another. There were undercurrents that ruined all the season's joy, and all the drinking was too steady and we couldn't face New Year's so we stayed at home."[38] There was also the death of their kitten, Alice Uhl. She was "always unhealthily tiny," Jean wrote Eleanor Taylor, but on Christmas Day Alice had fallen ill. Jean was for taking her to the vet's to be put away or having a farmer shoot her, but Cal would hear none of it. Instead, for three days he had "nursed her most tenderly, keeping her on a cushion in his study and tempting her with all sorts of things like liver broth," until at last she died.[39]

"There will be more wars," Lowell wrote Taylor two weeks later, with the Germans once more in retreat back across the Rhine and the end of the cataclysm beginning to seem thinkable. What was in store after the war was what troubled Cal now: the rise of a godless Russia and a "universal materialistic state" both there and in America, where Christians would "be driven underground." The time had come "to be very evident indeed about our Faith." Until the apocalypse came, however, he would try and enjoy the house Jean's money had bought.[40]

By February 1945, Jean was stuck in the writing of her new novel, *The Mountain Lion*. Sick of the Proustian/Jamesian structure of her old syntax and diction, she was hungry, like Cal, to find a "new and supple style," one filled with "concrete diction and colloquial juxtapositions." Once again she was on the wagon, so that she'd been reduced to a bundle of "filthy nerves."[41] She taught a course that spring in the short story at Queens College, which meant a long and time-consuming commute each Tuesday from Westport to Grand Central Station, then out to Queens by subway and bus, only to find her fourteen students sitting there "inert". The semester turned out to be a disaster.[42]

Then, in April, she was awarded a Guggenheim Fellowship for $2,000 and another $1,000 by the American Academy of Arts and Letters. *Boston Adventure* was even nominated for a Pulitzer. But now she found herself sinking into a deep depression following on her alcoholic dependency, trying to counter that by spending her days and nights cleaning her "foully dirty" house with its many nooks and crannies. It was, she sighed, "an endlessly hopeless task."[43] She was also fed up with Westport and its "fashionable, vulgar, anti-semitic, expensive, second-rate, bourgeoise, politically naive" ways. Then the Barn was sold and she and Cal were given just two months to find another place.[44]

At the end of April, Cal and Jean went to see his parents—a visit which turned out badly, with Mrs. Lowell giving them "the same lectures and moral generalizations and refusals to countenance the way we live and the dredging up of all the mistakes of the past." As for Jean, she felt herself "more thoroughly, more icily, more deeply disliked than ever on account of my book, even though it is generally admitted that it's a damn good thing Bobby married someone who makes money writing." Only in that way could writing be justified with Cal's parents. Mrs. Lowell had even gone so far as to tell Cal "that his poetry was nice but valueless since 'one must please the many, not the few.' "[45]

Originally, Cal and Jean had planned to spend the summer with the Tates in Tennessee. Instead, they began looking for a place deep in the Maine countryside where they could hole up and write. That June they travelled as far up the coast as the New Brunswick border and then began working their way south. By July they'd settled into a small furnished cottage in Boothbay Harbor, "a sort of Maine Monteagle," Cal wrote Tate, except that the nights were cool, "the scenery . . . beautiful and the summer people, to the number of 15,000 . . . atrocious."[46]

Jean's take on their Maine Monteagle differed appreciably from Cal's. The place was merely "a horrid cottage in a horrid town overrun by horrid large summer people, our landlord being the most horrid of all: a happy-go-lucky everyday-philosophy psychiatrist from Brooklyn Heights" whose wife had had a botched facelift.[47] But they loved Maine and were still looking for that summer house, preferably some fishing village "not blighted by Route 1." Meanwhile she and Cal were holed up and working fairly well (only "fairly" well because Cal was trying to write an omnibus review for the *Sewanee Review* "of all the rotten poetry that has come out recently," with the result that he was "pretty cross most of the time"). But at least Jean was steaming along on *The Mountain Lion* and Cal on a new book of poems. By the end of July, she had finished a hundred pages of her new novel, mostly because she was out of the Westport house and there were "no more interruptions by week-end visitors and neighborhood poker parties," and the cottage "so unattractive" she was not moved "to any sort of domesticity."[48]

The book Lowell was working on was *Lord Weary's Castle*, an expanded and radically revised version of *Land of Unlikeness*. That July he sent the manu-script to Jarrell, stationed at Davis-Monthan Field in Tucson, Arizona, where Jarrell was serving as a U.S. Army Air Force navigational instructor. During the first half of August, even as the war came to a horrifying but swift conclusion with the dropping of two atomic bombs on Japan, Jarrell pored through Cal's poems line by line and poem by poem. He was delighted with the new work, he wrote Cal, especially with the long poem which had appeared recently in *Partisan Review*, "The Quaker Graveyard in Nantucket." "I had rather read your poems than anybody else in the world who is writing now," he told Cal, for the general level of Cal's output was now up to the level of the best six or seven poems in *Land of Unlikeness*.

Like Cal a serious reader of theology—though he favored the Protestant over the Catholic writers—Jarrell was not sure Cal really had "the orthodox Catholic position about Grace" down in these poems.[49] But when Cal under-took to explain the subject to Jarrell by return, Jarrell replied that, while Cal's explanation was "much the most humane and sympathetic Catholic version" he'd heard, it didn't seem quite *true* to him. He found it odd, too, that, while the Christianity which Cal espoused in his letters was particularly attractive, none of that had come over into the poems themselves.[50]

Not that it mattered as far as the poems were concerned, for he still thought "Quaker Graveyard" the best poem Lowell had ever written, the ending so subtle and right it beat even William Empson at his own game of complex ambiguities.[51] The poem had begun, Lowell would remark years later, "un-likely as it seems—as a translation of a Corbière poem on Paris night life that was a little like the litter" in "Colloquy in Black Rock."[52] Actually, the gist of the poem had gone through dozens of transformations since that first summer on Nantucket eight years before, when he'd written "Jonah." Later it had been retitled and reworked as "The Death of the White Whale," then "To Herman Melville." By degrees, and though it had been years since he'd stared out into the Atlantic's depths off Madaket, he'd grown "drunker and drunker with the sea." At last he'd put all his chips on the poem's surging rhythms and let the undertow of the sea's music carry him as he would never allow it to carry him again.[53]

The operative poem behind Lowell's is Milton's *Lycidas,* though Lowell's is a more violent sea, more out of Hopkins's "Deutschland," meshed with Thoreau's meditations on a corpse pulled from the sea surge off Cape Cod, the buoy-bells and sinister rocks of Eliot's "Dry Salvages," and Hart Crane's paean to Melville. But even more, Lowell was listening to the rhythms of *Moby Dick* (for him *the* great American novel, and absolutely unrepeatable). Like *Lycidas,* Lowell's elegy is a palimpsest, in this instance borrowing largely from American history, even as it is shaped by the figure Lowell thought stood at the gateway to American poetry: John Milton. "Quaker Graveyard" is a "long symbolic elegy,"[54] not only for Lowell's cousin, Warren Winslow, a naval officer like his father, who had been killed in a naval accident at the Brooklyn Navy Yard, but for the millions lost, brother "hell-bent" on killing brother in the killing fields of the North Atlantic and the South Pacific.

From the poem's opening lines one feels the unyielding percussive strokes of the sea, and of the prophet who speaks now in the unforgiving rhythms of an ocean from which, if the dead rise, they rise only to be weighted in the steel scales of a green Christ/Poseidon before being returned to the hell-bent depths from which they came:

> *A brackish reach of shoal off Madaket,—*
> *The sea was still breaking violently and night*
> *Had steamed into our North Atlantic Fleet,*
> *When the drowned sailor clutched the drag-net. Light*
> *Flashed from his matted head and marble feet,*
> *He grappled at the net*
> *With the coiled, hurdling muscles of his thighs:*
> *The corpse was bloodless, a botch of reds and whites,*
> *Its open, staring eyes*
> *Were lustreless dead-lights*
> *Of cabin-windows on a stranded hulk*
> *Heavy with sand. . . .*

And the final lines, after the fruitless fury of the North Atlantic Fleet, after the wars, after human history will all have finally expended themselves, circling back once more to the waters off Nantucket, as unchanged now as on the first day of Creation or in the days after the Flood, when the sign of God's covenant appeared in the shape of a rainbow bridging the cruel waters:

You could cut the brackish winds with a knife
Here in Nantucket, and cast up the time
When the Lord God formed man from the sea's slime
And breathed into his face the breath of life,
And blue-lung'd combers lumbered to the kill.
The Lord survives the rainbow of His will.[55]

"A house is really the only solution for anyone," Jean would tell one friend that fall. "And certainly for me, who desire to immobilize myself like an eternal vegetable." The nesting instinct was strongly upon her, she who at thirty was finally going to have "a house and lawn and trees."[56] By August 20, Jean had what she wanted: a real New England find, white-clapboarded, green-shuttered, 1820, fifteen miles inland from Boothbay Harbor at a place called Damariscotta Mills. She bought it outright with money from her novel and began at once to fix it up. It would be *their* summer place, hers and Cal's, with winters in New York or in Tennessee with the Tates. It had three bedrooms, a dining room and living room, an upstairs study, four fireplaces (one of which still worked). It had plumbing and electricity (but no central heating), a gabled attic, a barn. It had three acres of land, elms and oaks, meadows, hemlocks, fresh air, and it stood high above the shores of the fourteen-mile-long bass-and-salmon-teeming Damariscotta Lake and the Damariscotta River, a tidal estuary that wandered lazily down to the mouth of the North Atlantic. The town itself consisted of a post office, a general store, a train depot, and the now-empty mills, which had provided the place with its name.

Once there had been the Penobscot and the Abenaki. Then the arrival of whites in the late 1630s, then the shipyards—twenty-nine of them—in the 1820s and '30s, until nearly all the great evergreens to the north of the town had been felled. By the time the Lowells arrived in Damariscotta Mills, the town was merely a backwater. The hotel was gone, along with the shipyards and the paddlewheeler which had once plied the lake. Now there was just the one general store around which the locals gathered, feet up on the stove, whittling. "They had the countenances and the clothes and the politics of cracker-barrel philosophers," Stafford would quip, "but I never heard one of them utter an epigram."[57]

There was other local color as well. The sheriff, for instance, whom Jean periodically paid to drive her the twenty miles to Bath to stock up on liquor, Damariscotta Mills being in a dry county. Or the woman they'd bought their house from—Miss Anna Glidden—who looked "like Uncle Sam and generally wears a carpenter's hat and a brown leather duster that goes to her ankles." Or Mrs. Cabot, their next-door neighbor, whose daughter was an Anglican nun. Across the road lived a bishop's widow with her six children. And to the east:

the Federal-style Kavanagh mansion, with its elegant octagonal cupola, named after one of the town's nineteenth-century lumber barons, where an old woman sat each day rocking in her wicker chair, alone.

Never had she been "so happy anywhere" in her life, Jean wrote Taylor a month after moving in, for the house was simply "too wonderful to be believed." True, at the moment it was "in pretty foul disorder with books and tools" and Cal's "blue socks and poem manuscripts all over the floors," and the night before he'd thrown "a piece of bread and honey down the stairs and just now he lost a filling." In her Heidelberg braids and black slacks and loafers, she oversaw the small army of local craftsmen, there to paint the walls and woodwork, lay new tile, assemble a stove, build bookcases, put in an oil burner, test the well, clean the chimneys, and putty the ancient windows. She spent hours poring over *House Beautiful* and Sears, Roebuck catalogues. Cal did his part by building her a bookcase out of a packing box, splitting five cords of wood, and doing "some creative work with a scythe." He also had the infuriating habit of asking Jean "halfway through each house improvement" if it wouldn't have been better to leave things the way they were.[58] In truth he was quietly seething with all her "nesting and neatening."[59]

Jean's study was downstairs, off the hallway between the kitchen and the parlor and under the main staircase, from which vantage she could keep an eye on her neighbors. Cal's was in the upstairs bedroom, where he could sprawl out on a working bed, as he had been in the habit of doing ever since St. Mark's. As soon as they arrived, Cal got some fishing in, borrowing a neighbor's boat and going out on the lake, where he'd caught "200 perch, 180 of which he threw back." He had no license, the season was over, and there were "duck hunters . . . out discharging their firearms all over the place," Jean recounted to Peter Taylor, but Cal somehow managed to be "neither arrested nor killed."[60] In the blue evenings, she would remember thirty years later, after it had all turned to dust, "they read at ease, hearing no sound but that of the night birds—the loons on the lake and the owls in the tops of the trees. When the days began to cool and shorten, a cricket came to bless their house, nightly singing behind the kitchen stove."[61]

A stone's throw from the house was St. Patrick's, the oldest Catholic church north of Maryland. But if the pastor, Father Lynch, turned out to be "a disappointment, being unintellectual and interested principally in prizefights," the church itself, a red brick structure with white wood trim built in the Federal style, was "too beautiful to believe." It was "full of paintings purloined from Spanish churches, an altar piece three hundred years old and a heavenly bell made by Paul Revere." Next to the church was a small cemetery where the early Irish Catholic settlers had been buried. And, while Father Lynch had been sent here a dozen years before for some offense to the hierarchy, he'd yet to unpack his books and still prayed daily for a parish closer to civilization.[62]

"I have reached the age"—she was thirty—"when I do not want to meet any new people," Jean confided to Taylor in late September. There were constant invitations—she called them "summonses"—to go swimming, dancing, or attend cocktail or dinner parties. But by then Cal had had enough of neighbors and was refusing all invitations, preferring instead to go on long walks in the surrounding hills and birdwatch, or lie on the couch and read the memoirs of Saint-Simon or the *New English Dictionary,* while Jean went alone to visit the neighbors. "Cal is always extremely difficult and makes me make up some horrendous lie," she complained, "or makes me go alone with an equally horrendous excuse for him." There were comic moments too, as when Jean attended a tea party given by Mrs. Cabot at the Kavanagh mansion. "Imagine," Mrs. Cabot had told her. "A bogus Cabot talking to a bogus Lowell."[63]

By then, Cal was ready to send both Randall and "Uncle" Ransom the final manuscript of *Lord Weary's Castle.* Ten poems had been salvaged from *Land of Unlikeness* and thirty new ones added. He also appended an ominous headnote to the collection: "Death comes when the house is built." Ransom responded immediately. "I don't know who has grown up in verse more than you these last few years," he wrote. "Mostly," he thought, "by way of giving up the effort to communicate more than was communicable, and by consulting the gentle reader's traditional range of intelligence rather than your own private article." These, he added with typical understatement, "are nice."[64]

It was six weeks before Randall could find the time to write Cal. But when he did, he'd done his homework carefully. "Mr. Edwards and the Spider," one of the new poems, was "tremendously effective," and "Where the Rainbow Ends" "one of the best religious poems in hundreds of years." But Cal should cut and cut, for it was "almost impossible to have a book of poems too short: the more poems, the more confused the reviewers and readers." It was important that Cal get this book absolutely right, for Randall was convinced that it would be "the best first book of poems since Auden's *Poems.*" The new poems were an incredible advance over *Land of Unlikeness,* the best nine or ten of them better than *anything* there. In fact, they were "some of the best poems anyone has written in our time and are sure to be read for hundreds of years."

This was heady praise, especially coming from Randall, who simply did not have it in him to fake praise of any kind. "You know how little contemporary poetry I like," he added. "If I'm affected this way—unless I've gone crazy—it must be the real thing." Cal was in fact "potentially a better poet than anybody writing in English." The main weakness of the poems was in their being "too little interested in people" and "more about the actions of you, God, the sea, and cemeteries." Cal's great strength, on the other hand, was that he wrote "more in the great tradition, the grand style, the real *middle* of English poetry, than anybody since Yeats."[65]

By September it was clear that the Tates' marriage—the one Jean had thought of as the model for her own—was in serious trouble, and now the Lowells heard from both. "I am not sure that you will want to come to Sewanee in October," Caroline wrote first. "I shall not be there and I am not sure Allen will." They would be getting a divorce that December. Allen had finally convinced himself that he could have "a brand new life," but only if he could "get hold of a brand new wife."[66] A few weeks later they heard from Tate. "Caroline has left me—permanently," he wrote, then reminded them of their promise to spend the winter with him in Monteagle.[67] By then Caroline, fed up with her husband's drunken philandering, had indeed gone. At the moment she was in Princeton.

In late October, Cal wrote Tate from Princeton. He and Jean had come down to find Caroline "the same person we have always known." He'd already invited her to stay with them in Maine, which he thought would be best for her, the country there being heavenly and the woods full of mushrooms. They would be delighted to have her.[68] And, though he hated becoming involved in domestic disputes, Jarrell nevertheless delivered himself of an icily precise opinion to Cal. Anything that might change Tate's life, he said, would "be good for him," for Tate had by then become his "own ruts." How little he'd changed in the last ten years, Randall added, compared to Ransom, who was ten years Tate's senior.[69]

But before the Lowells could return to Maine, Cal came down with acute appendicitis and had to be admitted to New York Hospital. For a few days, Jean stayed at the Murray Hill Hotel, then moved in with her friend, Cecile Starr, at her West 10th Street apartment, sleeping on the sofa for ten days until Cal could leave the hospital. She and Cal celebrated Thanksgiving in their room at the Seymour Hotel with two friends.[70] In the meantime, Caroline had gone ahead to Damariscotta Mills to work on her novel. But as winter settled in, the house began showing its age. The pipes, she wrote Jean, alarmed, were making strange noises in the night and seemed in danger of freezing, the bathroom was arctic, she was having difficulty keeping the wood stove going, and storms had already knocked out electric power on several occasions.

On November 25, while Cal continued his recovery in New York, Jean went back to Maine. "It is cold but the house is warm," she wrote Bill Mock. "We have stoves now in four rooms and I don't think there will be any danger of the pipes freezing for several months." She still loved it here, even liked "pouring hot water on top of the well to unfreeze it so that I can get drinking water."[71] But she'd been back only one day when there was a blow-out with Caroline, who'd been after Jean to tell her everything she knew about Allen's new girlfriend, until she'd finally gotten from Jean more than Jean had wanted to tell her. Then, over dinner, Caroline began calling her a busybody, saying that now there could be no hope of reconciling with her husband "and that up until that moment there had been and that I had thereby ruined the lives of two of the most valuable artists the world has ever known." Caroline had been screaming recriminations at Jean, when suddenly she threw a glass of water in her face and told her she meant "to break every goddamned thing in the goddamned house," and then began smashing everything she could lay her hands on: "dishes, glasses, pitchers, bottles of mayonnaise, peanut butter, the sugarbowl, a jar of maple syrup." Frightened, Jean ran next door to Mrs. Cabot's, whose daughter called for the doctor and, when he couldn't come, the sheriff.[72]

News like that travelled quickly around Damariscotta Mills; when she calmed down, Caroline called Tate, who told her to meet him in New York. For Jean, the rupture with the Tates, who would not forgive her for calling the police, would be final. Tate was also furious with Jean for confiding in Caroline his past transgressions. "Won't you please, Jean," he wrote her a few days later, treating her as if it had all been her fault, "never in the future mention my affairs to anybody, or even reply if the subject comes up?"[73] It was not the Tates she was most worried about now, however, but Cal, afraid she would crack up if he didn't take her side when he returned home. But Cal knew the Tates too well to question the truth of her story. As it was, the incident served to throw the Tates into one another's arms, at least for the moment.

Earlier that fall, the Lowells had had Delmore up for a weekend. Rather than go down to Tennessee to stay with Tate, he'd suggested, why not stay with him in Cambridge? Perhaps he could get Cal a Briggs-Copeland Fellowship to teach composition at Harvard for the next few years. And hadn't Jean been thinking of a winter townhouse in Cambridge, at least until they got used to the winters in Maine? Delmore wrote Cal from New York that he planned to be back in Cambridge in late January 1946 and hoped he and Jean would come then to visit for "as long as you like. The longer you stay," he added, "the longer I will like it." There were "two floors, two typewriters, beautiful pictures, too many books, but in fine, adequate provision for whatever solitude and privacy you as Jean may require." As for Tate, he added, *there* was a man who first exhausted his friends, then turned around and accused himself of lacking "charity, forbearance, and imaginative sympathy." Better to spend the winter with someone steadier, like him.[74]

By December the temperature at Damariscotta Mills had plummeted to twenty below, when the Lowells found icicles festooning the bathroom taps. Then the pipes burst. For two weeks they were without plumbing altogether, while the plumbers worked heroically to replace the ancient lead pipes. By the end of the month water was finally restored to the house, at least for the moment. "Practically all our time is taken up with tending fires but even so we are both getting a good bit of work done and Cal has sent off the ms. of his new book," Jean wrote the Taylors at year's end. They'd decided to spend February with Delmore "and give the carpenters a chance to lay the kitchen floor." In fact, the Lowells were "crazy about Delmore," Jean's first impressions of him having been all wrong, for Delmore had turned out to be wonderful fun. It would be "a trial run" to see if three writers could work out "a harmonious menage together."[75]

Sometime that December, when Cal and Jean were isolated in the big house, without a car, without running water, the event occurred which would signal the beginning of the end of their marriage. By then, Jean was once more "drinking like hell," Blair would remember, and driving Cal to distraction. "I really for the first time saw her as a drunk," Blair would recall, after he'd visited. "She was hardly drawing a sober breath. And clearly miserable." Taylor too would remember hearing that Cal had tried to force Jean to have sex against her will. He knew Cal "wanted to have children and that Jean didn't" and Cal had "tried to force the issue."[76]

And Parker would remember Jean telling him that one night, while she was dreaming of a former lover, Cal had awakened her to make love and, still half asleep, she'd repeated her lover's name.[77] In a perfect frenzy, Cal tried to strangle her. She woke up then, groggily aware that she had called out her lover's name, even as Cal's hands tightened on her throat. She began digging her nails into his wrists until suddenly he stopped and left the room. In an unpublished draft of "A Country Love Story," Jean would play the scene again, having the wife, alienated by her husband's absorption in his work, fantasize instead about an imaginary lover. "You bitch, you bitch, you bitch," he would say, "to torture me. Who is he?" And she would answer: "It's not worth it."

Lowell too would brood hard and long over that night, writing it over and over as the central moment of his long poem, *The Mills of the Kavanaughs*, which he began work on after he and Jean were separated. But in the two versions he finally published, though he tried to understand what had happened through Jean's eyes, and though the passage is filled with a kind of twilit sexual giddiness, he could not bring himself to speak even then of his attempt to take her against her will:

> *'Boy, your chin*
> *Is bristling. You have gored me black and blue.*
> *I am all prickle-tickle like the stars;*
> *I am a sleepy-foot, a dogfish skin*

Rubbed backwards, wrongways; you have made my hide
Split snakey, Bad one—one!' Then I was wide
Awake, and turning over. 'Who, who, who?'
You asked me, 'tell me who.' Then everything
Was roaring, Harry. Harry, I could feel
Nothing—it was so black—except your seal,
The stump with green shoots on your signet ring
                              . . . Harry, I am glad
You tried to kill me; it is out, you know;
I'll shout it from the housetops of the Mills;
I'll tell you, so remember, you are mad;
I'll tell them, listen Harry; husband kills
His wife for dreaming. . . .

And then Lowell, recalling his wife watching him in the kitchen in the pre-dawn hours, crouching, beside himself with confusion:

Spread-eagled back on your backless chair,
Inhaling the regardless, whirling air,
Rustling about you from the oven jets,
Sparkling and crackling on the cigarettes
Still burning in the saucer, where you'd tossed
Almost a carton, Love, before you lost
All sense of caring, and I saw your eyes
Looking in wonder at your bloody hand. . . .[78]

   In the winter of 1963, remarried and living in New York, Lowell would face that terrible night yet again in an unpublished draft of "The Old Flame." The summer before he'd detoured off the Maine Highway to drive up through Damariscotta Mills and see how the old house was faring, "Drawn by some magnet / forty miles from my route, as if we were still married."[79] The poem he published would end with an image of his sexual frustration that winter, as he and Jean listened to the enormous engine groaning and plowing just outside their window:

In one bed and apart,
we heard the plow
groaning up hill—
a red light, then a blue,
as it tossed off the snow
to the side of the road.[80]

But even then he would not be able to look back at what his hand had done. Instead he would have to settle for watching himself as if he were someone else, someone other than the man who had "reached at midnight / for your wind-pipe," then spent the rest of the night rocking back and forth "in blue-jeans / by the kitchen stove," waiting for the blue of morning.[81]

At the end of January 1946, the Lowells left Damariscotta Mills to the work-men and moved in with Delmore at 20 Ellery Street in Cambridge. Everyone would pitch in, Delmore decided. He would fix lunch, Jean dinner, and Cal would try to keep the coal furnace going. Four days after his guests had arrived, Delmore was lauding the arrangement. "In mid-morning the household resembles either a literary movement or a school for typists," he wrote his future wife, Elizabeth Pollet. "The only unpleasantness is that Jean gets most of the mail."[82] "Each morning in three rooms three authors compose literary works and two typewriters move from left to right," he wrote the same day to another correspondent. Cal did not type, and was even more than Delmore "a manual lunatic" who couldn't "even play the phonograph."[83]

A month later Jean could still report that she and Cal were having "a splendid time with Delmore," though they would have to be getting back to Maine soon "because a house doesn't like to be left alone too long."[84] But the Lowells also understood it would not be good for the two of them to be alone, and even when they went down to New York in late February to visit friends, they returned with "indigestion, bad nerves and great ill-nature," cross with everyone.[85] Back at Ellery Street, they found that Delmore had acquired a cat named Oranges in their absence. Delmore's company must have soothed them, for they decided to stay on into March, even though the country and the house were calling Jean now that spring was coming.

By mid-March Cal had planned to stay on in Cambridge until Easter, still six weeks away. They'd even taken to calling Delmore's place "Bert-haven," a place where Arms could feel at home. On the 19th, Delmore arranged for Cal to meet T. S. Eliot's older brother, Henry Ware Eliot, to see if a Briggs-Copeland Fellowship couldn't be managed for Cal, since, as Delmore explained, it was absolutely essential for any literary career to have one. "I have never been so charmed," Jean wrote the Taylors, "even though Mrs. Eliot confused me with Carson McCullers whose new book [*The Member of the Wedding*] had been reviewed in the morning's Times." Because Ware had turned out to be "stone deaf," conversation had been a bit difficult, she noted, but what "came through so beautifully was [Ware's] deep devotion to his brother." But even Delmore's comic, byzantine scheming produced no fellow-ship for Cal.[86]

Now that her son was so close by, Mrs. Lowell was eager to see more of him, was, in fact, rather put off that Cal had decided to stay with Delmore rather than with her. Luncheons were therefore *de rigueur* and frequent, though they left Jean nearly traumatized. She had not been "so persistently needled," she said, since before she and Cal had been married. "Your family is just a myth to me, Jean," Charlotte told her on one visit. "In our little community here, we all marry our third cousins and know everyone." And: "You are looking well, Jean, and putting on weight, but Bobby looks terribly thin and not at all well." And again: "Is it that you don't like us that you didn't stay with us instead of Mr. Schwartz?"[87] No wonder Jean felt a certain *schadenfreude* in hearing of an after-church coffee gathering at which an officious hostess had asked a certain Mrs. X if she knew Mrs. Lowell, and the woman had answered no, she didn't, but that she had enough troubles as things were.[88]

On March 16, Mrs. Lowell gave a cocktail party for seventy-five people, to which Bob Giroux—in Cambridge then to sign contracts for Cal's and Jean's new books—and Delmore were both invited. It was after this party that the Cambridge menage turned noticeably sour. Delmore, preternaturally suspicious of slights in any event, felt intimidated by the servants, heirlooms, and the palpable reserve of Cal's parents. Nor did it help matters that Cal more than once pointed to the portrait of Mordecai Myers, his nineteenth-century ancestor, and remarked that he too was Jewish. At least one-eighth Jewish. Nor that Bob Lowell had kept remarking how much Delmore sounded "like a Jew."[89]

As if that weren't enough, when Delmore had visited the Lowells in Maine the previous fall, Frank Parker and his English wife, Leslie, had also been there. After Delmore left, Leslie had told Cal she was sure something was going on between Delmore and Jean. When Jean learned of this, she was so upset, Parker recalled, that she told Cal to show the Parkers out. Parker himself did not think anything serious was going on, but Cal was furious.[90] Now, after the bruising he'd received at the hands of Cal's parents, Delmore began teasing Cal that Jean was interested in another man, perhaps even himself. Given the frayed tightrope Jean and Cal were dancing in their life together, it was a stupid and suicidal thing for Delmore to do.

Then, one night in late March, when they'd all been drinking, Delmore went too far and Cal, who already harbored suspicions about Delmore and Jean, hit him before Jean could break up the argument. Almost at once Cal was sorry for what he'd done, and tried to make it up with Delmore. But the Ellery Street experiment was over; it was time now for the Lowells to leave, Jean returning to Castine, and Cal to the Trappist monastery in Rhode Island to make a ten-day retreat. "The Lowells have departed," Delmore wrote Elizabeth Pollet on the 26th. "Calvin" had returned to the Trappist Fathers, "desiring silence after hearing what I had to say about the Holy Apostolic Church." And Jean was back in Maine, where there would also be silence. "Both," he sighed, "are so devoted to me now that I am ashamed."[91]

"A couple of days ago Delmore Schwartz died from a heart-attack," Lowell would write Elizabeth Bishop twenty years later. Delmore had collapsed "just outside his room in a cheap New York hotel—alone, out of touch, for a year, a shadow, a rumor seen here and there, gone underground, after he vanished and hid from Syracuse University, angry that he hadn't been given tenure. Maybe the heat killed him . . . but really his end was in the cards for long, too much drinking, a paranoia that cut him off from jobs, and even friends." Back in 1938, Caroline Gordon had once told him that Delmore was "the one mature young man" she'd met. At the time the comment had stung, but then Cal could feel he had been "dismissed with a great swarm of other young men." And besides, in 1938 there had been truth in her comment. *In Dreams Begin Responsibilities* "had just come out, and reasonable, intuitive essays, the old new criticism, but with a new touch, in all the Quarterlies." But by the time Lowell had come to know him well, in 1946, Delmore was "much more bruised and swollen." Looking back now, he could see that it had been

> an intimate gruelling year . . . Jean and he and I, sedentary, indoors souls, talking about books and literary gossip over glasses of milk, strengthened with Maine vodka. . . . Delmore in an unpressed mustard gaberdeen, a little winded, husky-voiced, unhealthy, but with a carton of varied vitamin bottles, the color of oil, quickening with Jewish humor, and in-the-knowness, and his own genius, every person, every book—motives for everything, Freud in his blood, great webs of causation, then suspicion, then rushes of rage. He was more reasonable then, but obsessed, a much better mind, but one already chasing the dust—it was like living with a sluggish, sometimes angry spider—no hurry, no motion, Delmore's voice, almost inaudible, dead, intuitive, pointing somewhere, then the strings tightening, the roar of rage—too much, too much for us! Nothing haunts me more than breaking with friends. I used to think he was the only one I broke with.[92]

"Rabelaisian, lubricious, drugged," Lowell would write in his poem, "To Delmore Schwartz," his elegy for a friendship. The qualifiers name the stuffed duck Delmore kept in his apartment, but point in reality to both Cal and Delmore, "Underseas fellows," both "nobly mad," talking away their friends, while a portrait of the paranoid Coleridge, convinced at one point that Napoleon's entire Navy was after him, gazed down on poor, paranoid Delmore in that mustard yellow room, the elegy's final broken lines signifying the slow, drunken dissolution of a friendship and of a world:

The room was filled
with cigarette smoke circling the paranoid,
inert gaze of Coleridge, back
from Malta—his eyes lost in flesh, lips baked and black.
Your tiger kitten, Oranges,
cartwheeled for joy in a ball of snarls.
You said:
"We poets in our youth begin in sadness;
thereof in the end come despondency and madness;
Stalin has had two cerebral hemorrhages!"
The Charles
River was turning silver. In the ebb-
light of morning, we stuck
the duck
-'s web-
foot, like a candle, in a quart of gin we'd killed.[93]

Randall, finally discharged from the Army in early 1946, had settled in New York by early April, ready to take over as poetry editor of *The Nation* during the year-long absence of Margaret Marshall. After four years in quonset huts in Arizona and Texas, he was hungry now for literary contact, and he took his job as editor very seriously. He also planned to teach part time at Sarah Lawrence that year, where Robert Fitzgerald—who would render magnificent translations of the *Iliad,* the *Odyssey,* and the *Aeneid* over the next forty years—was also teaching. Fitzgerald would remember Randall at thirty-two as "young and tallish and a bit gangling but with dignity, his long throat distinctly angled, his dark eyes in repose proud and solemn, the lids drooping slightly toward the outer corners . . . hooded eyes where memory and mockery lurked. . . . He loved his job at *The Nation,* or at least he certainly loved the game of matching reviewers and books, and he did it so well that in . . . Ransom's later judgment his editorship deserved a Pulitzer Prize."[94] It was useful being poetry editor of a magazine, Randall had told Cal, for "when the same readers read you steadily, you don't have to keep repeating your first principles in each new review."[95] Since he knew Cal's work so well, he meant to scoop everyone by asking for as many of the best new poems as he could get for *The Nation,* and began by printing "Colloquy in Black Rock," "At the Indian Killer's Grave," "The Exile's Return, and "Where the Rainbow Ends." By the time *Lord Weary's Castle* was published, *The Nation* had printed twelve of its poems.

After he finished his retreat in early April, Cal returned to Damariscotta Mills and the carpenters and paperhangers and painters for ten days, then decided to go off to New York to stay with Randall for a week. "I am again left here alone with the mice," Jean wrote Taylor on the 15th, the day Cal left.[96] Alone with the workers and the old house, she consoled herself with liquor, the very thing which had driven Cal away. Predictably, the New York week turned to two, then to three, so that Cal was still there on May 6, when the offices of *The Nation* were turned over to celebrate Jarrell's coming aboard. One of those invited to the party was John Berryman, Delmore's close friend and former colleague at Harvard, who for the past two years had been at Princeton, where he'd already briefly met Cal in company with the Blackmurs. But now, in New York, Cal was so taken by Berryman's combination of wit and intelligence (he seemed to Lowell to have read *everything*) that he invited the Berrymans to visit him and Jean in Maine that summer, an offer Berryman would take him up on. And, though Tate was no longer speaking to Jean, he managed to see Cal in New York, for, "unobserved," one New Yorker—Boden Broadwater, Mary McCarthy's husband—had watched "Cousin Tate—in the most faun-colored of suits—taking cocktails in the Algonquin lobby with Mad Lowell."[97] On the train back to Maine, Cal also stopped off in Cambridge to see Delmore.[98]

But the workmen were still at Damariscotta when Cal returned on May 9, making it almost impossible for him to move about in his own home. "When he came back and found the house fresh with all this wallpaper and this new paint," Stafford would tell Taylor, "he exploded and said that it was cheap, that it was immoral, and that I had done the whole thing out of a desire to stifle him."[99] Thirty years later, in "An Influx of Poets," she would repeat that it had been her "nesting and . . . neatening" that Cal had looked on "as plebeian, anti-intellectual, lace-curtain Irish." For solace Cal took to the open again, "birding with field glasses every day," and reading a series of books called *Birds of New England* "by a Mr. Forbrush who is the most eccentric writer of our times," and whose "running attack on the 'pernicious activities' of cats" set "Jean's teeth on edge."[100]

Over the Memorial Day weekend Cal's parents came up for a visit. Then Cal and Jean went down together to New York for a week-long visit with Randall and Taylor. But no sooner were the Lowells back in Damariscotta Mills than the summer guests began arriving in force. After a week of it Jean was already exhausted. "In some ways," she confided to her sister on June 13, "the problem is not terribly complex. I am suffering from years and years of ac-cumulated fatigue, not only from working hard but from spreading myself too thin and knowing too many people. Being a writer is a back-breaking job and now my back is broken."[101] Two weeks later she complained to Mock that so far 1946 had been awful and now she had "a million new neuroses and a bone-deep and permanent fatigue." By then, with full summer upon them, the house had at last been finished, along with *The Mountain Lion* and *Lord Weary's Castle*. But already she worried what the coming winter would bring, brooding about "the job of closing the house" and wondering why on earth they'd ever taken a house upon themselves, a house which had ruined them financially and her physically. By then too they had both made themselves "so eccentric" that she feared they would be "left alone by the absolutely *good* neighbors we have."[102]

In spite of which, between them, Cal and Jean managed to invite everyone to enjoy their house that summer. The list included: their old neighbors from Westport, their Boothbay Harbor landlord with his wife and her parents, Peter and Eleanor Taylor, Blair and Holly Clark, Frank and Leslie Parker, Robert Hightower and his wife, Delmore, the Blackmurs, the Berrymans, Bob Giroux, Richard Eberhart, the Rahvs. "That awful summer!", Jean would remember, when "every poet in America came to stay with us. It was the first summer after the war, when people once again had gasoline and could go where they liked. . . . At night, after supper, they'd read from their own works until four o'clock in the morning, drinking Cuba Libres. . . . And then all day I'd cook and wash the dishes and chop the ice and weed the garden and type my husband's poems and quarrel with him."[103]

Of all the guests who arrived that summer, the most important for Lowell's own poetry would be Berryman. John and Eileen arrived in Damariscotta Mills after a stay with the Blackmurs further up the coast in late July, and—though they were scheduled for just a weekend visit—Cal was so taken with his new-found Scholar Gypsy that the Berrymans stayed twelve days. Berryman would remember that time as "lazy, agreeable, interesting & alcoholic."[104] For Lowell's part, it was *this* Berryman, the young, clean-shaven scholar who had read everything and could quote at marvellous length from so many poets, and not the drunken, bearded Henry of the *Dream Songs*, whom he would think back on with such fondness.

"Too many guests had accepted," Lowell would recall twenty-five years later, after the Scholar Gypsy had preceded him to the Circle of Philosophers. And though he and Jean had been "inept and uncouth at getting the most out of the country," Berryman had been "all ease and light. We gossiped on the rocks of the millpond, baked things in shells on the sand, and drank, as was the appetite of our age." Over those twelve days Cal found himself in heaven, talking with one of his few peers on Browning, Arnold, Hopkins, Tennyson, Swift, Dunbar, Henryson, Alun Lewis, Chatterton, Chaucer, Gray, and the Newman who had written the *Apologia*. It was Berryman, he would remember, who had shown him how to read Shakespeare's late style and "what could be done with disrupted and mended syntax."[105] In the difficult poems Berryman himself was already writing, Cal would come to see, the syntax and diction of "Homage to Mistress Bradstreet" and of *The Dream Songs* was already beginning to form, to flower later in such swift and delicious surprises as:

But never did Henry, as he thought he did,
end anyone and hacks her body up
and hide the pieces, where they may be found.
He knows; he went over everyone, & nobody's missing.
Often he reckons, in the dawn, them up.
Nobody is ever missing.[106]

Setting the dishes after each meal as her mother had done at the boarding-house she'd run when Jean was a girl, Jean unburdened herself to Eileen. She'd fallen in love with Caligula, she told her, and now she was living with Calvin. During Lent he'd starved himself, and if he could have got his hands on one, he'd have worn a hair shirt. He wouldn't even drink with her. But that didn't stop Jean from keeping a secret stash and a cocaine nose-spray, or from sitting up all night alone in the dimly lit kitchen, an open bottle before her. By then she'd even stopped changing her clothes, donning the same checked slacks and black sweater each day.[107]

"Our well is almost dry and bathing is out of the question and has been for two weeks," Jean wrote the Taylors on August 7, "and it is possible to wash dishes only once a day so that by evening the kitchen is a sight." The Berrymans had left at nine that morning and by ten Bob Giroux and a friend had arrived. So it had gone. By then they'd had "regiments of people" and she was "weary and cross" at a house which refused to stay clean.[108] In early July, when the Rahvs had come up, they came bearing gifts from Delmore for Jean's thirty-first birthday. These were three kittens from Oranges' first litter, which Delmore had already named for her: Oranges Fish Jr., Comic Strip Cat, and Smarty Pants Schwartz. And though the kittens were a comfort to her, their incessant scampering about made things seem all the more crowded. After Giroux and his friend, she still had the Parkers, the Clarks, the Blackmurs, and Gertrude Buckman to look forward to, so that both her writing and her marriage had taken their toll. More than just the well had gone dry.

Then, on August 13, Lowell wrote Taylor a note so uncharacteristic for him that it clearly signalled a crisis. "I don't care for confessions," he wrote, "but I suppose I must tell you that everything is chaos between us. Jean is driving like a cyclone and we both have had about all we can stand and more." He thought he might go to New York in September and stay with the Jarrells, then "get a room to pick up some sort of temporary work." Jean had lots "of plans, none of them too good, including going to Hollywood." Anyway, he added, "we have got to *leave each other alone* and the future to time." Please, he added, "just be an ear for this letter, and don't say anything to me or anyone else."[109] Three days later Jean wrote in a similar but more scattered way to her sister. "It is quite impossible to determine what we shall do," she began. "We know only that we cannot live together next winter, but whether we shall yet make permanent arrangements, I don't know." It was hideous having to conceal from their visitors what was really going on, and worse—she added darkly—to "feel conspired against."[110]

The "conspiracy" must have seemed to Jean the mirror inversion of the Cambridge ménage, this time with Delmore's ex-wife, Gertrude Buckman, filling in for Delmore. On the day Cal wrote Taylor, while Jean was in Boston seeing her dentist (though Cal suspected she was seeing Delmore), Gertrude Buckman landed gloriously and dramatically, like some dea ex machina, by seaplane on Damariscotta Lake. "She came to us," Stafford would write, "quixotically and at the expense of her last host, in a Piper Cub, landing . . . behind us. . . . I was not there on that beautiful afternoon when her blithe plane banked and came bobbing to rest and she came swimming to our landing."

"The clever quicksilver, the heartless fey, the no-woman, the bedeviller," Jean would vilify Buckman for helping to end her marriage.[111] And though it was Jean who'd invited her up, it was Cal who monopolized Gertrude's company, going for long walks with her, or swimming in the lake, something the hydrophobic Jean was afraid to try. Bad as it was to have Gertrude around, criticizing Jean's cooking and housekeeping, it was gall to hear Cal agreeing with Gertrude on everything. But when, according to Buckman, she offered to leave, Jean begged her to stay, afraid now to be alone with Cal. Buckman would also insist that, all the while she was there, she and Cal never so much as held hands.[112]

Buckman's visit lasted three weeks, until after Labor Day, when she returned to her New York apartment, from whence she wrote long, fairylike, rambling letters which said in all but words how much she was in love with Cal, and how very beautiful and odd he was. She would also insist that it was Cal who had made the first move. But it hardly mattered by then, for the Lowells' marriage was over. There is a photograph from that summer, perhaps taken by Gertrude. It is an open field. In the garish midday sunlight, Jean, her hair in Heidelberg braids, looks pained, as if she wanted to be left alone. Cal, wearing a lumberjack shirt, squints toward the camera, likewise in pain. "It is just barely possible that if I can ever pull myself together something will work out for us," Jean told the Taylors at the end of August, trying to sound noble and detached, even as her sentences began to unravel. "But I love Cal too much now to allow him any longer to be subjected to what seems to amount almost to insanity. . . . I am almost altogether to blame for my life being the ruin that it is."[113] And that same day to Mock: "I am really on the verge of something and as soon as I have cleared the house I shall close it and go away, I don't know where yet. I am a hopeless mess."[114]

Just after Labor Day, when Gertrude, the last of the regular summer guests, departed, Jean could at last "rise to consciousness again." It was the second day now that she and Cal had seen no one and they would both sleep well because they'd had "a long row on the lake today." She'd rowed part of the time, "rattled and cross and resentful" at Cal, "for I saw no reason why I should be in the boat at all since I could not swim." For the moment, at least, alone in the quiet of their house, things between them seemed a little less hopeless.[115] But it was all wishful thinking, even the part about sleeping well. The truth was, as she confessed to Mock, that it had been one hell of a summer "and I drank to a mad extent and drove myself and fetched up with a first-class case of insomnia so that even now when everyone has gone and no one else is coming, I do not close my eyes on an average of two nights a week." The incessant drinking had left her in "dreadful nervous shape," and she was thinking of going off to Bermuda alone and then returning "in a month or so to whatever modest cold-water flat Cal has found for us in New York."[116]

But, though she tried not to think about it, by then she knew—they both knew—that she and Cal would never live in "Lord Weary's castle" or anywhere else together again. If they came back to the house her *Boston Adventure* had made possible, it would be in the spring, and it would be to get rid of the place. At the moment, only the Jarrells and the Taylors knew anything about all this, for the "Tatian demonstrations of last autumn" had taught them both "a few things."[117] When, on September 15, the Parkers arrived belatedly for a visit, Jean had already taken the curtains down and the rugs up. Then, when the Parkers had left, Cal at last told Jean the marriage was finished. On the evening of the 19th, their last night together in Maine, after Cal had gone to bed, Jean sat up before the fireplace dropping Cal's letters to her into the flames. In the dour, preternatural silence broken only by the cry of a loon on the lake, she looked out the window and thought she saw Father Lynch hiding in a tree, his outline highlighted by the light coming from the Kavanagh mansion. "Something was coming," she would remember. "I could smell it like the air before a hurricane and I thought, 'I can't take it.' "[118]

A priest looming in a tree, watching over the death of a marriage. It was a nightmarish omen for Jean as much as for Cal. For, if Lowell was about to leave Jean and take up with another woman, in a strange *ménage à quatre* linking himself to Gertrude, as he suspected Jean was linked to Delmore, then he would have to leave his Catholicism behind when he left for New York. When, the previous winter, Ransom had asked him to expand a review he'd done of Newman's *Apologia*, Cal had told him he no longer had the heart for such things and had grown tired of theological questions, though he still went to Mass.[119] But even there much of the zeal was gone, so that, walking to the 8:00 A.M. Mass one morning that summer, he'd complained to Jean that

Father Lynch would probably be even "more long-winded" than usual, "since he would have no prospect of breakfast" until he'd finished the ten.[120]

In August, when Eberhart had come over for a visit from Castine, the two of them had argued religion. But in truth, Lowell wrote him afterwards, he was no longer interested in pursuing such issues, especially by mail. True, he was "an old hand" at apologetics, this man who two years before had meant to spend his life defending the faith from a soapbox, but by the summer of '46 he'd learned by "sad experience" that nothing was "more futile" than arguing religion, unless it was "the current New York discussions of Stalinism. One says the same thing again and again, and everyone ends up where he started." From now on, God and the Church would have to be found everywhere. The upshot of it all, then—the daily masses, the year at LSU, the year at Sheed & Ward, the year at Monteagle, the two years at West Street and Danbury and Black Rock and Maine—the upshot of all that was that he was now "probably a little better person" than he might otherwise have been.[121]

On Friday morning, September 20, Cal—in Jean's recounting—rowed out halfway to Loon Islet on Damariscotta Lake and dropped the weighted gunnysack containing Oranges Fish Jr., Comic Strip Cat, and Smarty Pants Schwartz over the side of the boat. Then he and Jean locked up the house, took the taxi to the train station, and rode south together to New York. Jean would remember Cal sitting there, reading Augustine's *Confessions,* all the while knowing Gertrude was waiting for him in New York. One last time she confronted him about this on the train, only to have Cal tell her he was tired of wives and wanted a playmate.[122] When, at nightfall, their train pulled into Penn Station, they took a taxi across town to a dingy tenement on East 11th Street, a hangout for pimps and prostitutes. Cal's room—where Jean would spend just one night—was above a kosher butcher shop, reached by a side entrance down a dark, forbidding corridor called Slaughter Alley.[123]

PART II

6

A Bigger Stage

1946–1948

The following day—September 21— Jean moved into the New Weston Hotel in midtown Manhattan. Distraught, humiliated, psychically exhausted, she was still intent on saving her marriage. She would allow Cal to see Gertrude, even arranging for the three of them to visit the Bronx Zoo together. But Cal had plans of his own, and they did not include Jean. When he and Gertrude showed up at Jean's hotel, they made prickly little comments about overly possessive people, then left, "very much," Jean complained, "like two married people obliged to have dinner with a boring relative." Bad as it was, she needed the marriage, for it meant "roots, home, a safe place."[1] Soon she was drinking again, alone and incessantly, far into the lengthening nights, in her room, at the bar. Bob Giroux tried to help by sending her to a psychiatrist, who told her she would first have to stop drinking before he could help her. She did not go back.

Meanwhile, in spite of coming down first with crabs and then the flu in his miserable tenement, Cal's spirits continued to rise. Within a month of moving to New York, he took Randall down to Princeton to have dinner with the Berrymans to get to know his Scholar Gypsy better. But the night they went, Randall was suffering from food poisoning, so that the visit turned out to be a disaster. Nor did Randall much care for Cal's praising this interloper, especially when he himself was feeling like death. "So here's Randall walking up and down in my living room, miserable and witty," Berryman would remember. "And very malicious, as he could certainly be, making up a brand-new Lowell poem full of characteristic Lowell properties, Lowell's grandfather and Charon, and the man who did not find this funny at all was Lowell. . . . At last we calmed Randall down . . . and stationed him on the couch, and I gave him a book of photographs of the Russian ballet (he was very keen on the ballet). While the rest of us had dinner, he lay there and made witty remarks about the photographs of the Russian ballet."[2]

"My pilgrimage to Princeton with Randall . . . to have dinner with the Berrymans was not happy," Lowell would later admit. "Compared with other poets, John was a prodigy; compared with Randall, a slow starter. . . . John jarred the evening by playing his own favorite recordings on an immense machine constructed and formerly used" by the popular music critic, Bernard Haggin. Things worsened; Berryman tried ballet:

> One liked Covent Garden, the other Danilova, Markova, and the latest New York Balanchine. Berryman unfolded leather photograph books of enlarged British ballerinas he had almost dated. Jarrell made cool, odd evaluations drawn from his forty, recent, consecutive nights of New York ballet. He hinted that the English dancers he had never seen were on a level with the Danes. I suffered more than the fighters, and lost authority by trying not to take sides. . . . On the horrible New Jersey midnight local to Pennsylvania Station, Randall analyzed John's high, intense voice with surprise and coldness. "Why hasn't anyone told him?" Randall had the same high, keyed-up voice he criticized. Soon he developed chills and fevers, ever more violent, and I took my suit coat and covered him. He might have been a child. John, the host, the insulted one, recovered sooner. His admiration for Randall remained unsoured, but the dinner was never repeated.[3]

A season of disintegrations, a season of flights. In mid-October, Jean went out to Detroit to admit herself into a hospital for alcoholics, but the Gothic structure so reminded her of Yaddo that she stayed only ten hours, before fleeing to her sister's ranch. Even there she lasted just five days, unable to stop drinking. Defeated, she returned to New York, where she took a seedy hotel room in the Village and each night drank herself into a stupor. She who had once wanted to help Dorothy Day's derelicts now looked like one herself. Once she found Delmore sitting on a bench in Washington Square Park, but by then he was in worse shape even than she. Then, in late October, a letter from Cal arrived. He was asking for a divorce.

By late November she'd seen Cal twice about lawyers. Cal had moved into the shabby basement apartment of a tenement for men only over on Third

Avenue, with the El roaring overhead every ten minutes. Once he met Jean on neutral ground, a coffee shop on 14th Street, without ever asking her how she was faring. No doubt the answer was all too clear. Cal was requesting a divorce on grounds of adultery—hers—and refused to sign over the title of the house to her unless she agreed neither to contest the divorce nor to ask for alimony. He was "just as much a Lowell," she shuddered, as he'd always been.

It pained her too to learn that he'd really left the Church, "having used her up" just as he'd used her. It drove her to distraction to see Cal acting with such "calm, Olympian brutality" while she was going to pieces.[4] She'd married her father, she was beginning to see at last, just as Cal had his mother. Finally, in late November, she admitted herself to Payne Whitney—"the loony bin," she called it, "Luna Park," a "high-class booby-hatch"—for "psycho-alcoholic" treatment, and soon she was glad for the space to regroup. "The first thing we do in the morning," she wrote her sister after a month there, "is go out to a small courtyard where we walk round and round as fast as the mischief for half an hour. A high grille separates us from the free world and you feel that at any moment passersby will toss us peanuts."[5]

At Christmas, Peter Taylor tried to act as intermediary between two of his closest friends. He asked them to forget about lawyers and postpone the divorce for a year. During that time, they were not to "communicate with each other" except through him.[6] Cal was at Yaddo when the letter came, having gone up to spend Christmas there alone and get some writing done. "The time for considering and re-considering is long past," he wrote Taylor, and he would only be counting the days till the year was up. Moreover, what Peter remembered of Jean and what he himself had been through with her were far different realities. "You mustn't idealize what other people have to live," he ended. "You mustn't."[7] Jean too turned down the idea, for the plan would only free Cal to reject her again, and that would hurt more than she could bear.[8] Seeing how things stood, Taylor withdrew his offer.

With each rambling, disjointed letter she wrote, Jean seemed only to make matters worse. When Cal wrote her about working out a settlement, she accused him of being a Yankee trader. As abruptly, she changed her mind and told him not to worry about the money. Cal's response was simpler: they had to learn to leave each other alone. When Jean had entered the hospital, she'd told no one, hoping Cal would start looking for her. But when that strategy failed, she called the Jarrells, the only people in New York Cal was seeing besides Gertrude. Did Mackie think there was any chance for a reconciliation? She did not. Could Mackie ask Cal to see her at Payne Whitney? She would try. A few days later, back from a short stay at Yaddo, Cal visited her. But he was as distant as ever. He meant to marry Gertrude, he told her. He was also being advised by his father and his Cousin Alfred—those two "financial wizards," she called them—so that she was afraid of once more being "bested by Boston." Worse, the news of her being in the hospital was now "all over the damned town."[9]

One visit, then, and most of that spent hearing about Gertrude Buckman's "many virtues." (One of those virtues, incidentally, was Gertrude's ability to write little Blakean satires, like the one in the March issue of *Partisan Review,* which went: "So the symbolic wedding ring / Often does not mean a thing / And infidelity runs rife / While everyday is simply strife / And everyone loves another's mate / And looks upon his own with hate.")[10] We cannot know what Cal wrote Jean, because his letters were long ago turned to ash. Nor can everything Jean said in her letters be believed, for she was in very bad shape then, and even at her best had a penchant for rewriting history. But Cal believed the marriage was over, and if he saw no one but the Jarrells, it was because, as he told Taylor that March, he dreaded seeing anyone.

In October 1946 Tate had written Cal, astounded at the "immense advance" his protégé had made in his poetry in the three years between the writing of *Land of Unlikeness* and *Lord Weary's Castle.* It was, indeed, "one of the most astonishing things in modern poetry."[11] And Karl Shapiro, Poetry Consultant for the Library of Congress, had written Cal praising him for his "drunken control that old man Hopkins had."[12] So the praise had begun even before the publication of *Lord Weary* in December. Then, in early 1947, came Randall's stunning review in *The Nation,* speaking of "a unique fusion of modernist and traditional poetry," the presence of certain effects existing side by side "one would have thought mutually exclusive," something new, "a post- or anti-modernist poetry . . . certain to be influential." He spoke too of the "raised voice" of a new rhetoric, of a new poetry which resembled "a great deal of traditional English poetry" in contrast to the Imagist or Objectivist poetry of Pound, Eliot, Moore, and Williams.[13] (Eight months later he would see the book—perceptively—as at heart a "verse history of New England.")[14] Berryman, writing for the *Partisan Review,* saw in *Lord Weary* "a talent whose ceiling is invisible."[15] Selden Rodman in the *New York Times Book Review,* and Austin Warren in *Poetry,* were both laudatory, as was Howard Moss in the *Kenyon Review,* who spoke of "that surprising phenomenon: a religious poet who writes like a revolutionary."[16]

In February, by which time Cal had moved to his third New York address in five months—an apartment on East 15th Street—he learned that Louis Untermeyer was to include him in his next anthology of American poets. He was flattered, he told Untermeyer, since Untermeyer's anthologies had long become an institution. In fact, he'd first read modern poetry in one of Untermeyer's anthologies as far back as 1931, when he was in the Third Form at St. Mark's, and could still remember "declaiming James Whicomb Riley, and being baffled by Stephen Crane's grass. Why was each blade 'a singular knife,' or something of the sort." And though he'd only just been asked to "join" the anthology himself, he wondered if some of his friends might not keep him company: Karl Shapiro, Randall, Robert Penn Warren (the later work), and—a new friend—Elizabeth Bishop.[17]

Bishop, who at thirty-five had just published her first book of poems, *North & South,* was living in a garret on King Street in the Village that winter, and was visiting the Jarrells when she first met Cal. "I loved him at first sight," she would remember, thinking back to that January evening in 1947. "He was living in a basement room on Third Avenue . . . and he was rather untidy. He was wearing a rumpled dark blue suit; I remember the sad state of his shoes; he needed a hair cut, and he was very handsome and handsome in an almost old-fashioned poetic way. I took to him at once; I didn't feel the least bit afraid." It was the first time she had "ever actually talked with someone about how one writes poetry," and it was a friendship which quickly blossomed into the most important in Lowell's life.[18] It would, in fact, have a profound and lasting impact on the way Lowell would come to understand what a poem could do.

In early February, Jean received emergency leave from Payne Whitney to visit her dying mother in Oregon. By the time she reached her parents' home, however, her mother was gone. All the way out, she'd been terrified that she would drink herself to death, but except that she found her broken father "more stunningly boring" than ever, the trip passed without incident.[19] She was back in the hospital when Lowell's poem, "Her Dead Brother," appeared in *The Nation* on the 21st, just as advance copies of her novel, *The Mountain Lion,* also reached her. Since poem and novel both used the theme of latent incest between brother and sister, Jean took the fact of Cal's poem appearing just now personally, especially as her novel was dedicated both to Cal and to her dead brother.

How could he have published such a poem, she wrote him. It was "an act of so deep dishonor that it passes beyond dishonor and approaches madness. And I am trembling in the presence of your hate."[20] At some point Jean had confided to Cal that there'd been some sort of sexual intimacy between her and Dick as children. Like Dick, the brother in Cal's poem had also died in battle, and the sister mourns in a town (like Damariscotta Mills) near the ocean, for "a New England town is death / and incest." Jean, who understood well enough that the poems Cal was now writing were oblique autobiographies, believed that Cal was commenting on her relationship with the one man she probably ever loved without qualification, her brother:

We will forget that August twenty-third,
When Mother motored with the maids to Stowe,
And the pale summer shades were drawn—so low
No one could see us; no, nor catch your hissing word,
As false as Cressid! Let our deaths atone. . . .[21]

And Lowell, though he may have thought he'd changed what was irritating him enough that no one would catch on, seems to have fastened on Dick to get back at the man who in his imagination at least had superseded him in Jean's affections. "No one could see us," a draft of the poem now at Harvard reads, to show how accurate Jean's intuition was,

> *and you came to me*
> *Touching and almost touching there alone!*
> *Your face is closer than it was alive*
> *And night blots out the hard half of your smile.*

On March 20, 1947, Lowell took the train down to visit the Taylors at the Womans' College in Greensboro, North Carolina. Taylor had organized a Writers' Forum there, in effect a Kenyon reunion which included Robie Macauley, John Thompson, Warren, Cal, and himself. Cal spent a month in the South, much of it with the Taylors, some of it trying to find traces of the Devereauxs—his maternal grandmother's family—in and around Raleigh, North Carolina, without much success. At Easter (April 6) he was in Charleston, South Carolina, "admiring the old houses," and visiting Fort Sumter, "horrified by the flat, coastal desert that surrounds it."[22] That forbidding landscape, including the spit of submerged sand where the Confederates defending Battery Wagner had once stood off an attack by the Black Massachusetts 54th, would come to figure prominently in his great public poem written fifteen years later, "For the Union Dead."

When Lowell returned to New York late on Sunday, April 20, there was good news waiting for him. He'd received a Guggenheim Fellowship for $2,500, another $1,000 from his publisher for *Lord Weary's Castle*, a $1,000 grant from the American Academy of Arts and Letters, and the Pulitzer for poetry. He'd also been awarded a two-month stay at Yaddo, and *Life magazine* was doing a photofeature on "Young U.S. Writers," in which he would feature. (The issue, which appeared in mid-May, included Jean as well, touted as the "most brilliant of the new fiction writers" and "wife of Pulitzer Prize winning poet Robert Lowell.")[23] A Hollywood movie producer, seeing a photograph of the stunningly handsome poet, called Harcourt, Brace, to ask if Lowell had done any acting. When the *Boston Sunday Globe* followed up with a feature on Lowell, placing him higher than either of his prestigious forbears, they quoted Cal's father as saying that poets seemed "to see more in his work than most other people."[24]

In late April, Cal went up to Payne Whitney to see Jean about the settlement and to offer her some money, especially now that he had some. "I spent a long day with Cal," Jean wrote the Taylors on the 24th, "and I did not sleep at all that night." The meeting had been like the wake of her dead marriage, for Cal required "the behavior of his friends to conform to his wishes" and he did not make concessions. He really did seem to have changed, she noted, so that somehow over the years "his really bad habits" had transferred over to her. Now it was *she* who argued "in the most rhetorical and polemical fashion" and who sought "to order and direct."[25] Two weeks later she felt strong enough to go up to Damariscotta Mills to begin the job of dismantling and selling the house. But by the second night she was so unnerved by old ghosts that she began drinking again, and on her return to the hospital was forbidden once again to leave the grounds.

Late that April Giroux invited Cal to meet T. S. Eliot at his offices at Harcourt, Brace in Manhattan. Eliot was so taken by Cal that he asked to see him again when he went up to Harvard in early June. The author of *Prufrock, The Waste Land,* and *Four Quartets,* and the acknowledged legislator of modern poetry, Eliot was now nearly sixty, Lowell half that age. Years later, Cal would recall that meeting. "Behind us," he wrote,

> Harvard's Memorial Hall with its wasteful, irreplaceable Victorian architecture and scrolls of the Civil War dead. Before us, the rush-hour traffic. As we got stuck on the sidewalk, looking for an opening, Eliot out of the blue sky said, "Don't you loathe being compared with your relatives?" Pause, as I put the question to myself, groping for what I really felt, for what I should decently feel and what I should indecently feel. Eliot: "I do. . . . I was reading Poe's reviews the other day. He took up two of my family and wiped the floor with them. . . . I was delighted."[26]

Just how much Eliot meant to Lowell can be gleaned from a comment Lowell made just months before his own death, when he wrote of him: "There is no elder or contemporary, no parent or childhood blood relation, half a century's memory, that I more yearn to see return alive."[27]

On June 4, just back from Cambridge, Lowell wired Tate in Washington that he had decided to accept the Consultantship in Poetry for the coming year, beginning in September, with a salary of $5,000 a year. Then he wrote Iowa, withdrawing from the $3,000-a-year teaching position he'd just accepted there. That job, he figured, could wait. Then he went up to Yaddo to work on a translation of Racine's *Phèdre* and some poems, including "Falling Asleep Over the Aeneid" and a "symbolic monologue by an insane woman," which was the strained beginnings of *The Mills of the Kavanaughs.* That poem might come to 1,000 lines, he thought, for Yaddo was so conducive to work that he found himself moving ahead like "a steam engine." The speaker of the poem would be based partly on his mother, partly on his mother-surrogate, Jean.

He found most of his co-workers at Yaddo mere "goons," though "friendly and harmless" enough. Among them were several old acquaintances, including Mary McCarthy and her husband, Bowden Broadwater, and Marguerite Young, who had by now turned out to be "rather crucifyingly odd and garrulous." But he also made some new friends that summer, especially J. F. Powers, the Irish Catholic short story writer and later author of the National Book Award-winning novel *Morte D'Urban,* a man with a wonderfully mordant wit, and Powers's editor at Doubleday, Bucklin Moon. And then there was Theodore Roethke, ten years Cal's senior, "a ponderous, coarse, fattish, fortyish man," Cal called him, "well read, likes the same things I do, and is quite a competent poet."[28]

By the end of the month, Cal had become so taken by a new poem of Roethke's, "A Field of Light," that he labored over the typewriter for several hours to get a presentable copy off to Ransom at the *Kenyon Review.* The poem had been "typed by Master Robert Lowell," Roethke reminded Ransom, "who says you will recognize what a labor of love his typing is. He thinks you might break down on this one, but I remain cynical."[29] The following day Roethke wrote Allan Seager, his friend and future biographer, that the past few weeks had been "pretty good fun. A good deal of time spent with R. Lowell: fishing, drinking, playing croquet, tennis, etc." At night they "wambled" into Saratoga Springs with Buck Moon & Jim Powers. His feeding habits—he was after all capable of eating a full-course meal at one restaurant, then going to another restaurant to order another—seemed "a source of perpetual astonishment" to the others, a fact which bored Roethke.[30]

On the last day of the month he and Cal took a bus up to the Bread Loaf School of English in Ripton, Vermont, to visit Robert Frost at his farm there and read their poems on a double billing at the school. "Isn't it fine," Frost had written Cal earlier, "that the young promise I began to entertain hopes of when it visited me on Fayerweather Street Cambridge in 1936, should have come to so much and to so much more promise for the future?"[31] The day after he and Roethke left Bread Loaf, Cal sent Powers a postcard outlining his misadventures. They hadn't been able to get a drink in Ripton, and none of the locals knew where the world-famous Frost lived. Then, on top of that, he'd left his laundry bag and book behind in his hotel room in Rutland and his raincoat in the car that had dropped them at the bus station—and, since the bus stop had changed locations, it had cost him and Roethke a hundred dollars for a taxi down to Ipswich, Massachusetts, to see Frank Parker. They were both drinking heavily and had already had one bottle of champagne for lunch, after first using it to brush their teeth. Roethke had even reinforced his drink with brandy. He'd taken to calling Roethke "the Beast," Roethke to calling him "Rattleass from Boston, Mass."[32]

"Robt. Lowell I liked very much," Roethke would write his friend, the scholar-critic Kenneth Burke, in mid-September, when he was at last back in Seattle. "We did a lot of fishing and reading and beer-drinking." But he did not think Cal's ear was "especially subtle, and some areas of experience he doesn't seem to understand (Not very much intuitive perception; too much influence of A. Tate and not much concern and respect for formal (stanza-form) order)." Still, the "best of his stuff" had "a rough power." It might not be all "that R. Jarrell says it is, but so what."[33] As for Cal himself, he never forgot Roethke's telling him he had "a tin ear," and though he made light of it at the time, Cal was to repeat the comment to Stanley Kunitz long after Roethke himself was dead.[34] Cal's own "final judgment" on Roethke was delivered in a letter to Powers the following February: "a fairly small thing done, at its best, with remarkable clarity and freshness." The pity was that Ted was letting "careerism" get in the way of what talent he had. If only he could forget "about renown and arriving and all that," Lowell added, though he knew how easy it was to make such a judgment and how hard to practice it.[35]

As he prepared to leave Yaddo at the beginning of September 1947 to take up his duties in Washington, Cal wrote Gertrude Buckman that he'd now finished "another long poem of 127 lines and part of another of same length." These were "Mother Marie Therese" and "Thanksgiving's Over," and together with "Falling Asleep Over the Aeneid" made "½ of a book—not too bad for a summer."[36] Then he and Powers headed for Chicago in Powers's '31 Chevy coupe, stopping over at Kenyon to see Ransom. When he wasn't imitating bears, it was the sound of the old Chevy, Powers would remember, an imitation Cal did exceedingly well in the voice of a crabby old New Englander. He made the car sound "tired, out of sorts, critical of today's world."

After leaving Kenyon they spent a night on the Indiana dunes, facing Lake Michigan's southern shore. There they came upon a birdwatcher's resort where an elderly man in knickerbockers offered to put them up, until Cal asked where the bar was. They had to settle instead for a tourist cabin outside Chesterton, Indiana, next to the railroad tracks, so that the room shook every time a train roared by. "Martinis," Powers remembered Cal chanting, "martinis are good." In Chicago they parted, Powers going on to Minnesota, Cal out to Iowa City before heading to Washington and his job at the Library of Congress.[37]

Cal's study at the Library, Karl Shapiro had already written to advise him, resembled "a combination drawing room and the ante-chamber of a wealthy diagnostician's suite." There was "absolute quiet . . . and a view that is one of the most beautiful in Washington."[38] The Consultant in Poetry had been established by Congress in 1937, during the height of Roosevelt's Works Progress Administration, the duties remaining intentionally vague, perhaps because Congress was not really sure what to do with a poet. Lowell's duties would include talking with scholars and poets who wished to use the Library's vast collections, answering correspondence (some of it rather bizarre), and choosing which poets to invite down for Library recordings. He took his duties seriously, though by the spring of 1948 he could write Leonie Adams, who would follow him as Consultant in Poetry, that the job entailed being "neither a librarian nor a Washington official, but something odd, one of the Government's oversights."[39]

During his tenure as Consultant, Lowell would invite a number of poets down to Washington to record, among them Frost, Williams, Tate, Ransom, Jarrell, Berryman, Moore, Bishop, and Meredith. He would also undertake to bring many of his visitors out to St. Elizabeth's Hospital in the southeast quadrant of the capital to meet Ezra Pound, incarcerated there for the past two years on charges of treason against the United States for his wartime broadcasts out of Mussolini's Rome. (He was to remain there until 1958, when he was pardoned by President Eisenhower). With Tate's help, Cal secured a room at the Cosmos Club on Madison Street in the northwest corner of the city, a men's-only club, where most of his neighbors were so old they reminded Cal rather of "Marshal Pétain's uncles."[40] Naturally, it was not until late October that the Congressional Librarian, Luther Evans, learned that "normal personnel procedures" had failed to discover that Cal had been a conscientious objector during the war.[41] Had they discovered this, Lowell would not have been allowed to assume the duties of the Consultantship. As it was, Evans would have to make the best of an awkward situation.

Within days of his arrival, Cal heard from Jean, who was now asking $7,000 as a divorce settlement. When Cal wrote Gertrude about this latest complication in their own affairs, she wrote back that she was "baffled" and had never "thought to come up against such determined wickedness, such abandon of scruples, such calculated and unabashed gold-digging." But it was clear to her by then that her own relationship with Cal was in eclipse. "My good dear," she added, sensing his aloofness, "would you rather we didn't write?" Why, she wondered, did they communicate so badly by letter? Was it because she wrote "emotional things" that made him uneasy? Perhaps coming down to see him would be better?[42]

But when she tried to arrange a meeting, Cal begged off, failing to return her calls or answer her questions. He never explained to her what had happened to change his feelings toward her, but by the time he'd reached Washington he knew they were far too different temperamentally for marriage ever to work. Her major purpose, in a sense, had been to help him separate from Jean. That done, he wanted space to consider what his next step would be. "He was to the end of his life," Buckman would say, "emotionally undeveloped and irresponsible." And besides, she added, they'd never had much fun together anyway.[43]

In the summer 1947 issue of the *Sewanee Review* appeared Lowell's double review of Bishop's *North & South* and William Carlos Williams's *Paterson, Book I*. It was a thoughtful and favorable review of both books, and it initiated an exchange of letters between Lowell and Williams which in turn led to a lasting friendship. In early August, just back from giving a talk at Salt Lake City, the sixty-three-year-old Williams wrote to thank Cal for his review. He knew he'd had to come up from under in writing an epic of a debased, teeming city like Paterson; that compared to the great city cultures of the past—Athens, Rome, or Florence—Paterson, or any American city, for that matter, Boston included, would have a difficult time measuring up. But the American experience and the American language and places like Paterson, and Paterson's people, were after all his life's work. He saw Lowell as a potential friend, but he did not fool himself that the young Bostonian was as yet an ally in the struggle for a distinctively democratic American poetry.

Now he and his wife of thirty-five years, Floss, were reading *Lord Weary's Castle* and enjoying it. He was particularly impressed with how Lowell had managed to mention local place names—Nantucket, Madaket, Siasconset, Boston—without their jumping out at the reader. "It's very hard," he knew from experience, "to treat of American things and name them specifically without a sense of bathos, of bad sentimental overlap resulting, not only in something like Benét's *John Brown's Body,* but even in Thoreau, Henry Adams and Henry James." He noticed that Lowell had anchored his data "in ground common to Europe and to Christianity"—and though for his taste such anchoring aligned it too heavily with the European tradition (Eliot and Tate), he was willing to accept Lowell's uneasy compromise if it had to be. With this letter, the reeducation of Lowell—for too long engineered by Tate—began again in earnest.[44]

In the meantime, Williams—at Lowell's invitation—planned to come down to the Library to record his poems in mid-October. "What would you infer from the fact that I have Van Buren's *Autobiography* on my desk?", Lowell wrote him, acceding to Williams's gentle instruction.[45] "Yes, I once heard somebody mention Martin Van Buren," Williams wrote back, jokingly alluding to Pound's American *Cantos.* In fact, a grand-nephew of Van Buren's, who'd "made money in suits and cloaks," lived near Williams there in Rutherford. Perhaps Lowell was even "contemplating a visit to the author of *Jefferson and/or Mussolini?*"[46]

Which was in fact exactly what Cal was contemplating. By the end of October, he'd been out to St. Elizabeth's to see Pound, who had turned out to be "like his later prose and absolutely the most naive and simple man I ever met, sure that the world would be all right if people only read the right books."[47] "Horizontal in a deckchair on the bleak ward," he would write twenty years later:

> *some feeble-minded felon in pajamas, clawing*
> *a Social Credit broadside from your table, you saying,*
> *". . . here with a black suit and black briefcase; in the briefcase,*
> *an abomination, Possum's [Eliot's] hommage to Milton."*[48]

His first meeting with Pound had turned out to be "pathetic and touching."[49] Still, the more one saw of Pound, he was soon telling Powers, the more devoted one became to the "marvellous monster."[50]

In mid-November Cal went up to Rutherford to visit with Williams, who took him on his rounds to visit his patients, introducing him to some of the locals, including a garage proprietor, who presented the doctor with a mess of fresh mackerel. "Had a fine week-end with the Williamses," Cal wrote Elizabeth Bishop when he got back to Washington. Williams had even taken him to the local nursing home "to see his old Spanish mother, 91, and was like a Dickens character patting her hands and laughing and making her laugh and saying: 'Mama, would you rather look at us or 20 beautiful blonds!' " He'd read the galleys of *Paterson, Book II,* over four times while he'd been in Rutherford and found it "much better than Book I even." In fact, he was ready to judge it "the best poetry [written] by an American."[51] Twenty years later Lowell would combine this visit with several others to recreate a living portrait of the poet:[52]

> *Who loved more? William Carlos Williams,*
> *in collegiate black slacks, gabardine coat,*
> *and loafers polished like rosewood on yachts . . .*
> *his brown, horned eyes enlarged, an ant's, through glasses;*
> *his Mother, stonedeaf, her face a wrinkled talon,*

her hair the burnt-out ash of lush Puerto Rican grass;
her black, blind, bituminous eye inquisitorial.
"Mama," he says, "which would you rather see here,
me or two blondes?" Then later, "The old bitch
is over a hundred, I'll kick off tomorrow."
He said, "I am sixty-seven, and more
attractive to girls than when I was seventeen."[53]

There were also long uninterrupted hours when Lowell could read in his Washington office, and certainly in his room at the Cosmos Club, so that he was able to go through Henry Adams's *History of the United States During the Administrations of Jefferson and Madison* ("the only really first-rate long history by an American," he told Tate, "better—perhaps—than even the *Education*"),[54] Henry James's *The Awkward Age,* the *Cantos, The Canterbury Tales,* Marianne Moore's *What Are Years?,* Ransom's *Selected Poems,* Dickens's *Hard Times,* J. F. Powers's *Prince of Darkness.* He even tried reading Sophocles in Greek, with the help of an English trot.

While Bishop had been swimming and fishing in the tropical waters off Key West, he wrote her that November, he'd been busy paddling around an indoor pool in Washington, a pleasure he'd had to give up when he'd been "nearly drowned and murdered by children with foot-flippers and helmets and a ferocious mother doing the crawl." He'd seen Pound again and had "won his heart" by telling him he was "a collateral descendant of Aaron Burr." He'd heard Anaïs Nin read from her work and had found it thin. Bishop's new poems, on the other hand, were dazzling, especially "Faustina," which he praised for its brilliance and wit of eye. Already her work was coming to represent for him a halfway house between the hard classical rhetoric of Tate, which he was ready now to leave behind, and the more idiomatic and imagistic poems of Williams, whom he admired, but whom he had yet to learn how to emulate.[55]

At Thanksgiving, Randall came up from North Carolina to record his poems for the Library. There were long talks, the usual give and take, and a review of Cal's poetic progress, during which Randall even congratulated him on finally getting people into his poems. "The Jarrells have been here and gone," Cal wrote Powers on December 1. "I have been talking and listening steadily for five days." At one point they'd been talking about Marguerite Young's paintings, he told him, when Randall had commented rather casually that one couldn't really describe them, since there was too much of a muchness about them: "much animals—much everything; but mostly poetesses sprayed with radium."[56]

Randall was still on his mind when he wrote Bishop again. They'd been reading galleys of *Paterson, Book II,* he told her, and marvelling over Williams's extraordinary achievement there, when they'd been interrupted by a pomposity, some "professor of political economy at Harvard, who claimed to have started Ransom (whom he called Johnnie) writing poetry." When the professor asked what they were reading, Randall had looked at him with "quiet, contemptuous compassion." "You wouldn't understand it," Randall had told the professor, "but I think most people would." Such as, in case the professor missed his point, most of his undergraduates at the Woman's College. "This," Cal reported, "went on for about five hours on Thanksgiving till Mackie and I were almost dead."

When Lowell attended the symphony early that December, he found himself seated behind President Truman and his wife, both of whom sat rigidly throughout the performance. Next to them, Cal noticed, were Admiral Nimitz and his daughters, "smiling, craning around, saying 'This is it' (when the Tchaikowski came on) then—having ignored each other thru the music and a long intermission—the Trumans and Nimitzes suddenly recognized [each other] and shook hands with unnecessary heartiness."[57] Such were the protocols in the halls of power. Even his secretary, Miss Armstrong, he noticed, had a better understanding of how things ran in Washington. Once, when she'd been sick that fall, he'd realized just how helpless he was without her. If he'd *really* had anything to do, he told Powers, his job would have been "incomprehensible." As it was, "paper and chaos pile up and I'm out of stamps and every day a retired major calls me and asks me to identify obscure quotations which may help him to win a radio contest, whose answer last week was Clara Bow." Across the hall from his office a Senate committee had been moved into the Division for the Adult Blind. No one, he'd noticed, saw the joke.[58]

That October, after eleven months at Payne-Whitney, Jean was finally released and allowed to move into a one-room apartment with a Murphy bed on West 75th Street, just off Central Park. "Terribly slowly and terribly wonderfully," she wrote Cal, "I am growing up."[59] She was broke, owed $1,300 to various people, and in desperate need of work. Yet so resilient was she, that within two months she had signed a contract with her old publisher for a new novel, and had been given a $4,000 advance. In December she sold her first story to *The New Yorker,* thus beginning a long literary friendship with her editor there, Katharine White. Over the next ten years, in fact, she would publish twenty stories with the magazine. She even began attending parties again, though she was still terrified of meeting anyone from the old days, especially the Tates and "all the cutthroats from *Partisan Review.*"[60]

One of the people Cal had sent an inscribed copy of *Lord Weary's Castle* to was the philosopher George Santayana, then in his early eighties, and living in retirement in the convent of the Blue Nuns on the Via Santo Stefano Rotondo in Rome. Somehow the book had reached Santayana by the circuitous path of the American Embassy in Istanbul, so that he came under the impression that Lowell was attached to the embassy there in the role of diplomat. He also thought Lowell was still a practicing Catholic. With his static, turn-of-the-century ideas about poetic form, Santayana did not much care for poetry written since the heyday of Trumbull Stickney and Robert Bridges. For him poetry was something that could be scanned by numbers, something one might readily translate into prose to better get at the meaning.

Decades before, he'd taught at Harvard, had known or known of the young Stevens and Eliot and Frost as students there. An affirmed agnostic, Santayana had nevertheless maintained a rather decorous love affair over the years with the Catholicism of his youth. "There is no God, and Mary is His Mother," would be Lowell's way of summing up Santayana's stance. What Santayana found in this young man he knew as yet only through his poems were "flashes of Catholic piety" which he could relate to, and while he told his American friend, John Hall Wheelock, that he found Mr. Lowell's diction arcane and the verse cryptic, there was something about it that made him keep coming back to it. Surely he was no "Communist or Atheist," but more a "Voice Crying in the Wilderness."[61]

Santayana had also been struck by *Lord Weary's* "puritan . . . element of religious horror and warning of hell-fire." What he could not understand, though, was why Lowell should hate "the *nice* American world so much, especially King's Chapel in Boston, where my excellent friend and model Bostonian, Herbert Lyman, was a leading Elder." He was also puzzled by the shape of Lowell's Catholic piety, which seemed closer in fact to "some capricious Anglican."[62] That December Santayana wrote Lowell in care of the embassy in Istanbul, asking for some information on his background, noting that his poetry had a power "greater than any recent poetry" he'd read in English, and that he'd discovered there many beautiful passages.[63]

When Cal returned to Washington in January 1948, after spending Christmas and New Year's with the Jarrells and Taylors in North Carolina, he found Santayana's letter waiting for him. In his reply, he sketched out his background, then noted that he was no longer in the Church. "I think that what Catholics believe is true, in a way," he added, because it had "a world of experience behind it." But it was not *the* truth. Actually, he no longer knew what he believed, and was just as glad. He was probably "something of a mild, secular quietist—usually in trouble though—and an anarchical conservative." But he blushed "to toss these rude terms to a philosopher" of Santayana's stature. He'd been honored to hear from Santayana, whom he'd been reading for the past ten years—his *Character and Opinion in America,* his autobiography, his essays on Christ, as well as those on Browning and Whitman. Except for Plato, Lowell admitted, he'd read too little philosophy, though he'd read Santayana's *Dialogues in Limbo* with the same intensity with which he'd read Shakespeare. He enclosed copies of "Falling Asleep Over the Aeneid" and "Mother Marie Therese."[64]

"I can think of you only as a friend and not merely as a celebrity," Santayana replied. "In spite of the great differences in our ages—I could be your grandfather—in our backgrounds and also, no doubt, in our characters, there is a notable parallelism in our minds." In Lowell's stance toward the Church, for instance, "feeling its historic and moral authority, and yet seeing that its doctrine is not true," he had arrived at exactly the place where Santayana himself was. Then he turned to Lowell's imitation of Virgil in "Falling Asleep Over the Aeneid." Virgil was probably too mild for Lowell's taste, he could see, which perhaps explained why he'd turned the Roman poet's Trojans and Italian barbarians into American Indians. And surely, Santayana remonstrated, Virgil would never have called Venus a "whore." She had lovers, he explained, "no end of lovers, including the young Anchises," but that was "because she was the goddess of fecundity and beauty." But then, perhaps Lowell did not "feel the sacredness of nature in paganism"? And yet it was clear he did feel the sacredness of Catholicism, which, in its fundamental perceptions, "Jewish as well as Greek," was, at bottom, but another form of paganism.[65]

Lowell was delighted to have someone of Santayana's stature take his work so seriously, especially where his own relatives had only gaped blindly. Then, with all the overreaching vigor of the young, perhaps unaware that he was critiquing his own practice, he explained that he had set out in his own dramatic monologues to correct the deficiencies of the form as Browning had practiced it, since Browning, in spite of "all the right ideas about what the poetry of his time should take in," had "muffed it" with his "ingenious, terrific metrics," which in the long run only shook "the heart out of what he was saying." If only he'd been patient, Lowell added, Browning could have been "one of the great poets of the world." In spite of which, Browning had often enough managed to find himself on the side of the angels.[66]

"Falling Asleep Over the Aeneid" is the first of Lowell's Sunday Morning poems, his occasional meditations on the current state of affairs during the time usually given over to Church attendance. Here he turns away from Christianity and the Bible—Lowell's earlier preoccupations—to the classics. The speaker of this dramatic monologue (which employs, as Browning had, enjambed heroic couplets) is named Vergil, the name creating an immediate historical palimpsest which links this New World figure in Concord, Massachusetts, to the author of the *Aeneid,* the two worlds in the speaker's dream state having suddenly become very much like each other. The time is the present—

1945 or '46—eighty years after the end of the Civil War; and—in the wake of the destruction by fire of Dresden, Hamburg, and Nagasaki (figured by the terrible funeral pyre which dominates the poem)—one is reminded of the death of the thousand-year reign of the Third Reich, with its heilings and flickering torchlight rallies, the burnt corpse of Hitler in his Berlin bunker and the beginnings of an American Empire. For Lowell, the Republic is dead, as dead as Pallas, killed by Prince Turnus, as dead as Colonel Charles Russell Lowell, killed charging the entrenchments at the Wilderness, as dead too as Colonel Robert Shaw, killed in the assault on Fort Wagner.

Virgil foreshadowed it all—war and war's aftermath—in his bittersweet epic, weeping *(lacrimae rerum)* as he recalled the solid virtues of the Roman Republic, even as Caesar continued to consolidate his new Roman Empire. Santayana was right, of course: Lowell has whipped the quieter landscapes of Virgil into a frenzy, for much of the anger and despair of "Quaker Graveyard" has spilled over into this poem as well. Here in Lowell—as Robert Fitzgerald, himself a superb translator of the *Aeneid,* would note—"reanimated, plumed and clopping," one hears again "the barbaric Ausonian cavalry."[67] There is in fact a barbarous dignity about Lowell's language here, a language close to what Pound did in his Englishing of Propertius, and Lowell has been careful to play the Latin idiom ("With snapping twigs and flying" and "armored horses, bronze") against the American idiom ("Boy, it's late. Vergil must keep the Sabbath").

"History," Joyce's Stephen Daedalus says: "a nightmare from which I am trying to awake." And Lowell, in late 1947, from Washington: "When the next atom bombs fall, there won't be any more inhabitable Atlantic coast in our life-time."[68] So too, with Vergil, dreaming the deaths of good men and the unleashing of a new savagery upon the world as the infant Empire (Rome then, America now) begins to consolidate its gains:

> *Left foot, right foot—as they turn,*
> *More pyres are rising: armored horses, bronze,*
> *And gagged Italians, who must file by ones*
> *Across the bitter river, when my thumb*
> *Tightens into their wind-pipes. The beaks drum;*
> *Their headman's cow-horned death's-head bites its tongue,*
> *And stiffens, as it eyes the hero slung*
> *Inside his feathered hammock. . . .*[69]

Toward the end of January 1948, Cal attended a dinner party given by Caresse Crosby for the French poet, St. John Perse, and was introduced that evening to a wealthy Georgetown neighbor, Mrs. Carley Dawson. Dawson was seven years Cal's senior, had a ten-year-old son, and dabbled in fiction and poetry. Soon she and Cal were going to concerts together, then dating more seriously. "Have I written you about Robert Lowell?", Dawson wrote her friend, Joyce Grenfell, in mid-February. The boy seemed "head over ears in love" with her, had told her he honored her and was even in awe of her. The Sunday before they'd walked "along the still frozen canal . . . with sandwiches and apples," her heart "in tears at his touching—almost courtly—gesture, of turning back at every step to offer me his hand over the boggy places." As with Anne Dick a dozen years before, Cal was intent on educating his beloved in music and poetry, and reading to her all he could: "Hardy, Pope, Marvell, and others." He'd even confessed to her that he'd made love to only four women in his life—Anne Dick, Jean Stafford, Gertrude Buckman, and now her. In Washington, she added, four was something of a record for chastity, "especially for one of his temperament."[70]

Lowell was back in Greensboro in early March to give a reading and take part in the college's Spring Arts Forum with Randall, Taylor, and Ransom. He returned to Washington on the morning of the 15th, just in time to catch the nightwatchman at the Cosmos Club holding up a letter from Carley to the light, he told her, at the same time hearing the man remark, "There're so many swirls. I can't make out what's on the back of page two."[71] Five days later, with Washington springing into life again, "like a Garden of Adonis . . . the trees greenish and reddish and getting hard to see through and the magnolias out in front of the Library," Cal asked Dawson to marry him, though, he added, a lot of water would have to flow under the bridge before that could happen.

"Perhaps," he wrote her on the 22nd, "we've talked too little. You can't know much about what goes on inside me, and I know little about you." Yet what he felt was overwhelming. And though he was still "officially" engaged to Gertrude, in truth they were now nothing more than good friends. As for his marriage to "the dragon," Jean, that had "receded into limbo."[72] On the lighter side, he joked about their old friend, Arms of the Law. "I think he really thought of himself as a bear," Dawson would remember. And her ten-year-old son, watching him do his "Arms of the Law" act, actually thought Cal was nuts. It was Arms of the Law who one night made his abrupt appearance when Cal and Carley got into an argument over Shakespeare, for suddenly he was grabbing her by the neck and throwing her to the floor. Cal's face had gone completely white, she would remember, and he was no longer in there. She broke the spell by telling him she was uncomfortable with his hands around her neck like that, and they sat back down on the sofa to continue their conversation.[73]

"I've just been to *Tenebrae* at the [National] Cathedral," he wrote her in the middle of Holy Week. He'd listened to a choir of Franciscans in their brown habits, "awkward gangling young men, looking like minor employees at the Library," chanting the Psalms and Lamentations so effectively that he'd wondered why anyone who wanted to believe should have much trouble doing so. But then the long-winded "grim pomposity" of the Irish Catholic priest's sermon had jolted him back into reality. The sentiments had come right out of Joyce's *Portrait of the Artist as a Young Man*. Ah, "what a benign, cultured old world country this would be," he thought, if only the Irish clergy could all be made "illiterate mutes."[74] So it had all come full circle; in spite of that other Dawson—Christopher—and Maritain, and Dante and Hopkins, and even Powers, Catholicism had once again become for Cal a religion fit only for Irish serving girls.

At Easter the Jarrells returned to Washington, Randall, "in a gay mood," recording some of his war poems the following Monday. Cal had spent Good Friday with them, arguing over religion, then feasting on "a long Mexican dinner" until they were "crushed by food."[75] Easter Sunday itself Cal spent with his Winslow cousins in Virginia, though nothing had yet sprung except red-bush and forsythia.[76] Earlier that month he'd arranged for Carley to meet his parents when she made a trip up to Boston. And, though he assured her that his mother had spoken of the visit with "real spontaneous warmth," Carley had read the meeting otherwise, knowing all too well what Charlotte had implied when she referred to her as a "knowing" person. Worse, Bob had suffered a mild stroke the very day Carley had visited.[77]

On April 7, Cal took Carley with him up to Johns Hopkins for a symposium on the New Criticism. It was a distinguished group assembled there—Blackmur, Ransom, Tate, Herbert Read, Robert Fitzgerald, and Cal among them—and the papers covered such topics as the Poetics of Aristotle and Longinus. Carley was not only impressed; she was terrified. "My dear Robert in grey flannel managed to look, as Allen Tate said in front of him, as if he slept in his clothes," she wrote Joyce Grenfell. At least Cal had brushed his hair, "and his thoughtful, alert, concentrating face looked like some benign angel come down to study and observe." But he was anything but a benign angel when he stood up to question or say something. He "thinks and speaks well," she added, "impromptu, and was called on frequently by the moderator."[78]

"At a critical symposium that [Cal] and I attended at Johns Hopkins," Fitzgerald would remember, "a great scholar and critic"—he was probably referring to Herbert Read—"speaking at large on literary topics, deprecated, in Lowell's opinion too rapidly, the work of Matthew Arnold. Cal towered up in pain from his place in the audience and asserted with diffidence but authority that Arnold had been a great poet, an estimate that astonishingly became the subject of the lead editorial in the next day's *Baltimore Sun*. It was the kind of stir that Cal had been born to make."[79] But the public occasion also marked the beginning of the end of Cal's obsession with Carley, who was already beginning to prove an embarrassment to him. The trouble revealed itself first, perhaps, at breakfast at the hotel where they were staying, when Cal dragged her down to sit with Tate, Blackmur, and Read. The experience fairly shattered her, she admitted afterward, for she was not "at my brightest at breakfast." Or at any other time, Cal saw, for the experiment was never repeated.[80]

At the end of the month, he went up to Boston to give readings at Harvard and Radcliffe and visit with his parents and old friends—Frost, Eberhart, and Parker among them. On the way up, he stopped off in New York to see Gertrude and tell her about Carley. Gertrude was more like "his child" now, he'd told Carley, "a forlorn, confused, and unhappy" child and not a threat.[81] When he saw her now, Gertrude acted nervously, tearing up bits of paper, then playing with rubber bands. "Several times," he confided to Carley, "we were in tears though neither is given that way." Gertrude had played Bach on her phonograph for him, then told him that much of what had happened between them over the past twenty months had been good. But it was good too that it had ended now, as she knew it had to.[82]

Cal was back in Washington on May 3, in time for Elizabeth Bishop's recording. She'd arrived in the capital two days before, suitcases and pet canary and all, and stayed with Carley the five days she was there. Cal had asked Carley to put Elizabeth up, for she was, he explained, "an independent shy soul" and would welcome the invitation. What he really felt for Bishop, even now, he told no one, including himself.[83] Then, on the 11th, in spite of Cousin Harriet and his mother's objections, he formally proposed to Carley. It had been a "harmonious evening," Carley wrote Grenfell three days later. She liked his "intuitive knowledge on the big things, and his tenderness and understanding on the small ones": remarkable traits in "so conventional a young man." The marriage would take place after Cal finished up at the Library in September.[84] Then he went up to New York to read on a bill with Tate and Marianne Moore and, while he promised Carley he would not see Gertrude, he did visit with Bishop. Back in Washington again, he followed up by writing Bishop to say how warm and friendly he'd found her company, and how much he enjoyed being with her.[85]

At the same time that Cal was telling Gertrude that their relationship was over, Jean was preparing to fly down to St. Thomas for her "Virgin Island divorce." Before the divorce papers could be issued, the laws there required a stay of six weeks to establish legal residency. In the meantime, Jean put up at the ramshackle *Hotel 1829* in St. Thomas. "I lie under a sheet on a Sears, Roebuck bed in the best hotel in town and watch the lizards slither into my laundry bag," she wrote John Berryman on May 17. "This is the third week of my quarantine and each day I wonder why Cal and I, who are now so fond of one another, could have come to such a pass."⁸⁶ And to Cal in early June, as the six weeks came to a close: "I want us both to marry again, don't you? We'll be so much wiser and so much calmer."⁸⁷ She was gay, she joked, but in truth her feelings ran much deeper; one evening, while she was having dinner with some friends, she began thinking of Cal and of all that might have been. Then she began crying, unable to stop herself.

On June 14 the divorce became official. Jean would get a one-time settlement of $6,500, out of which she would pay her own legal fees. There was a witty caption in the *New York Daily News* which read: "WEARIES OF LORD LOWELL'S CASTLE; ENDS BOSTON ADVENTURE." "I still felt married to him, but memory stayed my hand," she wrote Taylor two weeks later, after she'd run into Cal in New York. In truth, she still found him "an altogether magnificent creature," and was so glad she would "never have to see him again" she could have danced." He had "a new girl in Washington," she'd learned, and one "very much older than he, natch."⁸⁸

But within a week she was writing Cal that she found *"no* advantages in not being married, not one." Not only was it "infinitely more complicated" but also "the most miserably lonely nightmare I've ever known." What fun was it, after all, to date a sixty-nine-year-old man "on Tuesday at the Plaza and the rest of the time to see fairies and get passed at by the husbands of one's friends?"⁸⁹ "Now I'm divorced and Jean and I are friendly again," Cal wrote Powers, "free" for the first time in years and a little at sea about it. His only plans now were to go to Yaddo in September and pick up on the Kavanaughs poem again. "It's a novel," he explained, "people, plot, as many as 3 consecutive lines that anyone might understand, if I explained a little."

He'd just been to the wedding of a friend, and now that he was thirty-one and unmarried, thinking about his own childlessness. All his friends, he noted, had children, except Randall, who had his cat, and Roethke, who had his mother. Some of his friends, in fact, were already "on their second round (daughters and wives)," he sighed, "and where am I, with only the muse?"⁹⁰ For by then he *knew* being married to Carley would never work. So, when her son went back to school in mid-June, Cal made no effort to see her. On one occasion, he promised to telephone her at noon but waited until six, calling briefly from a drugstore and breaking off the conversation, he explained, because his friends were outside waiting for him. He travelled up to New York with her on the train, yet—as he had with Jean two years earlier—hardly spoke the whole way, until Carley told him she really thought analysis might help him. Then she was on the train heading for upstate New York alone.⁹¹

Elizabeth Bishop, meanwhile, was vacationing in Wiscasset, Maine, a place Cal knew because he'd summered there as a young teenager. She'd been reading Cal's review of *Paterson Book II*, she wrote him, and felt strongly that

Williams had committed the unforgivable by quoting the real letters of a female correspondent. How mean to do that, she ended. But then Williams had always had "a streak of insensitivity."[92] Cal answered from Washington in early July. Bishop had to understand that *Paterson* was only half complete, and so the letters, which now seemed to overpower the lyrical elements of the poem, would settle into the poem's overall architecture. He disagreed with her on Williams's use of the letters (as he would again when he came to use another woman's letters—his wife's—in his own poems twenty-five years later). Williams had included them, he argued, because they were effectively *objets trouvées,* real artifacts that were "terrifyingly and typically real, and yet . . . monotonous, like the real thing." Besides, how could he—Cal—argue with the author of *Paterson,* who had been "like water" in showing him what poetry was capable of achieving.[93]

Now that he was divorced, he told Bishop, he felt as if he finally had his life once more in his own hands. And what he wanted to do now was to drive up to Maine and see her. What did she think of his coming up in early August? Though she was at Wiscasset more or less with an old friend (and possible lover) of hers from Key West, Tom Wanning, Bishop welcomed the idea. She also asked Cal to bring up some alcohol, which was proving hard to come by in that part of Maine.[94] Only when he'd heard from her did he finally write to Carley. Their relationship was over, he told her, and he'd considered leaving the States and going to Italy, except that in the eyes of the government, he was a convicted felon with no nationality, no citizenship, and no passport. It had been a long hot summer in Washington, and he was about to leave for Stonington, on the Maine coast, where Bishop had just relocated.[95] Carley decided to join them there.

He arrived there on August 7. He was "scared to death," Carley would write Grenfell five days later, on the eve of her departure, and he'd acted worse than her ten-year-old would have in the same situation. For the first three days, in fact, he would not even look at or talk to her, and had concentrated all his attention on Bishop, involving the poor woman in their personal affairs. On the 10th, the three of them had gone deep-sea fishing. The Atlantic waters were smooth, and they'd anchored and rolled for nearly five hours. Bishop had caught a five-foot shark, "which providentially got away as it got to the boat," and Cal had caught "something so big he couldn't pull it up." Mostly they'd caught dogfish. On the way back in, they'd seen seals sporting everywhere. The following day, Bishop contrived to have Cal and Carley go off to a nearby cove for lunch. "He was speechless all the two-mile walk except for the remarks I made," Carley noted. "Once there, I said, 'Oh for God's sake cheer up! If I can be happy, you certainly can! Life's too short for anything else.' " Bishop's presence, thank God, had turned out to be "a life-saver" for both Cal and her.[96]

What she did not say was that Cal had absolutely refused to let her go with him when he went down to visit a group of poets in Boston. So, early on the morning of the 13th, she woke Bishop, told her she and Cal were finished, and left with Tom Wanning, who drove her to the train station. It was the last time Carley ever saw Cal. He'd acted as if he were crazy, she wrote Grenfell a week later from Cummington, Massachusetts: unstable, infantile, egomaniacal, prone to violence.[97] On September 6, she added a postscript to the affair. She'd met Allen Tate at Cummington and had told him what had happened, and Tate had reciprocated by remarking that during his year in Monteagle, Cal had been in the habit of lying "on the floor, with his wife in bed, doing penance."[98] In truth, she felt awful she'd left Bishop, the "wisest woman" she knew, "so warm and human," with that horrible man.[99]

Which was, of course, exactly what Lowell had been hoping for all that week. It is no coincidence that the opening poem in *For the Union Dead* is "Water," a lyric which obliquely yet poignantly and wearily remembers his one day alone with Bishop that August of '48, for the ideal union for him, he now came to believe, should have been between him and this woman. But the day would pass without his finding the courage to make his intentions clear. "Remember?", his poem would ask, paying Bishop the compliment of echoing the scene of her own poem, "The Fishhouses," like his, set on the bleak North Atlantic, it too an elegy for a world lost:

> *We sat on a slab of rock.*
> *From this distance in time,*
> *it seems the color*
> *of iris, rotting and turning purpler,*
>
> *but it was only*
> *the usual gray rock*
> *turning the usual green*
> *when drenched by the sea. . . .*
>
> *We wished our two souls*
> *might return like gulls*
> *to the rock. In the end*
> *the water was too cold for us.*[100]

And yet, after he'd left Maine, Lowell would act as if he and Bishop had at last come to a new, more intimate understanding. He must have known that her proclivities were homosexual, though she'd had affairs with men when she was younger and was in fact with Tom Wanning when he arrived at Stonington. "Cal and Elizabeth never made love—Elizabeth was very explicit about that," a close friend has said. "She would joke and say that she never wanted to marry Cal but she would have liked to have a child with him."[101]

Now he went down to Ipswich to stay with the Parkers for a week. From there, in mid-August, he wrote Bishop in a strained, cheerful voice, saying she'd been "an angel" to put up with his "imbecility and bad behavior." Still, thanks to her ministrations, he was "almost a new man."[102] At her suggestion, he had gone into Boston on a sticky August afternoon with Parker to call on the painter Hyman Bloom at his studio on Huntington Avenue. Learning that Bishop had sent them, Bloom went to a bar to share five or six beers with them. And, though Bloom and Parker, both painters, would become friends, Bloom never took to Cal. When Frank showed Bloom a fiddle of his into the bowl of which Cal had etched a lewd verse—"something about rumps and bums"— Bloom permanently wrote off Cal as a barbarian for defacing an otherwise fine instrument.[103]

After Boston, Cal went down to New York to see Bob Giroux, then had a "long milk and lemonade session" with Jean at Grand Central Station, before returning to Washington. Over the next few weeks he dawdled, going to his office to read his mail, do the *Times* crossword puzzle, read Wyndham Lewis's *Apes of God,* and see a production of *Henry VIII.*[104] He wrote Robert Fitzgerald, praising his reviews of Tate and Pound, the latter "a masterpiece of tact"[105] (though he confessed to Berryman that he still found Fitzgerald's "Catholic" style "a bit florid and pious").[106]

Now that he was an invalid, Bob Lowell had moved out of Boston with Charlotte into what Cal called a "sheepish toy house" in Beverly Farms on Boston's North Shore, where Bob could spend his last years nearer the ocean. Late that August, Cal wrote his mother to explain that he'd written a will giving her everything he had during her lifetime, the money after her death to be split between Randall and Taylor, "the most needy of my friends."[107] He heard from both parents by return. His father wrote shakily to say how pleased he was that Cal had provided for his mother,[108] his mother to say that she'd cried, for the gesture had reminded her of the time Bobby had given her and Daddy all of his allowance "before starting to St. Mark's and we bought an electric toaster which we still use." Still, she was expecting *him* to inherit whatever "I may leave, as I really would not care to live without you and Daddy."[109]

Months earlier Berryman had sent Cal his first book of poems, *The Dispossessed.* Since he'd not heard from him, Berryman wrote now, wondering if Cal had ever received the book. "Many apologies for not thanking you for *The Possessed,*" Cal wrote back now, getting even the title wrong. The new and difficult poems, he thought, were "the most wonderful advance that anyone has made," though he had to agree with Randall that they seemed to exist only "in bits and passages—so many breaks, anacoloutha etc. that the whole poem usually escapes me." What the poems showed, however, was that Berryman now had "the equipment to do almost anything." All he needed was "some overwhelming and unifying" subject on which to focus his considerable energies.[110]

"My term here is drawing to an end," Lowell wrote Powers, seeing a resemblance between his sojourn in Washington and his year "of jail and floor-mopping—all intake, nothing much done, passing activity," though in the long run probably worth while.[111] His last weeks in the capital were being taken up with the "hack-work bibliography on 60 modern British poets for the Library." The trouble was that once you got past the top fifteen—Hopkins, Hardy, Yeats, some of Housman, Robert Bridges, Wallace Stevens, Frost, Williams, Marianne Moore, Tate, Crane, Auden, Ransom, Pound, and Eliot—the ranks thinned out rapidly. And yet, as he told Santayana, there were "more good writers of short poems" now "than at any time since the 17th century."

He still had to record his poems for the Library, "pack, induct the new consultant, be de-processed from the Library, say good-by to quantities of friends and relatives (usually at dinners)," and entertain two friends who had waited until the last minute to visit Washington. Then it would be off to Yaddo, carrying his house upon his back. Just before he left, he went out with Bob Giroux to St. Elizabeth's to say goodbye to Pound. Pound had been "full of gay obscenities, funny nutty jokes on notables," and at one point had demanded of Giroux, "If you're the Possum's [T. S. Eliot] publisher, why ain't you mine?" He had sung them some songs, read from his translations, and scribbled out lists of books he insisted had to be published. Then, as his visitors were leaving, Pound became serious again. "God go with you," he told Cal. "If you like the company."[112]

7

Lizzie

1948–1950

On September 20, 1948, Lowell returned to Yaddo, with its "run-down rose gardens, rotting cantaloupes, fountains, a bust of Dante with a hole in the head," its Ruskins, Balzacs, "pseudo-Poussins, pseudo-Titians, pseudo-Reynolds, pseudo and real English wood . . . like a church, like a museum."[1] At the heart of it all was the "Mansion," with its stained-glass windows, bad paintings, and pseudo-thrones, built "as a reproduction of another enormous house owned by a Roumanian queen (?) who flourished about 1900, and wrote verses." Yaddo, with its "famous race track, Negro bars [and] local literary people who seem as though they'd come out of one of Balzac's provincial novels." Cal knew that too much solitude turned him "fantastic and uncivilized,"[2] so that it was "puritanical and unimaginative" for him to keep returning to such a place.[3] And yet, here he was again, for the third time in as many years. He was given two rooms in the farmhouse: a small dark bedroom and a large bright study.

Among those at Yaddo when he arrived this time were Elizabeth Hardwick, a thirty-two-year-old novelist and writer and reviewer for the *Partisan Review*. A close friend of Mary McCarthy, Hardwick was an attractive, witty, acerbic Kentuckian. One of thirteen children, whose father had dealt in oil furnaces in Lexington, Hardwick had struck out on her own early on, heading for New York in 1939, age twenty-three, with a B.A. and an M.A. from the University of Kentucky, to begin Ph.D. work at Columbia. Since then New York had become her home. In 1941 she'd abandoned graduate studies to devote herself full time to writing, and had published her first novel, *The Ghostly Lover*, in 1945 to a scattering of reviews. Lowell had met her once during his year in Washington and had seen her at *Partisan Review* parties in New York when he'd gone with Jean several years earlier, though he'd been too shy then to strike up a conversation with her. In 1947, Hardwick had been awarded a Guggenheim, and by the time Cal saw her at Yaddo she had, like Mary McCarthy, become something of a force to be reckoned with at *Partisan Review*. Just that summer, in fact, she'd savaged Peter Taylor's stories in the pages of the magazine. Like McCarthy before her she'd been an intimate of Philip Rahv's and a close friend of Allen Tate's, and now, at Yaddo, she wickedly regaled Cal with stories of Tate's sexual indiscretions. Cal took to her brilliance and charm at once and—though Bishop was to half-jokingly warn him about her—he asked Hardwick to come back up to Yaddo for a stay as soon as she could arrange it. Hardwick promised to return after Christmas.

"The place swarms with Elizabeths," Cal wrote Bishop at the beginning of October, as Bishop prepared to leave Stonington. Besides Elizabeth Ames, who was in charge at Yaddo, there was Elizabeth Hardwick, who'd brought back to him "those days—when it was glorious and horrible to be alive—of the Tate divorce." There was also "an introverted and an extroverted colored man; a boy of 23 who experiments with dope"; and Malcolm Cowley, who was "nice but a little slow."[4] In truth, the place was a bit dim, he confided to Robie Macauley, and populated by some awfully strange people, like the fellow who was writing a history of Harvard, "who almost swallows himself when he misses a pingpong shot."[5] Once again Lowell returned to his long, ponderous *Mills of the Kavanaughs*. His plan was to do two new eighteen-line stanzas a week, and finish up the poem by the spring of '49. By the end of October, he had 900 lines of his "immense Maine-Catholic-dramatic narrative," and now thought it might stretch out to 2,000. "It goes steadily, but inch-meal," he wrote R. W. Flint, a young critic much interested in Lowell as a religious poet. As for his Catholicism, he explained to Flint, who had questioned him about it, it had been "one of the few ways of living" that had made any "sense and mystery" to him. Being "nothing much" in terms of any orthodoxy, as he now found himself, made less sense, though it too had its advantages.[6]

But by October's end, the solitude of Yaddo was beginning to get to him. "My quarters here remind me of wormwood," he confessed to Tate. "No cats, no dishes, no furnace, no 3-handed bridge," and "not much company in the evenings."[7] He and Tate got some fishing in down around Bennington, Vermont, and then it was a "big gang meeting of poets" at Bard during the first weekend in November. Bishop was there, along with Hardwick, Richard

Wilbur, Jean Garrigue, Louise Bogan, Mary McCarthy, William Carlos Williams, Eberhart (whom Cal roomed with), and—as Bishop told Dawson—"a wild man from California in a bright red shirt and yellow braces named [Kenneth] Rexroth who did his best to start a fight with everyone and considered us all effete and snobbish easterners. He never quite succeeded and finally had to prove his mettle or his reality or something by taking three of the prettiest undergraduates off for an evening in the cemetery."

Friday night Williams read, "talked, rather," Bishop reported, "in a completely scatterbrained way"; then Louise Bogan the following day, then "all the POETS were dragged up front and . . . made *points* and dragged in dynamos . . . & everyone kept saying it was the best thing that ever happened at Bard." Too shy to read herself, Bishop let Cal read her poem, "The Fish" to the others.[8] "Many odd things happened at Bard," Cal wrote Tate afterwards, the low point being imbibing too much vodka and a concoction called *Glugg* ("a gallon of boiling burgundy, a pint of whiskey, and every kind of rind, berry, nut and spice in the world"), the concoction drunk "on a hot Saturday night in a steamy crowded room."[9] Years later, he would remember being helped back to his room very drunk, holding Bishop's hand all the way. But Bishop would remember it differently. It was Hardwick and she both who had helped him negotiate the distance back to his room, where they had removed his shoes and loosened his tie and shirt, at which point Hardwick had commented, "Why, he's an Adonis," From then on, Bishop added, "I knew it was all over."[10]

The big event that fall was the Nobel-laureate T. S. Eliot's lecture on Poe at the Library of Congress in Washington on November 19, a happening which brought poets out from all over the country. Pound was particularly insistent that Williams finally meet his old enemy, Eliot, and had enlisted Lowell to see that the meeting took place. Williams would go, he said, but he remained skeptical. Why, after all, *should* they be brought together? It was better the way things were, "with this kind of antagonism." Eliot couldn't help him, "except by continuing to ignore" what he was doing for American poetry. "Let him do that at his own peril," the old warhorse insisted. "I'm indifferent to him or what he does." He knew he and Cal were different, and perhaps that was "a good thing," for they annoyed each other less that way, and he could speak more freely to him. In any event, what Williams wanted for American poetry required "a large frame of reference," large enough to "include two people as far apart as we are" in fact being its greatest virtue and "its main reason for being."[11]

On November 16, Cal left Yaddo for New York to stay with the Tates. The following night the Tates threw one of their wild parties, during which someone—perhaps Cal himself—tried (and failed) to spike Eliot's drink. Things had to be pretty dull at Yaddo for Cal to have drunk the way he did that night, Bishop noted, and he was having "a wonderful time making up for it" at Bard and now in New York. Still, there was "something so childlike about his enjoying himself" that she couldn't find it in her to take offense, though she did wish he'd looked a little better for the Washington affair.[12]

From New York and New Jersey they came to see Eliot: the Williamses, Auden, Lowell, the Tates, and Bishop with her Key West friend, Pauline, Hemingway's ex-wife. Eliot looked "white & hot & exhausted," Bishop wrote Carley Dawson afterwards, and managed to be funny, though the talk itself had been a bit of a disappointment. The poets had been placed in a reserved section and made "an impressive array," even though most of them had already been drinking and were "quite tight" by the time Eliot gave his lecture. Afterwards Cal introduced Williams to Eliot. He managed to see Bishop only briefly at the party given afterwards for the poets.[13]

Then Bishop and Pauline Hemingway went back to Dawson's apartment for the night. The following day, after she saw Pauline off, Bishop was to have had lunch with Lowell and Auden. But by mid-morning she'd discovered Dawson's cache of liquor and had begun drinking, so that by evening—having gone nowhere—she'd finished all the open bottles she could find (Dawson counted twelve, mostly wine). The following morning she called Alcoholics Anonymous and got herself to a detox center, where she spent the next five days drying out. Afterwards she wrote Dawson, filled with remorse. There'd been too much activity, she explained, too many parties, and she'd just done "too much." The truth was she flourished "better on boredom & adversity than on gaiety &, relatively speaking, success."[14]

But in the isolation of Yaddo that fall and winter, Lowell too was drinking much more than he ever had before. "Dear Uncle Tom," he wrote Eliot on Thanksgiving Day. "When we finally said goodbye" it was as if "a whole life-time had welled up and we knew each other for ever." He hoped Eliot and Williams got to see one another again, for he was sure they had much in common.[15] To Williams he wrote that Eliot had been disappointed to have seen so little of him, and meant to make a pilgrimage up to Rutherford if his schedule at Princeton allowed it.[16]

But the meeting had not been a success for Williams. Yes, he wrote Cal by return, Eliot was "cute as a pussycat," but Williams still didn't trust him. In fact, he thought the man "dull at some central point in his perceptions," paralyzed from the haunches down. Well, for that matter Poe had been maimed, too. So what? Williams would have liked Eliot too, if it wasn't that he was so "antipathetic" to everything the man stood for.[17] For, while Eliot himself remained above the fray with Williams, shrugging off Williams's attacks on him, at least in public, for Williams his poetic differences with Eliot were anything but some tiresome, imaginary war, as Jarrell would later claim they were.

This was war, a war to decide the future of American poetry, and Lowell must have been pleased to find himself caught between his old aristocratic and classical allegiance for Tate and Eliot and his growing democratic allegiance for Williams. It was, after all, heady stuff for someone less than half the age of either Williams or Eliot to find himself being courted by two of the great shapers of modern poetry. "If Bill Williams comes here next summer," he wrote Tate a bit coyly in December, "I'll probably be denouncing meter & God knows what."[18]

Improbably, it was Bishop who was the mediating point along which Cal was moving—inchmeal—toward a poetics closer to Williams. Six months earlier, he'd written Flint that it was "maturity of experience" which had made Williams such a wonderful poet, so that by comparison Dylan Thomas's gorgeous diction seemed "wordy, green . . . [and] living in an imaginative darkness." Only a man past fifty who knew his town and its people long and inside out could have written a poem of place like *Paterson,* he believed. Moreover, Williams was as much a "master of language" as the more recognized Eliot, the two of them "almost infallible" in their use of words, whether "the spoken, the conventional, the technical, the flat, the intense."[19]

In late November, the first Bollingen Poetry Award, recently established by Congress to be administered by the Fellows in American Literature of the Library of Congress, went to Pound for *The Pisan Cantos.* The award to an American many considered a traitor and an anti-Semite caused a furor in both the press and in Congress that would erupt periodically for decades and which resulted more immediately in the removal of the award from the Library to Yale. Lowell, who had voted with the majority to give the award to Pound, wrote the new Consultant in Poetry, Leonie Adams, suggesting they get Luther Evans, the Congressional Librarian, "to feel that he not the Fellows" was "being daring" in presenting the award to such a controversial figure, and then "emphasize that the press [would] be favorable as well." The Library Fellows had made their choice on aesthetic grounds—*The Pisan Cantos* was, after all, the best volume of poems to be published by an American in 1948—and now they would have to stick by their choice.[20]

But to Williams, Cal was far more ambivalent. "We're levelling all our guns on the Librarian," he wrote the same day he wrote Adams, though at the moment Evans was away and his subordinates "scared to death." True, Ezra's strange map of the world was rather like "an enormous Italian boot with a little fringe of lace at the top, labelled 'Europe,' " which was "damn little to offer us who face the terrible future—the Russian war!" As for Ezra's Jewish conspiracy theory, that was just "stuff." He'd seen plenty of people like that "in and out of jail—their minds toppling with it." Sure there was something to his ideas about Usury and the banks, but Pound was living out of a book now, and "our lives will *not* be right if we just read Ezra's hundred masters.' " The fact remained that, in spite of its shortcomings, Ezra had somehow managed to write a poem of extraordinary scope and power.[21]

Early in December, Bishop finally wrote to Lowell. She was still not feeling herself and had decided it would be better not to visit him at Yaddo just now, since she had to avoid "all intellectual excitement for a while."[22] But if Bishop required solitude, too much solitude at Yaddo, combined with too much drinking, was the undoing of Lowell. Three weeks before, he'd listed for Santayana some of the things he was reading in his cell. "Old things," he said, "very carefully and in small quantities—*Lear, Antony and Cleopatra, The Dunciad,* bits of Milton, a little of *Phèdre.*" He was even trying *Faust* in the original, though his German was "lousy even with a trot." Like Pound, and like his friend off there in Rome, he too was living in a cell.[23] For by then, as he told Pound, Yaddo had become for him a kind of "St. Elizabeth's without bars."[24]

Meanwhile he continued to work away at his long poem. But the more he grappled with the narrative, the more it seemed to slip from him. "I've got a long section, which I pompously call *Book Four,*" he wrote Powers in mid-November, by which time he'd written close to 500 lines since arriving, though ahead of him lay "plenty of revision."[25] Only five more books, and he'd be finished. By then he was thinking not of 1,000 lines, as he had in Washington, nor even the 2,000 he'd spoken of six weeks earlier, but of something closer to 3,000. It looked now as if it would take two years before the poem was ready. He knew he didn't really have much yet, but in the revisions he promised to "go to town." By then, he hoped, the poem would "be pretty hot," especially now that his own experience was at last beginning to flood up into the work.[26] As winter deepened, he cheered himself on more and more loudly. For the first time in his life, he felt, he was writing with everything he had. But by Christmas Eve he knew, as he told Bishop, that the poem was turning into his own "grapes of Tantalus."[27] The more he reached, the more it eluded his grasp.

Then, at the beginning of the new year, Yaddo was given an "injection of life." There was Flannery O'Connor, who had arrived the month before ("23 and only been writing about 3 years—I think she'll be hot in a few years"), Peter Taylor's brother-in-law, James Ross ("a benzedrine inhaler" and a "sort of unintellectual version of J. F. Powers"), and Hardwick ("full of talk and stir"), who returned to Yaddo on January 6.[28] "Everyone says I've gone from introversion to extroversion in the last few years," he wrote Santayana.[29] By then it was clear he needed company because his one companion for too many weeks now had been alcohol, mainly a cheap burgundy, which he could get for two dollars a gallon. By then, too, rumors were circulating around New York that Cal was becoming "wound-up." Just before Christmas, Jean had written Taylor that even Eliot was concerned with Cal's drinking. She couldn't believe that the Calvin she had known had let himself go to such an extent and she needed "reassurance" that he was all right.[30]

On New Year's 1949, she wrote Cal directly. "Is it true," she asked, "that you are drinking too much and going to pieces and that that ungainly bird Eliot is worried to death about you? So the story goes."[31] The story was true. "I was just nodding," he wrote Santayana on January 5, "and I saw an image of a fat, yellowish dog receding down the center of a country road—the center was grass and the ruts clam-shells; so much for flux." His mind was flooded now with just such weird associative images. Should he shut them out of his poem, he wondered, or let them come as they willed? "The other day I thought of weaving in a passage from Homer—after a day, all I had was 'Lycaon listened to Achilles speak.' This seemed the right time to knock off." Working month after month on his long poem, alone in his room in northern New York, and drinking, he was beginning to feel buffeted before this onslaught of the Muses.

Worse still was losing control over *The Mills of the Kavanaughs,* which seemed to be turning more and more into another *Ring and the Book.* At the moment he was working on a 700-line section spoken by his heroine. "The characters and action *are* the poem," he explained. "Lurid (gently treated, though, I hope) incest-suicide plot—descriptions of Maine (history and nature: setting), my characters' Catholic faith & practice—a lot of Greek and Christian myth (done dramatically), the war (the hero is a lieutenant-commander in the last war) but this only comes in by illusion—mainly the heroine imagining where he is. I try to stay to what I know."[32] "My poem grows," he wrote Powers on the 15th, "and I guess I'll be ages doing it and maybe publish separate parts. Vergil used [to] write a line a day, and Ted Roethke [wrote] 53 in two months (but Ted's [lines] were shorter) so I might as well go slow."[33]

With the poem yielding only one pseudo-Virgilian line a day by mid-January, Lowell decided to "knock off for a few days" and catch up on his reading: *The Tempest, Othello,* Thucydides, *The Georgics, Tartuffe, Le Misanthrope, Les Précieuses,* Ring Lardner, and A. D. Hope. He read Blackmur and found a real poet there, though "with a deep desire to labor and ruin his poetry," a habit which seemed endemic to the New England temperament: "harsh, earnest, loyal, sentimental, messy—it's all in [Henry] Adams, but somehow he does it forever while the others flounder." It was an astute if unself-conscious comment on the dismal state of his own work at that point.[34]

He wrote Eliot. After Washington, he told him, he'd spent two weeks writing trash before he could get back on track with his poem. And now, for some reason, he no longer even cared about its fate. Instead, he preferred to "brood over it like a mother bear, till the form flashes (another fine mixed figure)." The main reason for this, he explained, was that he was anxious to remake his post–*Lord Weary* style into something more open, organized, and gentle, which he could use to counter his penchant for the overly dramatic. He wanted a more accessible poetry, rather than the forced rhetoric he was writing. He knew he was beginning to ramble on now, but then everyone had to "blow off steam" at times. "FORGIVE ALL THIS CHATTER," he screamed. It was a "monk's life" here at Yaddo in the dead of winter, but he wanted Uncle Tom to know that he was not drinking here the way he had down in Washington in November. At least he'd learned that burgundy was "about perfect for the long run."[35] A few days later he wrote Bishop that that morning he'd stuffed a lighted cigarette into his pocket while making his bed.[36]

Then, on February 11, the *New York Times* carried a front-page story which involved Cal's fellow Yaddonian, Agnes Smedley. Cal, who was by then wound to the breaking point, began watching Smedley's moves more carefully. "TOKYO WAR SECRETS STOLEN BY SOVIET SPY RING IN *1941*," the headlines read. In the article which followed, Cal learned of a 1941 report by General Douglas MacArthur calling Smedley a spy and a Soviet agent. But eight days later the Army disowned the report, and the *Times* ran another story in an effort to save Smedley's name. This one was headed: "ARMY ADMITS SPY FAUX PAS; NO PROOF ON AGNES SMEDLEY." The following day, February 20, there was another story in which Smedley thanked the Army for clearing her name. On the same page, across from the announcement about her, was a headline. "BOLLINGEN AWARD TO POUND ANNOUNCED," it read. "POUND, IN MENTAL CLINIC, WINS PRIZE FOR POETRY PENNED IN TREASON CELL."

The following morning two FBI agents showed up at Yaddo. By then the guest list at Yaddo had shrunk to four: Lowell, Hardwick, Flannery O'Connor, and the novelist Edward Maisel. The agents asked for and were granted interviews by Hardwick and Maisel. Yaddo, Lowell and the others now learned, had been under investigation for some time, its administrator, Elizabeth Ames, being especially watched. The place was permeated by Communists, the agents explained to Lowell, for Mrs. Ames's secretary had been an FBI informer for the past five years. Worse, the woman who had welcomed him and kept him on long after his two-month stay had run out, the woman he had described to Santayana three months before as harmless and deaf and rather forgetful in her speech, a sort of "well-meaning early Hanoverian king," except that she was "a liberal and doesn't approve of kings," it now turned out, was now in Lowell's eyes at the very least a Communist sympathizer.[37]

Five days later, Lowell convened a meeting of Yaddo's board of directors and demanded Mrs. Ames be fired at once for her involvement with Agnes

Smedley. Yaddo, he said, was a body and Mrs. Ames "a diseased organ, chronically poisoning the whole system, sometimes more, sometimes less, sometimes almost imperceptibly, sometimes, as now, fatally." If the board did not fire Mrs. Ames, Lowell would confer with a number of people in New York, including Lionel Trilling, Philip Rahv, Sidney Hook, and Bernard Haggin. There were others as well on his list, a list which included nearly all of his literary friends: Santayana, Frost, Eliot, Williams, Ransom, Marianne Moore, Bishop, Tate, Blackmur, Warren, Auden, Leonie Adams, Louise Bogan, William Empson, Fitzgerald, Jarrell, Bishop, Shapiro, Taylor, Powers, Stafford, Berryman. Even Delmore. Regardless of what action the board took, however, Lowell and the other guests were leaving as soon as possible.

Badly shaken, Mrs. Ames tried to respond. On the morning after the FBI agents had questioned Hardwick and Maisel, she said, Lowell, Hardwick, and O'Connor had come to see her to ask her about the allegations against her. The following day—the 24th—she herself was interviewed by the FBI for two and a half hours, and, she noted, "when they left, thanked me for my cooperation." She could only attribute the whole affair to "fear and hysteria," then added that Hardwick herself had had "some experience with Communism" in the thirties and had by then become "disillusioned and bitter with the experiment." The board adjourned. It would take the matter up again in three weeks' time in New York. That would give things a chance to cool down.[38]

In mid-January he had had a long argument with Alfred Kazin over socialism, Lowell had told Santayana. In truth, he confessed to Santayana, he was antipathetic to socialism, which he dismissed as a mere technique, his own sensibility being closer to T. S. Eliot's conservatism than to anything else he could think of.[39] But Kazin's memory of Lowell at this time was sharper. When he'd met Lowell at Yaddo that January, Lowell had "sounded like Evelyn Waugh rampaging against the wartime alliance with Russia. . . . It was a gloomy time for me; listening to Lowell at his most blissfully high orating against Communist influences at Yaddo and boasting of the veneration in which he was held . . . by Pound and Santayana." He was "wonderful and frightening . . . he was in a state of grandeur not negotiable with lesser beings."[40] Kazin seems to have noticed everything except how terribly ill Lowell was by that point. "In the end nothing was done," Malcolm Cowley would note afterwards; "nothing could be done." First the guests left, "then I left too, feeling as if I had been at a meeting of the Russian Writers' Union during a big purge. Elizabeth [Ames] went to a nursing home. Her secretary resigned. Yaddo was left like a stricken battlefield."[41]

By then Cal was on a crusade against the devil himself. On Sunday— February 27—he went with Flannery to Mass for the first time in over a year. The following day, he and Hardwick and O'Connor went down to New York to confer with the Fitzgeralds, where Cal announced that he was once again back in the Church. That very morning, he told the Fitzgeralds, he'd received "an incredible outpouring of grace" and felt God was speaking through him. To Sally Fitzgerald, on the other hand, Cal seemed merely to be "shooting sparks in every direction." At nine twenty-five on the evening of March 1—his thirty-second birthday—he sent Tate, who was Visiting Professor of Humanities at the University of Chicago that semester, an urgent telegram from the lobby of the Earle Hotel, where he was staying. It read, simply, "PLEASE COME," which Tate interpreted to mean, "Come and help me fight this evil."[42]

The telegram was followed by a series of telephone calls. Cal was planning to travel out to the Midwest as soon as he could to gather his troops against the Communist evil he'd witnessed first hand at Yaddo. He would confer with Tate in Chicago, then with Taylor in Bloomington, then with Ransom at Kenyon. "Cal seems to have reconverted to the church and I for one think it is a good thing," Tate wrote Hardwick on the 3rd. But he and Caroline were also worried that, along with his conversion, Cal had now fallen in love with Lizzie and meant to marry her. And yet, he added, though it was clear that Cal was manic, he could scarcely believe Lizzie had lost her reason as well.[43]

At six-thirty on the morning of the 4th, Cal telephoned Fitzgerald. "I want you to get a pencil and paper and take some things down," he said urgently. Ash Wednesday—which had fallen on March 2—"was the day of the Word made Flesh," and on that day Cal had "received the shock of the eternal word."[44] Fitzgerald wrote at once to Tate. God, he believed, had touched Cal in a very special way. Perhaps he had been especially called on to bear witness to the truth more strenuously in these terrible times.[45] At week's end Cal went to confession, then took the train to the same Trappist monastery in Rhode Island he had visited several times during the war and remained there for a week-long retreat. But Tate was worried. "We want Cal to come out but it would be better after he cools off a bit," he wrote Lizzie on the 8th. As he saw it, Cal had got himself "boxed into the corner that he has always wanted to be in . . . the inescapably celibate corner." Tate had it all figured out. As a Catholic married in the Church, Cal couldn't marry again, and as a strict Catholic, he couldn't commit adultery. For some time now, he believed, Cal had been "trying to get himself in this dilemma." Now Tate figured he would probably become a monk like Thomas Merton.[46]

When he returned to New York on March 16, Cal seemed calmer. During that week, while he waited for the Yaddo board to convene in New York and discuss the charges he'd brought against Mrs. Ames, he and Lizzie took Flannery to dinner at the midtown apartment of Mary McCarthy and Bowden Broadwater. "Having me there was like having a dog present who had been trained to say a few words but overcome with inadequacy had forgotten them," Flannery would remember. "Well, toward morning the conversation turned on the Eucharist, which I, being the Catholic, was obviously supposed to defend." McCarthy—herself an ex-Catholic—thought of the Eucharist now merely as a symbol, though—she added—a pretty good one. Then, in a shaky voice, Flannery retorted, "Well, if it's a symbol, to hell with it." That, Flannery added, "was all the defense I was capable of but I realize now that this is all I will ever be able to say about it, outside of a story, except that it is the center of existence for me; all the rest of life is expendable."[47] Delighted by the warmth of Flannery's convictions, Cal began referring to her as his saint.

Ten years later, her body wracked with the lupus that would kill her, Flannery would recall this time with sadness. "Let me right now correct, stash & obliterate this revolting story about Lowell introducing me as a saint," she wrote a friend, for there was a deep "impropriety of repeating this kind of slop." When it had all happened, she noted with the sanity which was her benchmark,

> poor Cal was about three steps from the asylum. He had the delusion that he had been called on some kind of mission of purification and he was canonizing everybody that had anything to do with his situation then. . . . I was too inexperienced to know he was mad, I just thought that was the way poets acted. Even Robert [Fitzgerald] didn't know it, or at least didn't know how near collapse he was. In a couple of weeks he was safely locked up. It would be funny if it had not been so terrible. . . . Robert and I both made fun of him when he said such things, but there was no deterring him. He mixed it all in with his wild humor. Things went faster and faster and faster for him until I guess the shock table took care of it. It was a grief for me as if he had died. When he came out of it, he was no longer a Catholic.[48]

The Yaddo meeting took place on March 21. Mrs. Ames was exonerated and Lowell vilified in a circular letter for exemplifying "a frame of mind that represents a grave danger both to civil liberties and to the freedom necessary for the arts."[49] On the 26th, the board met to dismiss Lowell's charges. Mrs. Ames was reinstated with a word of admonition, especially for the impropriety of boarding Agnes Smedley until she'd become a fixture at Yaddo. After that the newspapers lost interest, though for a while still, as Cowley noted, Yaddo remained *the* topic to discuss while holding a martini, until the New York literary scene filled with other "slanders, rumors, accusations and counter-accusations."[50] Undoubtedly, the board had met to clear its own name and so had to turn Lowell into the villain, with little said about the FBI's awful handling of the whole affair. Lowell of course was deeply hurt by the committee's censure, incredulous that people he considered his friends would attack him as they did. No wonder, then, that just after the letter was circulated, the tenuous grasp Lowell still held over his own sanity at last let go. He did not attempt to answer the censoring letter, but he now found it impossible to sleep or to be alone.

On the 26th—the same day on which he was officially reprimanded—Lowell attended the Cultural and Scientific Conference for World Peace at the Waldorf-Astoria. The conference was meant to promote goodwill between the United States and the USSR, but in the light of the Cold War, the House Committee on Un-American Activities, loyalty oaths, lists of subversives, and the anti-Stalinism of the fragmented American left, to say nothing of the one thousand anti-Communist pickets organized by the Catholic War Veterans demonstrating outside the hotel, the Peace Conference was doomed from the start.

The Russian delegation was led by A. A. Fadayev, head of the Russian Writers' Union, and included, among others, the composer Shostakovich. The American panel included its organizer, Lillian Hellman, Leonard Bernstein, Dashiell Hammett, and Agnes Smedley, as well as three professors recently dismissed from the University of Washington for allegedly being Communists. The *Partisan Review* crowd was also out in force—Dwight Macdonald, Mary McCarthy, Lizzie, and Cal—there ostensibly to learn the fates of several Russian dissidents, among them Boris Pasternak and Isaac Babel. Cal and the others had come armed with umbrellas, to be used to pound the floor if they were not recognized from the dais. Finally, each was given two minutes in which to speak. When it came Cal's turn, he stood up and made a point of introducing himself as "a poet and a Roman Catholic," and, of course, a strong anti-Communist.[51]

On the morning of March 29, Cal sent Tate another telegram: "ARRIVING BY PLANE 435 THIS AFTERNOON WITHOUT OLD ROBERT [FITZGERALD] AND LIZZIE." It was signed, "LOVE UNCLE LIG."[52] The following day, Tate wrote Lizzie. Cal was now with him in Chicago, "and in 24 hours has flattened us out." Tate was at a loss what to do. Fundamentally Cal seemed to make a great deal of sense, but his mental condition was "very nearly psychotic." He was looking to Tate now as God's spokesman, hoping he would be able to tell him what to do next. It was pathetic, Tate said, to have Cal constantly embracing him and Caroline, asking them to "stand by him, since he is weak."[53] Twenty-four hours later, Tate sent another note. Cal had finally begun to quiet down. His sense of humor might save him yet.[54]

But it was Cal's sense of humor which was his immediate undoing. On Saturday night, April 2, he thought it might be great fun to present Caroline with a list of her husband's lovers, all those Tate had told him about over the years. Then he turned on Tate and told him to repent. All this he did in the voice of Arms of the Law, for good measure holding Tate out a second-story window while Arms recited Tate's "Ode to the Confederate Dead." Tate had had it. Though he'd broken with Stafford for once calling the sheriff on his wife, he now found himself calling the police as soon as Arms would let him. But there was more. Earlier that evening Cal had made such a scene in a restaurant that he and the Tates had had to leave. Then, back at the house, he'd opened the window and shouted profanities to anyone who would listen.

It took four policemen ten minutes to wrestle him into submission and handcuff him. Tate explained that Cal was sick and finally managed to talk the police out of arresting him. Instead, he got Cal to one of the University of Chicago's psychiatrists at Billing Hospital, who diagnosed Cal as having a "psychotic reaction, paranoid type," and thought he should be placed in custody immediately. Instead, Tate took Cal back to the house, where at three in the morning Cal finally fell asleep. At breakfast Cal told him he was leaving at once for Bloomington to see Taylor. "I saw no way to stop him short of calling the police and committing him. We put him on the train in great apprehension," Tate would explain afterwards. Then, with Cal on his way, Tate called Taylor to explain what had happened, suggesting the police be at the station to meet Cal. For good measure he added that Cal had tried to molest a child at the railroad station.[55]

Having handled Cal thus far badly, Tate fired a letter off to Lizzie. "Cal is dangerous," he warned; "there are definite homicidal implications in his world, particularly toward women and children. He has a purification mania, which frequently takes homicidal form." In Cal's condition, withholding full assent to what he said made one the enemy. As the police were subduing him, Tate added, Cal had kept shouting for them to cut off his balls. Much of Cal's trouble Tate was now willing to lay at the feet of Lizzie and Flannery for indulging Cal at Yaddo. Then he softened his admonishment with an insult. After all, they were just women, neither of whom "had the experience or knowledge to evaluate the situation in public terms."[56] Two weeks later, ever solicitous, Tate would explain Cal's malaise in a letter to one of Cal's relatives. "As I see Cal over the past twelve years," he wrote, "and no one I think knows him better, three things held him together: the Church, his marriage and his poetry. He gave up the Church; he gave up Jean; and some months ago he virtually gave up poetry. He had been pushed forward too rapidly as a poet and he had attempted a work"—he meant the *Kavanaughs*—"beyond his present powers. He couldn't finish it."[57]

When Cal arrived in Bloomington on the afternoon of April 3, Taylor met him—alone—at the station and put him up at the University of Indiana's Faculty Club. He could hardly believe what he was seeing. At dinner at the club that evening, he watched as Cal sniffed the air. "Do you smell that?", Cal asked, and when Taylor said he couldn't, told him it was the smell of brimstone. Then Cal began looking around the room, trying to locate the devil. He spotted him, finally, just behind a large potted fern. After dinner, Taylor took Cal back to his room and went home, but a short while later there was a call from the Faculty Club. Cal had left his room and "had run through the kitchen terrorizing the cooks, and then run out into the streets."

Soon he'd wandered over to a movie theater and decided it would be good fun to steal a roll of tickets. The police were called, and once more, feeling cornered, Lowell took on the arresting police officer and beat him up. More police arrived out of the shadows, beating him up in turn, then putting him in a straitjacket and taking him down to the station to be booked.[58] Lowell would recall this incident with a sense of amazement and self-deprecation as an attack of "pathological enthusiasm," when he roamed the streets crying out against homosexuals and devils. "I believed I could stop cars and paralyze their forces by merely standing in the middle of the highway with my arms outspread." In his wildly associative state Bloomington had come to represent Joyce's hero, Leopold Bloom, as well as Christian regeneration. "Indiana stood for the evil, unexorcised, aboriginal Indians. . . . To have known the glory, violence and banality of such an experience," Lowell would acknowledge, was surely "corrupting."[59]

Beside himself with worry, Taylor telephoned Merrill Moore, who then telephoned Mrs. Lowell. The following morning he went to visit Cal in his jail cell, where Cal insisted he get down on his knees and pray. *Now* couldn't he smell the sulfur and brimstone rising all around them? Taylor knelt down beside Cal, aware that the guards were watching him as well, wondering if he too was another religious nut. When he got up to go, Cal placed a rosary and a photograph of Bishop in his hands for safekeeping.[60] "If you were *really* a Christian," he accused Taylor, "you'd give me your identification, take my place, and let me go free."[61]

Later that day Moore and Mrs. Lowell arrived in Bloomington by plane, and Taylor helped them get Cal out to O'Hare, where John Thompson was waiting for them. By then Cal was foaming at the mouth and talking nonstop. At La Guardia in New York they had to wait hours for a plane to Boston, Thompson would recall, while Moore napped in his chair or wrote sonnets, and Cal sat on the floor.[62] From there Cal was taken to Baldpate, a small private hospital in Georgetown, Massachusetts, forty miles north of Boston, and placed in a padded cell. A few days later, he wrote Williams that he was resting and thought the doctors were learning as much as he was about himself. That was on April 10.[63] On the 16th, he wrote Berryman that he hoped Tate had explained what had happened. "I'm flourishing," he added, "in an odd way."[64]

That same day Charlotte wrote Taylor that her son was now on the road to recovery. The "attack" had been caused by "overwork, over-stimulation, under-eating and sleeping, lack of exercise and physical care."[65] But the truth was that Cal would not allow either his mother or Merrill Moore to see him. Charlotte was therefore driven to the expediency of asking Bob Giroux to act as intermediary. When Giroux arrived at Baldpate, what he saw reminded him of a prison, with locked doors and windowless rooms with leather-padded walls. The guard had peered through an open slit in the door and asked Cal if he wanted a visitor. Giroux would remember Cal, pale and drawn, telling him that, now that his mother finally had him where she wanted him, she would probably keep him there for the rest of his life and *never* let him go to Mass.[66]

"O dear!", Cal wrote Taylor on April 27. "The senile swindler who runs dear old Baldpate has been holding up my letters, or else you would have gotten a note." Being here had been rather like "a purging of the Augean stables," so that he was already on his way back in "mysteriously wonderful and rugged shape." He also wondered what Peter thought of Elizabeth Hardwick, for they had both decided now that they wanted to be together.[67] Lizzie was writing him and coming up from New York to see him whenever she could, though at the same time he was also writing Jean, insisting that their marriage was still sacramentally valid.[68]

By early May of 1949 Cal felt "in wonderful shape in all ways," though the days at Baldpate were "long, long, long!!!" He'd seen his parents and Robert Frost once, and Frank Parker many times, though the visit from Frost had been "worth all the others many times."[69] Once, when Parker came to visit, Cal's doctor, concerned that his patient wasn't getting enough exercise, asked Parker to wrestle with him. But Parker had gone that route before, at St. Mark's, and he told the doctor he would as soon go into a lion's den as wrestle Cal and have his head torn off. On another visit Cal asked Parker to bring him a Bible. The only one Parker could find was an old family Bible with a thick leather cover. When Parker saw it next, the cover had been battered beyond recognition, the result of Cal's ongoing dialogue with God.[70]

"Ah Randall, when shall I see you!!!", he wrote Jarrell six weeks into his confinement, trying desperately to pick up the old thread of discourse before it had been clipped by his illness. There were two people Randall had been "wrong as hell about." The first had been Gertrude Buckman, and now Lizzie. Randall had to learn to "love more of the *wonderful* people." It was twelve years now that they'd been learning from each other. Now he insisted that Randall reread Paul and the Gospels to see "that the truth is both with the Jews and the R.C. Church; or so God said." He thought Randall was "perhaps the best poet in America (where are there better poets?)," unless of course he himself was. But he was "poor, helpless and conceited here—so bear (Arms) with me."

He'd reread Vanzetti's letter to Sacco's son and saw now that their case was his own. "I'm sure the pro-Russian traitors are secretely supported by *certain* rich men—those who have sold us (the poor—who's worse paid than the poet—even carpenters get more and work less) sold us for a pair of shoes." When he got out of here and away from these electric shock treatments he was having, he was going to do everything in his power to get the Sacco case reopened, so that those responsible were imprisoned and electrocuted. "Mother of God, old Randible," he ended, "there's no *man* I love more than you."[71] It was too much for Jarrell. When he read Cal's letter—though he would keep his mask in place when he wrote him back—he was deeply shaken by what had happened to his broken, brilliant friend.[72]

By mid-June Cal seemed on the verge of release. Lizzie went up to Ipswich to stay with the Parker and wait. "I'm about pulled together and out, I guess," Cal wrote Leonie Adams, delighted that Bishop would be taking over as Consultant in Poetry after her. What an experience his illness had been: electric shock treatment, isolation, drugs. At least now he was "allowed to go out and away" for hours by himself. He was much as he'd always been, he guessed, except perhaps "a little worn."[73] A week later Lizzie wrote Berryman that Cal had now recovered "completely, marvellously," and looked wonderful and was "well in every way, as you will know when you see him." He was now in the convalescent part of the hospital, rather like "a small country club," and free to do as he wanted until bedtime. He could remember everything that had happened and talked "pretty freely about it," though he was still "a little shaken up and puzzled" by it all. It had been the shock treatments which had brought him around, and now she and Cal were taking walks together, swimming, talking. The doctors were advising psychotherapy once he was released, though nothing that might bring on another attack. At the moment, however, Cal did not want to see anyone but her. She was one of the few people he could trust because she'd been through it all with him. "We have very little money," Lizzie added, disgusted that Cal's parents were making him pay for his treatment and that she would have to find a "first-rate psychiatrist who would take him on for nothing."[74]

But that July Cal was still at Baldpate. On the 6th he wrote Lizzie, who had had to return to New York, about a visit from his parents. All had been "grave and tame," he told her, except for one patient—since transferred to St. Elizabeth's—who had insisted on calling his father "Daddy Bob." His mother was ready now to accept his wish to live with Lizzie, though "with cordial diffidence." Then he asked Lizzie if she was willing to become engaged. "WILL YOU?", he pleaded. "How happy we'll be together writing the world's masterpieces, swimming and washing dishes." With a twinkle he added that he was reading *The Idiot* again.[75]

"I'm well and about to leave," he wrote Taylor the following day, though he had to admit to still feeling "rather gravelled and grim and dull, perhaps from rooming with 2 alcoholics and 2 dope addicts and a television set in a room like your [Army] barrack in Chatanooga." At least out of all his delirium he'd come intact "with the Catholic Church and Elizabeth Hardwick—and my unfinished poem and the crazy plan (approved by the doctors) of getting a house somewhere and settling down for some time with Elizabeth—unmarried, because according to the Church Jean's divorce doesn't count unless annulled."[76] Three days later, after a stay of three months, Cal was finally discharged from Baldpate. By then he had decided to marry Lizzie in spite of the Church's canon law restriction on remarriage. Elizabeth Bishop wrote from Yaddo to wish him "great happiness." She hoped his troubles were over now for good.[77]

But—at his mother's insistence—Cal's father now urged caution. It would be better for Cal to wait before plunging into a precipitous relationship, he wrote his son three days after his release. However, if he did decide to go ahead and marry, Lizzie would be responsible for him. Better to come back home, then, and work on his long poem and convalesce, especially now, after his shock treatments. One way or the other, however, Cal was going to have to pay for his lengthy hospital stay. In fact, Bob had already deducted the bill from his trust, which now left Cal with a mere $600 to his name.[78] As for Lizzie, all she had was her one-bedroom apartment in Manhattan. The strain, on top of everything else, was too much for Lowell, and he began almost at once sliding into a deep depression. "No one can care for me," he shuddered. He had ruined his life. He would always be mad. "The hospital is still too near a memory for me to find much amusement or pleasure in describing it," he wrote Eliot on July 25 from his parents' home in Beverly Farms. He was getting married and then he and Lizzie would move to Red Hook, New York, on the Hudson, for the coming year. He felt ashamed of the way he'd behaved the previous year, and was looking for a retreat from the bustle of being too much in the limelight.[79]

On the 28th, Cal and Lizzie were married at his parents' home. Parker was best man, and Mary McCarthy, dressed in a black Balenciaga, maid of honor. The wedding itself was "a small heterogeneous" affair, he wrote Taylor, more like the Taylors' wedding at Monteagle six years before than any other wedding he could think of.[80] For a few days he and Lizzie stayed on at the Parkers, while Cal's depression deepened. One of those mornings, Parker remembers, Cal came downstairs announcing he'd just seen the Holy Ghost. He was holding up his pajamas and urging Parker to smell the brimstone in them.[81]

"Red Hook is a little way from the Hudson," Cal wrote Taylor, "not far from Bard College." The house itself, once the headquarters of General Israel Putnam of Revolutionary War fame, was both "picturesque and ancient." He and Lizzie had rented it from the critic Fred Dupee, and were now "learning everything from the beginning: cooking, burning garbage, lawn-mowing etc." They were very isolated here and saw no one and had "nothing to do but establish a routine and write." His pastoral life was quite different from the "comical mad period" he'd had "singing ballads (very badly and baldly with made-up tunes) and destroying furniture." That was before the shock treatments had begun. But he was still finding it hard to shake this overarching sense of unease and lethargy. In the meantime he kept busy editing a selection of his poetry for Eliot at Faber & Faber in London, tinkering with new poems, cutting the grass in the August calm, and puttering about the house, away from everything and everyone, without a car between them.[82]

But by the second week in September his depression had become so profound that he had to be admitted to the Payne Whitney Clinic on Manhattan's East Side, the same hospital to which Stafford had been confined two years earlier. "Dearest, dearest, dearest Lizzie," he wrote his wife of six weeks. "I think of you all the time, and worry so about all I have dumped on you. We are going to work it all out, dear, be as wonderful as you have been." Payne Whitney was "a thorough and solid place," he reassured her, and just what he needed to get better. In a week he was convinced the craziness and insecurity he was suffering from would begin to disappear. For the moment he was being kept under observation, encouraged to mix with other patients, play Badminton and Russian Bank, do elementary carpentry. Things, he ended, "are much the same, mornings, the unbearable; afternoons, the numb."[83]

He was rediagnosed now as manic-depressive, at the moment in the depression phase of his illness. "I seem to be . . . in the down-half of what you saw in Bloomington," he began a letter to Taylor, "self-enclosed, unable to function, depressed." But he decided against sending it.[84] It was not until late October that most of his friends even knew he was back in the hospital. Even his parents were not told, on Merrill Moore's counsel, since that would only make matters worse. Moore in fact wrote Lizzie to say that Bob Sr. was being "quite infantile and demanding and difficult" at the moment. On the other hand, he reassured her, Cal's parents were no longer necessary to Cal's well-being, but travelling their own "street car going to the end of the line where the car will stop and they will get off and walk the rest of the way."[85]

In early October, the Tates visited Cal at Payne Whitney. Caroline was dismayed to find the same Cal she'd found in Chicago, "only past the violent stage."[86] Tate, distraught at Cal's condition, came through by trying to cheer up his old protégé. "Tell yourself every morning, five times," he wrote him, "that you are one of the best poets and that your friends feel about you precisely as they always have; that is, devotedly."[87] By month's end the doctors were telling Lizzie that they did not think there would be any more episodes after this. But she was not taken in by their easy reassurances. "They like to look at you," she wrote Taylor caustically, "as if they were revealing a great discovery, and say, 'you know there is a lot of anxiety beneath the calm surface.' "[88] By then Cal was being allowed out of the hospital on Wednesdays and weekends. Since Red Hook was too far upstate for a young couple without a car, Lizzie found a tenement apartment for the two of them on West 104th Street.

Only in early November, certain he was on his way to recovery, did Cal write his parents. He'd been too ashamed, too puzzled, really, to write them earlier, he explained. But now he was beginning to learn something from his psychotherapy sessions. He was trying to understand his first six or seven years and had many questions to ask them.[89] For his part, Bob was happy his son was in treatment, and thought it a "sensible and responsible" move. "You had a wonderful career in college," he added inanely, "and we certainly don't want your health to interfere with a brilliant career."[90] As the weeks passed Cal seemed to be getting better, though, as he confessed to Taylor on November 21, from his room at Payne Whitney, "a mean streak in me somehow hates to admit it."[91] In truth, he was beginning to feel like a new man again, though one sorely in need of a job now. He wrote Paul Engle at Iowa, asking for the job he had put on hold two years before, and spent most of his afternoons at the New York Public Library, readying himself for teaching modern poetry at the Kenyon School of Letters the following summer. Then, at Thanksgiving, he and Lizzie went up to his parents for the holidays, though not without misgivings.

On his release from Payne Whitney in mid-December, Cal and Lizzie settled into their West Side apartment, decorating the spare rooms with white boughs and silver bells for the holidays. At last Cal began seeing old friends again—Blair Clark and John Thompson—and was interviewed in New York by Paul Engle for the Iowa position. He and Lizzie spent Christmas Eve with the Thompsons cutting out paper grotesques for the Thompsons' baby's tree. Afterwards they walked along Central Park and up through Harlem, "past churches and funeral parlors" to 125th Street, "like the street of a small town," Cal noted, "covered with colored lights."[92] The call from Iowa came on December 28. The job was his and would begin in a month. Once again Tate had written on his behalf. Lowell was relieved to have the job, though, as he told Taylor, he was afraid his Iowa students would be so "frightfully brilliant" that he was preparing for his classes "as if for one of those nightmare Ph.D. examinations."[93]

Just before Christmas, Lowell wrote Santayana. He was sorry for not having written earlier, he explained, but he'd been ill for most of the past year, the trouble being that his *"mystical* experiences and explosions" had "turned out to be pathological," leaving him feeling very much like Santayana's Oliver in *The Last Puritan:* "gloomy, aimless, vacant, self-locked." He had watched in fascination "the holocaust of irrationality and tormenting apathy" he had become, and had finally decided to shed his Catholicism if he was ever going to survive. He'd also remarried: a wonderful woman, a writer like himself, who was helping him recover.[94]

Cal's letter reached Santayana on the 29th, and he wrote back at once. His young friend was indeed the last puritan, he joked, and as such truly a part of the American experience. He joked too about the character of most Catholic converts. One could always play them, he'd found, for they were always looking for "arguments and edifying explanations." As for Cal, whether he wore his Catholicism "with a smile, or put it off quietly with a smile," it made no difference to him. Either way his thoughts were with his young friend.[95] The following day Santayana instructed John Hall Wheelock in New York to send the Lowells a check for $500 as a belated wedding gift. It was a magnanimous, courtly gesture, and it meant much to the Lowells in their straitened circumstances. "I assume," Santayana wrote Wheelock, "that you know of the curious telepathic friendship that has arisen between Robert Lowell and me in the last two or three years. Lately our correspondence ceased, because he had fallen under a cloud, a compound of over-excitement and profound depression. Yesterday I received a very calm letter, in the old manner."[96]

Almost it seemed as if Cal had come back from the dead. By New Year's, 1950, he was ready to travel for the first time in nine months. He spent the first weekend of the year at St. John's in Annapolis, giving readings and "answering the students' bright metaphysical questions," before going down to Washington for a meeting of the Fellows at the Library of Congress. When he returned home on the 8th, Santayana's letter and check were waiting. "Dear Uncle," he wrote, "The terms of your adoption were intended to *confine* you to a strictly spiritual relationship." Still, he'd endorsed the "embarrassing check anyway," feeling rather "like an imposter, though a happy one," who could now leave "with his wife for Iowa feeling bank-worthy and grand." As for his Catholicism, he was right back where he'd been when he started his correspondence with Santayana: "fallen or standing in disillusion." He'd stared into the mystery of his faith until his face had been seared. "Only the bull who has been burned out of a barn looks at the sunset and trembles. Often I long to walk in the great house of the church, but the candles would set my clothes on fire long before I reached the altar. I too can cry out 'O altitudo'—all Christ's violence and love, and all so instituted and work-a-day that a bee might be at home in that house. So I am back where I was with a difference having left the Church."[97]

"When I first heard that Lowell was to come [to Iowa]," the poet W. D. Snodgrass would recall forty years later, "I scarcely dared believe my ears." The poems in *Lord Weary's Castle*

> had overwhelmed young readers, much as . . . Swinburne's had an earlier genera-
> tion in England. I cannot say we understood them. . . . But after the dry,
> etiolated language and attitudes of Eliot, we were starved for vigor. A Lowell
> poem seemed like some massive generator, steel-jacketed in formal metrics
> against the throb of rhetoric and imagery. . . . Until his arrival he was the one
> topic of conversation: the time he'd done as a conscientious objector, his periods
> of madness, his past violence. We were surprised to find that, though tall and
> powerfully built, he seemed the gentlest of mortals, clumsily anxious to please.[98]

By mid-January, the Lowells had found a one-and-a-half-room apartment at 728 Bowery in Iowa City. Iowa City was "flat and ugly," Lizzie wrote her mother-in-law, and anything over fifty years old a landmark.[99] "Snow, mud, ice," Cal added. "But also the light, space and cleanness."[100] Far from finding his students dazzling, as he'd thought (and feared), he found a handful merely intelligent and talented; as for the rest ("poor things"), he would be happy if he could just teach them to read. But he too was learning, learning that there were "many pitfalls and confusions" for the beginning teacher. Some things he had to learn were of a purely mechanical nature, "such as arranging assign-ments and conferences." Other things would take longer, such as learning "how to organize a mass of scattered and casual information," or how to "speak clearly without redundancy." Hardest and most important of all was understanding what one was talking about. "To know how a poem is put together and what it *means*—no amount of enthusiasm or energy can relieve you of that duty." But so it was, he was learning, with everything.[101]

"I am well out of my extreme troubles," he could say by mid-March, though there was still "a stiffness, many old scars, the toil of building up new habits." By then he was working steadily again on the "Kavanaughs," and wishing the poem were behind him.[102] But at least he was back to writing poetry "with his old inspiration and fantastic concentration," Lizzie had writ-ten Charlotte in early February, so that even he had "had to admit that what he'd done was brilliant as ever."[103] But Lowell was also finding that the long poem had cohered not a jot more in his absence, and that, while it had some good lines, it was still mostly a "muddle,"[104] still too "fragmentary, allusive, tenuous and fantastic."[105] By spring he seemed to know that the poem was far too long on classical and biblical allusion and far too short on narrative. In truth, the poem had become all but unmanageable.

In mid-February, Robert Penn Warren came down from the University of Minnesota to give a reading, and three weeks later Lowell went up to Minneapolis to return the favor. There was the usual academic reception afterwards for him at which fifty people had showed up, he told Bishop, and he'd found himself spending most of the evening talking to "A) an old girl of Delmore Schwartz's B) a whaling authority C) an authority on Egyptian medicine."[106] In May he judged a poetry contest at the University of Chicago. Otherwise, he stayed close to Iowa City.

"All has turned out very well," he reassured Tate on March 15. "We are living in a large light room and kitchen, furnished with borrowings, pick-ups, and packing trunks—our own, and large as garages. . . . Every afternoon a pack of very harmless and sorry-looking stray dogs settles on our pathway." Dogs were a distinctive characteristic of the town. But then so were "high-brow movies, the new criticism, and the Benasek murder trial," which Lizzie was "moving heaven and earth to enter as an accredited reporter," and which would form the basis for her next novel.[107] The previous November, he explained to Taylor, a girl had been strangled and now there was a trial: "gruesome, blurred, silly, pitiful—sororities, fraternities, 'pinned,' 'chained,' 'they seemed happy' psychologists, Irish policemen—money, justice, and no good answer." Already, he noted wryly, Lizzie had "talked a book" about the thing.[108]

His writing class was held "in a *temporary* modern structure" with plants and an imitation Henry Moore statue in the window and student art on the walls. Each week he and his students arranged themselves "in a long empty, somehow dingey loop of chairs" and held mimeographed copies of the "poems of the week." All during class people had the irritating habit of drifting in and out, "looking for the sociology building, warming themselves, killing time, holding whispered conferences. No one comes to look at the art, but you never forget that it is attending you." As for his students' poems, they were about "everything from poetry society sonnets to the impenetrably dark— defended with passion, shyness, references to Kant and Empson, mysticism." Five or six of his twenty-five students had turned out to be "pretty good," by which he meant they could do things he couldn't, "and might become almost anything or nothing."[109]

As for the university, that was turning out to be rather like his teaching, he thought, both "tame and friendly," so that he was finding it "surprisingly easy to talk and argue" through his classes. Iowa City, on the other hand, was neither New York nor Boston: no fireworks, and none "of the icy lucidity" of the eastern professional. Teaching amounted to "boning up on what you can't use, then faking," he had discovered when he'd read Burns aloud to his class with a Scots accent to huge success. One learned, finally, by explaining oneself to others, and that had meant unlearning almost everything he'd ever been taught. On the other hand, it had taken him less than six weeks to decide he liked teaching and meant to dedicate himself to it.[110]

Ten days after the Lowells left New York for Iowa City, Jean Stafford remarried. Her new husband was Oliver Jensen, a rugged linebacker of a man, a staunch Republican, author of a book on the carrier war in the Pacific, and now editor and writer for *Life* magazine. Blair Clark, Cal's best man ten years before, gave the couple a reception at his New York apartment. "This letter is impossible to write," Jean had written Cal on the eve of her marriage, "since there lies behind it so very much emotion and so very much memory and about all I can say is God bless us all."[111] There would be a honeymoon in Haiti and a large colonial house in Westport to come back to, but in two years the marriage would fail. "Periods of black moods, and drinking," Jensen would recall long after, "plus endless rehashing of her troubles with Lowell. . . . After a while she came to disapprove of me too and my view on most subjects."[112]

In Iowa City, the Lowells saw Cal's old Kenyon classmate, Robie Macauley, and his wife Anne, and almost no one else. "The people are really quite pleasant, intelligent, and friendly," he told Taylor, "but it's a world of the new criticism, the young hatching into professors, the old hardening, and the virtues are very solid." Then, in late March, into that staid world roared Dylan Thomas, who seemed to live on beer and whiskey, beginning at seven in the morning and going past midnight, his only solid food ingested at breakfast. Thomas told "the best and dirtiest stories" he'd ever heard, Cal would remark, as he eyed this man with the dumpy, absurd body, hair "combed by a salad spoon," and "brown-button Welsh eyes" which moved about suspiciously or fixed "on the most modest person in the room." Thomas seemed almost an apparition, unlike anything else on the American poetry scene, except perhaps for Roethke. Here indeed was "a great explosion of life, and hell to handle."[113]

By semester's end the Lowells had saved enough from Cal's Guggenheim, his Iowa salary, and what he would make teaching at Kenyon that summer that they could plan now to spend the following year in Italy. Cal had proven he could teach and return to Iowa when he wanted to. In the meantime, he wanted "the time, freedom, and stimulation" to finish his long poem, and he wanted Italy. In June, he returned to Boston with Lizzie to visit his parents and deliver the Phi Beta Kappa Ode at Harvard.

Then it was out to Ohio for six weeks to teach at the Kenyon College School of Letters, founded two years before by the distinguished triad of Trilling, F. O. Matthiessen, and Ransom. The teaching staff that summer of 1950 was no less distinguished and included, besides Cal, William Empson, Kenneth Burke, Allen Tate, and Delmore Schwartz. Unfortunately, Cal managed to get stuck with the "worst house in Gambier" for the duration: "one with no porch, a two foot kitchen, and a surly theology-ridden black cat."[114] The teaching, on the other hand, he found "very easygoing, sociable, exciting . . . and not at all impossible." Besides his daily two-hour classes, he gave two public lectures—one on Frost and another on Browning—and finished a draft of the "Kavanaughs" without, somehow, having to rewrite "any of the old stuff."[115]

There were some awkward moments that summer, one being when Lowell went to the University of Akron to lecture on Frost. The paper had already been warmly received at Kenyon, but because he "poked a lot of fun at the academic philistine," the talk bombed in Akron. "Awful moment," he told Bishop, "when you realize you must read twenty more pages to a slowly vanishing wall of disapproving old ladies."[116] A second awkward moment came when Delmore attacked Tate at a cocktail party for backing Pound for the Bollingen. When Cal tried to placate him, Delmore stiffened and turned instead on Empson, who had also backed Pound, and was just back from China, still sporting a Mao suit. That was too much for Delmore, who shouted that Empson was a Communist and a traitor to England.[117] As for Cal, though he'd earlier told Santayana that the *Cantos* were "largely idiosyncratic trash, with lovely lyrical reminiscent and autobiographical stretches,"[118] he stuck by his vote for Pound during the exchange with Delmore. The Pound issue refused to die.[119]

After classes ended in early August, the Lowells went down to Lexington, Kentucky, for a two-day visit with Lizzie's mother and twelve brothers and sisters, before going on to Greensboro, North Carolina, to visit with the Taylors. Then it was on to Beverly Farms and a conference at Harvard. The conference, held from the 14th to the 16th, turned out to be "a crazy jumble" for Cal. It had included "the Canadians," as Lowell called them—Northrop Frye and Hugh Kenner—as well as Peter Viereck (who talked "like an incoherent manic Merrill Moore"), Stephen Spender, Marianne Moore ("our one belle"), and Randall. But Randall's talk on "The Obscurity of the Poet" so irked Cal that he broke with Randall over it. Randall had been too "tense and inspired," he wrote Bishop. And while the talk had been profound and cogent, with all Randall's "disgusts and enthusiasms," it had not escaped being rude as well.[120]

Indeed, there was enough in Randall's often witty and caustic, sometimes heavy-handed diatribe to offend everyone, but several passages had seemed aimed in particular at Cal. "When a person says accusingly that he can't understand Eliot," Jarrell had written,

> his tone implies that most of his happiest hours are spent at the fireside among worn copies of the *Agamemnon, Phèdre,* and the Symbolic books of William Blake; and it is melancholy to find [him] . . . pushing eagerly through the pages of *Gone with the Wind* or *Forever Amber,* where with head, hands, wings, or feet, this poor fiend pursues his way, and swims, or sinks, or wades, or creeps, or flies; that all his happiest memories of Shakespeare seem to come from a high school production of *As You Like It* in which he played the wrestler Charles; and that he has, by some obscure process of free association, combined James Russell, Amy, and Robert Lowell into one majestic whole: a bearded cigar-smoking ambassador to the Vatican who, after accompanying Theodore Roethke on his first African expedition, came home to dictate on his deathbed the "Concord Hymn."[121]

Even more to the point was Randall's comment that the dramatic monologue had somehow become the poetic norm, with poet and public staring "at each other with righteous indignation, till the poet said, 'Since you won't read me, I'll make sure you can't.' "[122] This, with a copy of *The Mills of the Kavanaughs* in Randall's room unread and all his "tennis tournaments, swimming and new enthusiasms," as Cal noted with disgust, beckoning for his attention, so that Randall had never gotten around to reading the *Kavanaughs* and—worse—hadn't even bothered to apologize.[123] That gesture in itself should have signalled for Cal what Randall really felt about the new work.

A month later Cal was still "boiling mad at Randall," he told Bishop, blaming the new Randall on his "fatal" immersion in Goethe, since the talk he'd delivered at Harvard amounted to "a tremendous philippic . . . against our culture that has no time or taste for poetry . . . something that would have made Jonathan Edwards sound like Montaigne."[124] Randall had become "a terror for his friends in public," Cal lamented, for one was "either corrected, ignored or expected to loudly agree," and ended up feeling like "a boor for supporting" him as much as one did, or "a hypocrite for not going further."[125]

Afterward, Cal and Lizzie spent a week with his parents, then went down to New York to prepare for the trip to Europe. Their ship, the Norwegian freighter *Fernhill,* was set to sail on August 30, 1950. Charlotte wrote with advice, telling them to remember "to contact the naval attaché at the appropriate American embassy and tell them that your father was a naval officer. That was helpful to us and gave us special attention." Both she and his father felt "very flat and lonely" with Cal gone, and it made her "sad to pass your little room and see it so empty." At the bottom of the page his father had scratched a note: "We miss you & . . . the house seems quite empty & quiet since you left. . . . We think it is nice to do well in your poems, but it is equally advisable to do well in a wife, & we think that you did."[126]

Then, on the very day of their departure for Europe, they received a telegram: "DADDY DIED VERY SUDDENLY AT THE BEVERLY HOSPITAL."[127] At once they returned to Massachusetts, leaving their luggage behind in New York. "I was the only person Mother permitted to lift the lid of the casket," Lowell would later recall. "Father was there. He wore his best sport-coat—pink, at ease, obedient."[128] After the funeral, his father's will was opened. To his dismay, Cal was not mentioned, though his mother later explained to him that, since he automatically came into a small trust with his father's death, there was no need to mention him in the will. But when Cal tried to talk to her about *her* future, Charlotte fainted and fell down the stairs.

"Three days after Father's death," Lowell would later remember, "the Beverly Farms house almost gave the impression of having once been lived in." His mother had bought it "as a compensation for Father, whose ten years' dream of moving from Boston to Puget Sound had been destroyed by a second heart attack." She of course had wanted to stay in Boston, "and dreaded Boston's mockery of this new house, which was so transparently a sheepish toy house for Father." Lowell would remember going into his father's bedroom and finding Volume I of Lafcadio Hearn's *Glimpses of Unfamiliar Japan*. On the flyleaf his father's mother had written: "Rob, from Mother. September 1908." On another page, she'd written: "This book had hard usage on the Yangzte River, China, when R.T.S.L. was on the gunboat *Villalobos*. It was left under an open porthole in a storm." A small room, he saw now. Like a sailor's quarters, its blue ceiling there to remind his father as he woke each day of all he had lost. And in the den: the "brown oak-and-iron escritoire brought back from Palermo by Grandfather Winslow," atop which lay his father's ivory slide rule and the framed photograph of the classmate—Billy Harkness—who had gone on to become an admiral. Everything neat, just as he'd left it, including his catastrophic actuarial charts worked out for private investments during the Depression, when step by step he'd become an investment counsellor, himself at last his only customer. "I feel awful," Bob had said that last morning, still trying to smile.[129]

"My father died quite suddenly . . . and we have been rusticating and maundering with my mother," Lowell wrote Bishop with the necessary detachment of a Flaubert.

His death was painless—not really tragic, for he had little besides filling the days to look forward to. He was not a suffering or heroic man, but rather as someone said "happy-seeming," always smiling or about to smile—and deep under, half-known to him: apathetic and soured. There was at least one great might-have-been—a first-rate naval career. The death seems almost meaningless, as is perhaps always the case when the life has long resigned itself to a terrible dim, diffused pathos.[130]

Toward the end of September, he and Lizzie went down to New York again, this time to sail aboard the freighter *Hopeville* on the 28th, their destination Genoa. He wrote Bishop, asking her to wave them off, as she in fact would. Then he wrote Santayana. The old philosopher in Rome could relax now, for—unlike his own father—he'd completed the work he'd set out to do sixty years before, though for a writer, of course, one's work ended only with one's death. He and his father had never really been close, Lowell knew, and now that Father was gone, his death seemed "illusive . . . and hard to take in," more like a cache of memories that emerged in the late afternoons.[131] Then he wrote Pound, still mouldering in his cell in Washington. It was the first time in a year and a half he'd written, but he wanted Ezra to know that he was about to discover Europe for himself. He'd spent a year "wading in the muck and weeds and backwash of a depression," and was well out of it now, though for a long time all had seemed lost to him. With America at war again—this time in Korea—and the interminable Cold War grinding along, everything in America seemed "clenched, and somehow nervous and muscle-bound." It seemed "a grand time to be off."[132]

8

Europe

1950–1952

Octber 10, 1950. A postcard from Tangiers to his mother, noting a "rainless, sea-sickless voyage so far."[1] Then disembarkation at Genoa. Then Florence. Santayana to Lowell on the 23rd, expressing regrets that he is now "too much crippled by cough, blindness and deafness" to be able to meet him there, then directions to Santo Stefano Rotondo, "through a round open doorway in the ruins of an aqueduct" just off the Colosseum.[2] Then Santayana to Dr. Luciano Sibille at Florence, asking him to ease the Lowells' way in Italy, Mr. Lowell being "a particular friend and sensitive in religious matters."[3]

Trapped by the war and unable to pay for hotel accommodations with the new money restrictions placed on foreigners, Santayana, nearing eighty, had moved in late 1941 to the Clinica della Piccola Compagna di Maria on the Caelian Hill at 6, via Santo Stefano Rotondo. In this way his bills could be paid for the duration of the war to the sister house of the Irish Blue Nuns in Chicago. As it was, the situation turned out to be ideal for the old bachelor, for the convent had the look of the "rustic ruinous Rome" of the 1840s, a library with English books, a rural aspect toward the south over the valley of the Tiber, French windows and balconies. As for the sisters, they had "the quality of provincial good people in Spain."[4] Best of all, Santayana found himself surrounded by women, with one old Irish priest—a patient—and the physician the only other men around. Even his meals were brought to him in his cell, where he could cogitate, or, with magnifying glass, green visor, pen, and large red crayon, he might write and correct galleys. He awaited his young friend.

Lowell had originally planned on staying in Florence for a week at most before heading south to see the one man he knew in all of Italy. But Florence, city of tyrannicides, held him that fall. The five-room apartment—"wonderfully furnished, beautiful dishes, sheets, silver, furniture and in a *chic* location" at Lungarno Amerigo Vespucci 2 (right off the Arno, with the Ponte Vecchio in the near distance), all for $200 a month, including food, rent, heating and a maid—helped him and Lizzie decide within days to stay on in Florence.[5]

"Out the window there is a statue of the 18th Century playwright Goldoni," Lowell wrote Bishop in early December. The statue looked like Alexander Hamilton, except wounded, its hand blown off five years before when the Ponte Alla Carraia (the Wagon Bridge) had been mined by Germans retreating across the Arno. (The Italians were still rebuilding the bridges in round-the-clock shifts.) Florence, with its "gray and sand-colored, Bostonish, compact" air: an emblem of "cultivated starkness," where one could live for about what it cost to live in a decent New York apartment, except "4 times as well." The language, the architecture, the art, the people, the politics, the places one might go for the history—one could not turn one's head "without starting up occupations, abundance in every direction." It was another world, and they were "floating" in it.

Florentine politics were "very up-to-date, fierce, irreconcilable," a "mixture of Dante's factions and . . . South America." Here were the old buildings, the Palazzo Vecchio, the churches, the dense layers of history, all in one compact square. And yet "the facts, necessities, and possibilities of life" were "rawer and more nervous" here than in America, even as Italy tried to forget that it had been reduced by the war to a sort of "provincial France." The city had its Communist mayor and its walls scribbled with anti-American slogans like "Out of Korea" and "Death to the Criminal MacArthur." And it had been an education for him to see the "boisterous, friendly, and fearfully orderly" Florentines walking the streets and then to suddenly come upon them in some square, assembled for a political meeting, as if in a flash one had walked from the world of the Medicis into the midst of "utter civil war or more likely a communist government." Having to tote their luggage from city to city had helped them decide to settle down as soon as possible. For her part, Lizzie could work on her Iowa novel without "the torture of the laundry, the cooking and the cleaning." And Cal, "in a daze about Italy," had already begun studying the very stones of Florence. Rome might be "much more lively socially and intellectually than Florence," but Florence was manageable; here was a city where one could "walk everywhere and learn your way about in a day."[6]

Among others they saw in Florence during their seven-month stay there was the expatriate Bostonian and specialist on Italian Renaissance art, Bernard Berenson, now in his mid-eighties, at his villa, *I Tatti,* set in the hilltown of Settignano: *I Tatti,* "with its splendid library, its pictures—its Sassetta and Domenico Veneziano," this "passable Italian villa, serviceable, comfortable, rather staid, with a good many brownish sofas and draperies," where so many Americans over the years had come to visit. But by 1950 Berenson was "too old, had been viewed and consulted far too much," Lizzie would write, and you had "a belated feeling you were seeing the matinée of a play that had been running for eight decades." From time to time, "one of Berenson's guests would take the night off and come to our apartment in Florence where we would drink too much or talk too much and the guest would return to his host, much too late, defiantly clanging the bell to have the gates of the villa opened."[7]

One night at dinner at *I Tatti,* Berenson, with patrician directness, had asked Cal about Jean Stafford with Lizzie sitting there at table. "He seems to approve of little in the arts or the world since 1900," Cal wrote Santayana, "which is natural enough, except that what must have most startled people about him once was (along with his energy) his up-to-datedness." Even so, the old gentleman's book on the Florentine painters, published fifty years before, was "still useful and fresh."[8]

Rain, Cal would remember of this time in Florence, incessant rain. And no one really worth talking to in the city except Berenson. "Our great companion was a fairy friend of Elizabeth's Tony Bower (I can still hear him saying, 'Ducky, my Dear!'), Italian literati rubbing you the wrong way, brash where Americans were polite, formal where Americans were simple, the 'experts' on Americana the worst." He would remember "a dreadful friend of the Frankenburgs from Lucca or Pistoia. Meetings with him were like being received by Prince Metternich's imbecile nephew," except that this fellow was even more easily offended. Still, Italy was *gloria mundi,* and after a while one had hit it "from many different angles, and made one or two of the best friends" one had anywhere, and the ice broke. He would have hated the American South, he would later confess to Tate, had it not been for the Tates and Ransom and Taylor. And so with a handful of friends made in Italy. Then, after a time one began to actually feel "that terrible wine, olive oil and soil power—the Italy of Vergil and Juvenal and Propertius." But what a film one had to go through before one could get at the core of Italy's casualness and force.[9]

In late November, Cal took Lizzie down to the Hotel Inghilterra in Rome, and then went out to see Santayana. Since Santayana did not feel at ease around women, Lizzie stayed behind when Cal made his daily visits out to Santo Stefano. "I would never have accompanied Cal to the nunnery," Lizzie would later explain, "because I know the deadening effect of visiting 'couples' and particularly for Santayana who would have been courteous and guarded and denied the free gossip, memories, queries that made the two-somes so engaging and original." Instead, courtly as always, Santayana arranged to meet the Lowells on a separate occasion in the Borghese Gardens, where he had a table reserved for them and a tea ordered.[10]

"The talk," Cal would report back to Bishop, "ranged from autobiography, philosophical theories on world politics, Aristotle's theory of sensation, Spanish quotations, ideas on Boston, lots of very catty and very good gossip and above all Boston and religion." The meetings proved to be "delightful . . . and perfect," except that Santayana was hard of hearing and could make out almost nothing of what Lowell said.[11] And yet, Santayana understood Lowell well enough. He'd seen him almost every day, he would write Wheelock afterwards, and had been reminded of no one so much as Rimbaud, "or like what Rimbaud might have become if he had remained devoted to his poetic genius." There were "dark and troubled depths in them both, with the same gift for lurid and mysterious images." He was not altogether sure what lay ahead for his young friend, but there was a good chance his future would be brilliant.[12]

The Lowells' trip to Rome coincided with Pius XII's proclamation of the Assumption of Mary, and, as Lowell explained, he and Lizzie managed to see many of the celebrations while missing the ceremonies. "Hurried and uninformed" as they negotiated the Eternal City, they also managed to miss both the Vatican and Capitoline museums and, "except for a tremendous feeling of having been there, probably had no new impressions, except that, in this post-War era, the Roman ruins looked at last contemporary."[13] Lowell would remember this time "When the Vatican made Mary's Assumption dogma," remember too the impact Santayana's Catholic skepticism had had on him and the Catholic faith he himself—the last puritan—had at last put behind him, if regretfully. Upon that image of Rome he would superimpose the grainy black and white film clips of the bodies of Benito Mussolini and his mistress, Clara, hanging like beef carcasses in the square in Milan in the spring of '45, conflating that scene with the human crush there in the Vatican in the fall of 1950, when

> *the crowds at San Pietro screamed Papá.*
> *The Holy Father dropped his shaving glass,*
> *and listened. His electric razor purred,*
> *his pet canary chirped on his left hand. . . .*
> *Pilgrims still kissed Saint Peter's brazen sandal.*
> *The Duce's lynched, bare, booted skull still spoke.*
> *God herded his people to the* coup de grâce—
> *the costumed Switzers sloped their pikes to push,*
> *O Pius, through the monstrous human crush. . . .*[14]

"A slow enjoyable life," he wrote the old philosopher when he'd returned to Florence in early December, sounding more like Henry James or Henry Adams or Santayana himself now. His days now were spent "reading, looking, going out two or three times a week," and analyzing the other Americans about him: the American heroines out of Henry James, but with jobs; the effeminate leisure class, "cultured, good gossips, a bit pathetic and flotsam-ish—the best once had great talents or ambitions"; professors on a jaunt, who'd brought "the graduate schools of Chicago with them."[15]

When proofs for *The Mills of the Kavanaughs* arrived from Ransom at the *Kenyon Review,* Lowell left them unchanged. But when the proofs for the new book of poems arrived, he began hammering hard "at the fuzzy places" in his long poem, adding stanzas, "filled with Miltonic mythology, hard for a rhetorician to resist."[16] He could only strike fire, he told Santayana, "when faced by the verbal, rhetorical . . . verses in front of me. Only at that point do I find significance among the narrows and obstacles."[17] In fact, he wound up spending November and December "massively rewriting the whole book in galley proofs,"[18] until he felt it had been "much improved," though—he would confess more truthfully to Bishop afterwards—not perhaps changed essentially.[19]

Looking out over the Arno from his rooms the day after Christmas, Lowell noted the white fog hiding the river, the light turning his room strangely gay. He felt slightly homesick just now, he wrote his mother, as he remembered "many things—mostly the New England coast, and many of our summers." In the square below, people were loitering or roistering, and there was the strange sensation that the war in Korea was somehow being fought "in the next county," so precisely did Florence "register every political vicissitude in the world." The Florentines themselves seemed "divided every which way . . . marking time—waiting for the giants, Russia and America, to act." Yet, as an American he felt buffered, and no one had actually been "unfriendly or truculent" toward him. In fact the city was coming to seem more and more like "a slightly older America," like the Washington and Philadelphia and Boston he remembered as a boy, the stones below alive each morning at five "with hundreds of scraping cart sounds—like blue crabs in a tub."[20]

"I have a theory that I can learn Italian simply by tossing about bizarre words and phrases," he wrote Taylor three weeks later, feeling more and more comfortable as an outsider in Italy. "A new language is a joy as soon as you can be incomprehensible to your friends. Already . . . I can say things to our maid that no one can understand; Elizabeth says things that I can't understand, and the maid says things that everyone in Italy can understand except us." On the Arno he could see long dugout boats poling up and down searching for the bodies of a woman and child, the men throwing out "weighted lines like Balearic slingers."[21]

At year's end, with Christmas money from his mother and his Cousin Harriet, Cal and Lizzie drove down to Monte Carlo for a three-day trip with some wealthy American acquaintances to see Frank Parker and his English wife, Leslie. "No gambling," he reassured his mother, "just sightseeing."[22] "We sound magnificently debauched," he joked with Cousin Harriet, "like Americans from the times of President Harding."[23] But the trip had met with "constant, mild obstinate ripples of conflict," he told Taylor afterwards, until it had turned hollow. Being with the Parkers had meant consuming "gallons of red wine, tons of raw red steak, Leslie sometimes silently and sometimes acidly fuming, no harmony among the wives," so that the meeting, "like many others with the Parkers, was and wasn't a success." First Lizzie had quarrelled with Leslie, then Cal had, until at last Lizzie had returned alone to Florence while Cal stayed on to see something of southern France.[24]

The Parkers were living in Cézanne country on a floor and a half of a big house—"part farm, part chateau—a sort of squire's bohemia—polo playing, nights of red wine, singing, Negro art students, dissolute sons of generals, deaf servants, groups in cafés—all muddled and jolly."[25] He'd also been to Avignon, he wrote Lizzie, and seen the palace of the antipopes, "a sheer pile of stone, cold and vaulting."[26] But by January 4, "after a long red wine evening with Frank" and "a night of indigestion and vomiting," Cal was forced to go through "a foodless and non-alcoholic day of aches and sweats."[27] Parker had shown him the engravings for the cover and frontispiece for *The Mills of the Kavanaughs.* One was of a swan hovering like a stalled elephant above Leda, Parker's uncanny reading of the crucial scene in the *Kavanaughs,* when Cal had tried to force Jean to make love. But Giroux would reject that for the other image of a great swan troubling the waters as it began to rise, an image out of Shelley and Yeats, and one which Lowell also admired.[28]

When he learned that Bishop was about to embark on a long cruise, a cruise which Crusoe-like would wash her up on the beaches of Brazil for the next eighteen years, Cal wrote asking her for the fifth time to join them instead in Italy. The opera season would begin in May with a production of *Macbeth.* In June they could go down to Ischia, looping through Venice on the way. Ischia was his idea of Bishop's Key West: "sand, sailing, primitivism and a horrible, brutal sport—spearing fish underwater." The three of them—he and his two Elizabeths—might live there together in "a smallish sand and windswept cottage." Come over, he pleaded.[29]

But with time on his hands, and the promise of spring already in the air, he began drinking again, heavily, as at Provence, as at Yaddo. "This is the day after the day after a night when I drank a good deal too much," a chastened Lowell wrote Santayana on the morning of February 1, 1951. The night before he'd "behaved stupidly and wandered about the streets alone" and come home "at four in the morning and woke everyone up and had an argument with my wife into daylight. So I am full of gray realizations and feel like the stylized young fool in the old plays who is usually called 'Mooncalf.' " Only, he knew, he was no longer a schoolboy and the situation, viewed in the cold hard light of morning, seemed both odd and senseless.

He, who had been called both the last puritan *and* Rimbaud by Santayana, tried now to make sense of his character to his father surrogate. When he looked at himself, what he saw was a bizarre mix of "stiffness and disorder," Plato's horses of reason and passion tangling each other up. Then he gave the best self-analysis he had ever proffered of his ten-year attraction with Catholicism. "When I came on the Catholic Church," he told Santayana, "it was a museum to contemplate," and he had contemplated. But what he really needed was "a way of life" he could actually live. Besides idealism, there was also truth to consider, but one "short of absolute, ideal, universal imaginative truth and literal historical factual truth." For the better part of ten years, he had thought he could "take such truth on trust if 1) the Catholic life could be lived by me and 2) I could respect and feel at home with that life."

So he had tried "discipline, gentleness, and understanding," without ever really getting at the heart of the matter, or rather not his heart, "or if at the heart it never circulated from there into the fingers." Maturity did not come to one by itself, he had had to learn, though he'd gone "as far as good sense allows the young with a certain sort of fierceness, violence, madness [and] enthusiasm," both in his poetry and in his life. Now, adrift from that discipline, and having experienced a serious breakdown following months of drinking, he had found himself repeating the pattern with two binges in a single month. If he was to survive, he knew now, he would have to find a way to live on a more even keel. To help him do that he was reading the French Catholic poet Desportes, in the hope that some of the poet's "calm polish" might somehow rub off on himself.

In the process of revising *The Mills of the Kavanaughs* that winter, he'd changed some 200 lines, until he thought he'd eliminated much of the poem's "obscurity and quaintness." At least the ending, he thought, was now "clearer and stronger." Still, he wondered if he'd really got at what was wrong with his poem, questioning whether there still wasn't too much "wonder, fierceness, and polish" left in it. Besides, as Santayana had already pointed out to him, the poem's real weakness was in its lack of dramatic motivation, which remained too "fuzzy, simplified, [and] unthought-out." What he lacked most, he realized, was the clarity of plot and the human experience of a Racine.[30] Alas, the poem read no better for him when he went over it again in April, for even at that remove he found it filled with an insufferably "dry, enamelled violence." How hard, he told Taylor, to be "humble enough to change for the better."[31]

Chastened, he began "casting about for a firm plot" on which to hinge his next poem, another narrative poem which would be based on the plot of Racine's *Phèdre,* which he'd started translating at Yaddo eighteen months before, even though he knew he'd already used its plot of incest and self-love in his poem, "Her Dead Brother." Perhaps he would do better now to attempt some family poems, focusing possibly on his father, whose image was already beginning to haunt him. But what plot could he really hope to find in that poor man's life? At the other extreme loomed Hitler. There, surely, was a life with all the plot one could wish for. All he would have to do was "use his head and saturate himself" (as he would the following winter in Amsterdam, when he read the twenty-volume proceedings of the Nuremberg Trials straight through). Each day now he followed the news coming out of Stalinist Russia, not only because, living in Florence, Korea seemed daily about "to flame into Europe," but because the Korean conflict itself seemed an emblem of the dualties of Manichean evil, "an Armageddon of the gods and the giants," the destruction he'd lived through with Germany in the last war replayed now with the Cold War.[32]

In April he and Lizzie visited Pisa and Siena and then spent ten days in the Roman countryside at the villa of the American Princess Caetani, founder and editor of the magazine *Botteghe Oscure.* Caetani turned out to be rather like "a mad, sympathetic aristocratic Mrs. Ames . . . really nice and kind, at least to us—so that though a grand and tireless manager, she thinks of nothing except her magazine—like an only child." By then, with Lizzie's novel and his poetry going nowhere, even after reading Tasso's epic *Gerusalemme liberata* in Italian ("a real technician's poem," he told Bishop, though "curiously anonymous in style, full of melancholy and tormented undertones, heroines like mine [in *The Mills of the Kavanaughs*], but less muddied"), it was time to put aside work and travel.[33]

For the trip he bought two thirty-dollar Italian suits and a trunk in which to store Lizzie's unfinished novels. By early May they were once again in Rome, Lizzie's good friend, Tony Bower, travelling with them. "A cultured harmless sort of fellow," Cal wrote of Bower,[34] and extremely interested in interviewing the ailing Santayana. But the interview did not go well, and Santayana dismissed Bower at once as someone not only uninteresting, but—worse— ugly.[35] Afterwards, the Lowells, with Bower, sailed from Brindisi to Turkey to encounter Constantinople, Bursa, Smyrna, and Ephesus, before sailing on to Greece (Priene, Delphi, Athens, Corinth, Sounion). "Turkey is strong on Americanizing and modernizing," he wrote his mother on June 13. "Even the faces and houses look more American than anything I've seen in Italy." Once Daddy had served as a naval attaché in Turkey, he reminded her. How he wished he could be with him now.[36]

Then on to Venice, Vienna, Paris, Versailles. On July 7, the Lowells met the
Macauleys in Paris and toured the city for two weeks. Cal even insisted on
marching in the Bastille Day parade with Bainville's Action Française history of
France in his jacket pocket.[37] Then a month-long trip down the Loire Valley
and Germany, before returning to Paris to meet Cal's mother to tour the
château country with her. It was while in Paris that Cal read *Paterson IV*. Parts
of *Paterson* III and IV had seemed "a bit spluttery and explosive" to him, he
wrote Williams in late July, though he could see how a poem about destruction
and regeneration by fire might well splutter. But on the whole the work was
terrific, the very image of America "for good or bad—force, disorder, aliveness
and pathos." He especially admired Williams's objective eye, which made
"most other poems seem like artifacts," including his own historical recon-
structions. In fact, *Paterson* had actually beat Whitman at the epic and was the
"American poem of our times."[38]

How much he envied Cal his seeing Europe now, Williams wrote back. It
was an odyssey from which, "not like some earlier American writers, I hope to
see you return to your Penelope (American) much enriched in your mind and
ready to take your fellows here in pushing forward the craft." After all, "assertion of origins" was "the more fertile basis for thought—and technique." He
urged Cal not to let himself be coaxed away from America, which would need
his voice.[39]

On August 20, Charlotte Lowell arrived in Paris, leaving wherever she went
"a wake of shattered chefs, ships-captains, hotel managers [and] Cook's
agents,"[40] so that by the time she and her son had been through southern
France and northern Spain together, Cal would write his mother with splendid
understatement that travelling together had meant "a great adjustment" for
them all.[41] No wonder that, after that visit, he was ready to go into hiberna-
tion. But Lizzie, who had set her heart on spending a second winter in Italy,
was stunned by Cal's decision now to spend it in Holland. It seemed a strange,
almost perverse choice on the surface of things, but Cal knew exactly what his
writing needed at this point: "an utterly unItalian and unLatin Europe," a
Europe closer to old Boston, really, and the city he wanted was Amsterdam.[42]

So, while he stayed on with his mother at the Hôtel Bristol in Pau, he sent a
most reluctant Lizzie on alone to Amsterdam to find them an apartment. "I
was scared and miserable," Hardwick would remember. ". . . I found it
absolutely terrifying—I didn't know anyone there, I didn't know what to look
for. . . . I was full of complaints—it all seemed so dour and hard to manage."[43]
And Lowell, trying to sympathize, but unwilling to give up his dream of a
northern European city, a Protestant city, wintry, one which would evoke the
landscapes of Vermeer, explaining: "We have both been so impatient and
wavering," euphemisms, he condescended to explain, "for the state we were in

when we parted." All he was asking for was "something within our means, in or near France, enough out of the swim for us to write, and enough in it for us not to be drowned in ourselves."[44]

Frustrated and at first unable to find such a place, Lizzie wrote how desperate she was to be south again. "Where the hell are we going," he shot back, "where is there any help for either of us to give or to take? Dear Uncle, I am at the end of my road. I want to be located as soon as possible, and preferably in Holland." For though he'd never even *seen* Holland, he had read Motley's *Rise of the Dutch Republic* "while still in short trousers"—it had given him nightmares then—and now, reading it again, he was finding it a "magnificent, rather obtusely and fiercely Macaulayish anti-Catholic affair."[45] Puritan that he was, he needed to get his love affair with Catholicism out of his system. He had learned—as he told Randall that fall—that Catholic apologetics were "more a splendid lawyer's harangue than the story of what happens."[46] What he needed, rather, was a Europe which would give him back his "own Protestant New England background."[47]

Too many Americans and English had worn the encounter with Italy and France to exhaustion. Holland would be new territory—wilderness, really— and it would give him "the freedom to pick and choose and the privacy . . . so necessary for reactions that are at all personal or profound."[48] Holland was worth the gamble. In the long run Lowell would be proven right, for what he would take from this transplanted eighteenth-century Boston with its "worldly, protestant, English speaking" citizens[49] would be nothing less than a new way of seeing, closer to the mode of the Dutch realists, with their transforming natural light, something akin to Williams's own sharply rendered pictures from Breughel.

Finally, on September 21, Lizzie wrote to say she'd located a shabby but adequate two-room apartment at 17 Nicholas Witsenkade in Amsterdam. Immediately Cal left his mother to the tourists and shops and cafés of Pau and travelled north to join his wife. The rooms were more than adequate for Cal's purposes, and even had a bay window overlooking the canal. At once he ensconced himself with Motley's *Rise of the Dutch Republic*. True, Amsterdam was "a much handsomer (less beautiful) city" than Florence, but already he was beginning to feel closer to America. Once again he was in control of his own destiny.[50]

At the beginning of October, the split between them now behind them, Cal wrote Randall to say he'd written a review of Randall's *The Seven League Crutches* for the *New York Times,* the editor there having told him that Jarrell deserved "a push or something of the sort." In it Lowell had called Jarrell America's "most talented poet under forty, and one whose wit, pathos, and grace remind us more of Pope or Matthew Arnold than of any of his contemporaries." Old friend Randall, he'd added with a mischievous touch: so "brutally serious about literature and so bewilderingly gifted" it was "almost impossible to comment on him without the humiliating thought that he himself could do it better."[51]

Seeing Europe firsthand, he told Randall, had meant learning European history all over again, and hanging "all one's facts and theories . . . onto new images." For the past year he'd been filling up on everything indiscriminately—"French and Italian poetry, even some German and Latin, thousands of paintings . . . history, plays, opera, ballet"—and he planned to let it all settle whenever it did. Writing again had proved tough going, he admitted, especially with so many more engaging distractions. He did not want to repeat himself again, and yet he had no idea *where* his new poems were heading. He had "six or seven medium length more or less historical things in mind—one on King Addullah of Trans-Jordan," whom he'd seen in Santa Sophia last spring. These messy new beginnings were still "comparatively hysterical and rhetorical" and lacking in life, but he was determined to get some new poems down on paper before he returned to America. Then he would "teach, have five daughters, a complete set of china, and join the Republican party."[52]

A month later Randall wrote Cal from Princeton with the news that he and Mackie were getting divorced. "I know how fond of Mackie you were," he explained, but the two of them had grown "further and further apart every year" and both would be better off staying so. Phrasing it that way had to sound "like the sayings of Spartans," Randall knew, but he seemed constitutionally unable to "write about such things very well." As for Cal's being worried about "losing his style," he, less than any poet alive, had to worry about that. Enough of it would always be there no matter what he wrote.[53]

After a short visit to Amsterdam to see her son's apartment, Charlotte returned to Paris, then sailed for America from Le Havre on October 28, with Cal at the pier to wave goodbye. After he'd said goodbye, he wrote his mother afterwards, he'd stolen back to catch a final glimpse of her "scarlet French hat buoyantly set for its long voyage to the statue of Liberty; I think Mrs. Brooks was leaning forward talking." He thanked her for treating him so royally in Paris, and for all "the newly discovered restaurants, operas and breakfasts in bed."[54] But to Bishop he offered another, more Vermeer-like portrait of his mother. She was "a very competent, stubborn, uncurious, unBohemian woman with a genius for squeezing luxury out of rocks," he told her, a woman with "a long memory for pre-war and pre-first-world war service," who thought "nothing of calling the American ambassador if there's no toilet-paper on the train." Under "the best conditions," he could not "begin to make sense out of her or to her," and each year since he'd turned eighteen it had only gotten worse. "I don't suppose you can imagine three months with the three of us," he joked, "all behaving very badly, then being very self-sacrificing, and fuming inside like the burning stuffings of an overstuffed Dutch chair."

Well, it was all over now, and he and Lizzie had emerged "triumphantly," though there'd been a minor scuffle between them, more like a relapse, really, "such as one gets from sulphur drugs." But at last he was writing again, and was already far into "the thin first drafts of a long monologue about a sort of 16th century Mrs. Dawson."[55] The poem he was working on—its form the heroic couplets of the *Kavanaughs,* its world borrowed from his reading of Motley and his European travels—would become "The Banker's Daughter," and its speaker—Marie de Medici, the Florentine noblewoman who became Henri IV of France's queen—would be based not so much on Mrs. Dawson (herself a mother surrogate) as on his own mother, as the anger and frustration he submerged in his letters now spilled over into his poem. In a very real sense, the poem suggests, his mother's overbearing ways had gone a long way toward killing his father and might, if her power was left unchecked, undo the son as well:

> *King Henry pirouetted on his heel*
> *and jested, "Look, my cow's producing veal. . . ."*
> *Alas, my brutal girlish mood-swings drove*
> *my husband, wrenched and giddy, from the Louvre,*
> *to sleep in single lodgings on the town. . . .*
> *I rock my nightmare son, and hear him cry*
> *for ball and sceptre; he asks the queen to die. . . .*

Amsterdam was quiet. Very quiet, as it mostly had been since its heyday three centuries before. Which was exactly what Cal needed. At last the young firebrand was well on his way to becoming, as he told Bishop, a happy bore. No one could "possibly survive on" into their forties, except as a hermit, without becoming a bore, he explained, which meant "having a line that [would] bore anyone of any age and in any circumstances." It would have to be a line that demanded "no spontaneous thought," and yet could find "openings everywhere" to blanket a conversation.[56] He was, after all, at bottom "a provincial New England creature," he wrote, elated, to the Macauleys in late February, when he blinked and saw that afternoons were finally returning. It had been the winter of his content, a groundhog winter, a time when he wrote no one and burrowed into his apartment, with its "flowered fuzzy walls, chairs and sofa, its dozen drapes covering each window," its bookcases "of standardized Chinese bibelots, its "solemn original" nineteenth-century King William III "gilt-framed oils of cats and roses and vulgarized Hobbemas," and sat by his stove, and read and read and read. Lizzie could usually be found next to him, curled up on the sofa, wrapped in his father's dull crimson peignoir.[57]

"We read continuously," he wrote Randall now, "except when interrupted, then we sigh querulously, 'But I never have any time to read.' " In that way he'd gone through the proceedings of the Nuremberg Trials ("I'm one-eighth Jewish myself, which I do feel is a saving grace," he would comment in an interview twelve years later. "It's not a lot . . . but I think it would have been enough to come under the Nuremberg laws").[58] He'd also read Bruno Bettelheim on the concentration camps, Hannah Arendt's *The Origins of Totalitarianism*, Macaulay's *History*, Motley, Clarendon, North's *Plutarch*, "and a thousand other things," all of which Randall "could no doubt have finished on a bus trip to North Carolina, and been at a loss for more" before he was half there. They'd even spent three weeks in London and become opera addicts, seeing performances of *Rosenkavalier, Fidelio,* and *Othello* ("thinking it would be *Otello* . . . in which Othello was the villain." Instead, Iago had turned out to be "a loveable Breughelesque extrovert"). But now, after four months in Amsterdam, the city, having "served its purpose," was at last turning itself back into "a flat country with a flat grey climate," one that reminded him of a cross between Mount Vernon and Columbus, Ohio.[59]

"Poor dear," Lizzie wrote the Macauleys on February 22, "he's got it into his head that he's a strong, simple and capable man of the people, like a Dutchman." Cal had borrowed their Dutch friend, Huyk van Leuwen's, houseboat as a daytime workplace, and she was worried now that he would leave "the gas on, trying to heat a can of soup." She would have to trudge down to the canal tomorrow to make sure he was still alive.[60] Cal had borrowed the houseboat in order to catch up on a long backlog of letters. Instead, he'd spent the time oiling his ski boots, reading books "in Dutch, French, English and German," and chasing away "some small boys who were making splashes outside his houseboat" (he could see them now through the portholes tampering with the moorings).[61]

During his stay on the houseboat, he'd not only "rummaged through all the books," but also "broken the filament of the oil reading lamp, unprimed the toilet-pump, let the furnace go out, had meals of cold oatmeal soaked in cold milk, and accomplished none of my fine resolutions," except to write three letters.[62] The first was to Randall. Three months after learning the news, he wrote to express his regrets over the divorce. In fact, he could hardly believe it. "You mustn't mind my saying," he told Randall, "that we all envied you and Mackie because your difficulties seemed to have nothing in common with the difficulties of other marriages."

He also took the occasion to defend the *Kavanaughs,* which Randall had reviewed the previous November for *Partisan Review.*[63] Yes, he *had* "poured every variety of feeling and technique into it," just as Randall had said. But it had been his *intention* to be "grandiose, melodramatic, carried on by a mixture of drama and shifting tones, rather like [Tennyson's] *Maud."* In spite of which he'd been delighted with Randall's review and had read "it many times out of vanity." Perhaps, he added, he even agreed with everything Randall had said there, but, as he'd really done nothing new since, he'd gone on overrating the book.[64]

Cousin Harriet had written to say she'd seen Jean at the Hotel Statler in Washington, where she'd been feted for the publication of her latest novel, *The Catherine Wheel.* She'd given a "short and amusing speech, well delivered," Harriet reported, and when she'd spoken to her afterwards, Jean had told her she was well and happy and had asked after Cal and Lizzie. But, Harriet added, Jean had been drinking again and her novel had accordingly suffered. For, though it was "sumptuously well written," there was "a certain slack quality" about it which augured "ill for her future."[65] Cal wrote back to say he'd not yet read the novel, with its Damariscotta Mills setting and its house much like the old Kavanagh mansion. Moreover, no one ever wrote him any more about Jean, so he'd been grateful for news of her, especially since Harriet had been one of the few Lowells or Winslows Jean had ever been able to abide.[66]

"I find that every day I less like writing letters and more like getting them," he wrote Bishop now. It was the same with his poems, which he'd taken to waiting to announce themselves in his dreams: "a first draft one night, uncanny revisions the next two." The Dutch, he'd found, were true polyglots, able to speak and read fluent French, English, and German. But their literature was, essentially, a commentary on other literatures. He and Lizzie had made some good friends in Amsterdam, but it was time now to move on. In England, they'd just missed the funeral of King George VI, though they'd listened to the news on the radio for ten days straight. Lizzie, "iconoclastic Calvinist" that she was, had been obsessed by it all, one "subtle, rarified theory" of the royalty following another. He could still picture her "brooding on her red plush sofa," her face suddenly lighting up, saying, "It's because they're more ordinary than other people."[67] Still, cooped up as they had been, he and Lizzie had seen too much of each other, which was why, really, he'd finally borrowed the houseboat. To Taylor, in fact, he admitted that during those "first rain-every-day months" in Amsterdam the two of them had "both suffered from the spleen and mastered . . . every wrinkle of domestic argument and sabotage." However, since their return from London and the return of sunlight, they'd "been merry," enjoying their "four o'clock smoked tea" together.[68]

Now too, after a hiatus of eight months, he picked up his dialogue again with Williams over the question of the American idiom. "I think I get what you mean about Eliot for the first time," he wrote now, fresh from reading Williams's *Autobiography.* "You say, I think, that at the time the *Waste Land* appeared a whole flood of 'American' poetry, that is poetry more in the present and more congenial to you was about to prevail. Then it was driven underground, into small privately printed editions, non-paying, ephemeral little magazines etc." And no doubt Williams was right.

Still, it had been "heroic of Eliot, whose personality and opinions [were] after all very special, not in tune with the times . . . by sheer artistry and sincerity to dominate." As for Williams, his way of writing needed the "eye, experience and sense" of the American idiom, something most of those who tried to write in his manner had failed successfully to imitate. And yet, he added, still stuck as he was in his own dead-end rhetoric, "I wish rather in vain that I could absorb something of your way of writing into mine."[69] As for his own work, it still remained, as he reported to Santayana that March, far too "mannered and too full of travel-impressions" for his own tastes.

He was growing worried about his old friend, who he sensed was at last feeling the weight of his eighty-nine years, and had asked anyone coming from Rome for news, though no one seemed really to know anything. As for his wintering in Holland, except for the climate, the overcrowding, "and an atmosphere that oozes toward the grossly mournful wastes of its inevitable future," the place had become for him "the ideal old international European country." His enforced inertia and idleness had been, he was convinced, not only helpful but necessary. And yet idleness was after all what it was: nothing.

Reading Bertrand Russell that winter on the history of Western philosophy, he found himself more and more sympathetic now with the "empiricist, mathematician, logician and old-fashioned liberal moralist" Russell seemed to embody. And yet there were shortcomings there too, in particular in Russell's reduction of all philosophy "to a few scattered accurately-stated and verifiable scientific laws, not necessarily very coherent or momentous in themselves." As far as Lowell could make out, "the old fixed wooden Aristotelian perennial philosophy" he'd "painfully studied as a Catholic" still remained viable. The trouble was that a "Macaulay-Whig" philosopher like Russell and a Catholic neo-scholastic like Jacques Maritain used "such different criteria" that each seemed irreconcilable with the other, so that finally the writer shrunk both from "the set mould of the Catholic and from the system-breaking of such a man as Russell who breaks all the great philosophers like clay pots." Whatever it was that made the imaginative writer timeless seemed to work poorly for the philosopher. The real strength of Santayana's own writing, he'd had to conclude, was that it oscillated "between the two noblest and most solid western intellectual and moral traditions": idealism and empiricism. That was where Lowell also hoped to situate himself. After a stint teaching in Salzburg that summer, he would work his way down to Vienna and Venice before settling in Rome in September. He promised to see Santayana then.[70]

In the spring of '52 the Lowells had also gone "music-mad." In London they'd heard "Bach's two Passions each twice," and now—in late April—they were on their way to Brussels to hear the Vienna Statsopera perform five Mozart operas in six nights. "I know," he crowed self-mockingly to Bishop, "all about the sonata form (a misnomer according to Tovey), canons, and modulations, but have difficulty in distinguishing them when heard, and have so far failed to convince the cynical and sceptical Eliz. H. Lowell that I am not tone-deaf. I always reply by asking her, 'Just what is a quaver?' or, 'When is Haydn going to modulate back into C minor?' Her replies are more airy than clear."

Now, after seven months, with the sun shining in the blue heavens and young leaves beginning to gauze the canal below his window, with the apartment half-filled with half-open suitcases and the radio at the moment "playing a sort of indian summer Mozart minuet," the Lowells prepared to leave Amsterdam. Their "long green coffin-like trunk" they'd counted on to hold almost everything was instead "brimful of books." They'd made several lasting friendships with the Dutch, "all very loving, urbane and hard-headed about each other," the way he sometimes liked "to picture, alas," the *Partisan Review* crowd acting toward each other. His friend Huyk, in particular, liked talking "intellectual shop" with him, their sessions often going from mid-morning of one day until early next morning, as together they read Dutch poetry to each other, Huyk—to Cal's amazement—quoting Goethe, Stendhal, La Bruyère, Auden, Yeats, Valéry, Randall, and Bishop to him by the hour.

But even after all this time, Cal lamented, Lizzie still refused to take Amsterdam to her bosom, Brazil being "the one trip taken by some one else" she could "bear to contemplate without envy." As for himself, Brazil sounded rather delightful. "You always make me feel that I have a rather obvious breezy, impersonal liking for the great and obvious," he confessed to Bishop, "in contrast with your adult feeling for the odd and genuine." True, Amsterdam wasn't "picturesque, healthy, spectacularly on the up or down," and "not very much anything except flat, canal-checkered and Dutch." But for oddness and genuineness his stay there, when he might have had Florence or Paris or Rome or Auden's Ischia. . . . Even Bishop hadn't matched that.[71]

"I think only of leaving the Netherlands, my only thought, in fact, for the last seven months," Lizzie confessed to Robie Macauley, so that she felt a rush of freedom when at last they left Amsterdam for good early in May and headed for Brussels and Mozart.[72] Then it was on to Paris, where they spent two weeks, part of it at "a big anti-totalitarian conference on Art of the Twentieth Century,"[73] to which every European writer and most of the Americans seemed to have flocked, among them Faulkner, Auden, Katherine Anne Porter, and Tate.

The Lowells were especially delighted to see Allen Tate, though the new pace of jumping into taxis or meeting him at "Champs Elysées cafés" took some adjusting to after their turtlelike winter. In fact, a bemused Lizzie noted, Cal seemed "quite shocked" to hear the fifty-two-year-old Tate refuse to "retire to his hotel room in the afternoon, carefully study the text, and attend, in gallery seats, an evening" at the *Comédie Française*. When Cal had suggested these things, Tate had merely stared at him "as if he had lost his mind." As for Lizzie, she was finally enjoying herself again, except that now Cal had her "so well trained" she felt as if she were failing all her school subjects. Cal's only comment on all of Tate's bustle was to note that Tate, who had recently become a Catholic, was acting instead as if he'd been "freed from all his inhibitions."[74]

By mid-June the Lowells were sailing down the Rhine, "coasting along on scenery and a little white wine and feeling rather refreshed," now that their "glorious Paris weeks" were behind them.[75] Then it was on to Vienna for three weeks of Mozart and Strauss, "the most dramatic show," Cal called it, "in the world."[76] From July 6 until August 20 he conducted classes at the Salzburg Seminar in American Civilization, located in an eighteenth-century rococo castle called the Schloss Leopoldskron. The Seminar had been founded by the late F. O. Matthiessen several years earlier and Jarrell himself had taught there only two years earlier. It was a vibrant, multi-lingual gathering of some one hundred poets, artists, and musicians from all over Europe. Shepherd Brooks, the Seminar's director, had met Cal at a cocktail party in Amsterdam that March and had invited him to participate, and Cal quickly developed a following of students fascinated by this brilliant, charming poet who seemed to have read everything.

In his six weeks there, as he later told Blair Clark, he managed to present not only "all American poetry from Emerson to Jarrell," but also organized readings in French, German, and Italian ("which meant studying the stuff pretty intensely myself"), as well as seminars on Chaucer, Pope, and Wordsworth. But his triumph (and "most pretentious moment") had been "a shot at Achilles' speech over one of Priam's sons," which he'd read in Greek, prefacing his reading with the comment that Greek quantities were anybody's guess, a way of saying that verve could always excuse sloppiness.[77] In late July, John McCormick, professor of Comparative Literature at Rutgers and Cal's colleague at Salzburg, interviewed Cal for *Poetry*, the first of many interviews Lowell would give over the next twenty-five years.

McCormick noted how the thirty-five-year-old Lowell, his hair already beginning to gray *(nel mezzo del cammin di nostra vita)*, walked "clumsily on the balls of his feet," like "an athlete slightly out of shape," his soft speech emphasizing auxiliaries and adverbs rather than nouns and verbs, the stress on words like "somehow," "quite," "unavoidable," and "too huge." He could see too that he was a serious man with serious interests who could also find room in his discourse for the frivolous. They spoke of history ("an art," Cal insisted, not a science), of the Nuremberg Trials, of Macaulay, of Adlai Stevenson and the Democratic Convention under way then back in the States.

A lunch, an off-the-cuff lecture on Hart Crane to an audience of students from a dozen countries, Lowell quoting from half a dozen of Crane's poems, while making such unexpected and brilliant observations as that Crane belonged in the company of the homosexual Arnaut Daniel in the *Purgatorio,* rather than with Brunetto Latini in the *Inferno.* At five, a seminar on American Poetry. Then a reading by nine poets from nine different countries, with Lowell introducing them all, his reading voice too high and lacking in range, though he read with feeling and inflection. Afterwards a visit to a German beer cellar to discuss Poe, Emerson, Melville. Chestnut trees lit by street lights, the splutter of single-cylinder Austrian motorcycles along the cobblestoned streets.

By then, tired and curt with any student who interrupted or disagreed with him, he paused to explain his abrupt behavior. "When I interrupt people," he offered, he was *not* "trying to be arrogant." Then reading aloud again, something he clearly enjoyed, this time Poe, Emerson, Melville. At ten Lizzie came by to announce that Adlai Stevenson had just been nominated, and so it was time to celebrate again by going into Salzburg to drink a bottle of *Gumpoldskirchner:* the Lowells, an Englishman, an Irishman, two Italians, McCormick. And now talk of Europe, Cal saying how good it was "to be away from home for a bit, to have a let-up from the unavoidable idea, a Promethean illusion perhaps, that the future of the world depends upon what your country does every day." Cal saying too how he was more conscious than ever of being an American abroad, that he could never live the expatriate life of a Pound, a Santayana, an Eliot, then bracketing that by adding that England alone might be possible for an American to settle in forever.

The greatest of his American elders were still Frost and Eliot, he went on. And then he was off ranking them in the calculus of his poetic hierarchy once more. Williams and Ransom and Tate and Pound and Crane and Marianne Moore and Stevens: all worthies in his great philosopher's circle, where they might all discuss poetry with Catullus and Tibullus and Ovid to their heart's content. And too the masters of prose: Fitzgerald, Hemingway, and—towering above the others—William Faulkner. And then a noisy Austrian band entering the *ratskellar* and Lowell and the others moving out into the heady summer night toward the railway station to continue their talk. At this velocity of verbal exchange, it was no wonder Cal had begun to speed up again.[78]

This time it takes the form of his falling in love again, as he had with Lizzie in 1949, only now it's an Italian music student named Giovanna Madonia, connected with La Scala, and he acts as if he's actually carefree and unattached, instead of there with a wife. Since, after three operas in London, five symphonies in Brussels, and another twenty at the Statsopera in Vienna, Cal now believes himself a serious student of music, in his illness he expects Lizzie to embrace his musical Giovanna. So, by the time the seminars are winding down, Cal is completely wound up. The lost puritan has metamorphosed into Rimbaud and Hart Crane again, and to hell with solid bourgeois values and the rest of it. To hell with the costs:

> *When the Pulitzers showered on some dope*
> *or screw who flushed our dry mouths out with soap,*
> *few people would consider why I took*
> *to stalking sailors, and scattered Uncle Sam's*
> *phoney gold-plated laurels to the birds.*
> *Because I knew my Whitman like a book,*
> *stranger in America, tell my country: I,*
> Catullus redivivus, *once the rage*
> *of the Village and Paris, used to play my role*
> *of homosexual, wolfing the stray lambs*
> *who hungered by the Place de la Concorde.*
> *My profit was a pocket with a hole.*
> *Who asks for me, the Shelley of my age,*
> *must lay his heart out for my bed and board.*[79]

One night toward the end of August he wanders from campus and is picked up by the Austrian police near the German border. Another scene: this one with police cars blocking the faculty complex at eleven o'clock one night, the professors huddled at one end, Cal at the other, where he's barricaded himself in his room, refusing to let anyone in. Jeeps, the Austrian police, and then American MPs. But Cal is adamant. He refuses to talk with anyone but Shepherd Brooks. Finally, one MP, a small southern kid, escorts Cal out of the building and deposits him in the American military hospital there in Salzburg, where Cal proceeds to pace up and down in his locked cell the rest of the night. The following day he is taken across the German border to the Army hospital in Munich, sixty miles away.

The transfer is accomplished in two cars, the first a tiny Hillman Minx with Shepherd Brooks behind the wheel, while a colleague keeps a tense eye on Cal, who sits alone in the back seat. And, at a safe distance behind the first car a second, with Brooks's wife at the wheel and Lizzie beside her. Cal himself is off in his own world, replete with Arms of the Law and other hypothetical, free-associative figures, while the two men up front wonder if he will try to grab the wheel along some mountain road. Suddenly Cal remembers that he has reports to do and begins rattling off bizarre profiles of each of his twenty as-yet-ungraded students. Then they're at the Munich Army Hospital, where Lizzie will begin her wearying vigil in a hotel on the Schillerstrasse nearby. "In Munich the zoo's rubble fumes with cats," Cal will write afterwards in his dramatic monologue, "A Mad Soldier Confined at Munich," itself a palimpsest of his earlier prison poem, "In the Cage":

> *hoydens with air-guns prowl the Koenigsplatz,*
> *and pink the pigeons on the mustard spire.*
> *Who but my girl-friend set the town on fire? . . .*

>   *Oh mama, mama, like a trolley-pole*
> *sparking at contact, her electric shock—*
> *the power house! . . . The doctor calls our roll—*
> *no knives, no forks. . . .*

In the hospital he passes the time discussing esoterica with the other patients as he has for the past two months with his university students and it seems a bizarre replaying of Pound in his gorilla cage at the Army's Detention Center in Pisa seven years before. The hospital, Lizzie can see, "is a terrible, terrible place for him." Nor do the other patients, being "of a very low mentality," care much for Cal or Cal's brand of highbrow, manic Boston humor. Still, there's a kind of grotesque vitality in all this. Now he is insisting on the innocence of Alger Hiss, calling Hiss's testimony before the House Un-American Activities a joke. Even Lizzie has to admit he's full "of a peculiar kind of wit" not unlike her own.[80] But when she visits him the following day, she herself has become the target. "Everybody," he tells her, "has noticed that you've been getting pretty dumb lately."

By then the commanding officer of the hospital has called Lizzie in to discuss her husband's case. He has some papers in front of him detailing Cal's refusal to serve in the Army during the war and he wants to know about Cal's military record. An Army doctor looks Cal over and tells her that Cal will not rejoin the Church, though he does seem ready now to join the Army. If he's willing to do that, he must be fine, he tells her. In spite of the gravity of the situation, she can't help smiling to herself, though she must be "sure he doesn't recover and get shipped to the Korean front."[81] The following day—August 26—she writes Mrs. Lowell, speaking only of Cal's strain from overwork. He has been "a huge success," she says, "a gift from heaven for the whole session." He is probably, "as much as anyone can be, a good representative of an intellectual American." And now, she adds, with her husband in love with another woman, and unable to resist the irony of the situation in which she has suddenly found herself, everything seems to have "paid off wonderfully."[82]

Within days Lizzie has Cal transferred to the Binswanger Sanatorium in Kreuzlingen, Switzerland. They travel there by rail (third class) with their beat-up old suitcases, which Lizzie must somehow carry by herself, with no money, and with Cal himself in terrible shape:

> *I watched our Paris pullman lunge*
> *mooning across the fallow Alpine snow. . . .*
> *Our mountain-climbing train had come to earth.*
> *Tired of the querulous hush-hush of the wheels,*
> *the blear-eyed ego kicking in my berth*
> *lay still. . . .*[83]

But the sanatarium itself is wonderful, and in ten days Cal is steady enough to be released. It has been a mild attack. "They clearly have the exquisite idea [at Kreuzlingen] that the only thing wrong with mental patients is that they haven't enough comfort, service and good hotel management," Lizzie will reassure the Macauleys afterwards. And in their case the hospital is right, "because we giggled all day long like a coal miner at the Ritz, in our connecting beautiful rooms, collapsed with sensuality in the deep baths," gasping "at the four meals a day. All this for both of us at $15 a day. The horrid Munich cost that much for Cal alone."[84]

The sanatarium "is how the world looks when a man subsides," Cal himself reassures the Macauleys on September 15. The place in fact looks like something Grandfather Winslow might have built out of Alpine and Adirondack stock. At the moment he and Lizzie are "snugly resting together and doing Sunday crossword puzzles in preparation for Venice, to which we go in two days."[85] He begs the Macauleys to forgive him "for being such a vehement bore," teaching having turned out to be strong medicine for someone as idle as he'd become after the "dark close quarters" of Holland, the cause, apparently, of his turning "people-and space-dizzy" in Salzburg.[86]

Blessedly, the entire episode has lasted less than a month this time, and the worst avoided. On September 17, he and Lizzie take the train down to Venice, where Tate and Spender and Blair Clark are vacationing, and where the Lowells will spend the next three weeks poring over, as Lizzie will phrase it, every stone of the city.[87] It is here too that Cal, walking with Blair on the Piazza San Marco, will tell Blair that he understands now that he will have to get serious treatment for his illness. He only hopes to God there is some way of getting at what is surely killing him.[88]

After Venice and Torcello, Lago di Garda with the Tates, then south again to Padua, Verona, and finally on to the "tremendous, quiet, slow tremendousness of Rome,"[89] where he and Lizzie could at last settle into the spacious rooms of the Pensione California on the Via Aurora to resume writing again. In mid-October, Cal went for the last time to see the monastery hospital near the Colosseum where, three weeks before, Santayana had died. "Lying outside the consecrated ground forever now," he would write of his dear, courtly, homosexual father,

>   *you smile*
> *like Ser Brunetto running for the green*
> *cloth at Verona—not like one*
> *who loses, but like one who'd won . . .*
> *as if your long pursuit of Socrates'*
> *demon, man-slaying Alcibiades,*
> *the demon of philosophy, at last had changed*
> *those fleeting virgins into friendly laurel trees*
> *at Santo Stefano Rotondo, when you died*
> *near ninety,*
> *still unbelieving, unconfessed and unreceived,*
> *true to your boyish shyness of the Bride.*
> *Old trooper, I see your child's red crayon pass,*
> *bleeding deletions on the galleys you hold*
> *under your throbbing magnifying glass,*
> *that worn arena, where the whirling sand*
> *and broken-hearted lions lick your hand*
> *refined by bile as yellow as a lump of gold.*[90]

"We're on the Pincian Hill," he wrote his mother on October 19 from the Pensione California, "just off the Via Veneto, between the Villa Borghese and the Piazza di Spagna . . . two smallish . . . immaculate rooms in a sort of Beacon St. going into the Fenway part of Rome." It was all so proper he feared he and Lizzie would "turn into two nineteenth century spinsters, deathly afraid of colds, and doing water colors of antiquity while waiting in vain for answers to letters of introduction." Only now did he feel strong enough to tell her what had really happened to him in August. It was "a very mild repetition of the trouble that reached its climax before in Chicago and Bald Pate [sic]," he wanted to reassure her. He'd spent a few days in a Munich hospital, then another ten "at a place that was something between an inn and a sanatarium on a Swiss lake." Thanks to Lizzie's watchfulness, the attack had never gone "much beyond a state of nervous excitement," so that he'd rapidly gone "through the three stages of exuberance, confusion and depression." It was over now, and "without any likelihood of relapse or return." He was certainly not interested in building up a reputation for poetic instability.[91]

Early in November the Republicans were ushered in. "Glum faces at the embassy listening to the election returns with the Foxes," Cal wrote Tate, just after Stevenson's defeat. "Best comment from a girl in back of us, 'It would have been thrilling to have had a bachelor in the White House.' " He and Lizzie were both blue about the outcome, for Eisenhower was for them "a sort of symbol . . . of America's unintelligent side—all fitness, muscles, smiles and banality." Even the *idea* of Stevenson, had been "so terribly better than one had a right to expect." They felt too bruised even to laugh.

From politics he turned to poetry. Tate had sent him a new long poem, "The Buried Lake," in terza rima, and Cal noted that younger poets who were at the moment turning to free verse would have to reckon with Tate's stunning new formal achievement. It had cheered Cal no end to see his former mentor using meter like that "to smash into new ground." What he particularly liked was how warm and vulnerable the new poem was, for nothing was harder than getting real conversation into a formal poem. He too was writing again, though everything he did still felt "pedestrian, pompous, or queer." But at least he and Lizzie were "working like monks" again, Lizzie on a Turkish story, he on half a dozen sonnets and two longish efforts.

One of these was an elegy for Santayana, an early version of what would eventually bifurcate into "For George Santayana" and "Beyond the Alps." The other poem was "Epitaph of a Fallen Poet," an early version of the Crane sonnet, where he knew he was at long last "going into new country," and not simply "repeating old tricks." Still, it was hell searching for a new idiom and not being able to find it, no matter how hard one tried, all the while having to watch "the petrified flotsam bits" of the old voice "bobbing up where you don't want them."[92]

Rome this fall, with its layer upon layer of history, had turned out to be heavenly, and he and Lizzie were having "a delightful dilettante's winter" reading Henry James and "drifting about with marked guide-books."[93] Still, there was "a bleak, detached loneliness" about beginning a third year in Europe.[94] No wonder that by mid-November they'd become so "fearfully Yankee about money and . . . undermined by homesickness" that they'd both decided it was time to return to America.[95] Cal would take over for Karl Shapiro and teach the spring term at Iowa. Maybe, he told Tate, it was "the puritan carping of my conscience saying I ought to be at work like everyone else."[96] Besides, they were "much too poor to be proud," he told Blair, which was "no fun and beyond the help of loans." There was too a sense "of deracinated idleness" entering their lives now, "or rather a vision of such feelings increasing in the future," such as lying in bed an extra two hours some half hungover morning, delighting in the first hour and "brooding greasily through the second and calling it pleasure or 'life' as Cousin Ghormley would say."[97]

There were new strains as well, like his break with one of his old Kenyon friends, Dave McDowell, who was in Rome that fall with his wife. Cal and Lizzie had been showing them Rome—"days of taking Dave on guided tours to the San Rocco Tintorettos, the Via Appia, etc." Then a "dinner with too much wine," during which Lizzie had told them "for ten minutes with devastating charm and mobile face that they talked too much," until "they dramatically strode into the Roman dark and out of our lives, as the rhetoricians would say." If they were "technically in the wrong," Cal defended himself, they were still "much the more sympathetic characters."[98] By December 7 he was writing Peter Taylor that he was frankly tired of Rome, and needed the solitude and sweat of another Amsterdam winter to consolidate his new poetry. Now Iowa City would have to serve that role.[99]

Two days after Christmas Cal and Lizzie left Rome by train for Paris, once again crossing the Alps. There they booked into a room at the Hôtel des Saintes-Pères to wait for their ship, which was scheduled to sail on January 9, their destination Iowa's "innumerable obscure manuscripts." Thoughts of his father had begun crowding his memory again, he wrote Cousin Harriet at year's end, so that he'd tried writing "a little elegy on him, but could only feel that he was alive and that I was a fool."[100] But there was also his other father, the one he'd come to Europe to see, and who was now gone as well. By then Santayana's Catholic skepticism had become his own, and when he left Rome, he left, like Aeneas leaving Troy, carrying Santayana's household gods with him. He had tried to scale the heights of the Sublime by force in his magnificent early poems and had failed, his "blear-eyed ego" kicking itself into a new birth which, he understood, also meant the death of the old.

Like Jonah before Nineveh, he'd waited for the violent collapse of the old world order, only to have to watch, appalled, the collapse instead of all that for so many years had sustained him. "There were no tickets for that altitude," he saw now, no language, no way of scaling those heights, those wasted Alps, those "fire-branded sockets of the Cyclops' eye," where even "the Swiss [mountain climbers] had thrown in the sponge." Impossible goddess of Wisdom, Athena, Our Lady of the Assumption, he would write,

> *prince, pope, philosopher and golden bough,*
> *pure mind and murder at the scything prow—*
> *Minerva, the miscarriage of the brain.*[101]

Better Paris, then. Paris, that black classic, irresponsible, lust-loving, modern Paris, who had taken the beautiful Helen, in spite of the disintegrations his irresponsible act had entailed. Better the Paris of Baudelaire and Rimbaud and Mallarmé, where—though the writing might seem as strange as the illegible symbols scratched on an Etruscan cup—at least the image of violence painted on the cup he planned to drink from would be clear enough. Clear at least as a mother skunk swilling in the garbage for a "cup / of sour cream,"[102] clear as those long-suppressed killer kings whose dark and violent forces ruled the world because they ruled (alas) the blood.

9

Boston

1953–1955

They sailed with five hundred seasick Canadians, Lowell would remember ("two years and two months of hoofing and gaping ending with three days of flu on a cockney steamer ventilated with blinding hot air"), and reached New York on January 19, 1953.[1] They were just in time for the inauguration of Dwight D. Eisenhower, for which Lowell wrote a sonnet, "On Stuyvesant Square During a Blizzard," later renamed "Inauguration Day: January 1953." In the poem, the pro-Stevenson Lowell saw the iced-over spirit of Ulysses S. Grant living on in Ike, both men having stepped into the presidency after serving as the country's commanding officers during two respective cataclysmic wars. He thought of Grant ordering his soldiers to move against the enemy barricades at Cold Harbor, of men in despair pinning their names to their uniforms so that at least their riddled bodies might be identified. Cold Harbor, birth of the dogtag, where in one hour ten thousand had died on the orders of an inept commanding officer. Ice, ice at the heart, a fitting metaphor for a Cold War administration:

> Ice, ice. Our wheels no longer move.
> Look, the fixed stars, all just alike
> as lack-land atoms, split apart,

and the Republic summons Ike,
the mausoleum in her heart.[2]

A visit from Berryman in New York, then a quick trip to Boston to see Mrs. Lowell, then out to Iowa City. Cal and Lizzie found a comfortable fourth-floor three-room apartment with "lots of light" at the Burlington Apartments. Cal taught Mondays and Tuesdays: a course in translation, in which he had to "acquire and give out scholarship almost simultaneously," and a poetry work-shop with twenty-three poets, each of whom brought him their "life-works" twice a week.[3] Allen Tate came out at the end of February to see him, and Cal in turn travelled to Oberlin to fill in for Tate, speaking twice, he noted, "in a New England Presbyterian church without alcohol or cigarettes" with his old adversary, Alfred Kazin. It was the first time he and Kazin had met since the Yaddo fiasco, and both, Cal noted, "had made an effort to be civil."[4] After-wards, Cal went down to Kenyon to talk away the night with the Taylors and Ransoms. But mostly he stayed close to Iowa City, where life soon settled into "a pretty dormant, day to day thing, a rather rustic pastoral after Europe."[5]

He spent all his spare time writing now, telling Tate that it broke "one's heart each time fighting one's verbiage and awkwardness to the real flesh." How he wanted "to do all the things" he couldn't yet do. The only thing which kept him going was looking into "the dim ahead" at his next book, where he really hoped to go to town. He was working on yet another "long monologue," though it was now against his beliefs, "in this age of mounting populations in print," for *any* poem to "go over 25 lines."[6] After all, he told Taylor, what did *War and Peace* have that wasn't "more pregnantly said in a one-line Japanese—what shall I call it?"[7] The memory of the failure of the *Kavanaughs* was still very much with him, and he wanted all that that poem represented behind him once and for all.

The trouble was, he knew, that writing was "only the inertia" of one's "old rhetorics and habits," the game being to push on and not be carried by one's "old jungle of used equipment." Part of the old jungle he still carried with him was being thought of even now as a Catholic writer, and getting "Catholic invitations to join their panel of authors," invitations he found it embarrassing to answer. The only act of faith he could make any more was a creed which stated, *"I don't know what I don't know."* Beyond that formulation lay "confu-sion and impossibility" for him.[8] So when Tate asked him to join him at a Catholic Worker conference in the summer of 1953 in Newburgh, Cal ex-plained that "art and religion *per se*" had "nothing to do with each other, though in this imperfect world they were forever colliding, "exploiting, avoid-ing and abusing each other." Which was perhaps as it should be. He would have liked to take some of the poets Tate was considering talking about at the conference and "muddy up the waters—sympathetically and intelligently"— then try to clear the waters "as far as the facts allow." It was very important to "condescend" to the skeptical spirit of Descartes "and be inexhaustibly fair to him," he had learned. Otherwise, there was "always the danger" Descartes would "be fair to us and annihilate our critiques."[9]

In late April he attended a poetry conference at Grinnell, then another at the University of Illinois. Then it was out to Champaign-Urbana to give a reading and visit with Randall, who seemed almost giggly to see him again. He signed on to teach at the University of Cincinnati as the Elliston Professor of Poetry for spring 1954, though he worried about having to prepare a series of public lectures for them. He was no critic, he confessed to Tate, and couldn't write, "as Caroline would say, a prose sentence." But unless he did the Cincinnati stint, he would never learn.[10] He caught up with Robert Fitzgerald, who was moving with his wife, Sally, and their million kids (as Flannery had phrased it), to Italy, and whom Cal hadn't seen since his "Yaddo mad-conversation business." For him the Fitzgeralds were "real heroes, lifting the population, taking care of all [their] good and needy friends"—like Berryman, like Flannery— "and doing hundreds of small hard man-of-letters ill-paid jobs." He was also worried about Flannery, who had lately been diagnosed with lupus, though she still wrote "gaily enough for her."[11]

In June, he and Lizzie bought a "green, glorious, sedate" 1937 Packard from an old professor, who had looked after it, Cal had been assured, "like a baby, or rather far better." He had just gotten his Iowa driver's licence, and was learning to drive now after a hiatus of fifteen years. He was, he reported to Bishop, both "slow and reliable," and took Lizzie for "pleasure drives along the unscenic Iowa River," the two of them "senile with joy and fatuousness." He loved driving that old car, and lay awake nights thinking up useless errands. And though he'd heard from friends that Brazil had turned out to be perfect for Bishop, he missed her terribly and wanted her back in the States for long visits. If she stayed in Brazil long enough, he planned to drive down and see her. Were there, he wondered, bridges over the Panama Canal?[12]

By early July, when he began lecturing at the Indiana School of Letters, he was deep into his "eight-day bicycle race" of teaching—Iowa-Indiana-Iowa-Cincinatti—and wistfully looking for a place near Boston where he and Lizzie could buy a house and he could get a job teaching. He'd lived nowhere for more than a year since 1940, and nowhere for more than six months since 1948, when he'd roomed at the Cosmos Club in Washington with a group of octogenarians, and he was tired of (Lizzie's) having to pack and unpack every six months. Nor was it fun any more having "books and duplicate kitchen equipment resting with . . . ten different friends and storage-houses."[13]

James Laughlin, founder of New Directions, in the 1940s. "Our only strong and avant-garde man [at Harvard in 1937] was James Laughlin," Lowell would write. "He was much taller and older then we were. He knew Henry Miller, and exotic young American poetesses in Paris, spent summers at Rapallo with Ezra Pound. . . . He knew the great, and he himself wrote deliberately flat and anecdotal poems. We were sarcastic about them, but they made us feel secretly that we didn't know what was up in poetry." These were free verse forms "based on the practice of W. C. Williams, a poet and pediatrician living in Rutherford, New Jersey." [*New Directions*]

William Carlos Williams at his typewriter, 1950. Reading the galleys of *Paterson,* Lowell judged it the "best poem written by an American" he'd ever seen. "Who loved more?", Lowell would write, recalling his visit to Williams's home in Rutherford in the fall of 1947, "William Carlos Williams,/ in collegiate black slacks, gabardine coat,/ and loafers polished like rosewood on yachts," Williams telling him, "I am sixty-seven, and more/ attractive to girls than when I was seventeen." [*New Directions*]

Lowell, thirty-four, at his typewriter in his apartment on the Lungarno Amerigo Vespucci, Florence, in the spring of 1951. Florence, he wrote Elizabeth Bishop, with its "gray and sand-colored, Bostonish, compact" air and "cultivated starkness," its graffiti denouncing the warmongering MacArthur's presence in Korea. Florence, city of tyrannicides, with its Palazzo Vecchio, its churches, its dense layers of history, its "boisterous, friendly, and fearfully orderly" citizens assembled in some square for a political meeting, where one might suddenly find oneself in the midst of "utter civil war or more likely a communist government." [*By permission of the Houghton Library, Harvard University*]

Harriet Winslow, Lowell's beloved Cousin Harriet, behind the house in Castine, Maine, which she bequeathed to Hardwick. The photo was taken in the early 1950s. "Harriet Winslow, who owned this house," he wrote a year before her death, "was more to me than my mother./ I think of you far off in Washington,/ breathing in the heat wave/ and air conditioning, knowing/ each drug that numbs alerts another nerve to pain." [*Harry Ransom Humanities Research Center, University of Texas*]

Robert Lowell, Mary McCarthy, her son Reuel, Elizabeth Hardwick, and McCarthy's second husband, Bowden Broadwater at the Club Zara on Tremont Street in Boston, 1956. "The weathered yeoman loveliness of a duchess," Lowell would write of McCarthy, "enlightenment in our dark age though Irish,/ our Diana, rash to awkwardness. . . ." [*Society Photo (concessionaires), Special Collections, Vassar College Libraries*]

Robert Lowell at forty with his daughter Harriet, spring 1957. Having little Harriet around was rather like "living on the moon" with a being as "simple as primordial matter." [*By permission of the Houghton Library, Harvard University*]

FACING PAGE: The Winslow house in Castine. Here and at the Barn, Lowell spent fifteen summers with his family, working on his poems, his plays, his prose pieces. "One must get used/ to the painted soft wood staying bright and clean," he wrote in the summer of 1963, "to the air blasting an all-white wall whiter,/ as it blows through curtain and screen/ touched with salt and evergreen." [*Harry Ransom Humanities Research Center, University of Texas*]

Robert Lowell with Harriet in Castine in the summer of 1960. He'd always suspected, he told Taylor that summer, that he and Lizzie "were curiously unlike other families, my multiple absent-mindedness, and Lizzie's way of investing small, domestic acts with the splendor of an early Verdi heroine." But "against the background of a normal child" like Harriet, he could measure how very strange he might seem to others. [*Rollie McKenna*]

Robert Lowell and Elizabeth Bishop in Rio de Janiero, August 1962. "We were giving an abraço, supposedly," Bishop wrote a friend about this photograph, "but 2 New Englanders get awfully gingerly and shy."
[*Special Collections, Vassar College Libraries*]

In early August, "seedy and subdued," he and Lizzie drove down to Kenyon to spend a month with the Taylors, Ransoms, and Macauleys. Then it was up to Boston to look for a house. Boston itself, they felt, would be *too* close to Mother, so they began looking along the lower Maine coast and southern Vermont before fixing on an old colonial house in Duxbury, forty miles south of Boston. In early September Lizzie returned to Iowa, while Cal spent two weeks at his mother's house at 33 Marlborough Street, meeting with the Duxbury owners, signing leases, battling constipation and a Boston heatwave, and having, as it turned out, the last long talks he would ever have with his mother. He found her "more human and relaxed" now than ever before, and that allowed him finally to relax a little with her as well. All in all he was having "a grand time being delicate and middle-aged, full of Back Boston thoughts."[14] He talked with her about everything, but especially about her upcoming trip to Italy (she would sail in six weeks, largely because she was unsure what else to do with herself). He even discussed Freud with her (thanks to her years working with Merrill Moore), so that Cal was in danger of himself becoming "a confused and slavish convert" to psychoanalysis. Every flaw in himself, he was learning, seemed to lead to "a goldmine of discoveries."[15]

He wanted roots now, wanted stability. At thirty-six, he wrote Flannery O'Connor, he was already "feeling very elderstatesmanish" and happy to be back in the States teaching.[16] And to Cousin Harriet, to whom he had begun turning more and more as to a wise mother, he wrote that with the acquisition of their Duxbury house and a car they had become "changed creatures." The house was "1740, with a 1950 oil furnace, a sun porch and three acres of land." His real home, he'd come to realize after two years abroad, was—after all—Boston, "the living twentieth century Boston at least as much as the old colonial" one. It was what he'd been born to and "only a sort of blind (O and I think necessary) rebellion" had made him turn away from it. Now, however, he was old enough to be "conventional if not 'proper' outwardly, and not shock (or be shocked by) people." Still, the Rimbaud in him asserted, one didn't "want to change too much."[17]

He'd had good students at Iowa in the spring, he told Tate, along with some "very confused ones" (usually the same people),[18] until he had begun feeling like a psychiatrist, "full of banal worldly wisdom." Still, this time round at Iowa had certainly been better than his first green experiment three years before, when he and Lizzie had arrived "as shy and lofty Eastern sea-board strangers." Part of the change was not only his having grown older, he realized, but growing smaller and more honest in the hand of God.[19] Now, in the fall of '53, he was teaching a workshop and a course in Homer in the original Greek, which he managed with the help of Gerald Else, a classicist.

"Sir Thomas Wyatt, Sir Walter Raleigh, John Milton's 'Lycidas,' Walter

Landor, Alfred Lord Tennyson's 'Tithonus'—week after week we came away staggered under a bombardment of ideas, ideas, ideas," W. D. Snodgrass would remember. "None of these works would ever look the same again; neither would our estimation of an adequate response to any work of art." When Lowell "did" a poem, a classmate of Snodgrass had said, "it was as if a muscle-bound octopus sat down over it. Then, deliberately, it stretched out one tentacle to haul Mythology, a second for Sociology, a third for Classical Literature, others for Religion, History, Psychology. Meantime, you sat there thinking, 'This man *is* as mad as they said; none of this has anything to do with my poor, little poem!' Then he began to tie these disciplines, one by one, into your text; you saw that it *did* have to do, had almost everything to do, with your poem."

Nor did it end there. "On the street two days later you would run into Lowell," who'd in the meantime been thinking of your poem and now had an altogether new reading for it. When he spoke, he had a habit of resting his cheek on his fist or his chin on the back of his hand, the elbow itself resting on thin air. Long, halting sentences, a downward-pointing, revolving forefinger which Randall had taken to calling "Cal stirring porridge." Then, slowly, "the mass and power of that mind overbore doubts or objections. You could never predict his opinion, what associations he might draw, toward any subject." "However high our expectations," Snodgrass summed up, "no one was disappointed by Lowell's teaching."[20]

Except perhaps for the young Phil Levine, down from working on a series of "stupid jobs" in Detroit's automobile factories:

> To say I was disappointed in Lowell as a teacher is an understatement, although never having taken a poetry workshop I had no idea what to expect. But a teacher who is visibly bored by his students and their poems is hard to admire. The students were a marvel: we were two future Pulitzer Prize winners, one Yale winner, one National Book Critics Circle Award winner, three Lamont Prize winners, one American Book Award winner. Some names: Donald Justice, W. D. Snodgrass, Jane Cooper, William Dickey, Robert Dana, Paul Petrie, Melvin Walker LaFollette, Henri Coulette, Donald Petersen . . . Shirley Eliason.

And of course Levine. Lowell also played favorites, Levine would remember, so that, "no matter how much they wrote like Lowell, some of the poets could do no wrong. . . . I could write nothing that pleased Lowell." At term's end Lowell gave Levine a B, at the same time telling him he'd come farthest in the class. "Then why the B?", Levine had asked. Because he'd already given the As out. "This was at our second and last fifteen-minute conference—which did not irritate me nearly as much as the first, when he accused me of stealing my

Freudian insights and vocabulary from Auden. 'Mr. Lowell,' I had responded (I never got more intimate than Mister and he never encouraged me to do so), 'I'm Jewish. I steal Freud directly from Freud; he was one of ours.' Mr. Lowell merely sighed."

But for Levine, Lowell's Modern Poetry course was even worse. "We expected him to misread our poems," Levine would recall with trenchant humor. "After all, most of them were confused and, with very few exceptions, only partly realized, but to see him bumbling in the face of 'real poetry' was discouraging. The day he assured the class that Housman's 'Loveliest of Trees, the Cherry Now' was about suicide, Melvin LaFollette leaned over and whispered in my ear, 'We know what *he's* thinking about.' " Lowell could also be fiercely competitive. "With the exceptions of Bishop and Jarrell he seemed to have little use for any practicing American poet, and he once labeled Roethke 'more of an old woman than Marianne Moore.' " Still, he was "master of a powerful and fierce voice that all of us respected, and though many of us were disappointed, none of us turned against the man or his poetry. As Don Petersen once put it, 'Can you imagine how hard it is to live as Robert Lowell, with that inner life?' "

But Lowell's worst offense, perhaps, was trying to overwhelm his classes with one of his own poems, a draft of "The Banker's Daughter." Levine would remember Lowell intoning the poem "'in that enervated voice we'd all become used to, a genteel Southern accent that suggested the least display of emotion was déclassé. . . . No one suggested a single cut, not even when Lowell asked if the piece might be a trifle too extended, a bit soft in places. Perish the thought; it was a masterpiece!"[21] Berryman, a Shakespearean scholar, Cal reminded his class, would be at Iowa in the spring, and they should look at his "Homage to Mistress Bradstreet" in the current issue of *Partisan Review,* strong evidence that he was coming into his own as a poet.[22] "In fairness to Lowell," Levine added, "he was teetering on the brink of a massive nervous breakdown. . . . Rumors of his hospitalization drifted back to Iowa City, and many of us felt guilty for damning him as a total loss."

But even for Levine, Lowell had his more attractive side. As when Lowell watched the 1953 World Series on television that October. "Once, before the workshop met, Melvin La Follette & I observed Lowell watching the Dodgers vs Yankees game. Outside of NYC I think everyone was pulling for Brooklyn. Before class began we went to the john & there as we pissed side by side we composed these parodies of famous Lowell poems, inserting the names of [Carl] Furillo, [PeeWee] Reese, [Yogi] Berra, [Roy] Campanella, Jackie Robinson, [Mickey] Mantle. Before we left Melvin noticed these familiar shoes under the door to one stall, pulled himself up so he could peer into the occupied one, & shouted, 'It's him.' " Later, when Cal came into the room, "he was all smiles & made reference to the game & the interesting poetic aftermath. I was surprised to see him so good natured about it. And relieved."[23]

Late November 1953, and already slow-falling drifting cotton snow, and the sedate Packard refusing to start. Out his apartment window Lowell watched the "bare tree trunks and the white snow of roof and street." He and Lizzie had had the Justices for Thanksgiving; a twelve-pound goose chased down with chocolate eggnog Alexanders. Verdi's *Falstaff* was playing on the phonograph, and he had just finished reading an article on smoking and lung cancer in *Time* magazine convincing enough that he had managed to stop smoking cold turkey for forty-eight hours and could crow to his mother that he was already feeling healthier and more virtuous. If he kept this up, he told her, he'd soon be drinking Overferein, walking a mile a day, and voting Republican. He made it for another smokeless twenty-four hours, before going back to his usual fifty cigarettes a day.[24]

Then, winter was upon him. Dylan Thomas, he wrote Bishop, had just died at thirty-nine, the victim of acute alcoholism. A life "short and shining," he added, as perhaps Thomas himself would have wanted it. He spoke too of Jarrell's college novel, *Pictures from an Institution,* with its too-pointed portrait of Mary McCarthy which even *Partisan Review* had refused to print. "They all say it is bad and not fiction etc., and wait with watering mouths for Mary to read it."[25] "Can you imagine anyone telling off either Mary or Randall?", Cal had written Bishop the year before from Holland. "At Harvard I once heard Mary say to Randall: 'I think your poetry is much more obscure than Cal's.' This was an obscure but hurting blow at both of us. Somehow I got caught between them. Randall laid down the law, but it wasn't a pleasure for anyone."[26]

He invited J. F. Powers to come out to read at Iowa in January. ("Your visit washed me out and put the fear of God into me," he would write after his friend had come and gone. "The prose workshop is ruefully stumbling to its feet—I think most of them are planning to enlist in the navy.")[27] He'd read one of Powers's recent stories with an especially dreary setting, wondering afterwards how anyone could be a Catholic, until he realized that the people Powers had described were uncannily like himself.[28] In early December he read at Yale, and visited afterwards with Brooks and Warren. Warren's *Brother to Dragons* he'd just reviewed for the *Kenyon Review;* but Warren, he worried, must have disliked what he'd said there, for during his entire stay at Yale Warren had never so much as mentioned it. And yet writing it had been "like pulling teeth" for him.[29]

After Yale he'd gone down to New York to attend the opera with Giroux and Berryman, the three of them in tuxedos, Lowell's borrowed from Giroux.

Then it was down to Washington to attend to Library business and visit with his Cousin Harriet and Pound. It was the first time he'd seen Pound in four years, and he was shocked to see "how unchanged he was," spouting "the same list of books . . . the same rhetoric." Still, Pound did seem fatter now and healthier, with fewer memory gaps, and jumping and dancing about like a bear, glad to be alive. Pound at sixty-nine was alive because he wanted to be, Lowell understood now, whereas Thomas had succeeded, terribly enough, in burning himself out as quickly as possible.[30]

New Year's Day, 1954, he wrote Bishop from Iowa, thanking her for the picture she'd sent him of herself holding a cat beyond the wheel of a car. The picture he'd perched high on his eighteen-inch Maine Christmas tree, a gift from Cousin Harriet. He had nine one-hour lectures on American Poetry to deliver in Cincinnati beginning in a month's time, of which not one had yet been written, and he wished he'd been "reading Americana instead of Homer and Pindar!" And though "Beyond the Alps," in his judgment the best poem he'd yet written, would be out in the summer issue of the *Kenyon Review,* most of the last three months had been spent merely reading. At the moment he was recovering from a three days' "head-inflaming cold," during which he'd read Carlyle's *French Revolution,* a book he'd found "overpowering, and almost as good as *Moby Dick."*[31]

When the Lowells moved up to Cincinnati at the beginning of February, they took the same apartment the Berrymans had occupied two years earlier. But they were hardly settled in when a cable arrived with the news that Charlotte Lowell had suffered a stroke in Rapallo and was now recovering in the local hospital. By the time Cal reached her, however—just after midnight on the 14th—his mother had just died of a second stroke. In her last days she had tried washing away the dark blotch which had pooled just above her right eye. Blair Clark had seen Cal between flights at Neuilly and had caught in Cal's eyes the unmistakable signs. No doubt about it. Cal was speeding up again. By the time he caught up with him in Rapallo, he knew he was right.

"I had a friend who had a formidable mother," Lizzie wrote the Clarks from her mother's home in Lexington, Kentucky, on the eve of Cal's return to the States. "And he said he used sometimes to stop in the street and say 'Is Mama *really* dead?' Not out of any sentimentality but from genuine wonder that such a strange force could suddenly vanish. In my heart I do four times a day pay Mrs. Lowell the compliment of profound disbelief in this latest event." And "such a real death too! On far-away, sunny shores struck down at noon."[32]

From his letters to Lizzie and Cousin Harriet and other relatives, Cal seemed to be coping well with Charlotte's death. He visited his mother's friends in Florence and Rapallo, attended a funeral service for the English-speaking community in Rapallo, visited with the Fitzgeralds and his Italian translator, Rolando Anzilotti, then went up to Genoa to order his mother an ornate casket. Then he made plans to sail on the 21st, which would bring him into New York on his thirty-seventh birthday. He hoped the sea journey would prove "a great easing."[33] But he said nothing to Lizzie about going to La Scala in Milan with Blair in tow, ostensibly to hear Elizabeth Schwarzkopf sing in *Figaro,* but in reality to see Giovanna Madonia, the Salzburg music student he'd fallen in love with eighteen months earlier, and now again, even though at the moment she was a bit inconveniently married.[34]

Disembarkation in New York,[35] then the body taken to Boston, then to the frozen wastes of Dunbarton for burial, with Charlotte's friends and a handful of Winslows to offer comfort. And Father, blackening in his best sports jacket, waiting for his sudden bride. "I guess I am a black sheep forever, but it's calming not to be for a moment," Cal wrote Blair on March 11, when he was at last back in Cincinnati and teaching.[36] He found himself looking back regretfully on the good talks he'd had with his mother six months earlier, talks which had helped take some of the bitterness out of his failure to get to his mother's bedside in time. That, and the knowledge that she'd "slipped far after her first stroke," so that he "would have only seen and talked to a part."[37] To Williams he wrote of his mother that it had taken "a lifetime to be off guard with each other."[38]

But it was clear at least to Lizzie that he was still speeding up. When he wrote Williams to congratulate him on *The Desert Music,* he told him he felt "rattle-brained and enthusiastic" just now.[39] Try as he might to maintain a certain distance from the fact of his mother's death, the loss had shattered him. To Tate he wrote that in her last months, "Mother really was trying to free herself from me. . . . Together, except sometimes when we were alone, we sat like stones on each other's heads—inhibiting and inhibited." But now that she was gone, he'd begun to see how many people loved her, and that, when she had been able to separate herself from him and his father, he had found "a boldness and humor" there that were all her own. Too late. Too late.[40]

Moreover, he found himself unhappy with his classes, and was beginning to see just how good his Iowa students had been. Here in Cincinnati it was mostly "old ladies, mean, mystical, vague, relentless," illiterate. Two students had dropped his course at the mere mention of Matthew Arnold. Two others were women in their fifties who'd given up housekeeping to write poetry and who thought more people should write poetry. He on the other hand did not. "Berryman, Spender, R. P. Coffin, Lowell come here," he sighed. But his students, though they took these classes, somehow remained "like God, unchanged."[41]

In the meantime, Giovanna was writing Cal of her love for him, a love which had been sparked again that night in Milan, so that no sooner was Lizzie back from Lexington than Cal told her the marriage was over. He and Lizzie were "perfectly friendly, oddly enough still, and both in very good spirits," he wrote the Taylors on March 19, so that there was little to tell. They were separating simply because they'd "exhausted each other."[42] Lizzie went off to New York, while Cal was "steadied" by a group of six faculty couples in Cincinnati. "When I had lunch with Giroux in Atlanta he told me about Cal's escapade," Flannery O'Connor would write Sally Fitzgerald at year's end. "It seems [Cal] convinced everybody it was Elizabeth who was going crazy. . . . Toward the end he gave a lecture at the university that was almost pure gibberish. I guess nobody noticed, thinking it was the new criticism."[43]

"It is better that I gabble on, and write badly, than that I say nothing," Lowell wrote Pound on March 20. He was "trying out a theory of translation as creative imitation on him," and had been reading Pound's *Homage to Sextus Propertius* again. The *Propertius,* he was discovering, was no more Propertius than Campion's Catullus was Catullus. It was something else: Pound himself, "a much more graceful, airy character," Propertius after all being "something of a Christian poète maudit, an iron, violent, paralysed, and pierced and piercing beyond belief man," whereas Pound's persona was "a man writing in the Occident of the first World War—humorous, skeptical, shocked that such a thing could happen."[44] What Lowell himself had discovered in reading Pound's translations was a way to move his own voice into new and foreign territory through an act of creative imitation. In his "enthusiasm," he was not yet fully aware of translation's links for him to schizophrenia and manic depression.

With his mother's death, Lowell's entire lifetime income doubled overnight, besides providing him with $50,000 in cash. "All very handy at this point," he told Blair, now that he was "orphaned," self-determined, and ready to start a new life. Ominously, he mentioned reading Henry Adams for what light Adams might shed on the New England manic-depressive character.[45] "Cal's love for me is more phissical [sic] than anything else," Giovanna wrote Blair in Paris, "(actually we talked very little, also because it is very hard for me to understand his English")[46] On the 25th, Cal finally told Pound about the Italian girl he intended to marry, and for whom he'd been "waiting half-dead" for the past two years.[47] To Berryman in Iowa City he sent an invitation asking him to stay with him in Cincinnati and be his Scholar Gypsy. Elizabeth, from whom he had now separated, was all right, he explained, but a bit too exuberant for his own tastes.[48]

"Poor Cal!", Lizzie wrote Blair. "He's really a great comic character! 'Uncle, honey, it's all over!' This was the way he announced the whole thing." She knew Cal was in another "elation," this one "brought about by guilt feelings over the relief" he felt at his mother's death, compounded by Giovanna's telling him "she would never have married [Luciano] Erba" if she'd known Cal had been waiting for her. For Lizzie, it was "like coming out of a cave to be free" of the burden of this marriage at last. All she wanted was to forget the whole thing "and start all over" with "a nice, sleepy old man" who snoozed "in front of the fire all day."⁴⁹

"For the moment you speak my language," he writes Pound on the 30th, madness staring hard at madness. He wants to talk verse, the one lifeline left him. "Not reading Vergil is your funeral, not his or mine . . . a man must sweat with his meters if he is ever going to be a *fabbro* [craftsman], and not just a prophet." He encloses two poems and tells Pound to "see what your cigarstore wooden Indian solid Kansas humor can do with it." One is an early version of "Words for Hart Crane." The other reads like some lost *Canto* and is called "Adolf Hitler von Linz (Siegfried)":

> *Hitler Adolfus? Shall I weigh him? . . .*
> *The lungs of Luther burn. You might say*
> *He laid his cards on the table face-up, and called the hands.*
>   *. . . I went to jail*
> In my own country *to save those German cities*
> *You smashed like racks of clay pigeons. . . .*
> *When they sent me down the Hudson, through neat Connecticut,*
> *Through an alchemist's autumn, and hand-cuffed to two two-bit*
> *Porto Ricans for Danbury, for my place of correction.*
> *You nothing, whom we might have called Lucifer,*
> *If only you'd lasted* un poco—
> una cosa picciola, animula blandula, *believing in Italy,*
> *Like no other German. . . .*⁵⁰

A few days later he is travelling down to Greensboro to see the Jarrells. There is a swollen look about him; he insists on wearing Randall's "Ferrari-red" sweater and his English tweed cap. He chain-smokes and downs beer after beer. He seems obsessed with the death of his mother. He is going to marry an Italian girl, he tells Randall, who congratulates him on getting rid of Lizzie. Randall wants to talk only of Malraux and Chekhov, Cal only of his girl. He has taken to wearing his father's Naval Academy ring with the Lowell crest on it and notices that Mary's daughter is also wearing a signet ring. He tells her that *his* family's motto is *"Occasionem cognosce,"* at which Randall lashes back: "Know the occasion indeed," and demands Cal return his cap and his sweater before he hustles Cal out the door and off to the railroad station with a surly goodbye.

Within days a call from Cal. He has been hospitalized again, and asks Randall to please write Giovanna and explain what has happened. He also asks him to receive Giovanna's letters, something that goes against Randall's abstemious grain, as later he will refuse to listen to either Tate or Taylor so much as talk about Cal's illness. Still, he promises to write Giovanna. When he hangs up, Randall stares at the phone. "So *that's* what it was. Oh, Randall," he tells himself, "you're so dumb."[51]

Next Cal writes Flannery O'Connor. He is not rejoining the faith this time, he tells her, for he believes he can do more outside the Church, at least for himself. Thus Flannery reports to the Fitzgeralds, adding that Cal has spoken "some other claptrap about Henry Adams being a Catholic anarchist and he was the same, only agnostic too. I wrote him that his not being in the Church was a grief to me and I knew no more to say about it. I said I severely doubted he would do any good to anybody else outside. . . . I said the Sacraments gave grace—and let it go at that. I got a postcard back saying thank you, that we did speak the same language but he wasn't as young as he used to be and not so quick on his feet anymore. Well, maybe he plans to get on them eventually."[52]

Now Cal's behavior begins escalating to the truly bizarre. He insults a guest at a party in his honor; he jumps from a moving cab because he realizes he doesn't have money with him; he begins visiting Cincinnati's strip joints; his eyes blaze and he chatters nonstop. Most of the faculty think he is just doing what poets do, and wink. But then, in the midst of one of his lectures, he suddenly stops speaking and begins looking about as if he means to attack one of the faculty, until even they finally realize that this is more than a Berryman or Dylan Thomas routine and that he may actually be mad. From then on they station the biggest men on the faculty in the front row as a precaution. For his final lecture, Cal expounds on Hitler and the idea of the Superman. When Lizzie hears this she knows it is time to return to Cincinnati, bringing John Thompson with her. The first thing she does is have Cal committed to Cincinnati's Jewish Hospital on a twenty-four-hour warrant, followed by a special court hearing meant to keep him there.

Meanwhile Blair contacts Giovanna in Nice and tells her not to fly to America just yet, for Cal has just suffered his third manic attack, this one a full-blown episode. By the time Peter Taylor sees him in early May, Cal is being treated with shock therapy: large doses of electricity to the brain. For a while Cal becomes calmer and more lucid, but by mid-June he is suffering once again from acute mania and has to be transferred out of Cincinnati to Payne Whitney in New York, where he is initially diagnosed as suffering from "acute schizophrenia" and given massive doses of chlorpromazine (Thorazine) until he feels as if his blood has turned to liquid lead.

He is placed in Payne Whitney's locked ward for three weeks. On June 26 there is a cable from Giovanna: "I am serene and I am waiting."[53] Then a note from Williams writing to reassure him, having himself suffered a similar break-down the year before. It is good, he tries to comfort his "brother under the skin,"[54] to have "such a place to go when we need it."[55] And Cal, as the fog begins to give way to the solidity of the hospital's white brick wall, asking, *Who am I?*, and the terrible struggle begins yet again to hold off the murk which threatens to engulf him.

By July 20 Cal is well enough to leave the grounds of the hospital for the first time and visit the Metropolitan Museum of Art with Lizzie. Afterwards, he writes Aunt Sarah and Cousin Harriet to reassure them that he has begun to feel himself again, though ahead there lie two years of "pretty uninterrupted therapy" to get to the bottom of his "blow-ups."[56] Life at the hospital, he adds, is "gentle and repetitious and gives one little opportunity for anec-dotes."[57] Nor is he in any hurry to talk about what's happened. Two weeks later he can tell Blair that he has been out of his "excitement" for a month now. Recovery this time has been like "recovering from some physical injury . . . a broken leg or jaundice, yet there's no disclaiming these outbursts—they are part of my character—me at moments." He has already written Giovanna that he plans to go back to Lizzie, and now "the whole business," though "sincere enough," seems like some "stupid pathological mirage, a magical orange grove in a nightmare." He knows he's made a terrible mess of things, and he feels "like a son of a bitch."[58]

He has been rediagnosed by the hospital staff. He is not schizophrenic after all but manic-depressive, and has responded well to a new drug, Thorazine, though the doctors have also told Lizzie they have doubts psychotherapy can work with Cal since he seems to lack the necessary insight into himself.[59] Finally, in late September he is discharged and moves with Lizzie into his mother's house at 33 Commonwealth Avenue in Boston, his "half palazzo and half lot" apartment. As an aid to his weekly sessions in psychotherapy, he begins writing down what he can remember of his early years, a project Merrill Moore had tried to interest him in a year earlier. Now he will try to analyze his past in thousands of polished prose sentences, a form of therapy which will occupy him for most of the next two years.

He is careful to keep as quiet as possible. "After months of walking in this maze," he tells Taylor, "one is a little speechless and surprised to have eyes."[60] He reads, borrows armfuls of records—Berg, Schubert, Gluck—from the Boston Public Library, attends the opera and the symphony, negotiates to procure a hundred-year-old portrait of a Winslow ancestor—an earlier Char-lotte—which he wants as an image to remind him of his young, reconstructed mother. By October, he and Lizzie are settled into the apartment, "the last

picture . . . hung, the last storehouse [having] disgorged its mildewed carton."
Depressed and pliable, he has had to learn to live on a regular schedule, to
function "like an old easy-going clock."[61] It's a "sunny-side of Commonwealth Ave. apartment" he lives in now, he tells Bishop, "three twenty foot
flights up," where he can look out onto "two decaying churches and Boston's
two hugest and most imperial life-insurance buildings." At last he is in a
position, he jokes, where he can "look down on society" from his tower and
watch "at least one parade" pass by each month.[62]

"We've been moving into two places at once," he writes Berryman that fall,
meaning Boston and Duxbury, "and discover that we are such nomads that
everything has to be learned from scratch. You wire a lamp and the disassem-
bled parts are worse than any Chinese puzzle; you paint a floor and find you've
sealed off your clothes for the day." He is also having his troubles with the
Boston police. Because he lost his Massachusetts driver's licence for drunken
driving in 1938 (the incident which cost Jean her face), he is now being
"investigated by a Mr. Hayton from station 16. Mr. Hayton doesn't exist, but
has always just left wherever you call. Each step in the process takes a month."
Lizzie's Iowa novel, *The Simple Truth,* has at last been published, and he has
"started messing around" with his "autobiographical monster," only to learn
that writing prose is hell. He wants to change every second word, but while he
toys with his revisions, "the subject sinks like a dead whale and lies in the mud
of the mind's bottom."[63]

A fall Sunday in Boston: in mid-morning the Lowells strolling down to
King's Chapel "(very white, sparsely attended and Unitarian)," in the afternoon Cal painting the halls black and stopping to puzzle at an old book of his
father's, then preparing for a symposium at Columbia on "The Unity of
Knowledge" three days off, when he will try to convince his audience that
"poetry really is a form of rational thought."[64] Another fall Sunday three weeks
later, when he writes Bishop for the first time in a year. "A lot of water has
gone under the millwheel," he hesitates, "since we were last writing." He's
been sick again, and somehow even with her shrinks "both from mentioning
and not mentioning." These things "come on with a gruesome, vulgar, blasting surge of 'enthusiasm,' " he tells her, until "one becomes a kind of man-
aping balloon in a parade—then you subside and eat bitter coffee-grounds" of
dullness and guilt.[65]

Byzantine negotiations to buy the portrait of his mother's namesake, including a trip to the old Stark mansion in Dunbarton, are finally concluded at
Thanksgiving, by which time Cal has learned that even among the Starks and
Winslows there are those, like Cousin John, from whom he is buying the
picture (actually Cousin Harriet will write the check), who are "real Sno-
peses."[66] He records into the void on a disk machine at Harvard, and in

reading over his old poems finds they now give him the twinges. It is almost as if someone else had written them. Lizzie works with him to keep his depression from grinding both of them down, for in spite of all their efforts to live a tranquil, upper-middle-class existence in Boston, both of them know now that the dark cloud will always be there, just over the horizon. Cal's prose reminiscences she approves of as a way of solidifying his "new, timetabled calm," since prose, unlike poetry, "need not thrive . . . on bouts of enthusiasm."[67]

Day by day, night by night, that winter and spring of 1955 Cal keeps to his regular-as-a-clock routine, taking long walks around the Charles Basin. He works at his desk each day for as many as sixteen hours, until Lizzie must almost take to "feeding him through a tube."[68] He writes a long and perceptive review of A. E. Watts's translation of the *Metamorphoses* for Ransom at the *Kenyon Review,* which sends him back to Ovid until once again he can sense the Roman poet's "great charm and power under the finish." No English poet, he says, has "ever translated hexameters into adequate pentameter couplets," and *"no* one in our century" has "written an interesting long poem in couplets." In that statement he quietly erases ten years of his own work.[69]

In February 1955 Cal had applied for—and got—a teaching slot at Boston University beginning in the fall. He was eager once more to keep his "hand green," his "mind mellow."[70] After a night of drinking, which left him in a "surly hangover mood," he vowed not to drink or smoke during Lent "in an attempt to reduce [his] level of excitement." Instead, he began consuming "a bearlike pound of honey every day" for his nerves and joined the Episcopal Church of the Advent in Boston.[71] The year before, reading at Yale, he'd wondered how Cleanth Brooks, that "lovely and absurd man," could become an Episcopalian. He could understand being "a Catholic or an atheist, or both in different moods, but Church of England in America when you weren't born to it!" Brooks's explanation had been that, living as he did now in New England, it was important to conform.[72]

Lowell, of course, was one of those born to the faith, and now he found himself returning to the middle way rather as a matter of good taste. "I shouldn't say this I suppose," he wrote rather sheepishly to Bishop in May, but "about two months ago after much irresolution I became an Episcopalian again (a high one). I used to think one had to be a Catholic or nothing. I guess I've rather rudely expected life to be a matter of harsh clear alternatives. I don't know what to say of my new faith; on the surface I feel eccentric, antiquarian, a superstitious, sceptical fussy old woman, but down under I feel something that makes sober sense and lets my eyes open."[73]

When Bishop questioned him about this, he tried to explain his position to her ex-Baptist, skeptical ears. "I think most people who are Christians find profession and practice something commonsensical, cow-like, customary," he began, and that was exactly how he wished to take it, since anything more in his fragile mental condition would be an extravagance. "It doesn't seem possible to act," he felt, "except for a few ritual motions, as though we really began to really believe. That God should really be Christ—that does seem strained, and so unlike our usual and soberest ways of seeing things as to be improper." Approaching forty, belief had become for him rather "a way of going to a country by not going, but by staying at home and buying a book of maps. Then you tell other people who also stay at home looking at maps that they are not getting anywhere because they have the wrong directions."[74]

In April he drove down to Newport, Rhode Island, with Lizzie to see the great houses, "all suffering the fate that Henry James said was waiting for them and all other 'disproportioned' things, i.e. to become Baptist retreat houses." Lizzie was learning to drive again, and they practiced together on the road between the Cambridge cemetery and the city dump, he telling Lizzie what to do for an hour, then she telling him "what not to do for an hour."[75] New England spring arrived at last, the magnolia blossoms freezing even as they decayed, and Cal was finally learning how to tell an oak from an ash and had even planted a hardy annual or two. They splurged on a new car, a 1955 Tudor Ford, "shark gray and robin's egg blue," which looked rather like "a tulip with chemicals injected in it."[76]

By mid-1955 their home had become a literary mecca of sorts. "Everyone seems to come here," Lizzie wrote Cousin Harriet. "And so we feel rather more in the literary world than usual." Among their guests: the Sitwells, Spender, Ransom, Lillian Hellman, T. S. Eliot, and magazine writers from "everywhere." Here in Boston, she was learning, "we are somehow expected to do our part and so we are always giving luncheons and cocktails for the visitors and actually enjoying it all." Boston did after all seem capable of being "alive . . . without being pulverizing like New York."[77]

Still, all in all, it did seem strange to Cal to find oneself back in one's native city after so long a hiatus. He'd left at seventeen, he told Pound, abandoning Harvard and his parents for the unknown, "full of passion and without words." He guessed all young men got up "the nerve to start moving by wrapping themselves like mummies from nose to toes in colored cloths, veils, dreams etc." But now, approaching forty, all that was behind him, and it was time to change, though shedding one's old "fancy dress" was rather like being flayed alive. Still, he was at last ready for "the pain and jolt of seeing things as they are."[78]

All that winter, he told Bishop, he'd been "playing at starting my autobiography," so that by May 1955 he had "a hundred pages of drafts," much of it "clumsy inaccurate and magical," though it might eventually work out passably. He even enjoyed being "off the high stilts of meter" for a change and writing in a form where there were no limits "to the prosiness and detail" he could go into.[79] When he wrote Taylor praising him for his autobiographical piece, "1939," a story recalling their early days together at Kenyon, he'd been initially "surprised and hurt" by the story's frankness. But it was important, this sort of new confessional writing, he could see, and he was "trying to do the same sort of thing . . . with scenes from my childhood with my grandfather, old Aunt Sarah, Cousin Belle." Invention and history. It was a splendid and imaginative combination.[80]

His first "grown-up" Boston spring was turning out to be an "idle rather sociable" affair, he told Blair in May. He'd been on several poetry panels, the kind where the audience looked at you as if you were "a special species, like the two-toed sloth." Most of the poets who headed these discussions, he thought, were formidably practical men like Richard Eberhart and Archibald MacLeish, who for some reason seemed driven to insist that poetry was something "sky-high." On these occasions, the Rimbaud in Cal rose instinctively to debunk, for it was only at poetry conferences that he became "a practical man, with several strings to my fiddle." He and Parker had just attended the twentieth reunion of the St. Mark's Class of '35, and he'd been "thinking back on his *break*" with his classmates, "a perhaps arbitrary dilemma, that of either sitting about inertly or of running blind." Nothing of course was "more tantalizing than re-shaping one's silly former self," though the voice of middle age had already warned him several times that most people—himself included—were "warped old dogs set on lying in the sun and changing as little as rocks."[81]

"A house-choosing summer," Cal wrote Bishop that August from Duxbury. "A house here and an apartment in Boston too expensive, too cramped, too cumbersome, too impermanent." And though they now had enough money to live "quite comfortably without earning anything at all," he didn't feel tempted to pursue such a life. So now he'd come home again, bought a house on Marlborough Street (No. 239), a block from where he'd grown up at 170: "gray stone, rather Parisian, four floors, two windows to a floor, white, neat, dainty Italian fire-places, a lovely foyer, a sort of stream-lined Victorian." At least one room—the dining room—of 239 was a "casual, frayed reconstruction" of his parents' house, made possible by the presence now of the senior Lowells' furniture: an English sideboard, a highboy topped with a gold eagle, colonial and Tiffany silver, a plain mahogany table (the one concession to contemporaneity Charlotte had made), and a wall full of eighteenth-century portraits of Lowell and Winslow ancestors. Still, the thought of returning to

Boston made him feel rather "like a flayed man, who stands quivering and shivering in his flesh, while holding out a hand for his old sheet of skin."[82]

In July they'd driven out to the Cape to visit Randall. "Brown, knotted, and with a great black beard with a white splash in the center. He blows hot and cold on one," Cal told Bishop. And both moods were disturbing. "Now he is chilly, and I think of him as a fencer who has defeated and scarred all his opponents so that the sport has come to be almost abandoned, and Randall stands leaning on his foil."[83] The reason for Randall's new coolness was that Cal had shown Lizzie a letter from Randall written during Cal's adventure with Giovanna, in which Randall had made the error of telling Cal how glad he was that he was finally leaving Lizzie. In spite of which, Randall wrote Bishop now, Lizzie had been "very cordial, poor disingenuous thing, and Cal was joylessly being good, good, the properest Bostonian imaginable, saying what a nice man MacLeish is, everybody is."[84] Fortunately, a second visit between the Lowells and the Jarrells three weeks later went more smoothly.

The Lowells spent that August and half of September in the seaport village of Castine, Maine, the first of many summers, as guests of Cousin Harriet. "Down over the Main Street knoll," the poet Philip Booth would recall, "the postoffice; and down below that—at the steep end of Main Street—the village drugstore, Ken's Market, the flagpole, the Town Wharf, and the sea." Cal and Lizzie stayed at the Barn behind Cousin Harriet's place, known as the Brick-yard House. Images: Cal, in blue buttondown and blue jeans, writing in the Barn. Cal playing round-robin doubles of tennis with the summer crowd by the High Road, winning one set against a woman in her sixties, losing against a teenage girl. And even when his strokes flail, he usually scores with his comic and brilliant monologue, one particular set somehow reminding him "of Philip of Macedonia, Jean Stafford, Aristophanes."

Cal's study in the Barn is complete with table, chair, typewriter, and a cot against the windows fronting Oakum Bay. When Philip Booth asks him to look at his poems, Cal suggests he study perhaps "three poets for a month, maybe copying-out poems" to see what he can use to extend his range: "Empson for intellect. Marianne Moore for observation. Frost for how to get a poem organized." Many of his touchstones are prose, but he also offers Arnold, Tennyson, Hardy, Wordsworth. Instinctively Booth knows that he is in the presence of "a master teacher" and that he is "the new boy taken out behind the gym by a Sixth Former," to be told "quietly that one isn't living up to the school's best traditions."[85]

By November, renovations at 239 Marlborough have been completed and the house, Cal tells Cousin Harriet, has become "a picture of repose." Even

Halloween has been restful, with "only good children, very small and escorted by their mothers," allowed to visit.[86] They have a heavyset Scots cook and maid named Anna. They are angry at the moment at Anna, he tells Bishop, because they think everything they have is tremendously grand and Anna doesn't.[87] He and Lizzie have just seen Jean Anouilh's *The Lark,* with Julie Harris as a "rather insufferably Peter Pannish" Joan of Arc. They plan on seeing the French mime, Marcel Marceau, the following week. At Harvard they have heard Arnold Toynbee and Edwin Muir.[88]

He and Lizzie feel "very lordly and pretentious" in their new home, he tells Taylor with deadpan humor, still a bit awkward in his new surroundings. They have even learned to "despise everyone whose nerve for cities has failed, all country people, all suburbanites, and all people who live in apartments." When they have guests, he and Lizzie prime themselves to show off.[89] They have become cultural fixtures around Boston, "very pretentious and sociable, sort of Pooh-bahs," and have taken to memorizing Lionel Trilling in defense of manners.[90] They have also become "fearfully conventional," he tells another friend, and he thinks he will "vote Republican (if my citizenship is restored) in local elections." He even has plans to take a course in the Massachusetts accent.[91]

Their house, in fact, has changed them in every way, so that Lizzie plans to write now for *The New Yorker* to help pay for the new maid, and he has decided that the only reason to go on writing his autobiography is for money. "So I do a page a day, put in all the corn I can think of, then take my page down to Elizabeth and implore her to think of more."[92] He is ready to explode into a frenzy of book buying because he has not been drinking since March, and because there are for once in his life so many empty shelves around him. He has hung pictures of his friends and family on the walls: Elizabeth Bishop holding her cat and driving. A bearded William Empson playing baseball. A bearded James Russell Lowell. Cousin Harriet. His father's pictures of Chinese temples and a Chinese battle. His father. His Grandfather Lowell, dead at twenty-seven. There are spaces allotted for Eliot, Pound, and Williams.

In December, after a silence of eighteen months, he writes Williams to thank him for his letter while he was in the sanatarium. Marlborough Street is "unimpassioned, darkish, bricky, Londonlike," he tells him, the very "mirror of propriety, though lately filling up with rooming houses and cramming schools," where schoolboys stand under his window making noise from nine in the morning until one the next. Most of his time is taken up trying to park his Ford out on the street. Still, it's the first year since 1940 he's "spent two successive autumns in the same city," and he is beginning to think he may never move again. "We might even become Boston worthies," he adds, if it weren't mercifully "for the worm of life in us."[93]

By year's end he has decided to stay on at Boston University and informs Iowa that he will not be returning. He writes Bishop to thank her for providing him with an example of what he wants to do if he ever gets down to poetry again: a "natural, easy tone, as if one were just talking in a full noisy room . . . until everyone is quiet." The antithesis, say, of Mary McCarthy, who is somehow rather "immense without her books ever being exactly good form or good imagination." Historians like himself, he has it on the word of Lord Acton, become so only by writing and not by reading. He knows he's been doing too much of the latter, until now he's been drugged by it, like Aunt Sarah's old friend telling him at a Christmas party that she'd become a television addict from staring into the screen hour after hour after hour.[94] It's time to start writing poems again, he knows. But how? And what?

10

Breakthrough

1956–1957

"**M**y old way of writing"—he meant the poems in *Lord Weary's Castle* and *The Mills of the Kavanaughs*— "wore out for me," Lowell would say in 1958, "and it seemed Sisiphean to continue." Symptomatic of the problem was finding himself "too crisply labeled" by "a writer on metrics in the *Kenyon [Review]*" who'd found that "all younger poets except me required new more flexible laws to be scanned." Now when he read his poems in public, he demanded "more humor, more immediate clarity, fewer symbols, more of the good prose writer's realistic direct glance." He wanted a way too of getting more of his own experience into the poem. His new style, he felt, would give him the extra string he needed for his fiddle.[1]

For too long a seemingly unending war had been going on "between Williams and his disciples and the principals and disciples of another school of poetry," Lowell would write in 1961, even as Williams's common style, his *American* style, was becoming the dominant force in contemporary American poetry. "The Beats are on one side," Lowell noted in an article in the *Hudson Review,* "the university poets on the other. Lately the gunfire has been hot. With such unlikely recruits as Karl Shapiro blasting away, it has become unpleasant to stand in the middle in a position of impartiality." It was an old war for Cal, begun at Kenyon in the mid-1930s under the tutelage of Ransom and Tate, when most English departments were still "clogged with worthy but outworn and backward-looking scholars whose tastes in the moderns were most often superficial, random, and vulgar." One studied the classics then rather "as monsters that were slowly losing their fur and feathers and leaking a little sawdust."

Like most poets, he'd had to learn the craft for himself, by trial and error, and that at a time when no profession had seemed "wispier and less needed than that of the poet." Moreover, in the wake of Eliot's insistence on the central place tradition played in shaping individual talent, it seemed that "almost anything, the Greek and Roman classics, Elizabethan dramatic poetry, seventeenth-century metaphysical verse, old and modern critics"—Aristotle, Horace, Longinus, Coleridge, Eliot, Blackmur, Winters—"could be suppled up and again made necessary." Seen from this vantage, the struggle had been one of reinvigorating the old metrical forms so that they might express the full depths of one's experience.

In all of this, Williams—that great revolutionary, "part of the great breath of our literature," as Lowell would phrase it—seemed for too long merely a byline, and one especially distrusted by Lowell's own mentor, Allen Tate. By the time Lowell arrived at Kenyon, Williams had become for him merely "secondary, minor," an example of what free verse at its poor best could do. But by the mid-1950s the Beats—though Lowell did not quite name them— had begun to change the rules of the game. "It's hard for me to see," he would acknowledge, "how I and the younger poets I was close to could at that time [1937] have learned much from Williams. It was all we could do to keep alive and follow our own heavy program." On the other hand, by 1955 Lowell had paid his debt to Tate and Ransom and Eliot and had become uncomfortably "conscious of the burden and the hardening" of the old New Formalism.

The essential element missing in the poetry championed by Tate, he'd come to see, was a sense of lived experience, that teeming culture Whitman had called for, a poetry that went beyond poetry to incorporate the living river of voices, rich and diverse in its sources, that made up this construct called America. It was just here, Lowell saw, that Williams had become the "model and liberator," though Lowell was still unsure where he himself stood in all this, since he did not care for the work of Williams's imitators and knew that, without Williams's speed and genius, most free verse verged too often on the dull and stillborn. He knew too, even as Eliot, Stevens, Pound, Moore, and Williams were leaving the stage, that a drastically new experimental art was needed. In truth, Williams—who looked so easy to imitate—could no more be replicated than Whitman could, "because neither the man nor the pressure" would ever be found again. Which meant that Lowell was on his own, to make what he could of the poetic revolution in the midst of which he now found himself.[2]

On the evening of January 16, 1956, he sat in the crowded aisle of a "wide-galleried hall" at Wellesley College along with three thousand students and others and listened to the seventy-two-year-old Williams, crippled by stroke after stroke, his right side paralyzed, "his voice just audible, and here and there a word misread. No one stirred." In that silence Williams read his long confessional poem for his wife of over forty years: "Asphodel, that Greeny Flower," the words falling among the young women listening there, a triumph "of simple confession," as the old man delivered, Lowell would remember with pride, "what was impossible, something that was both poetry and beyond poetry."[3]

The morning after the reading Cal wrote his Cousin Harriet. Out his window he could look down on his "hardly passionate" Marlborough Street at "an old-fashioned candy-box day," the "snowflakes as big as fingernails." That morning he had watched as Williams's train disappeared from the Boston station in a blinding flurry of snow. Since Lowell had last seen him nine years before, Williams had "nearly died four times, been psycho-analysed (at the age of 69 and on Merrill Moore's advice), been partially paralyzed," and might die—suddenly—at any time. "All this gnaws at him," Lowell knew, "and since he is a doctor, there is nothing that he can hide from himself. Still he is very gloriously alive, and says he had always had a mother-complex"—a familiar sound to that, no doubt, for Cal—"and no sense at all [of it] before his analysis."[4]

He himself was in the process now of analyzing himself and his background, and had been drawing up a great-rooted family tree, going back as far as he could, until, as he told Cousin Harriet, the roots of the tree had been lost in "the sands of the unknown."[5] He pored over his copy of Ferris Greenslet's *The Lowells and Their Seven Worlds* (1946), trying to trace as well his thin Jewish and Scots strains. He noted too the strain of mental illness in his great-grandfather's mother, Harriet, and her daughter, Rebecca. Had noted once again the mixed history of the Winslows: puritans, frontiersmen, Indian killers, colonial governors, a Revolutionary War general, even a reputed witch found in the tree. His favorite—the one he would have liked to have talked with, was of course Beau Sabreur, his anti-self, mortally wounded, yet strung by duty, ordering himself strapped to his horse, as he turned for the last time to lead his men into the Wilderness.

A white February and "a mild, dismal and colorless March," he tells Cousin Harriet, preparing to head south with Lizzie into the Shenandoah Valley, to Charlottesville, Williamsburg, Washington, Annapolis, Gettysburg. He thinks back to his trip with Robie and Anne Macauley that summer of '51, when he and Lizzie travelled through the Loire Valley, all of them broke, their car so small their suitcases "sagged on the roof and collected dust and rain." This time, more prosperous, they are travelling in a "big, luxurious Ford."[6] After the trip he will feel like a "scrapbook of Americana," having witnessed for himself the imposing public statues at Gettysburg, James Monroe's brass-bound furniture, Jefferson's inventions, all mixed up in his mind and taking "five or six history books and biographies to put them back in their reasonable places."[7] Driving through Maryland on their way back to Boston, he catches Randall's face on the front page of the *Washington Post,* and the announcement of his appointment as Consultant in Poetry. But as the day advances, the idea of a bearded poet seems to grab the attention of the newspaper editors, until by the evening editions Randall's face has grown "like a face on an expanding balloon."[8]

He has begun Lent, he tells Powers, "full of resolves: Dante's *Paradiso,* no sweets, sweet replies to Elizabeth's analysis of my driving."[9] At Easter, he writes Caroline Gordon about her new novel, *The Malefactors.* He feels, he says, a fury against the homosexuals she has portrayed there, yet knows "one's heart is hard and brainless" as long as one holds to such destructive anger. He recalls Dante's kindness toward his homosexuals, Brunetto Latini and Arnaut Daniel, "as though this were a very courtly and gentle vice, a shadow of gentleness." Then he thinks of Proust, boiling *his* homosexuals alive.[10]

By May, he and Lizzie are "in a state of tremendous excitement." He has just learned, he tells Powers, "that like almost all other mortals we are to have a child . . . months ahead, but for certain unless there is some accident. It's terrible discovering that your one moral plank, i.e. an undiluted horror of babies, has crumbled! We're so excited we can hardly speak, and expect a prodigy whose first words will be 'Partisan Review.' "[11] The baby is due in January, he tells Bishop, and already he and Lizzie are exhausted. "We lie about on sofas all day eating cornflakes, no-calory ginger-ale and yogurt. Elizabeth never moves except to turn the page of an English newspaper or buy a dress. I never move except to turn on my high-fi or to go on expeditions for second-hand books."

He is even learning at long last to act like a social being, carrying on what passes for conversation with people as diverse as his barber, his dentist, the head of the English Department at Boston University. Since Lizzie's rough first month, they have become "timid, delicate and ante-bellum."[12] They will stay in Boston all summer on orders of Lizzie's doctor, he tells Taylor, "not that he expects trouble," but because Lizzie is forty now, and "we are too old to try again." His mortality has also been brought home to him again not only by the news of the baby but by a friend's funeral: "a grim business, for one felt that he was like one's self, restless, imperfect, dissatisfied."[13]

For indeed a shadow has been following him during these past two years of solid Boston respectability. And it is this shadow Lowell has been at pains to articulate in a talk on "Art and Evil" which he has just delivered at Bard. In our time, he has told his audience, we have discovered an "ample and redeeming shadow of darkness" midway through "a second solid, sensible, wealthy, optimistic, child-bearing era, one not unlike the times of Queen Victoria and Prince Albert." It is a period in history he feels he too embodies in himself as he moves through these mid-decade Eisenhower years, hogging

> *a whole house on Boston's*
> *"hardly passionate Marlborough Street,"*
> *where even the man*
> *scavenging filth in the back alley trash cans,*
> *has two children, a beach wagon, a helpmate,*
> *and is a "young Republican."*[14]

It seems one of the time's necessary ironies that contemporary literature should be mining "the black earth of our evil authors and evil visions" as a necessary counter to the postwar boom, replete with its high standard of living and its dynasty of Republican presidents. For, he insists, even in the midst of a protracted Cold War and a national desire for things remaining comfortably middle class, "we are all looking for darkness visible, and we know that a realistic awe of evil is a . . . valuable thing for the writer to have." He offers examples: the criminal minds of Rimbaud and Satan; those cold, calculating visionaries, George Eliot's Grandcourt and Aeneas; comic criminals like Dickens's Sarah Gamp and Faulkner's Popeye; grand manipulators like Mephistopheles and Iago. He thinks of T. S. Eliot underwriting *The Waste Land* by calling upon the most violent of the Elizabethan tragedians as well as Baudelaire. Thinks too of America's "madcap experimental writers" of the 1920s: Pound, Williams, Faulkner, Hart Crane.[15]

It is a topic, this question of art and evil, which Lowell will keep circling back to with increasing fascination. Jarrell too, in spite of his Mercedes and his tennis matches and the rest, shares this fascination with him. "I'm sure I like bad men much better than you do," Cal teases him, for "they are God's creatures too, and I don't know what writing would have done without them." Have not the French poets from Baudelaire to Apollinaire really renewed poetry? In fact, except for Hardy and Hopkins, they *are* modern poetry. Rilke and Yeats "and all our own best people (except Frost) have come from them." Darkness "honestly lived through is a place of wonder and life," he is coming to understand, as he catches the visionary "moonstruck eyes' red fire" of predatory skunks refusing to turn their gaze from him.[16]

Except for two "gentle, dawdling weeks" at a friend's house in Duxbury, filled with "tepid moonlight swimming, croquet on a crooked court, corn, a dismal local fair . . . twenty-four hour television for the Democratic convention, clouds of mosquito-tox and a rereading of D. H. Lawrence," the summer of 1956 is spent close to home.[17] In late July there's a conference on the Little Magazine at Harvard, featuring Marianne Moore, one-time editor of *The Dial*, for whom the Lowells hold a tea. A "notable" tea, Moore will describe it to Bishop, adding how much she likes the "heartfelt, generous, genial, initiate and so prepossessing" Lowells and their "Boston-in-its-glory" Marlborough Street residence.[18]

After Labor Day, Lowell goes on a ten-day "highly modern and primitive fishing trip" up to Maine with a friend. The two of them are hydroplaned in to Lake Chamberlain near the village of Moosehead, to discover Thoreau's Maine woods: a world of "moose tracks, beaver dams, salted and drying bullet-punctured bearskins . . . machines for sawing, generating electricity, running sleds, squeezers, mixers, tying flies." And, of course, everywhere: fishermen. For hours, days, they track through forests to "five splendid brookmouths, the only places to fish in the whole endless area," accompanied by their guide, Junior, whose mouth "is usually open," and from which "sounds come we cannot always understand."

As usual, Cal has been reading to soak up the ambience for his trip. This time it's James Russell Lowell's *Moosehead Journal*, with its own "Dickensian and gin-drinking guide," who always brings the conversation "around to two subjects: his new raw-hide boots" and the old, forgotten Maine Aroostock War. He's also reading *Moby-Dick* and Hawthorne's "custom house memories" again and notes how the nineteenth-century Americans seem to wrap themselves "in enormous swathings of humor, whimsy, eloquence."[19] But also Flaubert's *Sentimental Education*, which he reads with a Blue Guide map of nineteenth-century Paris. Paris: so different from his own Boston, he tells Pound, which is really "just a lovely heap, Yankee, Italian, Negro, Irish, with its head, Harvard, cut off by the Charles River." What is Boston, after all, he sums up, but "a culture without being cultured." And what is Harvard but the obverse: something cultured, without being a culture.[20]

He watches Lizzie buy maternity clothes: "stork shop dresses," "slimmish one-piece" things imported by Senator Jack Kennedy's "poor wife for wearing at the Democratic convention." Each day now he and Lizzie notice the "little changes, stirrings, aches."[21] How strange, he tells Williams, to feel "autumn coming on and knowing that almost before the year is out we will have a child." It is "as though one were at last invited indoors after having slept outside on the ground all one's life as a stunt."[22]

He watches the World Series, the turning leaves, and teaches the Victorian poets. When his staunch Republican Aunt Sarah, his mother's sister, visits for a few days, he tries to hide the Adlai Stevenson sticker "rampant on the back window" of the Ford. He reads de Tocqueville, who noted a century ago that after a presidential election the election fever is once more "dispelled, calm returns, and the river, which had nearly broken its banks, sinks to its usual level."[23] He drives up to Dunbarton to hear what the Army Corps of Engineers plans to do about relocating the Winslow burial grounds before the river there floods the area, and images of raking the grounds with his grandfather thirty years before begin again to flood his memory. "I had been so looking forward to driving little Harriet Winslow Lowell or little Robert Traill Spence Lowell Fifth up to Dunbarton and letting her/him play about the graves just as I did," he writes Cousin Harriet. "I think I am more upset than anyone alive."[24]

In October 1956, he flies down to Washington for a Library meeting, once again visiting with Pound, Randall, and Cousin Harriet. When he stops by Randall's office at the Library—his own office nine years before—he finds prints by Degas, Munch, Klee, and Vuillard hanging on the walls. Randall, he notes, does seem to carry "his atmosphere with him" much as the earth itself does.[25] And once again Pound goes on about money and the Jews, so that afterwards Cal writes him that he has no mind for his anti-Semitism, that he is part Jewish himself and Pound must not talk to him any more on the subject.[26] Late that month and into November he watches on television the agony of Hungarian freedom fighters struggling against Russian tanks, NKVD quicklimed in the streets, boys with sten machine guns, Stalin's statue roped and toppled, civilians retreating. It is all, he tells his friend, the poet William Meredith, "a nightmare of guilt" to him. He has a Hungarian-American girl in his class at B.U. that semester who writes him "bad love poems," and whom he has had to order to memorize Marianne Moore instead. It is at least a gesture in the direction of maintaining civilized standards.[27]

"Five minutes old, Little Harriet looked strangely like both her parents and like you," Lowell wrote Cousin Harriet on January 10, 1957, six days after Harriet Winslow Lowell's birth. But then, he added quickly, she looked "more like Dylan Thomas than, say, Audrey Hepburn. Staring with glossy, bulging little eyes, she is withering with contempt some importunate bystander trying to make conversation by asking her if she accepts the universe."[28] How strange, being a parent at forty, when most of Lizzie's co-patients were "mothers 20 years younger and still doing college themes." Already their Irish cleaning lady had taken to comparing Lizzie and him to Mary and Joseph. Besides bottle warmers, bassinets, strollers, they had also hired a baby nurse: the formidable Miss Elsemore.[29]

From the first moment, Miss Elsemore—"carrot-haired, fifty-five, four foot eight, 150 pounds"—had made it clear just *who* would be in charge of little Harriet, letting neither parent "touch or in any way direct" the care of the baby.[30] They were, however, allowed to watch and be "in on every move," Lowell noted with a resigned sigh, including "the great stage of the daily bath" and "drilling for the first photograph." The worst trial by far had been "letting Harriet cry so that she can learn to drink her three hour meals when offered."[31]

The baby was "various," "sedate," and left her parents feeling rather "like infantile, stone-age cretins," he told Powers in February. To Bishop he wrote that it set his teeth on edge to hear Harriet crying upstairs "as rhythmically as breathing," because Miss Elsemore—unlike Lizzie—was a firm believer "in letting a baby cry before eating." Morning, noon, and night the house shook, though through it all it stood while the two women smouldered and warred. But Cal was in fact delirious about the existence of this little girl, as if up to this point in his life he'd been "lacking some prime faculty" like "eyesight, hearing, reason."[32] A rhapsode on the pleasures of domesticity: little Harriet bathing downstairs, bright sunshine and snow outside, he and Lizzie "living on the moon for the last two months"[33] with a being as "simple as primordial matter."[34] How he wished, he wrote Cousin Harriet, all this happiness could have happened ten years before, when he'd been at the Library of Congress. And yet, would he have been ready for a child then, so "narrow, intense, and undomesticated" had he been.[35]

Berryman wrote congratulating Cal and Lizzie on the baby's birth, then noted that Anne, his new young wife, was also about to give birth to their first. "I detect a sleek, seal-like smile," Cal replied on March 1. "But what are years? Will any of us equal the old master"—he meant Eliot—"and marry a generation and a half younger than ourselves? Today I am forty years old, and my baby daughter weighs ten pounds." Berryman had read "91 Revere Street," a section of Cal's autobiography, when it had appeared in *Partisan Review* the fall before, and had been particularly taken by the portrait of Cal's father. But, Cal answered, so many of his relatives had disliked the memoir that he'd been unable to go forward in the writing. Or so he reasoned now. The truth was that by 1957 he'd worked on his memoirs long enough and wanted now to "store up more drive and wisdom."[36]

In fact, he was feeling again the pressure of having done "so few poems in the last five years," especially now that the old ones seemed so far away, he confessed to Bishop, that he had real reservations about reading his poems on a three-week West Coast poetry tour that would begin in March. Still, he added, it would be awful to die without ever seeing the Pacific. Besides, he was only one of a number of "eastern poets"—Jarrell, Eberhart, Wilbur, Marianne Moore—who'd been "shipped west by [the] barrel-load to give readings."[37] He began the tour on the 20th, staying with Roethke in Seattle for four days before working his way down the California coast, "that thin effervescent strip of coast backed by a waste of mountains."[38]

Roethke now had "a lovely young (early thirties) Bennington student wife," Cal wrote Powers afterwards. Her name was Beatrice, and she was "much prettier and more mature and frailler than Ted." During the time Cal had been in Seattle, Beatrice had been "in a strange barbed wire hospital for TB, and Ted was on the town," serving only whiskey to his students and to Cal, so that after four days of it, Cal "was all but dead: eating, reciting poetry, hearing Roethke poetry, losing at bowls, inspecting a fifty thousand dollar modern house with Irish Victorian furniture that Ted, feeling he was Von Hindenberg, wished to buy from the painter Morris Graves." It had all been great fun, including the drinking, but he was vastly relieved to have it over. In September, Cal would get a wild letter from the Beast. "Well," it would read, "it's happened again! Same old routine: 4 or 5 city police (as the boogs say) dragging me off to the same old nut-bin." And: "I want *something* from Harvard quick either a promise or a final commitment about Archie's [Archibald MacLeish] job." And: "You may have got a garbled or semi-garbled letter from me." By then Cal knew he was looking into the furnace at his Doppelgänger, and could feel his own face searing.[39]

Cal caught Lizzie up on things from San Francisco. After his "grand rather too active stay" with Roethke, there'd been a hurried trip up to Vancouver, which he'd found "very calming" but "weak-teaish in tone," especially after Ted. San Francisco, city of Kenneth Rexroth and the Beats, however, had turned out to be a very different world altogether. A "glorious city," really, but with "too many readings . . . too many dull black magic poets," and Mrs. Witt-Diamant, in charge of the poetry circuit there, reminding him of Miss Elsemore—"utterly efficient, tireless, unpoetic, unprudish"—so that being with her was "a little like being in a pressure boiler with the metal top gabbing tirelessly and usefully away."[40] Then it was on to Carmel, then Yvor Winters at Stanford, then Santa Barbara. Before he returned to Boston on April 8, he spent a last drunken evening at Kenyon with the Ransoms and Taylors, writing afterwards to apologize for his behavior.[41]

Three weeks later he was apologizing again. This time to Bishop, who had flown up from Brazil and was staying in New York with her companion, Lota de Soares. By the time he'd gone down to New York to see her in late April, it was clear that he was becoming manic again, and soon he was making amorous advances toward Bishop once more. Back in Boston, repentant, he wrote that he'd acted "too much like myself!", that is, like some horny "centaur fusion" of Bishop's Rooster and Prodigal Son. The truth was, he admitted, that he'd been drinking far too many martinis and been "in a very foolish, exalted and exhausted state," the direct result of his West Coast trip. It would never happen again, he promised, adding that he was now "very tame," and would remain so when he and Lizzie visited Bishop and Lota in New York in a month's time.[42]

The West Coast readings had indeed been fierce, he would remember. Six days a week, sometimes two in a day. The San Francisco he'd found was "the era and setting of Allen Ginsberg and all about, very modest poets were waking up prophets." But he'd found such an explosion of poetry out there that he'd quickly become dissatisfied with how few poems he'd written—and those few finished three or four years earlier—so that now "their style seemed distant, symbol-ridden . . . willfully difficult."[43] When he read before an audience now, he found himself paraphrasing his Latin quotations and adding "extra syllables to a line to make it clearer and more colloquial."

Not that he was a convert to the Beats, for he knew too well "that the best poems are not necessarily poems that read aloud." Still, in the wake of the Beats, his early poems "now seemed like prehistoric monsters dragged down into the bog and death by their ponderous armor,"[44] so that reading his own work aloud during his West Coast tour, he found himself reciting what he no longer felt. No sooner was he back in Boston, then, than he began writing lines in a new style, lines like these from an early draft of "Man and Wife":

> On warm spring nights . . . we can hear the outcry,
> If our windows are open wide,
> I can hear the South End,
> The razor's edge
> Of Boston's negro culture. They as we
> Refine past culture's possibility,
> Fear homicide,
> Grow horny with alcohol, take the pledge. . . .[45]

But nothing cohered, and soon he "left off to forget the whole headache." Instead, he went back to Ford Madox Ford's free verse colloquial poems again, finding in them something of interest, something none of the poets writing in English at the moment seemed to be doing. He also found himself in full agreement with Williams, who'd been "right about our U.S. speech and emotional rhythms being unlike the British."[46] Then, in the Donald Hall and Louis Simpson anthology, he discovered new poems by his former student, W. D. Snodgrass: part of a long sequence called Heart's Needle. Incredibly, Snodgrass was doing better work than anyone except perhaps Philip Larkin in England.

Snodgrass's new work, at once so "amusing and heartbreaking," so modern in its idiom and yet "as measured as Herrick," stunned Lowell with its brilliance.[47]

In May, Lowell hosted Williams when he read at Brandeis. In June, it was Cummings, who read to an audience of eight thousand in the Boston Public Gardens, though it was the fifty-eight-year-old Tate, "gallant as the day is long and with a list of girls' addresses as long as Don Giovanni's," who stole the show by refusing to be civil to Archibald MacLeish, present to introduce Cummings.[48] So there they sat, Cal told Bishop afterwards, "a rather conspicuous and hateful row, [along with] the two Merwins [Bill and Dido], us, Allen [Tate], Moira Sweeney, Bill Alfred—all ages, all degrees of innocence and cynicism."[49] On June 22, at the helm of his Ford, Lowell drove Lizzie, Harriet, and Miss Elsemore the "six hour two hundred mile journey" up to Castine, pulling a U-Haul-It trailer which, "menacing as an armored tank," threatened to whiplash at any moment behind them. "If you don't read about us in the papers," he wrote Taylor on the eve of their departure, "we will have arrived. Inside the car is to be menacing too, I fear. We've just sacked our ferocious, wife-hating old dragon of a nurse. But she refused to be sacked and is forebearingly going with us to see us through the first two weeks."[50]

And yet Miss Elsemore really was an admirable woman, one in a thousand, who did love little Harriet and hadn't minded him so much as she had Lizzie. They were going back to Castine for the summer, this time staying in Cousin Harriet's house. On the trip up, the highways had been so hot they'd "shined and burned like electric irons," so that Cal had finally left the Maine Turnpike and taken the shore route, stopping at Wiscasset to go swimming by some old rotting schooners. Nor had the trip been made any easier by Miss Elsemore, who, "furious at her dismissal" and "loaded with token forebearance from a last minute reading of her *What Jesus Really Thinks,*" kept telling the baby that she was as fickle as the rest of them and would soon forget all about her.[51]

But Miss Elsemore's replacement, a local girl named Carol, aged seventeen, came with difficulties of her own. One was Carlos, her "terrifying" boyfriend, who liked taking Harriet out for spins in his car—or did until the Lowells put a stop to it. Then Harriet became ill—indigestion and fever—her "sad, colorless face, blue eyes . . . hand reaching for stethoscope, my glasses, the tail of an orange cat." It was enough to break a father's heart. She was on the mend now, yet his hair had thinned over this illness and had made of Lizzie "a statue of care in her new red hair and shattering summer ensembles."[52]

"I'm sitting in a little barn my Cousin Harriet made over and painted with aluminum paint a sort of pewter color inside," Cal wrote Williams just after their arrival. "It's on School Street right on the Village Common and looks out over the bay, which on one side looks like a print of Japan and on the other like a lake in Michigan as the rocky islands with pine trees ease off into birches and meadows."[53] The house itself was between two rivers and looked out over a thousand islands. The summer, with tennis, outings, yachting, was all very relaxing, almost "boy scoutish," he told Bishop as July wound down, "first with Fred Dupee and his children and then with the Merwins: picnics in small outboards, sails, a cruise with Eberhart in his cabin cruiser . . . drives to Bar Harbor, Stonington, Camden, cocktails, whisky sours." In light of the amount of alcohol he'd consumed since visiting with Roethke in March, Cal had seen the need to cut back drastically. In mid-July he stopped drinking altogether and didn't think he would try it again for at least another year. The first two days of his self-imposed abstinence had been "very rough and surly-making," he confessed, but now he was "through the roughest water." It was not the first time he'd gone cold turkey. Nor would it be the last.[54]

"I'm continually knocked over by the intensity of [Cal's] intelligence," Philip Booth confided to his journal that summer. "But Cal wants to hear the Maine voice in which I tell stories, or he wants to be taken sailing. To whatever experience I'm native, Cal is deferential, with innate Boston ease." After supper in the Lowells' barn, "that tall summerroom Cal's Cousin Harriet made from the old ell back of her house on the Common," there's an evening listening to Nadia Boulanger on Cousin Harriet's old Magnavox. *If there's another war,* Booth thinks, *this is the kind of civilization I'd want to remember.*[55]

At the beginning of August Bishop and Lota flew into Bangor for a month-long visit with the Lowells. Cal knew he owed Lota a debt of gratitude for having "saved and changed Elizabeth's life, taking care of her in Rio when she was very sick and curing [her] somehow of both drinking and asthma."[56] But Lota's presence no more stopped him from making protestations of love to Bishop than Lizzie's presence did. Whatever his intentions about remaining calm may have been, they were quickly forgotten. When he'd seen her in Boston in June, Bishop had looked "thin and beautiful and healthy," and they'd talked intimately together for hours, so that the old flame had once again been rekindled in him.

Before Bishop had left Boston to return to New York, they would tell each other "almost everything that had ever happened" to either of them. It delighted him that she really did seem to have risen "from the ocean's bottom."[57] But when he confided to her in Castine that he planned to come to Brazil alone the following year, Bishop had no choice but to tell Lizzie what was on Cal's mind. But even that did not put a stop to Cal's advances. So, a week after arriving, Bishop and Lota departed Castine, taking the Bangor plane back to

New York. Two months later, she returned to Brazil with Lota. "I see you to
your plane in Bangor," Lowell would write shortly afterwards:

> *You are thirty pounds lighter,*
> *Your uncertain fingers that float to your lips.*
> *And you kiss them to me, and our fellowship*
> *Resumes its old transcendence like a star.*[58]

A week later he wrote Bishop to apologize for his behavior. "I see clearly
now that for the last few days I have been living in a state of increasing mania,"
he confessed, knowing that by the end of her curtailed visit he'd been nearly
"off the rails" altogether. It was as if he could not be in her presence for "any
length of time without acting with abysmal myopia and lack of consideration.
My disease, alas, gives one (during its seizures) a headless heart." By then he
was on an anti-manic drug, Sparine, which meant he could neither drive nor
see anyone. The drug felt like "the slowing and ache of a medium fever," so
that the "terrible, overriding restlessness of one's system" was halted and the
mind saw life again as it was.[59] Bishop wrote back, telling him to take care of
himself and to continue to "be an ornament to the world (you are already that)
and a comfort to your friends." There were things, she urged him, that could
help. Among them were "sobriety & gaiety & patience & toughness."[60]

Relieved that she'd forgiven him, he sent her a long letter about his trip with
Eberhart and Booth to Sommes Sound, sailing up to Stonington, under Deer
Isle Bridge, past Eggommoggin and Blue Hill and Mount Desert, "a great
brown mountain" looming ahead like "Atlantis in Dante's Ulysses canto." At
night he could look out over the great lawns, the birch and elm groves along
Sommes Sound, until he'd felt he was "seeing the great Roman villas described
by Horace and Juvenal as examples of the glorious *sic transit gloria mundi.*"
But most of that day and the next he and the others on the yacht had steadily
drunk, Lizzie finishing, he said, a water tumbler of martinis by herself, after
which she had "sprawled on the fore-cabin and just out of hearing began sotto
voce an amazingly frank and detailed reappraisal of our entire marriage" that
had gone on for ninety minutes.

But there was something he had to tell Bishop if she was ever to understand
why he'd acted as he had. He reminded her of that day at Stonington nine
years before, after Carley had gone and the "infected hollowness" of the whole
business had begun to drain from his heart. It was then that Bishop had said to
him, "When you write my epitaph, you must say I was the loneliest person
who ever lived." At that moment, he realized, a new level of intimacy between
them had been reached, and it was just a matter of time before he proposed to
her and she would accept. "Really," he admitted, "for so callous (I fear) a

man, I was fearfully shy and scared of spoiling things and distrustful of being steady enough to be the least good." But he had wanted his proposal to have "the right build-up," and Stonington with Carley present had not been the place. In November, he'd been with her again at the Bard conference, but by then Lizzie too was on the scene.

Still, he'd meant to propose to Bishop that winter in Key West. But then had come the Yaddo explosion and Lizzie's care, and the best he could hope for from Bishop after that was a "disinterested friendship." Life allowed very few chances, if any, he saw now. He'd never really thought there was any choice about writing poetry. "But asking you [to marry me] "is *the* might have been for me, the one towering change, the other life that might have been." For the past nine years he'd kept that other life buried, but that spring, even before her arrival in New York, all the old unfinished business had finally "boiled to the surface." It would not happen again, he promised, though he would always feel "a great blytheness and easiness" with her. He really did love Lizzie as much as Bishop loved Lota, and he was sure now that it was "the will of the heavens that all is as it is." Then too there was the baby to make a safe haven for.[61]

It was in this new isolation, alone, confused, angry, repentant, that he found himself writing poetry again. In the fourteen weeks between mid-August and late November Lowell would write or heavily revise eleven poems in free verse, a number of them work he'd written years before in couplets. Out of this period would come final versions of "Beyond the Alps," "Words for Hart Crane," "Inauguration Day: January 1953" and "To Delmore Schwartz," the last begun in 1946. The new poems would be "Skunk Hour," "Man and Wife," "Memories of West Street and Lepke," "To Speak of Woe That Is in Marriage," "My Last Afternoon with Uncle Devereux Winslow," "Commander Lowell," and "Terminal Days at Beverly Farms." These last would form the core of *Life Studies*.

First came "Waiting for Skunktime," a title shortly replaced by the shorter, darker "Skunk Hour," a poem he experienced almost as a crucifixion. It would be written backwards, as Lowell himself phrased it, beginning with the dark night of the soul, and closing with the writing of the first four stanzas. He read Bishop's poems carefully now, "imitating the loose formality of her style" (breaking through at last, he told her in December, to where she'd always been by finally getting rid of his "medieval armor's undermining").[62] He used a six-line triple-rhymed stanza, the lines contracting and expanding as needed, as he felt his way toward the opening stanzas. "Cotton-nosed," he called them: a hook, a way of drawing the reader into the poem's landscape before driving into the heart of the matter.[63]

"Skunk Hour" is the quintessential poem of negative transcendence, a palinode to the poems of dark light in *Lord Weary's Castle,* the earlier image of the kingfisher breaking in flames giving way now to the "moonstruck eyes' red fire" of the skunks who have come to dominate Lowell's world. "One dark night," the heart of the vision begins, and Lowell at once establishes the reference point with St. John of the Cross's "una noche oscura." But it is a contemporary version of the Spanish Catholic mystic's vision of light streaming through in the midst of darkness. For this is Lowell's radically Calvinist vision reinstating itself in place of his earlier Catholic vision. It is no accident that he should be alone in his Tudor Ford, with all its complex associations with the English Protestant ascendancy under Henry VIII merging here with American capitalism and the machine romanticism envisioned by that son of American Protestantism, Henry Ford, "Tudor" reduced now to some tired advertiser's play on "two-door."

The poet climbs "the hill's skull" to spy out lovers as Whitman had before him, the voyeur leaving home to search desperately for the love he equates with sexual contact. In this infernal pastoral he hears only "A car radio" bleating on about "careless Love," in a place where cars seem to lie together in the darkness like boats in the harbor below, "hull to hull." The scene is as death-like and as surrealistic as Williams's wartime scene in "The Semblables," where cars parked across from the munitions factory seem to wait patiently outside the Catholic Church for their absent drivers who have gone to attend Sunday Mass.

Lowell's speaker seems to suffocate, his very body become the enemy his spirit cannot hope to escape from, his eye watching as his own hand seems to choke him, until, like Milton's Satan, he is out with it:

> *I hear*
> *my ill-spirit sob in each blood cell,*
> *as if my hand were at its throat. . . .*
> *I myself am hell;*
> *nobody's here. . . .*

Nobody, that is, except for his kin the skunks, hungry for garbage to eat. The image is appetitive, sexual, the poet on the prowl for something to fill his emptiness. As for the soul: that has been trampled underfoot, the word—like the word "Tudor"—drained of its deeper significance to become merely something on which to walk on up Main Street, the Romantic's "moonstruck eyes' red fire" replacing "the chalk-dry and spar spire / of the Trinitarian Church," which Lowell here likewise renounces, just as he had his Catholicism in "Crossing the Alps."

The transcendence he had sought in his earlier ascent to Rome or in the

Romantic ascent up the Alps is replaced now with the far more humble image of his own back porch, where he stands only at the "top / of our back steps," breathing in the rich sexual air of "a mother skunk with her column of kittens." And now he watches as the mother "jabs her wedge-head in a cup / of sour cream," and settles in to enjoy herself. The image is phallic, though it is the female who jabs and thrusts and "will not scare," and one wonders if Lowell's confusion of sexual roles hasn't something to do with his ambivalence toward Bishop: a simultaneous repulsion and powerful erotic attraction for what is at once forbidden and unattainable both because of his own marriage and even more so because of Bishop's own lesbianism.

Seen in this light, the first half of the poem is a wry, exhausted commentary on the breakdown of the poet's world. It is a world where nothing chimes with anything else, where everyone seems boxed in by his or her own isolation, from the old "hermit heiress" on Nautilus Island living in an inverted pastoral world through the harsh Maine winter "above the sea," and whose son is a "bishop" (the pun on Bishop's name immediately disturbing the valence of the poem), to the "fairy decorator" who has appropriated the lives of the local fishermen to make of them a work of art. It is also summer shelving into fall, he sees: the promise of a world with Bishop first sensed at Stonington shattered at last here at Castine. For now everything is sick, stained with the "red fox stain" of decay. He knows too that something in himself—call it the primal life force, call it perversity—will never let him recover the stabilities of the Victorian century of his parents which for a while he and Lizzie had tried desperately to enter for themselves.

When he'd written Bishop in August about sailing off the coast of Castine, he'd mentioned Eberhart's "old school-teacherish and skipperish" way of constantly correcting him about the way he had piloted Eberhart's *The Reve*. The yacht, he'd told her then, was "something from that last gasp of Victorian design when the old massive designs still held but when the quality of the old massive materials was fast falling."[64] In this description of Eberhart's craft rests the Old World view, and Lowell's need to replace that craft with a more direct kind of utterance which the latter half of "Skunk Hour" represents in its rhythms and oblique symbolic structures.

In October he would write Cousin Harriet about a visit he'd made with Lizzie and Bishop that June to see Bishop's Salem cousin and her Worcester aunt, the latter two "bubbling with bad taste, outrageous flattery and appeals to [Bishop] for money." They'd wanted her "to write like Ann[e] Lin[d]berg," he noted, understanding that most of the Lowells wanted the same thing from him: to be "like [Lindberg] too with a big house and simple desires."[65] But something in his blood had told him that the world of his parents, a world from which he had so violently rebelled in his search for God, and to which, after their deaths, he had tried for a while to return, arming himself with a wife and child and a new Boston respectability, could never hold him.

"Skunk Hour," then, is Lowell's "Dover Beach." In it we hear the slow withdrawal of all those stabilizing forces which seemed for a time to uphold him: the Sea of Faith, the world of Boston with its classical music, its operas, its museums, its dinner parties, its literati, its universities, his marriage, even his infant daughter. For the only thing which seemed any longer able to hold him was the sexual odor not of boxwood, as with Williams, but of skunk.[66] It is, then, the primal appetite to find what release the last puritan can in the machinelike jabbing of a "wedge-head in a cup," that cup echoing all the way back to the image that closed "Crossing the Alps": the image of "killer kings on an Etruscan cup," itself an image of instinctual survival even when the language on the cup, as on an urn, ceases any longer to communicate with those empty ciphers, words.

By early September 1957, Cal was back in Boston, "furiously writing at poems." He'd spent "whole blue and golden Maine days" in his bedroom "with a ghastly utility bedside lamp on," his pajamas "turning oily with sweat," and now had six poems well under way. They still "beat the big drum too much," he told Bishop now, but there was "one in a small voice that's fairly charmingly written I hope."[67] He was speaking of "Skunk Hour" and of its indebtedness to her more timid nightstalker in "The Armadillo."

And to Williams three weeks later: "I've been writing poems like a house a fire . . . five in six weeks, fifty versions of each," experimenting "with mixing loose and free meters with strict in order to get . . . accuracy, naturalness, and multiplicity of the prose."[68] Anything could be put "into this kind of poem," he would tell another correspondent, one's thought needing only to be "the most forceful words and word-order." Yet at the same time he also wanted "the surge of the old verse, the carpentry of definite meter that tells me when to stop rambling!"[69] No ideal form could do for any two poets, he knew, and while he understood Williams's attack on metrical form, meter too, "if decently used," had its place. Now that he was finally "growing young" in his forties, he felt more technically indebted to Williams than ever before.[70]

Then, at the beginning of October, he went "rummaging through a carton of old poems, envelopes, pictures etc.," and discovered some of his old poems from *Lord Weary's Castle,* "all marked up, stabbed, puffed, and dissected" by Jarrell. Now he wrote Jarrell to thank him for the "wit and patience and . . . generosity and justice" he had given his poems ten years before. Those times had come back for him all over again, and now he wanted to try out the new poems on him, having in the past two months loosened "up the meter . . . and hosing out all the old theology and symbolism and *verbal* violence." He would send Randall "Skunk Hour" and then, if he got "a peep" out of him, "four or five more."[71]

How wonderful, Jarrell wrote back, to have Cal writing poems again. He asked to see the others. Cal wrote back at once with a new poet for Randall: W. D. Snodgrass, whose poems in *Heart's Needle* he'd been marvelling over. "I'm sure you remember him with his silly name and his Mahler songs," Lowell wrote now. "I had him off and on in classes at Iowa for years and thought that he had done one or two of the best poems that my students had written there." But in his new poems Snodgrass had gone far beyond that; he was in fact another Laforgue, incomparably the best poet since Randall himself had begun writing, and the equal of Larkin.[72] ("I don't think I've gone off the deep end about him," he wrote Bishop ten days later, when he sent her some of Snodgrass's poems, though he had to admit he was already beginning to feel "a little shivery being all alone so far in discovering him.")[73] Meanwhile he was working "like a skunk, doggedly and happily," writing poems in "a sort of free verse"[74] that took off from his "Ford [Madox Ford]" poem, and—indeed— from Ford himself. He was sending them to Randall ("with fear and trepidation," he told Bishop) and would be very sad if the man who had critiqued *Lord Weary's Castle* so brilliantly did not like them.

Then he wrote Snodgrass himself to congratulate him on perfecting "a style that would be hard to better." What he liked about the poems in *Heart's Needle* especially were their "bits of autobiography, the clear measures," his "Herrick-like moderation and freshness" in a style which seemed "completely underivative" and which might "stand up in comparison" with any other American of his generation.[75] In November, he sent Pound a sheaf of his new poems, adding that he felt so "much bolder about meter" that he was no longer taking "count of the scansion" in the new work. After "twenty years of writing in harness," he did not think it "suicidal to cut loose a bit." On the other hand, compared to what Pound had achieved in the *Cantos,* his poems were still "small and self-centered" and needed "a certain tightness" if they were to come off.[76]

Three weeks later he sent Williams the new poems. "At forty," he told him, he'd written his "first unmeasured verse." For the new, deliberately prosy lines to work, he understood, they needed a "tremendous fire" under them, which he'd tried to supply in at least a few of the more personal poems. It felt great to have "no hurdle of rhyme and scansion between yourself and what you want to say most forcibly," he explained, for even the best poets had "much more trouble" than they liked to admit "getting our rhymed and metrical verse to even make clear sense." This was clear from his revaluation of Tate, and Tate, he added, was "surely one of the most passionate and practiced poets alive."⁷⁷ In this manner he was exorcising the figure he had had to leave behind if he were to write his new poems.

By the time he wrote Williams, he'd mailed copies of his poems to Bishop, Jarrell, Rahv, Pound, and Tate. Pound's response was so ambivalent that Lowell couldn't be sure if it was "enthusiastic flattery . . . or fierce abuse." Rahv, on the other hand, unequivocally liked them, calling them "the one real advance since Eliot," and immediately took four of them for the *Partisan Review*.⁷⁸ But Tate, sensing the break with his own poetic practice, was deeply disturbed by what he read and told Cal so in no uncertain terms. The new lines were arbitrary and rhythmless, Tate insisted, and merely "composed of unassimilated details, terribly intimate and coldly noted." "Skunk Hour" and "Inauguration Day" might do, but *all* the family poems were "definitely *bad"* and should not be published. In his best poems in *Lord Weary's Castle,* Cal had managed "a formal ordering of highly intractable materials," bound together into a unity by an underlying symbolic order. But these poems, because they lacked just such an order, at once dissolved into a chaos of "details presented in *causerie* and at random," without interest to any, perhaps, but the poet and a few friends.⁷⁹ In fact, Tate told others he was afraid the new poems showed symptoms of incipient mania in Lowell. His deepest fear, of course (though he did not say so), was that he had finally lost control over his former disciple.

Williams, though increasingly crippled by several new strokes, nevertheless responded at once to the new poems with three cheers, realizing that Cal had at last come over to his camp. As soon as the poems had arrived, Floss had sat down with him and read through the manuscript "in one sweep." It had been an "absorbing experience" and one he would not soon forget, for with these poems Cal had "tremendously" advanced himself "as an artist and a man in the world." He felt proud to have been taken into his friend's confidence, for Cal's new "occupation with unrhymed measures" would vastly broaden his "potentialities." For ten years now he had watched Cal, knowing he'd needed just this breaking free from the self-limiting restrictions of too close a dependence on formal verse. Suddenly Cal had become "one of the two or three major poets" of his generation whom Williams counted on to keep him "abreast of the times."⁸⁰

Bishop's response came just before Christmas. She'd found the entire family group of poems "superb," a "wonderful and impressive drama" in the new rhythm Cal had been searching for. She was, she confessed, "green with envy" at the new assurance found in these poems. After all, she too might have written in as much detail about her own Uncle Artie, say, but would it have mattered? Uncle Artie had become "a drunkard, fought with his wife, and spent most of his time fishing . . . and was ignorant as sin. It is sad; slightly more interesting than having an uncle practising law in Schenectady maybe, but that's about all." But all Cal had to do in his family poems was "put down the names. And the fact that it seems significant, illustrative, American, etc. gives you, I think, the confidence you display about tackling any idea or theme, *seriously,* in both writing and conversation." In some ways he was "the luckiest poet" she knew, though she also knew that in other ways—given his mental illness—he was not.[81]

On December 4, Cal flew down to Washington with Lizzie to read "Skunk Hour" as part of the Phi Beta Kappa convocation at William & Mary, and then visit with Randall—"sick with the flu"—and Pound—"who is not sick, just nutty as always"—and Cousin Harriet.[82] A week earlier Lizzie had written Cousin Harriet to assure her Cal was doing fine. "The happiest, healthiest couple are always writing the most brooding, neurasthenic works," Lizzie had explained to reassure her that Cal was *not* carrying the darkness of his poems over into his life.[83] But during the five days he was on the road, Cal began speeding up again, so that by the time he'd returned home, he'd decided to invite all of literary Boston to a party, without first informing Lizzie.

McGeorge Bundy was there, and I. A. Richards, and Frost, along with Edmund Wilson, Adrienne Rich, Arthur Schlesinger, Jr., Bill and Dido Merwin, and Gertrude Buckman in the kitchen. Bill Alfred, who taught Anglo-Saxon literature at Harvard and had become one of Cal's closest friends, was put in charge of mixing drinks. Cal meanwhile kept himself busy setting his guests at one another's throats, or clearing the coffee table of its glasses with a sweep of his foot. The extraordinary thing about it all, Dido Merwin would recall, "was that nobody seemed to realize that he was mad."[84]

Finally, after three sleepless days and nights, while she hoped Cal's mania would burn itself out, Lizzie called the police. At first, Cal refused to go, then said he would if he could be admitted to McLean's. A friend agreed to accompany him, and the two met at the police station. Afraid of shock treatments, afraid of being locked up again, afraid of what was happening to him, Cal appeared to be resisting arrest in the station and was once again treated roughly by the police, who even refused him water, until his friend demanded they stop treating him like some ape. Then he drove Cal out to McLean's, where Cal was admitted, isolated, and stripped to his underwear to keep him from hurting himself.

11

Life Studies

1958–1960

During his month-long stay at McLean's Cal met a young psychiatric fieldworker fresh out of Bennington named Ann Adden, and soon the pattern of infatuation with an attractive young woman who would help him start over began again. As he had with Anne Dick twenty years earlier, he started in on Ann Adden's education, prescribing Dante, Kant, and *Mein Kampf* for her to read.[1] He was so convincing and so adamant in his demands that soon Ann was even helping him play truant. At one point he could be found wandering around Boston Common, at another in his lawyer's office hammering out a divorce settlement.

"He was energized and concentrated and obsessive," his B.U. student, Donald Junkins, would remember when he visited Cal's locked cell at McLean's in mid-December 1957. "What do you think about God?" Lowell had asked him, as they looked out on the golf-linklike fairways. God did seem to be in the constitutionality of things, Junkins had offered. Did Junkins mean everything the way it was?

Cal picks up a drawing from his bed, a likeness done by someone who has been there just before. It is an intense, true image, revealing Cal's mental vigor and strained, eyeballing passion. Freud has freed the world, Cal insists, and he wants a divorce. In his typewriter is a draft of "Waking in the Blue," dedicated to Ann Adden.[2] Ann has been to see him and Cal has responded in verse which—like all references to her—will not survive into the published poem:

Ann, what use is my ability
for shooting the bull
far from your Valkyrie body,
your gold brown hair—
your robust uprightness—you, brisk
yet discreet in your conversation.[3]

After his release from the hospital in mid-January 1958, he rented a room at a motel on Harvard Square while he continued to meet his classes at Boston University. But he still continued to see Ann, at the same time begging Lizzie not to give up their home together. "These damned girls complicate everything," an exhausted Hardwick wrote Cousin Harriet on January 2. "They keep me from acting in his best interests often because I don't want to seem pushing or jealous."[4] On the 20th, Cal moved back to Marlborough Street. "The details are always like a Russian novel," Lizzie wrote Bishop that morning, "because of the immense *activity* of these states, the fact that things are happening, wildly, even from the hospital." Cal was still far from well and she did not know how she was going to cope with his being home. But he'd begged to be allowed to return to his study and routine, and Lizzie had relented, hoping he was ready now to settle down again. He was still taking sedatives and seeing a Dr. Rochlin, "the $30 hr man, a first-rate psychoanalyst on the staff at Boston City Hospital," who refused to believe Cal was psychotic. Meanwhile there was also little Harriet to think of, toddling about now, "very Lowell-like, very independent, strong, self-willed."[5]

But no sooner was Cal back home than Lizzie knew she'd made a mistake. "He is very, very far from well," she wrote Cousin Harriet. "On the telephone he sounds all right, calm and considerate, but in person the excitement, the unreal plans and demands, the unpredictability have hardly altered." Superficially, there'd been an alteration in his behavior because of his medication, but "the deep underlying unreality" was still there: his discounting of anyone else's feelings, his "wild projects." She had not *"taken him back*—awful phrase," but she could not refuse him refuge. He'd assured her he would not see Ann again, refusing to call her or answer her calls, so that even Ann had become "a basket case." In the meantime, he was telling Lizzie he'd found someone else altogether, who would make everything "so much better" between Lizzie and himself. This last revelation had not so much shaken as numbed Hardwick, especially as it showed how deep Cal's derangement went.[6]

During the week he was home Cal seemed for a while to be getting better. He wrote Williams that it had taken him "twenty writing years just to begin to understand" Williams's "refinements of metrical and idiomatic technique." He had no master, he noted, "only masters," and Williams was "about the first among them." At B.U. he'd been teaching the opening pages of *The House of the Seven Gables* and had found "enough economic history" there "to set the Commonwealth of Massachusetts (and Ezra too!) back on its toes again." "Anyone who could digest this much," he'd told his class, "wouldn't elect simpletons like Senator Saltonstall or the bone-headed Irish blow-hards that we seem content with." Why, he wondered, was New England, "once the flower and really Attica of American culture, now a museum useful mainly for drawing talent to it from other sections of the country?"[7]

But he was speeding up again, wondering aloud to Pound if he thought "a man who has been off his rocker as often as I have been could run for elective office and win?" He was thinking of running on the democratic ticket for state senator for his Back Bay district against some "inconspicuous Republican." What vistas would open before him as he "sat in the Boston State Capitol on my little $5,000 a year job that would cost me about $10,000."[8] By then, as Lizzie told Cousin Harriet, Cal was as "active as electricity," and had to be readmitted to McLean's for what Cal insisted now on calling a "voluntary stay."[9]

"This business at McLean's isn't exactly very serious," he wrote his cousin, Isabella Gardner. After all, he'd been having "periodic manic upsets" for the past nine years, and he was here now "voluntarily" to see if he couldn't get rid of them for good. He had a private room, a typewriter, an FM radio, "a door that will shut and frequent visitors." He read Kant and *Ulysses,* and finished a poem that I. A. Richards had admired. And while he wasn't teaching at the moment, several of his B.U. students had come out to see him with their poems. He still wanted a divorce, noting that both he and Lizzie were "very much of one mind in this decision, and feel harmonious about it." True, his marriage had in many ways been "gloriously successful," but there was the constant "jangling of nerves" which had nearly killed them both. Now, at least, he and Lizzie were at peace.[10]

But for Lizzie there was anything but peace. Exhausted with it all, she went down to New York to stay with the Clarks for a few days. Then, on the 14th, she visited Cal at McLean's, only to leave feeling as if someone had beaten her. He kept insisting that he had to get "to Reno immediately, marry someone or other, and *then* . . . take treatment." It was a "life or death matter" for him, the "only bearable plan for 'curing himself.' " She could see how frightened he was: calm and controlled on the surface, still unable to admit he was having another attack. And then the doctors, telling her that Cal's attachment to her was one of the few they could find in his life history, and that a divorce now would be a disaster.[11]

"For the future, the unimaginable, frightening future which seems awful no matter what happens about the present," she wrote Cousin Harriet, the doctors still thought Cal, in spite of his being under "the complete domination of childhood fantasies," could be cured, "but that it would be hard, take years of serious working out with a doctor of his profound problems and fears." It was "all very well to talk about cures, coping with problems, working it out, and so on," Lizzie had told them, but did they really believe it? Could they cure someone when he was middle-aged and had had as many breakdowns as her husband had? Yes, they assured her. In fact, in the past few years they'd begun "to get permanent cures" and Cal was surely not as bad as many others they'd treated.[12]

By early March he was spending weekends at home. "I am feeling much better and so at last is Bobby," Lizzie wrote Cousin Harriet. For his forty-first birthday they'd seen a movie, bathed the baby together, and dined by the fire listening to *The Marriage of Figaro* before he'd had to go back to the hospital. He was already "pretty much himself once more" and eager once again to return home.[13] "Elizabeth and I are happily back together," he wrote Bishop two weeks later. "All the late froth and delirium have blown away. One is left strangely dumb, and talking about the past is like a cat's trying to explain climbing down a ladder."

He was staying during the week now at Bowditch House, a place no man had apparently "entered since perhaps 1860," but which had just been made co-ed, so that he felt rather as if he were "entering some ancient deceased sultan's seraglio."[14] He and the other inmates had been treated, he told Taylor, "to a maze of tender fussy attentions suitable for very old ladies," such as chocolate-scented milk. His fellows there were all "ex-paranoid boys," including a Harvard Law professor in the room next door who kept shouting, "Decades, Oh Decades," or "Horror, Horror!", and—on the other side of him—several old men in their senility who wandered about "balmy and morose" dripping crumbs in front of the TV screen, "idly pushing the buttons, while the [attendants] would ask them jeeringly when they were born, or exclaim, 'I feel more and more like the custodian of a morgue.' " Besides, how *was* one to feel "after having been Henry VIII or even a cock of the walk weekly sheriff?"[15]

"After a hearty New England breakfast," he would write in "Waking in the Blue," seeing in both the Harvard Law professor and the senile " 'Bobbie,' / Porcellian '29 . . . / roly-poly as a sperm whale," strutting about the hospital "in his birthday suit," terrifying, bizarre images of what lay ahead for himself:

> *the shaky future grow[n] familiar*
> *in the pinched, indigenous faces*
> *of these thoroughbred mental cases,*
> *twice my age and half my weight.*

We are all old-timers,
each of us holds a locked razor.[16]

How good to be back home, he reassured Cousin Harriet, with Lizzie
napping and snow falling, and the street below empty "except for a bareheaded
man waiting on a toy city-snow-colored poodle." At least this time, he hoped,
he really did think therapy could help him. Good times lay ahead, he ended,
"and little Harriet will never see the shadow that has darkened us and gone."[17]
Lizzie had been terrific through it all, he told Taylor, and they were a family
once again, taking long strolls around the Public Garden on Sunday afternoons.[18] And to Roethke, who had been in mental states much like his, he
spoke of how one minute things would be "going swimmingly," and the next
of finding oneself in the hospital, being shot up with huge doses of Thorazine,
making "windy utterances," and creating "domestic chaos."[19] Ten weeks later
he sent off a second note to say that he was now much improved, but that
"getting out of the flats after a manic leap" was rather like those old crew races
at St. Mark's where, "when the course is half-finished, you know and so does
everybody else in the boat, that not another stroke can be taken," in spite of
which everyone went on pulling, while those on the wharf watching the race
saw nothing of the terrible struggle within.[20]

Among the casualties lost in the violent wake of Cal's latest episode was, of
course, Ann Adden. Not even her name survived the two poems Cal wrote at
the time, "Waking in the Blue" and "Home After Three Months Away." Nor
did it survive the sonnet he addressed to her ten years later in *Near the Ocean*,
which he titled "1958." Only in the revised version of *Notebook 1967–68*
would her name finally be allowed to surface. "Remember standing with me in
the dark, / Ann Adden?", he would write then, still filled with regret, confusion, and the vestiges of an old longing, as deep as the pilgrim's longing for
some ideal Jerusalem:

> *In the wild house? Everything—*
> *I mad, you mad for me? . . . Remember our playing*
> *Marian Anderson in Mozart's Shepherd King,*
> *Il Re Pastore there? O Hammerheaded Shark,*
> *the Rainbow Salmon of the World, your hand*
> *a rose—not there, a week earlier! We stand. . . .*
> *We ski-walked the eggshell at the Mittersill,*
> *Pascal's infinite, perfect, fearful sphere—*
> *the border nowhere, your center everywhere. . . .*
> *And if I forget you, Ann, may my right hand. . . .*

At the B.U. graduation that June he watched as the pianist and teacher Nadia Boulanger, a favorite of both his and Cousin Harriet, received an honorary degree, and listened to a "good dramatic harangue by Raymond Aron on President De Gaulle of France," followed by a "granity, steam-rollerish spiel by Secretary of Defense McElroy."[21] He spent a morning with Pound (released finally from St. Elizabeth's after twelve years confinement) and his wife Dorothy, driving them out to Quincy to see the John Adams House, "very grave and cool," Cal noted, after "the pealing traffic-wrung environs of Boston."[22] At month's end, he drove up to Castine with Lizzie in their "new, shining, gun-metal-gray and meekly utilitarian ranch wagon,"[23] Cal driving back to Boston a week later in Cousin Harriet's old Buick to begin his twice-a-week sessions with his therapist and to teach summer school in the "green, summery, slow world" of Harvard. "Time was when we used to drum up trade for poetry courses," he quipped. "Now one wishes for a dam." Even Eisenhower, he suspected, must have "a drawer of unintelligible imitations of Dylan Thomas." He had twenty-five students, the only problem being that there weren't twenty-five poets in the entire country.[24] By midsummer, he told Bishop, even his new poems were beginning to feel like "old lumber" which "somehow . . . won't light." Still, he had enough now for a book, and felt "half-happy to let it rest in a drawer until the next awakening." He still liked the language of the new poems, though he felt "fatigued by their fierceness," that "old serpent in the perfect garden," and rather wished his poetry could be described as "stubborn, hopeful, summery, utilitarian."[25]

That fall he read James Agee's *A Death in the Family,* Conrad's *Lord Jim,* and Boris Pasternak's *Dr. Zhivago,* its final pages reeling through his mind, so that for a while "the stone facades of the new Russia" had seemed to blow away "like gauze."[26] In spite of the bad translation, he told Bishop, *Dr. Zhivago* dwarfed "all other postwar novels except Mann." But the deeper truth was that in the figure of Dr. Zhivago he saw a shadow portrait of himself, so that he felt once again "shaken and haunted" by thoughts of his own mortality.[27] How sad to die in one's late fifties as Pasternak had, when one would rather be able to say, as Eliot could, that one felt as foolish at seventy as one did at seventeen.[28] He even rearranged one of his B.U. workshops in order to spend more time reading the Russian novelists. The result, he confided to Taylor, was that halfway through the course he was "at sea, trying to teach Tolstoy and Dostoifski [sic] to people who've read nothing."[29]

In September he wrote Roethke, congratulating him on his new poems, the "big style with all its roll, grandeur, order, licence and sudden jabs of observation" swooping down "so easily on your moments of darkness." By then Cal had finished his own book of poems, and for the moment was finding himself confronted with an overwhelming sense of "stylistic and logical helplessness, days of staring at ugly fragments." Still, out of the "armfuls of waste paper" he'd left behind—"exercises, confessions, confusion"—he thought he'd finally "discovered a way of getting something new and felt said."[30]

One of several special students Lowell admitted into his workshop that fall was Anne Sexton. "The class met . . . on Tuesdays from two to four in a dismal room the shape of a shoe box," Sexton would recall. "It was a bleak spot, as if it had been forgotten for years, like the spinning room in Sleeping Beauty's castle. We were not allowed to smoke, but everyone smoked anyhow, using their shoes as ashtrays." There were "twenty students—seventeen graduates, two other housewives (who were graduate somethings) and a boy who snuck over from M.I.T." Lowell was formal "in a rather awkward New England sense," his voice "soft and slow," as he went "through each line of a student's poem." Then he would read another poem evoked by the one in front of him. He seemed to work "with a cold chisel with no more mercy than a dentist."[31]

With the notable exception of Bishop, most of the poets Cal read were men, she noticed: Browning, Hopkins, Hart Crane, Williams. "I am very bitchy acting in class," she told Snodgrass. And why not, with the class just sitting there "like little doggies waggling their heads at his every statement."[32] But by the beginning of the following semester, impatient as she was to learn, she could see what Cal was really trying to teach her: "what *Not* to write," which she was learning to do now by "leaps and boundaries."[33] Two years earlier she'd never even heard of any poet but Edna St. Vincent Millay and now— with his help—she could "walk through lots of people's poetry and pick and pick over."[34]

In October, Lowell went out to Kenyon to receive an honorary doctor's degree. He saw Ransom there, an old man now, filled with a "lonely warm dignity." Most of Ransom's friends at the college were dead, and he'd tried to comfort Cal (and himself) by telling him there were "other things more important than companionship and intellectual conversation," though what they were he didn't say. Tate was courting Cal's cousin, Isabella Gardner, and the two of them came out to see him when Cal returned to Boston. How he wished Gardner might be more sophisticated in her enthusiasm for young poets, Cal told Randall, poets who already seemed to be "trailing heavy gray clouds of ennui and oblivion."[35] With Caroline Gordon he was even blunter. In pursuing Isabella, Lowell told her, Tate was acting like some aged Lord Byron pursuing some "bone stupid" Countess Guiciolli.[36]

On the positive side was his meeting Stanley Kunitz, teaching at Brandeis that fall. Kunitz was "a small, sharp, orderly Bohemian little gray man," he told Bishop, who looked "rather like Kenneth Burke," and whom he'd taken to at once. He was delighted by Kunitz's story of Roethke escaping from a sanatarium disguised as a woman. He read Bill Alfred's *Hogan's Goat* and thought it "a ferocious wonderful play in blank verse, full of Irish violence, Irish alcoholism, Irish politics, religion and Brooklyn Irish eloquence." His friend Adrienne Rich was having her third baby "and reading Simone de Beauvoir and bursting with benzedrine and emancipation." She and Lizzie had already had one glorious forty-five minute argument. And I. A. Richards was "glistening with mountain-climbing and his first book of poems—replies to Wittgenstein and Oppenheimer and Coleridge and the obscurer Plato," all written in Welsh rhyming schemes as intricate as Pound's Provençal poems in translation.[37]

He drove down to the Cape to stay with Edmund Wilson for their annual "boozy" Wellfleet weekend in November, when Wilson, "loaded to the gills," discoursed eloquently on Pasternak and Mosby's Civil War memoirs.[38] ("Wilson drinks like an ox, like Ted Roethke," Cal confided to Powers, "and yet it does no harm. Only at about 11:30, he becomes rather speechless. The rest of the time conversation pours back and forth. I know no one who has read so much and is so good company about what he has read.")[39] At Dartmouth he visited with the eighty-two-year-old Frost, still upset that the Nobel had gone to Pasternak rather than himself. Only when Frost recalled how little his past successes had done to help his family was he finally able to compose himself. What a "mountainous, marvellous man" he was, Cal told Bishop, the only friend he had who was genuinely interested in the details of his crack-ups, and in what he thought of girls.[40]

"Once I visited his [Lowell's] class at Boston University," Snodgrass would later recall. "It seemed this couldn't be the same man; I have seldom encountered anyone duller. I struggled to inject some life into the class, but my deference to him, my unfamiliarity with the students' work, my shock at his state—all conspired against that. As we left the building, he hovered over me much as before, saying, 'I always feel you should be as numb as possible in class—not say too much that's interesting. You ought to give the students a chance—not just obliterate them.' " During that same weekend, however, in spite of his intense dislike of Lizzie, Snodgrass spent a splendid evening going over Cal's translation of Rilke's "Orpheus, Eurydice, Hermes."[41] "We've just had a visit from Snodgrass," Cal told Bishop afterwards, and he'd found him both

> touched with the fire of heaven . . . in a few of his daughter [*Heart's Needle*] poems, but green and hysterical personally and rather unhinged by ten days in New York after three years of being buried and unknown at Rutgers. He wore plaid socks, wooly white underwearlike trousers, a coat made of white fibers and carbon and Ithaca New York tailoring, spoke in a profound persuasive, hypnotic

Jarrell-like whisper, then giggled. The Eberharts liked him unreservedly; Lizzie disliked him unreservedly.[42]

At Thanksgiving, Williams wrote Cal that Floss had just read him the completed *Life Studies,* the "heartbreaking statement of the human situation which has possessed you for the last ten years." This, Williams noted astutely, was language at its most "aristocratic," though he could see Cal was learning to speak more to people, the more so when he avoided complex formal devices, as now mostly he did. "There is no lying permitted to a man who writes that way," Williams added, as a huge compliment to his friend.[43] Cal wrote back at once. Yes, there'd been real terror in undergoing what he'd undergone, but great pleasure too in the writing. And the simple expediency of dropping rhyme had gotten rid "of a thick soapy cloth of artificiality." Truly, the spoken language seemed to beat "any scholarly alchemist's pseudo-language."[44]

He and Lizzie went down to New York a week later to see three Balanchine Stravinsky ballets (in one night), and visit with both Stanley Kunitz and Mary McCarthy, "beautifully, plainly dressed" with her black hair in a Quakerish knot, "collecting donations for Spanish Civil War derelicts, her Florence book done," *The Group* already begun, her "god now after Hannah Arendt" John Pope-Hennessy on Donatello. Then it was downtown to the borders of Little Italy to visit with Auden in his "two messy rooms," expensive Oxford Press books heaped on top of nondescript volumes, Chester Kallman in another room saying nothing, then suddenly turning on a recording "of the Brecht-Weill *Seven Deadly Sins* sung in German with the Auden-Kallman translation as a trot." Cal could not but admire the way Auden, in his "beefy, slow, eccentric normality," had been able to speak "worlds more" than McCarthy ever had about Italy in her "peculiarly highstrung" manner, a manner so many Americans seemed to share.

With *Life Studies* finished, Cal went back to reading: Laforgue, Lawrence, Chekhov, Tolstoy, Dostoievsky, then "a jag of Americana": James, Melville on Hawthorne, Williams, *The Great Gatsby, The Scarlet Letter.* "Being Harriet's father quite changes Pearl for me," he confided to Bishop, for he now saw her as "a rather realistic portrait of the Hawthornes' Una, bursting like the Congo on their shy seclusion." Old nineteenth-century New England, he told her, "must have been fearful—in what other country would Thoreau, Melville, Whitman and Dickinson have been so overlooked!" Still, this last of the puritans sighed, the New England of a century before had sprouted "in a way there are no signs of now, and so many of the best writers were hardly literary men—[Francis] Parkman, Motley, [John] Adams, even [Daniel] Webster."

And while mid-century Boston was a pleasant enough place to live, he and Lizzie were already beginning to find "the home product . . . all dendrification and jelly." All that seemed to have survived of the faded flower of New England was the "woodiness of the old caution, now these fifty years no longer sprouting," and "the jelly of *Vogue* and *Literary Digest* literary tastes."[45] In a year's time he would be speaking disparagingly of Boston's "provincial mind." It was time to consider moving.[46]

A year later Lizzie's "Boston: A Lost Ideal" would appear in *Harper's*, to the dismay of many Bostonians, summing up what both she and Cal had come to feel about the city. Boston's traditional importance, she would write there, had been intellectual, "and as its intellectual donations to the country have diminished, so it has declined from its lofty symbolic meaning, to become a more lowly image, a sort of farce of conservative exclusiveness." The city was Irish- and Italian-run, and run badly, a place where "the night comes down with an incredibly heavy, small-town finality." It did have the "brilliantly exciting Boston Arts Festival held in the Public Garden for two weeks in June," it had Symphony Hall, it had a wealth of lectures in Cambridge. But it had become merely "cozy, Victorian and gossipy," without even a hint of the "wild electric beauty of New York, of the marvellous excited rush of people in taxicabs at twilight, of the great avenues and streets, the restaurants, theaters, bars, hotels, delicatessan shops." By then it was clear where the Lowells planned to settle next.[47]

From Sylvia Plath's journal for January 20, 1959: "A moment with Elizabeth Hardwick and Robert Lowell: she charming and high-strung, mimicking their subnormal Irish house girl [Eileen]," Cal kissing Lizzie "tenderly before leaving, calling her he would be late, and all the winsome fondnesses of a devoted husband . . . his half-whisper and sliding glance. Peter Brooks, his tall wrinkled soft kind charming face . . . his iceblue-eyed pouty blond ballerina wife [Esther] . . . saying to [Lizzie], 'Next to me I hear you're the biggest bitch in Cambridge'." And Lowell: "You should tell her: you're boasting."[48] And two months later: "Criticism of 4 of my poems in Lowell's class: criticism of rhetoric. He sets me up with Anne Sexton, an honor, I suppose. Well, about time. She has very good things, and they get better, though there is a lot of loose stuff."[49] And two months after that, a student's lament: "How few of my superiors do I respect the opinions of anyhow? Lowell a case in point. How few, if any, will see what I am working at, overcoming? How ironic, that all my work to overcome my easy poeticisms merely convinces them that I am rough, anti-poetic, unpoetic. My God."[50] Lowell's meteoric revaluation would come only four years later, after Plath's suicide at thirty, when he read her posthumous poems in the *Times Literary Supplement*, stunned by what he'd read there.

In early February 1959 the Lowells went down to New York again, this time for an exhibition of the Abstract Expressionists. Cal read at the YMHA and saw Williams's *Modern Loves* performed Off-Broadway. He enjoyed the Pirandello-like opening, he wrote Williams afterwards, and "the wonderful, delicate, realistic long scene two," though he wasn't sure about the function of the poet-playwright.[51] When he'd gone out to Rutherford to visit Williams, Williams had just suffered another stroke, so that Lowell found him "mournful, enjoying one day out of seven, waiting for the end, the nervous system cracking but not the mind and courage."[52] Back in Boston he wrote Bishop, asking for a blurb for *Life Studies* and telling her he'd decided to add "91 Revere Street" to the book, "about fifty book pages and perhaps rather engulfing for the verse." He couldn't see himself "writing any more autobiography for ages," and hated "to see the piece yellowing away" in the pages of an old *Partisan Review,* where his Winslow relatives at least would have liked to keep it buried.[53]

Using various paperback Penguin anthologies of German, French, and Italian verse, Lowell worked that winter on a series of translations, some of which he'd begun during his confinement at McLean's the previous winter. Among the poets he translated were these: Rilke, Montale, Ungaretti, Baudelaire, Rimbaud, Heine, Der Wilde Alexander, Hebbel, Goethe, Hölderlin, Carossa, Pasternak. In late February he read with James Baldwin at Brandeis, "each paid $200," with "limp little audiences of about thirty wriggling students," he told Bishop. He liked Baldwin's "negro essays very much," more so than the "blarney" he'd found in Richard Wright, and he was trying now to obliterate his "abolishionist [sic] pangs before seeing Randall" in Greensboro in a few days, where he would once more read as part of the Arts Forum.[54]

"So much to chew on from my visit and little articulate to say," he wrote Randall on his return to Boston in mid-March. He'd liked seeing the South again and remembered how it had once saved his life. He'd also had a "wonderful visit" with the Taylors, "joshing, fussing, squabbling, much as we used to at Kenyon."[55] He and Randall had enjoyed themselves lamenting the times, he told Berryman, and he was now convinced that there really was something "curious, twisted and against the grain about the world poets of our generation have had to live in." What troubles Berryman and he and Roethke and Bishop and Delmore and Randall had all shared. He hoped the exhaustion Berryman was complaining of at the moment was "nothing very drastic," for the knocks they'd had were "almost a proof of intelligence and valor." He praised Berryman's new poems in *His Thought Made Pockets & the Plane Buckt,* though he still wondered if Berryman really did need "so much twisting, obscurity, archaisms, strange word orders, &-signs for *and.*" But his friend had at long last found his voice, and it was one which made the heart ache.[56]

For a while the oatmeal quotidian reality of Greensboro and Columbus even helped cure Lowell of his growing distaste for Boston. There was no one to talk to in such places, he complained to Bishop, "but the flat local English departments," and even staying with Randall had felt like "a Jesuit retreat." He would be lying on his bed "reading Randall's *St. Jerome* poem and in he would come, wrinkled brow, hypnotic eye, to talk of our doom," insisting that the two great facts which had emerged since World War II were "the decline of the west and our *probable* total nuclear extinction." Just now Randall seemed nuts on the subject, Cal told Bishop, but he was also right, for the country's growing reliance on the Bomb and "the crass commercial vulgarity of our country" did seem to go beyond belief.

Randall could be generous in his comments, Lowell noted, but he could also be obtuse, as when he'd told Cal he thought he and Jean Stafford "were more alike than any two people" he'd ever met and would have "been perhaps a little *too* spooky and haunted together." He'd rounded off that discussion by insisting that Jean was even "queerer" than Cal. Still, Cal treasured the man who had refreshed him for the past twenty years with his "pure, narrow steadiness." At least Randall stood by his intuitions, while all he seemed capable of doing was "flub and bull hither and thither."

He was still seeing his therapist three times a week, and hoped that another year would unsnarl the knot inside. "I do so want to live on into gray and white hairs, still growing," he told Bishop. And in fact "all the battering of the last ten years" did seem to be finally paying off. He knew that he had in him the "puritanical iron hand of constraint" side by side with "gushes of pure wildness," and that these two had to come to terms. It was "rather narrow walking" between such bi-polar opposites, either going "off the beam into hallucinations," or lying about, "aching and depressed for months." He had even managed to convince himself that he'd held off a depression for the past year by working and drinking as hard as he had.[57]

In late March Lowell had a visit from Allen Ginsberg, Gregory Corso, and Peter Orlovsky. Two thirty-nine Marlborough, he joked to Bishop, was "nothing if not pretentious," and meant to stun people like Ginsberg. At the door they'd been met by his and Lizzie's maid, Eileen, then taken off their wet shoes to tiptoe up to his fourth-floor study. Mostly, he thought, the Beats were phoneys who had "made a lot of publicity out of very little talent." How pathetic and doomed they all were, for how long could one recite "so-so verse to half-jeering swarms of college students?" Still, they did seem at least to be *trying* to write poetry, and their talk that evening had turned out to be agreeable enough. "There has been an awful lot of subdued talk about their being friends and lovers," Cal added, "and once Ginsberg and Orlofski disappeared in unison to the john and reappeared on each other's shoulders. I haven't had the heart to tell this to Lizzie or anyone else." His hunch was they would all "die of T.B."[58]

When the thirty-three-year-old Ginsberg said goodbye, he left behind some books and pamphlets for Lowell to look over, including a copy of Paul Carroll's magazine, *Big Table*. A few days later Lowell wrote him "a few, scattered, inconclusive thoughts on the various writings" he'd found there. He liked Edward Dahlberg's prose, found it "original, almost Plutarchan and Montaignelike." The poetry he liked less well, finding it "too atomized with single not entirely memorable epigrams." Jack Kerouac was "uninspired Joyce," and William Burroughs's interest lay partially in its "psycho-pathic" elements. The "paeons" Kerouac and Ginsberg had written were "a lot of bull" and "tactically unpersuasive." As for Corso, he was merely "a small attractive poet, and not in the same universe as Williams or Moore or Pound or many others that I like, such as Auden." He asked Ginsberg to forgive his bluntness, which he hoped was not "the usual famous New England kind."[59]

A long, rambling letter came back by return from Ginsberg, meant to shock. "You know, really," the bearded young man whom Williams had all but named his son in *Paterson IV* told this other son of Williams, "I see W. C. Williams as a big Goof, piddling around with his ideas, not at all the neat technician that you see him. I love him, and his poetry,—but I was amazed (enlightened) and shocked to see you apply New Criticism to his 'indented' houses," those late triadic step-down lines Williams had employed in "Asphodel" and elsewhere over the past six years.[60]

Lowell came back with a barrage. "I think letters ought to be written the way you think poetry ought be," he began. "So let this be breezy, brief, incomplete, but spontaneous and not dishonestly holding back." He'd now had a chance to read Robert Creeley and Denise Levertov and had found both of them "careful, disciplined," and "sensitive." But given "the rough and tumble" of what was truly alive in poetry at the moment, he thought Creeley the "tamest imitation of Williams' tricks, tone, mannerisms, rhythms," so that he could barely hear his "polite, dim, halting voice behind the barrage of Williams," but "not to much purpose, while Williams' manner drones at me in Creely [sic]." Levertov, who also appeared to derive from Williams, seemed to have more observation but less skill than Creeley. Everywhere he found in them both "a bit intangibly the humor and quirks of Pound—the hardest of masters, if you yourself are a quiet little person and so unlike him."

On the other hand, he'd found Ginsberg's *Kaddish* "really melodious, nostalgic, moving, liturgical," though too long ("the manner sometimes almost writes itself''), and there was probably "too much Whitman" there. It was also "a bit too conventional, eloquent and liturgical," the last term here assuming a negative cast. There was much in Ginsberg's letter he sympathized with, "and of course reams more" that he didn't. But what did the differences between them come to finally if not a difference of experience, "what one's mind, heart, soul and stamina have gone through"? If they argued for a million years, he saw, he would never get Ginsberg to agree with him, nor he with Ginsberg. Just maybe, however, they might learn to tolerate each other.

But Lowell had yet to say what really bothered him about the Beats. "A reason for the rough brusqueness of your"—he crossed that out and wrote "my"—"letter is this":

> I see a great deal that fascinates me in your wave of writers. Yet as a whole? There's so much that is timid, conservative, intolerant of other kinds of writing. The times are bad? But not as bad as you think. 10,000 noodles to one competent writer; 10,000 competent writers to one interesting writer; 10,000 interesting, honest writers to one inspired writer; 100 inspired writers to one of great moment. But why drown out what there is? Just to name Americans in this century: James, Frost, Robinson, Wharton, Dreiser, Ring Lardner, Fitzgerald, Hemingway, Nathaniel West, Salinger, Saul Bellow, Mary McCarthy, Flannery O'Connor, J. F. Powers, K. A. Porter, Pound, Williams, Ransom, Tate, Warren, Jarrell, Crane, Kunitz, Roethke, Elizabeth Bishop, Faulkner, Winters, Blackmur, James Baldwin, Santayana, Eliot? I've given these people in no particular order. They differ enormously in interest. There [are] others just as good I've intentionally or absent-mindedly passed over. But all these are first-rate, nor should they be taken for granted in the welter of commercial writing, movies etc that we live in. Your wave of people may add a name or two to this list—or more than a name or two; who can foretell the future?—you can't drown out what is already there.[61]

In April, the British reviews of *Life Studies* began pouring in. Bishop had already provided a touchstone of critical perspicacity in her blurb when she wrote that reading a poem by Lowell gave her the "chilling sensation of here-and-now, of exact contemporaneity: more aware of those 'ironies of American History,' grimmer about them, and yet hopeful. If more people read poetry, if it were more exportable and translatable, surely his poems would go far towards changing, or at least unsettling, minds made up against us [as poets]. Somehow or other, by fair means or foul, and in the middle of our worst century so far," America had produced a magnificent poet.[62] Now, he told Bishop, he'd received "rather a rave review from Alvarez in England," which would make it difficult for the English to ignore the book. And though many of the British reviews were mild in their praise, there were strong reviews as well by G. S. Fraser and Roy Fuller, and by Philip Larkin in *The Manchester Guardian Weekly,* who noted the "almost flippant humour not common in Mr. Lowell's previous work."[63]

When *Life Studies* was published in the States that May, it was reviewed by Eberhart in the *Times,* F. W. Dupee in the *Partisan Review,* John Thompson in the *Kenyon Review,* Stephen Spender in *The New Republic:* all friends who'd followed Lowell's work for years. But Alfred Kazin also wrote praising the new work. Among other things noticed by critics in these poems was the closer identification of the speaker with the poem, the opening of the poem to new dimensions of human experience, and the sense of a declining glory in the American experience. Somehow Cal had managed to speak of "the most desperate and sordid personal experience," Thompson wrote, and yet do it "with full dignity."[64] With characteristic humor Lowell wrote Tate that the reviews had all complimented him on his "desperation and harshness," which was "rather like being given Nessus' shirt with medals on it."[65]

Giroux had scheduled a party in New York at the end of April to celebrate Cal's first book in eight years. But as the date approached, Cal realized he was speeding up again when he began calling Caroline Gordon to try and "save" Tate from marrying Isabella Gardner. This time he had himself quietly admitted to McLean's, where he spent the next two months. It was his fifth breakdown. One of those who witnessed his collapse this time was Anne Sexton, who articulated the eerie transformation that many of his students over the years must have witnessed:

> *In the thin classroom, where your face*
> *was noble and your words were all things,*
> *I find this bodily creature in your place;*
>
> *find you disarranged, squatting on the window sill,*
> *irrefutably placed up there,*
> *like a hunk of some big frog*
> *watching us through the V*
> *of your woolen legs.*
>
> *Even so, I must admire your skill.*
> *You are so gracefully insane.*
> *We fidget in our plain chairs*
> *and pretend to catalogue*
> *our facts for your burly sorcery*

or ignore your fat blind eyes
or the prince you ate yesterday
who was wise, wise, wise.[66]

"You heard the subterranean note in [Cal's] voice correctly, I guess," Flannery O'Connor wrote Caroline Gordon on May 10. "Bob Giroux spent last Monday and Tuesday with us and said Cal hospitalized himself before the party. He thought it a good sign that he did it himself and didn't have to be forced to."[67] Tate of course was beside himself. And though he wrote Cal at once reassuring him that he would "be alright very soon" and that his book was "magnificent,"[68] he told his friend Andrew Lytle that Cal had complicated the matter of his own divorce by his further disclosures to Caroline.[69] It was Lizzie who was left to apologize to Tate. "If only these things of Cal's were simply distressing," she wrote him. But in truth they caused her and others "real suffering. And for what? I do not know the answer to the moral problems posed by a deranged person, but the dreadful fact is that in purely personal terms this deranged person does a lot of harm."[70]

Three weeks later she wrote Bishop. The new attack was not as bad as some of the earlier ones, except that Cal was passing the time "doing poor rewritings of all his early poems in preparation for a Collected."[71] She waited for the blessèd break when his judgment would return. And Cal, in a note to Edmund Wilson toward the end of May, saying he wanted to "improve" one of his poems, this one "diamond-pointed" on one of Wilson's window panes at Wellfleet, though how he meant to change a poem written on a hundred-year-old piece of glass he did not say. He enclosed the new version, "gnomic and round-headed enough, I hope, for any man's taste." Right now he was at Bowditch, he explained, "conditioning" for the last month, and "feel swimming, and looking forward to tanking up again on your conversation."[72]

After eight weeks Lowell was again released, having promised to continue his psychotherapy, though with this latest onslaught he had all but lost faith in the process. The summer of 1959 was a repeat of the previous summer, with Cal commuting back and forth to Castine, teaching at Harvard, and seeing his Boston therapist three times a week. "I feel rather creepy and paltry writing now to announce that I am all healed and stable again," he wrote Bishop from Castine in late July. But so it was. "Five attacks in ten years make you feel rather a basket-case." Maybe, when another ten years had passed, he would have become "a sort of monument of the norm—Eberhart and Wilbur combined."

Life in Castine was what it always was: "awfully tennis-playingish and beachy." Most of his days were spent typing, "surrounded by chintz and

Cousin Harriet's somber 19th century oils of Alpine valleys. The sun comes in the window." Once again he and Lizzie were "very happy and companionable," and somehow he still managed to click along. Nor could he believe that he'd spent "a mad month or more" at McLean's "rewriting *everything*" in his three books of poetry, arranging the poems chronologically, "starting in Greek and Roman times," before he'd finally risen for air with the present in *Life Studies*. Strangely, while he was rewriting his poems all had seemed to "hit the skies" and cohere. Now he could see that it was "mostly waste."[73] It would not be the last time he would attempt to shape his life's work into an epic history.

That summer he worked on translations of Heine and Baudelaire, and wrote a piece for the *Sewanee Review* in honor of Tate's sixtieth birthday. It would become the fine prose memoir of his starting out as a poet, "Visiting the Tates," and that fall he would tell Tate that Tate had been the only influence who'd ever "really got deeply and closely" under his skin. "I don't suppose I would ever have written again," he added, if it hadn't been for that year in 1942–43 in Monteagle. For the past twelve months he'd been writing prose and doing translations, but only because new poems refused to come.[74] In truth, he felt drained of new poems, he confessed to Cousin Harriet, so that everything he wrote now seemed but "a dry repetitious version of something sufficiently and better said in *Life Studies*."

Instead, like Candide, he passed his days gardening, playing tennis at four, and going on the annual Blue Hill yawl race up the Deer Isle Reach. He had become a survivor, with a knack—much like his skunks—"for surviving and drawing much happiness."[75] When William Meredith apologized for not getting in touch with him during his sickness, Cal reassured him there would have been no point in doing so while he was absent from the world, since he knew all too well "about the uninstructed heart" and how "wearisome and . . . fruitless" it was "for human ears to try and catch its clamorous babble."[76]

A short list of Lowell's students at Boston University would include at least the following: Kathleen Spivack, Henry Braun, Donald Junkins, Hilda Raz, Helen Chasin, Stephen Berg, Jean Valentine, George Starbuck, Anne Sexton, Sylvia Plath. If we add those whom Lowell later taught at Harvard, the list would expand to include James Atlas, Sidney Goldfarb, Robert Grenier, Lloyd Schwartz, Gail Mazur, Jonathan Galassi, Andrew Wylie, Robert Siegel, Alan Williamson, Richard Tillinghast, Steven Sandy, Jane Shore, Bill Byrom, Anne Hussey, Robert Pinsky, and Frank Bidart. These, added to Justice, Levine, Snodgrass, and the others, known and unknown, suggests the impact Lowell had in the classroom, to say nothing of the untold thousands he would influence through his prose, his poetry, his very presence as a voice for American poetry. But in the class it is one on one that the teacher must work, as with Matthew Arnold, as with Hopkins, Berryman, Bishop, Jarrell, and Lowell.

In September he was back teaching at Boston University. Tate and Belle Gardner were in town the weekend of the 12th, and Tate visited Lowell's classes. "One day Cal brought Allen Tate to class and we did one of Tate's poems," Donald Junkins would remember. "Something about a well and a descent. . . . There was a British graduate student in the class who was far and ahead the most incisive and articulate talker, and when Lowell asked for comments on Tate's poem this fellow started in on it quite heavily." When he "apologized to Tate for being harsh, Lowell quickly interrupted his apology with something like 'no, go ahead, say it.' He [wanted] good talk and comment."

One night, when Junkins and Henry Braun were walking home, Braun told Junkins he was afraid Cal would be angry with him for criticizing a poem Cal had written and then slipped anonymously into the class discussion. "We had just done a Snodgrass poem," Junkins would remember, "everyone praising its delicacies and phrasings, and Cal passed out 'The Drinker,' " the one poem he'd managed to write in the past year. ("Neither thunder nor the muse has struck me for ages," Cal had lamented to Bishop the previous spring, and the drought still held.)[77] "Henry and I were pretty rough on it, but Henry actually banged his fist on the long table we were all sitting around and said 'This simply won't do!' Then Henry praised the Snodgrass poem more." Actually Cal was delighted by the outburst, though he did refrain from printing the poem until he'd greatly revised it.[78]

Late one evening he had another of Berryman's phone calls, this one bemoaning his separation from his second wife and his two-year-old son. "I have been thinking much about you all summer," Cal wrote him the following day,

> and how we have gone through the same troubles, visiting the bottom of the world. I have wanted to stretch out a hand, and tell you that I have been there too, and how it all lightens and life swims back. . . . I've thought of your dazzling brilliance so astonishing to your friends, of reading in Chicago two years ago and hearing the uproar of admiration you had left behind you. . . . Then our talks in Maine, meeting in New York. There's been so much fellow feeling between us, and for so long now. . . . The night is now passed, and I feel certain that your fire and loyalty, and all-outedness carry you buoyantly on. The dark moment comes, it comes and goes.[79]

The dark moment comes and goes. In his more recent poems, he told one critic, he'd tried to avoid religious imagery. And yet, the "dramatic dark" of his

Calvinist upbringing still persisted. It was "a strange thing" to linger on, "long after its iron web of theory and fiercely debated and lived theology" had perished, and he would have much preferred to write more in the style of Yeats's "Labour is blossoming or dancing where / The body is not bruised to pleasure soul." Yet, in spite of his encounters with Flaubert, Montale, and Rilke, he knew he was still a puritan at heart.

Only in the last ten years, with his second marriage and later the birth of his daughter, had he begun to write what he'd really had to say. And yet in these same ten years he'd had five breakdowns: "short weeks of a Messianic rather bestial glow, when I have to be in the hospital, then dark months of indecision, emptiness," so that "the dark and light are not mere decoration and poetic imagery, but something altogether lived, inescapable." Now had come the need to be more impersonal again, and with it the need for yet another style, a style he was still searching for.[80]

Meanwhile, there was Harriet, growing under his gaze. Harriet, his child, "extraordinary, full of little courtesies and whimsies . . . noticing more than we do." Often he mused "it all in," and he knew Lizzie's eagle eye missed little. In two days Harriet would begin nursery school, "the first step, a mild one but dramatic, toward her own separate life," though at first Lizzie would go with her, "with a crowd of new nursery school mothers, all circled about as a council for the teacher."[81] Three times a week, doubtfully, wistfully, he would note over that first month, his little daughter set off into the blue of Boston and Charles Street for school at 9:00 A.M., "like an art student," bringing home her Abstract Expressionist paintings looking like nothing so much as "chalky spaghetti-like swirls."[82]

He flew out to the University of Buffalo to see the library's holdings of the great moderns and to read in the Exhibit Room, surrounded by the notebooks and manuscripts of Joyce, Yeats, Thomas, Williams, even Elizabeth Bishop, so that he left feeling rather like "a small, hardened, purified vestige of literary history."[83] It must have seemed strange, then, to find himself a few days later sitting on the stage of the 92nd Street YMHA introducing T. S. Eliot. And stranger still, as Stanley Kunitz noted, for the great literary statesman to signal to Cal to stay on stage after the introduction. At that moment, Kunitz noted, the mantle of the poet seemed to shift from the High Modern to the Middle Generation, for the request, coming from Eliot, "had the authority of a dynastic gesture."[84]

"I went on a weird trip yesterday with Aunt Sarah and [Cousin] Emily to Concord New Hampshire," he wrote Cousin Harriet on January 8, 1960. "The object was to confer with the Historical Society and the army engineers

about the [Winslow] graveyard . . . three vague Winslows full of family reminiscence, three suave, friendly engineers full of facts . . . three New Hampshire
people, country New England accents, folk-lore, a sinewy hold on regional
history. . . . Well, the flood-control floods must come." The graves, if left
where they were, would be covered by a foot of water every five years, and so
had to be moved to higher ground.[85]

So much of his past was fading from him. He prepared two new courses,
one on the Eighteenth-Century Novel (which he would soon enough decide
he did not like), took daily walks, and got ready for brief reading trips to
Amherst ("idyllic in its whiteness," he reported to Tate, "only no one wants to
be there"), New York, Chicago.[86] At the moment his three-year-old daughter
was trying to decide "whether to be a cook (specializing in tea), or a zoo
keeper, or a parent keeper."[87]

The problem of a new style continued to vex. "I have been thinking," he
wrote Flannery O'Connor, that master of the Southern Gothic, "that we
perhaps have something of the same problem—how to hold to one's true,
though extreme vein, without repetition; how to master conventional controls
and content normal expectations without washing out all one has to say. This
hurried way of saying it sounds cynical, but I think something like this happened to Shakespeare in moving from his clotted, odd, inspired *Troilus and
Cressida* to the madder but more conventional *Lear.*" For the past year he'd
tried to free himself of the style he'd perfected in *Life Studies,* a style that would
continue to shift toward the even plainer style of his new poems. Only recently—in the past month, in fact—had he managed several confusing new
poems "that somehow, impossibly, make little sense and are nakedly and dryly
clear in style."[88] A month later he was telling Randall that he wanted "a whole
new deck of cards to play with, or at least new rules for the old ones. Maybe it's
the times, or maybe it's being well in one's forties, or maybe it's all a private
thing with me: but I feel wrung with altered views and standards—more than I
can swallow. So many questions, one is almost speechless."[89]

On the morning of March 3 Lowell was interviewed in his Marlborough
Street study by the twenty-four-year-old Frederick Seidel for the *Paris Review*.
"I've just finished a long, long morning of giving a recorded interview for the
Paris Review," he wrote Meredith later that day, "one in which strain gave no
edge, and hesitation no civilized tolerance. I feel flat and flattened."[90] It was a
good interview, and many subjects had been covered. Jarrell, he had insisted,
was still the best critic writing in the States at the time, in the direct line which
included Tate, Eliot, Blackmur, and Winters. He spoke of the difficulty of
writing in meter, of sculpting the poems of *Life Studies* out of his autobiographical prose. Spoke too of his inability to know if his earlier poems had really
been religious or had just used religious imagery, so that anyone reading them

would never have been able to guess what creed he believed in. What *was* common to all his poems—he hoped—was the sense of lived experience. After all, nothing else—not politics, not theology—made a poem.[91]

He and Meredith had just received grants from the Ford Foundation to study opera in New York for a year beginning in September, and he had just reread Herman Melville's "Benito Cereno" from *The Piazza Tales* with the idea of translating that story into an opera. With the civil rights issue taking on new impetus, he'd been struck by Melville's portrait of Captain Delano's "growing saturation"—not unlike his own—in this "new Spanish and negro world," Delano's "false guesses, his darkening suspicions." The question was "how to handle the whole plot so as not to make it rather shockingly anti-negro." Like Flaubert, like the recording angel of history, he wanted to write from as neutral a position as he could, watching as wrong blazed "into a holocaust," with no one—black or white—completely innocent.

The trouble was that in Melville "the negroes with their bloodthirsty servility" were little more than "symbolic demons," so that on the stage they would be even "more unbearable than read, or even worse, likely to seem a sadistic unfelt farce." The old abolitionist strain in him was anything but "anti-negro," yet he wanted to be careful *not* to err "on the easy side of optimism" in race relations. How to render the complex truth, then, was the problem. Perhaps, he added, there was something to be learned from the way Georg Büchner had dealt with the revolutionary theme in *Danton's Death,* which he thought "the best modern political play" he'd read. Over the next several years the race issue would continue to loom large in his work.[92]

On March 23 he was awarded the *National Book Award* for *Life Studies.* In his acceptance speech he spoke of cooked poetry and of raw, contrasting the more radical poets represented by Donald Allen's *The New American Poetry 1945–60* to the more mainstream poets represented by *New Poets of England and America,* which Donald Hall, Louis Simpson, and Robert Pack had assembled. "Something earth-shaking was started about fifty years ago by the generation of Eliot, Frost, and William Carlos Williams," Lowell said that evening. "We have had a run of poetry as inspired, and perhaps as important and sadly brief, as that of Baudelaire and his early successors, or that of the dying [Roman] Republic and early Empire." There were two kinds of poetry: one that could only be studied, and one that could only be declaimed, "a poetry of pedantry and a poetry of scandal." The problem was that the cooked, "expert and remote," seemed constructed "as a sort of mechanical or catnip mouse for graduate seminars," while the raw, "jerry-built and forensically deadly," seemed "often like an unscored libretto by some bearded but vegetarian Castro." Where, then, should poetry be heading as he and others entered the sixties? The truth was he didn't yet know himself.[93]

The following month he flew down to Washington to visit Cousin Harriet, confined now by strokes to her apartment. Beneath her "calm strength," he wrote her when he was back in Boston, he'd felt her struggling under the weight of her disabilities like a salmon pushing upstream against the terrible odds. What was life after all but a mix of "light and shadow," he told her, "as much light as God and nature allow," so that often now he too found himself "staring at some memory, or something going on" under his eyes. "If I look long enough, I think, a clue will appear—I will see the future and what it is." And yet, he'd lived long enough now to understand that one never saw "the truth or ourselves."[94]

When, at month's end, Roethke came east to read at Wellesley and Harvard, the Lowells threw a party for him. It was a party too for I. A. Richards, Roethke's Harvard mentor of twenty-five years before. Philip Booth was there, and Adrienne Rich, and Anne Sexton, and Bill Alfred, and Don Junkins and his wife Mardi. Junkins would remember Lowell climbing up to his study and returning with an armful of books by the poets assembled there that evening and calling for an impromptu poetry reading. He was "a wonderful host . . . clear-eyed and celebrative in his self-admonishing friendliness, solicitous of each poet that he introduced." He was neither drinking nor smoking at the time, and Lizzie "was gay and wonderfully verbal and southern." Richards, in his seventies—"white-haired, tensile, eloquent"—began the reading by quipping that he'd written "a lifetime of poetry criticism that ought not be applied to his own poetry."

Around midnight, sitting on the couch with Mardi Junkins, Roethke proceeded to place his hand on her thigh. Cal gently removed the offending hand without saying a word. Roethke tried again. Again Cal removed it. Later, after Bill Alfred had left, Roethke remarked what a nice man he was, and Cal told him that, yes, Bill Alfred was his best friend. Roethke looked at Cal. "Cal," he said, "you're my best friend." Roethke seemed at that moment, Junkins remembered, particularly lonely and vulnerable, and it was difficult to say just what he'd meant by his comment. Then Cal put his hand on Roethke's leg and assured him. "Ted," he said, "you're my best friend."[95]

Before an audience of several thousand in the Boston Public Garden that June, Lowell read his public poem, "For the Union Dead," to thunderous applause, the echoes of which Bishop told him she'd heard as far away as Brazil.[96] He'd begun the poem in January and had worked hard at it for months. One can believe it, for the poem is a powerful public utterance layered with a series of interlocking images and three hundred years of Boston's history, ranging from its earlier promise as a beacon on a hill to its present moral and physical decline.

At the center of the poem is Boston, and at the heart of Lowell's Boston is the fine Saint-Gaudens bas-relief which stands in the shadow of the State House and which commemorates Colonel Robert Shaw and his regiment of African-American volunteers, the famed Massachusetts 54th. The relief remembers the men who walked into the face of death in a charge against Confederates waiting behind palmetto logs for them at Fort Wagner, amazed that armed "niggers" would actually march against them. That monument had stood there all these years, Cal knew, while he'd played as a boy on Boston Common, or later, when he'd walked there with his daughter and Lizzie, the monument barely noticed in the blur of traffic, its unfulfilled dream sticking "like a fishbone / in the city's throat."

Here in the poem Lowell recalls himself as a boy in the Boston of the 1920s, face pressed against the glass of the "old South Boston Aquarium," watching "the bubbles / drifting from the noses of the cowed, compliant fish." But times have changed. The aquarium lies empty now, "its broken windows boarded," the fish having devolved downwards into the "giant finned cars" which slide by on grease. Lowell knows how easy it is to avoid the issue of racial injustice, to sigh instead "for the dark downward and vegetating kingdom / of the fish and reptile," and look for American progress elsewhere, as in the construction of new buildings, as in the new garage being dug under the Boston Common.

"One morning last March," he writes, repeating his childhood gesture of pressing against the glass of the aquarium, but now weighted with the knowledge of the general devolution of his century, the century of the Final Solution and of the Gulags, of Hiroshima, of his own prison experience which prevented nothing:

> *I pressed against the new barbed and galvanized*
> *fence on the Boston Common. Behind their cage,*
> *yellow dinosaur steamshovels were grunting*
> *as they cropped up tons of mush and grass*
> *to gouge their underworld garage.*

When he sees the very heart of old Boston being carved to make room for cars, he cannot help but think of those sandpiles and dunes he'd seen with the Taylors a dozen years before where Fort Wagner had once stood, protecting the flanks of Fort Sumter out in Charleston Harbor. He thinks too of Colonel Shaw's "bell-cheeked Negro infantry" marching through Boston in the late spring of 1863, "half the regiment . . . dead" two months later. Shaw, like his own ancestor, Beau Sabreur: the flower of his puritan, abolitionist heritage, "lean / as a compass needle," a sterner Lowell with his "angry wrenlike vigilance, / a greyhound's gentle tautness," who seems like Lowell himself "to wince at pleasure, / and suffocate for privacy."

Well, Shaw is "out of bounds now." Like Lowell, he can rejoice "in man's lovely, / peculiar power to choose life and die." Not "choose life *or* die," and the paradox seems to ring true: that it is in consciously choosing the higher path which may mean death that one experiences life most fully. Even as with these nameless black soldiers, who at the monument's dedication William James said he "could almost hear breathe," and who even now seem more fully alive than anything in this claustrophobic Boston landscape. We have lost the real meaning of the sacrifice of those who died in the Civil War, Lowell says, for the "old white churches" on "a thousand small town New England greens" barely "hold their air / of sparse, sincere rebellion" any more, and the flags which "quilt the graveyards of the Grand Army of the Republic" have frayed all the more over the intervening years. For time only mellows history, washes over it, makes the "stone statues of the abstract Union soldiers / grow slimmer and younger each year," as they seem to doze now over their muskets.

But in truth reality is harsher, and the ditch nearer, the ditch where Colonel Shaw's "body was thrown / and lost with his 'niggers,' " as here in the heart of Boston, here in the fact of the Cold War, in the fact of "Hiroshima boiling" over other people of color. Again Lowell crouches, in fear and disbelief, this time before the "drained faces of Negro school-children" on his television set, as their drained faces "rise like balloons," like bubbles ready to break, the struggle for the true union of all Americans, black and white, more lost than ever a century after the sacrifice of Colonel Shaw and his soldiers. Instead, it is the Mosler Safe which has become our true "Rock of Ages," money and its special interests the eternal survivors as in all wars.

"I wake up thinking I have perhaps twenty more years," Cal would write Taylor after reading his poem on the Boston Common. "That they are whizzing by—soon a network of vexing physical disorders. I think about my ragged conduct, unreality, squabbling uncontrollable desires etc. and feel . . . why not be a Catholic and hold all this together." But he no longer believed, "and couldn't be one anyway." ("I feel very Montaigne-like about faith now—it's true as a possible vision such as *War and Peace* or *Antony* [*and Cleopatra*]— no more though," he'd confided to Bishop the year before.)[97] What was left him, then, was merely a "hollowness and airy disorder," which would have to do in place of faith.[98] As with his shadow portrait, Colonel Shaw, what would be left to prod him from now on would be duty, riding the bubble of his dream, as he too waited for the "blessèd break" of sure oblivion.

PART III

12

Opéra Bouffe

1960–1962

By working steadily for six hours each day that summer, Lowell managed to translate Racine's *Phèdre* in just two months. He was "churning away," he told Taylor, "much more busily than I have for years, and love it all, yet feel rather in a treadmill of declamation and heroic clichés."[1] In this one summer, he realized, he'd doubled his entire poetic output by rendering hundreds of French couplets into their English equivalents. In his foreword to the play, he would raise some of the problems he'd had in trying to bring Racine over into his own idiom. His meter had been based by necessity, he explained, on what would be familiar to an audience raised on Dryden and Pope rather than on the Court of Louis XIV, the difference between *his* couplets and Dryden's being that Dryden had used "an end-stopped couplet, loaded with inversions, heavily alliterated, and varied by short unrhymed lines," whereas his own were run on, avoided inversions and alliteration, and loosened the rhythm with shifted accents and occasional extra syllables. Another problem was that Racine, perhaps the "greatest poet in the French language," had used a smaller vocabulary than any English poet he could think of.[2] What he was bringing over into English, then, would be a highly charged syntax, with enjambed couplets which more often evoked the high tensile strength of Browning than they did the balanced and classical Racine. As with all of his translations, Lowell's own preoccupations could be everywhere felt.[3]

At Castine that summer he and Lizzie looked after Lizzie's twelve-year-old Kentucky niece. Because she still took "a doggie to bed with her," he told Taylor, his niece had given his "imperious baffled" three-year-old daughter "an opening to treat her as another child." He'd always suspected that he and Lizzie "were curiously unlike other families, my multiple absent-mindedness, and Lizzie's way of investing small, domestic acts with the splendor of an early Verdi heroine." But now, "against the background of a normal child," he could measure how very strange both he and his wife really were.[4]

"The full summer is here now," he wrote Cousin Harriet from the parlor of the Brickyard House that July. Their handyman, Mr. Farley, "and a dignified elderly assistant" had been hard at work on the Barn—Cal's workplace a short drive away on the Bagaduce River overlooking the bay—so that it now looked "very new and strong." The cement piles were set, a new floor installed, the barn door reduced by half.[5] The Barn was spartan: a table, some battered chairs, a portable typewriter, the only splotch of color provided by a new Franklin stove, puritan-pumpkin orange.

It turned out to be "a shifting, kaleidoscopic, colorful outdoors summer," he would remember, with tennis, swimming, island picnics, teenage dances for his young nurse and niece, and woodfires at night. The big drama of the season was the removal of two hornets' nests from the house on School Street, using paper bags, somehow accomplished "without bloodshed for us."[6] He watched the Republican Convention on television and was astounded to hear "a style of oratory" in use "in which, not only truth, but even meaning" was "well-nigh impossible." Still, Henry Cabot Lodge had been almost persuasive enough to convert him back to the Republicans, he told Cousin Harriet, until he'd heard Nelson Rockefeller and Richard Nixon.[7] Before returning to Boston en route to New York, the Lowells spent Labor Day Weekend at Mattapoisett, where they "lay swimming and mooning for three days." He saw faces there he hadn't "seen for twenty-five years," including old Macdonald, Grandfather Winslow's farmer, "just moving out of his house to an old people's home." Macdonald had obliged Cal by remembering the old days, and had given him his grandfather's old mining pick as a parting gift.[8]

Beginning that September, the Lowells had arranged to swap their Boston house on even terms with Eric Bentley for his Manhattan apartment at 194 Riverside Drive, thus drowning "the ache of moving, its searches and uncertainties."[9] ("Upper Broadway, Riverside Drive," Lizzie would later write, "the ulcerated side streets hanging on the edge of the academic plateau, shuddering over the abyss of Harlem and the gully of Amsterdam Avenue.")[10] Anthony Hecht and Richard Wilbur had also won Ford Foundation grants to work with various repertory companies, and had been sent to the American provinces, while Peter Taylor had been offered the chance to work in London with the Royal Court Theatre. But since Cal and Meredith had both specifically expressed an interest in opera, they'd been assigned to work with the New York City Opera Company at the Metropolitan for the regular season, which opened just as the Lowells arrived in New York in mid-September.

At first Cal and Meredith were rather at sea, neither poet nor opera official knowing quite what to do with the other. "I am literally being paid to listen to opera rehearsals," Lowell reported to T. S. Eliot on October 12. "God knows what will come of it, supposedly a libretto, but I sit lapping it all in and staring at immense Natalie Rahvlike blondined divas and tenors looking like Dick Tracy antagonists. The opera people . . . haven't the remotest idea who I am or what I am doing. It's all a great refreshment after the huge dose of myself and self-contemplation in *Life Studies*."[11]

In truth Cal knew almost nothing about either music *or* the opera. Nevertheless, he found the rehearsals "great fun—full of things like Stokowski walking out and Christopher West walking out." He and Meredith had unfortunately told the Met officials that they were "just absorbing opera," which had not endeared them at all. Still, somehow, they managed to make important contacts, and soon Lincoln Kirstein was showing Cal's *Phaedra* to the British producer, George Devine. It was rather fantastic even to think of Laurence Olivier or Maria Callas or Melina Mercouri starring in something he had written. The major problem now was "whether any actor could deliver and any audience hear reams of heroic couplets of a rather pseudo 17th century grandiosity."[12] By mid-November he was writing Adrienne Rich that he'd made "some 200 corrections" in the play since she'd seen it in September. Several speeches had been rewritten and he'd taken about half of Bishop's suggestions, until he was weary of patching the thing. He even had a producer now, a Mrs. Bel Geddes: "blond, sixtyish, looks rather like Mrs. Adlai Stevenson . . . rich and full of energy and sympathetic."[13]

In November, an Englishman read the play aloud "to a small softspoken group of friends" in Cal's apartment—a rather level, monotonous, and intellectual drone—at the end of which the idea of an acting play "seemed thousands of miles away."[14] By Thanksgiving, Cal had immersed himself in "5 Puccinis, 3 Mozarts, 3 Verdi's, three Strauss's, *Carmen, Boris,* Della Piccola, Monteverdi, Eck, and more things than I can remember, and at every stage of imperfection." In one week alone, "sitting humbly in the dark at rehearsals," he'd heard enough Puccini to compose a libretto for the dead. But though the opera was "good fun" and even "an obsession" with him, it all faded if he missed a few days of rehearsal. In truth, the world of the Met had "about as much connection with writing as a grant to watch the Yankees practice for a season."

He shared with Rich some of the rather "grotesque scenes" he'd been

witness to as honorary phantom of the opera: "Strauss's *Arabella* being done
in an English translation by a German by singers who only know German," the
diva asking, "Ist es *leeps* or *lips?*" The translatorese of "we come perhaps from
very dubious people," Italian tenors looking like "comic strip goons" as they
chattered away "in little groups about their income taxes and singing teachers
and mothers," then having to be told "by the choir master not to put their feet
up on the Met's plush seats" and yelling bravo whenever everything went
haywire. He watched as stage directors tried "to make the opera into plays"
even as the conductors tried "to make them into oratorios, both very keyed up
and oblivious of the other's world." He watched astonished as Cherubino
jumped through a window without the sound of breaking glass. "The great
people," like Rudolph Bing, took "great pride in being able to tell" him and
Meredith apart and getting it right "about half the time."[15]

Obviously neither Lowell nor Meredith was taken very seriously by the
opera people, Meredith would recall. The one time they actually did speak with
Bing, he suggested the two of them go up to Columbia and take an introduc-
tory course on opera, to which Cal had answered very sweetly, "You must
understand, Mr. Bing, that Mr. Meredith and I are already professionals.
We've come for some help in seeing how the opera company works." Bing had
shrugged, but saw that they got house passes, could watch live rehearsals, and
hang around backstage.[16] But there was never anything like a real collaboration
between the poets and the New York Met, as the Ford Foundation had perhaps too naively envisioned.

Though Cal had made his final "truce" with Boston in "For the Union
Dead," and though the city of his birth still held pleasant memories for him,
after just two months in Manhattan he and Lizzie had decided to move there
permanently, so that by December Lizzie was looking for a place of their own.
After Christmas she went back up to Boston with Harriet to sell the house on
Marlborough Street while Cal wrote Boston University that he would not be
coming back to teach. There was real excitement to the "queer jumbled
world" of New York, he told Rich: Dag Hammarskjöld at the United Nations
reading his poems; Kenneth Koch and Ginsberg disputing which was "the
dullest of the other's poems," Bill Williams in the audience at the YMHA on
92nd Street as he and Mary McCarthy's actor brother, Kevin, read from
Paterson. He and Lizzie seemed to be "the only gentiles" at every party they
went to, and loved New York, and felt gloriously seedy about being part of that
world.[17]

Election night at the Riverside apartment turned out to be a scene of heavy
drinking with Kunitz and the Tates, a night when Cal became "so plastered"
he couldn't remember what he'd said or done afterwards and felt on the plane
down to Washington next day as if he were still "living in an aquarium."

(Kunitz would later tell Cal that he couldn't decide whether Cal or Tate had made the least sense that evening.) The reason for the noisy night was that a Democrat was about to enter the White House for the first time in eight years, and both Cal and Lizzie had stayed up till six in the morning "waiting for the Minnesota returns that never came." They were beside themselves that John F. Kennedy, the forty-three-year-old senator from Massachusetts, Cal's age exactly, had edged out Nixon, a politician Cal had intensely disliked for the past ten years.[18]

Three days after Christmas Cal signed the lease for their apartment at 15 West 67th Street. His friend and financial adviser, Bob Gardner, Isabella's former husband, thought the signing "required more ceremonial than entering the Tavern Club."[19] Both Lowells would have to meet with the co-owners on January 9, 1961, and, if that went well, the apartment would be theirs. It was an extraordinary find, with its wonderfully individual two-story turn-of-the-century skylighted artists' studio interior, in a building just off Central Park. "Our new apartment is absolutely definite now," Lizzie wrote Cousin Harriet the day after the meeting. "More than that—irrevocable. I had some misgivings and clung a bit to Boston just because we were there. On the other hand, there was no profound reason why we shouldn't make the move."[20] The place had four bedrooms, Cal told Bishop, "kitchen, dining-room, and one huge room, two stories high, with a two-story window, fireplace, beams, etc. Miles away on the top of the house," was "an old servants' room" which he meant to use for his study.[21]

There was even a playground for Harriet in Central Park, and they were very near Broadway and the new Lincoln Center. The apartment ("baronial," Lizzie called it)[22] was eight stories up—reached by a small, dark, wooden elevator—and looked across on some picturesque old police stables, which would soon give way to a nondescript modern building. Living in New York after Boston, Cal added, was "like discovering . . . oxygen in the air—people to talk to, plays, opera, and something in the air that somehow makes the same people very different here from what they are in Boston." Everything seemed "merrier, easier and more serious."[23] With some rather pronounced vicissitudes, it would remain Lowell's New York address for the rest of his life.

Cal's star was now clearly in the ascendancy. Just after the New Year he introduced Eliot at the YMHA, telling him beforehand that he felt very close to him, though he was not sure "how to say this from the platform."[24] On January 21 Cal and Lizzie, along with 170 other invited guests, went to Washington for Kennedy's inauguration. There'd been some "strange scenes" there, Cal would recall, such as Tate in tails and white gloves, and Belle Gardner looking rather like a "sponge wrapped in a quilt." Later, when he was introduced to the new President, he had received "the kind of compliment that indicated [Kennedy had] really read *Life Studies."* He was, Cal told him as a Boston Yankee sizing up a Boston Irishman, the first President to treat his "peers as equals." The Kennedy business had been very inspiring, he reported afterwards to Bishop. "With a lot of reservations, I feel like a patriot for the first time in my life. I wrote in the Kennedy guest-book, *Robert Lowell, happy that at long last the Goths have left the White House.*"[25]

By late 1960 Lowell could count fifty "free translations" he'd done over the past three years: "11 or 12 Montale, 4 Rilke, 15 Baudelaire (the hardest and done in rhyme and meter) 3 Leopardi, 3 Heine, 5 or six Pasternak." Some of these, he told Eliot, were "almost original poems and . . . some of my best work."[26] But he was still adding to his manuscript: three by Rimbaud— "Mémoire," "Bâteau Ivre," "Des Chercheuses"—Baudelaire's "Le Voyage," a Victor Hugo, and twelve pages of Villon's *The Great Testament,* "probably my best translations along with the Baudelaire."[27] The *Phaedra* would be out in April, *Imitations* in September.

But by his forty-fourth birthday he was ill again. Once again there was a girl, this time a young New York poet named Sandra Hochman. Again he an-nounced a new beginning. Along with leaving Boston, he would leave Lizzie behind as well. It was all familiar, of course, but what complicated matters this time was that his New York psychiatrist, Dr. Viola Bernard, took a decidedly different tack from the doctors at McLean's and began searching for the existential causes behind Cal's sickness. So, when Cal insisted on starting over again with a new apartment and a new woman, Dr. Bernard went along with his plan. On the evening of March 3, 1961, Cal showed up with Hochman at Blair Clark's brownstone on East 48th Street. "Cal was in terrible physical shape, shaking, panicky," Clark would remember. "He was on drugs and sweating, lighting cigarettes, talking non-stop. They both stayed overnight at my house. I locked my door and in the middle of the night [Hochman] started beating on it. . . . She was worried about him, because he was breathing badly, and drinking. So I spent the rest of the night trying to calm everything down, trying to get him to sleep."[28]

The next day Cal was admitted by Dr. Bernard to the Neurological Institute at Columbia-Presbyterian Medical Center. There he was taken to the twelfth floor and placed in a locked ward behind two sets of locked doors. When Meredith visited him two weeks later, he found Cal still obstreperous, eating two pounds of chocolates and smoking several packs of cigarettes a day. "He was a factory of energy," Meredith would recall, though he was also strangely very gentle, spending his days writing and revising his translations "furiously and with a kind of crooked brilliance," talking about himself "in connection with Achilles, Alexander, Hart Crane, Hitler and Christ," all of which broke Meredith's heart.[29]

Cal's sixth attack was relatively mild, and by the end of the month he was discharged from the hospital. But by then the humiliation and strain of it all had proven too much. "Cal and I have come to the end of the road," Lizzie had informed Tate and Gardner on April 18, and she was getting a divorce as soon as she could. Cal was in one of his "half-well, half-sick states" at the moment, a condition very hard to gauge, when he felt both "confident and shallow about the future."[30] Worse, even after he left the hospital he still thought he was in love with Sandra. Lizzie and Harriet were wonderful, he told Lizzie, but he meant to set up an apartment with Sandra over on the East Side. That meant four apartments and four rents: the new apartment at 85 East End Avenue with Sandra, the Riverside apartment, the Boston apartment, and the West 67th Street apartment, still empty, still awaiting its new owners.

When Dr. Bernard continued to support Cal in his delusion, Lizzie went back to Boston. That simple tactic was enough, apparently, for reality to begin flooding back into Cal. Within days he was calling Dr. Bernard to say he wanted to go back home. Then he simply walked out on Hochman. When he returned to Lizzie this time he was shattered. A year later he would speak of the affair to Bishop as "a slightly malarial memory," though he could see that Hochman herself had had a "surprising energy and freshness, a slice of the new age, full of references, interests and rhythms," a way of seeing that until then had been utterly strange to him.[31] But he and Lizzie were "very much back together and both feel as if we had been tossed in blankets," he wrote the Tates at the end of May 1961, "particularly now as we stare at the mountain of a four-fold move: New York to Boston, New York to Maine, the Boston house to our new New York apartment, Boston to Maine." He'd turned in the manuscript of *Imitations* and found himself momentarily unemployed "and in one of those dreadful empty vacation periods between bursts of writing." The following evening, he added, he planned to attend the American Academy festival, where he would wind up sitting between Phyllis McGinley and Rolfe Humphries, "old enemies that I go thru the ritual of being very polite to."[32]

On the morning of June 15 he found himself walking down the street from his East End apartment, only to see a figure walking toward him: "a dirty untucked shirt, red, bulging, drink-gone face, a sort of pirate, all shapeless red and waiting—and when I got nearer it held a dollar bill and asked me to buy him a bottle of wine." But his "puritan morals and squeamishness" had joined forces and he'd moved on. By sharp contrast, he found himself one day later staying in a luxurious room at the Beverly Hills Hotel in Los Angeles, taking part in a CBS film about Boris Pasternak. He'd been flown out first class, "a second vodka martini brought without asking, two sparkling burgundies, part of a chicken stuffed with butter," and had dwelt on the distances separating Dr. Zhivago riding across the vast spaces of Russia by train and himself looking down on "1000 miles (ten miles a minute) of uninhabited Rockies and deserts—real dust oceans," feeling like the "last parasite of the Tsars." The Boston house had just been sold and he was feeling "dull and grieved" about the death of his Boston years. "All that life!", he sighed.[33]

But Lizzie too was thinking. Thinking "about the winter and trying to see how" she could "learn to manage it." She wondered about her own disintegration in New York, and worried about the estrangement she and Cal still felt toward each other. She hoped Cal would not be so horrified by the idea of settling into their new home that he would want to flee it. For her part, she would do what she could to make his home and daily life such that he would never be sick again.[34]

By July, though over his mania by then, Lowell was still obsessed with the idea of writing an epic poem on Hitler and World War II, "done more or less chronologically, short scenes, prose, strict and free verse . . . many styles." It would take "many years to do," he wrote Bishop, and would free him at last of writing about himself. In this way he could bring in history and "perhaps catch a great chunk of the times we have endured." By the time he did come to write his epic poem about evil in the modern world, he would call it *History*. As for his latest breakdown, he told Bishop he'd been okay for the past two months. But this sort of thing had happened to him so often now that he felt "a little cut off" from the human race.

This time he'd been "less high and [less] in an allegorical world . . . and not so broken down afterwards." During these periods, he felt as if his mother's moralizing were wrestling in him with his father's optimism. Somewhere along the way he'd decided both his parents had been wrong and that the truth lay elsewhere, only to find himself talking "like both of them at once."[35] He spoke of his book of translations, bigger now, and better worth dedicating to Bishop. But the last poem, ostensibly dedicated to Hannah Arendt, would really be dedicated to Lizzie. A translation of Rilke's *"Die Tauben"* ("Pigeons"), Lowell wrenched it from the chronology of the rest of the volume to place it last. It was a poem about the need to go home again, in effect a glossing on what he'd said in "Skunk Hour." "The same old flights," it began wearily, the same old rounds,

> the same old homecomings,
> dozens of each per day,
> but at last the pigeon gets clear of the pigeon-house . . .
> What is home, but a feeling of homesickness
> for the flight's lost moment of fluttering terror?
>
> Back in the dovecote, there's another bird,
> by all odds the most beautiful,

one that never flew out, and can know nothing of gentleness . . .
Still, only by suffering the rat-race in the arena
can the heart learn to beat. . . .

Over non-existence arches the all-being—
thence the ball thrown almost out of bounds
stings the hand with the momentum of its drop—
body and gravity,
miraculously multiplied by its mania to return.[36]

The previous fall Lowell had written Powers that he'd spent twelve hours one Sunday squiring Harriet and her four-year-old friend, Jacob Epstein, around the Bronx Zoo. "They began by a long dialogue on how they would destroy each other, down the chimney with the fire going, into the river with a rock etc. and ended chasing each other under chairs at the Central Park Tavern through angry dignified M. Hulot waiters." At three and a half, Harriet was already full of interruptions, insisting her father speak into her toy telephone, then clopping about in Lizzie's high heels. Mostly she spoke an "unintelligible dialogue, made up of contralto laughs." After a day with her, Lizzie had taken to quoting Leslie Fiedler's maxim that children were moral imbeciles.[37]

But now, in the high summer of '61, and back in Castine, he could report to Cousin Harriet how much his little daughter had matured: "Last week after an outburst, she said, 'I've been thinking and I'm going to be much better'—no more thumb-sucking, finger-smelling, demands for between meal pink cupcakes etc." Then at the end, she'd added, "I've been doing a lot of thinking, and there are ways you could improve, Mama." So, he could see, the age of criticism had begun, and they were "no longer seen through a glass darkly, as gods, but as we are." More frighteningly, they were surrounded now by a "great whirl of children: 3 Gardners from the Brickyard, 3 Philip Booths . . . four Canon John Pyles, two boys to seven girls . . . while their parents sat in the barn, sipping gin and tonic and musing profundities."[38]

"Cal has no native talent," Booth wrote in his journal that Fourth of July weekend. "His natural frames of reference are as historical-literary as my dream. Even his most pedestrian associations are freestyle." As when they'd gone down to the Town Wharf to visit a Navy submarine tied up alongside *The State of Maine,* which had been opened to the public for the day. Vertical ladders, narrow passages. "Tell me," Cal asks Booth afterwards, "are the men who sail that thing *Marines?*" Booth explains; Cal shakes his head: "Oh, I should have *known* that." He is momentarily embarrassed. "But it is by just such associative leaps that some of Cal's best poems get written."[39]

Cal was back in New York for two weeks in mid-July to teach and settle the furniture into the new apartment. Then, back in Castine, he began work on his trilogy of plays, *The Old Glory*, starting with a version of Melville's *Benito Cereno*. Cereno is yet another shadow portrait of Lowell, the story, as he explained to Cousin Harriet, centering on "an honest but rather thick-skulled American sea-captain from Duxbury, Mass., who spends the day on board a Spanish slave ship in 1799, unaware that the slaves have seized the ship and killed most of the Spaniards. The hero is a sort of Henry Jamesian innocent abroad."[40] He was writing the play to satisfy the spirit at least of his Ford opera grant. Within a week he had a draft of the whole finished: forty-seven pages of "a sort of iambic free verse with a lot of show and charade and horror, more action than language."[41] All along he'd had in mind something with "grand Gerontionlike Elizabethan monologues." Instead, all had turned out "terse, rapid and direct." Moreover, he'd written it so quickly he'd stunned even himself.[42]

"For the last two weeks," he wrote Bishop on August 7, "I haven't had a drop to drink. . . . I have so many holes in my souls [sic], I imagine this is the only way for me to go through the rich jungle of New York on my own feet." The truth was that he'd had "too gay a time" in New York in July with an old Kenyon classmate and Leonie Adams. Earlier that summer he'd gone out to Staten Island to take part in a writers' conference at Wagner College. Saul Bellow was there as representative novelist, Edward Albee as playwright, he as poet. In the *New York Times* that morning as he rode the Lexington Avenue local downtown, he'd read that Kennedy had just called up the reserves. Directly across from those headlines was another article noting that 70 million people might be killed if the United States and Russia went to war. With Kennedy in office, there was this weird sense that the common man no longer intended either to be pushed around as he had with Eisenhower, or to be embarrassed by American U-2 spy planes downed over Russia.

Then, at the ferry docking he'd met "the conference leech and two conference morons," had given his two-hour class, all the while maintaining a "very distant, ascetic and philosophical" posture. Afterwards he'd had dinner with the conference leech and a beard announcing himself as "the best poet of 24 in America," followed by a night of "stifling sleepless heat, sounds of intimacy, outrage and drinking." When he'd tried to go swimming along the beach that afternoon, he'd found condoms floating at six-inch intervals on the tide and five-year-old boys blowing them up like balloons. Out on the horizon he could see the Brooklyn skyline and the *Queen Mary* making for Manhattan.[43] It was all rather amusing, except for the fact that along these same Staten Island beaches—though he did not say so—his young mother had walked forty-five years before, carrying him, her only child, and so unhappy, she'd later told him, she wanted to die.

He himself felt now as if he'd been "washed up on land and given a new suit, after six months of floating." The "cancerous impatience" he'd inherited from his mother and which had eaten at him for so long was at last wearing away, and life was becoming for him "much too lovely not to live out."[44] Especially in Castine, a world altogether different from New York, though it too was near the all-devouring ocean. To Taylor he described a trip out to Mount Desert Island with Lizzie, Harriet, and Betty Dawson, their New Jersey "colored nurse," slow, afraid of snakes and nature in general, and carrying her $175 Polaroid camera with her wherever she went. One day he'd driven up to Bar Harbor to show Betty the beauties of the Maine landscape, but her only comment had been: "They have dinky roads like this down in Virginia."

Mostly he spent his days writing and living "an awfully staid and scarecrowish non-drinking life," reading Harriet "stories about Aunt Jemima's home life and the eel who wanted red slippers." At night he and Lizzie fell asleep at ten wondering how they would ever unpack their new apartment—"80 cartons of books, shelves that go to the ceiling."[45] By late August he was finished with the third play of *The Old Glory* trilogy: "Endecott and the Red Cross." Like the second, "My Kinsman, Major Molineux," it was based on one of Hawthorne's tales. Together the three plays, 110 pages in manuscript, would make an evening in the theater and a book. "God knows if they are any good," he wrote Meredith on September 8, "but change is fascinating after short poems." He'd always wondered why someone like Eliot had written plays, but could see now that there was "a sea of energy inside one that can't come out in poems and will come out this way."[46]

Leaving Castine to return to New York that fall, he told Adrienne Rich, was like coming back from the moon. He'd spent whole days that delicious summer conversing with his daughter, "limitlessly amused" by her wonderfully cumbersome syntax, content to read week-old newspapers and *Time* magazines filled with news "that never happened." One article had noted—without a hint of irony—that in a nuclear age it was impossible to write like either Jane Austen or Tolstoy. He'd also read of some young American telling P. G. Wodehouse that atomic bombs had the capacity to destroy a third of the world, to which Wodehouse had responded, "I can't wait!" How pleasant then to be back in New York, "the center of things, a place where things really happen and surely a must on any list of Russian atomic targets."[47]

By month's end the Lowells were settled into their new 67th Street apartment and Cal was teaching Milton and a writing workshop at the New School for Social Research downtown on 12th Street. He loved going to Central Park with his daughter, or even crossing it as he did that fall on his three-times-a-week schedule to see his psychiatrist on the East Side. Harriet began school, going "off alone . . . on the school bus with one of those frightened but determined looks she is now old enough to have," Lizzie wrote Rich. "I wept, for just what I don't know." She was exhausting herself just trying to stay "calm and subdued" with Cal in New York.[48]

But for Lizzie as for him a lot was over now, "or begun to be over," Lowell wrote Bishop, "the sweat of moving in, the nervousness of facing the damage of last year and facing it down here in New York." After ten weeks he was still drinking nothing stronger than Welsh's grape juice mixed with ginger ale, though he still felt "a little grudging and unsociable around six o'clock," his usual cocktail hour. But what really had him on edge that fall was the "queer, half apocalyptic, nuclear feeling in the air, as tho nations had died and were now anachronistic, yet in their anarchic death-throes would live on for ages troubling us, threatening the likelihood of life continuing."

He did not at all like feeling autumnal. And yet what was life, after all, but "our one-way trip to the dust"? Well, we would all "get there, still not understanding, for all's incomplete and not to be understood." Waiting for a haircut at the Boston Ritz in early September, he'd picked up a copy of *Life* to read about "megalitonic warfare, the 96 per cent that we and Russia could destroy of each other, the planes with bombs 24 hours in the air, any one able to get jittery or answer a false warning and let go." Once in the chair, however, he noted that the barber, "a brownish, baldish, spectacled man," looked rather like William Carlos Williams, and—amidst all the fever of atomic warfare in the air—was talking about something as simple as "fishing for flounder in Boston harbor," the day always "spoiled by one or two drunks." The world's fine, the fellow had reassured Cal, "except for the people in it."[49]

But the nuclear fever was still very much on Cal's mind at month's end, when he told Meredith it seemed "a hideous comedy" for the two superpowers to be charging "the globe with so much ruin." He'd felt that way about the bombings in the last war, but now the issue had come to a head, and seemed to be on everyone's mind. He'd considered joining the unilateral disarmament group, but had so far avoided that option because he hated "the arid, logic-chopping debater's world of the righteous cause."[50] What was this nuclear situation after all, he told Mary McCarthy, but "an historical grimace of terror." He did not mean that the whole house was "about to blow up in our faces, but rather that unless things change and nations step down from their stockpiles, this will happen." Somehow, just now, the cards had been dealt all wrong.[51]

One day that October, he told Jarrell, Anton Webern's music had been playing on the radio. "It's like wild animals through the woods walking," four-year-old Harriet had said to him. And then, "It's like a lot of spiders crying together, but without tears."[52] She had just hit on what he'd been feeling all that fall. Spiders, like those in his Jonathan Edwards poem of twenty years before, suspended above the fire, and crying without tears. "Back and forth," he wrote now, in the first lyric he'd written since "For the Union Dead" more than a year before, as he stared into the uncomprehending face of the grandfather clock in his apartment:

> *back and forth*
> *goes the tock, tock, tock*
> *of the orange, bland, ambassadorial*
> *face of the moon*
> *on the grandfather clock.*
>
> *All autumn, the chafe and jar*
> *of nuclear war;*
> *we have talked our extinction to death.*
> *I swim like a minnow*
> *behind my studio window.*
>
> *Our end drifts nearer,*
> *the moon lifts,*
> *radiant with terror.*
> *The state*
> *is a diver under a glass bell.*
>
> *A father's no shield*
> *for his child.*
> *We are a lot of wild*
> *spiders crying together,*
> *but without tears. . . .*[53]

He spent much of the fall reworking *The Old Glory* so that it would act, and waited for word of the reception of *Imitations*. "I seem to be getting a rain of mangling reviews," he wrote Randall in early November, *"Time Magazine* and now Dudley Fitts [in the *New York Times*] who says my [*Imitations*] should be read in a salt mine with a grain of salt."[54] He complained to Alvarez about the "longish panning review" in *Time* which had dismissed half his poems as bearing "the smudge of translation" and the other half as the work of "some talented foreigner." Then there were the "three hysterical Frenchmen" who had written to *Encounter* to say that his Rimbaud translations were "an insane slaughter and hopeless trash." On the other hand, "every decent judge from Edmund Wilson down" had liked at least some of them. He felt misunderstood, which was after all, he figured, not such a bad feeling.[55] What he'd attempted in these poems was something akin to Thomas Wyatt's lyric versions of Petrarch: imitations inspired by the original rather than strict translations. In spite of the adverse criticisms, however, *Imitations* would win the Bollingen Prize for translation in 1962.

He began writing again, completing seven new poems between mid-October and year's end: an elegy to one of his St. Mark's classmates, "Alfred Corning Clark," "Eye and Tooth" (a farewell to his contact lenses), a poem for Jean called "Old Flame," two for Bishop ("Water" and "The Scream"), "Middle Age," and "Fall 1961." "Writing's hell, isn't it?", he'd complained to Isabella Gardner that October. "I tire of my turmoil and feel everyone else has, and long for a Horatian calm." The new poems, however, were anything but that.[56]

The Lowells spent New Year's Eve, 1961, with the Taylors in Columbus, Ohio, playing "a sleepy rubber of bridge" before retiring at eleven-thirty.[57] In early January, Cal went up to Yale for a Bollingen Committee meeting, then threw a party for Tate which lasted far into the evening, at the end of which Tate seemed "transfixed by bourbon."[58] Whenever Belle left the room, he wrote Taylor afterwards, all Tate could talk about was trying to bed Spender's wife, Natasha. At one point Tate asked Lizzie for a kiss; at another, he embraced Cal and told him he was his best man friend, his only faults being that he was too generous and had no sense of reality.

Then, wearing one of Harriet's green cardboard birthday derbies, Tate summoned the little girl to his side with great pomp. "You are a Kentucky Belle because your mother is a Kentucky Belle," he told her. "You are very dear to me because your parents are very dear to me. You will be dear to me when you are older." ("One had a feeling she would be much more dear to him then," Cal couldn't help noting.) Harriet had looked him over, then answered, *"If* you're still alive." Later still in the evening, when Tate began describing himself as at heart a southern puritan, Lizzie retorted that he was about as puritanical as an ape. "All fun to tell," Cal had to admit, "but rather deadly to live through." The man was "so smart and alive sober," he sighed, but what he saw mostly now was Tate's "vacation evening side."[59]

But Tate wasn't the only poet who showed Lowell his "vacation evening side" that winter. On the evening of February 9, 1962, in snow, Cal crossed over to Staten Island on the ferry to read on a bill at Wagner College with the thirty-five-year-old New York poet Frank O'Hara. Willard Maas had arranged the mismatch, perhaps not knowing—as certainly Lowell did not—that for various reasons, including a perception that Lowell was one of those stuffy New England poets, O'Hara was "pissed off" at Lowell. In the news that day the tabloids had headlined Lana Turner's collapse at a party, so that on the ferry ride over to Staten Island, O'Hara had composed one of his readymades. It was called, simply, "Poem," and began: "Lana Turner has collapsed." The audience was delighted with it. Then, instead of reading for his allotted twenty minutes, O'Hara went on for nearly an hour. The gesture was dazzling, defiant, then tedious and bitchy, as O'Hara had no doubt intended. When Lowell got up, he began by saying pointedly that he would only be reading for a few minutes. He also apologized for not having written a poem on the spot.[60]

Just after the New Year Lowell was offered a two-year Boyleston Professorship at Harvard, after Richard Wilbur had turned down a full-time position there. Harvard had a lot of advantages for him, Lowell wrote Wilbur that January. He could teach one semester each year, two classes, two days a week, from September through December, for $8,500 a year, about double what he made now teaching twice that number of courses at the New School. Moreover, he would have better students and could keep a foot in Boston, which he was already beginning to miss. He wished he cared more about teaching, and admired Wilbur's ability to stay content at Wesleyan, for he knew how hard it was "for most people—almost everyone at times—not to gorge and guzzle and drink all the whiskey in the bottle." It was the sort of self-control over unlimited ambition, he added, which he admired in Hardy, Walter de la Mare, and E. M. Forster.[61]

On March 1, Cal celebrated his forty-fifth birthday in Portland, Connecticut, with Wilbur, whose birthday fell on the same day. Cal must have been feeling the touch of mortality on his shoulder now, Wilbur would recall, for at one point he told Wilbur that his father had died in his early sixties, which meant that he himself had fifteen years more to get said what he needed to say. He needed that party, for the winter of '62 had brought one illness after another for the Lowells: chicken pox, flu, tonsilitis, bronchitis, piles, coughs, scarlet fever. By March Cal was down to 173 pounds, less, he told Bishop, "than at any time since school," and looked "all too much like a poet." As for his mental health, he was using Bishop's physician now, Dr. Annie Baumann. "Brisk sunny visits," he noted, "pills, shots, conferences behind closed doors, conversations with her all-German nursing staff." It almost made "illness a treat."[62]

But some deep change seemed to be taking place in him now, he confided to Berryman, so that all winter he'd had the "uncomfortable feeling of dying into rebirth." But this was not "the sick, dizzy allegorized thing such words suggest and which I've felt going off my rocker," he explained. No, this was "the flat prose of coming to the end of one way of life—whittled down and whittled down, and picking up nothing new though always about to." It seemed to have something to do with his dream about Philip Rahv, in which Rahv had "just married a society lady and bought a house on Beacon Street.

[Rahv] was picking up everything I had carefully thrown away all my life—golden keys of social ease, till at the end, his two [imaginary] sons had just entered Groton."[63] To Bishop he expanded on the dream in another letter later that same day. Rahv was ascending "the social ladder rung by rung," he told her, even as he was climbing down, and had decided to send his boys to Groton because, as he'd said in his New York accent, it was "de only place to send them," while his Harriet was about to graduate instead from some local public school. Was he whittling away his inheritance, he wondered? His last words to Rahv had been: "Is this what *Partisan Review* was all about?" To which Rahv had replied, "Of course." How snobbish these old rebel bohemians really were, he saw, for who else besides Rahv—and Mary McCarthy—believed in society any more?[64] Cal's whole way of life seemed to be slipping away from him.

Similarly, he confided to Bishop, he was finding even Henry Adams (his old Bible), and the whole New England style which had so shaped his autobiography and *Life Studies,* a terrible bore now. Writing in that fashion seemed rather like bringing coals to Newcastle, though he would not have wanted anyone else to say it. Adams himself, he knew, must have understood the limitations of a Boston-centered view of things, known too it was "a real illness in him—one he loved to exploit." What was that style, after all, but "a state anyone from our background should go through to be honest and alive, and then drop"? But to maintain it after a certain point was rather "like calling malaria life . . . real malaria under the jokes, exaggerations and epigrams, a sort of Baudelairian gallantry. But who could *want* what Empson says somewhere to learn a style from a despair?"[65]

In March he went up to Yale for a literary gathering and sat in a corner with Norman Holmes Pearson, ignoring everyone and talking about Pound, whom Pearson had recently visited in Italy. Pound, nearing eighty, and deeply depressed, was down now to 130 pounds and had all but stopped talking. He'd asked Pearson to be remembered by his friends in the States, and to be "forgiven his harshness to each."[66] Now Lowell wrote Pound himself. He remembered those long afternoons in Washington fourteen years before, "the cookies, the arguments, the dangerous rides home with other visitors."[67] And though just that day he'd written Kazin that Pound's anti-Semitism was "like the voice of a drunkard telling people in cars to drive through the pedestrians,"[68] a voice which nothing could condone, still, Pound as poet was "a hero, full of courage, and humor and compassion." Now, however, that Ezra was approaching the end, Cal fondly hoped he might feel happy about his life, "and the thousands of kindnesses you have done your friends, and how you've been a fountain to them." So, he added, "you've been to me, and I miss the old voice." He was sending along a copy of *Imitations,* "real translations," like

Pound's own, the Leopardi, Villon, and Rimbaud "first read by me after reading your criticism."

On March 19 Lowell flew down to Puerto Rico with his family for ten days "to bake away our colds and the midwinter grayness and grind of the city."[69] It was wonderful, he wrote Bishop afterwards, especially San Juan, "a lovely old sort of southern town," and "the millionaire hotel world which we saw on visits to Blair Clark and Lillian Hellman." It had all been very soothing, even the "two fruitless days" he'd spent big-game fishing.[70] Back in New York at the end of the month, he found himself "shaken," he confessed to Edmund Wilson, partly by the beauty of Puerto Rico, "with its sun and water," partly by "all the creeping Puerto Rican life, which is all around us here on the West Side, but which is revealed there in greater purity." It was a teeming, vibrant, foreign way of life, he could feel, and one which just might be around long after his culture—and Wilson's—had been completely swallowed up.[71]

In early April he flew out to Minneapolis for a reading and a visit with the Tates, Berryman, and Powers. The Tates seemed more themselves in Minneapolis than they did in New York, he told Bishop, and he could see that Belle Gardner had "saved Allen's life from the long inspired nightmare" of Caroline Gordon. Belle might be slow and imperious, but "not to Allen, and sane—no crazy agrarian axe to grind!" Berryman, on the other hand, whom he'd not seen in ten years, seemed "utterly spooky, teaching brilliant classes, spending week-ends in the sanitarium, drinking, seedy, a little bald, often drunk, married to a girl of twenty-one from a Catholic parochial college, white, innocent beyond belief, just pregnant." Berryman was living in two modest cinderblock rooms near the university, and when Cal had visited there, Kate was asleep in one, "getting through the first child pains," and John in the other, among "a thousand books . . . going into the 7th year on a long poem that fills a suitcase and is all spoken by John's first son (seven) from his second marriage." These were drafts for *The Dream Songs,* a long sequence of poems as strange as Berryman himself. The *Songs* were "a maddening work of genius, or half genius, in John's later obscure, tortured, wandering style, full of parentheses, slang no one ever spoke, jagged haunting lyrical moments etc." One shuddered, he added, "to think of the child's birth."[72]

Among the books Lowell read that spring were Katherine Anne Porter's *Ship of Fools,* "very grim" and "the only *long* novel by an American since *An American Tragedy* that needed to be long"; Jarrell's new collection of essays, "very dashing and satirical and sad, "a sort of American *Culture and Anarchy;* and Edmund Wilson's *Patriotic Gore,* his best book so far, with "Plutarchan portraits" of Lincoln, Grant, and Oliver Wendell Holmes. But, really, he wondered, who read any more? After giving his students at the New School "a laborious six weeks on Pope, Dryden, Dr. Johnson, Goldsmith etc.," he'd been appalled to learn that they'd read "only one poet before Hopkins—Donne of course." He had felt "taken in the flank" because he'd been "all pointed to explain the new poetry as a continuation, change and revolution of the old." Except, of course, that no one knew the tradition any more with the exception, perhaps, of a few English professors.[73] Just now he was "on a Wordsworth and Blake jag," and was hoping to learn from them how to do poems "that would hit all in one flash, though loaded with subtleties of art and passion underneath." He was even studying "great clumsy structures like Wordsworth's *Leech Gatherer,* that somehow lift the great sail and catch the wind." But where were there poets in the States with the old "brute energy, flash, power," poets who could drive "a sentence or a stanza to its mark"? Poetry seemed now in the hands of pedants who merely bored one to death.[74]

On May 11, 1962, he was one of two hundred guests who attended a dinner at the White House in honor of André Malraux, French Minister of Culture and author of *Man's Fate.* It was a gracious Kennedy evening, and Lowell was high on the list of those invited. He was Kennedy's exact contemporary; both had been at Harvard in 1936, and both were friends of Blair Clark. Among those present that evening were Bobby Kennedy, Marilyn Monroe, Arthur Miller, Arthur Schlesinger, Jr., "absolutely top of the world squiring the Kennedy sisters," Archibald MacLeish, "who told me the trumpets made his heart beat, New York types like Marc Rothko, [McGeorge] Bundy drunk, Mrs. [Anne] Lin[d]bergh, Red Warren with whom I had a frantic search for the men's room. . . . Three wines, champagne, Stern and Istomin playing a long Schubert trio." At one point Kennedy had made a rather graceful joke that "the White House was becoming almost a café for intellectuals." The whole event had been rather frivolous and glamorous and Camelot-like, and Malraux himself had somehow "refrained from saying anything objectionable."[75]

But when he thought more about that evening, Lowell became troubled. "Except for you," he wrote Edmund Wilson at the end of May, "everyone there seemed addled with adulation at having been invited. It was all good fun but next morning you read that the President had sent the 7th fleet to Laos, or"—Lowell was thinking of the Bay of Pigs fiasco of the spring before—"he might have invaded Cuba again—not that he will, but I feel we intellectuals play a very pompous and frivolous role." After all, it was the writer's duty to be a window, "not window-dressing." Now "of all times," he added, "the sword hangs over us and our children, and not a voice is lifted."[76]

On June 4, the Lowells flew off with Harriet (now five) and Harriet's young guardian, a Radcliffe student named Toni Kern, to spend the summer in Latin

America as guests of the Cultural Congress: Lowell as poet, Hardwick as prose writer. Their first stop would be a ten-day layover in Trinidad, then Belem for another ten days, then on to Rio de Janiero on June 25 for six weeks (the stay would get longer), before flying on to Argentina, Chile, and Peru. Cal had prepared a one hundred-poem anthology of English and American poetry translated into Spanish and Portuguese which he planned to read in Brazil, the American section beginning with Frost and ending with Snodgrass and Rich, the English beginning with Hardy and ending with Larkin and Ted Hughes. But how little he or even his best American students knew about Latin American poetry, he confessed to Bishop. He was especially nervous about addressing highly cultivated audiences in Rio de Janiero. Despite his best efforts, he was afraid he would be too "shabbily prepared" to meet them, and was sure that, particularly with the Brazilian intellectuals' knowledge of French and Latin culture, he would be dismissed as little better than some North American barbarian.[77]

The first stopover was Trinidad, where they spent the weekend with Derek Walcott and his family in a beach cabin high on a cliff overlooking the Atlantic. Walcott would remember meeting the Lowells at the Queen's Park Hotel and being so flustered he'd mistakenly called Lizzie Edna St. Vincent Millay, to which she'd replied, "I'm not that old yet." But soon they had all warmed to each other. That night, after everyone else had gone to bed, Cal showed Walcott some of his poems from *Imitations,* which they read together by gaslight. He would remember Cal pointing to the Hugo and Rilke translations, and asking Walcott what he thought. "It was a very flattering and warm feeling to have this fine man with his great reputation really asking me what I thought," Walcott would recall. "He did that with a lot of people, very honestly, humbly, and directly. . . . He kept a picture of Peter, my son, and Harriet for a long time in his wallet."[78]

On June 18 the Lowells were met in Para by Keith Botsford of the Cultural Congress. With him they travelled down the coast of Brazil via Recife and Bahia to Rio de Janiero, where they took up residence at the Copacabana Palace. Cal's job was to give interviews and press conferences and attend dinners. In the volatile political situation of the moment, his presence was meant to counteract leftist writers like Pablo Neruda. Over the next two months he performed his duties well, but by late August he had begun to speed up again, and as he did so, he told Elizabeth Bishop once again that he was in love with her. That Bishop had confessed to her psychiatrist that she too loved him, "next best to Lota," did not make things easy for her either.[79]

By mid-August, however, Bishop was aware that Cal was drinking far too much. He was obsessed with the Cold War, found both the United States and the USSR equally culpable, and spoke continually of the Bomb. He repeated himself and would listen to no one. At one point Bishop asked him not to come to her apartment before mid-afternoon, but he insisted on coming anyway, at all hours, because, he said, he found it soothing. He protested his love and eternal friendship over and over. But Bishop had heard it all before and by now knew the routine by heart.

She even wondered if Cal *knew* he was becoming ill and was doing nothing to stop it. One night he got into a heated argument over the subject of Sartre. On another he disappeared with a woman novelist. Lizzie was frantic with worry and went over the signs of incipient mania step by step with Bishop and Lota. There was a blow-up on the phone with Cal when Bishop tried to tell him that she was having dinner with someone else. "I'm important too," he had told her, accusingly. More than once she broke down and cried with the strain of it all. Then, on September 1, Lizzie, Harriet, and Toni sailed for home while Cal stayed on, insisting on going on to Argentina.

On the 4th he flew to Buenos Aires with Botsford in attendance as his "lieutenant," treating him as his flunky, making him pay for everything, and calling him a homosexual. He was drinking constantly now and even managed to get Botsford drunk. He insulted the U.S. Ambassador to Argentina by bringing along a group of Communists to a party in his honor, and then— more dangerously—tweaked the general who was about to become Argentina's president. He accused the cultural attaché of being an illiterate. He waxed eloquently on the subject of Hitler. He decided he would not teach that fall at Harvard, but stay on in Buenos Aires for another month until Mary McCarthy and Stephen Spender arrived for the PEN Conference. He read the entire volume of *Life Studies* to an audience, without a single comment. On a boulevard in the capital, he undressed and climbed up onto an equestrian statue. He threw away his anti-manic pills. He began asking for his old girlfriend, Sandra Hochman, again.

Four days later Botsford was so exhausted he flew back to Rio alone, leaving Cal to fend for himself. On the morning of September 10, Bishop called Botsford and learned that Cal was now alone in Buenos Aires. Botsford was having a party the following night, he explained, but planned to return for Cal after that. Furious that Botsford would leave Cal alone in his condition, she told him to get hold of Niles Bond at the embassy in Rio and inform the Argentinian embassy just how sick Cal was.

Bond called Bishop back that afternoon. He'd contacted Buenos Aires about Cal, then Dr. Bernard in New York, and located a psychiatrist in Buenos Aires. Bernard gave Botsford the name of the medicine Cal was to take, and insisted that he be flown to New York at once. The next day Bishop received a cable from Cal. "DEAREST ELIZABETH," it read, "COME HERE AND JOIN ME ITS PARADISE!"[80]

Cal meanwhile was partying (and arm-wrestling) with the exiled left-wing Spanish poet Rafael Alberti somewhere in Buenos Aires. When Botsford tried to contact Cal, Alberti's friends hid him from what they saw as a CIA attempt to kidnap their friend. Finally, when Cal returned to his hotel with an Argentine woman named Luisa, an ambulance was called. In his full-blown manic state, it took six paramedics to wrestle him into a straitjacket. Then he was taken to the Clinica Bethlehem, where his arms and legs were strapped and he was injected with 2,000 milligrams of Thorazine four times a day until his blood turned once more to lead. As he lay there, struggling helplessly, confused and afraid, he begged Botsford to help calm him by whistling.

13

For the Union Dead

1962–1964

On October 1, 1962, accompanied by a doctor and nurse, Blair Clark arrived at the Clinica Bethlehem and escorted a heavily sedated Cal back to New York. Even on the trip back, however, Cal managed to fall in love with the stewardess, who left the aircraft at Asunción. It took everything to restrain him from following her so that he could marry her and begin a new life.[1] At Idlewild he was met by Lizzie and Dr. Bernard and driven directly to the Institute for Living in Hartford, where he would remain for the next six weeks. While still in Buenos Aires, he'd written Bill Alfred, saying he was at death's door with flu and malaria, and asking him to get someone to take over his classes at Harvard until the end of October. As it turned out, he would not begin teaching there until the following spring.[2]

"I come home days now from the hospital," he wrote Bishop in early November, "and will be entirely finished with the hospital in four days. So all has passed over, not too gruellingly." He'd put off everything for the moment, even readings, to sit in his study "and read and snooze, or listen to records." It sounded like old age, he knew, but wasn't. He'd been run down from "over-exuberance" and a lung infection contracted in Argentina, the latter now happily gone without a trace. During his illness, he realized, he'd managed to avoid both the Washington conference of poets *and* the Cuban missile crisis. Stanley Kunitz had caught him up on the conference. Delmore had been jailed "for shouting while drinking by himself," and later rescued by, of all people, John Berryman; Kunitz had been insulted by Oscar Williams and in turn had called Williams a worm, then nearly hit him; and Randall had read a tribute to both Cal and Bishop. Each poet Cal had seen had given him a different account "of what was good, odd or great."[3]

To make up for his "long summer vacation," Lowell buried himself once again in his work "like a mole,"[4] he told Berryman, writing new poems and translating Horace, Góngora, and Quevedo, as well as Juvenal's Tenth Satire, all of which would appear in his catch-all book, *Near the Ocean,* five years later. Among the new poems he worked on that fall were "Water," "Dropping South" (about dropping in a dream on the Copacabana beach in Rio, where he had in fact stayed), and "Caligula," a "long unfinished dramatic monologue on my namesake,"[5] which rehearsed his recent madness:

> *Your mind burned, you were God, a thousand plans*
> *ran zig-zag, zig-zag. You began to dance*
> *for joy, and called your menials to arrange*
> *deaths for the gods. You worshipped your great change,*
> *took a cold bath, and rolled your genitals*
> *until they shrank to marbles. . . .*
>
> > *Animals*
> *fattened for your arena suffered less*
> *than you in dying—yours the lawlessness*
> *of something simple that has lost its law,*
> *my namesake, and the last Caligula.*[6]

To his surprise, he told Bishop, he was once again writing in strict meter, even sonnets, "not at all to my intention, and a fact that I find disturbing to my theories of how poetry should be written." He was even working on poems he knew he could never use, such as ten sonnets of Gérard de Nerval that vanished "to nothing in English, words for a symphony for the dead, that Leonard Bernstein wanted me to try," having so far produced only "a bilge of declamation." Was it, he wondered, the muse who had seized him now, or merely "the spirit of rhetoric"?[7]

For four months he wrote almost no one. It was only on Christmas Eve, with the sound of snow chisels banging through the sidewalk ice to the concrete pavement below, that he broke his long silence to return to the world by writing to Bishop. Harriet was now attending the prestigious Dalton School on the East Side, he told her. And the night before Jack Thompson had brought over a Mexican poet and a young Brazilian play director whom he'd met in Belem, decked out in a gray muscovite hat, who had proceeded to attack the United States' exploitation of South America.

On the larger political scene, the Cuban missile crisis had overnight altered the charged atmosphere of New York from the depression and unnamed fear he'd felt so strongly only the year before. With the Kennedy-Khrushchev confrontation over the presence of missiles in Cuba, everyone had been "either exalted or scared out of [their] wits . . . and then relieved." Now—suddenly—there was "no criticism, and I think no government in my life time has been less hated."[8] Yet within a month he would be calling Kennedy's response to the crisis "the great gambler's stroke of luck on Cuba." Like most Americans, Lowell felt stunned and grateful for the lull in the Cold War, though "feeling strangely that we had little to do with it."[9]

Christmas Day he dined with his family and relatives at a hotel in New York, "overlooked by a small rotating Santa Claus." He'd dressed as Santa Claus for his daughter, he told Cousin Harriet, but had made the mistake of taking his costume off in front of her. At least, though, she still believed in God. When he looked at her now he already saw "a long-limbed restless girl in her teens, the last day I will lift her up. How long childhood is for a child, and how short for parents."[10]

Late January 1963: From his study Cal could look out on the yellow brick of the buildings surrounding him and on the season's "smoke-colored sky." He'd worked each day for the past three months at his poems and had at last finished them all. Now he was ready to come up for air. Recovering from his seventh attack had been rather like wrestling with a giant, he confided to Cousin Harriet. And though the struggle had been monstrous, at least he'd avoided being tossed completely out of the ring. In a week he would begin teaching the nineteenth-century American poets at Harvard: Emerson, Long-fellow, Bryant, James Russell Lowell, figures "so far in the past, that they are certainly no longer what one is trying to get away from."[11]

During the long winter strike of the *New York Times*, a number of New York writers, Hardwick among them, had begun a new magazine meant to rival the *Times's* book section in substance and format. It was called the *New York Review of Books*, and Lowell had personally guaranteed the bank loan to ensure its undertaking. "All the most distinguished and lively book reviewers and essayists in the country have been written or phoned for pieces," he told Bishop. "Now after two weeks they have almost all come through." The idea was "to make the first number so dazzling that even after *The New York Times* returns, people will want to keep the new magazine floating." The upside of the new venture was watching Lizzie's "wonderful energies" working for a new standard of excellence. The downside was the rushing around him of people with excoriated nerves, until he felt as if he were "in the fire and burnt-outness of some political or religious movement."[12]

Only now did he write Keith Botsford a letter of apology. He felt "a bit like the cat painfully backing down the telephone-pole it scooted up," he confessed, and thanked Botsford for seeing him "through the rough-house and phantasmagoria at the end in Argentina." He hoped some good at least had come out of the tour. "I am ashamed," he added simply, "of what I did." And though it was only seven above in New York, Brazil was everywhere around him in his apartment: "yellow, blue and red boat streamers" hanging from the second-story balcony," their "big silver slave's bangles" on display to impress visitors. Two poems had already come out of his trip south: "Dropping South," and "Buenos Aires," the latter about walking through the city "and trying to guess its history, present and past, from its statuary."[13]

That winter the deaths of the Elders began to mount. In late January 1963 came news of Frost's death at eighty-eight. "Walking by his house in Cambridge last Thanksgiving," Cal told Bishop, "I thought with some shame about how wrong I was to be bothered by his notoriety and showing off," for in truth the man's life had been "bounded and simple."[14] Though, as he noted in a piece he wrote now for the *New York Review of Books,* "under the camouflage" of the almost-farmer "there was always the Brahma crouching, a Whitman, a great-mannered bard. If God had stood in his sunlight, he would have elbowed God away with a thrust or a joke."[15]

Then, in early March, came the long-expected news of the death of William Carlos Williams. But Lowell had already bid his goodbyes to his old friend a year earlier, when he'd ended his essay on Williams with the memory of "seeing him out strolling on a Sunday after a heart-attack," the town seeming "to know him and love him and take him in its stride, as we will do with his great outpouring of books, his part in the air we breathe and will breathe."[16]

In February had come news of the suicide of his former student, Sylvia Plath, in her apartment in London. The full impact of that death would touch him only in the fall, when Lowell would read her "terrifying and stunning" posthumous poems in the British magazine, *Encounter.* It was an experience which left him (as it did Berryman) feeling as if "almost all other poetry were about nothing."[17] In his Preface to Plath's *Ariel* a year later, Lowell would speak of how, in her last poems, she had finally entered into herself, becoming "something imaginary, newly, wildly and subtly created—hardly a person at all, or a woman, certainly not another 'poetess,' but one of those super-real, hypnotic, great classical heroines." For him, Plath represented the "feminine rather than the female," he explained, though it was also true that Plath had managed to turn everything one thought of as "feminine" on its head.[18]

That winter Lowell did not find it easy having to face "18 frozen introverts" in his writing class at Harvard, and he wound up talking "too much poetry to too many embryonic poets." (By term's end his estimate of his Harvard students, as earlier with his Iowa students, would rise dramatically.) He had a room in Quincy House, he told Bishop, "very modern, all glass, with walls of unfinished cement brick," and received newspapers with titles like *India News* which came for the former occupant, a Mr. Sinha, "who has left behind something I've always dreamed of, a library made up of books I've never read." Each of his weeks was divided now into two short weeks, "each with its own air and space, instead of my old all of one cloth New York weeks." Each Monday morning he flew to Boston to teach, each Wednesday night he flew back to New York to write.[19]

By February 1963 he had enough work for a new book: twenty-two poems and twelve translations. He thought of calling it *An Eye for an Eye* (he would settle on *For the Union Dead* after his 1960 poem), and didn't know yet what he thought of this post–*Life Studies* work. Too often it seemed to him "all acid and mannerisms." Had he merely acquired a "mechanical appetite for publishing," doing what dozens of other writers were doing, only worse?[20] He had written much of the book against his imminent collapse and come out, he hoped, "more or less healed," beginning with free verse, then moving to more metrical poems, "more plated, far from conversation, metaphysical," the subjects more personal. Lastly he'd written in a surrealistic vein, these latest poems, he feared, being also the thinnest.[21]

But the deeper change for Lowell in these New York years was in his becoming, almost in spite of himself, more and more of a public figure. When he wrote Powers at the end of May to congratulate him for winning the National Book Award for *Morte D'Urban,* he spoke about the novel's central figure, a priest forced by circumstances to deal with all sorts of issues for which he was not prepared to deal. In fact Lowell was speaking of himself when he spoke of a "man forced by his position to have opinions and make decisions on all sorts of things he is really foggy about, forced to live through the alternatives of dropping out of life or forever talking through his hat, two infinities of nothingness." That at heart was his own situation, as it had been Dr. Zhivago's, though he was also aware that Powers had mercifully given his character a life set solidly in quotidian surroundings, surroundings which at least gave one "a kind of peace."[22]

In April he spent a weekend with the Ransoms at Kenyon. He heard Jarrell read at the 92nd Street YMHA, and was much taken by "The Lost World," Randall's long terza rima poem on his growing up in Hollywood. It was good, after so many years, he told Bishop, to see Randall finally on the brink of reaching "a gentle honest and inspired state of life."[23] Marianne Moore, approaching eighty now, was his guest at West 67th Street, and he wrote her afterwards to say that her "freshness and imagination" still left other poets, including himself, on "old derivative and used up roads."[24] In June he read with William Meredith at the Boston Arts Festival in memory of Frost; though the two had found themselves, he quipped to Anne Sexton, reading to an audience who'd been expecting Peter Ustinov and which had hardly heard of Frost let alone them.[25]

That summer he watched his six-year-old daughter ride around the yard of their house in Castine on her first trainer-wheel bicycle, and watched her too as she acted out her part in a pyramid in the local Fourth of July Parade. He was off alcohol again, though he wondered if it really were possible to live the unnatural strain of some other life "that could be thrown into your own and remove all its inertia and blindness." He wrote a poem for Cousin Harriet, completely incapacitated now by strokes and slowly dying in her steamy Washington apartment. He thought of the poem as "tender, peaceful and sad," and titled it "Soft Wood."[26] Somehow his Scholar Gypsy seals, returning each year to Castine as regularly as the seasons, caught the essential truth of downeast Maine in a mode altogether softer and more healing than the world he'd offered in "Skunk Hour":

> Sometimes I have supposed seals
> must live as long as the Scholar Gypsy.
> Even in their barred pond at the zoo they are happy,
> and no sunflower turns
> more delicately to the sun
> without a wincing of the will.
>
> Here too in Maine things bend to the wind forever.
> After two years away, one must get used
> to the painted soft wood staying bright and clean,
> to the air blasting an all-white wall whiter,
> as it blows through curtain and screen
> touched with salt and evergreen. . . .
>
> Harriet Winslow, who owned this house,
> was more to me than my mother.
> I think of you far off in Washington,
> breathing in the heat wave
> and air-conditioning, knowing
> each drug that numbs alerts another nerve to pain.[27]

In July he flew first class, courtesy of the State Department, to England for the Poetry International festival, attended a party in his honor given by Eliot at

Faber & Faber, ate "Mongol food at the Empsons," had a Cambridge reunion with Frank Parker and Bill Alfred in London, and saw, among others, John Wain, Sonia Orwell, and Louis MacNeice (who would be dead within a month). In two days, he lamented, he'd turned down "about $1000 in drinks." London, he would tell Eliot afterwards, had turned out to be "an almost unbroken chain of microscopic, little visits for little luncheons for little rehearsals of little performances." He viewed two Mantegnas at the National Gallery, bought two Scots dresses for Harriet, and got to see "one silly play." Yet London, in spite of its "architectural and habit hurdles" which were so much more byzantine than New York, was still glorious.[28] He even managed an afternoon talking poetry with Jarrell on a park bench in Kensington Gardens. "Cal was for Plath that day," Mary Jarrell would recall, "and [Tom] Gunn—and Larkin. Randall was for Larkin, Larkin, and Larkin: that was normal. . . . Like two physicists on different hemispheres who advance their own knowledge on each other's papers, Cal and Randall (when their initial resistance passed) . . . pushed with their paws and found something palatable in each other's latest enthusiasms."[29]

On July 24 Cal flew on to Paris, where his and Mary McCarthy's both being on the wagon seemed to hang "like a plague" over the city. He went with McCarthy to see the Delacroix exhibit at the Louvre, then enjoyed a marvellous dinner which had taken McCarthy days to prepare. At Saint-Cloud a photographer from *Life* snapped pictures of Lowell and McCarthy and others outdoors at a picnic in the afternoon light. "I think of being twice met at Orly with waits," Lowell would thank her afterwards, "the Church at Senlis, St. Genevieve, the somehow huge Turkish bath bareness of the Pantheon, then your apartment with every inch shining with the dash and care of your selection, and finally the shadows deepening on the grass of Saint Cloud, the dachshund trotting off to safety, and the fruit still holding out and lasting with Flemish splendour."[30] After Paris he flew down to Nice to take part in a Fulbright seminar. "Imagine Monte Carlo," he wrote Lizzie. "Nice is nice, but somehow I've seen it before." By month's end he was back in Castine.[31]

On August 1, 1963, at Puget Sound, on the other side of the continent, Theodore Roethke died of a heart attack while diving into a swimming pool. He was fifty-six. Cal was deeply shaken by the news. As chance would have it, he'd written Roethke just before leaving for England to talk about an issue Roethke had raised again: the relative poetic merit of their contemporaries. "I remember Edwin Muir arguing with me that there is no rivalry in poetry," Cal had written back. "Well, there is. No matter what one has done or hasn't done . . . one feels each blow, each turning of the wind, each up and down grading of the critics. . . . Each week brings some pat on the back or some brisk, righteous slur, till one rather longs for the old oblivion." He supposed that in any age there had to be "many frogs in the pond, and even many toads," and he was glad that Roethke "made up part of the great chorus of poets, and could do so many big things" he himself had no gift for. How different their two musics were, and yet "how weirdly" their lives had paralleled. "Let's say we are brothers," he ended,

> have gone the same journey and know far more about each other than we have ever said or will say. . . . To write we seem to have to go at it with such single-minded intensity that we are always on the point of drowning. I've seen this so many times, and year after year with students, that I feel it's something almost unavoidable, some flaw in the motor. There must be a kind of glory to it all that people coming later will wonder at. I can see us all being written up in some huge book of the age. But under what title?[32]

Roethke was the first of Cal's American generation of poets to go, and, as poets have done for the past three thousand years, he wrote an elegy for this lost singer. He would remember with pain the Beast telling him at Yaddo fifteen years before that he had "an ear like a meat-grinder," remember too that glistening bald head,

> *focussed like a torpedo on the croquet game at Yaddo,*
> *the folder with all the reviews of your books*
> *listed from* A *to* Z,
> *our first two champagne bottles popping at breakfast.*
>
> *All night you wallowed through my sleep,*
> *then in the morning you were lost*
> *in the Maine sky. . . .*[33]

"Two days ago," he wrote Mary McCarthy, "we heard that Ted Roethke had died apparently of a heart attack in a swimming pool." Actually, he'd been expecting the news of Ted's death for months now, since Roethke had looked

> so bruised and overcast when we last saw him in New York. And yet he seemed to live with a kind of knowingness, as if he saw all the holes in the road better than we did. Last June, I was reading the stage-directions to a German play that used historical characters. The directions said one should forget all about photographs, and remember the actions and essence of these people. But I think it must have been hard for Ted to forget what he looked like, all the awe and comedy he necessarily carried about with him, all that delicacy of ear and touch under the great wallow, all the suffering and phosphorescence of his last years. It's hard to get used to knowing that it's not just the very remote and old that die, but someone who used to beat you at croquet a few months ago.[34]

For months Cal had feared that the Muse had at last abandoned him for good. "I really want to write in a new way," he'd told Bishop in May, "one I can't describe, but one that is free from a kind of shadow I still often walk under but no longer believe."[35] Three months later he reiterated this concern. "Forgive me for saying that I felt comforted by your saying your Muse is dead," he wrote her now. "Mine is dead as lead, and when I try to write I feel full of a hollow aimlessness, though otherwise happy."[36]

That was in August, when he turned again to translating. This time it was Dante—the Brunetto Latini Canto, the one Eliot had Englished so beautifully in "Little Gidding" twenty years before. "By magical, intuitive and tactful touches," Lowell would write among the manuscript pages of *Near the Ocean*, "Eliot made Dante charming in English. By innovations on Dante, he made him contemporary. And by a life-long dedication, he made his own collective poems a single journey through hell, purgatory and Paradise. The two poets seem fibered together." How he wished his own poetic journey might have had that sort of terrain, however one read Paradise.[37]

The turn to Dante in turn inspired him to try "a nightmarish terza rima thing"[38] called "The Severed Head," but even that had stuck. It had stuck because the Muse, as every poet must fear at some point, had abandoned him to the hell of making revision upon fruitless revision. He felt now as if he'd been left pouring out his own heart's blood over words which refused to flare into life. Gasping for air in the air-locked room of the self, he watched his shadow self approach:

> *Then*
> *a man came toward me with a manuscript,*
> *scratching in last revisions with a pen*
> *that left no markings on the page, yet dripped*
> *a red ink dribble on us, as he pressed*
> *the little strip of plastic tubing clipped*
> *to feed it from his heart. His hand caressed*
> *my hand a moment, settled like a toad,*
> *lay clammy, comfortable, helpless, and at rest,*
> *although his veins seemed pulsing to explode.*[39]

And Derek Walcott, in New York that September in Lowell's apartment, about to go out somewhere with him, fixing the knot of Cal's tie. "He returns the knot to its loose tilt. 'Casual elegance,' he says, his hands too large to be those of a *boulevardier*. The correction is technical, one moment's revelation of style."[40] What Walcott does not yet see is that the severed head is gasping for air.

"Great flurry," Cal wrote Bishop on September 20,[41] back in sticky New York. He'd been made poetry editor of the *New York Review of Books* for the moment, and had spent part of August in Castine asking friends for poems. Now the issue was about to appear. Classes were also about to begin again. Still, after three years of living in New York, he felt better prepared for its onslaughts than before. With Kunitz he did a TV show honoring Roethke. Then it was Lowell's formal introduction by Bob Giroux to the New York Metropolitan's Committee at an Opera Club dinner. With Marianne Moore and George Plimpton he attended the second game of the 1963 World Series at Yankee Stadium, the year the Dodgers beat the Yankees four straight.

But that fall he was disturbed too by attacks on two of his friends. The first was against Mary McCarthy for her novel, *The Group,* which Norman Mailer attacked in *Newsweek* and then in the *New York Review of Books*—attacks so personal, Cal wrote McCarthy, that it was as if Mailer had "taken up the boxing fight he had proposed . . . at Edinburgh and taken a swipe" at her when her head was turned. He urged her to counter with her own review of Mailer's work. The second attack was against Hannah Arendt for her documentary, *Eichmann in Jerusalem,* a book savaged by Lionel Abel in *Partisan Review* and then by Norman Podhoretz in *Commentary.* Alas, that the entire *Partisan Review* world should be throwing bricks at one another, Lowell lamented. It was all rather "vexing and sometimes distressing, though one does fall asleep somehow." As for Rahv and Jason Epstein at the *Partisan Review,* he wished someone would send those two "on a goodwill trip around the world."[42]

In October, Irving Howe, editor of *Dissent,* presided over an evening focusing on Arendt's *Eichmann.* Since Marie Syrkin had already offered a damning critique of the book in Howe's magazine, Arendt declined the invitation to attend what she knew would be a hostile gathering. Syrkin lined up with Lionel Abel (who had already dubbed Arendt "the Rosa Luxemburg of nothingness") against Daniel Bell and Raul Hilberg. In the audience that evening were Lowell and Hardwick. As expected, most of the talk had gone against Arendt, Lowell would report to Bishop, stunned by what he'd witnessed.

He had found himself in a strikingly different New York that night, "a pure Jewish or Arabic world, people hardly speaking English, declaiming, confessing, orating in New Yorkese, in Yiddish, booing and clapping." The gathering, in fact, had felt rather like "a mixture of Irish nationalists and an Alcoholics Anonymous meeting with contending sides." Still, by the time the meeting broke up, a catharsis had been reached, with everyone feeling friendly and relieved. There was nothing "like the New York Jews," he added with a mixture of amazement and admiration at so much unrestrained forthrightness and energy. "Odd that this is so, and that other American groups are so speechless and dead."[43]

But there was also something haughty and cold about this infighting among the New York intellectuals which disturbed him, something he distrusted in the aloof, disdainful *New Yorker/Partisan Review* stance he caught in the clipped quasi-British accents of Irving Howe (who would write the 1968 essay entitled "The New York Intellectual"). That same year in his own *Notebook* Lowell would juxtapose the chill brilliance of Howe with his own example of the true democratic radical, William Carlos Williams. "How often was this last salute recast?", Lowell probed, pointing to Howe's iced-over rhetoric:

> *Did Irving really want three hundred words,*
> *such tact and tough, ascetic resonance,*
> *the preposition* for, *five times in parallel,*
> *to find himself 'a beleaguered minority,*
> *without fantasies of martyrdom,'*
> *facing the graves of the New York Intellectuals,*
> *'without joy, but neither with dismay'? . . .*
> *How often one would choose the poor man's provincial*
> *out of town West Side intellectual*
> *for the great brazen rhetorician serpent,*
> *swimming the current with his iron smile!*[44]

Against that poem he placed the figure of another Jew, unnamed, but in the true American grain, joking about Wasps and praising Williams, the perpetual outsider, a figure rather like Lowell, himself part Jewish, both grown weary of the New York enlightenment, where

> *what Wall Street prints, the mafia distributes;*
> *when talent starves in a garret, they buy the garret.*
> *Williams made less than neckties on his writing,*
> *he could never learn the King's English of* The New Yorker.
> *Sooner or later, everything good gets printed;*
> *time even stoops to merit.* Dr. Williams
> *saw the germ on every flower, and knew*
> *the snake is a petty, rather pathetic creature.*[45]

Lowell was in New York that November 22, finishing a day of rehearsals for the spring performance of *The Old Glory,* when he heard the news that President Kennedy had been shot in Dallas. The death affected him so deeply that he later came to believe it was the immediate cause of his eighth manic episode. "Kennedy's murder was a terrible trauma for all of us," he would write Bishop the following January, after he'd been released from the hospital. "At first it

Lowell, forty-seven, presenting John Berryman, forty-nine, with the Russell Loines Award in New York, 20 May 1964. Berryman was so upset by Lowell's review of *77 Dream Songs* in the *New York Review of Books* that he nearly failed to show up for the award. "I love him," Berryman had written in "Dream Song 177" nine days earlier. "I may perish in his grins/ & grip. I would he liked me less." And Lowell, three years later, having by then adjusted to the startling idiom of the *Dream Songs,* in a poem addressed to Berryman: "I feel I know what you have worked through, you/ know what I have worked through . . . / John, we used the language as if we made it." [*University of Minnesota*]

Robert Lowell with Ezra Pound in Rapallo, late March 1965. "I can't see him as a bad man, except in the ways we all are," Lowell would say at Pound's memorial service in New York on January 4, 1973. "I do see him as a generous man to other artists, and this in a way none of us will touch." He recalled the last time he'd seen *il miglior fabbro:* emaciated, "neat in blacks and whites, silver beard," looking like "the covers of one of his own books, or like an El Greco, some old mural, aristocratic and flaking." [*Harry Ransom Humanities Research Center, University of Texas*]

Lowell, fifty-five; Caroline Blackwood, forty; Sheridan; and Caroline's youngest daughter, Ivana, at Milgate, late 1972. "In an otherwise discreet review" of *For Lizzie & Harriet* and *The Dolphin*, Lowell wrote Elizabeth Bishop in July 1973, *Newsweek* had published an unflattering photograph of Lizzie, together with "a family portrait photograph" taken by Thomas Victor and given without Lowell's permission to *Newsweek*. The photo, he thought, made the four of them look rather "like a secret polygamous poor white family." But in truth Victor has caught in the instant of the camera's shutter some of the conflicting tensions inherent in Lowell's marriage to his dolphin. [*Thomas Victor*]

Robert Sheridan Lowell, age four, in gladiatorial helmet and robe, 1975. An image of his father and a force for the aging father to contend with. "I'm afraid he is rather a University of Virginia type," Lowell wrote Peter Taylor in August 1972, as Sheridan approached his first birthday, "blond, dirty, lacking in feminine delicacy, already thirsty for the fraternities. He managed to short-circuit a third of the house one night, in one unobserved second; he tipped over a twenty-pound part of the fireplace . . . he wet his little sister [Ivana] who was nice enough to invite him to her bed in the early turbulent morning." [*Harry Ransom Humanities Research Center, University of Texas*]

Lowell with students from the University of Tennessee, Knoxville. The photograph was taken by Gina Pera at Newfound Gap in Great Smoky National Park on the afternoon of 12 May 1977. The students, Alicia Randisi, Kathy Shorr, and Franklin Jones, had offered to take Lowell up the mountain path, but after walking thirty feet, he gave up, citing heart problems.

Robert Lowell at Castine in August 1977, a month before his death. Back after an absence of seven years, he circled round once more to his New England roots, writing from memory about the "old New England classics, Thoreau, Melville, etc." Even if he did nothing with the essays he was writing, he'd told himself in the summer of '65, he hoped at least the reading would "sink into dry sand," or—better—"dry fertile earth." In the summer of 1977 he stood very near the ocean, a place where water was both "heaven and allegory," and wrote as well as he'd ever written. [*Photograph by Elizabeth Hoffman. Harry Ransom Humanities Research Center, University of Texas*]

seemed the work of a Southern fanatic, then of a leftist plot. I found myself weeping through the first afternoon, then three days of television uninterrupted by advertising till the grand, almost unbearable funeral. . . . The country went through a moment of terror and passionate chaos with everyone talking wildly, and deeply fearful and suspicious."[46]

To Adrienne Rich he would recall how he'd stepped directly from St. Clement's, where rehearsals had been going on, into a taxi. "The radio was going in a confused way," he would remember, "and the driver was grinning and giggling in a compulsive way, and saying, 'The President has been shot.' The death hadn't been announced, but seemed probable. I asked the driver why he was smiling, and he said 'Because it hurts so, it just hurts.' . . . I must have been very wrought up anyway, because I lay for a long time on my bed listening to the reports and weeping. One felt as if a civil war were beginning. No rational daylight law seemed to hold, and it's easy to see how Johnson rushing to his plane feared lest an atomic war might be beginning." What a world one lived in, where one walked constantly in the shadow of instant nuclear armageddon, though in fact from the outside one's life might seem "comfortable, safe and controlled."[47]

Meredith would remember seeing Cal at the Opera Club a week after the assassination and Cal telling him with a smile that President Johnson had just asked him to be in his cabinet. He seemed to act as if he really had been asked, knowing full well that others would find it hard to believe.[48] He began bombarding Eliot with transatlantic telephone calls, for which he later apologized, explaining later that the onslaught of an "enthusiasm" was always "accompanied by a feverish reaching to my friends."[49]

In early December, he was driven once again to the Institute for Living in Hartford. This time it was a relatively mild attack, and by early January 1964 he was judged well enough to fly down to Washington to deliver a short speech on the Gettysburg Address at the Library of Congress. Lowell was particularly anxious not to exceed the 270 words of the address he was there to honor. In his remarks he noted that only Lincoln, Jefferson, and Kennedy of all the presidents had been genuinely able to use words. (Kennedy's name had not been in the original draft, but after reading the address the dead President was to have delivered in Dallas the day he was shot, Lowell belatedly added his name.) Lowell also outlined America's "struggles with four almost insoluble spiritual problems" which the Gettysburg Address had somehow adumbrated: "how to join equality with excellence, how to join liberty with justice, how to avoid destroying or being destroyed by nuclear power, and how to complete the emancipation of the slaves."[50]

On January 9, 1964, Lizzie wrote Tate that Cal was almost better again and would soon be home. This time the attack had come on him without warning, which was "most discouraging because he tried awfully hard to push it away." He hadn't had a drink for the past year; he'd gone to the doctor and done whatever was suggested. In truth, the attack did not "seem to be under the control of the will, not even a little bit," so that he was now "very *triste*" and "utterly bewildered."[51] When he came home in mid-January, he was in fact in a state of post-manic pathological self-abasement. Something organic was the matter with her husband, Lizzie knew, something truly beyond his control. For his part, Cal tried to make light of this latest episode. In fact, when he'd gone to the hospital, he told Rich, he'd armed himself "with a suitcase of classics: Freud, the complete Aristotle, Dante," only to pass his time staring at the TV, waiting breathlessly for the next episode of *Dr. Kildare.*[52]

The hospital stay this time had been "rather soft and subdued," he wrote Mary McCarthy. "I was never very sick and the recovery was gentle and gradual: a dull fairly agreeable month of small crafts, chaff with the other patients and popular television," something which softened "the critical mind for a while," but otherwise did no harm.[53] But the attacks had become a permanent part of Lowell now, so much so that Richard Wilbur, walking beside Mary McCarthy with Cal a few steps in front of them, a frail nobility still evident in Cal's gait, in the heft of his phrases, would remember her whispering to him, "Poor Cal, one day in seven he's as God intended him to be."[54]

Afterwards, it was always a little painful "prodding the formless, embarrassed mind to pick up the pieces."[55] The attacks did seem really to "come from the air," Cal had to admit to Bishop. "The stir of a feather can start them, though no doubt I would be immune, if I had a different soul." Still, they seemed to throw him less and less off balance now, and if he was "spiritless and loggy" at the moment, it was rather from commenting on too many term papers and poems. Lizzie was still "up to her neck in controversy," first with Mary McCarthy for her parody of *The Group,* something McCarthy had not found at all funny, and now with Arthur Schlesinger, Jr., for a satirical piece Lizzie had written about the Washington scene. "Hornets buzz outside," he added, "but we are at peace at home."[56]

In February the English critic, A. Alvarez, interviewed Lowell for *Encounter* at the West 67th Street apartment. Alvarez noted the backs of the tall buildings, the water towers, airshafts, backyards, the creak and banging of the central heating system, as well as the silence of Lowell's study, where, fortunately, the honking of car horns never seemed to penetrate. He noted too the hugeness and frailty of the man sitting across from him, the gentleness laced with "a mixture of stringency and tartness," a man who seemed relaxed *and* reserved, the "slightly tentative directness and openness, that curiously new-born quality" which went with Lowell's convalescence. It was a tone, Alvarez astutely noted, which matched "very precisely the raw, nervous atmosphere of New York in the period following Kennedy's assassination."

Why did so many American artists identify with the dead President, he wondered? Perhaps because, Lowell suggested, Kennedy had represented "a side of America" that was "appealing to the artist in retrospect, a certain heroism." Kennedy's had been a martyr's death, for he had been reckless, had gone further than the office called for, so that he seemed "fated to be killed." As such, Kennedy's larger than life image was something one could treasure and be stirred by. Here in America, at least, the artist was free to speak freely, to articulate "the confusion and sadness and incoherence of the human condition." Everything seemed on the table these days, even "one's family life."

Sick as Cal was, it was Freud who most moved him now, "his case histories," and *The Interpretation of Dreams* in particular, which read "like a late Russian novel." He had been especially taken by Freud's very human color, by his sadness, by that long German-Austrian and Jewish culture Freud seemed to embody, that "beautiful and sad and intricate" side of things which seemed to have disappeared from psychoanalysis. Now, after his Episcopalian youth and his Catholic years, Lowell had found Freud "the only religious teacher" possible for him any more. True, he was not a strict Freudian, but Freud *was* very much a part of his life, a figure who somehow contained in himself the Jewish *and* the Christian traditions, and who had placed both, perhaps, "in a much more rational position." It was Freud, really, who had provided the conditions for modern thought, especially here in New York, where Jewish culture seemed to serve as a leaven for all American culture.[57]

That February the Lowells also attended a Town Hall Meeting in New York at which Lee Harvey Oswald's mother was the keynote speaker. "There was the sad, fierce, unattractive, provincial and somehow pathetic Stalinish crowd, vague declamatory speeches that wouldn't have worked with any other crowd, a hugely for the moment effective and fact-drenched speech" arguing for a conspiracy in the death of Kennedy by Mark Lane, "delivered with a professional defense lawyer's fluency and sarcasm—then at last Mrs. Oswald rather frightened and stage-struck talking nonsense about the American way." But in spite of Lane's theory, Cal told Mary McCarthy, he was still convinced that Oswald had acted alone in killing Kennedy, "otherwise not only the Dallas police, but the FBI would have had to plot, frame and lie." Still, he had to admit, the investigation had been "handled in a cruel, sloppy, hit-or-miss hustle of confusion."[58]

Election to the inner circle of the Academy of Arts and Letters to fill the slot left vacant by Frost's death, then rehearsals again for *The Old Glory*, postponed when he had become ill the previous November. "I know so little about what will act and what won't," he wrote Rich, "that this might as well be my first manuscript."[59] The play would have its New York premier in early November 1964. But, after "a baffling week" of hearing it read aloud by actors and finding himself "talking like some of my more pompous and farcical characters," he confessed to Eliot that he feared the "foolishness" he heard in their speeches might well be a reflection of "some held-down slice of my character that I've tried to banish from my poems." In March he was on the road again, with "a broken series of teaching and reading trips."[60] He did not much care for such readings any more, knowing too well, as he told Wilbur, the "saturation, the bewilderment of new names and works . . . the jaundiced eye for one's own efforts," the feeling that came during the question period after a reading of being "a ventriloquist puppet that has lost its master." But such things came, he understood, with the territory.[61] He began his duties on March 6 with a reading at Connecticut College at the invitation of William Meredith. It was his first public appearance in four months.

Several times that spring he saw Randall, first in Greensboro, then at Kenyon. Randall seemed older now, "smaller, and grayer, and still rather shaken by the jaundice he had over a year ago," he told Bishop, yet somehow "noble and a little sad." Still, it was evident that they were all growing older. He'd just received his twenty-fifth reunion classbook from Harvard, he wrote Randall that May. "Face after unremembered face tells how it married so-and-so luckily after a 'protracted siege,' has three children who will soon be ahead of it at golf and fishing, joys in an 18th century farm, is fighting a losing battle against the lawn and the waist, is conservative in religion, politics and the community."

How good to think of Randall, then, "still so honest and hopeful and full of brilliant talk and knowledge, able to judge and to make," to think too of Randall's "great parade of women" poems with their "delicate splendor," more like "bits of Tolstoy than other poets." He was glad too that Randall had liked the poems in *For the Union Dead,* especially now, when he himself too often found in them "a mean tameness and sour monotony." Everything since *Life Studies,* he confessed to his closest and toughest critic, had been a hunt, rarely successful, "for the knack and power to fly."[62]

But even as Jarrell's star began to fade, Berryman's began suddenly to rise, and he was about to make the game of writing poetry even more demanding and exciting. Berryman might wonder why Lowell of all people would want to review his *77 Dream Songs* for the *New York Review of Books,* but Cal had his reasons. One of them was to better understand what Berryman had achieved there, the other to keep abreast of the man who had suddenly become Cal's strongest competition. It was a strong if mixed review, and—as Lowell confessed to Meredith—he'd left in his doubts, "burying them in a froth of enthusiasm." But even with all his "larger, more enthusiastic impressions" tossed in, Cal was sure cagey John would think he'd "hemmed him in with barbs."[63] Why not say, then, what he thought?

In June, Lowell drove up to Boston to accept the Golden Rose of the New England Poetry Society award. He was so nervous about driving again after so many months that the trip had turned out to be "an expedition" for him. Afterwards, he'd gone out to Cambridge to talk with Adrienne Rich "about various people, Berryman, Susan Sontag." He recalled "the Dutch paper on the table, and near you, all around you, your house, your children at school . . . your recurrent images of the doomed elms." But foremost on his mind was Berryman. "Almost everyone is caught in the dilemma of either starting again, a little threadbare, having junked too much in desperation, and the desire to be fresh, or there is a hardening, a sticking to the old good, but predictable, means." Unable to proceed with his own poems, he had turned to translating: a sequence of Anna Akhmatova's poems on her son's exile to Siberia, coming out in *The Atlantic;* the Brunetto Latini coming out in *Encounter;* his Juvenal in *Arion.* But what he really wanted were new poems, a torrent of new poems, such as Berryman had written over the past ten years.

He thought of Berryman, of "his troubles and his power, and with what smash and vehemence he carries himself." But that sort of daimonic energy was too near him, he knew, and would have crushed him "in a minute," which was why Berryman's poems had elated and troubled him so much more than they did Rich, who had just written a favorable review for *The Nation.* The truth was, he admitted to Rich, that parts of Berryman's poetic character were so close to him he could not bear to "look on him even in the imagination without a drowning feeling." He could feel the surge of "oxygen coming into my lungs and then failing."[64] In truth, *The Dream Songs* were nothing less than a new planet swimming into view in the near ether, and instinctively Lowell knew that they had caused a fundamental disturbance in the universe of American poetry.

Equally, what was causing a major disturbance in American society in 1964 was the issue of civil rights. A year earlier, Lowell had been appalled by the race riots in Birmingham, Alabama. He knew the position of the southerners—how could he not, knowing Tate and Taylor and Randall—but what the South was doing in opposing civil rights was "barbarous, and all for a nightmare of the nerves, something that exists there, but not in fact."[65] For him, on the other hand, civil rights seemed "the clearest of black and white issues," though the road to seeing civil rights legislation enacted, he told Bishop, would be "a rough one."

In truth, one walked the streets of New York these days "with a perhaps silly feeling of dread," in which it was all too easy to summon up the specter of "rich and poor, black and white, liberal and conservative . . . at each other's throats." And though the least likely place for such an apocalyptic scenario would be New York, even here people were "beginning to be afraid of each other." Each day television flashed the message home, though television itself was not the cause. He'd been reading something on the Spanish Civil War, noting how tensions had "simmered and simmered" in Madrid until "overnight it became merciless on both sides." If twenty-five years earlier he had chosen Franco's forces in that conflict, his liberal instincts now were on the side of the Spanish Republicans, though considering the blood both sides had spilt, not with very much conviction.[66]

In Castine that July he watched on television as the Republican Party nominated Barry Goldwater. "Goldwater's speech was ominously alive," he wrote Blair Clark at the beginning of August:

> I had a feeling that I was watching a dark little forlorn movement, the black splinter of an already shrunken party. But who knows? What you say about his possible election is true and dire. We would soon have a fascist state, for I think the Goldwater people would soon find themselves lurching into further extremes to keep going, and our country would be fearful to ourselves and the world. Sometimes now you get a little innocent gleam, innocent though dirtied with much brutality, jobbing and falseness, of someone genuinely wanting to move back to the old simpler times.[67]

It was his own wish, of course, and within a year, as Lyndon Johnson escalated the war in View Nam, what he'd feared most about Goldwater's foreign policy would be realized, to his consternation, by Johnson.

A cold summer in Castine, he wrote Bishop as the season wound down. "A sort of Dutch April of overcast cold days, maybe five in the last forty . . . sunny," during which he'd worked daily in the Barn on the *Oresteia* trilogy—a project he was doing for Elia Kazan and the Lincoln Center. By then he had a draft of the first and longest part, the *Agamemnon*, already completed. He wanted an acting draft, and so had cut a third of the original text, turning what was "noble, cloudy and deep" into an actable libretto, something "rapid, clear and forceful." But working at it there in the splendid isolation of the Barn had left him feeling rather "like a soldier who has left the field to mould archaic lead spearmen." He'd also gone through the galleys of *For the Union Dead* and also "sliced with Lizzie's help ten or fifteen pages" from *The Old Glory*,[68] sharpening its Zhivago-like theme of the ruined aristocrat (rather like himself) in the wake of the social displacements caused by revolution.

After a fifteen-year struggle, Flannery O'Connor—not yet forty—had finally succumbed to lupus in Milledgeville, Georgia, surrounded by her mother and her beloved hundred-eyed peacocks. The clearest image Lowell could make of her was of the young writer just starting out, when they'd been at Yaddo together, "always in a blue jean suit, working on the last chapters of *Wise Blood,* suffering from undiagnosed pains, a face formless at times, then very strong and young and right." Even that early on she had "found her themes and style, knew she wouldn't marry, would be Southern, shocking and disciplined," he told Bishop that August. "In a blunt, disdainful yet somehow very unpretentious and modest way . . . she knew how good she was," and must have known even then "dimly about the future, the pain, the brevity, the peacocks, the life with her mother."

To him Flannery had always seemed a "commanding, grim, witty child, who knew she was destined to live painfully and in earnest, a hero, rather like a nun or Catholic saint with a tough innocence, well able to take on her brief, hardworking, hard, steady, splendid and inconspicuous life." And yet, he marvelled, in spite of living under the scrutiny of her mother and her doctors there in the heart of rural America all those years, Flannery had remained "less passive and dependent than anyone" he could think of.[69]

"Boston is all history and recollection; New York is ahead of one." Thus Lowell, speaking with Stanley Kunitz for an interview that September. In New York one found "a whole community of the arts, an endless stimulating fellowship . . . at times too stimulating." No one was too great for New York. No one. There was "something frightening" about a city that consumed its own past at such an alarming rate. And yet it was the only American city that could still provide "an intellectual human continuum to live in." Remove New York and you cut "the heart out of American culture."[70]

That October *For the Union Dead* received, to Lowell's immense relief, front-page reviews in the *New York Times* and the *Herald Tribune,* as well as a spread in *Newsweek,* together with interviews in all three. It was all "very occupying and exciting," he confided to Bishop, seeing he'd won through once more. But what, after all, did it really mean? "More invitations to be on dull committees, more books in the mails for blurbs, more tiresome doctor's degrees. Thank god, it can't go very far for a poet."[71]

At month's end Lowell introduced Jarrell at the Guggenheim, who read and commented on Bishop's poems (Randall, he noted, seemed interested in only two poets these days: Bishop and Dickinson). The reading itself had been "odd and mannered," he reported back to Bishop in Brazil, but Randall's comments had been "inspired and gave a generous and very deserved and accurate personal portrait of you—I mean through the poetry. . . . We both said you were the best poet of our generation."[72] He himself was feeling overworked just now, having "heard too many rehearsals, read too many letters, dipped quickly into too many books and articles," all the while trying to avoid becoming overexcited.[73]

Then, as the November 1 premier of *The Old Glory* approached, rehearsals intensified. Lowell turned his study over to the English director Jonathan Miller, so that he and Miller could work on the play together more easily. The rehearsals were held at the 180-seat St. Clement's Episcopal Church in the Hell's Kitchen section of New York, a large, rather drab brick mission church which served, thanks to its vicar, the Reverend Sidney Lanier, as a church on Sunday for the theater community and—for the past year—as The American Place Theater, Lowell's play being the first major production put on by the theater. All his days seemed spent now, he told Bishop, "lying sitting standing listening reading, rather like a horse on a carousel up and down through the gay dance." So much to do, he complained, until it felt as if nothing were being well done.[74]

"I don't think Lowell had a really intrinsic sense of the theatre," Miller would recall. "I don't think he had a good visual sense either, of how things might look. He was tremendously open to suggestion, totally humble about that." But here Lizzie proved useful, for she'd reviewed drama for *Partisan Review* back in the 1940s and understood the theater far better than Cal. What she had was "a very sharp, *Variety*-reading, Broadway sense" of what would and wouldn't work for the critics.[75] *The Old Glory* would win five Obies for the 1964–65 season, including Best Off-Broadway Play. It would run into January 1965, when the second part, and the play's real force, *Benito Cereno,* would be transferred to the *Theatre de Lys* in Greenwich Village for a regular Off-Broadway run.

W. D. Snodgrass, reviewing *The Old Glory* for the *New York Review of Books,* was so struck by the force of what he'd seen that he wrote that Americans might "yet have a theatre of our own."[76] And Jarrell wrote a letter which appeared in the *Times* on November 29, saying he'd never "seen a better American play than Benito Cereno," and that the "humor and terror of the writing" had been "no greater than those of the acting and directing." In short, what he'd witnessed had been "a masterpiece of imaginative knowledge."[77] Two weeks after the play opened, Cal wrote Bishop that it had been a "raving *succès d'estime,*" despite patronizing reviews from the daily critics, and that Randall, that hard taskmaster, "strangely malleable and boyish without his beard," had called *Benito Cereno* "the best thing" he'd ever done.[78]

Indeed, the directing and acting were superb, with Frank Langella as Benito Cereno, Lester Rawlins as Captain Amanda Delano, and Roscoe Lee Browne as Babu, the African-American slave, whose electric performance gave white audiences a nightmare image of servility, rage, and icy self-control in which the black slave–white master roles were played out to their terrifying logical conclusions. But when someone in *The Village Voice* accused Lowell of wanting to put down the present black revolution by guns, Lowell felt compelled to respond. The play, he reminded his accuser, was set "in Jefferson's time, and the remarks so outrageously attributed to my own feelings are meant to show the ambivalence toward slavery, even in the mind of a Northerner like Captain Delano," who literally could not see what was before his eyes because he thought "of the Negroes only as servants and primitives." He wanted it to be known that, as far as he was concerned, he lamented "the loss of the old Abolitionist spirit," since "the terrible injustice, in the past and in the present, of the American treatment of the Negro" was of the greatest urgency to him both as a man and as a writer.[79]

In spite of his yearly cycle of manic attacks, and in spite of his intense activity that fall, Lowell had so far managed to weather his excitement. "It's partly Milltown," he told Bishop, "a drug that somehow soothes without heaviness," and which was able to depress "preliminary panic." Then, on October 22, 1964, Cousin Harriet died. It was a loss, he said, felt even more keenly than the loss of his own mother, and one which had similar repercussions. He was seeing his therapist and trying to keep busy—his way of dealing with personal sorrow—and wrote Bishop in mid-November that he'd somehow managed thus far to weather Cousin Harriet's loss without panicking "into excitement." He'd learned something from his previous breakdowns, he supposed, so that "a huge hunk of health" had "survived and somehow increased" over the past fifteen years and might see him through now. "Pray god," he told her, "there'll be no more."[80]

But by Thanksgiving it was already clear that Cal was once more escalating out of control. He began asking Miller to stay up later and later at night to keep him company, passing the time by inventing hypothetical vacation weekends, in which all of history became a replica of Pound's *Cantos,* a cubist framework of simultanieties where anyone might meet anyone. It was a world, Miller would recall, populated by tyrants and geniuses all jostling with one another. "How would it be if you had a weekend with Joinville and Lionel Trilling?", Cal asked Miller on one occasion. "Who'd be the best chess player?"

He began feverishly revising his work again, this time writing whole new acts for his plays, including new ones for *Endecott and the Red Cross,* in which Sir Walter Raleigh's wife came on stage holding the severed head of her husband. It was a nightmarish symbol, perhaps, for Cal's own sense of lost connections. One night in Cal's study Miller pulled down a copy of *Les Fleurs du Mal,* only to find under the cover *Mein Kampf.* And once, at Idlewild Airport, seeing four Hasidic rabbis walk by, Cal had winked and told Miller that it was not the Germans who'd been responsible for World War II.[81]

Back in May, Cal had learned that Jean Stafford was at the moment hospitalized in New York and wrote to tell her how often he'd wanted to say just how sorry he was for his blindness during their marriage. On May 6, she'd written back. "There's no possible way of thanking you for your concern," she wrote him, "for your lovely letters, for the books. . . . My dear, never castigate yourself for what you call blindness—how blind we both were, how green we were, how countless were our individual torments we didn't know the names of. All we can do is forgive ourselves and now be good friends—how I should cherish that."[82] That same month he'd set about helping secure a Wesleyan fellowship for her, which she had begun in September.[83] Now, in early December, he had a chance to see her. His *Phaedra* was premiering at Wesleyan University, and Jean was there as a Fellow of the Center for Advanced Studies. When Cal asked her to attend a performance of the play with him, she accepted. Her third husband, the writer Joe Liebling, to whom she'd been especially devoted, had died the year before, and her own writing had by then slowed to a trickle. Now here was Cal, trying to hold hands with her during the performance, then telling her afterwards that she had to straighten out her life. When Blair Clark told her during intermission that Cal was smitten at the moment with Jackie Kennedy, Jean quipped that what Jackie had and she and Lizzie didn't "was an assassinated husband and if he didn't watch his step, we would be three peas in a pod."[84]

Vera Zorina, the wife of Goddard Lieberson, president of CBS Records, played Phaedra in that production. As Richard Wilbur and Jean sat together in the lobby of the Center, Wilbur recalled, Jean had leaned over and told him "that Cal had just ascended to the second floor where the Liebersons' bedroom was, under the deluded impression that Zorina wished to have an affair with him."[85] Whether that was another of Jean's fictions or not, by that point Cal was definitely on the prowl again. One night at St. Clement's, he watched a Latvian dancer named Vija Vetra rehearsing Indian sacred dances for the liturgy and introduced himself. The topics ran to the Russian presence in Latvia, Esthonia, Lithuania, before turning to more intimate aggrandizements. Then he was inviting Vetra back to his apartment for drinks and to meet Lizzie, who was not impressed. And then, like that, he was setting up an apartment with his sacred dancer over on West 16th Street and buying furniture, once more intent on starting over again.

14

Public Spokesman
1965–1967

"**I** begin to think perhaps Cal should make one last effort to cure himself or at least to be happier, if only temporarily, than he is with me," Lizzie wrote Blair Clark in early January 1965. Always before, when he'd gone through these episodes, she'd felt that he still loved her, or, she insisted, "I would not have fought so hard."[1] Now she was no longer so sure. Once again it was Blair who intervened by taking Vetra to talk with Dr. Bernard, who in turn explained that Cal would have to be committed. So, on January 25, as Cal sat quietly between Blair and Vetra in the back seat of the limousine Blair had hired, the three of them holding hands all the way, Cal was driven back to the Institute for Living in Hartford. There was fear in his eyes, Blair would remember, as if he were being led to a slaughterhouse. Each day Cal wrote Vetra, in care of the West 67th Street apartment, then called her to find out why she was not writing back. But Vetra had seen no letters because Lizzie had been in no mood to act as a clearinghouse for her husband's mistress, and not until he insisted did Lizzie wrap up his letters and send them downtown.

Soon after being admitted, Cal was writing Lizzie how bored he was. He was taking leather appreciation, ceramics appreciation, and watching basketball games for an hour at a time without smoking. He spoke of his fellow inmates at the Institute: the old man who continually read Francis Bacon, the college freshman who carried the *Modern Library Giant Collected Keats & Shelley* around with him but who had never heard of "Ode to a Nightingale." He kept busy grading his students' papers. Surely there was some terrible flaw that blew a bubble into his head every year. He could not go on this way, he complained, though he knew that that was only partly up to him "and partly up to fate, nature, God and whatever."[2]

Again—amazingly—Lowell recovered rapidly. By February 9 he was writing chattily to Lizzie, trying again "to feel important and dignified to hide what a mess I've made of my human ties. If you and Harriet want me," he added, "I am yours."[3] "Cal, my heart bleeds for you," Lizzie wrote him now, asking him to remember the greatness he'd made of his life. She wanted only to do what was best for them all.[4] When Vetra came up to Hartford to see Cal, he broke the news to her that he was going home again. She had no choice but to acquiesce, though she did ask if she could have Cal's shirt as a souvenir. Two weeks later, Lowell's attorneys, Migdal Low & Tenny, sent Vetra a letter ordering her to relinquish the 16th Street apartment. Vetra sent the bills on to Lowell, who stared at them before dropping them on the floor. Not only was he crestfallen by what he'd done, this time he felt embarrassed and humiliated. It was left to Lizzie to see that the bills were paid.

It had been a quiet stay this time, he wrote Bishop afterwards. He'd gone in "almost well and so had little" in the way of a "jolting re-evaluation." Now, after so many attacks, he rather thought of them as "something woven in my nervous system and one of the ingredients of my blood-stream, and I blame them less on some fatal personal psychotic flaw. Who knows? They are nothing to be blythe about, but I feel rather composed about it all. Here I am back in the bosom of my family, and back in my study, and getting ready to finish the *Oresteia*. Life and work go on."[5]

When Eliot died on January 4, Cal had been too keyed up to be able to respond. But now, in late February, he wrote Charles Monteith, his editor at Faber & Faber, to say that though many of his friends had died in the past two years, Eliot's death, "though long on the verge," seemed "the most impossible and intolerable of all."[6] Two months later, he would tell Giroux he was still finding it hard to reconcile himself to the fact that he'd now reached an age when *all* his Elders were beginning to disappear. Of all of them, none had spoken "with such authority as Tom," who had "so little played the role of the great man." He'd been "a good and patient friend," and no other man had "so touched something personal" in his depths.[7] In March 1965 he and Lizzie flew to Egypt, where he lectured on poetry at the University of Cairo. Afterwards he travelled to Rapallo to visit Pound, "emaciated, neat in blacks and whites, silver beard," looking like "the covers of one of his own books, or like an El Greco, some old mural, aristocratic and flaking."

But he could also feel the graying of his own generation. Randall at fifty, he'd told Bishop in February, had softened, and he was pleased that his friend had finally shaved his beard and now deigned to walk "the same earth we do." Gone now was "the noble air of pained, aloof nobility. Something touching and imposing to look at is gone, but what a relief for his friends!" He felt somewhat ambivalent about Randall's new volume, "The Lost World," liking much of it, yet finding there a "repetition of a style and subject, as though Housman had written rather voluminously and slopped up his meter, and strung individual poems out." Then too there were the "endless women, done with a slightly mannered directness, repeated verbal and syntactical tricks, an often perverse and sadistic tenderness." Still, when Randall was hot, he preferred him to anyone except Bishop.[8]

Then in April came news of Randall's nervous breakdown. "I have thought twice about intruding on you," Cal wrote his friend now, "but I must say that I am heart-broken to hear that you have been sick. Your courage, brilliance and generosity should have saved you from this, but of course all good qualities are unavailing." He himself had been through this sort of thing so often now that he felt he understood something of what Randall must be going through. The worst part was the "grovelling, low as dirt purgatorial feelings with which one emerges." But those too would pass, he promised, and "what looks as though it were simply you, and therefore would never pass, does turn out to be not you and will pass." *Courage,* he cheered his old friend.[9]

By late spring Lowell had a draft of the second part of the *Oresteia,* and was hoping to have all three parts put on at Lincoln Center in another year. He doubted if his versing had much inspiration, though he felt he'd at least caught some of the "barbarous archaic grandeur" of the *Agamemnon.* He wrote an essay on Eliot for *Sewanee Review,* and began "a rambling impressionistic prose essay" on emblematic New England figures: Mather, Melville, Colonel Shaw, and others.[10] His summer's work was already blocked out for him. In April he flew out to Seattle to give the Theodore Roethke Memorial Reading. Six weeks earlier he wrote Bishop that he would have to work himself "into the proper state of awe," having known Ted too well to miss his faults, especially his "tender hard-heartedness" and his "too great a wish to be big, so that much of the poetry is a little dead under the ringing cadences." But then Roethke really had been big, and it had taken courage "to burn out with such a big flare."[11] But it was the cadences of Auden and Yeats which would ring for him that summer in Castine as he composed a group of public and declamatory poems in response to President Lyndon Johnson's rhetoric defending America's increasing involvement in the hundred year-war raging half way around the world.

In February 1965 Johnson had begun exponentially escalating the war in

Viet Nam by ordering air strikes on Communist targets over the North. In March he began sending in large numbers of American troops. In response, anti-war demonstrations began mounting not only in Washington but on campuses all across the country. Although there were less than 100,000 American troops in Viet Nam (the figure would grow to six times that figure over the next three years), Cal was already "outraged by it," Blair Clark would recall; "and I—a much more 'political' person than Cal—I pooh-poohed it, and said to Cal I didn't think Johnson would get caught in that trap. Of course, [Cal] was right."[12]

In May, Eric Goldman, special consultant to the President, organized a gathering of artists to visit the White House, much as Kennedy had two years earlier. There would be painters, sculptors, writers, musicians, movie stars, photographers. Among the writers invited were Saul Bellow, John Hersey, Edmund Wilson, and Lowell. Johnson himself thought of the gathering rather as a way to spend a pleasant afternoon. For his part, Wilson, outraged at Johnson's foreign policy in Viet Nam, at once and categorically refused to attend. When Lowell was telephoned, however, he agreed to give a poetry reading. But after thinking it over for a few days, he decided in good conscience that he too could not attend and wrote the President directly in late May. "I am afraid I accepted somewhat rapidly and greedily," he explained. "I thought of such an occasion as a purely artistic flourish, even though every serious artist knows that he cannot enjoy public celebration without making subtle public commitments." Since, therefore, he viewed the President's foreign policy with the "greatest dismay and distrust," he had decided to decline his "courteous invitation" after all. As Lowell had done twenty years before when he'd told Roosevelt he would have to decline the honor of being invited to serve in the armed forces, he once again sent copies of his letter to the newspapers, including the *New York Times*. Then it had been B-17 strikes over the Ruhr. This time it was B-52s over Hanoi.[13]

On June 2, Goldman called Lowell to try to dissuade him from publishing his letter in the *Times* the following day. Lowell was gracious, Goldman would recall, "free of self-righteousness about the position he was taking, and thoroughly understanding of the complications he was causing. I hung up the telephone with the impression of a fine human being. I also hung up with the feeling that all hell was about to break loose."[14] At once Goldman wrote a reply to Lowell and sent it on to Johnson for his signature. It spoke of the President's full and deep respect for Lowell's disagreement with "certain phases of the Administration's foreign policy." But Johnson, baffled and outraged, would have nothing to do with the letter. He told Goldman to answer Lowell directly, and under his own signature.

The next day, Lowell's letter made the front page of the *Times*. "We are in danger," he had written, "of imperceptibly becoming an explosive and suddenly chauvinistic nation, and may even be drifting on our way to the last nuclear ruin. I know it is hard for the responsible man to act; it is also painful for the private and irresolute man to dare criticism."[15] But that was not the end of the matter. The following day the *Times* ran another front-page story under the heading: "Twenty Writers and Artists Endorse Poet's Rebuff of President." Robert Silvers and Stanley Kunitz had organized a telegram to the President, and it was signed by an impressive array of figures: Hannah Arendt, John Berryman, Alan Dugan, Alfred Kazin, Stanley Kunitz, Dwight Macdonald, Bernard Malamud, Mary McCarthy, Larry Rivers, Henry Roth, Mark Rothko, Louis Simpson, W. D. Snodgrass, William Styron, Peter Taylor, Robert Penn Warren.

The telegram served only to further infuriate Johnson, who called the signers a bunch of fools and sons of bitches and half-baked traitors. The White House Arts' Festival would turn out to be a fiasco, and Dwight Macdonald, who did attend, would bring with him a petition signed by nine others who had been invited to the White House urging Johnson to get out of Viet Nam. Before the festivities were over, Macdonald would nearly come to blows with Charlton Heston. Even mild Mark Van Doren of Columbia University would tell the press that Cal had been conscience-bound to stay away. Infuriated by this attack in his own house, Johnson ordered a blackout of the festival. Nor did this open hostility to his policy by a group of intellectuals deter him from escalating the war. That August he would ask Congress for an additional one billion to carry on the fighting.

He'd "stumbled into accepting an invitation to read at the White House Arts' Festival, a rather meaningless melange with Phyllis McGinley as my fellow poet," Cal would tell Bishop afterwards, and had then written "a public letter of refusal." The papers had been "full of headlines such as *Poet Snubs President*, letters piled in and invitations to address all sorts of protesting groups." But he'd had his say and wanted to go no further, though he was finding it hard to avoid being a lightning rod on the topic. So, in early June, when he received an honorary degree from Williams College, along with Allen Dulles, Henry Luce, and Adlai Stevenson, Luce had told him that he liked Cal's poetry a lot better than his politics. But he was gratified when his old hero, Stevenson, told him that he was following Cal's new public life with interest *and* satisfaction.[16]

Several months later, Lowell would thank J. F. Powers for his review of Gordon Zahn's *In Solitary Witness: The Life and Death of Franz Jägerstätter*, the story of an Austrian CO executed by the Nazis in 1943 for refusing to serve in Hitler's army. The review had brought back for Lowell his own experiences during the war, when he'd searched so desperately "for authorities on just and unjust wars." He knew from hard experience how difficult it was actually to define a just war, knew too that absolute pacifism seemed "possible to few, and usually under conditions that make it either easy or inconsequential." But he also knew that in reality few wars were ever just, and that what might begin as a just war had "a habit of deteriorating" into something else. He was still troubled by what he thought of as the Church's relative silence during World War II. "Anyway," he added, "there ought to be an unrelenting chaos of people kicking against wars, people frequently risking and giving their lives to prevent or soften wars." He knew he'd "risked little" by going to jail twenty years before, and believed now he'd had little enough help "from either our society, American priests, or the vague sublimities of Pius XII." As for the White House business, he finished, nothing he'd ever done had had such approval, and he'd been "plagued ever since to sound off on Viet Nam programs till I wish I could go to sleep for 100 years like Rip Van Winkle."[17]

On June 21 the Lowells returned to Castine. But rather than work on the *Oresteia* or his New England essays, as he had planned, Lowell worked instead on a group of poems in an eight-line stanza and octosyllabic line borrowed from W. H. Auden, W. B. Yeats, and Andrew Marvell, the "steady, hypnotic couplet beat" following him "like a dog" all summer.[18] The poems he wrote that summer would make up the first section of his next book, *Near the Ocean*. Among these were "Waking Early Sunday Morning," "Fourth of July in Maine," "Central Park," and "Near the Ocean," the last of which he described as "a nightmarish, obscure reverie on marriage, both vengeful and apologetic," set "in our small eastern seaboard America." It would be his own version of "Dover Beach," and also his "most ambitious and least public" poem of that summer. And because he'd received more publicity for refusing to attend the White House affair than for all the poems he'd ever written, it was no wonder he now felt "miscast" and "burdened to write on the great theme, private," and at the same time "global."[19]

For the past year he'd "finished nothing worth keeping," he wrote Bishop in mid-July. But now, in spite of all sorts of long-distance calls "still swarming in about my White House business," he had a 112-line poem which he thought "rather witty and tragic."[20] The manuscripts for "Waking Early Sunday Morning," another of his "Sunday Morning" poems, reveal much of what was on Lowell's mind as he tried to counter the gigantism and disinformation coming out of the White House that summer of 1965, and they show just how concerned he was that, if he were not careful, he too might end up countering one false rhetoric with another:

> *I am sick*
> *of stretching for the rhetoric*
> *and hammering allegoric splendor*
> *that forged Goliath's brazen armor,*
> *and shook his Brobdignagian staff*
> *that made the chosen fly like chaff—*
> *so gross the confidence that shone*
> *in meter and iambic line!*
>
> *I think with loathing on the year's*
> *dotage, and output of tame verse:*
> *coy whimsy, turgid indignation,*
> *stealings, endless self-imitation,*
> *whole days when I can hardly speak,*
> *yet blunder home, unshaven, weak*
> *enough to offer anyone*
> *stuff done before and better done.*

What he wanted was somehow "to break loose, like the chinook / salmon jumping and falling back, / nosing up to the impossible / stone and bone-crushing waterfall."[21] He wanted what he'd wanted in "Quaker Graveyard"—transcendence—and thought again of Eliot, the language's public spokesman who was gone from the scene now, in effect passing the mantle on to him. But in the face of television and radio and the newspapers, wasn't his own voice in danger of becoming a thin, frightened shadow, "Prufrock in love with Dionysius"? He thought of the big Texan in the White House as he must be this same Sunday morning, puffed up with power as Cal himself was when delusions of grandeur overwhelmed him:

> *free to chaff*
> *his own thoughts with his bear-cuffed staff,*
> *swimming nude, unbuttoned, sick*
> *of his ghost-written rhetoric. . . .*
>
> *Pity the planet, all joy gone*
> *from this sweet volcanic cone;*
> *peace to our children when they fall*
> *in small war on the heels of small*
> *war—until the end of time*
> *to police the earth, a ghost*

> *orbiting forever lost*
> *in our monotonous sublime.*[22]

In early August, Lowell flew down to Washington to address a huge crowd of students assembled to protest the war. But he was tired, and afterwards he tried to escape the war for the moment by driving up into New Brunswick and Nova Scotia for some salmon fishing. Back in Castine, he visited with the Booths, Eberharts, and Hoffmans again, and sailed as he did once annually with Eberhart in *The Reve,* this time out to Spectacle Island.

That same month he was invited to meet Ted Kennedy at Philip Booth's place. Kennedy, along with several other young congressmen and their wives, had been sailing along the Maine coast and had docked in Castine for the night. Lizzie decided to stay home, having seen all she wanted to "of those jet-set Kennedy women in their tight pants." But Cal was amused, curious, pleased. Those who gathered at the Booths that evening were all younger than Cal, though they seemed to know his work certainly better than President Johnson did. "All so young and running things," he would tell Bishop afterwards, all "looking like Bill Merwin. I felt like a white Racoon!"[23] At one point Kennedy asked Cal why he'd turned down the White House invitation, and again Cal tried to answer. He had not wanted "to lend even tacit approval" to what Johnson had "begun to do to us." He didn't know what to do about the war. That was up to those in power. What he did know was that what was happening in Viet Name was "only more terrible, and more visible," than what the United States was probably also doing in Chile. Not only were we corrupting other countries, he added, even more terribly we were "corrupting ourselves."[24]

By late August he had finished two more poems: "The Opposite House," a "20-line poem reduced from 72," and "Fourth of July in Maine," a "long piece in 17 eight-line stanzas on Cousin Harriet that Lizzie finds beautiful and self-indulgent. Such, and a bunch of [Osip] Mandelstam translations."[25] "The Opposite House" is one of two New York poems he wrote that summer. In the poem, the speaker imagines himself looking out from his study window on West 67th at the deserted police stables across the street. It is a poem with links to his play, *Benito Cereno,* here too Lowell revealing his fears that racial tensions in New York were turning the city into another Madrid on the eve of civil war. "Everyone speaks Spanish here," he wrote. "Everyone is black. . . . We are afraid of each other."[26]

Like the other poems of that summer, "Central Park" had also begun in octosyllabic couplets, before Lowell compressed it and added a number of triplet rhymes, thus heightening the poem's sense of exacerbation and claustrophobia. It is a poem with echoes of Williams's wanderings through the public park in *Paterson*, Book II, and stresses even more than Williams the obscene dichotomies between the lives of the rich and the poor one finds in New York, that brittle lightning rod for the rest of the country:

> *Then night, the night—the jungle hour,*
> *the rich in his slit-windowed tower . . .*
> *Old Pharaohs starving in your foxholes,*
> *with painted banquets on the walls,*
> *fists knotted in your captives' hair,*
> *tyrants with little food to spare. . . .*
> *We beg delinquents for our life.*
> *Behind each bush, perhaps a knife;*
> *each landscaped crag, each flowering shrub,*
> *hides a policeman with a club.*[27]

In early October, Lowell was shocked to learn that Jarrell was once again in the hospital. "Poor Dear Randall," he wrote Eleanor Taylor on the 6th. "I feel he is our own special thorn and pearl, vexing and noble beyond any of our acquaintance! He's had a hell year. May it be over."[28] Earlier that year, in a depressed state, Randall had put his hand through a glass window, cutting his wrist so deeply that even after surgery the hand had refused to uncurl. Now another depression had descended on him, and he had left his wife. Then, on October 14, walking alone at night near the campus of Chapel Hill, he came in contact with a passing vehicle and was killed instantly. Peter Taylor and Lowell, as two of Randall's oldest friends, were pallbearers at Holy Trinity Episcopal Church in Greensboro when Randall was laid to rest in a Quaker graveyard on the 17th. Lowell had just dedicated *The Old Glory* to him, and when Mary Jarrell received the book, she saw that Cal had written on the title page that he was "heart-broken" his poor friend could not "have this book he loved—and helped."[29]

"I imagine you may have heard by now of Randall's death," Lowell wrote Bishop two days later. "He was undergoing treatment of an injured wrist at Chapel Hill, and 'lunged' in front of a car on a main highway near a bypass. He had a bottle of pain-killer [Demerol] in his pocket." No one could tell "for certain whether the death was suicide or an accident. I think suicide, but I'm not sure, and Mary's version, the official version, is accident. . . . Poor dear, he wanted to take care of himself!"[30] Within a week Lowell had written a ten-page eulogy for the *New York Review of Books*. "Randall's mind," he wrote there, "unearthly in its quickness, was a little boyish, disembodied, and brittle. . . . He had the harsh luminosity of Shelley—like Shelley, every inch a poet, and like Shelley, imperiled perhaps by an arid, abstracting preciosity."

And yet wasn't he also "the most heartbreaking English poet of his generation," a "poet-critic of genius" at a time when, as Randall himself had said,
most criticism was "astonishingly graceless, joyless, humorless, long-winded,
niggling, blinkered, methodical, self-important, cliché-ridden, prestige-
obsessed, and almost autonomous"? Lowell was especially thankful that Randall's community in Greensboro had given him "a compact, tangible, personal
reverence that was incomparably more substantial and poignant than the
empty, numerical long-distance blaze of national publicity." "Twice or
thrice," he added, "he must have thrown me a lifeline."[31] His elegy for Randall
would be even more guilt-laden and haunting. "They come this path," he
would write there,

> *old friends, old buffs of death.*
> *Tonight it's Randall, the spark of fire though humbled,*
> *his gnawed wrist cradled like* Kitten. *"What kept you so long,*
> *racing your cooling grindstone to ambition?*
> *You didn't write, you re*wrote. . . . *But tell me,*
> *Cal, why did we live? Why do we die?"*[32]

November saw the Battle of the Ia Drang Valley, the costliest of the entire
Viet Nam War, when the Seventh Cavalry, Custer's old unit, was chopped up
by two North Vietnamese battalions, much as Varus's Legions had been deci-
mated in the Rhine Valley two thousand years before. It was history spiralling
around once more. That same month Lowell read at Sanders Theater in Cambridge as part of a benefit for an anti-war organization called Massachusetts
PAX. During the question period, Alan Williamson would recall, a man, probably a reporter, rose from the second row and said, "You speak in your poem of
'man thinning out his kind.' Do you regard the . . . UNITED STATES OF AMERICA
as the agent of this thinning out?" Lowell had answered the question with a
question. "Don't you?," he asked. He let at least two minutes go by in total
silence, then insisted, "I asked you a question, and I'd like an answer." Another minute of silence; then, his point made, Lowell continued very softly, "I
said *man* thinning out his kind; and that's what I meant; and it's going on all
around us; and pray God it will stop."[33]

The year before, Lowell had sent Jackie Kennedy copies of some of his
books, and she had graciously acknowledged his gifts. Now, on the second
anniversary of Kennedy's assassination, he dropped off a signed copy of *The
Old Glory* at her East Side apartment, leaving it with a member of the Secret
Service. Why, she wrote him, hadn't he told her he was coming by? Was he
playing Santa Claus, leaving presents and running off? She could just hear the

"brilliant Secret Service saying—'Robert Lowell? We don't know anyone by that name!' "[34] "Home from you," he would write, remembering how he had walked back across Central Park to his own apartment after dropping off the book,

> *and through the trodden tangle,*
> *the corny birdwalk, the pubescent knoll,*
> *the dirtwood rowboats docked three deep . . . .*
> *I in my Dickensian muffler, snow-sugared, unraveling—*
> *so you phantasized—in the waste thaw of loss:*
> *winter and then a winter; unseared, your true voice seared,*
> *still yearningly young; and I, though never young*
> *in all our years, am younger when we meet.*

On December 1, he escorted Jackie to the opening night of Bill Alfred's play, *Hogan's Goat*, in New York. He also began telephoning friends about his new admiration. Then he bought an 1854 bust of the Indian chief Tecumseh for $3,500 for her and placed it on the dining-room table at West 67th, where it replaced a bust of Napoleon. Once more he was beginning to speed up.

Episodes at the opera: Giroux, the Fred Dupees, and Cal at the Met for a black-tie performance of *The Queen of Spades*. When Cal arrives at the Club Met, his talk is all of "brilliant women"—Lizzie, Mary McCarthy, Jackie Kennedy. It is nonstop talk, and it is dazzling. Then, in the opening minutes of the opera, he falls asleep. Another evening: *Don Carlos*. A shot rings out from the stage during the performance and Cal shouts out, "Oswald." He is driven back to his apartment and from there to New York Hospital. The following day Sidney Nolan, his new illustrator, drives him up to Boston where he is admitted to McLean's.

"One has to laugh at his antics," Peter Taylor writes Allen Tate on the 7th, "but it is heartbreaking." He wonders if anything more can be done for Cal than is already being done.[35] "I was in N.Y. last week and heard a play-by-play account of the purchase of Tecumseh," Tate writes back. He's heard that Cal stood up at the Met to conduct the opera, and knows what everyone by now knows: that the seizures are becoming more frequent, though "the crush on Madame Jacqueline is an improvement in the direction of sublimation."[36] Auden writes Charles Monteith at Faber on the 20th, supporting Cal's nomination for the Oxford Poetry Chair, but warns Monteith that Cal has times when he "has to go into the bin. The warning signals are three a) He announces that he is the *only* living poet b) [there is] a romantic and usually platonic attraction to a young girl and c) he gives a huge party."[37] And Jackie

Kennedy at year's end, from Sun Valley, to Cal at McLean's, who is there she thinks on a "retreat" for the holidays, thanking him for the book he has sent her on Alexander the Great, and also for putting her onto Joinville and Cato.[38]

It was a mild episode this time, and by February Cal was back at work. At the end of the month he and Lizzie gave a dinner for Jackie and Bobby Kennedy, and though Bobby failed to show, Cal told Bishop afterwards, Jackie showed up, "full of wild vignettes spoken in her breathless, almost parody voice. I thought Lizzie was horrified and discovered she was charmed. Once in a blue moon . . . . one from the grand world is really delightful. Sometimes, I think I would die, if it weren't for a few platonic relations with women. Adrienne Rich used to come out twice a week to see me [at McLean's] and a couple of hours would whirl by in what seemed like a few minutes of talk."[39]

Bobby too courted Cal, sending him a note in which he quoted a passage from Pushkin: "That hour is blessed," it read, "when we meet a poet. The poet is brother to the dervish."[40] "I have always been fascinated by poets like Wyatt and Ralegh," Cal wrote Kennedy on the 25th, by poets who were not only poets but also "statesmen and showed a double inspiration." Perhaps the greatest of these had been Dante, "who ruled Florence for a moment, and would never have written about Farinata and Manfred, without this experience." In fact, it seemed to him, whole sections of the *Commedia* read rather like a Ghibelline epic. Then there were statesmen like Lincoln and Edmund Burke, who had also been great writers. He was delighted to see Kennedy "putting into practice that kind of courage and ability that your brother so subtly praised in his *Profiles* [*of Courage*]," and for knowing "how to be brave without becoming simple-minded. What more could one ask for in my slothful, wondering profession?"[41]

Snodgrass would recall meeting Lowell that spring of 1966. He'd run into Iowa's Paul Engle at the New York City Ballet during intermission, then into Cal outside Lincoln Center, and Cal had invited them both back to his apartment. When Engle had been hospitalized in New York several years before, Cal had visited him there, and their friendship had resumed, though each still walked on eggs around the other. The reunion with Snodgrass and Engle went on into the early hours of the morning, until Lizzie, standing on the second-story balcony of the apartment in her nightrobe and socks, called out: "Cal! Cal! Don't you know the time? You'll be an absolute wreck!" Snodgrass and Engle had both tried to tiptoe out, but as soon as Lizzie had disappeared, Cal winked and urged them to join him for one more drink.[42]

In New York that sweltering July, in what must have seemed a million miles from the Lowells' West Side apartment, destiny finally caught up with Delmore

Schwartz, whose body was discovered in the corridor of a seedy hotel off Times Square. For three days it remained unclaimed, before Delmore's death was finally reported in the *New York Times* on the 14th. "Oh destiny, where is it?", Lowell wrote Meredith from Castine two days later.

> You probably heard of his death, a heart-attack, alone, outside a cheap hotel room in New York. I felt frightened to be with him for years—needlessly, in a way, but I was sure it would lead to confusion and pain. Then I think back on his low voice, so intuitive, reasonable, a great jag of my education, from weak hands into weak hands perhaps, more than I could use, but much of it has stayed. Two things had hold of him, when I knew him best, the first dark rays of his paranoia, often lighting up things, but unbearable to friends, and his long effort to write in [a] quiet, underwritten style—maybe a crippling venture, maybe not. . . . His destiny seemed the most hopeful of any young poet in 1940, then the downward road, some germ in the mind, the most dismal story of our generation perhaps, and maybe a lot more to the writing than one knew.[43]

"A clear day, bush and grass in the sun, bush and grass in the shadow, the sea high, like a lake shore, a few feet off now from my window," he wrote Bishop that same day. Harriet was a very big nine-and-a-half-year-old now, who took sailing lessons one morning and tennis the next, and did her homework "wedged in between jig-saw puzzles and bottles of pop." He had a seventy-page draft of *Prometheus* done, and had begun to wonder why he'd buried himself "in it so, five days a week, and sometimes six." Could "any truth come through the old Greek plot, the few, ever-recurring words?" He'd been "thinking of Whitman's huge sweep, mostly in his thirties and forties, lines pouring out, a hundred poems a year, yet with long, idle afternoons of sauntering, chatting, at ease nearly with what the eye fell on," whereas for him whatever was near at hand seemed to leave him glazed with anxieties.[44]

It was a summer "almost without event or narrative," and soon he would be back in New York again. A day of writing in the Barn, a packed lunch beside him, then two hours of tennis doubles in the afternoon, and an evening at home or with his "undrama-torn Castine friends." The only eruption in his schedule had occurred in late July (he told Bishop later) when, following his "desire and ignoring [his] better judgment," he'd flown down to Hyannis for Jackie Kennedy's thirty-seventh birthday party:

> white turrety inn building at Cotuit . . . women with hair a foot high . . . drinking guests . . . Mike Nichols, Charles Addams, and Jerome Robbins. . . . After a while, Jackie suddenly present . . . both senator Kennedys, [Robert] McNamara. Later, a luxuriously simple dinner . . . Mike Nichols next to Jackie, later, middle-aged people dancing the new dances, not very wildly, but too young for me, a

slightly tawdry untimely Marie Antionette feeling of a festival when the age for being whole-hearted about such things had passed, the flash of the jet-set, a little lurid and in bad taste in a world of poverty and blood.

Later in the evening he'd met McNamara, and Jackie had had to put her hand over Cal's mouth and tell him to be polite—Cal "saying something awkward about liking him, but not his policy, then Jackie saying, 'How impossibly banal. You should say you adore his policy, but find him dull.' A few minutes talk with [William] Styron and me arguing with McNamara, no great impact on either side, except that McNamara seemed a simple brilliant administrative soul," who'd "given little thought to moral complications, and who might have even taken the usual liberal line against Viet Nam more easily than I would." He'd sensed too a "vague feeling" of anti-Johnson sentiment there. The "most interesting person to talk to had been Bobby Kennedy," though there too one sensed "a scary feeling of ambition and power . . . along with frankness."

The following day, driving "rather dull and stunned" out to Provincetown along Route 6 to see the Kunitzes, Cal found himself stopped in traffic, looking at a roadmap for an alternate road, "something more like the backwater of Castine," when suddenly he'd moved "forward with a jolt, found the car had stopped, a hole through the windshield, a little of my hair in the spider web of smashed glass, the car no longer able to move. The car ahead of me wasn't damaged, no blood drawn from me, though $500 injury to my car," which his Hertz insurance would cover. Then, after "hours of waiting, papers, police, a wrecker," he was off again for Provincetown, this time in an Avis car. Two days later he was back in Barnstable Court on charges of "inattentive driving, a roomful of indicted, adolescent carelessness, I by now in fear of losing my licence, taking from my pocket a birthday poem written by William Jay Smith to Francis Biddle, beginning, 'In life's great court, all men are judged.' " He pleaded *nolo contendere* and paid a twenty-five-dollar fine. By evening he was in Cambridge, lecturing "on the dead: Randall, Roethke, and Delmore Schwartz," and suddenly realizing that he too "might have been dead without knowing it."[45]

That September, he read Berryman's beyond-the-grave sequence—the "Opus Posthumous" poems—in the *Times Literary Supplement* and was so impressed with them that he sent Berryman, then in Dublin on a Guggenheim, a telegram calling them "a tremendous and living triumph." Three weeks later he wrote again to say that the sequence was indeed the "crown" of Berryman's "wonderful work, witty, heart-breaking," so that "somehow one believes you on this huge matter of looking at death and your whole life." He was sure it would be read for a long time to come, "one of the lovely things in our literature."[46] But to Philip Booth he spoke more frankly. Berryman was "very very sick, spiritually and physically," he felt. Everywhere in his work he could feel the man's anguish. He knew that being a poet made it impossible to dodge such despair, that the poet as a species was "marked and fretted." Nevertheless, the poet also had a duty to "somehow keep even-tempered, amused, and in control. Berryman in his mad way keeps talking about something evil stalking us poets." It was a bad way to talk, and yet he also knew there was truth in it.[47]

That fall at Harvard Lowell taught another workshop. And, while office hours were open ostensibly to all, they were kept a closely guarded secret by his students. One either knew when they were, or one didn't. During those years, Alan Williamson would remember, office hours were held on Wednesday mornings, from nine-thirty to noon, in a "windowless, cement-block seminar room in Quincy House, followed by lunch at the Iruña, beginning with gazpachos or garlic soup."[48] Students and other poets sat around a seminar table, waiting for their poems to be judged. Sometimes Lowell read his own work, or talked about history, religion, politics. Then the student would read the poem aloud, after which Lowell would read it, circling over the page to the passages where the poem suddenly flared into life, constructing on the spot the new poem he thought could be salvaged from the rest. He worked by intuition, Robert Seigel would remember, refusing to employ prosodic terminology, and speaking instead of "lucky lines," or "happy lines," or of getting the "rot" out of a poem. From the way his voice and face changed in the poem's presence, Lowell made his students understand instinctively how rarely they came in contact with real poetry.[49]

His teaching assistant in the fall of 1966 was an Irish earl named Grey Gowrie, part of Cambridge's student jet set who, some felt, both flattered and tended to overexcite Cal. Gowrie's admiration at the moment was for Charles Olson and the Black Mountain school, an enthusiasm not shared by Cal.[50] But halfway through the term Cal himself began to look more like the disshevelled Olson, drinking glass after glass of vodka cut with milk and breathing like a bull. He began making dark jokes about Olson and Henry Kissinger, jokes about Harvard's Law School and School of Government and its connections with the Johnson administration. He offered soliloquies on issues of power and rambled on about his own war experience as a CO.

Powerless to enact the change he felt the country so sorely needed, and in truth terrified of the excesses of tyrants, Lowell tried to protect himself as the mania once again overwhelmed him by speaking of the need for a strong man to take charge of the government, until at last he was once again seeing himself as Napoleon or—variously—as Hitler. He began calling the Kennedys to give them his ideas on how the government should be run. He made caustic remarks to his friends which cut to the core, comments like: "You're so stupid you never should have taken up writing." Or: "It's a pity your husband never sleeps with you."

Once again he was on the edge of committing physical violence. He woke now long before dawn, lamenting his hurtful comments of the night before, but seemingly unable to stop them. By 10:00 A.M. he was drinking to anesthetize himself. He knew he should enter McLean's again, but he was up for tenure now, and had to show Harvard he could make it through a full term. Seigel would remember Cal inviting him and half a dozen other students he met on the street to a party in Cambridge for some twenty-five Harvard faculty. He and the students were met at the door, and the hostess, even as her face paled, graciously asked them in, whereupon Cal proceeded to monopolize the conversation.[51]

Just before Christmas, Grey Gowrie flew down to New York with Cal in tow. But Lizzie had had it with the Cambridge crowd and told Gowrie to handle this one himself up at McLean's. "I took him in a Fleetwood Cadillac," Gowrie would recall ". . . an enormous thing, something hired for corporation presidents. I got him to the airport, and on the way I thought he'd died. He went completely out and I really thought he was dying. When I got to the airport, I went looking for a stretcher for an ambulance. And then to my amazement, I saw that he'd got out of the car and was at the news stall buying *Playboy.*"[52]

On Christmas Eve, Cal visited Bill Alfred in Cambridge, until he decided that Alfred's household—which consisted of Alfred, his father, and his male dog—was too monosexual for him (Alfred wondered if he meant "homosexual"), and left to stay at Frank Parker's house across town.[53] Liberty Dick, Anne Dick's sister and Parker's cousin, was living in Parker's house while Parker was staying in Boston, and she called Parker to say Cal was at the house and in very bad shape. Parker drove out, got Cal to bed, then went back into Boston. But in the middle of the night there was another call. Cal was up again and drinking, and trying to get a phone call through to Jackie Kennedy. Parker drove back out to Cambridge to spend the night with Cal.

Christmas morning Cal's friends rallied to get him to McLean's. Bill Alfred was there and Grey Gowrie and his wife, Xandra, but it was Esther Brooks who called the police. Soon there were eight of them outside Parker's house, guns drawn on this quiet residential street in Cambridge. Parker asked them to wait outside until he could find a way to tie Cal up. And there was Cal, leaning against the sink and staring about him. It was just incredibly sad, Parker remembered, and by then everyone was exhausted. Cal kept promising to leave for McLean's soon, but the hours kept ticking by. In truth he was terrified by the police, and when at last Parker seemed to make a move for him, Cal swung and knocked him up against the kitchen table. Then the police were coming through the door in blue verticals, and Cal was throwing a milk bottle at one of them, before he was overwhelmed and taken to the hospital.[54]

Since his 1954 attack, Cal had been treated with Thorazine, which relieved the symptoms of mania, though it made one feel like a sleepwalker and did nothing to prevent the disease from recurring. Now a new drug was tried: lithium carbonate, which worked by keeping the patient suspended between the poles of mania and depression, leaving one feeling detached, apart from the daily pressures which assaulted one. The drug itself was a salt formed by the reaction of lithium with carbonic acid, the theory behind it being that manic-depressives had too little of this salt. Blood tests had to be taken regularly to establish how great the salt deficiency was and then the appropriate lithium dosage would be administered. In theory, at least, a patient might be monitored and stabilized for life. When Cal was released from the hospital in February 1967, he was put on the new drug.

After his release, he and Lizzie took a short winter vacation down to Guadeloupe, then returned to New York at month's end. On March 1, when Cal turned fifty, Lizzie invited thirty guests to help celebrate his birthday. Just being "around and hale," he told Bishop, was "a triumph for our stricken generation of poets."[55] Once again, he returned to his work, revising and retyping his *Prometheus,* something he was convinced would either stun or stupefy his audience. It was "a sort of Shelley, or generic European declamatory romantic poem—alive maybe, if anything can breathe under the formidable armor of its rhetoric and stance."[56] Sometimes, he felt, it was as if a ghost had translated the play and he had merely signed his name to it. He also wrote his first poem in six months, a lyric about "the inner stirrings of a character, half me and part Gérard Nerval."[57] The new poem had several titles: "Prometheus (For My Fiftieth Birthday)," "March 1 1967," "Fifty," "Surviving Fifty." Over the next six months the poem would change from a hundred lines of free verse in irregular stanzas to a sequence of five sonnets entitled "Half a Century Gone."

On March 12 he was in London for the opening of *Benito Cereno* at the Mermaid, with Jonathan Miller once again directing. John Gale interviewed Lowell that afternoon for *The Observer,* during which Lowell spoke of several things that continued to trouble him, not least the conflict still raging in Viet Nam. Five months before, he'd told Bishop that American politics were (not unlike himself) "in a state of groggy confusion." For, while everyone hated Johnson, most feared something worse if he were to be removed from power. Perhaps too the intensity of the war would at last taper off.[58] But by the spring of 1967 the situation seemed more hopeless than ever.

He and the British philosopher Isaiah Berlin had been talking at breakfast of the slim chances of Bobby Kennedy running against Johnson in the next election, he told Gale. Which was too bad, since Kennedy now seemed the country's best chance for ending the war, especially as Kennedy was about "as open morally as a politician could be." As for the war: it was not being fought to keep America safe. Moreover, it would take "a million years for North Vietnam to have done as much harm to us as we've done to ourselves." What he was most afraid of was America's lurching into another world war as Europe had in 1914, or seeing one of the great nations—he did not exclude the United States—embracing fascism in an effort to control internal dissent. What was Russia, after all, but an enormous machine waiting for a disaster to happen? Perhaps, then, the best one could hope for the future was the creation of some sort of "Pax Americo-Russiana."

Asked if he would ever write another play, Lowell answered that he might like to do one on Trotsky's last days, or one on Malcolm X, assassinated two years before by Black Muslins in New York. The main difficulty in writing either play, however, was in getting one's characters to speak. If he did write about Malcolm X, that "most fascinating of the Negro leaders," whose autobiography he'd recently read, there would be the enormous difficulties of writing a convincing black dialogue. He thought he could probably get Malcolm talking, "but all the Negroes around him—I don't know how they'd talk. And there's the problem of Negroes murdered by Negroes. What sort of public would follow that?"[59]

That spring the Yale School of Drama received a $25,000 grant from the National Endowment for the Humanities (NEH) for a production of *Prometheus Bound,* of which Cal was awarded $10,000 for his translation. Once again he chose Jonathan Miller to direct his play. Rumor had it that President Johnson had been enraged to learn that a government agency had awarded money to someone who had insulted him, and that Johnson had demanded the award be withdrawn. To his credit, Roger Stevens, chairman of the NEH, had refused. Worse, the play contained in the figure of the tyrannical and spiteful Zeus someone very close to Lowell's idea of Johnson propounding on Viet Nam. At one point Lowell had Prometheus castigating his tormenter, Zeus, as if he were off in the White House, surrounded by his advisers, while napalm smashed against hamlets ten thousand miles away. The links with the portrait of Johnson which Lowell had written in "Waking Early Sunday Morning" were obvious:

[Zeus] sits in the heaven of his assurance and our folly. There, the wings of birds never reach him, he is hidden from other gods, and is free to play with his thunderbolts, each day another sublime crash of fireworks, another mountain range broken beyond repair. His brilliance blinds, his greatness whirs in his ears. He has no time to look down and smile on the slaves who work for him in the depths. He sleeps through the submissive bird-song of their praise. And yet he wakes, and rejoices whenever one of these slaves and obedient instruments is caught on the wheels of his perfection.[60]

In his Author's Note to the play, Lowell admitted that his own concerns and worries and those of the times had inevitably seeped in. "Using prose instead of verse, I was free to tone down the poetic eloquence, and shove in any thought that occurred to me and seemed to fit."[61] Among those at the premiere in New Haven on May 9 were David Merrick, Robert Motherwell, Stephen Spender, Philip Roth, George Plimpton, Susan Sontag, and of course Lowell himself. That spring, he confessed to Bishop, he'd seen "a lot of his Io," played by Irene Worth, "who surely made my play at Yale." She was a gallant actress, one of the best, though "living from hand to mouth." But the whole production had been "lovely, a wonderful Prometheus, Kenneth Haigh, and Miller's marvellous direction." It took two long hours to perform, but seemed to work, if—he added—one liked that sort of thing.[62]

In May too he was on national television to introduce the Russian poet Andrei Voznesensky, visiting the States as a way of fostering goodwill between the United States and the USSR. "In this chafing and often terrifying moment for [Voznesensky's] country and ours," Lowell remarked, "a yearning is felt on both sides to break through. We are dissatisfied with the present lull, surly, torpid, distrustful" of "two big powers with the power to hurt." Sometimes, he added, "each country seems like an invention of the other." So tense were events just now, he noted, that one listened to the news even while shaving. He recalled "an impatient, just-lit cigarette" sighting him "down from the soap dish, and the bathroom door . . . ajar to catch messages from the world news roundup."[63] Not that there was much accord between those two monoliths, China and Russia. In fact, he'd learned from several Russian writers themselves how much they actually loathed Mao. Nor did they much care about either Ho Chi Minh or the American presence there. "One wishes," he added, "that in another year there would be a third poet here—a Chinese and a good poet, and one more detached than Chairman Mao." But later in the broadcast, when he told Voznesensky that both the United States and the USSR had "really terrible governments," and that one had to do the best one could with both governments or there might not *be* a world to govern, there was an "audible sharp intake of breath" from the audience, and perhaps from the CIA and KGB agents watching. Not surprisingly, when it dawned on him what Lowell had said, Voznesensky refused Lowell's offer to comment.[64]

Lowell's disembodied laurelled head floats from the cover of the June 2 issue of *Time* magazine, the title, "Poetry in an Age of Prose," emblazoned in the corner. "There's poetry all over the place," the article has Robert Lowell saying. "I think more people write it, and there are more ways to write it. It's almost pointless—there's no money in it—but a lot of them become teachers, and a lot of them write good poems and read to a lot of people." "The strength of the novel is that it tells a story and has real people," he is reduced to offering in *Timese*. "But poetry has the wonderful short thrust. By the time you get to the end of a poem, there's a whole interpretation of life in 70 lines or less." Edmund Wilson says Lowell has achieved a poetic career on the old nineteenth-century scale. One learns that Lowell's poetry is "seared with a fiery desperation," and "fed by rage and self-laceration."

"The *Time* thing had me almost out of my mind," Lowell wrote Taylor on June 4. "They questioned dozens of people, asked impertinent personal questions"—Blair tape-recorded his interview—"things like how hard were my breakdowns on my wife (Lizzie by the way wonders why *she*, not Jean, wasn't described as beautiful and gifted). I called up, apoplectic with fear and fury, and they promised not to annihilate me. And they didn't." Nor would any stranger in the street "ever thank God recognize" him from the cover. Such, then, was Fame, American style.

And yet here he was, at fifty, reduced to wearing three pairs of glasses: "far, reading, and my old good for nothing which I prefer." He was taking pills now for high blood pressure, and could no longer play tennis singles. All depressing news, particularly since both his parents had also suffered from heart trouble. Still, he insisted, he was in terrific shape. He even had lithium pills now to prevent manic attacks, "something (probably a sugar pill unnoticed when taken or after but) which supplies some salt lack in some obscure part of the brain, and now for the rest of my life, I can drink and be a valetudinarian and pontificate nonsense."[65]

"This year they are guinea-pigs," Philip Booth notes that July, "long-haired guinea pigs. Bringing ice out from the kitchen, Cal stops in the warm gloom of the unpainted passageway (between house and barn], puts the ice-bucket down on the plank floor, and scootches [stoops] to the fruit-crate level inhabited by Harriet's pets. As Harriet tends them, Cal tends her. All this is all but wordless, as basic as pats and murmurs . . . he must once have been as small, as needful, and as largely adoring, as this half-hidden Harriet. Under the one dull lightbulb hung in the passage he hugs her to his shoulder. . . . Then, with no perceptible transition, he picks up the ice-bucket, and lugs his whole grizzly-bear frame back over the transom into the adult barn.[66]

"I've been in a coma of sloth and industry, writing to *no*-one, answering no-one," he wrote Adrienne Rich that August, when for a moment he came up for air. He'd "been poetizing (hideous word, shades of Richard Eberhart) furiously," and now had "three poems, all *memento moris* about summer and being fifty. One, long, about a hundred lines, takes phrases and more from Simone Weil, and somehow I connect it with you mostly," though the lines he quoted to her seemed rather to focus on the cover portrait in *Time* magazine:

> *this circlet of friable laurel,*
> *a funeral wreath from the despotic gangster.*[67]

That summer he had come back again to the long poem he'd begun on his fiftieth birthday, going on from there to write several poems which had their inception with Harriet's ten-and-a-half birthday, celebrated that Fourth of July. He'd begun by writing a free verse draft of what would become the opening poem in *Notebook 1967–68,* then revised it to take the shape of a blank verse sonnet. Then another sonnet and another: improvisations, short bursts opening and rounding to a conclusion. Not unlike the impulse behind Berryman's *Dream Songs.*

In fact, he had Berryman very much on his mind as he settled on the idea now of writing a sonnet sequence. In an unpublished draft of his "Afterthought" to the completed volume, two years later, he would acknowledge Berryman's influence before erasing his tracks: "I can think of us working in much the same way: the intense shaping of a short section, free yet dependent, in that it pointed towards sections already written and suggested others half intuited."[68] The sonnet stanza would obsess him as the shape of the *Dream Songs* had obsessed Berryman for so many years, except that Lowell's sonnets would come much faster than Berryman's had first come to him, and in much larger gulps, so that by Christmas, Lowell would already have seventy sonnets.

"My summer's poem is now 800 lines," he would tell Mary McCarthy then, "practically an *Iliad* for my short-winded symbolist talent. It has . . . all my usual stuff, plus Napoleon, Cato, the Duc de Guise etc. Things seem to swim out of the happenings of the day, including distant things, the ponderings and vagaries of thought."[69] In the coming year—1968—he would write an average of four sonnets a week, so that by 1969 he would have 4,000 publishable lines. In effect, the sonnets became for him an improvisational form, a day book, something by turns loose and strict, rhyming or not, a form forever hungry to devour whatever events washed up along the sands. There would come poems on time and the passage of time, on fog, on the lost key to things, on the search for God amidst the age-old repetitions of Thales, Pythagoras, Parmenides, and Heraclitus, the Promethean poet under the iron rule of forces only dimly understood if at all, the poet's Procrustean guesses no surer than his brilliant small daughter's:

> *Half a year, then a year and a half, then*
> *ten and a half—the pathos of a child's fractions, turn-*
> *ing up each each summer, God a seaslug, God a queen*
> *with forty servants, God . . . she gave up—things whirl*
> *in the chainsaw bite of whatever squares*
> *the universe by name and number. For*
> *the hundredth time, I slice through fog, and round*
> *the village with my headlights on the ground,*
> *as if I were the first philosopher,*
> *as if I were trying to pick up a car*
> *key . . . It can't be here, and so it must be there*
> *behind the next crook in the road or growth*
> *of fog—there blinded by our feeble beams,*
> *a face, clock-white, still friendly to the earth.*[70]

He was back in New York in late July for a check-up and saw Bishop, who was now living in Greenwich Village, "temporarily separated from Lota by Lota's doctor's orders," he told Rich, "but to be reunited in September. We had a lovely afternoon walking through [Central] Park, for once cool, and discussing, reminiscing—unable to believe our ages." Mary McCarthy West had bought a large house next to theirs in Castine and was "very much," with her husband's family, a presence there. So now there was the additional strain of trying to equal McCarthy's dinners, and making their "rather run-down Spanish maid sound like [Mary's] spick French-speaking Polish maid." How strange to have *"two* Margaret Fullers"—Lizzie *and* Mary McCarthy—"in one little village!"[71] There were also the weekly readings of old French orchestrated by the Lowells' friend, Mary Thomas, who taught French at Exeter, the whole tenor of these casual gatherings where one was used to guessing at the meaning of a word all "rather frighteningly improved" now by McCarthy, who *always* did her homework.[72]

There was one picnic in particular at Smith's Mill, Philip Booth would remember, at "a millrace cove with a clamshell beach . . . three miles across the harbor from Cal's Barn." Twenty people speaking twenty dialects on a spit of Maine coast: Harris and Mary Thomas from Exeter speaking French, Priscilla Barnum trading Georgia talk for Lizzie's Kentucky drawl, Olga Carlisle explaining the nuances of Pasternak's Russian to Cal, a classics professor telling

Booth that *xai on,* the name of his boat, was bad Greek, Sonia Orwell's English English, James West speaking Polish to his housemaid Maria, who insisted on answering in proper French. All this, here, in the land of the Penobscots, as the children, Harriet among them, went on digging for flintheads in the old Penobscot shellheap.[73]

Once more that fall Cal divided his week between New York and Harvard where, newly tenured, he taught (as he had the year before) a seminar on the Bible and another workshop. In September, Lota came up to New York to be with Bishop, only to overdose her first night there on barbiturates in Bishop's apartment and become comatose. A week later she was dead. "The mournful end of a marriage," a stunned Cal wrote Eleanor Taylor.[74] And to Bishop afterwards: "It's been a joy to sit chatting with you, even in this sad time. . . . You make most people, even the most charming, seem as if seen through a glaze, as if they lived in a glaze." And though he admitted he had no rights in the matter, he felt as much for Lota's loss as he had after his Cousin Harriet had died.[75]

In mid-October 1967 he went down to Washington, along with those seasoned veterans of the defiant gesture—Norman Mailer, Dwight Macdonald, and Paul Goodman—to protest the Viet Nam War. On the evening of the 19th he watched as Mailer, drunk, harangued the crowds with obscure jokes. As always, Lowell was uncomfortable in such surroundings, but he felt duty-bound to be there ("I find an elephantiasis in [Mailer] that is contemptible," he'd told Kazin five years before, "then a real mind and real energy that leaves me envious and empty.")[76] On the 20th, linked arm in arm with Mailer, Noam Chomsky, and Dr. Spock at the head of five hundred draft resisters, sympathizers, and media personnel, Lowell marched to the steps of the Department of Justice and from there addressed the assembled crowd. "I was asked earlier this afternoon by a reporter why I was not handing in my draft card," he spoke into the microphone, knowing it was not *his* life on the line, but rather thousands of nineteen- and twenty-year-olds. It had been a stupid, taunting question, he knew. But these were serious men he was linked with and they would not avoid whatever might arise "in the way of retribution."[77]

Shortly afterwards, the forty-four-year-old Mailer was arrested for crossing a police line, while Lowell and Macdonald allowed themselves to be turned back by green-helmeted MPs. "Under the too white marmoreal Lincoln Memorial," Lowell would write of his part in the march on the Pentagon,

> *the too tall marmoreal Washington Obelisk,*
> *gazing into the too long reflecting pool,*
> *the reddish trees, the withering autumn sky,*

> *the remorseless, amplified harangues for peace—*
> *lovely to lock arms, to march absurdly locked*
> *(unlocking to keep my wet glasses from slipping)*
> *to see the cigarette match quaking in my fingers,*
> *then to step off like green Union Army recruits*
> *for the first Bull Run, sped by photographers,*
> *the notables, the girls . . . fear, glory, chaos, rout . . .*
> *our green army staggered out on the miles-long green fields,*
> *met by the other army, the Martians, the ape, the hero,*
> *his new-fangled rifle, his green new steel helmet.*[78]

What Lowell caught in his poem was a palimpsest of American history: the half-holiday atmosphere of that first Bull Run in the summer of 1861, when green Union soldiers had marched out from Washington for a picnic war against the rebels, against Stonewall Jackson, only to return, those who could, bloodied and defeated. Now Lowell was comparing those soldiers with green civilians like himself, linked arm in arm with him, so unlike Colonel Charles Russell Lowell, Beau Sabreur, his ancestor, facing the enemy at the Battle of the Wilderness, twelve horses shot from under him by the time the Confederate slug smashed his tubercular lung. And now, in the fall of 1967, these superannuated liberal spokesmen—himself among them—joining in a sit-down demonstration outside the West Wall of the Pentagon. Then, even as Noam Chomsky was seized by the police, Lowell prepared to fly home—to Mailer's amusement and annoyance—to a New York dinner engagement with Edmund Wilson. "In Boston they think I'm Norman Mailer," Cal wrote Lizzie afterwards. "And in New York they think I'm Robert Lowell."[79]

Unlike Mailer, Lowell would later quip, he was less interested in running for mayor of New York than in simply being "a voyeur" in his poems. And yet he had to acknowledge that Mailer had shown "an awful lot of courage" in assuming the role of public spokesman, even as he himself began more and more to avoid the public spotlight. Mainly, his reaction to the march had been "fragility," the "fragility of a person caught in this situation . . . as in that poem of Horace's where you throw away your little sword at the battle of Philippi and get out of the thing."[80] That was his honest reaction, then: fear before the naked force of American MPs, in spite of which he still believed in heroic action, had in fact, in spite of his trembling hands and three pairs of glasses and high blood pressure, acted once again with courage.

One November morning, returning to New York after teaching at Harvard, Cal found Elizabeth Bishop in his apartment, disconsolate over the death of Lota and drunk on vodka. She'd been taken upstairs to his study, undressed, and put to bed by Lizzie and their maid, Nicole. But by the time he arrived home Bishop was sitting dazed in the kitchen with a can of beer. During the night, she'd made "a foraging trip downstairs over the barricade of Harriet's bicycle" looking for some hard liquor. Now Cal himself "put her to bed with a sleeping pill (mild). Later, going to the bathroom, she slipped and broke her shoulder, quite badly. A worse injury maybe than anyone's in the [Pentagon] marches and demonstrations." Then the "ambulances, waits in the hospital, calls to Dr. [Annie] Baumann."

In the twenty years he'd known her, he'd seen Bishop drunk only two or three times. What helped her through her depressions, he knew, was "an ox-like power of character and imagination" which nothing seemed strong enough to break. Mary McCarthy had called her a poet of terror, and that seemed right, he thought, for until now he'd never "been able to quite connect what I know of her life with the seemingly dispassionate coolness of the poems." Within weeks of the accident Bishop was back in Brazil to settle Lota's and her estate before moving to San Francisco with a young woman, "about thirty," whom she'd met in Seattle, "divorced, perhaps because of Elizabeth, with a child of two," a "very decent and good sort."[81]

Early in December the Lowells flew down to Caracas to attend another Congress for Cultural Freedom event. With them were Jason Epstein, Jules Feiffer, and Lillian Hellman. In several sonnets written that fall, Cal would capture the contrast between the slab on which the grizzly corpse of the martyred Che Guevera had been photographed two months before ("the last armed prophet / laid out on a sink in a shed, displayed by flashlight")[82] and the obscene palatial surroundings of the mafialike president of Caracas:

> *his small men with 18-*
> *inch repeating pistols, firing 45 bullets a minute,*
> *the two armed guards petrified beside us, while we had champagne,*
> *and someone bugging the President: "Where are the girls?"*
> *And the enclosed leader, quite a fellow, saying,*
> *"I don't know where yours are, but I know where to find mine." . . .*
> *This house, this pioneer democracy, built*
> *on foundations, not of rock, but blood as hard as rock.*[83]

Violence, then. Violence everywhere, a violence as old as the Mayans, the Aztecs, the Incas, Lowell had come to understand. Violence in the blood, leading to mania, self-destruction, overdosing, wrist-slashings, unslakable thirst. Violence as old as the Caesars, as old as Nebuchadnezzar and Abraham. As old as the pocked face of man himself caught in the mirror of a haggard moon.

15.

Notebook

1968–1970

On December 29, 1967, Lowell flew to Cuernavaca for a ten-day visit to Ivan Illich's Center for Intercultural Documentation. He'd met Father Illich in Venezuela and been impressed and delighted by what he'd read of the ascetic, cosmopolitan Yugoslav Jesuit's work in the *New York Review of Books*. At first Lowell had intended to combine the trip to Mexico with one to Cuba, until the State Department had refused to authorize his passport to Cuba as a journalist. It was just as well, he told Bishop, because in Mexico he could forget about everything. The Center had made for a "queer gathering," though, for one moment he'd been "talking to heavy Chicago nuns, and the next to Brazilian refugees with forty year sentences waiting for them." He'd even managed to climb among the Toltec ruins, and had watched the flamboyant fireworks in the marketplace usher in the New Year.[1]

What he did not tell her about was the young Irish woman he'd fallen in love with, Mary Keelan, twenty-seven, employed at the monastery of Emmaus in Cuernavaca as one of Father Illich's assistants. One thing that came out of the brief, intense affair was a sequence of twelve sonnets, and the first poems in which Lowell was able to give a woman a viable and dramatic life of her own. As for the religious life of the monastery, he rendered that as if he were seeing it through the eyes of a Malcolm Lowry or a Fellini:

A Papal Commission camped on them two years,
ruling analysis cannot be compulsory,
their cool Belgian prior was heretical, a fairy. . . .
barbwired in spotless whitewashed cabins, named
Sigmund *and* Karl. . . .²

Then too there was his portrait of the "two immovable nuns" across the hall from him and his girl, both nuns

> *. . . out of habit, too fat to leave*
> *the dormitory, living for ten days on tea,*
> *bouillon cubes, cookies bought and brought from Boston.*
> *You curl in your metal bunk-bed like my child,*
> *I sprawl at your elbow pillowed from the dead floor—*
> *nuns packing, nuns ringing the circular iron stair,*
> *nuns in pajamas scalloped through their wrappers,*
> *nuns boiling bouillon, tea or cookies—nuns*
> *brewing and blanketing reproval. . . .*
> *The soul groans and laughs at its lack of stature—*
> *if you want to make the frozen serpent dance,*
> *you must sing it the music of its mouth.*³

By then his long poem came to 1,000 lines and would "probably go on another 500" until the year he was journalling had come full circle in June. Then he would polish the poem through the summer. "I am writing it as if it were my last work," he told Bishop. "Someone asked me if I expected to die when I finished it."⁴ The "someone" had been Monsignor Illich, like Christ in his earliest portrait an "ascetic donkey," braying to Lowell the night he'd read his sonnets at the monastery, "Will you die, when the book is done?" And Lowell, "Old lapsed R.C. / lacking half-way to atheist," caught by surprise, replying, "I have begun to wonder."⁵

On January 8, 1968, he left Eden to return to New York, "back to the cold, draft-evader protests, jury duty, my last trip to Harvard." The indictment of Dr. Spock and the others for their protests had been "a bad tactical error by the government," he believed, for now "all sorts of tepid withdrawn people, like Auden," were signing protests. He too had signed something pledging his support "to the men indicted—saying we will take their places if they go to jail." Honor demanded that he do this, but how he hated "the claptrap, the polemical stirrers one, alas, must agree with!" And yet there was a thrill of sorts to all this stir, rather like "being a soldier one day a month, then sunning and gossiping the rest."

And here it was midwinter in New York, which he'd reached without having another manic episode. The lithium pills really did seem to be helping. It would take two or three years to know for sure, but already the "critical months" had passed and he was still functioning. "Ordinarily I would certainly have been in a hospital by now," he told Bishop. "The great thing is that even my well life is much changed, as tho I'd once been in danger of falling with every step I took." Thousands of hours of psychiatry and therapy, he sighed, "almost 19 years" of it, and all of it "as irrelevant as it would have been for a broken leg."[6]

Then, on January 31st, the Viet Cong launched their Tet Offensive, over-running every major city in South Viet Nam, including Saigon, and the war, which had been going on with increasing fury for the past three years, and which the White House had assured the American people was finally being won, now seemed to spiral completely out of control. "Hasn't the last week been hideous?", Cal wrote Mary McCarthy on February 5. "I think somehow of the Indians throwing their lives away with scornful courage, and often my eyes water."[7] He'd been to a draft resistance meeting a few days before and had prepared a statement which would appear in the *New York Review of Books* under the heading: "Day of Mourning." "We should have a national day of mourning," it read, "or better our own day of mourning, for the people we have sent to misery, desperation—that we have sent out of life; for our soldiers, for the pro-American Vietnamese, and for the anti-American Vietnamese, those who are fighting with unequalled ferocity and probably hopeless cour-age, because they prefer annihilation to the disgrace of an American con-quest." But the crowds had kept drowning him out, until at last he'd left the podium and the rally.[8]

He'd been to several such meetings, "somewhat arranged by Mitch Good-man, Denise Levertov's husband, and one of those indicted with Spock." But honesty seemed impossible at such gatherings, where "little groups of non-G.I.s [and] draft-evaders" were "placed on the stage (samplings of the com-mon man)," and few could "speak at all, except in erroneous clichés." The one who'd gotten the most applause in fact was "an oldish boy, obviously on dope, with a rented Viet-Cong uniform, a Viet Cong flag he waved, and an unintelligible story of facing a 23-year sentence for being caught with the needle, instead of attending a resistance rally."[9]

The previous November Minnesota Senator Eugene McCarthy, with Blair Clark for his campaign manager, had quietly entered the Democratic race against Johnson and the war. In 1966, Lizzie had written a piece on U.S. senators for the *New York Review of Books* and McCarthy, it turned out, had been one of the few senators Lizzie (and Cal) had been able to meet. "I liked him from the start," Cal would later say, and "felt a temperamental affinity" with him, together with a common bond of shared attitudes and values.[10] But it was his dry Irish wit, which reminded Lowell so much of Powers's deadpan humor, which finally won him over. For his part, McCarthy admired Lowell's poetry and the public stance he'd taken against Lyndon Johnson. So, when Clark asked Cal to speak on McCarthy's behalf at several New York fund raisers, he agreed. But it was a strange, fatalistic sort of support he would offer, as when, introducing McCarthy to a crowd at a posh town house in Manhattan two weeks before the New Hampshire primary, Lowell began by saying that McCarthy didn't stand a chance of winning.

But McCarthy, who had been expected to receive 10 percent of the New Hampshire vote, stunned everyone by garnering 42 to Johnson's 49, in large part because of the fierce, dedicated work of his young supporters, his Child Crusaders. "I've been all over the place," Cal wrote Peter Taylor after the primary, "and followed McCarthy three days in New Hampshire, going through two sweater factories, one shoe factory, one wood factory, one Lions and Kiwanis club, two ladies clubs. . . . My line was that if I spoke he'd lose the few votes he had." (True to his word, Cal did almost lose him votes when he told the owners of several New Hampshire sweater factories that workers in the shoe factories seemed much happier than their own employees.) But it had been nothing short of a miracle to Cal "how such a quiet and in many ways soporific campaign [had] worked." Moreover, it was "hard to imagine anyone less like a great statesman . . . and more like a good writer" than McCarthy. Just ten days ago, the campaign had looked hopeless, and still did, though "much less so" now, and in a way McCarthy had "already succeeded by smashing light into New Hampshire."

Then, three days after New Hampshire, Bobby Kennedy entered the presidential race. On the night of March 14, Lowell had been talking to someone at McCarthy headquarters in New York and had rashly asked if he could do anything, "intending to get out of a suggestion that I address 3 New Jersey country clubs to raise money (wouldn't I be expelled from the [American] Institute if I did such a thing)—my rosette ground to powder—and was asked to call the senator Kennedy. So I did and left my number, and he called (leaving no stone unturned)." It took only a few moments for Lowell to sense the currency of power and determination in Kennedy, the edge, the directness, the willingness to cut short the conversation if there was nothing more to be said. Bobby told him what he was about to do the next morning, Cal wrote Taylor, "only the [public] tone was somehow much gentler and more reassuring."[11]

For years now Lowell had been intrigued by the image of Robert Kennedy as some driven, fated prince out of the pages of Shakespeare. Himself he saw rather as "an aristocratic, Christian atheist," a sort of post-Christian anti-Machiavellian counsellor to princes who might be able to counsel a man like

Kennedy.[12] So, three years before, he'd given Jackie Kennedy a marked copy of Plutarch's *Lives,* and was delighted to learn that Bobby was reading it, for Bobby was larger than life, and in fact the man he'd all along hoped would bring down Johnson. Clearly he would have liked to work for him. Now, he realized, it was too late for that. His heart would have "to be with McCarthy to the end, personally, & because he is much the better candidate as far as I can judge." More importantly, McCarthy had "hoped and dared when no other politician in the whole country hoped or dared, when there was no hope."[13]

At month's end Cal told a reporter for the *New York Times* that, "of the announced or seriously offered Democratic or Republican candidates, only Senators Kennedy and McCarthy [seemed] morally or intellectually allowable." Of these, McCarthy was "preferable, first for his negative qualities: lack of excessive charisma, driving ambition, machinelike drive, and the too great wish to be president."[14] But two weeks later he told another reporter that if McCarthy didn't make it, Kennedy would be his choice. He knew Bobby "fairly well," he added, and he was "a lot better than he seems to a lot of people."[15] And so, with his long poem "all but finished" and the inspiration which had kept him writing for the past nine months momentarily stalled, Cal was going to Milwaukee on March 21 to stump for McCarthy.[16] (From there he wrote Lizzie dejectedly that it looked now as if the odds were "against our getting any but the two worst candidates," by whom he meant Johnson and Nixon. What a nightmare it was to be in the midst of all this.)[17]

Then, on the evening of March 31, Johnson announced he would not seek reelection. So it would be McCarthy, Kennedy, and Vice President Hubert Humphrey battling for the Democratic Primary, with McCarthy taking Wisconsin and Oregon. But the key confrontation would come in California in June. In the midst of all this flurry had come the unthinkable: the assassination of Martin Luther King, Jr., on April 4. "Somewhere a white wall faces a white wall," Lowell wrote, capturing the nightmare sense of strangulation which much of the nation felt at the news. For a while he even feared he would go over the edge again, as he had when John Kennedy had been killed. He was doubly thankful now for his lithium:

> *one wakes the other, the other wakes the first. . . .*
> *the walls, once woken, are forced to go on talking,*
> *their color looks much alike, two shadings of white,*
> *each living in the shadow of the other.*
> *How fine these distinctions when we cannot choose. . . .*
> *At this point of civilization, this point of the world,*
> *the only satisfactory companion we*

can imagine is death—this morning, skin lumping in my throat,
I lie here, heavily breathing, the soul of New York.[18]

He wrote Mary McCarthy, thanking her for her letter in support of Gene McCarthy. "I loved it all," he said, including "the horrible vision" of John Kennedy's old New Frontier returning to power, "the sheer wood a little grayer—tarnished by power, discredited and famished by exile." Like Gene McCarthy, Lowell too was coming to dislike "the rich, polite East" more and more. Only the night before he'd been at a gathering and watched one woman, dressed "in a half transparent black mourning dress" for Martin Luther King, "loving *all* three candidates of the Democratic Party." It was a symbol of the liberal covering all bets so as not to be disappointed by the Democratic choice: "working for Kennedy, favoring Humphrey, charmed by McCarthy, tho embarrassed by his voting record." Robert Silvers at the *New York Review of Books* was thinking of asking Mary to cover the Indiana campaign once she finished her Hanoi piece and Cal urged her to do it. She would "see strange things," just as he had or would: "the Lions Club of Spring Point, Oregon, sweater factories. All very merry and trivial in this sad world." Yet, in spite of his joking, the democratic process *did* matter, and sometimes his eyes watered "in anticipation of the inevitable defeat."[19]

In late April students at Columbia protesting the war and the draft occupied several campus buildings, including President Grayson Kirk's office, effectively shutting down the school for a week. Lowell had been at Columbia earlier that month and had spoken then for "four or five minutes against President Johnson's Vietnam war," for which he'd received "tame applause." But he'd not been there when the police moved in to end the takeover at Kirk's request.[20] Upset by the use of so much force against unarmed students, Lowell saw Kirk not as some "branch of the Scotch Church," but merely as "some poor, odious, pitiful creature."[21] "The old king enters his study with the police," he wrote in "The Restoration," a room

> *much like mine left in my hands a month:*
> *unopened letters, the thousand cigarettes,*
> *open books, yogurt cups in the unmade bed—*
> *the old king enters his study with the police,*
> *but all in all, his study is much worse than mine;*
> *an edge of malice puts the seal of man:*
> *frames smashed, their honorary honors lost,*
> *all the unopened letters have been answered.*
> *He halts at woman things that can't be his,*

he says, "To think that human beings did this!"
The sergeant picks up a defiled White Goddess, *or is it*
Secret Memoirs of the Courts of Europe?
"Would a human beings do this things to these book?"[22]

In late May Lowell was in Oregon, attacking the now-faded New Frontier of John F. Kennedy with arguments close to Mary McCarthy's. By then he'd become sharply opposed to what he called Bobby's "shy, calculating delay in declaring himself," and then "the shaggy rudeness of his final entrance." Who really wished now for a "return of the old new frontiersmen?" After eight years, Jack Kennedy's men seemed "tarnished with power" and "thirsting to return to that power." Nor could he forgive Bobby "for trying to bury us under a pile of gold."[23]

On June 3, Lowell joined the McCarthy entourage at the Fairmont Hotel in San Francisco. By that point he'd definitely come to the decision that if McCarthy lost California, McCarthy should support Kennedy, and vice versa. Then, without consulting McCarthy, Lowell arranged to meet with Kennedy, who was staying at the same hotel. "They had a fairly unsatisfactory talk," Arthur Schlesinger, Jr., would recall. Cal thought Bobby was making debater's points and told him, "You musn't talk to me this way." Bobby replied by saying he guessed there wasn't much more to say. Cal wished he could think of some joke to cheer Bobby up, though he knew even that wouldn't do much good. Afterward, Cal told McCarthy he'd felt rather "like Rudolf Hess parachuting into Scotland."[24]

Then the televised debate between McCarthy and Kennedy. But even as McCarthy was being prepped for the debate, Cal walked into the room and took him downstairs for a drink. Afterwards the two of them took a limousine down to the waterfront, so that McCarthy could get a glimpse of Alcatraz, the two of them passing the time composing a modern version of "Ode to St. Cecilia's Day." "By the time he got to the [television] studio," McCarthy's chief adviser in California, Tom Finney recalled, "McCarthy was more like Henry V at Agincourt."[25] His poor ratings afterwards showed it, though McCarthy blamed his performance on not knowing what lies Kennedy would come up with. For his part, Blair Clark would maintain that McCarthy lost the debate (and California) because he did not want to win it, and also out of some contorted resentment of the Kennedys.[26]

Lowell had already returned to New York when Bobby Kennedy was shot as he moved through the kitchen of the Hotel Ambassador late on the evening of the 5th, just moments after the announcement that he'd won California. With Kennedy's death, Lowell's heart went out of the race. (Moreover, though

Lowell did not live long enough to learn this, Clark would later insist that McCarthy gave up on the campaign when, only four days after Kennedy's death, he secretly told Hubert Humphrey that it was now up to Humphrey to carry the banner. Humphrey, who was certainly no match for Johnson, would (alas) soon allow himself to be bullied into accepting the status quo in Viet Nam.)[27] "Doom was woven in your nerves, your shirt, / woven in the great clan," Lowell would write, the New England of Henry Adams paying its respects to the Irish aristocracy of the doomed Kennedys:

> they too were loyal,
> and you more than loyal to them, to death.
> For them like a prince, you daily left your tower
> to walk through dirt in your best cloth. Untouched,
> alone in my Plutarchan bubble, I miss
> you, you out of Plutarch, made by hand—
> forever approaching our maturity.[28]

That September, after the poem had appeared in the *New Republic,* Lowell would hear from Donald Junkins, as staunch a supporter of Bobby Kennedy as Lowell had been of McCarthy, who had taken exception to the line, "forever approaching our maturity." Not *"our"* maturity, Junkins argued, but *"your"* maturity—Bobby's maturity. Cal countered: he'd known both McCarthy and Kennedy well and both were "very ugly on each other long before they were running against. Gene at least had the advantage of putting his Bobby-criticism in the form of sardonic jokes, which had the advantage of being imaginative and polemically true. Bobby's were frontal slurs, sometimes true, sometimes untrue and platitudes." As for that last line, he added, Junkins had simply misunderstood it. *"Our* is not an editorial we," he explained, "the secondary meaning the only possible one, would give *our* the meaning of *man's* or *mankind's,* or the future maturity of our country." Bobby, he conceded, "may have been our hero; he was never mature; nor would anyone who knew him well and love[d] him, have thought so. To say that he was our maturity robs him of most of his true seriousness and pathos."[29]

In June, Lowell received an honorary degree from Yale, but even on that occasion he felt the need to make his disapproval of the war known. On May 30 he'd written President Brewster of Yale that he wanted to make a statement—one as "uninflammatory, unrhetorical and unembarrassing as possible"—after he received his degree. "I know," the statement read, "that I am being honored mostly, and probably entirely, for my poetry; still I wish to express my gratitude to this University for now honoring me, when I stand in much the same position, and perhaps in some of the same danger as William Coffin of Yale and Benjamin Spock of Yale, and the other defendants at Boston."[30]

Two weeks later he was back in Castine, glad for the retreat after a spring of campaigning. "God, what ease to be here," he wrote Rich on June 18. "Ache and fatigue have been running out of my body like discharged swill. Two tree swallows nest outside my barn door in a forbidding little wooden house bought at last year's yacht club affair. A family of skunk paid us a visit last night—smelled but not seen."[31] And to Eberhart a week later: "I've come up here very tired from the life and vicissitudes of the spring. Now we are thawing, you couldn't call it warming in this Maine spring. Harriet goes to camp day after tomorrow, and we're all somber, but I think she'll like it."[32]

It would be the first time Harriet, now eleven and a half, would spend the summer away from her parents, staying at Camp Alamoosook, forty miles from Castine, on a lake island. But Lowell was so desolate after dropping her off that he wrote his only child soon after he got back to Castine: "As we were driving from the camp, a small, cow-brown but long-haired rabbit rushed across the dirt road. He was smaller and darker than the one we saw at the hatchery man's house." What to say to a young girl? Sally Austen's poodle had offered to keep him company in the Barn, but he'd been too busy. "Today," he brought her up to date, "I have corrected and typed and retyped a hundred lines." He'd gone out to the rail along the ocean's edge and had spotted a circle of stones down on the beach, a remnant from one of their picnics. "I was sad. I am sad. I wish you were back. . . . Are you still alive and undrowned?"[33]

"Warm days, warm days," he wrote her two weeks later. He and Mother had picnicked with the Wests and the Hoffmans and had come upon a young dead seal, which the children had buried afterwards. "It was the color of a pig, and had its head eaten off. . . . That night it was so hot in our upstairs rooms, we could hardly move. I sat for a while late at night on a lawn chair, and watched the trees under the stars."[34] And at the end of the month, again: "Bright dry days, good tennis, a pretty dinner prepared by Mother, and broiled steaks by me over the fire for the Wests." He'd been lying on his bed in the bedroom, he told her, "watching the tops of the elms, tossing high in the wind and sunshine—by themselves," and had written a poem about it all: "you playing your own [Nocturne], the trees tossing in the wind, and that other wind . . . the wind of inspiration, what blows in your mind when you compose or just think":[35]

Downstairs, you correct notes at the upright piano . . .
the loose tap beats time, you hammer the formidable
chords of The Nocturne, *your second composition.*
Since you first began to bawl and crawl
from sheltered lawn to this shady room, how often
these winds have crossed the winds of inspiration—
in these too, the unreliable touch of all.[36]

"Harriet is quite happy in her camp," he told Adrienne Rich. "A little shy but full of it, full of jargon." It had been sad seeing her rowed away after their visit. On the other hand, Lizzie's relations with Harriet's guinea pig, Muffie, had "improved alarmingly since Harriet left."

On July 10 he and Lizzie were in Boston for the sentencing of Spock and the other defendants. It was now too that Cal "more or less" made up with the voluble activist Mitch Goodman. Nothing would happen, he thought, to the defendants for another year, and "after an acute moment of pang one felt almost nothing." Still, a two-year sentence was "an ugly acquisition for the future." Suddenly the election and the country's future seemed "almost a dream."[37] "Far from our treasonable, reasonable taunts to save the country," he wrote after the sentences had been handed down,

> *soft conventions of discourse with lawyers, judge and jury;*
> *"We have had all we can have, and have ruined*
> *so much we cannot safely ruin this."*[38]

That same month Lowell heard from Tate, married for a third time and now in his mid-sixties, that he and his young wife, Helen, had just lost one of their year-old twin sons, Michael, in a crib death. Even this would lend itself to journal entry and elegy:

> *Things no longer possible to our faith*
> *go on routinely usable in nature;*
> *the worst is the child's death. Even his stone,*
> *the very, very old one, one century, two,*
> *his one-year date common in auld lang syne*
> *is no longer for faith's eye-scale. . . .*[39]

"I remember my Harriet at much the same age going down Marlborough Street in her carriage," Cal wrote to console his old friend. "She wore a cumbersome ribbed hood, like Charles Bovary's famous hat; she had a hideous, heavy frown that probably meant she wanted sleep—and she was every-thing! Poor Allen, poor Helen, poor little lost boy! I am almost crying myself, and wish I could help."[40]

From August 5 through the 9th he watched the Republican Convention out of Miami on television, and thought of what kind of an America was being bequeathed to his daughter. "Brotherly, stacked and mean, the great Conven-tion, / throws out its Americana like dead flowers," he wrote midway through the rallies, as the Republicans gathered behind "the mortician," Nixon, who had promised to end the war with honor:

> *one summer, two summers, young breasts escape the rib;*
> *the future is only standing on our feet,*
> *and what can be is only what will be—*
> *the sun warms the mortician, unpolluted.*[41]

Everyone of course was for peace and against war. But history had taught him otherwise. He thought back to his undergraduate years when the West had stared at the appeasements offered Hitler at Munich, all in the name of maintaining peace. Now it was Russia pitted against the United States, their shadows playing over the killing fields of Viet Nam. All of the candidates were pledged to bringing peace, but who would deliver on the promise? And then suddenly, in late August, in Czechoslovakia, Russian troops and tanks were moving in to quell an uprising by the people, effectively ending whatever chances McCarthy might still have had to win the nomination:

> *Hitler, Mussolini, Daladier, Chamberlain:*
> *that historic confrontation of the great—*
> *firm on one thing, they were against the war;*
> *each won there, by shoving the war ahead twelve months.*
> *Is it worse to choke on the vomit of cowardice,*
> *or blow the world up on a point of honor? . . .*
> *John Crowe Ransom at Kenyon College, Gambier, Ohio,*
> *looking at primitive African art on loan:*
> *gleam-bottomed naked warriors of oiled brown wood,*
> *makeshift tin straws in their hands for spears;*
> *far from the bearded, armored, all-profile hoplite*
> *on the Greek vase; not distant maybe in their gods—*
> *John saying, "Well, they may not have been good neighbors,*
> *but they never troubled the rest of the world."*[42]

When Harriet returned to Castine, Cal and a neighbor took her and some of the other children up to the local cemetery, where the neighbor "appeared sheeted (but with a visible dog and car) as a ghost." As a rule, he didn't do "much of this sort of thing," he admitted to Rich, so doing it had been fun. Earlier in the month he'd read with Adrienne Rich, Miroslav Holub, and Galway Kinnell in Vermont, one more poetry reading for peace. But now he was bone tired of it all. In truth, readings of any sort had long ceased to amuse him.[43] One half of hell, he'd told Bishop that winter, was the specter of "forever meeting a new English faculty, coed, all older than one is, cup of coffee in a paper cup, in the other hand a cookie and cigarette, and always standing, and signing copies of one's least liked book." The other half was "the pre-reading cocktail party meant to last half an hour and lasting two, so that you can hardly walk or see."[44] Now, he told Rich, readings even for peace or for "any cause on earth, except free alcohol," were neither fun nor "morally permissible." True, there was the "last ditch argument" that they made money for a good cause, "but never in proportion to the energy killed and the affliction inflicted."[45]

On August 24 he and Lizzie flew to Washington to meet Eugene McCarthy and from there flew on to Chicago. By then Lowell was sure they would be "licked" worse than Nelson Rockefeller had been in Miami. He supposed he still loved New York, he told Bishop, but he was very tired just now and would as soon stick his head in a plastic sack as return to the political fever that awaited him there.[46] But Chicago was no better. Amidst riots and the Chicago police the bizarre drama of the Democratic Convention unfolded at the end of August. There was fear everywhere in the city, fear so palpable Lowell wrote that he could feel it even in the muddy music on the grand piano, in the very look of the nervous house plants, the singed back of a Siamese cat, the Louis Quinze order in the decor of McCarthy's wealthy Chicago brother, fear in the vertiginous yachts and car garages below.[47] Senator Ralph Yarborough, on the same Chicago-bound plane with Lowell and McCarthy, wrote Cal that "not even the lift of seeing you could hold up against the depression witnessing the police brutality that followed," the "ultimate indignity" coming when McCarthy headquarters on the fifteenth floor of the Conrad-Hilton Hotel were broken into by the police, who began indiscriminately beating the students gathered there.[48] Cal, watching the events unfolding on television, could only stare in disbelief when, following Mayor Richard Daley's orders to "preserve disorder," the Chicago police charged McCarthy's young supporters:

> *In our staff headquarters, three heads smashed, one club.*
> *Five days the Hilton was liberated with troops and cars—*
> *a fallen government. The youth for McCarthy*

knew and blew too much; their children's crusade!
Waste fell from the windows at the end of the party. . . .
"How can you have a Convention, if you can't throw out a beer-can?"[49]

"After five nights of Chicago, police and mob," a spiritually exhausted Lowell wrote when he had finally made it back to Castine:

I am so tired and bad, clichés are wisdom,
the clichés of paranoia. On this shore,
the fall of the high tide waves is a straggling, joshing
march of soldiers . . . on the march for me. . . .[50]

"When I look inside it's sad and acid," he wrote Bishop four days later. "Age, death of friends, aging of everything in sight, the bad immediate future of this country, most countries, talents and decency misused etc. The stuff of life always." Chicago really *had* been as bad as it had looked on television, he told her. He had stayed away from the rallies at the Amphitheater and out of the marches this time round, instead spending most of his waking hours in McCarthy's apartment, "chatting, watching him throw an orange to his brother, hearing his rather beatnik daughter say we would have to have our gas and pistols now, and maybe, tanks." The rest of the time he'd spent with Lizzie, William Styron, and Mailer drinking in the bars.

Yet every so often he'd gone out "into the park and sidewalks by the Hilton. One night boys with bloodied heads were brought into staff headquarters, the next our staff headquarters were raided by about twenty policemen, because some probably imaginary beer cans were thrown out the window." It was like "the old Gestapo movies," and he and the others had been effectively terrorized. And yet, the youthful demonstrators, he thought, had for the most part "behaved beautifully" and had been "about as dangerous as a church congregation." Still, he had no sympathy for the Democratic Party organizers who had sent those kids in "to be bashed."

McCarthy himself had done nobly, "the only man of importance in either party to defy the parties, nor did he overdo it." And while his defeat had come as no surprise, the violence had. Well, it was time now to read Shakespeare and prepare for his fall classes, though it would be hard "as giving up whiskey to give up hearing and seeing live things at every turn of the head." He felt particularly bruised by how the young had been treated, their poor heads smashed by police clubs. It was, he said, "as if a man had hit Harriet."[51]

Everything about New York seemed insufferable that fall: "the election, talk about the election, the depression, the frustration, the moisture,—and there's noise twenty hours a day. Such the insight of my jaundiced eye, my jaundiced ear." He was having "strange moods of testiness" which were proving "very productive" for his long poem, but which did not make him very sociable. Looking back now, it was still "quite likely" that, whoever won the election, the next few years would be "desultory, depressed and moist, and maybe peaceful." The only "completely dangerous 'leader' " out there stumping seemed to be George Wallace, "a man of perhaps too little articulation to win power." After all, both Nixon and Humphrey had by then sworn themselves to peace—with honor—in Viet Nam.[52]

He wrote Berryman congratulating him on the publication of the second and last part of the *Dream Songs*. His admiration for the poems was "still rolling up," he told Berryman, and he was "dumbfounded at how many of the same things" both their long poems had: "rough iambic lines, often pentameter (for me mostly), short sections that are not stanzas; wife, wives, child, old flames, new ones, sex, love, loves, portraits of writers . . . landscape (I have more of this), portraits of the dead, full middle age, humor, death etc."[53]

But then Berryman had a hundred things he didn't: "jokes, rhymes, Henry, more jokes, Delmore," and enough of Ireland to make Berryman "the best Irish poet since Yeats." He especially liked the way Berryman got his thought and personality onto the page. Both their long poems, he thought, had "a good deal of gaiety and desperation," though Berryman's world was more comic and Lowell's "16 months of time" perhaps more tragic. He did not mean the speakers of the poems, for neither was "tragic, except mostly as all men are, and rather less." Most poets dwindled in force as they aged, he noted. But Berryman just got better and better. Like him, Cal too wanted to go out of this world "walking."[54]

With Kennedy dead and McCarthy out of the race, Lowell buried himself once more in his poem, "finishing and extending" it, not even allowing himself to open unimportant mail. By early November he had 3,000 lines or 215 sonnets, and still he wasn't finished. It was like reading *The Faerie Queene,* he told Taylor. By the time you'd finished reading it you'd forgotten the beginning, so that it could be "safely repeated." It was Election Day, and he did not even want to think of politics, much less vote, though he thought he might wear a black armband to class.[55] Instead, he opted for a dark blue tie. "Election Night, the last Election Night," he wrote, with Nixon now the next president of the country:

> *My daughter telephones me from New York,*
> *she talks* New Statesman, *"Then we're cop-outs! Isn't*
> *not voting Humphrey a vote for Nixon and Wallace?"*
> *And I, "Not voting Nixon is my vote for Humphrey."*
> *It's funny-awkward; I don't come off too well;*

"You mustn't tease me, we were clubbed in Chicago."
We must rouse our broken forces and save the country:
we often said this, now the fallen angels
open old wounds and hunger for the blood-feud
hidden like contraband and loved like whiskey.[56]

As winter came on he found solace and amnesia in drinking and in writing, and saw almost no one. "I've done so little, sociable or practical, this year," he wrote Tate at year's end. "My poem possesses and obsesses—like whiskey, that other inspirer. When I know I'm through, another small section pushes out." If history was after all a fiction, it was unfortunately also "stubbornly bound to shadowy fact."[57]

There were grievous difficulties at home now, due in large part to his continued infidelities and his drinking, drinking which he believed his poem demanded. Early in January 1969 he went up to Canada to give a reading, and from there wrote Lizzie a revealing note. "I have been hard going the last couple of years," he admitted, though when hadn't he been? Could he again "become the pillar never absent from the family hearth?" In spite of everything, he did still love her, he added tamely, loved her "varied interests," her "refreshing teaching," her "neat clothes," her "capacity for keen conversation and argument and most for our lovely child." Somehow he'd connected "almost unstopping composition with drinking. Nothing was written drunk, at least nothing was perfected and finished, but I have looked forward to whatever one gets from drinking, a stirring and a blurring?" Now he promised, "as a child might say," to try and change, cut back on his alcoholic intake, stop if he had to, though "even the Trinity" couldn't "make the crooked stick straight—or young again."[58]

But in truth he was also suffering from high blood pressure and a hyperthyroid condition exacerbated by the lithium he was taking. He found himself apologizing to Marcia Nardi (the "Cress" of Williams's *Paterson*) for not being able to do more for her poems. "The reason why this is so," he offered, "is that all fall I've suffered from some sort of thyroid excess or deficiency,[59] both at once in different 'areas,' I think. It leaves me with waves of languor; I can't sit through a movie, my meagre preparation for classes is a toil etc. Probably the thing isn't serious or dangerous but absolutely nothing can be done till more tests are made. I think I am even forwarding science. . . . Everything has gone unattended to." Everything, that is, except work on his long poem. Here the weariness left him unaffected, so that he could still get in fifteen-hour workdays.[60]

In late February he was in Gibraltar, where he visited Tangiers with Meredith before flying on to Israel on March 6. From Tel Aviv he had planned to head north to Nazareth, visiting the Golan Heights, then travelling south again to Jericho and Jerusalem. His tour would include readings, visiting libraries, and meeting Israeli literary figures. But in Tel Aviv he found his body shaking terribly when he tried to raise a cup of coffee to his lips. "God, have mercy on me—may I not die far from you!", he wrote Lizzie. How lovely it would be to just fall asleep now and wake "a 100 years younger. My hand almost shakes too much to write. . . . I only pray to God that I see you and Harriet again, dearest!"[61] When Lizzie received this letter on March 9, she was frantic. Luckily, Barbara Epstein at the *New York Review of Books* was able to help her reach Cal at the King David Hotel in Jerusalem, and Lizzie was "ecstatic" to find him better. "Darling," she ended, "I won't let you go so far away ever again."[62] The trouble, he wrote her now, had been his blood pressure again, "trembling of foot and hand." The remedy too had been simple enough: "Don't climb high places, overdrink, stay up too late (all the old things)." Including not forgetting—as he had—to take his high blood pressure pills.[63]

At the University of Jerusalem he met with students and was invited to stay on an extra week to meet several important Israelis, among them David Ben Gurion, now living in retirement. When someone had asked him the year before how he approached the Bible as literature, Lowell had answered that the Old Testament God was a "war-god, often a criminal tyrant." And yet that God was "close to the nature of things, ergo profound," and "more real than God usually is in writing." At least the "odious God of Job, unlike Milton's," was "alive, an Arab god, almost an African god; somehow . . . a necessary tho mostly vile and barbarous ancestor of Christ, who really does stand up."[64] Now he picked up the theme again in a sonnet. "The sun still burns in Israel," he wrote now, his three weeks in Israel long enough to allow him to see that the God of Jeremiah and Isaiah and the minor prophets was still very much alive in the new state of Israel:

> *I could have stayed there*
> *a month longer and even stood conscription,*
> *though almost a pacifist, and still not sure*
> *if Arabs are black . . . no Jew, and thirty years*
> *too old. I loved the country, her briskness, danger,*
> *jolting between salvation and demolition. . . .*
> *the ways of Israel's God are military;*
> *from X to X, the prophets, unto Marx. . . .*[65]

On March 21 he flew to Madrid, where his family and William Meredith were waiting to begin a ten-day sightseeing vacation through Andalusia with him. Then he returned to New York alone. "Empty house," he wrote Lizzie on the 31st, "except for the dry water-dropping sounds of Muffin [the angora] munching newspaper." The rabbits, Jump and Jump Junior, had (alas) "lapsed into silence," so that he had "no speaking family!"[66] In mid-April he was off on another tour—two weeks this time—first to "riot-torn and police-torn Harvard," then down to "pastoral Charlottesville."[67] But he was very tired now, and felt as if frayed wires were running through his body.[68]

In June, his "long poem" (274 sonnets) was published as *Notebook 1967–68*. Over the next year it would be met with a mixture of accolades and bafflements. William Meredith set the tone for the book's reception with his front-page review for the *New York Times Book Review*. Though "complex and imperfect," this was major work, Meredith offered, a propitiatory offering of fragments of a created order to "the modern god of chaos." The various sections of the poem were a combination of the public and the intensely private which had managed to escape the "weary assets" of the sonnet sequence through their freely expanding images and unexpected resolutions.[69] But perhaps Robert Boyers was most on target when he wrote a year later that for the first time in his poetry Lowell had found a form equal to everything he described, no matter how quotidian or how grisly. The result was nothing less than the creation of a "comprehensive and essential document" of twentieth-century consciousness.[70]

How had Lowell achieved this? By stepping down from the aloof, ironic vantage of Flaubert which he'd assumed in *Life Studies,* or the Marvellian octosyllabics of the public spokesman in *Near the Ocean,* to immerse himself in the troubled, chaotic, muddled world of the present, from that vantage addressing his audience in a language which reflected the radical shifts and anacolutha of the contemporary sensibility: a rapid-fire advance from thought to thought, public and private, as quickly as one might shift stations on a radio or channels on a television. And yet a poetic world in which the random and the myopic caught in a flash of insight the essence and import of the event under scrutiny. Indeed, the radical shifts which had given Lowell so much trouble three years before in Berryman's *77 Dream Songs* had by 1967 become an essential part of Lowell's own poetic.

Now, having discovered a form flexible enough to digest everything and anything, Lowell could no more give it up than Berryman had been able to give up his Dream Songs. So, all that "slow, out of things summer" of 1969 in Castine he continued revising and adding to his poem, ostensibly, he told himself, for "a definitive(?) English edition."[71] Again he wrote almost no one, and nearly wept when summer ended and he had to return once more to New York. Somehow, he told Tate, "one . . . never needed asylum more from the rub and grandeur of the serious city." The summer had quickly disappeared for him "on a sliding green carpet, and painfully soon," while he'd revised thirty poems and added twenty-two new ones, fitting them all into their proper slots.[72]

He had his misgivings, he confessed to Ransom, about all this "floundering of revision, a flaw removed and three added, the good things mislaid along the road, the chances missed through blindness, hardness etc."[73] And yet, mending the lines of his poetry to catch more of the flux of reality had turned out to be a "great joy." By then he had become, he told Kazin that October, first and foremost a voice for his times, an historian, a sort of novelist, "more firmly hooked to fact and records, freed from the usual plots of romance." And while it was true that the historian (he was speaking here specifically of his beloved Henry Adams, but he meant any historian, including—if he was fortunate enough—himself) didn't "quite *make* history," it was equally true that most lived history was "dull, petty, hardly worth preserving, until the great historian" entered the mass of facts to shape them.[74]

"I've come to New York for some reason with feet of stone," he wrote Berryman that September. He was tired now, tired of the routine of dividing his week between New York and Cambridge, and ached for some country place to which he might escape. And yet he knew he could never take the Maine winter. His feet dragged, and his blood pressure was acting up again. That summer he'd felt "embarrassed and hesitant about getting on the tennis court," and there'd been that episode too in Tel Aviv when he thought he was going to die. "These wretched little black splinters mortality hits us with," he sighed. How he would have liked to scorn the problem of old age, though not quite the way Yeats had done, since it seemed "silly to triumph that much" over growing old. And even Yeats—that old poseur—must have known underneath it all that for all his storming what he was really afraid of was dying.

His *Notebook 1967–68* did seem to have to be read through as one would read a novel, he confessed to Berryman, and a "very short, dense, rather difficult novel" at that. During the past summer, in spite of himself, he'd done nothing but work on it, scattering new and revised poems through the book, unable "to judge their effect or effectiveness," though he guessed they were "up to the others and enough different." He didn't know whether he had "anything more in me worth adding," though he could see Berryman at least was still going strong. "There were new and top Dream Songs in the [*Harvard] Advocate*. If you can go on that way, why stop ever?" In truth, he would rather have Berryman's praise now than anyone else's, he confessed. And then, what was deeply troubling him surfacing for a moment before it dived back under the black waters again. "Sometimes, it's only love that lets air in our lungs."[75]

That summer Richard Tillinghast, Lowell's former student, had written offering him a visiting professorship at Berkeley for the following spring. Tillinghast's letter, like so much else, revised, would find its way into Lowell's poem:

> *"We're in a prerevolutionary situation*
> *at Berkeley, an incredible, refreshing relief*
> *from your rather hot-house, good prep-school Harvard riots.*
> *The main thing is our exposure to politics;*
> *whether this a priori will determine*
> *the revolutionary's murder in the streets,*
> *or the death of the haves by the have-nots, I don't know;*
> *but anyway you should be in on it—*
> *only in imagination can we lose the battle."*[76]

"Your saying that I 'should be in on it,' " Lowell answered, "is as tho I were to offer you Castine by saying 'we seem likely to have a tidal wave and you should see the morale of a village in danger.' " But by then he no longer had faith in either the government *or* the student radicals, "tho some in some things." Besides, it was "a joy this summer to be back to real life (real rest?). The contentions, the revolution, the counter-revolution will all come back to me. I cannot doubt it, and perhaps they'll be welcome."[77]

But that fall they were not welcome, as he shuttled to and fro between New York and Harvard, where once again he taught Shakespeare—the English Histories—and another workshop. Bill Alfred was still there, a blessing as always, but many of Lowell's best students were gone now, including Alan Williamson, Richard Tillinghast, Robert Seigel, even Grey Gowrie, back now in England. All Harvard seemed to be able to offer now, he wrote Berryman, were the "riches of solitary speculation—too much." But was there anything more last man alive than dinner with oneself? "One resolves to stop doing what one doesn't enjoy. But of course it's not that easy. It's not that easy to say one now knows better what one wants than in earlier days. Still, it's pretty good, if we could only slow and hurry time at will." Then he added: "I think anyone who cared for your book would for mine. Anyway, we're accomplished beyond jealousy. Without your book"—then he crossed that out—"without *you* I would find writing more puzzling."[78]

Nevertheless that fall he did manage to consolidate a new and important working relationship with one of his graduate students, Frank Bidart. Remarkably, Bidart seemed to know *Notebook 1967–68* as well as Lowell himself. Moreover, Bidart was already an accomplished-enough poet that Lowell trusted him sufficiently to listen to his advice on revising his poems, a gesture of confidence which Bidart sometimes found unnerving. In January 1970 he would spend a week in Cal's 67th Street study working on the massive revisions for the book which would now be called—simply—*Notebook*. Cal worked in one room, Bidart in another, splicing the hundreds of one-, two-, and three-line revisions into copies of the book so the printer could make the necessary changes. In truth, it seemed more and more impossible for Cal to read or type out a poem without making changes. As Jarrell had told him, he did not write. Language in Cal's hands was too volatile, too protean, for that. Instead, he rewrote.

"These girls," Lizzie had said ten years before in exasperation over Ann Adden. Yet for the past several years there seemed always to be a girl waiting for Cal at Harvard, and the arrangement was undoubtedly causing a deep fault line in the Lowells' marriage. In the fall of '68 it was a Cambridge poet, in '69 a twenty-one-year-old senior named Martha Ritter who was writing her thesis on *Notebook 1967–68*. At first she worked along with Lowell and Bidart, but by October she was seeing Cal alone. "I would go and cook things and type up poems and make typographical errors and invent new words," she would remember, and soon they were making love. The fact that she was a virgin had fascinated him, and he'd been touched that she could love him—a man thirty years her senior—as she did, though he also explained to her that he would never leave Lizzie. That is, unless he got sick again. That, at least, had always been the pattern.[79]

"The optimistic James Dickey is one of the most desperate souls I know of," Cal had once confided to Bishop, "dreaded by the faculties where he has read." In spite of which, he was a "rather good poet . . . particularly on horrible things like firebombing." Next to Dickey, Cal really did have "a much less agonized German existentialist life," though it was probably also less frivolous.[80] In the late 1960s the bearlike ex-football player and ex–World War II fighter pilot was often paired with Lowell as his equal in popularity and standing. Richard Tillinghast would remember having lunch with these two forces at the Chez Dreyfus in Cambridge in the fall of '67. In the undertow of the conversation that day was the shadow of Robert Bly's recent attack on both poets. Then, as the drinks flowed, Dickey spun out a yarn of being attacked by a bear and of killing it with his bow and arrow. "But the bear wasn't dead, Jim," Cal said, suddenly bearlike himself and laughing: "When you got back to your office, the bear was sitting at your desk. It was Bly."[81]

Now, in the fall of 1969, Dickey had asked Cal to take part in an interview

with a film crew from the *Encyclopaedia Britannica,* to which Cal had assented, *if* the thing could be done "painlessly and freely—without rehearsing,
redoing, standing around in the studio while something else is on." These
things were death, he told Dickey, and "fill the swill pail with chafed flesh and
nerve."[82] The filming went off on schedule in Cal's New York apartment, and
afterwards the camera crew commented on Cal's hospitality and graciousness.
"Every so often," Lowell told Bishop, Dickey, who had begun drinking at
9:30 A.M., "would say loathesome things like 'The future of American poetry is
in this room.' Or 'my problems are worse than yours.' " No doubt they were.
And yet he also felt Dickey's "great energy to say something, so lacking in
most writers."[83]

After a year in office, Nixon had done little to end the war in Viet Nam. So,
for three days that November Lowell once again took part in the anti-war
demonstrations, this time driving down to Washington from New York with
Blair Clark and Mary McCarthy. It was all part of "Washington March Week,"
he wrote Bishop afterwards. "Slightly unlikely people in the van. Mary
McCarthy, here from Paris for dentistry, marshalling signatures for a proclamation; my old friend Blair Clark, speaking at Purdue, Chicago and Washington." As for himself, he was getting "less leftist, if that were possible," with
each passing day, though he had already promised to march again with Dwight
Macdonald. These demonstrations seemed to amount to little more than "a
mammoth ball," he knew, "fed and checked by hopes of danger," though he
hoped it would all stay "mostly tame."[84]

Yet all in all, he told Meredith at year's end, it had been a happy autumn for
him. "Better health, greater ease of soul, 60 new poems added to *Notebook* and
hundreds . . . of revisions," and now the revised manuscript at last turned in.
His family was doing quite well. At the moment Harriet was downstairs playing chess with a friend, the friend winning "except when both cheat, then no
one can." He would be teaching at All Souls, Oxford, beginning in mid-April
1970, for two months, and would return to the States in late June. Then
Castine, then Harvard again in the fall. But now, for a bit, a taste of "New York
idleness."[85]

Still, it was time for a change, and Lowell's two months in England would
stretch to a year, then two. Lizzie too was tired of New York, which after ten
years had devolved into a strange amalgam of the quiet and the exhausting.
"The phone rings all day," she sighed, and then there were the interminable

> plays one is urged to go to in the freezing night, an occasional unwanted invita-
> tion, malignant growths of mail, bills, anxiety about the cost of things, the look
> of things. . . . You feel as if you'd been in a play running for years and then it
> closed and you went uptown and no one called. That is the feel of the political

scene, an utter, odd, shambles, a nothing. And you can't find any re-entry point anywhere. I suppose it is the Johnson destructiveness, and in addition the destructiveness of youth."[86]

So the New York apartment would be let to Carlos Fuentes. Lizzie would take a year's leave from her teaching at Barnard College, where she had been teaching since the fall of 1965, and Harriet would go to school in England.

Lowell had planned on going to Moscow in January 1970 with Blair Clark and his wife Olga, but at the last minute the Russians had cancelled Olga's visa, probably because she knew the Russian language and the Russian literary scene too well for a writer of Lowell's stature to be allowed to go about freely, and the trip had to be cancelled. Instead, Cal read at the University of Connecticut at Stephen Spender's invitation, then in February at the University of Rochester at Anthony Hecht's. He wrote fan letters to Marianne Moore, Mary McCarthy, Mona Van Duyn, and tried to cheer up Meredith, who was suffering from depression.

"Probably you've never had a *real* depression," he wrote Meredith in mid-February. "Tensing at the thought of each new meeting, never speaking more than one sentence, and that dull. . . . Two happy moments a day, that of falling asleep, of waking with a dream I thought would continue (if I were in luck). None seemed to mind, tho occasionally I was chided by people for being restrained." Since he'd last seen him, his own life had had "many shadows and slips," but he'd been "too generally happy to really remember."[87]

In late February 1970, he and Harriet spent an afternoon going through piles of old photos which Harriet was gluing into three scrapbooks. "They go from my grandmother as a bride to last summer," he wrote Bishop. There was even one of Harriet in a "festal Indian suit and boots," gifts from Bishop herself. Now he was returning the favor, sending Bishop three poems, all written for her: the old "Water" poem rearranged "as blank verse with some care. Then the old Castine poem ["Flying from Bangor to Rio 1957"] and an all new one."[88]

The new one—"Letter with Poems for a Letter with Poems"—was particularly risky, because it revealed Bishop at her most vulnerable and quite unlike the figure of reticence she had offered in her own poems. But the best lines would come in yet a fourth poem, lines uncannily right, still unwritten, still unrevised. "Have you ever seen an inchworm crawl on a leaf," it would end:

> *cling to the very end, revolve in air,*
> *feeling for something to reach to something? Do*
> *you still hand your words in air, ten years*
> *unfinished, glued to your notice board, with gaps*

or empties for the unimaginable phrase—
unerring Muse who makes the casual perfect?[89]

On March 2 Cal was at the National Book Award ceremonies in New York to accept an award for Bishop's *Collected Poems*. "I like to make a cut at boldness occasionally," he wrote her afterwards. "This I think I had to do. The rather curious jury, due to [Kenneth] Rexroth, left Pound off the listings of poets to be considered (Meredith put him on)." No one had noted the omission, he added, though there'd been a great clamor about Vladimir Nabokov's *Ada* and Philip Roth's *Portnoy* being left off:

> I came from the wings to the bright stage (first twenty red plush rows absolutely empty) as "recipients" do and said more or less this: That I felt very shy receiving the award for you, that you had always been my favorite poet and friend. . . . I spoke of your enormous powers of realistic observation and of something seldom found with observation, luminism (meaning radiance and compression etc.) and so on for a few sentences. Then I said I was going to say something perhaps ungracious, but that I cared not, because I would consider myself dishonored if I didn't say it. Then I spoke of the complaints (named no names) and said that on the whole I agreed with the complainers, but that a much more important author, Ezra Pound, who had published a little book in June, one of his good books and quite possibly his last [*Drafts & Fragments of Cantos CX–CXII*], had been mentioned by no one. . . .
>
> I read your [*Visits to St. Elizabeth's*]. . . . I said it was a clear poem [about Pound] whose meaning was hard to determine, but the tone was reverential mockery or mocking reverence. I went back to my seat on stage—decent applause. Behind me a voice saying, "I announce that I sever myself from this antisemitic fascist performance." Rexroth in sideburns, tho I didn't know at the time. Well, the master of ceremonies . . . saved my life by instantly saying: "I want to announce that I disassociate myself from anyone who could say what you've just heard was antisemitic or Fascist." There was faint applause for Rexroth and more for the master of ceremonies.[90]

But that did not end the matter. Immediately afterwards, Lowell had gone up to Cambridge and Provincetown to give readings, but in his absence (and though the Lowells' phone was unlisted), someone called the apartment at five-thirty in the morning "and a voice, quite calm and clear, said 'This is the voice of the shofar.' (The Jewish ramshorn for war.) Quite good music; Lizzie listened for a minute or so, then expecting it to change to the usual anonymous obscenities, hung up." The following morning, again at five-thirty, there was another call, obviously long distance. Then the operator saying, "Do you want to speak to Mr. Levin?" Then the line disconnected.

An hour later there was a third call, a voice saying it was time for Lowell "to make peace with his God," to which Lizzie had countered, "I never heard anything so impertinent and absurd. He is at peace with God." Then the voice saying something about "last rites" and that on that day Lowell would die. "Vain threat!", Lowell joked, and it did all sound rather "buffoonish" telling the story now. Yet at the time it had all seemed so "dignified and terrifying." Since then there'd been no more calls, but it had been an awful week for Lizzie and Harriet. "Tell them," Harriet told her mother, "if they call again, Dad is off on his trip to Israel." Then she added, "What do they mean by *his* God, there's only one God."[91]

On March 19, the day the Lowells left for Italy, and after delaying for over a year on the festschrift for Tate's seventieth birthday Lowell had promised reluctantly to edit, Cal wrote apologizing for losing all the essays and reviews Tate had sent him. Somehow, Cal lamely offered, his study had been cleaned "all too thoroughly by the maid," so that he felt "like Mill with Carlyle's *French Revolution.*" Perhaps, though, the clean sweep was all for the best, he added, since Tate's poetry "and probably everything else" Tate had written needed "a fresh angle, a new word." He mailed the letter on his way to the airport.[92]

Venice was high on the Lowells' agenda, especially for Harriet, though she was not, Cal joked, about to spend much time visiting such places of superstition as the city's venerable churches.[93] Cal, on the other hand, had every intention of visiting the churches, "avidly seeking out work by the great masters," Lowell's friend, Esther Brooks, would remember. But this was no longer the same Lowell who had written so movingly of the awesome silence of Our Lady of Walsingham twenty-five years before, and he was visibly impatient with any religious work not done by a recognized master. "If over there in some small chapel within a great church you found a madonna and her infant sitting tranquilly as she had these last three hundred years or more under a perfectly carved cupola, touched by a beam of unexpected sunlight, and he found you there almost hypnotized, moved nearly to tears, he would pause to ask 'Who is it by?' and if it was not by some famous master or was simply *ignoto,* he would pass it by as though blind."

At one point Brooks became so impatient with his asking her to locate a masterpiece for him that she refused to tell him where it was. They were in the Basilica of the Frari then, and Cal was looking for the Titian housed there. He should find it by looking, she insisted. She was being childish, he retorted, for "that Titian was more important than guessing games, etc. But when he understood that I was not going to locate it for him he intercepted a monk hurrying to his prayers and asked him *'Dov'e Tiziano?'* [Where's Titian?] and the monk pointing to heaven replied *'In Paradiso, speriamo bene'* [In heaven, I hope], crossed himself and hurried on. I was trying to stifle my laughter when Cal asked, 'Is he a friend of yours?' "

Later, when she finally did locate the painting for him and he was once more on familiar ground, he began discoursing on its merits, "on Titian and his times, on Titian and beautiful women, on old men, on the works of old men." He was "riveting, fascinating, funny, odd, and completely, interestingly original and serious." That was Cal's way, Brooks saw: to turn experience into thought, then into a metaphor, and then to react with feeling toward the metaphor he had created.[94] Now, as he journeyed toward the brave new world of England, he was about to do the same thing with his marriage of twenty years.

PART IV

16

Dolphin

1970–1971

Toward the end of April, Lowell sent Lizzie a postcard from Amsterdam to say he'd now seen all their old friends from that winter of twenty years before. Most of them were still "old left," he noted, "but without the unpleasant features" of the old *Partisan Review* crowd. He'd also had a letter from the chairman of the English Department at the University of Essex offering him a teaching position for the upcoming year (£4,000, about what he made at Harvard, the same courses, and about the same travelling time as it took to get from New York up to Cambridge). He would be "replacing" Donald Davie, who'd left Essex two years before to teach at Stanford.[1]

Essex, outside Colchester, an hour from London by train: one of the new universities built by the British government in the 1930s. And the scene more recently of student unrest, until Davie had left in disgust, convinced that the school was overrun by Trotskyites and leftist sociologists, so that during the student riots of 1968 he'd found himself on one side of the issues and most of his colleagues on the other. "I have despaired of my country," he wrote Lowell, "as perhaps you have despaired of yours."[2]

If Lowell had not quite despaired of America, he was certainly tired and disillusioned with the direction the country had taken since the death of Bobby Kennedy and the defeat of Gene McCarthy and he needed time now away.

Essex seemed to offer that respite, and he decided to act at once, using the back of the letter offering him the job to tell Lizzie where they might live during their English year. She should sell the car and look after his literary papers, lying now at the University of Stonybrook out in "the wastes" of Long Island. Maybe, "God help us," she would also come upon the Tate material while she was rummaging, for he'd just got the worst letter from his old mentor he'd ever received.[3]

"Your Napoleonic stance permits you to confess other people's lives," Tate had written, meaning to wound, and not forgetting the grudge he'd held for the past twenty years, when Cal had suffered his first breakdown. "I hope that you will not again confess mine." At least *he* knew why Cal hadn't carried through on the festschrift.[4] On April 25, the day after he arrived at All Souls, Oxford, Cal wrote Tate. "You have plenty to be sore about," he began. "My stumbling block was writing the essay." But, he asked, how could Tate claim "a mysterious intuition" into motives he himself did not possess? Surely Tate knew why one didn't write something: for the same reasons Tate hadn't written his novel in 1942, or Cal his Jonathan Edwards book. "It would be hard to say, but our motives were nothing sinister; neither were mine in again writing poetry and putting off the essay. . . . Ah Allen, which of us has insulted the other more? You have, as is right. I was your student and younger friend." Tate's angry missive was certainly not "a good way to keep friends," though Cal wanted Tate to know he still loved him.[5]

"Here I am," he wrote Lizzie later that day, "a half lost soul in All Souls." It was a bachelor's world, but very beautiful, rather "like Bath . . . and Yale, quite Italian. I have eaten in gown and handled a 14th century psalm book."[6] For the next several days he basked in the strangeness and the glory of it all, "windows on the Warden's garden close, roused by the knock of the maid, my gown taken from my back at Commons and rushed up two flights of stairs by my scout to my lodgings . . . letters stamped and mailed for me." The only drawback was that, since the second sex didn't exist here, he felt fourteen and once again back at St. Mark's. Davie had written to assure him that the Essex English department was "one of the best he'd ever seen," naturally enough, since Davie had virtually handpicked it. Moreover the English could under-stand why, just now, an American might want to get away from America for a while.[7]

A week after Cal's arrival, Faber & Faber held a party for him in London. When his publisher had asked for a guest list from him, Cal had named Jona-than Miller, the Grey Gowries, the Alvarezes, the Isaiah Berlins, the William Empsons, and the Stephen Spenders. But he had also invited Lady Caroline Blackwood, whom he'd first met in New York five years before when she was seeing Bob Silvers. One night Cal had had her to dinner at West 67th Street, but, hearing that Cal would talk of nothing but poetry, Blackwood had elected to remain silent that evening. Besides, he was just on the edge of a manic episode at the time, she remembered. Once, looking out from the back seat of a taxi, she'd watched a man weaving through city traffic, and staring straight ahead. The cab she was in had almost hit him. It was Cal.[8]

In 1970 Blackwood was thirty-eight and twice married. She was the eldest child of Maureen Guinness, Marchioness of Dufferin and Ava, and Basil Sheridan Hamilton-Temple-Blackwood, 4th Marquis of Dufferin and Ava, who had been killed in the Burmese theater of operations in 1945. Blackwood was therefore a member of the wealthy Guinness clan, though, as Cal later told Powers, she had long ago learned to loathe "the stout which was fed her as nourishment as a child."[9] Her first marriage had been to the painter Lucien Freud; her second—still nominally in effect—to the musician Israel Citkowitz, by whom she had had three daughters. She was an essayist and a budding novelist, and had already published articles and stories in *Encounter* and *London Magazine*. She was stunning, vital, and had the easy self-possession of the aristocrat.

After the Faber party, and already fed up with his week of imposed monosexuality, Cal insisted on going back with Blackwood to her house on Redcliffe Square in Kensington, where he promptly made himself at home, explaining that Bob Silvers had given him her telephone number so that he and she could get married. For the first month, they saw each other clandestinely at All Souls and on trips to Ireland and the Lake District, while Lizzie, back home, kept waiting for news of the London apartment her husband was supposed to be finding for her and Harriet, now that he'd signed on at Essex for the next *two* years.

Italy had been lovely, he wrote Bill Alfred, and—miraculously—when he'd left Lizzie and Harriet everyone was still speaking, though Harriet had "set her teeth firmly against art except for Carpaccio's dragon," which she wished would devour "Saint George and wear a dove armband." After New York, England seemed "too good to be true," and the English Department at Essex as good as any he'd seen: "young, scholarly, Bohemian and interested in literature—a quality almost unheard of in an English department." He was anxious just now to get away from America for one reason in particular: to forget for a while "the grit and steel and wind of our now atmosphere," and learn to breathe again.[10]

For in truth America in the spring of 1970 was in turmoil. Nixon had sent troops into Cambodia and stepped up the bombing of North Viet Nam in an escalation of the war, and there were now riots on hundreds of campuses around the country, including Harvard. Students at Kent State had been killed by national guardsmen, and violence was escalating in cities like New York and

Los Angeles. Lowell had already seen "pictures of Nixon's agony plastered over every front page," and wondered now if the war would be allowed to "grind on longer than our lives."[11] "At home, the colleges are closed for summer," Lowell's sonnet, "America from Oxford," dated May 5, reads:

> *the students march . . . [Operation] Brassman lances Cambodia,*
> *[Nixon] has lost his pen, the sword folds in his hand like felt. . . .*
> *Is truth here with you, if I sleep well,*
> *Bystander? The peacock spins, the Revolution*
> *hasn't involved us . . . a heat that moves*
> *air so estranged and hot I might be home. . . .*
> *We have climbed above the wind to breathe.*[12]

That May he worked on the galleys for the revised and expanded edition of *Notebook* (with the help of Grey Gowrie, he told Lizzie), then travelled up to Manchester and Bristol for readings and to Leeds for an honorary degree. He spent his time in Bristol with Mary McCarthy, strolling about the countryside, and at Oxford walked about "under Arnold's Cumner Hills." By then news of the invasion of Cambodia by American troops had begun to simmer down. For a while "the very name of America disappeared from half the papers," he wrote Lizzie on May 17. "Even at the height, people changed the subject to Oxford gossip." But soon he and his family would all be together, "and find, God willing, more leisure to breathe."[13]

"I don't know how to describe the England I am hoping you will see and love next fall," he wrote Harriet now. "Think of a much larger New York State, thousands of green fields everywhere, stone house villages." He felt America everywhere here, until "some often small detail of accent or architecture" reminded him that he was in England, the big difference being that here one could run about "much more—more parks." It was also a country almost without thugs.[14]

But for all his breeziness, Lizzie knew something was wrong. "What's up? Such boiling messages, all as public as possible on cables and unenclosed postcards," Cal wrote her on the 26th, trying to stare her down. "It's chafing to have the wicked, doddering, genial All Souls porter take down your stinging cable." He laid her suspicions on her pressures there in New York. Of course he was still looking for a place, and at the moment had the Gowries house-hunting for him in the "parkish" sections of Regent Park and Hampstead. He let on about nothing.[15]

"Very Oxford day," he wrote Lizzie on the last day of May. He'd watched along with hundreds of others as boats were bumped in the races along the Isis, had had lunch with Iris Murdoch and her husband; Lord David Cecil; and Father Peter Levi, S.J.; had attended the funeral at St. Mary the Virgin of Enid

Starkie (who had been in large part responsible for his failure to get the Oxford Chair in Poetry four years before); and had spent an afternoon reading Warden Sparrow's Shakespeare books. The day before he'd walked with his illustrator, Sidney Nolan, all the way from Godstow to Oxford "over a three mile meadow covered with buttercups, peacocks, cattle and skylarks." He'd read Marianne Moore's poems to the Oxford Poetry Society, answered questions, and felt as if he were about to get his St. Mark's Sixth-Form certificate all over again.[16]

His duties would end on June 24. On the 14th he wrote Lizzie that he would be coming home immediately afterwards. In the meantime, he told her, he'd been to the Lake Country with Grey Gowrie and to Poland with Blair Clark. In the company of Omar Pound, Dorothy Pound's son and an old friend of Cal's, he'd visited Basil Bunting and then Dorothy Pound, "a debt to old times."[17] But time was running out. Either he returned to the States, or he stayed in England with Blackwood. Finally, on the 20th, he telegrammed Lizzie from Maidstone, Kent, Blackwood's country estate. "PERSONAL DIFFI-CULTIES," it read, "MAKE TRIP TO NEW YORK IMPOSSIBLE RIGHT AWAY LOVE CAL."[18] When Lizzie learned who Cal was seeing, she thought he had to be sick again, though when she called him about it, he seemed low-keyed, even solicitous for her and Harriet. Distraught and betrayed, Lizzie fired off a letter at once. "I want to add my absolute horror that you two people have taken away something I loved and needed. My job at Barnard, which I tried to get back, but it is filled for this year and their budget is filled." Then she said what was really on her mind: "My utter contempt for both of you for the misery you have brought to two people who had never hurt you knows no bounds."[19]

Lizzie was right. Cal was on the edge of another attack, as even Blackwood could see. At All Souls Cal had made advances toward one of the dons' wives, and his conversation at high table, usually so brilliant, had degenerated into drunken boorishness. In early July he locked Caroline into one of the flats at her Redcliffe Square house. Finally, on the 9th, he had to be admitted to Greenways Nursing Home in St. John's Wood. Mary McCarthy heard the news from Sonia Orwell and telephoned Lizzie from Paris. A week later Sonia telephoned Blair with the news that Cal could leave Greenways if Caroline would take responsibility for him. But by then Caroline, too fragile herself, had fled to Ireland, sending Cal a note which would find its way into a poem: "I think of you every minute of the day; / I love you every minute of the day."[20] But she also told him she would not see him again until he'd fully recovered. "I love you with my heart and mind," he wrote back; "what can I do, if you give me nothing to go on?"[21] As was his pattern, he pursued her with letters, until finally he left Greenways to look for her at Redcliffe Square. The only person he found there was the cleaning lady, and his unexpected grizzly appearance so frightened her that she quit her job on the spot.

In late July Lizzie flew to London, taking Bill Alfred with her. She had little faith in the doctors at Greenways, who had allowed Cal to come and go at will, stopping in the local pubs to drink to his heart's content. Cal was no ape on display, she told Blair Clark, but a "brilliant, proud, dignified man."[22] The woman was secondary. Let him marry her if he wanted. But if he kept drinking on top of the drugs he was taking, she was afraid he would kill himself.

As for Greenways, though at first it had seemed seedy, she could see it really was a hospital. Cal looked awful, his hair shoulder-length (which she cut for him, along with having his clothes cleaned and pressed), and he was kept heavily sedated at all times, so that he could only go about for an hour or so before he collapsed. She took him to lunch and to see *Patton,* and—watching the wreck her husband had become—could not hold back her tears. For the most part he said nothing, or spoke only in jokes, unaware of what others were doing for him, except when "a look of unutterable depression" would flash for a moment across his face. It was like a nightmare here in London, she told Mary McCarthy, especially having to watch Cal surrounded by the Gowries, Israel Citkowitz, Caroline, and above all Sonia Orwell, all of them "hapless, helpless, unhelpful."[23] As for her and Bill Alfred's ministrations, Cal accepted those as if he were some "invalid archbishop, seeing nothing extraordinary in the service."[24]

When Blackwood, then in Scotland, heard that Lizzie was in London, she returned at once to be with Cal. All remained muted and dazed between Lizzie and Cal, Lizzie refusing even to bring up Caroline's name. But as she was leaving to return to New York on August 5, she handed him a note. "If you need me," it read, "I'll always be there. If you don't, I'll not be there." When Cal read this, he came back down the stairs of the hospital. He was crying.

The following day he wrote her in an unsteady hand. "You[r] last not[e] and much else that you said and have said through the years go through my heart," it read. "You couldn't have been more loyal and witty. I can't give you anything of equal value. Still much happened that we both loved in the long marriage."[25] Then, three days later, still groggy, again: "I bubble on, saying nothing because I am thinking more contentedly than ever of your long and yet rushed visit. A heart here thinks of you always." It turned out to be a mild attack of mania this time, and he was expecting to leave the hospital in a week, though "nothing since the rainbow of Noah's flood" was certain.[26]

When Cal was in fact released a week later, Caroline refused to let him return to her flat on Redcliffe Square. "I assume *ceteris paribus,*" he wrote her, "that when I am in a certain state you are too. I could come out in a week or two, if I could have a place to stay. Do come and see me."[27] But she insisted he find his own apartment. Moreover Israel Citkovitz, her estranged husband, who lived in one of the three apartments which made up the Redcliffe Square house, insisted that no madman was going to stay with his children. Cal settled on an apartment at 33 Pont Street, a five-minute taxi ride from Redcliffe Square.

"I've been rambling about getting a studio, toying with revisions, feeling the deadest poet as so often, and getting my textbooks ordered for Essex," he wrote Lizzie at the end of August.[28] To Harriet, growing suddenly and mysteriously into a young woman in his absence, he wrote: "I don't know what a father so far away can say to you. My life except for you and mother is naturally much as it always was. Writing, teaching, enjoying myself as much as I dare. . . . A girl your age must grow older and wiser, which isn't always true of the old." He wanted very much for her to be able to talk and feel at ease with him. "All is as it was," he closed. "Tho not quite."[29]

That fall, with Cal at Essex, Bishop began teaching in his place at Harvard. "I am living in a silly Back Bay part of London," he wrote her in September, explaining that he was now separated from Lizzie. The apartment, he joked, was "near the Cadogan Hotel where Wilde was arrested," and he too was "leading a silly but not unhappy life." The future looked cheerful, but who at their age could know? As for her teaching at Harvard, she would find "drawbacks and deadwood" there, but the work would be "light and exciting." He had many friends in Cambridge, two of whom he especially recommended: Bill Alfred, whom he'd come to depend on, and Frank Bidart, "American Basque . . . who knows my poems much better than I do."[30]

Three weeks later he wrote Bishop again with an update on the new sequence of poems he was working on. In the past four months he'd written thirty new sonnets "in the meter of *Notebook*, but somehow unlike *Notebook* in tone—more strained, the Romantic romance of a married man in a hospital." These would go into *The Dolphin*, the book of poems which would follow the course of his new life with Caroline. Mostly, he had to admit, he was "not very forthright" in the new poems. A few might be good, but in truth he was "disheartened by the whole," and was trying to comb out "the unnecessary grand obscurities."

Caroline, he explained, was a writer, had three "very pretty daughters, oldest ten, and was once years ago married to Freud's grandson, Lucien." She'd lived in San Francisco and New York and was "very beautiful and saw me through the chafes and embarrassments of my sickness with wonderful kindness." As for his own family, guilt clouded each morning, and though things were "not embattled," neither was anything settled. "If only," he sighed, "life could be as manageable as teaching."[31]

That fall at Essex he taught a workshop and Shakespeare's Roman plays. He missed his library, he complained to Lizzie, though he'd always "more or less gotten on without using one, except for the random, accidental offerings of Quincy House." Unfortunately, "instead of Hazlitt's characters," he had

"Professor Dorch's defense of the character of Julius Caesar."[32] "When Lowell joined us," Dudley Young, Lowell's young colleague at Essex, would remember, the music of the sixties

> had begun to turn sour, and many of the causes were looking lost. But the energy was still high (just turning vicious), and . . . normalcy nowhere in sight: politics, dope, music, poetry, sex, apocalypse, mysticism, and more politics. . . . The students were brash, unbuttoned, and street-wise; and though suspicious of anyone as old or as famous as Lowell, they enjoyed telling him [Bob] Dylan's stuff was more important (an argument he would engage with some ferocity). It was a measure of the lateness of the hour that his radical credentials, which would have appeared impeccable in 1967, were by then looking dubious to many.

Once again Cal's week was divided into two mini-weeks: three days at Essex, then four in London. At Essex he stayed with Dudley Young. "From the outset our relationship was a fierce one," Young would recall. "We had so much in common, and so much to fight about. The Candlemas Bear, lacking a middle register, insisted on a blow-out every night. . . . At submanic velocity the man was truly amazing, the range dazzling, the anecdotes endless and funny and fine. To bring us back from high talk, or just to silence some bore, he would ask Deg, my sagacious labrador, lying by the fire, what *he* thought; and there would follow a doggy discourse, regal and hilarious, usually along the lines, 'What fools these mortals be.' "[33]

The young American poet Michael Waters, studying at the University of Nottingham that fall, at one point learned that Lowell would be reading at Essex, though the event had received almost no attention and there were no posters anywhere on campus when Waters and a group of other Americans arrived. In fact, the room where the reading took place held only a handful of professors. Soon Lowell walked in with several other dons, was introduced, and read. Afterwards, the don who'd introduced Cal asked if there were any questions and, when no one raised their hand, Waters raised his hand and asked Lowell about his confessional poems. At once the don interrupted to explain that Mr. Lowell did not write confessional poetry, and that if that was the sort of question his guest was to be subjected to, there would be no more. Lowell, still at the podium, interjected. If there were to be no more questions, could he read another poem? Fine, the don agreed. "Then I'd like to read 'Skunk Hour,' " Lowell drawled. "It's one of my confessional poems."[34]

October 11, to Lizzie: "A gray warm Sunday until now at twilight it is cool and clear. For the last three or four hours, I have been home and in bed reading forty of fifty pages of Emerson's poems for teaching. The unease of distance and severance are on me." Incredibly, he wondered why she didn't write him and tell him what she was thinking. After a week of teaching, he was finding Essex "enough like Harvard to sometimes seem mirage. The same students, tho half audible from their good manners and foreign idiom, the same old classes, the same with fresh textbooks, a taxi drive along the Thames that is like the East River and even the Charles." Home and not-home.[35]

But soon enough the oatmeal reality of teaching at Essex began to sink in. "Queues for the only cafeterias," he wrote Bishop, "often no sitting space, long, tan, narrow, uniform corridors, only manageable by eccentric numbers that go up to six figures—my room 603, 113." The university had been built at a time "of some sensational failure in architectural design, all asbestos white without a red brick in sight." And his classes, he'd discovered, were minute "to the point of insult." To Lizzie he was even more direct. After teaching at Harvard, his Essex students seemed "rather retarded."[36]

Within a year he would try an experiment with them. He'd been teaching them the poems of Wallace Stevens, and—sensing their boredom—had asked them what they would rather be reading. The Beatles and Rod McKuen, the answer came back. "So we read pop for a month," Lowell would remember— perhaps the only one who took the assignment seriously—only to discover that the Beatles were "a cross between Noel Coward and Gilbert, more polished and idiomatic than most poets," and that McKuen had offered him nothing. Bob Dylan he found alloy: "true folk and fake folk," with lines, but no whole poems, someone who leaned too heavily "on the crutch of his guitar."[37]

Bill Alfred, worried about Lizzie, wrote to tell Cal to stop waffling and come to some decision as to what he intended to do: stay with Caroline or return home to Lizzie. Picking up the challenge, Cal wrote Lizzie. "I feel like a man walking on two ever more widely splitting roads at once," he told her, "as if . . . being torn apart and still preferring that state to making a decision." Besides, what decision was left to make? "After all I have done, and all that seven months have done, can I go back to you and Harriet?" Besides, he'd changed. He was soberer now, "cooler, more displeasing to myself in many little ways, but mostly about you."

A copy of *Notebook* had just arrived and he'd "read through all the new and more heavily revised poems," the sense dawning on him that the new poems were really about him and Lizzie and Harriet, the "endurance" of his twenty- year marriage "being the spine which despite many bendings and blows finally held." And yet . . . he did not think he could come back to Lizzie this time, couldn't "weigh the dear, troubled past, so many illnesses, which weren't due to you, in which you saved everything," couldn't "compare this memory with the future, unseen and beyond recollection" with Caroline, whom, he told Lizzie, he loved very much. If she would give him "this short space" before he arrived in New York "to wobble in his mind," it would help. If, finally, he did turn from her, he would be "turning from the longest realest and most loved fragment of my life."[38]

"There's an old picture somewhere, mostly as frontispieces, where Dante stands against an elaborate tapering tower with galleries," he wrote Adrienne Rich now. "It is Purgatory, and it seems to lean." That was how the last twenty-one years seemed to him: a kind of purgatorial ascent. And to Lizzie again: "Even if I returned for good, if that has meaning, almost all would be unsolved," since their past few years together had been like living "a depression." At the moment he was going through the "usual, once annual depression, lighter than most," but enough to make him "peculiarly indecisive and useless." He understood that remaining in England with Caroline meant de facto he'd made his choice, but she had to understand that Caroline wasn't just one more manic crush.[39]

"I do not want Cal back under any circumstances," Lizzie wrote Blair in near despair. "This is the last time he will see me. . . . In all the months he has been gone . . . he has never answered one question I have put to him, or discussed really anything, me or Harriet or practical things or Caroline— except himself." If he dared to bring Caroline to New York, she would take Harriet and leave for the Caribbean.[40] When Cal learned how Lizzie felt about things, he promised to make his intentions "absolutely clear" when he saw her. He also promised to come to New York alone.

Besides, he was not so sure after all that he wanted a divorce. By November he was writing Taylor that he would probably go back to Lizzie.[41] And to Mary McCarthy: "I've done great harm to everyone and bemused myself." To marry Caroline would cut "against the grain, the circumstances, our characters." Besides, it was more hubris than could ever be got away with, as even Caroline seemed to understand. And then: "Even for such a careless person as me one is cemented in habits beyond belief. I had to come to England and live with practically a new wife to learn my whole being is repetition of things once done."[42]

So, after mulling it over, he wrote Lizzie, asking if it wasn't too late to start over again. "A cold way of putting it," he explained, "is that long burned-in and accepted habits never leave us. One can make out with the family he has long endured, which has a long time suffered him and his ways." In the meantime he'd been "pouring out poems," and almost had a book now "in the same form as *Notebook,* but much smaller."[43] It was his first reference to Lizzie of *The Dolphin.* He did not yet have the nerve to tell her that the book was about their failed marriage.

Late in the month he read before "a record small audience" at the Mermaid in London, "scene of *Benito*'s triumph," he wrote sardonically to Lizzie. Essex University was at the moment "in great disgrace, a protest with bonfires, then the next day . . . a long-prepared *Daily Telegram* attack on our leniency." The protest had not even been over the long, protracted war in Viet Nam but merely over the use of marijuana. "Not much to arouse the demons," he thought, or even "amuse them."

He was still writing with every spare moment he could find and living a molelike existence, burying his indecisions "in many many poems." By then he had ninety new ones "and a tall house of draft and discard," so that he was "very bad company" just now, and no longer even tried to keep up with what was happening in America.[44] In the past five years, he had honed a poetics of the quotidian, an equivalent to Mailer's New Journalism, in which whatever chance tossed up he had snatched at for his subject. But in 1970, exhausted by the civil rights movement and the interminable war in Viet Nam, and afloat from his own country, he found himself shifting even more to the subject of himself, and at the moment that meant dealing with the death of one relationship and the birth of another.

By the time he was ready to fly home on December 14, Lowell had written Bishop that the break with Lizzie seemed inevitable after all.[45] As he was leaving, Caroline slipped him a note, several lines of which found their way into yet another poem, "With Caroline at the Air Terminal": "If I have had hysterical drunken seizures, / it's from loving you too much. It makes me wild, / I fear." Even if they never met again, she wrote, what Cal had given her was unique.[46] Back in New York, he sent her a short, terse cable: "I AM NOT A CRIPPLE."[47] Lizzie had been waiting at Kennedy for Cal, waiting expectantly. But she could see at once that he was wearing Caroline's ring, and almost the first thing he said to her, after explaining that he would be staying with Blair, was that he'd stopped waffling and had made up his mind. He was going back to Caroline.

A week before Christmas he met Berryman at the Chelsea Hotel in Manhattan. *Love & Fame* had just been published, and Berryman, at the end of a long reading tour, was drinking heavily once more. "He had been phoning poems and invitations to people at three in the morning," Cal would remember,

and I felt a weariness about seeing him. . . . We met one noon during the taxi strike at the Chelsea Hotel, dusty with donated, avant-garde constructs, and dismal with personal recollections, Bohemia, and the death of [Dylan] Thomas. . . . We settled for the huge, varnished unwelcome of an empty cafeteria-bar. John addressed me with an awareness of his dignity, as if he were Ezra Pound at St. Elizabeth's emphatic without pertinence, then brownly inaudible . . . at the end we were high without assurance, and speechless. I said, "When will I see you again?" meaning, in the next few days before I flew to England. John said, "Cal, I was thinking through lunch that I'll never see you again." I wondered how in the murk of our conversation I had hurt him, but he explained that his doctor had told him one more drunken binge would kill him.[48]

Two days after Christmas, he wrote Berryman that he'd now had a chance to read his new "Eleven Addresses to the Lord" at the end of *Love & Fame* and could "hardly find words to praise it." It was both "cunning in its scepticism" and yet somehow felt "like a Catholic prayer to a personal God." He applauded "the humorous, anguished admission of faults, somewhat like Corbière," somewhat like Verlaine. "Anyway, it's one of the great poems of the age, a puzzle and triumph to anyone who wants to write a personal devotional poem." And then: "You write close to death—I mean in your imagination. Don't take it from your heart into life. Don't say we won't meet again." He enclosed his London address. "A new life. One to be envied, but today it fills me with uncertainties that mount up [to] terror. Well, may your God and mine bless you and our families." It was the last letter between them.[49]

After Christmas, Frank Bidart came down to New York to talk about Lowell's new poems. In early January 1971, at the height of a blizzard, Cal managed to see Bishop, who was again in New York. He celebrated Harriet's fourteenth birthday. Then, armed with a redwood bear named Arms of the Law, a gift from his daughter, he flew back to London and to Caroline. "In my thoughts I planned a much more ample personal and bread and butter letter," he wrote Lizzie on the 7th, "but still feel the jar, loss of sleep etc. of the flight." He thought of all the "kind charming things" she'd done to make his trip special: standing there at the airport with her "curled hair and beautiful smile that survived the long dull wait," the "blue wash cloths, the buttermilk, the calm Christmas day, and the wonderful wit and good spirits of Harriet, surely rather owing to you—I mean your old undeviating loyalty."[50]

Then, in February, Caroline learned she was pregnant with Cal's child. It took six weeks to break the news to Lizzie, who told him he would have to tell Harriet himself. "It's hell trying to talk on the transAtlantic phone," he wrote his daughter on March 14. "I don't know whether Mother has told you what I am going to write. I want anyway to tell you myself and try and keep you from feeling lonely and hurt." He and Caroline were going to have a baby. It was already visible and was due in early October. But there would never be "a second you in my heart," he told his Harriet, "not even a second little girl, to say nothing of a boy." She was always with him, she and her mother. He wanted her to visit them whenever she could. "We're not ogres," he felt the need to add.[51]

A few days later he had a letter from Blair, who had disliked Caroline from

the first, when he'd seen them together in London over lunch and had reminded them that Lizzie would need a decent settlement for herself and
Harriet. When he asked Caroline if she would be willing to see that Lizzie was
taken care of, Caroline had told him no.[52] "You can't expect help from Elizabeth," he wrote Cal now. "That well is poisoned." As for Harriet, he would
be on his own in an uphill battle for her affections.[53] But then, to Cal's
immense relief and happiness, Lizzie wrote to say she was planning on sending
Harriet over to London in June. "She will be long looked forward-to and
embraced with warmth," he wrote back. "There are many things, good
weather, sights, countryside, my play, etc. to make her stay happy. And I hope
yours."[54]

He flew to Norway for readings at the Universities of Bergen and Oslo, and
found a landscape with bits of Oregon, Colorado, and Vermont tossed together. Then it was on to Copenhagen and Amsterdam. Hotel accommodations in Norway had turned out to be rather like living in a Volkswagen, he told
Lizzie: "efficient, uncomfortable, cheap and small," though breakfast had
been electrified for him by "a cheerful middleclass man in spectacles" chanting
Danish hymns.[55] And to Rich: "I'll spare you a lecture on repetition and
change based on a trip to Norway and reading the *Burnt Njal Saga*. What
could be less like our lives than [the Vikings] of honor and hack." And yet "at
every point a responsive chord" had been struck.[56]

But there was an undercurrent of terseness and defensiveness in his letter to
Rich. On his return from Norway he'd found her angry, "haunting letter"
waiting for him, the subtext of which was Lowell's abandonment of Lizzie.
The women's issue, he remarked to Lizzie, had apparently ousted the blacks
now for Rich's attention. But the questions she posed him were exactly those
she herself was most concerned with just then. Why, she wondered, did poetry
have to be difficult? What would the poetry of the future look like? What was a
woman's role in poetry?

Cal groped for answers. Difficulty in poetry was not something one put on
like a coat, he told her. Rather, it came with the material one worked with. As
for the "poetry of the future," he wasn't sure he'd read any. But then again
he'd probably read a lot: "Rimbaud, Othello, whatever poetry is straining to its
uttermost. Most art, even the best, hardens to convention, yet the very best
can't be imitated by the future, no second *Moby Dick*, and hundreds more."
On the woman's issue, given his present situation and Rich's friendship with
Lizzie, he preferred instead to discount the underlying seriousness of her
question. "Randall and Peter [Taylor] and I found them [women] even in our
Kenyon exile, we were all more or less engaged. I know," he ended, "too
much about women to be entangled into an argument."

As for his fathering a child at fifty-four, he explained, he was having the baby because he and Caroline had "stumbled into it and then found we wanted one, and had a moral horror of abortion—I mean for ourselves, not for others." In fact, he felt "calm and awe" before the fact of the child. "Why shouldn't our having a child be profound?", he asked Rich. "The times are difficult, almost impossible today, yesterday, always. If one lived in East Pakistan, Biafra, or Vietnam. Character and private conditions may make having children fearful, but I don't believe the *times* make it harder for anyone we know." Then he added: "In sad moments it seems that man and woman advance from one black bog to another. To look at the worst, as Hardy says. And the joy is incredible too. Please forgive my chaffing."[57]

For ten weeks there was no response from Rich. When she did answer, it was to signal the end of their friendship. "I feel we are losing touch with each other, which I don't want," she wrote. "I feel a kind of romanticism in your recent decisions, a kind of sexual romanticism with which it is very hard for me to feel sympathy . . . my affection and admiration for Elizabeth make it difficult to be debonair about something which—however good for her it may ultimately be—has made her suffer."[58] When she wrote again, it would be in a public forum, and the sting of her rebuttal would last until Cal's death.[59]

At the end of March, Cal and Lizzie began preparations for a legal separation. "It's all very sad," he told Tate, "I have no wish to talk about it now. . . . We've done our best, and at least Harriet won't experience a divorce in which her parents hate each other." He also pleaded with Tate not to quarrel with him any more. "You and I have held on to each other for almost thirty-five years. I have always, or almost always, been charmed by you and thought of you with reverence and gratitude."[60] Tate answered by return. "I don't think we've quarrelled," he wrote. "We were temporarily at cross-purposes." He even offered to stand as godfather to the baby. He also wondered if Cal had seen the blistering attack on him in the *Times Literary Supplement*.[61]

That attack would be answered in the *TLS* by both Conrad Aiken and Berryman (with whom Tate had recently and decisively broken). Now, however, Cal wrote Tate to reassure his ailing mentor that he was more than just a man of letters; he was in fact a Dionysius. Last term, he'd given his Essex students "a day on sonnets, reading them you, Longfellow and [Frederick Goddard] Tuckerman." Of the three, only Tate's were filled with "fury, music and wit, not a word to be dropped or moved in whole poems." As for the *TLS* attack, poetry and its critics in this post-Blackmur, post-Jarrell age were rather like "twenty moving currents ceaselessly sloshing and twisting against each [other] in a bucket. . . . So many parties each with its heroes." A pity to have "so little [critical] talent" now, "and that so buried, and so stepped on often by the rude hacks. Everything liked till nothing's liked." Again he apologized for failing to come through on the festschrift. "I was writing all the time," he explained, "as if I might die before I gave out." He was not exaggerating.⁶²

Harriet would not be coming to see her father after all, Lizzie wrote Cal at the end of March. Instead, she would go to Mexico with The Experiment in International Living, together with several classmates. He was keenly disappointed, for he missed his daughter terribly. "I feel I've more than half lost Harriet through distance," he told Peter Taylor. "It's more than I can bear sometimes."⁶³ "Dear Little Harriet," he wrote his daughter early in May.

> *Little,* for so I think of you through all the years since the day when I carried you a limp almost boneless lump from the maternity hospital to Aunt Sarah's car and the long times when I could carry you a squat-nosed snubbles refusing to walk home from our walks in Central Park. . . . It breaks my heart that you are so far away [and] so hard to get to. Sometimes when I am thinking a little absentmindedly and sadly, it seems almost as though I were a clay statue and part of my side had dropped at my feet like a lump.

He needed to see her, he said, if for no other reason than to remind him that he was still "a great American moral leader, and not a reactionary sybarite."⁶⁴

Caroline's daughters—Natalia (ten), Eugenia (seven), and Ivana (five)—were waiting for a visit from Harriet as if she were Elvis Presley, he told her. In June, his *Prometheus Bound* would be performed in London and he wanted her to see it. It was all about a man "tied to a rock [who] talks for two hours." He knew he was "a very unresponsive, humorless conventional man, seldom giving voice to my emotions." He was beginning to sound now like his shadow portrait of Jonathan Edwards ("My deffects are well known; / I have a constitution / peculiarly unhappy: // flaccid solids, / vapid, sizzy, scarse fluids, / causing a childish weakness, / a low tide of spirits. // I am contemptible, / stiff and dull"). "You can guess," he ended, "what it costs me to tell you I more or less wept with joy reading your card, the one letter in a pile of complimentary books, bills, requests to do things I didn't want to do."

He'd just been to the London Dolphinarium on Oxford Street "to see two performing dolphins, Baby and Brandy. . . . They can jump twenty feet, bat a ball back to their trainer, pretend to cry for fish." They were smarter even than Sumner their cat, "bigger-brained than man and much more peaceful and humorous." Like Harriet, like himself as a boy, Caroline's daughters had many pets: two kittens, "a hideous large white rabbit, Snowdrop, a beautiful small black rabbit, Flopsy," and a nervous "tiny gerbil named Gertrude Buckman."⁶⁵

In fact dolphins had by then become Cal's new obsession, a sure indication, as with the Tecumseh statue he'd bought for Jackie Kennedy, that he was speeding up again. He went out to the Kings Road and bought several stone dolphins from the Antique Hypermarket, where they sold for several hundred pounds apiece. These he shipped to Caroline's country house at Maidstone and had placed at either side of the front door; others he had placed in the garden. Somehow he managed to hold off his incipient attack by sheer will, Caroline, terrified, treating him with the too-pronounced tact and delicacy one might show toward a dangerous drunk.

"The air is full of returning Englishmen and American visitors," he wrote Lizzie at the beginning of May. "Yesterday I heard [Richard] Poirier in a labored perverse lecture blast Saul Bellow at the [American] embassy." He was going to Rome at the end of the month for ten days to take part in a Fulbright symposium to speak on contemporary American poetry and planned to "just read people I like, such as Wallace Stevens, Randall, etc." The trip would be fun, and afterwards he would go up to Ravenna and Urbino with Rolando Anzilotti.[66]

In June he and Caroline attended their "first woman's [sic] Lib" event, a play in London, to which Sonia Orwell had invited them. This, he told Harriet afterwards, turned out to be a "God-awful . . . avant guard [sic] all woman's cast play" which perhaps she would have enjoyed more. Sonia had presided, "and couldn't keep the women in the after-play discussion from talking all at once and shouting obscenities at each other. Aren't you glad," he added, "you are a lady?"[67] A month later *The Listener* published an "impious" piece by Caroline on the play, with the result that "menacing and armed bull-dykes," Lowell told Taylor, were now marching outside his London apartment.[68] ("I've hardly met the real Lesbian storm troops," he would tell Lizzie later, "but I think they talk like hysterical negroes and other fanatics—the meaning of words, the object they denote mean nothing.")[69]

With the warm weather he and Caroline and the girls were spending more of their time at Milgate—Caroline's country estate in Maidstone, Kent, fifty miles southeast of London. Cal got some trout fishing in at a nearby reservoir, and watched enviously as his neighbors made record casts, while he himself caught nothing. By then Caroline was five months pregnant, he told Taylor, and looked nine. They were thinking of calling the baby Lowell Guinness until after the divorce. He loved England and was sure an old southerner like Taylor would too: "safe schools, no negroes, quaint old people, absolutely nutty ones our age, whiskey without ice."

After working frantically, "sometimes six days a week," he had nearly finished his new book of poems and felt "utterly empty."[70] Yet, all in all, he felt happier than he ever had in his life. Since returning to England and learning he was to be a father again, he'd been at peace and had quarrelled with no one for the past four months, "an absolute record for me with anyone." If he and Caroline were both "slovenly," he added, at least they were "essentially sane." All, then, was well, at least "as far as mortality and one's large failings allow."[71]

But he struck the same note of ambivalence with Blair Clark: an undercurrent sense "of not seeing something through." It was not "the kind of thing I usually bedevil myself with," he admitted, but a twenty-year marriage was rather like "a full life time, one never to be filled."[72]

"O to be young!", he wrote Lizzie in late May. "I was reading a review by [V. S.] Pritchett of the Magny dinners. The people were young when they began, and ten years later dead or very old." His own fears were very much the subtext of that comment. He'd been seeing the old lately and had two delightful almost alone evenings with Jorge Luis Borges, "talking about Tennyson, James, and Kipling," nearly weeping when Borges talked "without pity to an audience about his blindness." He'd also spent a long afternoon in the hospital with the Welsh poet, David Jones, and an evening with Hannah Arendt, now "on the verge of old and frail."[73] By late June, the droves of "vecchi" had expanded to include Alberto Moravia, Peter Quennell, Mrs. Ian Fleming, Elizabeth Bowen, Hugh MacDiarmid, Mario Praz, Cyril Connolly. The only trouble with the old, he told Taylor, was that they all liked "to talk and didn't like to listen." He wondered if Lowell Guinness would help make him feel "like a Kenyon junior" all over again.[74]

Dudley Young gave a party for Lowell in London at term's end so that he could "square off" against R. D. Laing, the Scottish psychiatrist and author of *The Divided Self,* with William Burroughs in a banker's suit standing in as referee. Young would remember "two warrior wives and five discerning hippoids" that evening, Laing sitting in the lotus position, while Cal cleaned his glasses and drank. Then Burroughs opening the evening with a story of being arrested on a murder rap and fearing he might be gang-raped by the inmates. Silence. Then Cal's resonant ironic southern drawl, ready to take on all comers, intoning, "You evah bin gang-fucked, Bill?"[75]

Prometheus Bound, once again directed by Jonathan Miller, opened at the Mermaid on June 24 with "the same lead actor, all the same almost," he wrote Harriet, "only it's being done in a former warehouse . . . on the muddy Thames River, and we are doing without scenery, except for a bucket and a rag."[76] He'd been through it three times, he told Lizzie, "brisking it up, making Zeus a little more like God or nature and less like a gestapo boss."[77] He'd seen the dress rehearsal, he wrote her on the eve of opening night, "very finished, except Ocean improvised his lines—maybe he should, but we hope he won't. Io very good, but less than Irene [Worth], and young. Hermes better. Gulls better." Reading the text over to speed "it with little changes," he kept coming upon Lizzie's old suggestions "like a hailstorm of gifts."[78]

But he was afraid of the reviews, which had panned *Benito Cereno* when it had opened at the Mermaid several years before. And he was right to fear, for

Prometheus "got the worst and most superficial and most [number of] reviews of anything I've written," he complained afterwards, "with only one good one in the lot, though that was *TLS.*"[79] In spite of which the play managed to fill the theater for six weeks.[80]

By then Cal's papers—up through 1968—were being actively sought after by both Harvard and Stony Brook so fiercely that in half a minute of negotiations, he told Lizzie, Harvard "had upped their price to 130 thousand from 90," with Stony Brook going to $150,000 two days later. But in spite of the numbers and the need for cash, he was not keen on the auction, and was relieved when his lawyer suggested he wait until after the divorce and birth of the baby. What he was hoping for from the sale was an annual income so that he might "give up teaching, something in the range of $8,000–12,000 year." Besides, having his papers at Stony Brook was rather like burying them in the Veterans' Cemetery out there, whereas his connections at least with Harvard were real.[81] Two years later the papers would go to Harvard for $141,000.

On July 1 he left for Scotland with Jonathan Raban, a young English critic who had already written favorably about Lowell's work and who would edit his *Selected Poems* for Faber and Faber in 1975. Together they spent six days in Edinburgh and the Orkneys, "home of the Spence negligence." Lowell's plan called for visiting Hugh MacDiarmid in Scotland, seeing his "ancestral islands," and getting some fishing in.[82] He recorded his poems with the Orkney poet George MacKay Brown, in the studio of Gareth Browne, Caroline's Scottish cousin. But the trip was primarily a genealogical adventure for Cal, Raban would recall, as he looked up whatever Trails and Spences he could find. Then, taking the taxi from the airport to Stromness, Cal asked the driver what he knew about these families, and sensed immediately that both branches had disgraced themselves: rackrents forced to flee the country for the New World. The news cut short Cal's trip by several days.[83]

In mid-July he was interviewed by Ian Hamilton for *The Review*. All the poems he'd published since *Life Studies,* Lowell pointed out, seemed to center on four places: Harvard, Boston, New York, and Maine. These were symbols, really: Boston and New York standing for the city; Maine for nature; and Harvard something "between, the university." It was too late in his career, he knew, for London ever to be the culture of his blood. Even if he spent summers in the Orkneys and winters in London, he might eventually "find a contrast similar to Maine and New York," but it would only be "a more slovenly repetition" of what New York and Maine had already come to mean for to him.

As for his public poems, those belonged to the past. He was older now, and his friends—those who were still alive—were also older, and he had at last entered something like his "total character." At fifty-four he'd already lived as long as most of the old writers. It was time then to sit back and ruminate.

Besides, public poetry—such as he'd written—had to come naturally, inevitably. His models in this were Eliot and Picasso, both of whom had worked "in one surprising style for some years, then surprised with another—maturing without becoming public voices or portents." It was his way of preparing his readers for the change his poetry was taking, and would continue to take, toward the domestic drama of modern love.

After all, who wanted to be on call to society, or come up with "a resonant poem for each great issue"? When he'd begun finding Marvell's "elegant baroque stanza too smooth," he had moved on instead to the roomier stanzas of the blank verse sonnet. True, sonnets were hardly "a prosodist's darling," but he'd found he could say "almost anything" with them that either conversation or letters could say. Still, he'd used the form nonstop now for the past four years and knew he could not "tempt" it much longer without falling into Parnassian. What he'd gained with the form, Lowell believed, was the ability to be more himself, ingesting more of the world, even if he did so more "clumsily" that he'd allowed himself in his earlier styles. In any event, writing that way had not been any sort of program he'd set for himself, but something he'd come to haltingly step by step. What the sonnet had given him in return for his serenading it was "rhetoric, formal construction, quick breaks."

Unlike the polished Flaubertian surfaces of *Life Studies,* the sonnet sequence had allowed him a way of mixing the instant with the deeper horizons of history, what he called the "flash of haiku to lighten the distant." Each stanza (or sonnet), while self-contained, might yet lead to the next stanza, and he could move there in a variety of styles, monologizing on stilts, or merely talking. True, the sonnet form was constricting, but then what form wasn't? Besides, he'd gained far more than he'd lost. After all, variation could be just as monotonous as using the same pattern over and over, and formlessness might have "crowded" him "toward consecutive narrative," something he was anxious to avoid for a turn-and-cut method. In four years he'd written four hundred sonnets, until it almost seemed as if he'd done nothing in that time but write, "thinking lines even when teaching or playing tennis."

Yet, like Whitman, perhaps, he'd managed long, idle patches for himself, "though drawn to spend more hours working than I ever had or perhaps will. Ideas sprang from the bushes, my head; five or six sonnets started or reworked in a day." If he saw something one day, he wrote it "that day, or the next, or the next. Things I felt or saw, or read, were drift in the whirlpool, the squeeze of the sonnet" counterpointed against "the loose ravel of blank verse."[84]

In July, Caroline moved her family—and Cal—to Milgate, keeping Redcliffe Square for her London address. Milgate was even "bigger and older and shaggier" than Mary McCarthy's house in Castine, Cal told Harriet. They had "a trout stream about five inches deep at its deepest, a lake? about as big as my Castine barn area and solid reeds right now, herds of cattle and sheep can be seen from my study window (a neighboring farmer's) . . . hundreds of birds with harsh, horrid early morning voices—pigeons, rooks, sparrows." In some ways, being here was like a chapter out of the past. He had "a bed to write on, about half the books I need, the same time commuting to where I teach as it was from London or New York."[85] And to Blair: "No more weekly full family stampedes from London to Kent. . . . Also it attenuates our uneasy closeness with poor Israel [Citkowitz]." He described the landscape as "a mixture of Connecticut semi-suburban and Pennsylvania professional farming," the house itself "early eighteenth-century Palladian and very old-South messy," a fact which sorely challenged his "New England creed" that morality was equivalent to tidiness.[86]

"Events," he wrote Lizzie in early August. "This morning two [barn] swallows flew in my window and out," like "those old friends" who used to scare him into his old barn, and a rabbit who dogged him "around the house, and can't be housebroken." First Bob Silvers and then Gene McCarthy had visited, "Gene rather pricking up his ears toward campaigning, or backing someone." Having Silvers, Caroline's former lover, at Milgate might have proved difficult, he knew, but all had gone well, for Bob, he said, was a real friend. It was he who had told Cal about Harriet's grown-up letters to Lizzie, at which Cal was still rubbing his eyes. "Suddenly from cats and [angora] pigs to full adolescence." How quickly the flower had come to her, "about five years earlier than anything came to me."[87]

For now he'd stopped writing sonnets and was reading again: the letters of Jane Welsh, reams of Dickens. He praised the new work of Lizzie's he'd seen, the essays on women writers which would make up *Seduction & Betrayal*. The subject, he noted, was still one "untouched in our time by anyone of critical and literary vocation," and he was delighted Lizzie was trying it. The single advantage he'd found in women's lib, he added, was that he could start "a humorous or angry argument with *any* woman. Last winter, a Lady Norwich stopped speaking to me with the furious remark, 'I have as much right as a man to crank a car.' I said I had always prayed for such a woman."[88]

"After the first grindings," he wrote Philip Booth, "I think we are all much calmer, much happier than two years ago. . . . I think of Lizzie and Harriet hourly, yet the strain of the motor was shaking us screwloose." The climate in Kent was much like Castine, he said, as he attempted to measure gains against losses. "Clouds by day and fires by night . . . drifting sheep and cattle . . . this morning, two grouse on the walk . . . still, no ocean, no many summers-tried neighbours."[89]

But a week later he was telling Bill Alfred how lonely and out of touch he felt. In the two months he'd been at Milgate he'd made only one trip to London and had had a mere handful of visitors. Moreover, maintaining a three-hundred-year-old house was a total mystery to him. "We see workmen, tremendous conference with the white collar superior, then for seasons no action, then a lone workman making puzzled noises for part of a day—then gone forever. . . . Worst is the sandman, who comes with the noisiest machine known to man—he may come at 4 AM or 6 PM, he quits at will, he is usually waiting contemplatively for a machine he forgets, to be brought by someone who also forgets."[90]

By the end of September Lizzie had learned of the existence of *The Dolphin* and was furious. "I only partly understand your second paragraph about 'recent shocks,' " Cal wrote her, with the baby expected imminently. "One of course is my book, but it doesn't have a publication date, need not come out ever. It's not defamatory." After all, the story he'd told there was "both a composition and alas, a rather grinding autobiography." Besides, poetry was always a fiction. He would send the manuscript along for her to read when it was cleaned up a bit, and promised her she would not feel "betrayed or exploited," though he could not imagine her wanting "to scrape through the sadness and breakage now."

Everything had fallen on them in the past few days: "false labor pains, rushed midnight trip to hospital, discovery that the child is upside down, and must be turned feet-first." For the past week he'd had "continual nosebleeds (high blood pressure?) now stopped and cured by an expert." To top everything, everyone was catching scabies from Bosun, their dachshund.[91]

Then labor pains in earnest, Caroline taken to the hospital in Maidstone, then transferred by midnight ambulance to University College Hospital in London because of possible complications. On the 28th, after twelve hours of labor, the baby was finally induced. It was a boy, a big boy, uncannily resembling his father, and given the name Robert Sheridan Lowell. "My blood survived the tense last two weeks," he wrote Lizzie at the beginning of October. It had been his "old high wavery blood pressure" acting up again. Now he was back on medication and having further tests. "All's well, heart, liver, etc. Only the blood goes high then drops—not with inner anguish, but mysteriously." He supposed the illness—like himself—couldn't be too serious.[92]

He chose Harriet to tell about the baby. "After 12 hours of labor pains, Robert was born in thirty seconds, no time to go to the delivery room. He looked like a lobster-red stiff gingersnap man, in crimson mud," rather "dignified, despite looking like a bartender, one who imbibes as well as sells."[93] And to Taylor: "I have a doctor's and psychiatrist's statement exempting me from ever throwing a football."[94] "Little Gingersnap Man, homoform," he would write in *The Dolphin:*

flat and sore and alcoholic red,
only like us in owning to middle-age.
"If you touch him, he'll burn your fingers."
"It's health, not fever. Why are the other babies so pallid?
His navy-blue eyes tip with his head. . . . Darling,
we have escaped our death-struggle with our lives."[95]

They returned to Milgate to find themselves in the midst of a Gothic tale. Bill, their ex-Royal Navy reliable young chauffeur, "who fixed everything, tirelessly, window panes, light switches, parts of the car, cleaned, drove without fatigue," he told Bill Alfred, one afternoon suddenly and "rather murderously beat a man who had been painting in our house—in front of this man's wife and son. For nothing, unfounded paranoid jealousy, because the painter had taken tea with his nanny."

There was surely some insanity there, so that Lowell had had "to fire the man and the nanny went with him. And somehow after having groves of people working for us, we had none. Rather tough, two little girls, one baby, a big house—none in any way (including the house which hardly pulled its weight in the crisis) anything but dependent." And so here they were, "limping along with an 18 year old local boy and his girl friend."

They'd interviewed couples endlessly, but found no one to fit in: "the man who'll do nothing but garden, the ruthless Italians with a friend who doesn't speak English, a husband who dresses for dinner and polished silver for Lord Butler, two Irish fairies, two feeble minded orphans brought up by Sister Colat in a Catholic convent." Now they were about to settle on a young Canadian couple, hippies, "but solid and with degrees."[96]

In truth, anything that took "hard work and a clear mind in England" these days, he wrote Taylor, "has to be done by Canadians or Pakistanis." But the worst was the isolation, for both he and Caroline had expired American licenses, and it was better that, with his driving record and quixotic health, he not try to renew his. As for Caroline, alas, she had just failed not one but *two* driving tests. There was also the unsettling vision of Bill the chauffeur somewhere out there, "wandering the downs of Kent."[97]

Cal invited Frank Bidart to come to Milgate after Christmas to help him with the work of revising *Notebook* yet again. This time he meant to divide the book in two: the more public poems making up a volume called *History;* the story of the disintegration of his marriage into another, smaller volume to be called *For Lizzie and Harriet.* As for his new book, *The Dolphin,* made up of some eighty poems, it was shorter now than when Bidart had seen it the year before, "but with many new poems." At the moment it ended "in a long pregnancy and birth—one poem—sequence, everything endlessly rewritten, and about 40 poems about England [sic] statuary, demos, etc. taken out, not because they are bad but because they clog the romance."

For *Lizzie and Harriet* had been reduced to personal narrative—"mostly the historic, the metaphysical and the political go . . . then go too the personal poems that fit well enough but are inflated, uninspired or redundant." All this revising had begun, he explained, "by trying to get round the mounting pressure on me not to publish *The Dolphin* (for moral reasons)." That book, it seemed, would have to wait.[98]

"You will come here," he wrote on the eve of Bidart's departure, "in a moment of comparative calm for us. In the way one does, we've piled up an incredible number of people at Christmas time: our four children, two of their friends—one called the naughty Armstrong—two Spenders who make each other age, the Mary McCarthys with a depressed son, the Grey Gowries, separated but momentarily reunited with son—and then The Staff, more than I dare name, all eccentric or nervous, with friends, imbecile mothers. When you come all that will be gone, except for us, almost enough for a village."

By then it was clear to Lowell that England was beginning to look rather like something out of the Brontës, and within a year he would be anxious to get back to the States to resume his teaching duties at Harvard. The English experiment had lasted so far for only a year and a half, and already America was beginning to have "the glamor of a foreign country" for him, a wildness, an appealing strangeness all its own.[99]

17

Milgate

1972–1976

Shortly after New Year's, 1972, Frank Bidart arrived at Milgate for a working visit which would last five weeks. He would remember Cal's English copy of *Notebook,* which Cal had carried around with him for the past two years, and the numerous revisions on every page. By then Lowell had become deeply dissatisfied with the aesthetic that had originally informed his *Notebook* poems: an aesthetic of the immediate, one that captured the flash of the moment. In 1967, after following Berryman's progress with the *Dream Songs,* Lowell had pressed for an art that would be less photographic and finished for one more closely linked to stream of consciousness, a poetry which could capture one's fleeting impressions, feelings, marginal half-thoughts. But neither he nor the reviewers (except for the most adventurous and perceptive) had been particularly happy with such an aesthetic, especially coming after the Flaubertian finish of *Life Studies.* Nor, obviously, was Lowell himself satisfied with the kaleidoscopic turns and shifting styles of his notebook sonnets. But since publishing a *third* revision of the *Notebook* seemed unworkable—even for him—he had decided instead to split the book into two.

He would do this by first separating out the fifty or so historical subjects from *Notebook*—the poems on writers, the poems on Attila, Clytemnestra, Roland, Alexander, Anne Boleyn, Robespierre, Lincoln, and others—and give these a chronological order. For a while he considered calling this volume *Heroes*, but found the title too constricting. Instead he settled on *History*, which had—after all—been his lifelong obsession. "Essentially," Bidart would recall, "almost everything that was not family poems from *Notebook* could go into *History*," along with the forty or so new "historical" poems Lowell had eliminated from *The Dolphin*.

The family drama poems, together with the sequence on "Mexico," now became *For Lizzie and Harriet*. Martha Ritter, Lowell's young lover at Harvard, would become Lowell's particular "dolphin" in *For Lizzie and Harriet*. This would remind Lowell's readers that while the dolphin of the title was Caroline, in a larger sense he was invoking the erotic muse which had renewed him. It was this same Muse, of course, which would also help destroy him.

Lowell and Bidart worked in this fashion: as Bidart cut sonnets from a clean copy of *Notebook*, Cal told him which poems he wanted, and in what order. Those Cal wanted were then clipped to legal-size sheets of paper. Then Cal, lying on his workbed with his marked copy of *Notebook* before him, would dictate across the room the revisions he wanted made, and Bidart would write these into the margin across from the clean copy of the poem.

"Usually he would dictate about four changes to a sheet," Bidart would recall, "and then I would read them and we'd talk about them and argue about them. And sometimes he would change the order, or he would make more revisions, or sometimes he would go back to what he had before." Bidart was free to say what he really thought about the changes, otherwise, as he knew, he would have been of no use to Cal. Caroline too offered her criticisms and suggestions.[1]

When Bidart flew back to Boston in early February, there were three texts: *History, For Lizzie and Harriet*, and *The Dolphin*, the last of which ended with Sheridan's birth and "essentially followed the real chronology of what happened." Bidart, however, had had little to do with that volume. He knew, as Cal did, that the very mention of the book had already caused Lizzie a great deal of anxiety, and that its publication, which would incorporate many of Lizzie's recent letters to Cal, would certainly cause her more.

But he also knew, again like Cal, that the book's theme—the disintegration of one marriage and the creation of another—was central to contemporary society. Indeed, Williams had already shown as much in *Paterson*, a poem which had also used another woman's letters. Both poems, Cal and Bidart believed, had as much right to exist as any other. What posterity would *not* forgive Cal for was Cal's writing a bad book. Moreover, Olwyn Hughes, Ted Hughes's sister, was already considering publishing *The Dolphin* in a private edition of 100 copies. When he returned to Boston, Bidart had a copy of the manuscript with him to share with both Alfred and Bishop.

"I think Frank and I revised 405 poems in a month," Cal wrote Bishop in February. "That's no way to write, but it was made more sensible by Frank's amazing filing code." The three books were his "magnum opus," he believed, and the best he would ever do. By then he'd decided to go ahead and publish *The Dolphin,* and now he needed her advice. Lizzie wouldn't like it, but what else could he offer her but this book? Besides, there was "something creepy about deliberately writing something posthumous."

He thought again of Berryman, who had finally killed himself by jumping from a bridge in Minneapolis that January. A month later, Marianne Moore would die at the age of eighty-five. She'd become a star in Lowell's sky "35 years ago" when he'd first read R. P. Blackmur's essay on her. Indeed, a week before she'd died he'd taught her "to my poor dim students, along with Cummings whom they of course liked and got much better." Marianne's death would make "little stir, unlike Berryman's—on whom each English weekly or arts page" had a bad elegy. This was right, he admitted, "tho I thought him doomed too ever since I ate with him last year—then it was drink, later he must have died from not drinking." In the long view, Moore had been the "much more inspired" of the two. But Berryman had played perhaps for higher stakes, his real heroism revealing itself in the way he'd leapt "into himself in his last years bravely." Cal's circle of friends was drawing tighter and tighter.[2]

"Anecdotes about John could be made up for miles by his cronies and students," Cal would write Lizzie. And the anecdotes would be "monotonous, wearying, like Dylan Thomas's, because the escapades even when they happened, lived on the imagination." He'd recently gone up to London for a program honoring Berryman, in which the BBC film Alvarez had made five years before when he'd interviewed Berryman in Ballsbridge, Ireland, had been shown. He'd watched John, larger than life on the screen, "close-up, just off drunkenness, mannered, booming, like an old fashioned star professor. His worst." Then he thought back to his Scholar Gypsy, "the young, beardless man, simple, brilliant, the enthusiast . . . buried somewhere with the older."[3]

"Do you wake dazed like me," he would write in his final poem for his friend,

> *and find your lost glasses in a shoe?*
> *Something so heavy lies on my heart—*
> *there, still there, the good days*
> *when we sat by a cold lake in Maine,*
> *talking about the* Winter's Tale,
> *Leontes' jealousy*
> *in Shakespeare's broken syntax.*
> *You got there first.*

Just the other day,
I discovered how we differ—humor. . . .
To my surprise, John,
I pray to not for you,
think of you not myself,
smile and fall asleep.[4]

That January there had also been a crisis at home. Six-year-old Ivana had tipped a kettle of boiling water over, critically scalding herself. For a while it looked like "touch and go," Cal told Lizzie, made worse by "the difficult drives through one of England's worst snow storms (nothing to ours, but looking like Napoleon's retreat from Moscow to the English eye). Then the skin-stripping operation; then next the plastic surgery."[5] Ivana would spend the next two months in the hospital and then return for yet more surgery. "Small-soul-pleasing," he would write of her,

> *loved with condescension,*
> *even through the cro-magnon tirades of six. . . .*
> *Though burned, you are hopeful, experience cannot tell you*
> *experience is what you do not want to experience.*[6]

February 1972 saw the "dark tunnel" of the miners' strike. "You probably didn't hear much of it in New York," he wrote Harriet on the 22nd,

> but here it held the whole stage. You'd be cooking an egg or reading Shakespeare or absorbing an interesting news reel about the stike on television, when all would fold into darkness. As this continued into the second hour, a chill settled down, you went to look for your overcoats. Other resources were tried, coal fires, wood fires, oil lamps, very dangerous, but which made the night like day with their luminous, glowing "mantels." Doom snowballed in the daily news, 2 million unemployed, armed pickets, polluted water, deaths in stopped elevators, dentist drills stopping mid-tooth. Worst for me, threats of a total milk cut-off. We were nearing the dark ages, when it all suddenly stopped. In two days, it disappeared even from the back pages of the newspapers.

Yet his heart was warm because she was coming to see him and he would be waiting for her at "Heathcliff [sic] airport" in a month's time.[7]

Lizzie wrote him detailed plans about how to keep their fifteen-year-old daughter happy, until he felt constrained to write back that even Napoleon's Italian Campaign, while "controlled by fast despatches from the *Directoire* in Paris," had to leave *"something* to Napoleon, who was there."[8] Now he wrote

Harriet to prepare her to meet her new brother. At five months Sheridan had become a turbine engine, "more and more distressingly extrovert." Already he was lifting "heavy steel standing lamps," racing "past speed-limits on down corridors in his walker," and talking "an unintelligible mash and gulp which he considers great conversation. He only smiles at me, though, because I never hold him over my head, and say, 'You're so manly, manly.' He has so many bigger women to survive."[9]

In mid-March Lowell heard from both William Alfred and Bishop their thoughts on *The Dolphin*. Certain of the poems were bound to tear Lizzie apart, Alfred wrote first, "important though . . . they are to the wholeness of the book." Auden, whom he'd just met for the first time, had told Alfred he was no longer speaking to Cal because of the book. "When I said he sounded like God the Father," Alfred added, "he gave me a tight smile. I write to warn you."[10] "DEAR WYSTAN ASTOUNDED BY YOUR INSULT TO ME WITH WILLIAM ALFRED," Cal cabled Auden soon after. "How could [Auden] stop speaking to me about a book he hadn't seen?," he asked Alfred. "I think he's not a snubber and has never stopped talking to anyone, except Rudolph Bing, even then I think it was the Met he stopped talking to. Pretty rough to me, unpleasant too to wait for his appearance in England . . . to be cut."[11]

Then came Bishop's letter. She'd spent an evening with Bidart reading *The Dolphin* and since then many times again. It was better even than *Notebook,* she thought: "every 14 lines have some marvels of image and expression, and also they are all much clearer." But she could not bear to have him publish something she regretted and that he might "live to regret, too." The book was a "terrible mixture of fact and fiction," and, even worse, he'd changed the text of some of Lizzie's letters. She didn't "give a damn what someone like Mailer writes about his wives & marriages," but she did give a damn about what Cal wrote. In the long run Mailer and Dickey and Mary McCarthy wouldn't count, but what Cal wrote mattered. The truth was that she could not bear "to have anything you write tell—perhaps—what we're really like in 1972." Perhaps it was as simple as that.[12]

Cal wrote back on the 28th. He could see that Caroline's pregnancy did seem to crowd on the heels of his goodbye to Lizzie in New York, though that was exactly the way things had happened. As for using Lizzie's letters, he did not "see them as slander, but as sympathetic, tho necessarily awful for her to read." After all, he insisted, Lizzie was the real "poignance of the book." Besides, he'd edited the letters, cutting, doctoring, and fictionalizing them. Moreover, he'd attributed things to Lizzie he himself had said, or which had been uttered by someone else, in order to comb out "abuse, hysteria, repetition." He'd even removed "the worst things" written against himself, "so as not to give myself a case and seem self-pitying." The real reason for including the letters was that they made Lizzie real beyond anything he could have invented.[13] But if he expected someone as private as Bishop to agree with him, he was mistaken. Even after twenty-five years she had yet to forgive Williams for using a real woman's letters in *Paterson,* and she'd winced when Cal had taken the liberty of appropriating one of her own letters in a poem he'd dedicated to her.

"Let me rephrase for myself your moral objections," he tried again with Bishop. "It's the revelation (with documents?) of a wife wanting her husband not to leave her and who does leave her." That was the real problem, "not the mixture of truth and fiction." He had not altered the truth of the letters, only cut them to their essence and softened them, for the originals, though heart-breaking, had been interminable. Still, he was willing to make changes, at-tributing many of the lines instead to himself, though he knew "making the poem unwounding" would be impossible.[14]

On April 10 he wrote Bidart about his decision to change the narrative of *The Dolphin.* He would move Sheridan's birth forward in the story, so that the fact of a new child would act as the determining factor in Cal's visit home to Lizzie. Bishop's objections were, he admitted, "a kind of masterpiece of criti-cism, though her extreme paranoia (for God's sake don't repeat this) about revelations gives it a wildness." The book, with whatever changes, would still be painful to Lizzie, and would never completely satisfy Bishop, for, as Caro-line had said, it couldn't "be otherwise with the book's donnée."[15] He also rehearsed his changes with (among others) Peter Taylor (who found nothing morally objectionable with them), and with Stanley Kunitz, telling him that the letter poems could now go back to Kunitz's "old plan, a mixture of my voice, and another voice in my head, part me, part Lizzie, italicized, paraphrased, imperfectly, obsessively heard."[16]

Now it was Bidart who was dissatisfied with the changes, for the real crisis for him had been over whether the poet would remain with his wife of twenty years, or start over at fifty-three in a foreign country with another woman. But by then Bishop's arguments had won out. Lowell would change the narrative so that Caroline's being pregnant when he returned to New York at Christmas would make it all but inevitable that he would have to return to her.[17]

By the time these changes had been decided upon, Harriet had made her visit to London and Kent and was already gone. It was the first time in fifteen months Lowell had seen her, and she'd carried the visit off well. The moment, he knew, would not come again. "I love you for liking both your father and mother," he wrote his daughter, "that's why they are such extraordinarily normal, healthy and modest people—and for never talking too much except on women and politics, particularly your theories of socialism."[18]

But the "mastering element" in his household now was his small son, who had somehow "learned to talk without using words—interminably, a blessing to the insomniac." At seven months he was "eating everything in sight: blanket, rug, small dog, our fingers," and seemed "a microcosm of James Dickey, but on the wagon." That was to Kunitz.[19] And to Bishop: "Do you believe in Woman Power? I do. The shadow at the end of history. However my son feels the opposite, has broken a kitchen chair, shovels everything (rugs, blankets, silver toys, the little dachshund, Caroline and my fingers) into his two-tooth mouth. Our family of women braces itself."[20]

A week later Lowell was in another auto accident, this one while in "a safe taxi" on the way with Caroline into Maidstone to see a Sunday matinee. Without warning, a car, "about twenty feet in front and going in the opposite direction, turned without looking into a filling station on our side of the road—that awful few slow seconds when you know you'll—and we hit. No injuries except I soon had a huge lump on my shin." It would "last far into the summer," but was not, he reassured Lizzie, otherwise "dangerous or painful." And while the accident had shaken him, it had also proven "handy to persuade people to fetch . . . things" like his cigarette lighter.[21]

Besides, he hardly ever got up to London any more, or anywhere, except Essex to teach, and that appointment had long ago soured for him. Rather than the one hour door-to-door trip he had imagined, it usually took four hours by train through London each way, and even getting there in a chauffeur-driven car was tedious. Moreover, his estimate of the students had sunk to a new low. Few of his university students—deferential, "inaudible and sluggish"—could have gotten "into a good American high school," he believed, much less Harvard. All he seemed to be doing these days was read books on subjects he'd just finished teaching "without sufficient preparation," and which he would never teach again. Moreover, if the teaching load was light, "the nervous burden" was heavy. So, when he'd asked a student if he didn't think "that Act Two Scene Four in *Lear* [had] most of the play's struggles," the students had all started "mutely mumbling their text." How was one to teach, he puzzled, "if the students don't do your work?"[22]

In mid-June, Frank Bidart returned once again to England for the "final tidying" of Lowell's three books. By then Lowell had revised *The Dolphin* enough that Bidart thought the narrative changes possible, if still less acceptable than the old order. "I have been working like a steamshovel, if a steamshovel works, for the last month and have been too slothful, unversatile or self-indulgent to do anything else," he wrote Harriet. George McGovern was running against Nixon, but it was hard "for old Eugene McCarthyites to rave about McGovern . . . the sentimental Irish lost cause passion that's somewhere in all of us." Nor did he think McGovern, even if he was picked by the party in Miami, could beat Nixon in November.[23]

As for Sheridan, he was continuing to devolve at an alarming rate, crawling "wide halls in seconds," and taking great joy in destroying things. He amused, fascinated, and terrified Cal. The day before he'd "stuck his tongue out all day, with a meditative, profound, or stupid expression." At ten months he'd managed "to short-circuit a third of the house." For her part, Caroline had taken to handling him rather like a fish-puppy.[24]

"I'm afraid he is rather a University of Virginia type," he wrote Taylor in late August: "blond, dirty, lacking in feminine delicacy, already thirsty for the fraternities." In the past day or so he'd tipped over "a twenty-pound part of the fireplace" and wet his youngest sister who'd been "nice enough to invite him to her bed in the early turbulent morning."[25] Two weeks later Sheridan had learned to walk, but very destructively, "even to books," he told Alfred, "and even after Milton appeared to him in a vision saying: 'If you kill a man you only kill a body, but if you destroy a book you destroy an immortal soul.' "[26]

He and Caroline spent whole days now writing on their beds in different rooms, revising, seeing no one "till six or later with wine," then hinting that "the best train back to London" was the 10:05.[27] But even as the baby exploded with life, every third thought of Lowell's turned to his own physical and creative demise. "Is dying harder than being already dead?" he wrote late that summer in a disturbing poem about coming upon his still-familiar corpse behind a closet door:

> *I came to my first class without a textbook,*
> *saw the watch I mailed my daughter didn't run;*
> *I opened an old closet door, and found myself*
> *covered with quicklime, my face deliquescent . . .*
> *by oversight still recognizable.*
> *Thank God, I was the first to find myself.*
> *Ah the swift vanishing of my older*
> *generation—the deaths, suicide, madness*
> *of Roethke, Berryman, Jarrell and Lowell,*
> *"the last the most discouraging of all*
> *surviving to dissipate* Lord Weary's Castle
> *and nine subsequent useful poems*
> *in the seedy grandiloquence of* Notebook."[28]

"I've been writing rather steadily all summer," he wrote Harriet on September 28, 1972, Sheridan's first birthday, "and now when I look up the tops of trees are yellow, and it is cold." Her brother had surpassed himself at his birthday party by ramming his musical lawn mower into his birthday cake, then finishing off the destruction by dropping a large ball into the middle of the remains.²⁹ Alas, he wrote Alfred, that his son should be so unlike himself, he who had become a "gentle Levantine diaspora man of meditations." Luckily Sheridan's nanny was "a nurse, a blond Australian girl, secretly a wrestling champion," so that he was confident the boy could be contained for the six-hour flight to America for the divorce.³⁰

On October 8, he and Caroline and Sheridan and the Australian nanny flew to New York and stayed at the Gramercy Park Hotel for a week, while the divorce proceedings were worked out. After that Lowell went up to Cambridge to see friends—Bishop, Taylor, Bill Alfred, Frank Bidart—and work out his teaching schedule at Harvard for the following fall. Then it was back to New York, down to Santo Domingo for a double divorce (Cal from Lizzie, Caroline from Israel Citkowitz), and Cal's marriage to Caroline (all of this taking place within forty-eight hours, among the clack of typewriters in a shed and a ceremony conducted in Spanish), then back to London for a wedding party on the 21st hosted by Sonia Orwell. Among those present at the reception were Cyril Connolly, Stephen Spender, Seamus Heaney, and Philip Larkin.

The financial agreement with Lizzie had been drawn up with Blair's help. Lizzie and Harriet would get most of the income from the interest on Cal's trust fund, which came to about $20,000 a year. Lizzie would get the West 67th Street apartment with all its "tangible personal property—furnishings, works of art, household goods." "We went through our divorce and marriage on schedule," Lowell wrote his daughter afterwards. As usual, there'd been "a few errors, such as not having any passports or identification when we stood before the divorcing judge." Santo Domingo itself had been "much like Porto Rico, only the Spanish speaking people are at least half negro, and the blessings and disadvantages of America are hidden." At Bill Alfred's apartment in Cambridge, Sheridan had performed a vaudeville act with Alfred's "hat, a carrot-grater and a milk bottle. . . . Just as we were leaving, the last hour, he realized what a chance he had missed and rushed for the dishes on low shelves." It was now early November, and with the election just days away, he could only wish the agony of another Democratic defeat might be over with. McGovern himself, he added, "must feel that he is living a walking nightmare that he can't stop."³¹

To Blair he wrote an altogether different letter. In truth, he told him, he felt like going about "in black mourning" for "the disgrace of lost alimony, like soldiers who lose a redoubt." He felt taken by the "barracuda settlement," though powerless to do anything about it. Still, it was worth the costs just to have the ordeal over with. He would have to keep up with Lizzie "to keep up with Harriet—and a thousand good memories."³² But he was angry, and told

Bishop he felt like one of Mailer's boxers "who is punished for ten rounds." He could keep his salary and royalties and what he made from the sale of his papers to Harvard. But everything he'd inherited—his trust interest, the New York apartment, the Maine house *and* the Barn, including all the furniture he'd grown up with—all that was gone.

As for Harriet, the settlement would take her through graduate school and beyond, but everything would be handled from now on by Lizzie. It was almost as if Harriet had been stolen from him "like the dozen silver spoons." He'd been so upset by the divorce settlement, in fact, as well as by a tension he perceived in Bishop now that he was returning to Harvard (she was sixty-one, and worried about her job, now that Cal was returning), that the two had parted in Cambridge on a rather sour note. For that he wrote now to apologize. He could not afford to lose one of his oldest and dearest friends.[33]

In late November he wrote Alfred to say he and Caroline were thinking of having Sheridan baptized in the Catholic Church by Father Peter Levi, S.J., the poet. "One Godfather has to be Catholic (and responsible for the child's religious growth) since we are not," he added. "I know this sounds rattletrap, but it has meaning for me (like the unbelieving Pound's Catholic burial). Somewhere in my memory the Church remains real, a suspension of disbelief, tho never more, probably."[34] Cal had already asked Bishop to stand in as godmother, and Taylor to double as godfather with Alfred.[35] But after Cal's hurried note to Alfred, nothing more was heard of the matter.

Then, at the beginning of December, the unexpected happened once again. "Things never stay safe," Cal wrote Bidart. "This morning, the nurse, about the best driver we've had, didn't look carefully enough coming out the driveway taking the children to school. Our doomed Volva [sic] was hit more or less in the middle and spun across the other lane into the barbed wire fence, which it broke. No injuries really by miracle, except for an eyelid cut on Ivana. Three side windows were either smashed or fell out. The car is beyond repair. So close."

By then galleys for all three of his books had arrived, and once more Lowell was busy making changes in the texts, "mostly slight, in four out of five poems," so that he had to promise to make no changes when the page proofs arrived, except for printers' errors. And yet what joy he found in revising himself. Teaching was going better this term, and Caroline had just written "an attack on New York free schools—Beats, Belfast, women's Lib, negroes, new left Jews—what has she left to demolish?"[36]

At year's end he wrote Taylor to say he would be in New York in early January to speak for ten minutes on Ezra Pound, who had died November 1. "I am trying to connect his Usura Social credit with alimony," he half joked. "It can be done maybe, except that Pound had two wives and no alimony and most of his life almost no support—maybe that's Social credit. Anyway, I'm a changed man, and may be heard about ten o'clock of an evening grousing *soak the rich.*"[37]

"It's not my duty as fellow poet, critic and his friend to defend or clear Pound's record." Thus Lowell at a memorial gathering for Pound at the American Academy of Arts and Letters in New York on January 4, 1973, honoring his old friend. "I can't see him as a bad man, except in the ways we all are," he continued. "I do see him as a generous man to other artists, and this in a way none of us will touch." He recalled his last meeting with Pound nearly eight years before, in Rapallo, on his way back from Cairo. Pound was "emaciated," he remembered, "neat in blacks and whites, silver beard," and "looked like the covers of one of his own books, or like an El Greco, some old mural, aristocratic and flaking." The last of the great Modernist poets was gone.

He stopped by the 67th Street apartment to see Harriet and patch things up with Lizzie. Happily, things did work out pleasantly enough, since, he joked, both he and Lizzie were "so disappointed with how little we got from the alimony" that each could afford to "sympathize" with the other. He also visited with Jean Stafford, twice in the past year alone hospitalized for alcoholism, and had a good talk with her. He could see the ravages of alcohol plainly on her scarred face, but had already decided that cutting out drinking would kill him as certainly as he was convinced total withdrawal had killed Berryman. Then he went up to Cambridge to talk things over with Bishop. "She and I had a rather sharp two months [of bickering] about my teaching at Harvard," he confessed to Taylor afterwards. Now, thank goodness, all that was finally over. "We got quite drunk at Harvard," he added, and "that set us at peace." A relief no doubt, since Bishop, like Taylor, had been his "dearest friend" forever.[38]

Now that his three books were off his hands, he was finished with sonnets, even though for the moment nothing new seemed to come to him, not "even as desire." He thought again of collecting his essays and calling them half-jokingly *Men* since, to his embarrassment, nearly every piece he'd written was about men. Just now he was reviewing Larkin's *Oxford Book of 20th Century Poetry* for *Encounter,* he told Lizzie, because it might give him "an opening to write unpretentiously about the poetry of the century . . . all British, Americans only used to point up differences." He had thought all poets of his generation considered themselves Modernist, but here was Larkin, in whose poems the whole movement might never even have existed.[39]

The review did in fact give Lowell a chance to look back over thirty-five years of working at the craft. "When I was a student," he wrote now, "our anthologies backed a dozen American revolutions, and had the clarity of posters.

Reckless with omissions and careless with dates, they often began with Walt Whitman, our best, and the wind of the great dream let loose." As for that other great precursor, Emily Dickinson, her "nervous sentences made the professionals' good poetry sound like translation." He spoke of the Chicago school of Vachel Lindsay, Carl Sandburg, and Edgar Lee Masters, "anti-capitalists, populists, wasters of words, inspired by accident, craftsmen with luck." Of the Modernists—Pound, Eliot, Marianne Moore, Williams, Hart Crane—he noted that all had written "far from the common, and in styles close to the difficulties of art and the mind's unreason." Behind all their work he could still feel something of the brilliant "outrage of the Vandals."

But to the English, of course, American literature must have seemed almost like "a sequence of demolitions, the bravado of perpetual revolution, break-through with the stereotype of nothing preserved." After all, as he too well understood, the central figure in American history and literature had been Prometheus, Satan, the firebringer, the Rebel. For years Lowell had seen him-self in the dual roles of prophet and rebel, though in truth he was feeling now far more like some chastened Prometheus, tied to this formidable outcrop called England.

More and more now he found his mind turning toward the quiet example of Hardy, undoubtedly the greatest English poet of the century, writing his best poems when he was already past seventy. "He had to be old to find natural inspiration in nostalgia, things changing, the days of his courtship, eternal then quickly gone, when love turned terrible and the marriage endured. . . . They are like the music then fashionable—so true they are—or like the period photographs, if a photograph had feeling."[40] He would have to remember that when he got over his "after-book blues" and began writing again.[41]

Now too, in late January 1973, after too many years, the American presence in Viet Nam was about to end. "All afternoon we have been under the belief that peace in Vietnam has at last been made," he wrote Bidart. "Somehow, I'm not sure why, the burial of a bad chapter never to be salvaged, is like a funeral." Suddenly, there seemed "nothing to do after so much occupation and purpose," either with the country or with himself. "While you are naked and running," he added, "you don't feel your nakedness." The servant situa-tion at Milgate was better now, though he wished he hadn't read Truman Capote's *In Cold Blood* out in this country. He'd also been reading various tracts on hermeticism, and was bracing to have Milgate "famed and visited as a Fludd shrine," since the founder of hermeticism had once lived in the very rooms he now occupied. He half wondered if he might not convince Fludd's ghost to become a sort of tutelary spirit for his too-huge, sprawling house-hold.[42]

Contrary to what he'd promised his publishers, he went on making revisions on his sonnets even in galleys, until he was sure he was freezing his editor's blood. "I haven't written a letter for a month," he told Bidart on February 9, "the perverse but comforting inertia towards most things while I finish correcting." Not only was he tinkering with words, he was adding yet more poems to his books, even after he'd promised himself to hand in everything ahead of time, "stop, and forget."[43] But a week later, all the revisions had finally been revised. "Page proofs finished, the text irrevocable." That over, he turned to Balzac for guidance, a writer who had "often finished as many as six novels in a year."[44] It was a time now for endings, for "de-effervescing," for finishing unfinished business: "writing, teaching, divorce, alimony, strife." All along he'd thought of *The Dolphin* as his last and perhaps best book, a problematic breaking through into a new life. Now, when phrases came into his head, he no longer pencilled them down, but bade them go elsewhere.

That winter and spring he and Caroline negotiated to buy up a hundred acres of grazing land around Milgate to stop it from being turned into either football fields or a golf course. Already, alas, the hoary woods behind the kitchen garden had been chain-sawed off, with only three trees saved. Perhaps if Caroline sold her two Francis Bacons they could keep the estate from becoming suburbanized. After all, this was Gainsborough country, and he liked seeing his neighbor's sheep and cattle grazing in such easy, gentle spaces. Money could also be expected from the final sale of his papers to Harvard (though he generously gave Lizzie $10,000 for her share in the papers and Bishop $5,000 for hers). He'd read a few of his own letters among all that paper. They weren't much, perhaps, he told Bishop, but they did "have words and sentences written seriously and unlike" anything he'd printed.[45]

"If only age could stop and inspiration be an irregular constant," he wrote her in March.[46] Caroline had just finished her first collection of essays, *For All That I Found There*, its title borrowed from the Ulster Protestant anthem. In truth, it was rather like a novel, he told Bidart, filled with New York and California characters, women's libbers and radical black schools. And while Caroline could be "a very formidable person," with heads falling "at night over the restaurant table," it had been like taking Harriet to the dentist to see how shyly Caroline had interacted with her publisher.[47]

Once again, Harriet arrived in England for spring vacation, and soon she was gone. "It's that we remain the same," he wrote Lizzie afterwards, "and she changes, almost while one watches." She was sixteen now, "her character and characteristics" already shaped, he knew, and yet her next years still lost in fog.[48] But he'd enjoyed the visit, he told Taylor, and Harriet had told him she felt just like him, which was what he felt too, down to his "illegible writing, ineptitude with everything done with the hands, imbecility in mathematics, a flair for practical jokes, incredible boasting, shyness and charm."[49]

Sheridan, on the other hand, remained pure chaos. At a year and a half he had decided to give up speech entirely for walking and entertainment. "He continuously makes a sound like a pot of boiling water wheezing and thumping," Cal explained to Harriet. "A month ago he had five words, now he has none and puts the energy into forever running (he never walks), refusing to go where we want him, and bringing us the wrong objects."[50] In June he came down with chickenpox of the mouth.

At the beginning of February Lowell had gone up to Hull for a weekend to visit with Philip Larkin. Since 1957, when he'd read Larkin's poems in *The Less Deceived,* he'd followed his career with intense interest. Larkin, however, who liked almost no one and nothing, had already dismissed *Life Studies* as merely "curious, hurried, offhand vignettes, seeming too personal to be practised, yet nonetheless accurate and original."[51] In the elections for the Oxford Chair of Poetry in 1966, in fact, Larkin had told Robert Conquest that, though he hadn't voted, he would have voted for Edmund Blunden, "who was a faint amount of good once, not like old R.L. who's never looked like being a single iota of good in all his born days. Lord Hairy's Arsehole."[52] That weekend in Hull, however, Larkin was at least outwardly cordial. But the following day, after an evening of drinking and listening to Lowell's poems, Larkin wrote his mother that Lowell was "a creature that has talked too much, drunk too much, and stayed up too late!"[53]

Then, in late April, Larkin came down to Milgate for a visit. At fifty-two, Larkin already "looked older than Eliot," Lowell told Bishop, "six foot one, low-spoken, bald, deaf, deathbrooding, a sculptured statue of his poems. He made me feel almost an undergraduate in health, and somehow old as the hills." At one point he'd asked Larkin about his poem, "Wild Oats," and "of the girl he speaks of there he met in his 20s, and had kept 2 photos of her in his billfold—and there they were, passport pictures." As far as Cal was concerned, Larkin was "the best poet still writing" in England, "perhaps by far."

By then Lowell was also hungry for and appalled by the news of Nixon's involvement with the Watergate break-ins, complaining that he could find no Americans to talk to about the fast-breaking scandal. The English were glad to oblige, he told Bishop, "but without one's own anguish and fervor. Sickening, fascinating gobbets come out in each paper. But it's too much, unless the country can somehow be cleaned up. I think the corruption has been going on long before Nixon, yet he is a criminal silhouette on things—government almost by the mafia." So many "worse things have been happening to our country for the last—but what is the precise date?—years."[54]

In fact, he was exhilarated by Senator Sam Ervin's investigations into the Watergate scandal and with Nixon's part in it all. "It gets to be rather too much doesn't it," he wrote Lizzie. "The dull endless roster of German names"—Haldeman, Erlichman, Kissinger—"and advertising experts. And the really much greater war crimes of Nixon and Johnson passing by unatoned." The only "human touch" he'd found so far among the accused had been that between Attorney John Mitchell and his wife Martha, who had refused to keep silent about what she knew. Couldn't "the last election be declared fraudulent—that would get around [Vice President Spiro] Agnew succeeding. Or maybe Nixon will ride it—I don't see how, except that the actual bugging seems secondary to the perjuries." Augean stables. Were they ever clean?

In April he'd gone fishing up north in Westmorland, "a sort of inland New England draining population county," he told Lizzie, and was at the moment leading a "wonderfully worthless life" of magazines, fiction, the movies. He read briefly "in behalf of paralytics and repairing the old Banqueting Hall" in Maidstone, then went with Caroline for three days to Paris, before going on alone to Florence and Pisa for a round of poetry readings and visits with Rolando Anzilotti and Peter Brooks. "After twenty years, city, country and tongue" seemed less foreign to him. "Again the twenty course dinners with the poets; again Gian Bologna—Orcagna restored, the halls of the Campo Santo [at Pisa] we saw in 1950 covered." How he wished they were arriving there together again.[55]

In mid-June he took part in the Rotterdam Poetry Festival. Rotterdam: another place he and Lizzie had visited back in the early 1950s. "The old center of the city," he told her, which then had been "just a messy, grassy open space" where the seventeenth-century city had once stood until bombed into oblivion, was now all "sleeplessly new, very pleasant, tho inhuman." The "high point of incongruity" there had been a meeting between Allen Ginsberg and Gunther Grass on a poetry barge, Grass saying, "Why, he doesn't even have cymbals." Offstage, however, Cal had found Ginsberg "rather quiet and . . . soothing."[56]

There was another momentary flare-up with Lizzie over the house in Castine. Lizzie had decided to sell it and do the Barn over into a house. Since Cousin Harriet had deeded it all to her for practical reasons, Cal knew he had no legal rights in the matter. Still, it was sad for him to see the place sold. "Should I let it go without worries and suggestions," he half-pleaded with her, "as if it had only been air to me?" How desolate to have to consider that all he had from the past in the wake of his divorce was his grandfather's "gold watch and . . . fifteen books."[57] He wondered if he might at least have an access agreement to the place, though he "would be too shy to live there" until after his death.

Milgate, too, seemed to be crumbling all about him. "In the last month," he complained, "we've had two flooded cellars, the removal of a partition, leadshallows stolen from an outbuilding, a dog lost, an unfindable fuse, a skylight leak, the disappearance of all our napkins and handkerchiefs, a plastering job . . . a three days' cook with a son who went insane—the mother . . . married to a hippy buying a donkey without asking us—the donkey had a bad cold and had the vet for six pounds, the dryer stopped, and so on. Houses really ail more than we do, they never cure themselves." Like Lizzie, he too watched as the years went by, thought of her, thought of her writing.

He pored over the scrapbook Lizzie had sent him. All that history, "artfully arranged pages, sequences, like my long poems, full of profundity for me if [for] no one else": Tate and Biala Ford, "Peter [Taylor] and me and Jean in New Orleans, looking hung over, except unbelievably for Jean." He had no old ones of Lizzie any more "because two and a half years ago I left my billfold in a restaurant or taxi—early in the evening going home—and lost about eight small snapshots and a hundred dollars in Per's Norwegian money." He especially missed "a wonderful wild one" of Lizzie smoking, taken on the Loire by Robie Macauley.[58]

But on the eve of the publication of his three books, he became increasingly worried about the reviews. "It's the twinges of mortality," he wrote Bishop, "one's length of life that keeps swimming into eyesight." He thought of Pasternak's *To live a life is not to cross a field*. "We cannot cross the field," he knew, "only walk it . . . finishing or not finishing this or that along the way. An image of all this is watching children and step-children growing into their futures I cannot see, and all from forty to fifty-five years younger than I even while I live."[59] He drank less now, "a bottle of wine a day," he told Taylor, "and most often half a bottle. My hands no longer shake over coffee, I can leave a taxi deftly like a man of forty."[60]

Then, in late June, the reviews began pouring in. Lowell's revisions came to a kind of gaming with words, as if words were merely billiard balls, one critic noted. Others failed to see a pattern emeging from the plethora of experience. And William Pritchard, writing in the *Hudson Review*, was convinced that Lowell had gone too far.[61] Worst of all was Marjorie Perloff's review in the *New Republic* in early July: "Poor Harriet," she wrote, "emerges from these passages as one of the most unpleasant child figures in history," adding that Lizzie and Harriet seemed "to get no more than they deserve."[62]

For Lowell, Perloff's review was too much, and he cabled Lizzie at once: "THE REVIEWS FRIENDLY OR UNFRIENDLY ARE MORE OR LESS ONLY CRUEL PUBLICITY POSTERS GOD HELP US AND SPARE US."[63] They were lampoons rather than reviews, he wrote Bishop on the 12th. "I think they all have a jarring effect on Lizzie, but one by a Miss Perloff in *The New Republic* has been a calamity for Lizzie—what it says about her and Harriet. The distortion of the 'fictional' characters becomes a slander on the people themselves." The week before, in fact, Lizzie had been almost "suicidal and friends had to drop in and telephone to see that she didn't take too many pills." Now, though she was quieter, he dreaded what the telephone might bring.

Then, *Newsweek,* "in an otherwise discreet review," had published an unflattering photo of Lizzie, "and above it a family portrait photograph (taken by [Thomas] Victor when he was here and given without our knowledge to *Newsweek*), Caroline, I, Ivana (labelled Harriet) and Sheridan looking like a secret polygamous poor white family." This last, however, had been "so grotesque that Lizzie seems to have thought it was funny."[64] He called Lizzie on July 7, then waited five days before writing. "I never in all this business have wanted to hurt you," he told her. In fact he'd meant the very opposite. "Most of the hurting reviews . . . will look very dim by September," he tried to comfort her. As for Perloff, he guessed she was some "instructor or young professor, earnestly, waspishly pursuing her career, too stiff to be much of a critic," though he could not overlook what he took to be her "stupid cruelty." He was sorry he'd ever brought this on Lizzie, "the ghastly transient voices, the lights."[65]

But in the close, sultry, fungal English summer of Milgate he felt trapped. If he looked out his study window he saw cows, fields, trees, a world "becalmed." If he strolled up and down his long study, he felt Lizzie with him in the room, with no escape from her attacks but rather arguing with her, as so often in the past, "though the past all in all gives a more joyful picture . . . and the future is only dread of what will happen." Bishop had been right after all, he thought, in warning him of the storm. Obviously, he'd never solved the problem of incorporating Lizzie's letters, or of meshing fact with fiction.

Still, even the reviewers had pointed out that the letters made Lizzie "brilliant and loveable, more than anyone in the book," he argued, though perhaps "not enough." Nor had he sufficiently considered the big circulation magazines, which would be hungry to reduce his complex plot "to news or scandal," as if he was merely some politician or actor. Publishing the letters was not, he still insisted, a question of immorality. For no one in *The Dolphin,* not even himself, was "perversely torn and twisted," and nothing had been made "dishonestly worse or better than it was. My sin (mistake?) was publishing the book at all." And yet he could not bear "to have my book (my life) wait inside me like a dead child."[66] Having done what she could to protect him from publishing in the first place, Bishop wrote to console him now. "We all have irreparable and awful actions on our consciences," she reassured him. No one was immune.[67]

But painful as Perloff's review had been, the review that hurt most was Adrienne Rich's in the *American Poetry Review* that fall. "There's a kind of aggrandized and merciless masculinity at work in these books," she wrote there. And what, finally, did "one say about a poet who, having left his wife and daughter for another marriage, then titles a book with their names, and goes on to appropriate his ex-wife's letters written under the stress and pain of desertion, into a book of poems nominally addressed to the new wife? . . . I have to say that I think this is bullshit eloquence, a poor excuse for a cruel and shallow book, that it is presumptuous to balance injury done to others with injury done to myself." Though Cal dismissed Rich's review as nothing more than dogmatic feminism, in truth he was deeply wounded by the attack, for Rich had been a close friend and the review put an end to that friendship forever.[68] Discussing her poetry back at Harvard with his students, he would henceforth relegate her to the "minor, definitely minor" category.[69]

Harriet had been visiting with Cal when the reviews began to appear, but thought the tension she sensed between her parents had to do with the property settlement. At the end of July she went off on a bicycle tour through Ireland with a friend. For her part, Lizzie left Castine on July 27 and travelled to northern Italy for a month to get as far away from the buzzing as she could. The day she left, she wrote Bishop to say she'd been hurt by the book as much as by anything in her life. How sad too that *The Dolphin* should turn out to be such an "inane, empty, unnecessary" book. She could not understand "how three years of work could have left so many fatuities, indiscretions, bad lines still there on the page."[70] ("I can't tell you how I dread the future with biographies and *Lizzie,*" she would write Bishop again three months later, "to say nothing of Cal, who will never be even touched with the truth of his own being and nature. Fortunately I'll be dead before most of them come.")[71]

To Cal she wrote simply that she never wanted to hear from him again. Then she wrote his American and English publishers to tell them how contemptible they were. "I have hardly had one real, uninsulting review in America," Cal wrote Blair, "but many of the English [reviews] are all I could ask." Some of them had even compared his poems with Yeats's last poems. But was any of it worth it to see his dear Lizzie hurt like this?[72]

"The summer's end and the month's end," he wrote Bill Alfred on August 31, as he prepared to return to Harvard after an absence of nearly four years. Harvard seemed rather like "a recovered universe" after all that time away. "If I looked in a mirror, I imagine I would have the white beard of father time." Relations with Lizzie had broken off completely, he confessed, and he'd heard nothing from her for the past two months. "The reviews fanned the fire," he knew, but publishing the book, he realized, had been bound to do it. "Was it Calvin or Harry Levin," he wondered, who had said that doing was "a choice of evils"? He and Caroline had rented a house in Brookline and he was looking forward once more to students who actually talked, to his "long religious and gossipy talks" with Alfred, and to seeing Frank Bidart, who would meet him and his family at the airport, "weary, plane-squashed, all ages, hardly able to speak our language."[73]

If he sounded autumnal, it was because, except for a few sonnets which would never be part of his books but which he'd written simply to show that life moved on, he'd composed nothing in nearly a year. But that fall at Harvard he wrote nine poems, all in free verse, all autobiographical. One of these was "Exile's Return," an early version of "Ulysses and Circe," a poem about returning home to circle the geography of the life he was finding he could not leave behind. He also wrote poems to the memory of his mother and father, to his son, and even one on his own "Afterlife."

Mostly it was a low-keyed autumn. In early November he gave a reading at the Pierpont Morgan Library, where he was introduced by Stanley Kunitz, who spoke of Cal's new poems as refusing to overpower the reader with their show of strength and instead showed one "the time in the right kind of voice for the day."[74] Harriet came up to Boston for a visit, and at term's end he went back down to New York for a short vacation. By then Lizzie had relented enough that Cal could talk to her before flying back to England. "Since my second fatherhood / and stay in England," he wrote that December, as he summed up his gains and losses,

> *I am a generation older.*
> *We are dangerously happy—*
> *our book-bled faces*
> *streak unstably,*
> *ears cocked to catch*
> *the first shy whisper of deafness. . . .*[75]

Not yet fifty-seven and already he seemed old, his hair long and white now and uncombed, his clothes worn and rumpled, his every second thought on death. In December, Peter Taylor suffered a heart attack. Then, in January 1974, a "deluge of strokes": Hannah Arendt in Scotland, Lillian Hellman in Paris, Frank Parker in Cambridge. He was so shaken by these casualties that he even considered giving up cigarettes, then reconsidered. At Christmas, Philip Rahv died in Boston. "Delighted with your Philip," Cal wrote Lizzie in mid-January, when he saw her prose elegy for their old friend. "It seems to say everything for and against imaginable in your short space—and more than what is possible in a funeral speech." Cal too had begun a piece on Rahv, but Lizzie's essay had made that redundant.[76]

After Brookline, it was good to be back at Milgate, sitting before a coal fire and writing again, even if "without much steam."[77] He was still writing in free verse and revising some of the "perversely wild translations" he'd allowed a place in *Imitations,* particularly the Montales, for it had been, he confessed to Bidart, "a mistake to invent something of one's translating" when faithfulness to the text could do it better, though he also knew that a faithful translation might do nothing for a poem, if all it did was make it "undistinguishable from another of the kind." Still, he added, "I did shockingly turn, twist, some of the translations to my own morbid purposes."[78]

Cambridge that fall had seemed more crowded than ever, he wrote Bishop now, with "too much brushing from one friend to another, too many shifts of attitude," too many academics. Yet spending time with her had allowed their friendship to pass "out of some shadow." The reviews hadn't, after all, turned out too badly: "about three to two unfavorable, many of these journalism, too little tested in poetry to know very much." He'd "spent days and days, like other revisers, spoiling by polishing," he admitted. But the "great fault" had been his reliance on a kind of "rhetorical melodrama," played and laboriously replayed.

He'd noticed that Bishop in an interview had written off confession and irony as suitable for poetry. But confession and irony, he told her, were his staples. What was confession, after all, but "the use or exploitation of painful experience that gets on one's conscience." And what was irony but the "being amusing (or worse acid) about what we can't understand." He didn't see how he could ever write now without using both, though neither strategy was going to "get one to heaven." On the other hand the new free verse poems he was writing, he assured her, told nothing, "except the most intimate of things." In his new work he had been at pains to tone down the rhetoric and so avoid the excesses of the sonnets. "This had to be," he explained, "though one's style, one's self really must not change."[79]

In April 1974, in spite of the adverse criticism it had received, *The Dolphin* was awarded a Pulitzer. It was Lowell's third. Nothing since refusing to go to the White House Arts Festival had brought him so much correspondence as this award, he wrote Bill Alfred, who had been on the nominating committee. Everyone was writing him: his "Japanese translator (Shozo), Ralph Lowell, Cousin Alice and many more."[80] He returned to the States for three weeks of readings, an itinerary which included Vanderbilt, the universities of Virginia and South Carolina (where he visited with James Dickey), then north to Washington, Skidmore, and Harvard, where he visited again with Bishop and Alfred.

In New York he had a good visit with Lizzie, marred only by an argument as he was leaving. Still, he wrote her, "nothing could have been more tender and considerate of old 'patriarchal' than your treatment of me—your treatment and Harriet's."[81] Back in England in early May he returned to Essex to read and talk about translation in support of three students jailed for striking. Then, on his return to Milgate, he and Caroline discovered that Israel Citkowitz was not answering his telephone. The fire brigade finally broke into his flat and found him lying in his bed, stone cold, having suffered a heart attack.

"Your father died last month," he wrote for his stepdaughters that June. "He is buried . . . not too deep to lie / alive like a feather / on the top of the mind."[82] The funeral itself had been "ghastly," he wrote Taylor, "with artificial sward, and a . . . minister saying in the style of the Church of England prayerbook but not the spirit."[83] For a month they lived under the shadow of Citkowitz's death, made even more palpable when they went up to Redcliffe Square to clear the apartment. It had been "filled with rubbish, plunder, a piano, books in French and German, piano things. Unlike most flats, it was as much him as the shell of a turtle, so that its end was like the last sigh of a soul."[84]

On June 25, Lowell flew to Italy to take part in the Spoleto Arts Festival. "We made a three hour trip to Spoleto that took three days," he wrote Taylor. "Waiting at Orly Caroline had a last minute cup of French coffee (the 1000 other mistakes were mine), we missed our plane and had to wait seven and a half hours; I had to carry two fifty pound suitcases past the douanne up and down a frozen escalator, seven and a half times." He was not well and the exertion had been too much for him, so that now he would not even allow himself "to lift a pencil or a briefcase" and dreamt often of a cane and "showy non-functioning crutches."[85]

Taylor had just suffered a second stroke (twenty years ahead of calendar, Cal wrote Tate)[86] and the news made him think again of his own mortality, especially when he was away from the comforts of home. Once more he tried to give up drinking and smoking. "I too go over my life trying to understand it," he told Taylor. "I think in a way, I never understood it, that it is addition not to be understood, just completed." Yet, puritan that he was, he couldn't really live that way, but had to believe that there was some "point to be reached— even a reward card to be won."

In July, John Crowe Ransom, Lowell's first real "intellectual father," died quietly in his sleep at the age of eighty-six. Ransom's death seemed right, he told Taylor, "an untroubling anyone courtesy. He was my teacher and kept me from breaking myself."[87] In his short memoir, published that August in *The New Review,* Lowell would recall the strange prewar world of Vanderbilt and Kenyon. Ransom's hopes had been based on "the decentralist provincial hopes of Tennessee agrarians and traditionalists," Cal wrote now, "a cause as impractical and permanent as socialism, though for now fallen away from the sunlight." Over the years he'd seen Ransom's "Southern first-love" dim into an "unoptimistic Northern liberalism." Had watched too as Ransom "rewrote his early perfect poems into a disastrously new style." Well, he knew from too much experience that one had "a thousand opportunities to misrevise."

Once he'd asked "the master photographer Walker Evans how Vermeer's *View of Delft* (that perhaps first trompel'oeil of landscape verisimilitude) differed from a photograph." Evans had "paused, staring, as if his eye could not give the answer. His answer was Ransom's—art demands the intelligent pain or care behind each speck of brick, each spot of paint."[88] In this short anecdote, Lowell touched on the urgencies of what was to be the final phase of his own poetry. "Pray for the grace of accuracy," he would write in his "Epilogue," in lines more deeply religious perhaps than any he'd written as a fire-breathing young Catholic CO, quiet, humble lines with a lifetime of learned experience behind them:

> Pray for the grace of accuracy
> Vermeer gave to the sun's illumination
> stealing like a tide across a map
> to his girl solid with yearning.
> We are poor passing facts,
> warned by that to give
> each figure in the photograph
> his living name.[89]

In August 1974, faced with impeachment proceedings, Richard Nixon, Lowell's great *bête noire*, was at last forced to resign. "A great pollution has been removed from our country, almost in a Biblical or Greek classical sense," he wrote Lizzie. "Wasn't Nixon good on *au revoir*, the smallest citron ranch, and his mother who was a saint?"[90] Even eighteen months later he could still taste the bitterness of Nixon's legacy. "You feel that America today is beyond prophecy in its state of indecision and chaos," he told one interviewer. "We've just had one of the most disastrous wars we have ever fought . . . and one of the most disastrous Presidents who has ever served. It is almost as if an invincible cavalryman"—he meant America—"had stopped dead against a wall. But it's only temporary. America will go on again and keep going, because it is so big and prosperous and has so much ability."[91] And amidst all the hoopla for the American Bicentennial he would remind America, in a poem printed in *Newsweek*, of what it had just come through, as he linked Nixon to poor, mad King George III:

> once a reigning monarch like Nixon,
> and more exhausting to dethrone . . .
>
> Could Nixon's court,
> could Haldeman, Erlichman, or Kissinger

blame their king's behavior
on an insane wetnurse? . . .

yet how modern George is,
wandering vacated chambers of his White House,

addressing imaginary congresses,
reviewing imaginary combat troops. . . .

mercifully unable to hear
his drab tapes play back his own voice to him,

morning, noon, and night.[92]

Mostly that summer of '74 he read, "Latin and French—last 6 books of the *Aeneid* and Horace and Racine," enjoying "the slow pace of reading languages" he didn't know, so that he could "floor the next monolingual English intellectual I meet," as well as Frank Bidart, who was about to arrive at Milgate for a two-week visit, "still having read nothing in English before Elizabeth Bishop." For months now he'd avoided drinking, taking Antabuse along with his lithium, so that his blood pressure had finally returned to normal, though he did have "cooling extremities," which left the soles of his feet feeling "like dry leaves." In general, though, he told Taylor, his health was as bad as the economy, what with a sagging stock market and runaway inflation, so that he half-joked about "trying to recover and sharpen" his objections to Margaret Thatcher's "totalitarian socialism."[93]

But the economy was no joke, for the depression was indeed hurting his family, he told Bishop. Perhaps it was time now to return to the States where he could earn a living and be nearer his friends. As for Harvard, he didn't feel "particularly persona grata there," he had to admit, not with his record. But it seemed "weak and demoralized not to do something . . . more" for his family than what his royalties might bring in. He also knew there wasn't much he could do in England. On top of which Caroline was now in the middle of "an old-fashioned nervous breakdown," full of "jerks, up and downs, panics, moments of excitement . . . tho most of the time . . . calm and full." Here he was, fifty-seven and still virtually helpless and impractical. How he wished there were something more he could *do* for his wife and children.[94]

In late September he was attending a publisher's party in London when suddenly, he told Taylor, he felt "an acute nausea (as if I had been drinking heavily,) then a rather comforting feeling of changing inside to ice, then I was being rolled about by six merry people on a low table, like a gentle practical joke. I had fainted. It may have been from accidentally drinking something like vodka in orange juice, or it may not."[95] "Last night I fainted at dinner," he addressed Taylor in a poem,

> *and came nearer to your sickness,*
> *nearer to the angels in nausea.*
> *The room turned upside-down,*
> *I was my interrupted sentence,*
> *a misdirection tumbled back alive*
> *on a low, cooling black table.*
>
> *The doctors come more thickly,*
> *they use exact language*
> *even when they disagree on the mal-diagnosis*
> *in the surgeon's feather touch. . . .*
>
> *The old boys drop like wasps*
> *from windowsill and pane.*
> *In a church,*
> *the Psalmist's glass mosaic Shepherd*
> *and bright green pastures*
> *seem to wait*
> *with the modish faithlessness*
> *and erotic daydream*
> *of art nouveau for our funeral.*[96]

A week later he was examined by a London heart specialist and "cleared of any heart trouble, as earlier of lung trouble." So now, he joked to Lizzie, "I am pushing crates and carrying buckets of coal upstairs." Since he was planning to teach that spring at Harvard, he was particularly upset by the news of race riots in South Boston. He knew that, though the riots would die down, the underlying resentments would "remain smouldering in the air." He would probably come over alone this time to save the expense of transporting his family, staying on at Quincy House as he had in the past. He wondered if he might stop a couple of days with her and Harriet and "disturb" his studio.[97]

The previous June, Jean Stafford had sent a picture of a balding, grey-haired, bespectacled Lowell to a friend with the note: "I enclose a new photograph of the reason we first met. Eve Auchincloss sent it to me saying, 'The Ben Franklin *de nos jours*. Yuch!' It's impossible to believe that this is the raving beauty I knew as a young man."[98] But three months later she was writing Cal that he'd saved her "from being taken by the black Maria to debtor's prison."

With "sorrow and regret," she'd sold her copy of *Land of Unlikeness* for a tidy sum and blessed him from the bottom of her heart.

"Quite frankly," she told Cal, "I want to make some more money out of you. May I? Can we collude as we were accused of doing when my head got busted?" Here was the deal. Not all her copies of Cal's books were inscribed. She also had his copy of an Oxford University Press anthology with "dense annotations in your hand of Collins' 'Ode to Evening' and even denser ones of [Wordsworth's] 'Intimations of Immortality' and I can sell that for more if you wrote your name under mine." She still drank, she told him, but only "as an insulation against boredom and impatience, or to exalt my feeling of camaraderie against boredom and impatience." From time to time she fell down and broke something, otherwise she was fine.[99] They would meet in Boston in the spring and he would autograph the books, he assured her. He also sent her a check.

He did not at all like the idea of coming to America without Caroline, he told Bishop. It would mean learning to cook dinner "of a kind," for "dinner alone in a restaurant" was for him both "fascinating and a torture."[100] Then, in December, Caroline changed her mind and flew to the States to find a place large enough for her and Cal and the children. Bidart was there to help her, and by the time she returned to Milgate she'd rented a brick town house on Cypress Avenue in Brookline. "I did not want to force her hand about coming to Boston," Cal thanked Bidart, "or even try to make a delightful prospect, until she had seen and judged for herself both the kind of house and the whole atmosphere." But he had to admit that everyone coming with him meant more to him than he could say.[101]

In truth he was sounding more and more ancient. "For several years I haven't felt my 'true self,'" he joked halfheartedly to Taylor:

> Most embarrassing, when I get out of one of the large taxis, the driver sometimes asks if I need help; I take stairs too with a considered seriousness, I forget names and faces as always only more; if I give someone a comical name, like Nemo or Lynhurst, I am liable to think it is his name. I forget things, have no memory of where I put my cigarette lighter after a few minutes, no recollection even after I find it irrationally lying on a distant bureau. I act, as all flesh must, my age.

It all seemed "ghastly brevity," he said of the news of yet another friend's death, "everything ending frayed and unfinished as usual, the fraying of health, more grand and final than Christian after-life."[102] And to Lizzie: "I was always rather a parody of other people. Now I am a parody of my old self."[103]

A week before Christmas he wrote Bishop that both of them, friends for twenty-five years, seemed near the finish of their lives now, even as Milgate prepared once more for a festive holiday with small children running about. "I see us still when we first met, both at Randall's," she "tall, long brown-haired, shy but full of ideas and anecdote as now," he "largely invisible" even to himself, both "swimming in our young age, with the water coming down on us, and we were gulping."[104]

But Bishop, six years Cal's senior, did not like this sort of talk at all, and she told him so. She refused to "feel ancient," wished Auden "hadn't gone on about it so in his last years," and hoped Cal wouldn't. Why, she had a friend in Florida who had just remarried for the third time at seventy-six and liked to walk hand in hand with her husband on the beach, the two of them "happy as clams."[105]

Just before he flew to Boston in early February 1975, Cal saw his London doctor, Paul Brass, to ask for a medical report for his Boston doctor, Curtis Prout. Since he was anxious to know the truth about his condition, he refused to give Brass his Boston physician's address, so that Brass finally handed him a sealed envelope to give to Prout. On the flight over, Lowell opened the letter to read what he'd both suspected and feared. "This delightful man has been a patient of mine since his arrival in England," the letter began:

> He suffers from chronic manic depression controlled with large doses of lithium, and he also has had raised blood pressure over the last four years. The blood pressure is controlled at about 150/100 on three tablets of methyl dopa 250 mgm per day. His pulse remains at 100 per minute and I must say he never really looks particularly well. You probably know that he had a tendency in the past to drink excessive amounts of alcohol and to smoke too much. Of his own accord he has been taking Abstem tablets [Antabuse] one daily and has more or less been on the wagon for the last four months. He has even cut down on his cigarette smoking to about 20 a day.

Brass also commented on the results of tests conducted by an eminent cardiologist after Cal's fainting spell in September. The chest X-ray had shown "a slightly odd-shaped heart, but . . . within ordinary limits." His ECGs showed "left axis deviation compatible with left anterior block." There was "some delay in right ventricular conduction," but this did not "amount to bundle branch block." If Lowell's dizziness recurred, Brass suggested, a pacemaker might have to be considered. The patient was also subject to "severe chest pains . . . starting in his back and radiating round to the right side," and X-rays had shown "considerable osteo-arthritis in his dorsal spine."

He had discussed none of this with Mr. Lowell, who was "extremely apprehensive" about his health, and knew the news "would certainly make him very worried."[106] In Boston, Prout would reassure Lowell that his not drinking made him look twenty years younger. But Cal was shaken. For years now he'd told himself—and others—that since both his parents had died in their early sixties of heart failure, he too would go at sixty. Now there were pictures to confirm that he did indeed have an enlarged and damaged heart.

The spring term at Harvard was not easy for Caroline, who found her husband continually on edge, "encouraged by all those hangers-on who tried to make him sit up all night drinking." It had been almost five years since his last manic attack, but—in spite of the lithium—she worried he might go off at any moment.[107] Then, in late April, while he was in New York to attend the opera and visit with his New York friends, Cal collapsed a second time. Robert Silvers would remember him at a restaurant after the opera, looking "exhausted, excited, incoherent," as he slumped over the table drinking glass after glass of orange juice.[108]

The following day Cal had lunch with Bob Giroux at an Armenian restaurant called the *Dardanelles,* a favorite of his when he was in the Village. "After we ordered our food (he did not ask for a drink)," Giroux would recall, "to my horror his head fell forward and he slumped down in his seat."[109] He was rushed to Mount Sinai Hospital, where the cause of the collapse was determined to be lithium toxicity. What had happened was this: feeling the onslaught of another attack, Cal had tried to check it by taking additional amounts of lithium. Later he equivocated with Tate, saying that what he'd had was some virus which "overcomes antibiotics and wanders from brain to eye to ear, then mostly to stomach. It can return. For a couple of days, my life was all in flakes in my mind . . . among other things our Monteagle in stormy sunlit vignettes."[110]

Less and less he wrote anyone now. "Lizzie once said that if I didn't move more and more usefully, my arms or legs would drop off," he joked with Taylor that July. It was his first real letter since returning to England six weeks before, and by then he'd lost touch with everyone. "Coming out of the furnace of 34 Cypress St. we found our house heated by one terminating coal fire. . . . Then heaven, on the afternoon the Common Market went through, we have had sun every day. The fields are turning whitish green. Our nights are October nights in Tennessee; our days summer days in Maine." Didn't "a happy country have no history?" Well, so it seemed with him and Caroline.

By then he had almost a new book of poems "all in the same style and meter": short lines, unrhymed, unscanned, its theme the facing of "time and age without hysteria." No longer were his subjects the historical great—Alexander, Cato, Joinville, the Kennedys—but "lower things now, the fetus, turtles, ants, destroyed English houses and a Princess executed by Communists."[111] It was, in fact, another turn in the spiral staircase downward, even further away from his earlier high, public style. "I have stood too long on a chair or ladder," he'd written five years before, already sounding like Yeats in old age,

> *branch-lightning forking through my thought and veins—*
> *I cannot hang my heavy picture straight.*
> *I can't see myself. . . .*[112]

Or like Hardy. For more and more it was the older Hardy, the septuagenarian, one heard now behind Lowell's poems—Milgate his Wessex, heartbreak and loss the theme of his last years.

With Bidart's help in rummaging through his papers at Harvard, and Giroux's help in having his old critical pieces and reviews retyped, Lowell had also come up with a prose book of nearly 200 pages, "longer than anything" he'd ever submitted. But to his astonishment, Giroux spoke only "of the *makings* of a fine book." Makings? Cal wondered if Taylor didn't have some rejected book reviews he might sell him.[113] He wrote Tate, on oxygen now and confined to his bed, and forced to dictate his letters; "I hate to think of the afflictions the summer may have brought you," he wrote, thanking him for the encouragement about his prose book. "There are a lot, but not enough, and not enough order," he told Tate, though he despaired just now of adding anything more, especially as each essay had cost him far "more qualms and trouble than any poem."[114]

Kunitz paid him a good visit in June. "He knew far more about the English than me but that's an understatement," he told Taylor. He could hardly believe the man was twelve years his senior, so agile was he. Lowell "missed playing tennis," but at Milgate could "find no one good enough to play, who plays badly enough for me." He got up to London once a week now, though he was so "un-practised" with new faces he could hardly open his mouth. On one trip he'd seen Robert Graves, eighty years old, "amnesiac after a stomach operation, looking like old Wordsworth, beautiful and gallant." As for himself, he was beginning to sound more Victorian than the Victorians with their endless lists of ailments: "coughs, pinkeye and palpitations." And yet, having stopped taking anything but lithium and digitalis—the latter for depression and heart trouble—"Lassitude and Nod [had] gone into the air, not to be found."[115]

Then there was that summer's prolonged heatwave, so that even at Milgate, he wrote Bidart, windows had been pried open that hadn't been open "since the age of Gladstone."[116] At the moment, he was preparing a *Selected Poems* and reading everything: Heine ("one of the greatest and funniest writers in his prose"), Flannery O'Connor's *Wise Blood* ("very much better than Updike"),

Vanity Fair, The Trial, and the parts of *War and Peace* that the BBC had recently televised. Prose was "so entertaining after poetry," he wrote Lizzie, "and so easy to read—simple language, plots, a style simple enough to draw you on for hundreds of pages."[117] Prose was a movie, to be run through, unlike poetry, a still life meant to be gazed at.

In late August he flew to Ireland for the poetry festival at Kilkenny to which Seamus Heaney had invited him. As Cal feared, the Kilkenny event turned out to be a week of drunken and contentious readings. "Just because one loves writing doesn't mean one likes what goes with it," he'd told Lizzie on the eve of his departure.[118] Still, salmon fishing on the river had been glorious, though there too the summer drought had driven the fish into the wilds, and he'd hated having to climb three or four gates to get to the water. Since he no longer felt twenty-five, he sighed, he had found himself circling about "looking for the easiest fence to surmount."[119]

Harriet, who began classes that fall at Columbia, had her own apartment now, and Cal worried aloud to Lizzie that she might be tempted to party too much. "But what can one do, children are so soon on their own as we are— independent in all ways except financially." Then, realizing he was beginning to sound like "the worst of old maids," he stopped. Perhaps, he wondered, he talked this way because he was actually clinically depressed and had been confusing that condition with his "steady beaverlike revision and writing." But then everyone seemed depressed these days. He wasn't changing. He was simply growing old. "Last week my youngest step-daughter, Ivana, the one who was burned, went off to boarding school. . . . It brought back my second form at St. Mark's. All those trees and old boys, old girls!" How could he have a daughter old enough to be at Columbia?[120]

Then, suddenly, another summer was gone. "Colder days, longer nights, gloom of children going back to school and teachers to college," he wrote Taylor. Except for Sheridan. "When Lulu our small mixed dog one night gave birth to seven puppies," Sheridan had wanted to know why the father hadn't been there. Moreover, Sheridan's "bicentennial experiences in America" had taught him "more than all his nursery schools, the ambivalence, which is really balance of power, of taking both sides." Here in England, people were still "a little bewildered" when Sheridan stood up for King George.[121]

There was a comic evening with Mary McCarthy in early October. She was, Lowell told Lizzie, rather like Henry James's description "of being taken for an automobile tour by Edith Wharton." He'd planned on taking her to the London theater, but three times they'd gone to the wrong theater, so that "by the time we arrived at the right one our tickets had been sold. In retaliation, she took us and the Mostyn-Owens and a Dutchman to a very bad play, then a very slow, expensive dinner, where we searched endlessly for the meaning of the meaningless play. I don't see how her energy, money or courage hold out, but how can sloth deflect to a torpedo?"[122]

The manic episode he had tried so hard to avoid finally hit him in November. It began with the onslaught of tyrant delusions, and then he could feel the mania crawling up his spine. "Honey, Christ," he pleaded with Caroline, "I'm going to have an attack." Since neither could drive, they boarded the train for London, but by the time they reached Victoria Station, Cal was gone. Caroline got him to the Redcliffe Square apartment where Dr. Brass began administering massive doses of Valium. All night he kept giving him more, unable to believe the amounts Cal was taking. He'd seen people have their noses taken off and their legs amputated with the doses he'd given Cal, he told her, and yet there he was, "walking around talking and waving his arms." The next day he was taken by ambulance to the Priory, a private hospital in Roehampton, south of London.[123]

Jonathan Raban visited Cal there a week later, only to find him on the lawn carrying a piece of steel, some engine part or piece of a central heating system. "The Chief Engineer gave me this," Cal told him. It was "the Totentanz . . . what Hitler used to eliminate the Jews." When Raban told him it was just a piece of steel and had nothing to do with the Jews, Cal got "this awful sad, glazed look in his eyes, and said something like 'It's just my way. It's only a joke.' "[124] Cal spent two difficult weeks at the Priory before signing himself out and returning to Milgate. Caroline, under terrible physical pain herself, made worse by the uncertainty of Cal's breakdown, was taking acupuncture treatments for her nagging back. Now Cal insisted on giving up lithium and replacing it with acupuncture, telling Caroline that, after a single treatment, he was cured.[125] But even Lizzie wondered if acupuncture might not help. "I have doubts, in my provinciality," she wrote Mary McCarthy at year's end, "about anything Asian, but I can't help but hope that some relief from the long, long lithium years might give Cal a period of at least physical lightness. It has always seemed improper to me that he should appear so old, walk so slowly, when lithium is not supposed to be a downer in that sense."[126]

For much of December he seemed calm. Then, just after Christmas, the mania flared up again and he had to be readmitted, this time to Greenways, where he'd been treated five years before. But after a week, he discharged himself again and went to Redcliffe Square, where he was treated with homeopathy and acupuncture and looked after by nurses. "I was so desperate at that point," Caroline would explain, "I would have gone to a miracle worker."[127] Unable and unwilling to stay with someone who was disintegrating before her eyes, she took the children back to Milgate and then commuted up to London to do what she could. Given her own distractions, she had no choice but to turn Cal over to round-the-clock nurses.

"I went with him in January 1976 to two acupuncturists in Harley Street," Seamus Heaney would recall:

> He was at that time confined in a small private hospital where I had called to see him earlier in the afternoon and had been given a restorative nip from his Imperial After Shave bottle, which he had assured me contained Benedictine. Then, almost it would seem to atone, he carried me away in a taxi, with his ever present male nurse. And the next thing we had penetrated to the inner sanctum of two friendly and . . . slightly quackish acupuncturists, stealthy, stooped and vaguely insinuating elders from the city of Leeds. They called him Professor. They spoke calmingly to him and he became calm. He answered their questions about what they called his tension with an unexpected childlike candor. He allowed them to palp along the line of his neck and over his temples and down the back of his skull. He took off his shirt. He bowed a little and accepted the needles, one by one, in a delicate gleaming line, from the point of his shoulder to the back of his ear.

"Gulliver in Lilliput," the image came then to Heaney. "Disabled, pinned down, yet essentially magnificent. . . . An emblem of his afflicted life, his great native strength and his sorrowful, invigilated helplessness. Richard not himself, then Richard himself again."[128]

"The professor must not be left alone at any time," the Nurse's Daybook for Lowell reads. "The day nurse must go out with him and the night nurse must sit in his room. He must not be allowed to touch alcohol in any form." But he smoked constantly, forgetting continually where he'd put his lighter and cigarette holder. He drank gallons of orange juice (one time mixing it with olive oil) and of course gallons of milk. He rubbed hair lacquer into his pubic area. Once he visited Westminster Abbey and Poets' Corner and spoke of becoming an Englishman so that he too could have a place among the great. He had lunch with his literary agent and three others and ordered wine. Before long he was enlisting those in the restaurant—including the waiters—to help him compile an anthology of world poetry.

He told people that, though he was in reality King of Scotland, he pledged to be democratic. Once, he managed to leave the flat undetected, take a taxi over to the Portobello Road, and come back with some bundles, including a large knife, which he began pointing at the nurse, trying to calm her by explaining it was just his way of joking. He remained unkempt and dirty, much as he'd been at St. Mark's forty years before.[129] So it went for two weeks, until Caroline was forced to call the police and have him taken by ambulance to St. Andrew's Hospital in Northampton, sixty miles northwest of London.

"To no good / they enter at angles and on the run," he would write afterwards, in a poem which brilliantly captures the sickening disorientation of mania, the free association, the weird punning, the fear of being straitjacketed:

two black verticals are suddenly four
ambulance drivers in blue serge,
or the police doing double-duty. . . .
When they regroup in my room, I know
their eyes have never left their watches.
"Come on, sir." "Easy, sir."
"Dr. Brown will be here in ten minutes, sir."
Instead, a metal chair unfolds into a stretcher.
I lie secured there, but for my skipping mind.
They keep bustling.
"Where you are going, Professor,
you won't need your Dante." . . .
I follow my own removal,
stiffly, gratefully even, but without feeling.
Why has my talkative
teasing tongue stopped talking?[130]

— 18 —

Exile's Return

1976–1977

Amazingly, after just two weeks Lowell was well enough to return to Milgate. "So good to hear your voice," he wrote Frank Bidart in mid-February 1976. "I had just been talking to Lizzie and felt a rush of health. My recovery has been easy in most ways, but I am weighed down by the new frequency of attacks. How can one function, if one is regularly sick? Shades of the future prison. But all's well for the present. The doctors differ somewhat but are optimistic. So am I. We sit by the fire paying bills. Caroline has written three chapters of a novel. I've written a short, heartfelt poem."[1]

The poem was "Home," and it was heartbreaking. *If he has gone mad with her,* he wrote, knowing what Caroline and others were thinking, and using the third person to distance himself, *the poor man can't have been very happy:*

> *Less than ever I expect to be alive*
> *six months from now,*
> *1976,*
> *a date I dare not affix to my grave.*
> *The Queen of Heaven, I miss her,*
> *we were divorced. She never doubted*
> *the divided, stricken soul*

could call her Maria,
and rob the devil with a word.[2]

"Where you are going, Professor, / you won't need your Dante," the police-man had taunted him. On the contrary, that was exactly what he would need, as he recalled here his own translation of the last-breath-penitent in Dante's *Purgatorio:*

No one prays for me . . . Giovanna or the others." . . .
the war lost, and wounded in the throat—
flying on foot and splashing the field with blood.
There I lost sight and speech, and died saying Maria. . . .
I'll tell you the truth, tell it to the living,
an angel and devil fought with claws for my soul:
You angel, why do you rob me for his last word?
The rain fell, then the hail, my body froze,
until the raging Archiano snatched me,
and loosened my arms I'd folded like the cross.[3]

In early March, down once more with flu, he wrote Taylor "a shamefaced & gloomy letter." Taylor had been in London that winter and had gone to see Cal during the latter stages of his manic attack. "I got well shortly after your visit," Cal wrote now, "and wish to god it had been sooner so that you would have been spared my antics." At the moment he was "the most halting and tedious person on earth," which—as in the past—was at least a spur to his writing.

Since his illness he'd written several new poems, "one a repeat of something in *For the Union Dead,* the same plot in another style." He was referring to "The Downlook," a palimpsest of his earlier poem, "Night Sweat," but in another register. "A long passage of darkness," he called it,[4] at the end of which he'd awakened to find a wife next to him in bed, offering her—as once Lizzie and now Caroline—his "huddle of . . . flesh":

nothing lovelier than waking to find
another breathing body in my bed . . .
glowshadow halfcovered with dayclothes like my own,
caught in my arms.

Except that this time he could see the pattern of elusive sexual consolation for the hopeless delusion it had by then become. The poem turned again, spiral-ling downward:

Last summer nothing dared impede
the flow of the body's thousand rivulets of welcome. . . .
Now the downlook, the downlook—small fuss,
nothing that could earn a line or picture
in the responsible daily paper we'll be reading,
an anthology of the unredeemable world. . . .
There's no greater happiness in days of the downlook
than to turn back to recapture former joy.

Ah loved perhaps before I knew you,
others have been lost like this,
yet found foothold
by winning the dolphin from the humming water.

And then, the lost puritan's admission of failure and deceit and moral culpability even as he desperately tried to right himself:

How often have my antics
and insupportable, trespassing tongue
gone astray and led me to prison . . .
to lying . . . kneeling . . . standing.[5]

Reading now through his *Selected Poems,* he told Taylor, "a whole book, 300 pages, more saturated in me than I myself, proves that I always do this, even in the overall plotting of a book." He was half-amused to think he could ever have thought of himself "as a tireless surpriser."[6]

That he had had another attack *in spite of* the lithium deeply troubled him. "I finally deciphered the crucial word 'tricky' in your lithium warning," he wrote Blair Clark now. "I think you mean the blood has to be taken every month or so to check the amount of lithium in the system. I've been doing that, though hating the blood needle." Worse, the air now was "full of rumours against lithium, hard to check on because it is almost a universal faith with English doctors." How he dreaded the thought of *two* attacks in a single year. True, this last had been "drawn out," but otherwise not too bad, and he'd been home a month now, "rather downlooking at first, then thawing, all the while writing with furious persistence."[7]

His new book of poems, tentatively titled *The Day,* was almost entirely free verse, he told Bishop, though his next, if there ever was a next, would probably be metrical. He admired the new villanelle she'd sent him—"One Art"—and could see how he too needed "to hold a shield" before his too-raw feelings and his reader. Meter might do that, though he also knew that writing finally came down to "a matter of character and imagination."[8]

But spring was coming, and with it things might soon look up again. The sun was shining and Harriet, now nineteen, would soon be arriving for another visit. "A coal and wood fire warms the large bright-window room," he wrote Blair in early March, and we swim along happily writing and rewriting." He was still thinking of returning permanently to the States, where he thought he and Caroline would both be better off, though the move would no doubt be "a shattering one for us as a family, getting the children resettled etc. or paying them flying visits, the groaning effort of abandoning houses, finding something new." Still, something had to be done if he was to avoid feeling like some "expensive, parasitical burden."⁹

In April he and Caroline flew to New York for the opening of the Bicentennial performance of *The Old Glory* at The American Place Theatre. Interviewed by Alvarez for the New york *Times*, Lowell noted that what he'd written about race relations fifteen years before seemed tame compared to what he felt in New York now, or anywhere for that matter, though he thought he'd made it "rather worse than it was at the time."¹⁰ The performance, which lasted from 6:00 P.M. until 11:30 and included all three plays, had been "rather splendid . . . and magnificently endless," he reported back to Bishop afterwards. "The actor playing Captain Delano looked into the audience, perhaps with his telescope, and saw five people in a row asleep. I was in mortal fear I might be one of them, and kept crossing and recrossing my legs, moving to the edge of my seat then almost through the back . . . and never nodded, but must have seemed afflicted. Or did I wink and was seen? Anyway, a bicentennial production, fifty players and more than fifty costumes and always the problem of racing the plays beyond their rhythm or killing the audience."¹¹ But without Jonathan Miller's direction, he confided to Lizzie, the production this time had seemed like "the original coin restamped in plaster."¹²

For a while he'd thought of living in New York when he next taught at Harvard, commuting back and forth as he had in years past. But now, after a week in the city, he told Bishop, he knew it had become both "too fast and fallen" for him ever to live there again. The whole trip had been too "driven, exciting, crowded as all such trips are. . . . The small smoke-drenched bedroom, the noisy stopping and starting trucks worst at dawn, the cross-biased friends who could only be warily mentioned to one another, the warmth of many dear meetings, the nervous publisher with many page-proof errors."¹³ Even the elevators at Farrar, Straus & Giroux had been jammed and the building's one stairway permanently locked "even to Bob Giroux because of dangerous school children." Having vegetated for so long in the English countryside, he would have to settle for living near Harvard.¹⁴

"I miss having you to talk to," he wrote Lizzie at the end of April, when he was back in England. "I feel deeply all you had to put up with me for so many years." He thanked her for his visit. And in a poem remembering that visit, he asked now why any artist, having found his true subject, would ever want to leave his familiar landscape, any more than Cézanne would have left his:

> *The sun of comfort shines on the artist,*
> *the same Academician from our building . . .*
> *he is repeating his* Mont-Saint-Victoire—
> *why should a landscape painter*
> *ever leave Central Park?*
> *his subject lies under his nose . . .*
> *his prison?*[15]

A time now for "terminal honors." An honorary degree in Dublin, a Robert Lowell Day at some high school in Ohio, a plaque to be placed at 91 Revere Street, "a maddening, pushing man . . . bringing out without my cooperation a book on two Lowells: James Russell and Robert Lowell, 2 aristocrats. Elegy, slander, and scandal." And yet he was "not saddened to be noticed."[16]

In June, in the midst of yet another English heatwave, he attended the Aldeburgh Festival, where Benjamin Britten's dramatic cantata for Lowell's *Phaedra* was performed. Lowell had first met the British composer in 1968, when they'd made arrangements for Britten to set some lines for his play. Now, with Britten only months from his own death, the piece was finally to be performed. The cantata, "imagined by Britten in the flower of his health," Lowell would recall, had been completed in extreme sickness. "It was one of the most beautiful settings I have ever heard, and for me an honor beyond all prizes."[17]

But all seemed more and more ghostly now, and he wondered if he even existed any more.[18] In late May he wrote Marcia Nardi, troubled that—despite his efforts—he had been even less able to find a publisher for her poems than Williams had thirty years earlier. "I doubt if I will outlive you many a year," he wrote the seventy-five-year-old Nardi, "but surely I don't want to leave you in the dark and shattered by my neglecting your appeal. It's a little like the drowned helping the drowned. I have had two breakdowns, and stays in hospitals in the last twelve months. My wife is very ill at the moment. One prays for strength to meet the day. Well, it will all work out, won't it? One goes on; good season follows bad."[19]

By then Caroline had been ill for three months. It was not back pain this time—the result of a car accident in Connemara many years before—he told Lizzie, but rather "some obscure stomach trouble, difficulty in swallowing, difficulty in keeping food down. As hospitals and tests approached and receded, first London, then Zurich, she rapidly got better—is almost well now but not quite."

And now, in June, Bishop was about to arrive for a visit, one not to be taken lightly. The dog would have to be sent away because of Bishop's asthma, yet half their chairs were "tainted" with dog hairs. He worried that his old friend would be critical of everything from "the dissheveled garden" to the "carefree garden man," to their care of Sheridan. Should Sheridan be sent away too, he wondered? "So many things down to my not writing in meter, making errors in description. Of course no one is more wonderful, but so fussy and hazardous now. Her set subject in person and letters is scolding with affectionate fury over Frank Bidart (whom she half-depends on) a safe thing though grating."[20] His worries turned out to be groundless, however, and he and Bishop had "talked on and on," he reported afterwards to Taylor, as if no time had passed since that day at Randall's thirty years before. "We weren't too accepting then," he admitted, "but accepted each other." And when she'd left, she'd seemed "almost ready to write autobiography in free verse."

But this problem of writing about the "I" continued to vex. "Have you ever tried to stop writing?", he asked Taylor now. "It's harder than alcohol, which I also foreswear as the very early sun crashes at about four through faults in the blinds." Over the years as a spokesman for poetry, he'd become "a sort of orange-squeezer expected to produce new and better juices." And while his method was "formidable enough to turn out new poems," it was not so easy—or even possible—to turn out new subjects. Then too there was the nagging fear that one might simply repeat oneself, playing—as he'd written of Nixon—one's "drab tapes" back to oneself, "morning, noon, and night."

How strange to "hit on something marvelous," his spirits for the moment lifting, "something impossible [to write for] anyone much under sixty." And then his voice falling: "only to find you had already printed it?"[21] Was he merely doing the same work over and over, "plough-pushing, if there's such an archaic idiom?", he asked Lizzie. And here he was, about to send off another book into the world, feeling "in this ebb of the European heatwave as if all the grass" had likewise been burned off his view of things. How he would love to "pause and be wise" now. But instead poems just kept "clanking in the head."[22]

Day by Day already came to "over three years work," he told Bill Meredith that July, all of it "written poem by poem, one not easily leading to the next, though finally in the last months sprawling (over a third of them) into a long sequence." The long sequence consisted of poems written since his recovery in March, and dealt with his last two "hospital lacunae." All the poems were "free of the sonnet and blank verse," all of them "painful yet I hope easily coasting to their natural stops."

Now that his *Selected Poems* were out, he could more easily see the curve of his life's work. It all came down, finally, to the making of some "small continuous *Prelude."* Even *Day by Day* sank into the overall story with its breakdown and recovery, as well as "many other more important things repeated in the old altering voice."[23] But he was not yet finished with the new book. Six weeks after sending Giroux the manuscript, he asked him to hold off sending it on to the printers, since he'd made so many changes—new poems, heavy revisions— that it would be simpler if he just sent him a new manuscript in October.

That summer, while Harriet stayed in New York, setting up a new apartment, Lizzie went up to Castine alone. From there she'd watched on television the Bicentennial celebrations and the parade of Tall Ships streaming up New York Harbor. No more long drives, as in the old days, she wrote. Now one could take a one-hour non-stop flight from New York to Bangor. At last their old, rundown Columbus Avenue was becoming more interesting, "a bit like old Third Avenue with shops and restaurants." But there was a sadness in the air as things went on—inevitably—changing.[24] "I remember the last passenger train to Bangor," Cal wrote Lizzie back. And now non-stop flights! Well, if the clock couldn't be put back, at least it might be put ahead.

Lizzie would be in England in mid-August as part of an International PEN meeting, and Cal wrote now with the news that Stephen Spender wanted him on the same panel with her. It would be their "first official appearance" together "since Greensboro before Randall's death," he reminded her, and he was delighted.[25] Unfortunately, the meeting itself—on the topic of "The Truth of the Imagination"—turned out to be "dreadfully pedestrian," and all he'd learned was that middle-aged people who'd published two books but couldn't write also couldn't talk, "but want to talk or at least hear people who can't talk talk."

By far the best thing about the conference, he told Bishop, was seeing and hearing Lizzie. "It couldn't have gone off more happily," he added, except of course for "the immanent sorrow" of any such visit.[26] And to Lizzie: "how comforting and enjoyable" to see her, and how strange to see her and Caroline "easily (?) together." He thanked her too for not showing the strain she must have felt. He'd also been pleasantly surprised by Susan Sontag's politeness toward him at the conference. "Sometimes," he confessed, "I think I am the enemy of womankind."[27]

After her visit to Milgate, Lowell learned from Bidart, Bishop's asthma had once again acted up, so that she'd returned to Boston confined to a wheelchair. Still, it had been a good visit, Lowell wrote her now. He was relieved to know that she really did like the new autobiographical poems in *Day by Day.* With that book all but finished, he had little to do these days but watch Milgate fall down around him, and think of how Grandfather Winslow would have pulled the place into order.[28]

But more than just Milgate was falling apart. "Losing friends always kills me," he had written Meredith in July, "and guilts me terribly, all the more now in one's 'maturity' when one feels it may be the pattern. Even the dead sometimes feel like friends we have deliberately lost."²⁹ That pervasive sense of loss could be felt everywhere in Cal's new book, where so many of the poems were goodbyes. Goodbyes to Peter Taylor, to Robert Penn Warren, to John Berryman, to his parents, to Cousin Harriet, to Jean, to Lizzie, to Caroline's former husband, to Caroline herself. Now, at the beginning of September, 1976, as he prepared to return to Harvard, he wrote a series of goodbye letters.

One was to Jean. It would be his last, and the only one of the many he wrote which she would save. "I have been thinking of you daily since our phone talk in New York," he wrote now, filled with old memories. Memories of Baton Rouge thirty-five years before, "Peter and I in pajamas sick over taking out Cinina's cat-shit, waiting still in pajamas outrageously for you to return from the office to get our lunch, Christmas with Red [Warren] staring long at a sheep that looked like Cinina [Warren's wife] and saying it reminded [him] of someone he couldn't place." Could she see that now, after all these years, he was trying to thank her for the past?³⁰ It was good he wrote when he did, for two months later Jean would suffer a stroke that would leave her unable to speak or write even the simplest sentence.

When he'd spoken to her in May, he'd told Taylor, Jean had been "under oxygen . . . had difficulty in talking and was low-spirited." "Sorry to sadden you," she'd said then, "but the truth is I am good for NOTHING." Yet next day she was back home. In truth, things had been "a terrible hurdle race for her" since Joe Liebling's death. When he'd seen her in Cambridge for the book signing, she'd been "dazzlingly charming and kind" to him and Caroline and—dressed in a red beret—had given them dinner, "palatial (but homely) food." She'd even told Caroline she was her "favorite Cal's wife."³¹

Now, he told Jean, he'd just written "a very warm, reminiscing, farewell to one's times poem to her," hoping she might be "solaced a little." But he could not muster the courage to send it. "Our days of the great books, scraping and Roman mass," his unsent "Letter" read:

your confessions had such a vocabulary
you were congratulated by the priests—
I pretended my impatience was concision. . . .

You have spoken so many words and well,
being a woman and you . . . someone must still hear
whatever I have forgotten
*or never heard, being a man.*³²

Like Wordsworth, he knew the past was all the currency he had to draw on. Yet he also knew that memory alone was not enough for art. What happened—history—was "always there with its riches of inharmonious material," he told Taylor, "its fragmented sharpness—the stuff of life with (weirdly) its artificial imposed limits like a hard rhyme scheme, or a novel plot. At sixty, we are in Mother Nature's hands, God help us."[33]

For months now Milgate had come to resemble some "Irish house or something in Gogol, trembling on the edge of extinction by the socialist state."[34] Now, in the fall of '76, with taxes under the Thatcher government becoming unmanageable for an estate the size of Milgate, Caroline decided she would have to sell. It had grown just "too expensive to run," Lowell confided to Taylor: "nine hundred pounds a quarter for electricity, etc." Instead, they would look for a smaller place, perhaps near Oxford, "costing as much, but cheaper to run." But for Cal the loss of Milgate would be like a death, "very sad and autumnal."[35]

Day by Day was finally done, he told Bishop, and the opposite of her own thin last volume, *Geography III:* "bulky, rearranged, added-to, deleted two months after submission—as though the unsatiated appetite were demanding a solid extra course, when dinner was meant to be over." Once again he picked up the issue of metrical verse with her. After reading Richard Wilbur's new book of poems, *The Mind Reader,* in June, he'd found himself "musing in iambics, not meaning to," and had "spent days even trying rhyme." This time, however, the formal experiments had failed to graft, and the poems he'd written had wound up sounding more "like parody." He knew rhyme and meter had "nothing at all to do with truth, just as ballet steps are of no use on a hike." They were merely "puzzles, hurdles, obstacles, expertise" that cried out "for invention, and of course in the end for truth, whatever that is." After all, Lawrence's free verse "Figs" was *"de gustibus* as true and surprising as Herbert's more formal 'Affliction.' "" Formalism or free verse: it was the writing finally that mattered.[36] For now he would have to stick with the free verse poems his muse seemed intent on offering him.

"We arrive Flight BA 561 2:05 P.M. on Wednesday the 15th," he wrote Bidart at the beginning of September, preparing to teach the Victorian poets and another workshop. He was still revising *Day by Day.* "How often writing takes the ache away, takes time away. You start in the morning, and look up to see the windows darkening. . . . I think in the end, there is no end, the thread frays rather than is cut." But how glad he was just now "to be getting back to Harvard . . . and to you the center of it." His beloved Milgate was on the block. It would not go soon, he supposed, but this foreboding sense of an "unfixed future" bewildered him.[37] "This week the house went on the market," he wrote now, recalling Castine and Damariscotta Mills, recalling too the losses Bishop had catalogued in her villanelle:

When I look back, I see a collapsing
accordion of my receding houses,
and myself receding
to a boy of twenty-five or thirty,
too shopworn for less, too impressionable for more—
blackmaned, illmade
in a washed blue workshirt and coalblack trousers,
moving from house to house,
still seeking a boy's license
to see the countryside without arrival. . . .
terror in happiness may not cure the hungry future,
the time when any illness is chronic,
and the years of discretion are spent on complaint—
until the wristwatch is taken from the wrist.[38]

Convalescents—that was what he'd called Caroline and himself that summer. She was still losing weight and having difficulty eating, he told Taylor, while every so often "twinges of . . . postmanic depression" seemed to descend over him again.[39] Now, as he prepared to leave for America, he had his second manic episode in a year and had to be readmitted to Greenways. Caroline was beside herself. She knew she was useless to him at such times, when he became an animal, or something possessed.[40] Since he was in no shape to teach, his classes had to be postponed till the spring. He spent six weeks in the hospital this time, and by the time he was released in late October, Caroline had already taken Sheridan and Ivana and fled to Boston, where she took up residence in the Cambridge house she'd rented for them for the fall.

On the 30th, a shaken Lowell wrote Alfred: "Two years ago I lived under the shadow of a false (?) but undiagnosed heart attack—one relief was Dr. Prout saying 'Walk a mile a day.' " But how could *anyone* walk a mile a day? He was coming over to Cambridge at once and was writing to warn Alfred that Caroline was very sick just now "with habitual overdrinking," though she was known to make "miraculous turnabouts." As for himself, at the moment he felt "ninety percent certified healthy."[41]

"Out of your wreckage, beauty, wealth, / gallantries, wildness, came your book," he wrote now in a poem addressed to Caroline,

your father's betrayal of you,
rushing to his military death in Burma,
annexed for England
by his father's father, the Viceroy . . .
There's so much else—our life.

At the sick times, our slashing,
drastic decisions made us runaways.[42]

He stayed with Caroline in Cambridge for the next three weeks, until the situation there became untenable. Then he moved in with Bidart to get away from the strain of Caroline's drunken tirades, which so shook him that he suffered a mild heart attack. It was "decided" that Caroline would go back to England with the children on December 3 and that Cal would wait word from Caroline to let him know if and when he could return to England. In any case it would have to be after his reading at the 92nd Street Y on December 8. In New York he would stay with Blair. Truly he seemed a beaten man now, and Bidart would remember how strangely quiet he had become. "He was just unbelievably grateful and relieved" to get out of that apartment, and into an atmosphere "that was not this terrific turmoil, anger, drama, tension."[43]

It was Bidart who introduced Cal at the 92nd Street reading that December. Having just learned that Jean was in New York Hospital again, suffering from the effects of yet another stroke, Cal read two poems that night in her honor: "The Old Flame" and "Jean Stafford, a Letter." His first wife could punctuate and do all sorts of things, he told his audience jokingly that evening, and then—more seriously—added that she was "one of our best writers, and her talent developed early."

Bob Giroux, who was in the audience, went the following day to visit Jean in the hospital and mentioned Cal's new poem for her. Fumbling with her oxygen mask, she managed to summon up enough strength to wring her hands and call Cal a "son of a bitch!" By her bedside, Giroux noticed, was her copy of *The Mills of the Kavanaughs,* the one book of Cal's she would not part with, and which she'd begun annotating heavily with biographical comments. It was *her* book, she said, the one Cal had spent years on trying to anatomize the breakdown of their marriage, as Cal's later books would anatomize the highs and lows of his subsequent marriages. "My only role," she sputtered through the tubes dangling from her crushed nose, "was typing for him."[44]

Lizzie had to be in Boston on business sometime around December 10 and while there, she told Mary McCarthy, she'd "spent three or four hours with [Cal], where he was weeping and saying he would do anything he could to make the marriage work." He spoke too of his "deep love for Caroline."[45] Then, in mid-December, he heard from Caroline, and—with fear and trepidation—flew back to England. They spent Christmas in Scotland with the Mostyn-Owens and Mary McCarthy's family: "seven children, seven-hour train trips and seven-hour dinners."[46] It had been "a serene and happy Christmas," he wrote Bill Alfred on January 11, when he was once more at Milgate, though he feared this interlude was "the sweet time before the fall," knowing the house might be sold at any moment, when they would "have to find . . . a new country" in which to live.[47]

If he was ever going to finish the *Eumenides*, the final part of the *Oresteia* trilogy which he'd left off translating twelve years before, it would have to be now. Using an annotated Greek text of the play which Alfred had lent him, along with a bad translation, one, he complained, "that makes Gilbert Murray look like Milton," he managed—in spite of ill health—to translate much of the play before returning to Boston in mid-January 1977. It was Joseph Papp who had read Lowell's *Agamemnon* years before and found it "naturalistic, simple, not flowery," and Papp who had encouraged Lowell to finish the trilogy for the Lincoln Repertory Theater. Now, however, when Lowell called Papp to tell him the translation was ready, Papp had to tell him that Andrei Serban, his director, had decided to go with Edith Hamilton's translation instead. Papp would remember how "terribly disappointed and hurt" Cal had been by the news.[48]

"My socialist-anarchist earned income half-person will be at Harvard by the first of February with a room or rooms in Dunster House," he'd told Lizzie on January 11.[49] Instead, he flew to Boston two weeks early, arriving on January 17, expecting to stay with Frank Bidart until it was time to take up residency at Dunster. But at 2:00 A.M. on his second night in Cambridge, Cal was knocking on Bidart's bedroom door, saying that he had to get to the infirmary right away. It was very cold that night, Bidart would remember, and he could not get his car started. So Cal waited, quiet and resigned, until a cab could be summoned. He was given a battery of tests at McLean's before being transferred to Phillips House at Massachusetts General for ten days, intrigued by the coincidence that forty years before Grandfather Arthur Winslow should have died in "almost" the same room he was in now. Lizzie flew up from New York to see him, and knowing that time was short, called his octogenarian Aunt Sarah, his mother's sister, who had refused to talk to him ever since his marriage to Caroline. Now he asked her to forgive him and visit him in the hospital, both of which—to his great relief—she did.

Helen Vendler, who had taken over Cal's classes while he was ill, remembers that Cal was not a very good patient. "He didn't particularly obey the instructions given to him by the hospital." For while "he did take the diuretics that he was supposed to take," he did not stop drinking or smoking.[50] "Something sinister and comforting / in this return after forty years' arrears / to death and Phillips House," he wrote now:

> *this irreverent absence of pain,*
> *less than the ordinary that daily irks—*
> *except I cannot entirely get my breath,*

> *as if I were muffled in snow,*
> *our winter's inverted gray sky*
> *of frozen slush,*
> *its usual luminous lack of warmth. . . .*[51]

After the water was drained from his lungs, Lowell was released and moved into Dunster House. The place was "very small," he complained to Caroline. "Two rooms, fireplace, view of the Charles, two desks, bookcases, third floor, meals if I want them," rather like an "old student among students." Never in his life had he been so on his own, "so firmly pinned down to emptiness." He could feel his mind going numb "reading through about thirty student poems," and the body too going numb "in its little room, too enervated to read through *Anna Karenina* as one resolved."[52]

After his cardiograph at McLean's had come out irregular, he told her, he'd "waited a long moment, then was practically handcuffed in a sort of sitting up stretcher, bounced down a stairless gangway . . . then banged in an ambulance to Mass. General. More waits, while I absorbed the imaginable seriousness of my condition. . . . What gentler thing could one ask for, except, though painless, it had absolutely no meaning, no long private message." He'd been diagnosed as having congestive heart failure, where "the lungs filled with water because the heart can't squeeze enough." This whole "hospital business" had been "painless eventless; perhaps what death might be at best. A feeling that one was doomed like Ivan Illich, but without suffering." Well, if that was all life was, it was "a coldly smiling anti-climax. Gone the great apocalypse of departure" he had for so long feared.[53]

Helen Vendler has left us her impressions of Lowell's Victorian Poetry class in what would turn out to be his last term of teaching. "I felt, always, that a scanning faculty quite unlike anything I could describe was reviewing and judging and annotating the lines or stanzas he took up; it made one feel like a rather backward evolutionary form confronted by an unknown but superior species." Lowell was "indolent, speculative, and altogether selective" in his remarks on the poetry. For what he offered his students, whether he spoke of Tennyson, Browning, or Arnold, was "a real life, a real mind, fixed in historical circumstance and quotidian abrasions." Often he spoke in parables, in a kind of veiled autobiography, rearranging "poetic features till they resembled his own." He noted Coleridge's way of rendering "the domestic, in all its tangles and dailiness and anguish, in a language aspiring to the casualness of intimate exchange and unemphatic realism."[54] It is a trenchant description of the underlying poetics informing *Day by Day*.

In late February he went down to New York to give a reading at St. Mark's-in-the-Bowery, on a double bill with Allen Ginsberg. How strange to be here again, where forty years earlier he and Jean had been married. For the first time in public, and in a pained whisper, he read "Ulysses and Circe," with its shadow portrait of himself as the grizzled wanderer locked in the prison of the self and drowning, a man who had caused so much mayhem in the wake of his domestic upheavals:

> *he circles as a shark circles*
> *visibly behind the window—*
> *flesh-proud, sore-eyed, scar-proud,*
> *a vocational killer*
> *in the machismo of senility,*
> *foretasting the apogee of mayhem—*
> *breaking water to destroy his wake.*
> *He is oversize. To her suitors*
> *he is Tom, Dick, or Harry—*
> *his gills are pleated and aligned—*
> *unnatural ventilation-vents*
> *closed by a single lever*
> *like cells in a jail—*
> *ten years fro and ten years to.*[55]

There was an awkward exchange that night with Gregory Corso, sitting out in the audience with his wife and baby and acting rather like a Visigoth before Ginsberg asked him to settle down and he left. When Lowell finished his reading, he was given a standing ovation. Then, before heading back up to Cambridge, Lizzie and Harriet helped him celebrate his sixtieth birthday. When Lowell returned to Cambridge, Bidart also had a party for him, for which Bishop wrote a funny quatrain, the two joking with each other about what their common dentist had said about the plight of the other's teeth.

He heard from Caroline that Milgate had at last been sold and that she'd taken an apartment at Castletown House, the largest and grandest of Ireland's Palladian country houses. Located twenty miles west of Dublin, the mansion, much of it begun two hundred and fifty years before, had recently been restored by the Irish Georgian Society, which had made Castletown their headquarters. The original plan after selling Milgate had called for Blackwood and Lowell to relocate in the States, but she had decided instead to make the move to Ireland. After all, the society's president, Desmond Guinness, was her cousin, and the tax savings she could realize by the move were substantial.

Still, Cal was understandably upset that he'd not been consulted on the final sale of the house or, more importantly, on the location of his new home. London was one thing, Dublin another, and he began having nightmares now of infinitely receding rooms. "What strikes me in this order is the teenager flat," he wrote Caroline on March 2, "the likeness to the Louvre (a vague feeling that we will live there as old royal Louvre pensioners), and the nearness of the Liffey." On the other hand the resettlement had at last "taken away a huge, undefined vagueness, my only way since I left of imagining our future— an infinite stairway of Dunster House cafeteria dining halls." He promised to join her and the children at Castletown during spring vacation.[56]

He knew from hard experience that he and the transcontinental telephone were enemies, and that it was no way to carry on a marriage. "I love you so much and I wish I could do everything for you," he wrote her. "What did you mean on the phone that I had nearly lost you?" He tried to screw up the courage to say he really *was* excited about the prospect of living at Castletown, where he would know no one but the Heaneys. After his last breakdown, she'd told him the marriage was over. Now she sounded as if she wanted him back. "But do you really want me back? Sometimes, you sound indifferent. I'm not," he wrote her on March 18, "though my voice may sound low and subdued coming from so far."[57]

At the end of the month he flew to Dublin for a ten-day visit. But the visit was not a success, and by the time he left he knew the marriage was over. Castletown was too isolated and the mansion too grand and overwhelming ever to feel like home. Even going to Dublin to see the Heaneys for lunch had been rather like making state arrangements. "I don't know what to say," he wrote Caroline when he was back in Cambridge, "our problems have become so many-headed and insuperable. Nothing like the sunshine of the years we had together—when it shone, as so often—so blindingly."[58]

Momentary sunshine amid the ever-changing weather of Ireland, turning suddenly to a splotch of blinding snow, such as he'd felt in the hospital, then nothing. "That unhoped-for Irish sunspoiled April day," he wrote, thinking of the fate of two royal Irish swans—both speeding out of control down the river—a parable for his marriage:

> *. . . We could even imagine*
> *we enjoyed our life's great change then—*
> *hand in hand with balmy smiles*
> *graciously belittling our headlong reverse. . . .*
> *We sat and watched the mother swan*
> *enthroned like a colossal head of Pharoah*
> *on her messy double goose-egg nest of sticks.*
> *The male swan had escaped*
> *their safe, stagnant, matriarchal pond*
> *and gallanted down the stout-enriched rapids to Dublin,*

smirking drunkenly, racing bumping,
as if to show a king had a right to be too happy. . . .
seven years, now nothing but a diverting smile,
dalliance by a river, a speeding swan . . .
the misleading promise
to last with joy as long as our bodies,
nostalgia pulverized by thought,
nomadic as yesterday's whirling snow,
all whiteness splotched.[59]

Yet he was still in love with Caroline and kept a picture of her looking out at him from a gondola—his dolphin, his unattainable mermaid—something to look at each day there in his cell in Cambridge. Yes, once—once—there'd been a time when "nothing dared impede / the flow of the body's thousand rivulets of welcome."[60] "He was as 'well' as Cal can be," Lizzie would tell Mary McCarthy, "most pleasing in being close to his feelings, serious about someone else, grieving for [Caroline's] love."[61] But the marriage he knew was over. And what he needed now more than ever was the companionship of the one woman who had been there for him all those years. Back from Ireland, he found himself each day on the phone with Lizzie, the two of them talking like the old friends they were, relieved to be close to her again, grateful too after all he'd done to smash his wake that she should still be there for him. If he had no place to go, Lizzie told him as the semester came to a close, he would be welcome to use his old 67th Street studio.

In mid-April he had lunch with Blair Clark at the Italian Pavilion. There, in a flat, matter-of-fact manner, he explained that complications had arisen over the Redcliffe Square apartment because of taxes. Castletown offered a host of Guinness relatives, he noted with a tinge of irony, with much visiting back and forth and parties for children. It was all pleasant enough, but it was no life for him. Worse, Caroline had told him too many times over that she could no longer take his mania and wanted the marriage over. He was "sort of moving back with Lizzie," he told Blair, and wanted his studio back, which Blair had been renting since September from Lizzie. Then he added that he would also be returning to Castine with Lizzie and Harriet that summer. It was not as if he were formally going back to Lizzie, Blair recalled, but "some other kind of arrangement, looser, vaguer."[62]

Within weeks of Cal's leaving, Caroline had changed her mind again. She was expecting Cal to return to Ireland after classes ended in May, and his new arrangements created a fury. "Us?", he wrote. "Aren't we too heady and dangerous for each other? I love you, am more dazzled by you, than anyone I've known, but can't I be a constant visitor?" At least then there would be "no wrinkles to steam-iron out." In truth Ireland seemed "so far from home and help . . . who and what I know," though it would be "a kind of paradise to come to with you and Sheridan and all the girls there, and the big winey dinner in the big rotting house."[63] And again, three days later: "And us? I really feel too weak and battered by it all. I fear I do you more harm than good. I think your blackness would pass if you didn't live in fear of [my] manic attacks. And they don't seem curable—almost thirty years. How's that for persistence?"[64]

When spring term ended at Harvard, Caroline called Cal to say she was joining him in New York to see what could be done to save their marriage. He wrote back confused, "not knowing how or what to say." In truth he was afraid of her visit

> because I am afraid nothing will be done except causing pain. How many lovely moments, weeks, months, we had. Sunday I sat by the Charles River watching the strollers, the joggers, the sunners—and the river. And I seemed to follow it back through our seven years, the great multitude of restaurants, the moment when everyone was in the bathroom when I bathed, the long summer of your swelling pregnancy, the rush to London, the little red man's appearance—or earlier trapped in All Souls, and a thousand things more.

But the last two years had been terrifying for both of them, he thought, and neither had "made it any better for the other." It was not even a quarrel any more, but "two eruptions, two earthquakes crashing." Of course they should talk. But when? There was little he could do until late May in Cambridge or June in New York, or in Ireland later that summer. Besides, hadn't she ended things during his last visit, "ended them wisely," so that they couldn't go back? "I have had so much dread," he ended, "the worst in my life, that I would do something, by my mere presence I would do something to hurt you, to drive you to despair. Who knows cause?"[65]

On April 30th he gave his last public reading at Harvard. It was held in Sanders Theater, where he'd read so often before. Again he read poems which spanned his entire career: "Bringing a Turtle Home," "Returning Turtle," "Memories of West Street and Lepke," "Central Park" (all these for Lizzie and Harriet); "Mr. Edwards and the Spider," "The March I," "The March II"; and two for old friends, like himself, hurt, he thought, by too much drink. One was "For John Berryman," the other "To Frank Parker."

For three days in mid-May—from the 10th till the 13th—he was at the University of Tennessee in Knoxville for a lecture and reading. Kathy Shorr, the nineteen-year-old undergraduate who was given primary responsibility for his stay, would remember picking him up at the airport and thinking how "big, strong, and physically frail" he seemed "all at the same time." For the two and a half days he was in Knoxville he wore the same clothes: "a dusky rose-pink Oxford cloth shirt, a mossy green sports jacket and pants, and Wallabees." When he learned there would be no alcohol served at the president's reception before his reading Saturday night, he became fidgity but kept his peace. Didn't they understand that one needed a drink before going on? But he'd been through this sort of thing with too many academics too many times before to think of it as more than a mild irritant.

The following afternoon—May 12th—he was relieved when Shorr and three other students borrowed a car and drove him up into the Great Smokies. When, after an hour and a half, their car had climbed as far as Newfound Gap, they got out to admire the view and took a group photo. It had been twenty years since he'd been up into these mountains and he was clearly pleased to be here again. The group began strolling up the mountain path. But before Lowell had gone fifty feet he stopped. He was sorry, he said, but he had a little problem with his heart.

It was no big deal, Shorr would recall. They all laughed, walked back down to the car, then drove back to Knoxville, where Lowell took Shorr and another co-ed to a cellar restaurant for some Planter's Punch and to talk baseball. "He was the first person I'd ever met," Shorr would recall, who seemed both normal and at the same time "a genius—not well-educated, or articulate, but something beyond that." Before he left, she shoplifted a copy of *History* for him to sign.[66]

Then it was back to New York to receive the $10,000 National Gold Medal for Literature from the American Academy, an award given only once every five years. It was another figure from the past, his first mentor, Richard Eberhart, who introduced him.

Caroline flew over for the presentation and stayed the week in a New York hotel with him. "It was absolute hell on earth," Blair would remember, "because she was doing everything to get him back and he was not saying yes." For his part, Cal really was "afraid that she would kill herself. But she didn't and she went back to England." On the evening of Cal's arrival Lizzie had a call from Cal. He was at Lenox Hill Hospital, where Caroline had been taken by stretcher after passing out in the hotel lobby. When she regained consciousness, she simply got up and left the hospital. Nor did it help matters when five-year-old Sheridan, after watching a documentary on Hitler on television, drew an imitation Hitler mustache on his upper lip, nor that Cal had joked about it, for Caroline was sure Cal's laughter signalled the onslaught of another manic attack.[67]

Lizzie would remember how terrified Cal was by Caroline's tenuous grasp on things, his coming up to the West 67th Street studio to be with Lizzie for an hour, then rushing out to be with Caroline. For her part, too, Lizzie marvelled at how much care he showed Caroline during this time, especially knowing how careless with people he had been in the past. Caroline kept insisting he return with her to Ireland, but this he refused to do, though he promised to come over in early September before classes began again at Harvard. He also found a doctor for her in Dublin to monitor her severe depression. When he returned to Boston at the end of May, she flew back to Ireland.

But he was returning to America for good, he told Esther Brooks when he saw her in Cambridge. In truth, it—and Harvard—were his "life's water." He did not want to divide what time was left him "between two continents and two cultures." He was also going back to Lizzie, who'd been "awfully good about all this," and "awfully good" to him "through all these difficult seven years."[68]

After he finished up at Harvard, he returned to New York and the 67th Street studio to be with Lizzie and Harriet. There was "no great renewed romance," Lizzie told Mary McCarthy in mid-June, "but a kind of friendship, and listening to his grief." What he wanted now was his old home, the old life, a piece of Boston transplanted to Manhattan, "the books, the records." One could say, she explained, that she and Cal were back together again, but the phrase was "not really meaningful—at least in the way it is commonly used." Nor did he talk of getting a divorce. Instead, there was "a general peacefulness . . . and a great preoccupation with Caroline, her future, the children."

As for Lizzie, she had made her adjustments to living alone and was not as "vulnerable" to Cal as she had been, though she still cared for him. The unrequited passion and grief he'd had from Caroline, his dolphin, had humbled him, "made him more like the rest of us." At sixty, he had finally learned something about love, Lizzie told McCarthy, especially since his return from Ireland in April, something after all about what it felt like to be "unwanted."[69] Unwanted: his earliest sense of things, reinforced by what Merrill Moore, perhaps his mother's lover, and his own psychiatrist, had told him forty years before. And now, at the end, in spite of everything, to be again unwanted, this time by his elusive, all-consuming dolphin.

He returned broken to Castine with Lizzie and Harriet. Cousin Harriet's old house on School Street was gone, sold in the wake of the divorce, but Lizzie had had the Barn made quite comfortable. He rented a small boathouse to write in, and returned to the prose pieces he'd put aside a dozen years earlier, pieces which would later be published as "Epic" and "New England and Further," short trenchant essays halfway between Williams's *In the American Grain* and his own sonnet portraits. Back in the summer of 1965, he had written a note to himself that he hoped to "quietly reread old New England classics, Thoreau, Melville, etc. with the idea of writing a New England essay." If he did nothing with it, he had added then, he hoped at least the reading would "sink into dry sand," or—better—"dry fertile earth."[70] Now, after an absence of seven years, he stood at the edge of the Atlantic once more, a place, he'd once said, both "sheer and perfect," where water itself became "heaven and allegory," and wrote as well as he'd ever written.[71]

"I haven't quite lost my muse," he would write Caroline at summer's end. By then he had nineteen pages with as many again to write. "Because I'm working on it," he added, "I think it my best critical prose."[72] Like Hawthorne, like Santayana, like Eliot, those other belated puritans, he was looking once more into his American past to discover himself and his country. "They taunt us," he wrote of the fathers and the legacy they'd left him, "they taunt us with their unattainable avoidance of dust, vacillation, the manmade apocalypse we ourselves have grown reckless enough to accept."

These were not the received portraits of the country's founders he was offering, but something darker, discovered through a lifetime of hard experience. Of Cotton Mather he wrote: "a power-crazed mind bent on destroying darkness with darkness, on applying his cruel, high-minded, obsessed intellect to the extermination of witch and neurotic." Of the American Revolution, he thought how quickly the populism of a radical like Sam Adams had calcified— like so much else—to "the marmoreal dignity of [a] George Washington." He called Emerson the country's "greatest nonfiction writer," his poems filled with the "lovely, complaining, weary music of Matthew Arnold," and, again: "a Blake in fetters." D. H. Lawrence had once dubbed Ben Franklin "the first American dummy," but wasn't he rather, Lowell offered instead, an eighteenth-century European worldly Quaker imbued with Swiftian savagery? More like Horace in his "open sense of human limitation"? But who, except someone who had spent a lifetime reading widely in American and world literature, someone in the habit of making such bold associations, would wish to take on such a dazzling, brilliant raconteur?[73]

The first ten days of July Cal and Lizzie were in Moscow as members of the American delegation to the Union of Soviet Writers, a trip sponsored by the Kettering Foundation. Others in the delegation included Edward Albee, William Styron, Nathan Scott, and Norman Gould Cousins of the *Saturday Review*. Even now Cal was still Cal. On the flight over, Styron would remember, Cal had chain-smoked in the non-smoking section of the plane. He'd asked for a seat in the smoking section, in spite of which Pan Am had mis-seated him. When someone complained, he merely shrugged, called him an "environmentalist," and continued smoking. Styron would remember an officious bureaucrat reminding the group that they would be staying in a very expensive hotel in Moscow and to be careful about ordering meals. Cal's response—as usual— was to order four bottles of a very expensive German white wine.[74]

But he was very tired and very quiet in Moscow, and to Scott he seemed "utterly spent and exhausted." On their return to the States, Cal and Lizzie went up to Cambridge, where Cal had more tests done on his heart before returning to Castine. The tests appeared negative, Cal was told, his heart in good shape. That summer Bishop was summering at nearby North Haven on the Maine coast. She'd already asked Cal not to visit her there, afraid that seeing him under his present conditions would only upset her. But he had to see her, and went anyway.

"A voice inside me says all might be well if I could be with you," he wrote Caroline in mid-July. "And another voice says all would be ruin, and that I would be drowned in the confusion I made worse." What effect, he fretted, would his visit have on her—or on him? Would it not be rather "like a nightmare we all have in which each motion of foot or hand troubles the turmoil it tries to calm"?[75] Then he heard from his oldest stepdaughter that her mother was "on the verge of tears all day, and needed a rest." He wrote Caroline again, reassuring her that she was with him,"—deep and in rapid images." He promised again to come over in September.[76]

In mid-August there was a front-page rave review of *Day by Day* by Helen Vendler in the *New York Times Book Review*. Months earlier he'd told Bidart with a mixture of pride and despair that he didn't know what the value of his work would finally be, but he did know he'd somehow "changed the game."[77] Now, in late August, when Bidart visited Cal and Lizzie in Castine, he noticed how "extremely warm and comfortable" the two were with each other, although Cal still seemed emotionally suspended. He was still carrying Caroline's letters around with him in an envelope, letters "very sort of ironic and full of jokes," saying she wanted him back. Yes, he was going to spend a week with Caroline and Sheridan, he told Bidart, but he was not going back. When Blair told Cal it would be a "fatal mistake" for him to return just now to Ireland, Cal told him he had to go to settle things.[78] But in truth, he was afraid of going.

He wrote only two poems that summer, both in the same free verse he'd used in *Day by Day*. One of them was "Summer Tides," a dejection ode, a reworking of Arnold's "Dover Beach." In the poem he situated himself looking out over the vast Atlantic as he stood by the shaky railing fronting the sheer precipice, beginning to crumble now into the waves below. "Tonight, / I watch the incoming moon swim / under three agate veins of cloud," he wrote that August,

> *casting crisps of false silver-plate*
> *to the thirsty granite fringe of the shore. . . .*
> *All this spendthrift, in-the-house summer,*
> *our yacht-jammed harbor*
> *lay unattempted—*

pictorial to me like your portrait.
I wonder who posed you so artfully
for it in the prow of his Italian skiff,
like a maiden figurehead without legs to fly.
Time lent its wings. Last year
our drunken quarrels had no explanation,
except everything, except everything.
Did the oak provoke the lightning,
when we heard its boughs and foliage fall? . . .
My wooden beach-ladder swings by one bolt,
and repeats its single creaking rhythm—
I cannot go down to the sea.
After so much logical interrogation,
I can do nothing that matters. . . .
I think of my son and daughter,
and three stepdaughters
on far-out ledges
washed by the dreaded clock-clock of the waves . . .
gradually rotting the bulwark where I stand.
Their father's unmotherly touch
trembles on a loosened rail.[79]

On the eve of his departure for Ireland, he saw Bidart in Boston and gave him copies of both his new poems as well as Caroline's letters to safeguard until he returned. That night they and Vendler had dinner in his favorite Boston restaurant, the *Athens Olympia,* just across from the Commons, on the edge of Boston's combat zone. He was afraid, he confessed, because he wanted very much to see his son and knew how desperate Caroline was to have him back. He talked about Dunbarton Cemetery, how the graves had been moved to higher ground by the Army Corps of Engineers before they'd flooded the area. He'd already arranged in his will to be buried there, preceded by a solemn High Mass at the Church of the Advent. The idea shocked and amused Vendler, but Cal only smiled. "That's how we're buried," he told her. When they saw him off at Logan, he was holding a big ship model for Sheridan.[80]

On September 2, 1977, Lowell arrived in Dublin, staying at Castletown for another ten-day visit. Initially he seemed happy to be back, though from the first he explained to Caroline that he would be returning to America. But Caroline kept after him until he became more and more agitated. "He'd gone back to Lizzie, publicly," she would say afterwards. "He'd made a mess.

Would there be more letters, another *Dolphin?* It was too awful. And he knew that."[81] On September 6, Seamus Heaney remembered, Cal and Caroline spent "a happy, bantering evening" with them at their suburban County Wicklow cottage.[82]

But Caroline, Blair Clark would learn, turned out to be at her absolute worst.[83] Cal, depressed and exhausted by the visit, decided to cut it short. He'd originally planned to fly back to Boston on the 15th. But when it became clear that he really did mean to return to the States, Caroline left Castletown and flew back to London. That was on Sunday the 11th.

Left with the children and a nanny, Cal called Lizzie to tell her that the Irish visit had turned out to be "sheer torture" and that he was returning to New York the following day. That evening, after the children had left, Cal wrote Caroline that he had "spent until about two with Sheridan." They'd had "a merry amiable time, except that he (wisely) preferred people to swans and a rubber tire swing to people."

Alone that night in Castletown House, Cal became trapped in the receding vastnesses of the mansion. First the telephone failed, then the electricity. When he tried to leave the darkened house to make a call from the village, he could not find his way out, and had to grope back up the stairs to his top-floor apartment. In the morning, it was the cleaning woman who released him. Still shaken, he told her that Castletown "was a very bad place" and needed an elevator. Then he carried his own suitcases down, climbed back up, and handed her three dollars. In his room he left behind some lines he'd written in the last few days. They were either a prayer or an expletive, or both. "Christ," he wrote,

> *May I die at night*
> *With a semblance of my senses*
> *Like the full moon that fails.*

Monday afternoon his plane touched down at Kennedy Airport and he hailed a taxi to take him to West 67th Street. He was holding a large brown paper parcel—a portrait of Caroline by her first husband, Lucien Freud, which Caroline wanted appraised in Manhattan. Somewhere, as the cab drove through the humming city that afternoon, perhaps beneath the canopy of late summer leaves as they passed through Central Park, Cal fell asleep, his last prayer answered.

Lizzie was called from her apartment by the elevator man and rushed down to the street below. A crowd had already begun to form when she looked into the back seat and saw him slumped there, his great frame very still. There seemed no sign of struggle. They raced through the city streets to the Emergency Room of Roosevelt Hospital, with Cal very still. By then she knew he was gone.[84]

On Friday, September 16, at 11:00 A.M., there was, just as Lowell had requested, a solemn funeral Mass at the Church of the Advent on lower Beacon Hill in Boston, very near where he had been born. Six hundred mourners crammed into the church, including many friends and notables. At communion, Lizzie and Harriet waited for Caroline to go up to receive, only to see her turn and walk out with her children, then return later. Cal was interred at Dunbarton, next to his parents, only the second Lowell to be laid to rest among so many Winslows and Starks. "The family graveyard . . . lay under a mist of rain," Lizzie wrote Mary McCarthy afterwards, "great trees and a few autumn leaves on the ground and the old gravestones, beginning with General Stark and ending with Dear Cal."[85] There were ten pallbearers, all friends, many of whom had seen him through all stages of a tumultuous and brilliant life: Peter Brooks, Robert Fitzgerald, Grey Gowrie, Frank Parker, Bob Giroux, Bob Gardner, John Thompson, Peter Taylor, Blair Clark, Frank Bidart.

For a while, Jean Stafford, ill as she was, considered dressing in widow's weeds, hiring a limousine, and driving up from Long Island to the funeral as the *first* Mrs. Lowell, until Giroux managed to dissuade her. After the funeral, Bill Alfred invited Caroline and the children back to his home on Athens Street. Noticing that five-year-old Sheridan had disappeared, he went looking for him and found him upstairs, talking to himself in clipped English accents. "You know," he told Alfred, "you Americans seem very nice. But why did you kill our King George?"[86]

There were many moving tributes to Lowell, many elegies then and later, as the enormity of his loss to American letters began to make itself felt. "In life we looked at that large head, heard his soft jokes," Derek Walcott would write by way of eulogy, "watched his circling hands, knowing that he would become one of the great dead. . . . The head was square but noble, but it was also an ordinary American head, and it was this unrelenting ordinariness that denied itself any sort of halo. He was a man of enormous pride and fanatical humility."[87]

When Andrei Voznesensky visited America in the summer of '78, he asked to be driven up to Dunbarton. There he took a sprig of berries which had grown above the grave of Pasternak and placed it now on Cal's.

And Frank Bidart, his faithful friend. "Valéry's words about Mallarmé come irresistibly to mind," Bidart would write. "Near him while he was still alive, I thought of his destiny as already realized."[88]

"I am looking over the harbor imagining I see North Haven," Lizzie wrote Bishop from Castine the summer following Cal's death, "but I probably don't reach that far in the blessed little bit of fog today." Frank Bidart had just read "North Haven" to her over the phone and she'd wept when she'd gone "to sit outside and think about it." When Harriet had come up to Castine with her that May, she added, "Cal seemed to be about everywhere: his red shirt and socks were a painful discovery. The death is unacceptable and yet I know he has gone and it is very difficult to bring the two together ever."[89]

"Years ago," Bishop had written in her moving elegy to her lost friend of three splendid, difficult decades:

> *Years ago, you told me it was here*
> *(in 1932?) you first "discovered girls"*
> *and learned to sail, and learned to kiss.*
> *You had "such fun," you said, that classic summer.*
> *("Fun"—it always seemed to leave you at a loss . . .)*
>
> *You left North Haven, anchored in its rock,*
> *afloat in mystic blue . . . And now—you've left*
> *for good. You can't derange, or re-arrange,*
> *your poems again. (But the Sparrows can their song.)*
> *The words won't change again. Sad friend, you cannot*
> *change.*[90]

But Lowell's words had already changed forever the American literary landscape. In his forty-year search to define himself in words, Lowell had somehow managed to do what only a handful of American writers have been able to do and do decisively: define and redefine ourselves.

Notes

The following are the repositories of Lowell or Lowell-related manuscripts cited in the biography, preceded by the symbols used in the Notes:

Amherst. Amherst College, Amherst, Massachusetts

Berg. The Henry W. and Albert A. Berg Collection, New York Public Library, Lenox and Tilden Foundation, New York, New York

Colorado. Jean Stafford Collection. Special Collections. The University Colorado at Boulder

Columbia. Columbia University Library, New York City

Dartmouth. Dartmouth College Library, Hanover, New Hampshire

Houghton. Houghton Library, Harvard University, Cambridge, Massachusetts

Indiana. Manuscripts Department, Lilly Library, Indiana University, Blooington, Indiana

Kenyon. The Greenslade Special Collections, Olin and Chalmers Libraries, Kenyon College, Gambier, Ohio

Minnesota. University of Minnesota Libraries, Manuscripts Division, Minneapolis, Minnesota

Oregon. University of Oregon Library, Eugene, Oregon

Princeton. Firestone Library, Princeton University, Princeton, New Jersey

Rosenbach. Marianne Moore Papers. Rosenbach Museum and Library, Philadelphia, Pennsylvania

Seattle. University of Washington Libraries, Manuscripts Collection, Seattle, Washington

Texas. Harry Ransom Humanities Research Center, University of Texas, Austin, Texas

Vassar. Vassar College Library Special Collections, Poughkeepsie, New York

Washington U. Washington University Library Special Collections, St. Louis, Missouri

Yale. Beinecke Library. Yale University, New Haven, Connecticut

PROLOGUE

1. I begin the story where Lowell began it: with his prose autobiographical fragments written between his thirty-eighth and fortieth years, as he began to remake his style in the image of Flaubert's *Education Sentimentale.* Much of the information here is taken from the unpublished memoirs at the Houghton Library, as well as from his memoir, "Near the Unbalanced Aquarium," posthumously published in Lowell's *Collected Prose,* edited and introduced by Robert Giroux (New York: Farrar, Straus & Giroux, 1987), pp. 346–363. Hereafter *CP.*
2. Cf. "Near the Unbalanced Aquarium," *CP,* p. 350, and the poem, "Sailing Home from Rapallo," *Selected Poems,* rev. ed (New York Farrar, Straus & Giroux, 1977), pp. 83–84. Hereafter *SP.*
3. Elizabeth Hardwick to Blair Clark, 27 March 1954. Ian Hamilton, *Robert Lowell: A Biography* (New York: Random House, 1982), p. 207. Hereafter Hamilton.
4. "Near the Unbalanced Aquarium," *CP,* p. 350.
5. *Ibid.,* pp. 352–353 and passim.
6. Esther Brooks, "Remembering Cal," reprinted in Jeffrey Meyers, ed., *Robert Lowell: Interviews and Memoirs* (Ann Arbor, MI: University of Michigan Press, 1988), pp. 283–284. Hereafter Meyers.
7. "Near the Unbalanced Aquarium," *CP,* pp. 362–363.

PART I

CHAPTER 1

1. Cf. Lowell's "Unwanted," in *Day by Day,* his last book of poems (New York: Farrar, Straus & Giroux, 1977).
2. Following the death of his father in 1950 and of his mother four years later, Lowell began in early 1955 to write steadily at a prose autobiography, providing variant readings and emendations of his childhood and adolescence in an attempt to better understand himself in his particular historical context. Many of the "facts" which I have selected for these early years come from collating and choosing from these multiple variants against what other information I could find, much as Lowell himself—or any of us—must do in reconstructing the past. But a word of caution in the use of such material. The poet Daniel Hoffman, reading Lowell's prose memoir, "91 Revere Street," when it was first published in *Partisan Review* in 1956, was struck by Lowell's comment that as a boy he had cherished a friend's "solid lead soldiers made to order in Dijon, France." Hoffman happened to be in Dijon at the time he read the memoir and sent several lead toy soldiers he found in a local shop to Lowell as a Christmas gift. When Lowell wrote back in mid-December to thank Hoffman, he confessed that he had "stuck the Dijon in blindly, on the Flaubertian principle of always being particular, as in the wonderful opening of the *Education* [*Sentimentale*]. And lo, there really are hand-molded lead Napoleonic soldiers from Dijon." Cf. Daniel Hoffman's memoir, "Afternoons with Robert Lowell," *Gettysburg Review* (Summer 1993), 6, 3, p. 482. Lowell's autobiographical drafts, which run to over three hundred pages, form part of the extensive Lowell collection at the Houghton Library.
3. For a good overview of the Lowell fortunes in America, cf. C. David Heymann's *American Aristocracy: The Lives and Times of James Russell, Amy, and Robert Lowell* (New York: Dodd, Mead & Co., 1980), to which Lowell himself somewhat reluctantly contributed.
4. Cf. Ian Hamilton's "A Conversation with Robert Lowell," *The Review 26* (Summer 1971), 10–29. Reprinted in Meyers, pp. 154–172.

5. Interview with Frank Parker, September 1992.

6. *Autobiography*. Houghton.

7. *Autobiography*. Houghton.

8. Lowell quoting from his mother's diary. Cf. *Autobiography*. Houghton.

9. The memoir was published posthumously in 1987 as part of his *Collected Prose,* pp. 291–308.

10. *CP,* p. 302.

11. "Antebellum Boston," with several facts, suppressed there, taken from the unpublished autobiography.

12. *CP,* pp. 303–304.

13. *Ibid.,* p. 304.

14. *Ibid.,* pp. 305–306.

15. Cf. *Autobiography,* and the *Life Studies* poem, "My Last Afternoon with Uncle Devereux Winslow":

> *I cowered in terror.*
> *I wasn't a child at all—*
> *unseen and all-seeing, I was Agrippina*
> *in the Golden House of Nero. . . .*

16. *CP,* pp. 307–308.

17. *Autobiography*. Houghton.

18. Cf. "91 Revere Street" and *Autobiography*. Houghton.

19. *CP,* pp. 321–323.

20. "91 Revere Street," *CP,* pp. 335 and *passim*.

21. *Autobiography*. Houghton.

22. "91 Revere Street," *CP,* p. 325.

23. *Ibid.,* pp. 325–326.

24. Cf. the sonnet sequence, "Nineteen Thirties," in Lowell's *Selected Poems,* p. 187.

25. Lowell to Mary McCarthy, 7 August 1963. Vassar.

26. Lowell to Arthur Winslow, n.d., late September 1930. Houghton. In all cases throughout the text where a date is not supplied, I have given what seems to be the most plausible one from internal evidence or cross-referencing with other information.

27. Lowell to Arthur Winslow, 22 October 1930. Houghton.

28. Lowell to Arthur Winslow, 7 November 1930. Houghton.

29. Lowell to Arthur Winslow, 20 November 1930. Houghton.

30. *SP,* p. 190.

31. *Autobiography*. Houghton.

32. *Day by Day,* pp. 89–90.

33. Blair Clark in Hamilton, pp. 22 ff. Also author's interview with Clark, March 1992.

34. Frank Parker, *Harvard Advocate* 113 (November 1979), 8. Reprinted in Meyers, pp. 252–253.

35. Parker, *Harvard Advocate*. Meyers, pp. 252–253.

36. *Day by Day,* p. 91.

37. Parker, *Harvard Advocate*. Meyers, pp. 252–253.

CHAPTER 2

1. Letter from Richard Eberhart to Steven Gould Axelrod, 14 July 1977. Quoted in Axelrod, *Robert Lowell: Life and Art* (Princeton: University of Princeton, 1978), p. 16.

2. Blair Clark to author, 1992.

3. "War: A Justification," *Vindex* 59 (1935), 156–158.

4. Lowell to Arthur Winslow, 18 May 1935. Houghton.

5. Lowell first made his attack on St. Mark's on 16 February 1940 in a speech titled "Mould-

ing the Golden Spoon" for a contest sponsored by the Ohio Inter-Collegiate Oratory Association. Houghton.

6. *Vindex* 59 (1935), 205–210.
7. *Ibid.,* 129.
8. Frank Parker and Blair Clark to author, 1992.
9. Lowell to Richard Eberhart, 10 July 1935. Dartmouth.
10. This book of manuscript poems is now at the Houghton.
11. Lowell to Eberhart, August 1935. Dartmouth.
12. Lowell in conversation with Helen Vendler. Cf. her memoir, "Lowell in the Classroom," *Harvard Advocate* 113 (November 1979). Reprinted in Meyers, p. 291.
13. Manuscript collection of poems. Houghton.
14. Early manuscript book of poems. Houghton.
15. "I had a friend," Lowell told an interviewer more than twenty years later, "Harry Brown [1917–1986], who writes dialogue for movies and has been in Hollywood for years. He was a terribly promising poet. He came to Harvard with a long correspondence with Harriet Monroe [editor of *Poetry*] and was much more advanced than anyone else. He could write in the style of Auden or Webster or Eliot or Crane. He'd never graduated from high school, and wasn't a student, but he was the person I felt closest to." *Paris Review 7* (Winter–Spring 1961), reprinted in Meyers, pp. 63–64. During World War II, Brown wrote for *Yank* and in 1944 he published a novel about the war in Italy called *A Walk in the Sun.* It was made into a movie. Brown was at Kenyon with Lowell and Peter Taylor in the fall of 1937 for two months before leaving to go on to other things. Peter Taylor has given us a fascinating cameo of Brown in his short story "1939."
16. Hamilton, p. 30.
17. Ibid., pp. 31–32.
18. Anne Dick to Charlotte Lowell, n.d., but late June 1936. Houghton.
19. Blair Clark to author, 1992.
20. Lowell to Frank Parker, about 1 July 1936. Houghton.
21. Hamilton, p. 24. Also Parker to author, 1992.
22. Hamilton, pp. 37–38.
23. Charlotte Lowell to Lowell, n.d., but early August 1936. Houghton.
24. Postcard from Lowell to Charlotte Lowell, 7 August 1936. Houghton.
25. Lowell to his parents, 9 August 1936. Houghton.
26. Lowell to Eberhart, 23 August 1936. Dartmouth.
27. Cf. Lowell's "Visiting the Tates," *Sewanee Review* LXVII (Autumn 1959), 557–559, reprinted in *CP*, pp. 58–59.
28. "William Carlos Williams," *Hudson Review* (Winter 1961–62), 530–536. *CP*, pp. 38–39.
29. Houghton.
30. Robert Lowell, Sr., to Mrs. Anne Dick, 22 December 1936. Houghton.
31. Letter from Charlotte Lowell to Anne Dick, n.d., but about 21 December 1936. Houghton.
32. Robert Lowell, Sr., to Evans Dick, 23 December 1936. Houghton.
33. Evans Dick to Robert Lowell, Sr., 27 December 1936. Houghton.
34. "Anne Dick 1. 1936," *SP*, p. 194.
35. "Father," *SP*, p. 195.
36. "Anne Dick 2. 1936," *SP*, p. 194.
37. "Mother and Father 1," *SP*, p. 195.
38. Frank Parker, interview for BBC, 1978, quoted in Hamilton, p. 41.
39. Lowell to Aunt Sarah [Winslow] Cotting, 10 Otis Place, Boston. Houghton.
40. Lowell to his grandmother, Mary Devereux Winslow, 10 Otis Place, Boston, 24 March 1937. Houghton.
41. *Ibid.*
42. Cf. Allen Tate's essay, "Techniques of Fiction" (1944).

43. Lowell's "Preface" to Ford's *Buckshee* (Cambridge, MA: Pym-Randall Press, 1966), reprinted in *CP*, p. 3.
44. Hamilton, pp. 42–43, and Parker and Clark to author, 1992.
45. Robert Lowell, BBC radio portrait of Ford Madox Ford, about 1960. Quoted in Hamilton, p. 43.
46. Lowell to Anne Dick, from a Pittsburgh hotel, n.d., but late April 1937. Houghton.
47. Lowell, "Visiting the Tates," *CP*, p. 58.
48. Caroline Gordon to Sally Wood. *The Southern Mandarins: Letters of Caroline Gordon to Sally Wood, 1924–1937,* ed. Sally Wood (Baton Rouge: Louisiana State University Press, 1984), p. 209. Cf. also William Doreski's useful *The Years of Our Friendship: Robert Lowell and Allen Tate* (Jackson, MS: University Press of Mississippi, 1990).
49. Allen Tate to Andrew Lytle, 19 May 1937. *The Lytle-Tate Letters,* ed. Thomas Daniel Young and Elizabeth Sarcone (Jackson, MS: University Press of Mississippi, 1987), p. 108.
50. "Visiting the Tates," *CP*, p. 59.
51. Tate's Open Letter of 24 May 1937. Reprinted in Hamilton, pp. 45–46.
52. Lowell to Charlotte Lowell, 24 May 1937. Houghton.
53. Lowell to Robert Lowell, Sr., 30 May 1937, from Nashville. Houghton.
54. Lowell to his grandmother, Mary Devereux Winslow, and Aunt Sarah Cotting, 30 May 1937. Houghton.
55. "Visiting the Tates," *CP*, p. 60.
56. Cf. Alan Judd, *Ford Madox Ford* (Cambridge, Engl.: Cambridge University Press, 1990), p. 431.
57. Janice Biala to George Davis at *Harper's Bazaar,* quoted in Judd, p. 429.
58. "Visiting the Tates," *CP*, p. 60.
59. Lowell to Eberhart, n.d., but June 1937. Dartmouth.
60. Lowell's ms. book of poems. Houghton.
61. William Carlos Williams, "To Ford Madox Ford in Heaven," *The Collected Poems of William Carlos Williams,* Vol. II (1939–1962), ed. Christopher MacGowan (New York: New Directions, 1988), pp. 95–96.
62. "Ford Madox Ford, 1873–1939," *CP*, pp. 59–60.
63. Harry Brown to George Marion O'Donnell, 8 June 1937. "Pure gold Blue Book, every last one of them." University of Washington.
64. Blair Clark to author, 1992.
65. Lowell to Charlotte Lowell, 5 July 1937. Houghton.

CHAPTER 3

1. Lowell to Charlotte Lowell, Tuesday, 27 July 1937. Houghton.
2. Cf. Lowell's Foreword to the republication of Ford's *Buckshee (Last Poems)* by the Pym-Randall Press (Cambridge, 1966), p. xii. *CP*, p. 4, has quietly slimmed the audience down to "several hundred." There were about 650 in the audience that afternoon.
3. Quoted in Judd's *Ford Madox Ford*, pp. 431–432.
4. John Crowe Ransom to Allen Tate, 1 January 1938. *The Selected Letters of John Crowe Ransom,* ed. Thomas Daniel Young and George Core (Baton Rouge: Louisiana State University Press, 1985), pp. 236–237.
5. Robert Lowell to Charlotte Lowell, Monday, 24 August 1937. Houghton.
6. Quoted in Arthur Mizener, *The Saddest Story* (London: The Bodley Head, 1971), p. 598.
7. Lowell to Charlotte Lowell, 24 August 1937. Houghton.
8. Merrill Moore to Ezra Pound, 13 September 1937. Yale.
9. Merrill Moore to Ezra Pound, 12 October 1937. Yale.
10. Lowell to John Crowe Ransom, 8 December 1961. Kenyon.
11. *CP*, p. 22. Also, cf. Lowell's comments to Frederick Seidel in 1960: "Before going to

Kenyon I talked to Ford Madox Ford and Ransom, and Ransom said you've got to take philosophy and logic, which I did. The other thing he suggested was classics. Ford was rather flippant about it, said of course you've got to learn the classics, you'll just cut yourself off from humanity if you don't. I think it's always given me some yardstick for English." *Paris Review* interview (Winter–Spring 1961). Reprinted in Meyers, pp. 61–62.

12. "A Look Backwards and a Note of Hope," *Harvard Advocate* 145 (November 1961): 22–23. Reprinted in Meyers, pp. 175–177.
13. Ransom to Tate, 10 October 1937. *Letters of Ransom,* p. 256.
14. "John Crowe Ransom 1888–1974," in *CP,* p. 20.
15. *Ibid.,* pp. 23–24.
16. Lowell, "Randall Jarrell, 1914–1965," in *New York Review of Books,* November 25, 1965, reprinted in *CP,* pp. 94–95 and *passim.*
17. Lowell to Charlotte Lowell, 11 October 1937. Houghton.
18. Lowell to Frank Parker, dated Tuesday [9 November 1937]. Papers of Frank Parker.
19. "Randall Jarrell, 1914–1965," *CP,* p. 90.
20. Lowell to Richard Eberhart, 12 November 1937. In Hamilton. This letter is no longer among the Eberhart Papers on loan at Dartmouth.
21. Richard Eberhart to Lowell, n.d., but mid-November 1937. Houghton.
22. Lowell to Eberhart, 27 November 1937. This letter, which Hamilton quotes (p. 58), is also not among the Eberhart Papers on loan at Dartmouth.
23. Jean Stafford to James Robert Hightower, 29 September 1937. Quoted in David Roberts, *Jean Stafford: The Life of a Writer* (New York: St. Martin's Press, 1988), p. 128.
24. Stafford to Hightower, 29 September 1937. Quoted in Charlotte Margolis Goodman, *Jean Stafford: The Savage Heart* (Austin: University of Texas Press, 1990), p. 61.
25. Ransom to Tate, 1 January 1938, *Letters of Ransom,* p. 263.
26. Robert Lowell in *Paris Review* interview, *CP,* p. 51.
27. Lowell to Charlotte Winslow, 8 February 1938. Houghton.
28. Frank Parker to author, 1992.
29. Autobiographical fragment. Houghton.
30. Peter Taylor to Hamilton, 1980. Hamilton, p. 54.
31. Stafford to Hightower, 3 October 1938. Roberts, p. 152.
32. Goodman interview with Mock, 1985. Charlotte Goodman, *Jean Stafford: The Savage Heart* (Austin: University of Texas Press, 1990), p. 85.
33. Evelyn Scott to Stafford, n.d. 1938. Quoted in Goodman, pp. 85–86.
34. Lowell to Stafford, 20 November 1938. Colorado. Quoted in Roberts, p. 155. Hightower interview with Roberts.
35. Stafford to Hightower, 23 November 1938. Roberts, p. 136.
36. Cf. Peter Taylor's short story, "1939," based on this trip. *The Collected Stories of Peter Taylor* (New York: Farrar, Straus & Giroux, 1971), pp. 326–359.
37. Stafford to William Mock, 27 November 1938. Dartmouth.
38. Stafford to Mock, 6 December 1938. Dartmouth.
39. Parker to author, 1992.
40. Stafford to Mock, 17 January 1939. Dartmouth.
41. "The Interior Castle," in *The Collected Stories of Jean Stafford* (Austin: University of Texas Press, 1992), pp. 179–193.
42. Quoted in Roberts, p. 178.
43. Stafford to Mock, 1 February 1939. Dartmouth.
44. Stafford to Mock, 20 March 1939. Dartmouth.
45. Stafford to Mock, 18 April 1939. Dartmouth.
46. Stafford to Mock, 22 May 1939. Dartmouth.
47. Blair Clark to author, 1992.
48. Merrill Moore to Lowell, 11 July 1939. Houghton.
49. Lowell to Merrill Moore, n.d., but late June 1939. Houghton.

50. Merrill Moore to Robert Lowell, Sr., 27 June 1939. Houghton.
51. Cf. Lowell's late poem, "Unwanted," in *Day by Day,* p. 122.
52. Lowell to Robert Lowell, Sr., 19 July 1939. Charlotte wrote on the letter itself, "This made Bob see red." Houghton.
53. Merrill Moore to Charlotte Lowell, 20 July 1939. Houghton.
54. Stafford to Hightower, letter postmarked 29 July 1939. Colorado. Evarts's dislike of the Lowells was noted by Parker in an interview with Roberts, p. 168.
55. Lowell to Robert Lowell, Sr., n.d., but August 1939. Houghton.
56. John Thompson in interview with David Roberts. Roberts, p. 174.
57. Peter Taylor in conversation with David Roberts, Roberts, pp. 174–175.
58. Anne White, interview with David Roberts, Roberts, pp. 175–176.
59. Stafford to Hightower, 19 December 1939. Colorado.
60. Cf. Roberts, pp. 157, 179–180, and *passim.* "It was then," Roberts writes, in the month before her marriage to Lowell, that Stafford confessed to Hightower "the truth about her gonorrhea." Since Stafford was adept at covering her tracks and constantly reinventing her past, as Peter Taylor, who knew her as well as anyone, has insisted, it is difficult to know at this distance the exact truth of Stafford's private life, whether indeed she had actually contracted gonorrhea (or worse, syphilis, as Roberts suggests), or indeed whether she was clinically frigid. At various times Stafford mentioned an Italian she'd met in Italy, an American baseball player in Heidelberg, and—to a friend of Lowell's (probably Blair Clark)—a German pilot who flew in support of Franco. Certainly in large part her admissions to and complex evasive tactics toward Hightower, Mock, and Lowell seem to have been ways of protecting herself. Cf. also Ann Hulbert, *The Interior Castle: The Art and Life of Jean Stafford* (New York: Knopf, 1992), pp. 51–53, and *passim* on this subject: "Throughout [Stafford's] life her illnesses often seemed to inspire imaginative elaboration and collaboration."
61. Stafford to Hightower, 27 March 1939. Colorado.
62. Stafford to Hightower, 27 March 1940. Colorado.
63. Hamilton, p. 68.
64. Lowell to A. Lawrence Lowell, February 1940. Houghton.
65. A. Lawrence Lowell to Lowell, 21 February 1940. Houghton.
66. Merrill Moore to Lowell, 28 February 1940. Houghton.
67. Robert Lowell, Sr., to Lowell, n.d., but April 1937. Houghton.
68. Stafford to Hightower, 30 March 1940. Colorado.
69. Stafford to Hightower, 31 March 1940. Colorado.
70. Stafford to Hightower, n.d., but 1 April 1940. Colorado.
71. Blair Clark, interview with Roberts, p. 180.
72. Stafford to Hightower, postcard, 2 April 1940. Colorado.

CHAPTER 4

1. Jean Stafford to James Robert Hightower, 4 April 1940, mailed from Chicago. Colorado.
2. Stafford to Hightower, 23 April 1940. Colorado.
3. Allen Tate to Charlotte Lowell, 17 April 1940. Houghton.
4. Tate to Merrill Moore, 17 April 1940. Houghton.
5. Lowell to Robert and Charlotte Lowell, 22 April 1940. Houghton. In a letter written the following day, Stafford complained to Hightower that to date she'd received but one letter from her husband, and that one had chilled her to the bone. But Lowell, adrift and without the emotional or financial support of his parents, may well have sounded merely forceful and determined about the course he was expecting both of them to take now that they were married.
6. Stafford to Hightower from Hayden, Colorado, 24 April 1940. Colorado.

7. Stafford to Peter Taylor, n.d., but May 1940. Vanderbilt.
8. Lowell to Charlotte Lowell, n.d., but about 20 June 1940. Houghton.
9. Lowell's graduation remarks, 9 June 1940. Houghton.
10. John Crowe Ransom to Cleanth Brooks, 15 Jan 1940. Cf. Thomas Cutrer, *Parnassus on the Mississippi: The Southern Review and the Baton Rouge Literary Community, 1935–1942* (Baton Rouge: Louisiana State University Press, 1984), p. 196.
11. "Louisiana State University in 1940," in *Day by Day*, pp. 25–26. Lowell wrote the poem as part of a festschrift in honor of Robert Penn Warren's seventieth birthday in 1975.
12. Stafford to Taylor, n.d., but about 25 June 1940. "I doubt if Cal will *ever* write to you," she added. "He is reading French, mss., and wrapping old *Southern Reviews* at the latter of which he is not terribly handy. It is hot and steamy but there are no snakes. There are, however, cockroaches. Cal killed one as big as a calf last night and I didn't sleep all night or rather did but very badly and dreamed incessantly of Blair [Clark]." Vanderbilt.
13. Lowell to Charlotte Lowell, about 20 June 1940. Houghton.
14. Lowell to his grandmother, Mary Devereux Winslow, dated "Monday." Probably late August 1940. Houghton.
15. Lowell to Grandmother Winslow. Houghton. Also cf. letter from Lowell to Robie Macauley, n.d., but late June 1940, that LSU was "a mushroom fake Mexican set-up, very relieving after the Gothic-heavy North."
16. Stafford to Hightower, 21 June 1940. Colorado.
17. Stafford to Taylor, n.d., but about 25 June 1940. Vanderbilt.
18. Quoted in Cutrer, *Parnassus on the Mississippi*, p. 56.
19. Stafford to Hightower, 26 June 1940. Colorado.
20. Lowell to Robie Macauley, n.d., but July 1940. Texas.
21. Lowell to Mary Devereux Winslow, n.d., but late August 1940. Houghton.
22. Stafford to Hightower, 31 October 1940. Colorado.
23. Stafford to Robie Macauley, n.d., but October 1940. Texas.
24. Taylor interview with David Roberts, Roberts, p. 191.
25. Stafford to Hightower, 31 October 1940. Colorado.
26. Stafford to Hightower, 31 October 1940. Colorado.
27. Clark and Parker to author, 1992. Cf. also Hamilton, p. 80.
28. Stafford to Hightower, 15 November 1940. Colorado.
29. Lowell to Robie Macauley, n.d., but July 1940. Hamilton, pp. 75–76.
30. Robert Penn Warren, interview with David Farrell. Quoted in Cutrer, *Parnassus on the Mississippi*, p. 199.
31. Jean Stafford, "An Influx of Poets," *The New Yorker*, 6 November 1978, p. 49. Hereafter "An Influx of Poets."
32. Stafford to Hightower, 10 February 1941. Colorado.
33. Stafford to Hightower, 4 March 1941. Colorado.
34. Hamilton, interview with Quinn, in Hamilton, p. 79. (Hamilton misspells Father Schexnayder's name as Shexnayder.)
35. Taylor, in 1980 interview with Hamilton, p. 79.
36. Stafford to Joan Stillman in 1952 interview, cited in Hamilton, p. 80. As Hamilton points out, there is no evidence—nor can there be—for Stafford's claim that she and Lowell had no sexual relations from the time they were remarried in the Catholic Church. Allen Tate would later spread the story that Cal often slept on the floor when Cal and Stafford were living with the Tates at Monteagle.
37. Stafford to Taylor, 14 April 1941. Vanderbilt.
38. Stafford to Hightower, 17 April 1941. Colorado.
39. Stafford to Hightower, 6 August 1941. Colorado.
40. "Jean Stafford, a Letter," in *Day by Day*, p. 29.
41. Stafford to Taylor, n.d., but August 1941. Vanderbilt.
42. Unpublished mss. Houghton.

43. Unpublished mss. Houghton. Also, cf. Eileen Simpson's memoir, *Poets in Their Youth* (New York: Random House, 1982), p. 131: "Jean claimed that Cal was the world's champion reviser, sometimes with startling results. A poem which had begun with the title, 'To Jean: On her Confirmation' . . . finished by being called, 'To a Whore at the Brooklyn Navy Yard.'" The poem already shows the strong influence of Hopkins on Lowell's poetry of the time. Cf., for example, Lowell's lines with the opening of Hopkins's "The Bugler's First Communion."

44. Parker to author, 1992.

45. From notes in the Stafford Collection. Colorado. Quoted in Hulbert, p. 139.

46. Stafford to Hightower, 9 September 1941. Colorado.

47. Stafford to Taylor, from Hotel Albert, n.d., but about 9 September 1941. Vanderbilt.

48. Stafford to Taylor, n.d., but October 1941. Vanderbilt.

49. Stafford to Taylor, n.d., but October 1941. Vanderbilt. What Stafford was trying to recall in her letter to Taylor was Catherine de Hueck Doherty's lay Catholic community, Friendship House, based in Harlem. Born into an aristocratic Russian family, de Hueck was referred to familiarly as "the Baroness." In 1941, prior to entering the Abbey of Our Lady of Gethsemane, Thomas Merton had spent a good deal of time working at Friendship House. The vicious racism he found directed by the city at large against Harlem's black community left a mark on Merton he was never able to forget.

50. Lowell to Richard Eberhart, n.d., but about mid-February 1942. Dartmouth.

51. Stafford to Taylor, n.d., but early May 1942. Vanderbilt.

52. Prose fragment, written early in 1974, shortly after Philip Rahv's death. Texas.

53. Stafford to Paul and Dorothy Thompson, 10 June 1942. Quoted in Hulbert, p. 141.

54. Stafford to Taylor, October 1942. Vanderbilt. What Jean's dream may have been telling her was that she felt "rooked," i.e., "cheated" by her husband's preoccupation with religion. Sadly, neither Jean nor Cal made the connection.

55. Cf. "An Influx of Poets," p. 49: "[Cal] once told me that I was going through the dark night of the spirit and I should meditate and read John of the Cross. I did, with a certain kind of recognition, read St. John's friend Teresa's 'Interior Castle.'"

56. Stafford to Taylor, n.d., but August 1942. Vanderbilt.

57. Parker to author, 1992.

58. Stafford to Taylor, n.d., but November 1942. Vanderbilt.

59. *Ibid.*

60. "On the Eve of the Feast of the Immaculate Conception," in *Land of Unlikeness* (Cummington, MA: The Cummington Press, 1944), unpaginated. The original version of these stanzas includes some half dozen variants. Both early and late Lowell was an inveterate reviser of his poetry, usually for the better, though not invariably.

61. Early unpublished poetry manuscripts. Houghton. In the poem of this name which appeared in *Land of Unlikeness,* none of these lines survive.

62. Unpublished talk on poetry, about 1960. Houghton. Quoted in Hamilton, p. 85.

63. Stafford to Taylor, n.d., but February 1943. Vanderbilt.

64. Stafford to Taylor, n.d., October 1942. Vanderbilt.

65. Stafford to Taylor, n.d., but April 1943. Vanderbilt.

66. Thus Stafford wrote to Lowell in early 1947, months after they had separated. Houghton.

67. Lowell to Charlotte Lowell, n.d., but about 20 August 1943. Houghton.

68. Stafford to Taylor, 6 July 1943, from the Hotel Van Rensselaer, 11th Street and Fifth Avenue. Vanderbilt.

69. Stafford to Taylor, 9 July 1943. Vanderbilt.

70. Stafford to Taylor, 5 August 1943. Vanderbilt.

71. Stafford to Taylor, 3 August 1943. Vanderbilt.

72. Lowell to Taylor, 18 July 1943. Vanderbilt.

73. Stafford to Taylor, 30 March 1943. Vanderbilt.

74. Manuscript note in his poetry notebook. Houghton.

75. Lowell's interview with V. S. Naipaul, published in *The Listener 82* (September 1969). Reprinted in Meyers, p. 143.
76. Cf. Lowell's "Declaration of Personal Responsibility," reprinted in *CP*, p. 370.
77. *Ibid.*, pp. 367–370.
78. Lowell to Charlotte Lowell, 7 September 1943. Houghton.
79. Lowell to Mary Devereux Winslow, 7 September 1943. Houghton.
80. Lowell to Mary Devereux Winslow, 11 October 1943. Houghton.
81. Lowell to Taylor, 13 October 1943. Vanderbilt.
82. Stafford to Eleanor and Peter Taylor, 13 October 1943. Vanderbilt.
83. Stafford to Taylor, 18 October 1943. Vanderbilt.
84. Jim Peck, in interview with Ian Hamilton. Hamilton, p. 91.
85. Spoken comments during reading at Dartmouth, November 1968. Tape at Dartmouth.
86. "Memories of West Street and Lepke," *Life Studies* (New York: Farrar, Straus & Cudahy, 1959), p. 86.
87. Autobiographical fragment and poem. Houghton.

CHAPTER 5

1. Charlotte Lowell to Jean Stafford, 31 October 1943. Blair Clark files. Quoted in Roberts, pp. 212–213. Cf. also Charlotte Lowell's letter to Stafford of 10 November 1943: "I am glad to hear you say that you can, and are willing to support yourself while Bobby is in prison. I have just heard of a woman whose husband was recently sent to prison for 3 years, after first losing her entire fortune. . . . I hope, Jean, for your own sake, as well as for Bobby's that you will see in the present situation an opportunity for courage, selfdevelopment, and integrity of purpose." Blair Clark files. Quoted in Roberts, p. 213. On Stafford's living expenses, cf. letter from Stafford to Tates, n.d., but late October 1943. Princeton.
2. Allen Tate, from Washington, D.C., to Stafford, 19 November 1943. Colorado.
3. Stafford to Taylors, 21 November 1943. Vanderbilt.
4. Stafford to Taylors, 5 December 1943. Vanderbilt.
5. Parker and Clark to author, 1992.
6. Lowell's 1975 interview with James Atlas for Atlas's biography of Delmore Schwartz.
7. Stafford to Peter Taylor, 22 December 1943. Vanderbilt.
8. Cf. Lowell's unpublished autobiographical fragment. Quoted in Hamilton, pp. 93–94.
9. In October 1962, while at Presbyterian Hospital on the Upper West Side being treated for manic depression, Lowell would write "From the Presbyterian Hospital Windows," an early draft of the poem which would later become "Sunset on the Hudson," then "An Anniversary: 1963" (the twentieth anniversary of his incarceration at the West Side Jail), and finally "The Mouth of the Hudson," collected in *For the Union Dead* (New York: Farrar, Straus & Giroux, 1964). It was in the early drafts that he remembered being on the masons' gang that January morning in 1944, transferring his lonely African-American prophet to the Hudson landscape to keep him imaginative company in the hospital. In the summer of 1954 he told his doctor at Payne Whitney that Israel's comment "summed up my morals and aesthetics."
10. Cf. Hamilton, pp. 92–93.
11. Stafford to Taylor, 11 February 1944. Vanderbilt.
12. Lowell to Cleanth Brooks, n.d., but about 6 April 1944. Yale.
13. Lowell to Ransom, 10 July 1944. Kenyon.
14. Stafford to Eleanor Taylor, 5 April 1944. Vanderbilt.
15. In 1946, Lowell told the critic Richard Chase that his wife's story, "The Home Front," was "about where we lived in Black Rock—next to a huge dump and a horrible inlet of mud and refuse." Columbia. "It stood behind a high brick wall," Stafford wrote in her

story, "its back windows overlooking an arm of the sea which, at low tide, was a black and stinking mud-flat." Originally published in *Partisan Review* 13 (Spring 1945).

16. Stafford to Eleanor Taylor, 5 April 1944. Vanderbilt.
17. Stafford to Peter Taylor, 22 June 1944. James Agee was also present, and "completely disarmed Cal" as he earlier had Stafford. Vanderbilt.
18. Stafford to Eleanor Taylor, 29 June 1944. Vanderbilt.
19. Manuscript poem. Houghton.
20. Stafford to Eleanor Taylor, 29 June 1944. Vanderbilt.
21. Stafford to Peter Taylor, 26 July 1944. By then, she added, she was reading St. Francis in preparation for her next novel. She and Cal were also planning "a modernization" of Dame Juliana of Norwich.
22. Lowell to Babette Deutsch, 24 February 1955. Berg.
23. Lowell knew that whatever the virtues of his Catholic baroque style in poems like this and "Quaker Graveyard," its vice was "the lashing a subject to death." Cf. letter from Lowell to Selden Rodman, n.d., but early September 1945. Selden Rodman.
24. Stafford to Peter Taylor, 12 July 1944. Vanderbilt. "I don't think Cal is any too well," she added, "but it may be only the heat and the tedium of mopping floors." The day after the seizure Lowell wrote Ransom that he felt "disorganized and rushed for time, very tired and wanting to loaf after mopping." Lowell to Ransom, 10 July 1944. Kenyon.
25. Lowell to Tate, 31 July 1944. Princeton.
26. Lowell to Ransom, 10 July 1944. Kenyon.
27. Lowell to Ransom, 6 August 1944. Kenyon.
28. "A Note (on Gerard Manley Hopkins)," *Kenyon Review* VI (Autumn 1944), 583–586. Reprinted in The Kenyon Critics' *Gerard Manley Hopkins* (New York: New Directions, 1945), pp. 89–93 as "Hopkins' Sanctity." *CP*, pp. 166–170. Cf. also Lowell's perceptive comment to R. W. Flint, in his letter of 16 January 1949, which reflects back on the poems he himself was writing during the mid-1940s: "I . . . like the Terrible Sonnets best; there's a technical joy and a deeper energy (that might be called joy) that saves them from being morbid."
29. Stafford to Hightower, 13 September 1944. Colorado.
30. Lowell to Ransom, 6 August 1944. Kenyon.
31. Introduction to *Land of Unlikeness* (Cummington, MA: The Cummington Press, 1944) pp. i–ii.
32. R. P. Blackmur, "Notes on Eleven Poets," *Kenyon Review* 7 (Spring 1944), 339–352.
33. Randall Jarrell, "Poetry in War and Peace," *Partisan Review* 12 (Winter 1945), 120–126. Reprinted in Jarrell's *Kipling, Auden & Co.: Essays and Reviews 1935–1964* (New York: Farrar, Straus & Giroux, 1980).
34. Stafford to Joe Chay, 12 October 1945. Colorado.
35. Stafford to Mary Lee Frichtel, 8 October 1944. Colorado.
36. Stafford to Eleanor Taylor, 16 November 1944. Vanderbilt.
37. Stafford to Joe Chay, 12 October 1944. Dartmouth.
38. Stafford to Joe Chay, 11 January 1945. New Year's Eve they stayed home, though the night before was as bizarre as Christmas Day, when they went "to a queer dinner party at a rich woman's house where all the ladies, after dinner, were obliged to get dressed up in our hostess's old evening frocks, to everyone's bewilderment. Afterwards we all sang Jingle Bells into a costly recording machine." Dartmouth.
39. Stafford to Eleanor Taylor, 29 December 1944. Vanderbilt.
40. Lowell to Taylor, 12 January 1945. Vanderbilt.
41. Stafford to Joe Chay, 4 February 1945. Colorado.
42. Cf. letters to Hightower, n.d., but May–June 1945. Colorado.
43. Stafford to Joe Chay, 14 April 1945. Colorado.
44. Stafford to Hightower, 2 May 1945. Colorado.
45. Stafford to Cecile Starr, 5 May 1945. Quoted in Hulbert, p. 184. Cal himself tried to

excuse his mother's haughtiness and chilliness by explaining that she was merely apprehensive.

46. Lowell to Tate, 7 July 1945. Princeton.
47. Stafford to Bill Mock, 15 July 1945. Dartmouth.
48. Stafford to Joe Chay, 28 July 1945. Colorado.
49. Jarrell to Lowell, n.d., but about 3–17 August 1945. Mary Jarrell, ed., *Randall Jarrell's Letters* (Boston: Houghton Mifflin, 1983), pp. 127–129. Hereafter *Jarrell Letters.*
50. Jarrell to Lowell, n.d., but September 1945. *Jarrell Letters,* p. 131.
51. Jarrell to Lowell, 3–17 August 1945. *Jarrell Letters,* p. 129.
52. Lowell to Babette Deutsch, 24 February 1955. Berg. Cf. Lowell's comment to John Berryman twenty-five years later, after having read Berryman's "Eleven Addresses to the Lord," that, while "cunning in its scepticism," the sequence felt "like a Catholic prayer to a personal God. I like the humorous, anguished admission of faults, somewhat like Corbière to whom your book is appealingly dedicated." Lowell to Berryman, 27 December 1970. Quoted in Paul Mariani, *Dream Song: The Life of John Berryman* (New York: William Morrow, 1990), pp. 474–475.
53. Lowell to Deutsch, 24 February 1955. Berg.
54. Lowell used this phrase in a letter to Selden Rodman, n.d., but June 1945. Selden Rodman.
55. "The Quaker Graveyard in Nantucket," *Lord Weary's Castle* (New York: Harcourt Brace Jovanovich, 1977), pp. 14–20.
56. Stafford to Joe Chay, 12 October 1945. Colorado.
57. Stafford, "New England Winter," *Holiday* 15 (February 1954), 34–36, quoted in Roberts, p. 230.
58. Stafford to Peter Taylor, 28 September 1945. Vanderbilt.
59. Stafford to Hightower, 1 October 1945. "If we stayed here, I would never write another line and I am afraid it will be many years before I can trust myself to do anything here besides think up new expensive jobs for the carpenter." Colorado.
60. Stafford to Taylor, 28 September 1945. Vanderbilt.
61. Stafford, "An Influx of Poets."
62. Stafford to Taylor, 28 September 1945. Vanderbilt.
63. Nancy Booth in interview with Charlotte Goodman, 14 April 1984. Quoted in Goodman, p. 153.
64. Ransom to Lowell, 5 October 1945. Houghton.
65. Jarrell to Lowell, n.d., but November 1945. *Jarrell Letters,* pp. 136–140.
66. Caroline Gordon to Lowells, n.d., October 1945. Houghton.
67. Allen Tate to Lowells, n.d., October 1945. Houghton.
68. Lowell to Tate, n.d., but late October 1945. Princeton.
69. Jarrell to Lowell, November 1945. *Jarrell Letters,* p. 138.
70. Stafford to Bill Mock, from Damariscotta Mills, 27 November 1945. Dartmouth.
71. *Ibid.*
72. Stafford to her sister, Mary Lee Frichtel, 27 November 1945. Colorado.
73. Allen Tate to Stafford, 1 December 1945. Houghton.
74. Delmore Schwartz to Lowells, 15 December 1945. *Letters of Delmore Schwartz,* sel. and ed. by Robert Phillips (Princeton, NJ: Ontario Press Review, 1984), p. 223. Hereafter *Schwartz Letters.*
75. Stafford to Taylors, 30 December 1945. Vanderbilt.
76. Clark to author, 1992. Also, cf. Hamilton, pp. 114–116.
77. Roberts says it was the dead German pilot's name Jean uttered. Perhaps it was someone else's, perhaps even her dead brother. Lowell's poem, "Her Dead Brother," in *The Mills of the Kavanaughs* seems to allude to a mildly incestuous episode between Jean and her brother Dick when they were adolescents.
78. *Lord Weary's Castle* and *The Mills of the Kavanaughs* (New York: Harcourt Brace Jovanovitch, 1977), pp. 92–93.

79. Poetry mss. Houghton.

80. "The Old Flame," in *For the Union Dead,* pp. 5–6.

81. Mss. version of "The Mills of the Kavanaughs." Houghton.

82. Delmore Schwartz to Elizabeth Pollet, 2 February 1946. *Schwartz Letters,* p. 231.

83. Delmore Schwartz to Helen Blackmur, 2 February 1946. Quoted in James Atlas, *Delmore Schwartz: The Life of an American Poet* (New York: Farrar, Straus & Giroux, 1977), p. 263. Cf. letter to R. P. Blackmur [February? 1946]: "Cal and Jean, who are very pleasant to live with, have taken to calling me THE BOY. Boy!" *Schwartz Letters,* p. 234.

84. Stafford to Taylor, 3 March 1946. Vanderbilt.

85. Stafford to Mock, n.d., but late February 1946. Dartmouth.

86. Stafford to Taylor, 21 March 1946. Vanderbilt.

87. Stafford to Cecile Starr, n.d., but mid-February 1946. Colorado.

88. Stafford to Taylor, 21 March 1946. Vanderbilt.

89. Cf. Atlas, *Delmore Schwartz,* p. 265.

90. Interview with Frank Parker, 1992.

91. Schwartz to Elizabeth Pollet, 26 March 1946. *Schwartz,* p. 236.

92. Lowell to Elizabeth Bishop, 16 July 66. Vassar.

93. "To Delmore Schwartz," *SP,* pp. 63–64. After the publication of the poem in *Life Studies* in the spring of 1959, Delmore, down and out on his luck, wrote Lowell from a rooming house in the Village to thank him for the poem and for some money Lowell had sent him. He'd been "touched and flattered" by the poem, and then added two bits of information. The stuffed duck had belonged to a friend of his—"one of the most unfortunate and unhappy beings" he'd ever known—who had finally shot himself a few months before. And as for the revision of Wordsworth's lines, he'd looked up the anthology he'd been reading at the time and found that what he'd actually written then was:

> We poets in our youth begin in sadness
> But thereof come, for some, exaltation,
> ascendancy and gladness.

With the hindsight of the breakdowns which both men had experienced, Lowell's revision sadly comes closer to the truth of the matter. Cf. *Schwartz Letters,* pp. 353–354.

94. Robert Fitzgerald, in *Randall Jarrell, 1914–1965* (New York: Farrar, Straus & Giroux, 1967), p. 72.

95. Jarrell to Lowell, 15 October 1945. *Jarrell Letters,* p. 135.

96. Stafford to Taylor, 15 April 1946. Vanderbilt.

97. Bowden Broadwater to Mary McCarthy, 25 May 1946. Quoted in Carol Brightman, *Writing Dangerously: Mary McCarthy and Her World* (New York: Clarkson Potter, 1992), p. 286.

98. "Cal stopped by yesterday on his way to Maine and said you had asked him [about] doing an *Introduction to Criticism* for Holt." Schwartz to Tate, 9 May 1946. *Schwartz Letters,* p. 241.

99. Stafford to Taylor, 19 December 1946. Vanderbilt.

100. Lowell to Taylor, 23 May 1946. Vanderbilt.

101. Stafford to Mary Lee Frichtel, 13 June 1946. Colorado.

102. Stafford to Mock, 25 June 1946. Dartmouth.

103. "An Influx of Poets."

104. Berryman to his mother, 4 August 1946. Quoted in Mariani, *Dream Song,* p. 177.

105. "For John Berryman, 1914–1972," *New York Review of Books* (30 March 1972), in *CP,* p. 112.

106. *Dream Song* 29, in John Berryman, *The Dream Songs* (New York: Farrar, Straus & Giroux, 1969), p. 33.

107. Simpson, *Poets in Their Youth,* pp. 115 ff.

108. Stafford to Taylors, 7 August 1946. Vanderbilt.

109. Lowell to Taylor, 13 August 1946. Vanderbilt.

110. Stafford to Mary Lee Frichtel, 16 August 1946. Colorado.

111. "An Influx of Poets."

112. In an interview with Ian Hamilton in 1980, Buckman insisted that nothing had happened during the three weeks she and Cal were together in Damariscotta Mills. Jean, she said, "was drinking herself into a stupor. . . . Most of the time she was just drinking—madly, madly, staying up all night and drinking." If a closeness developed between her and Lowell, it was Stafford who had forced it on them by her behavior. As for Lowell's feelings toward her, she insisted she had no way of knowing. "How could I tell that? I suppose we were drawn to each other. He was so beautiful then. But I did think he was a very odd character, I must say. Unlike anyone else I've ever known." Hamilton, p. 118.

113. Stafford to Taylors, 28 August 1946. "I have wanted to write you ever since Cal told me he had written but there have been so many people here and besides I have been rather too miserable to be coherent." Vanderbilt.

114. Stafford to Mock, 28 August 1946. Dartmouth. "This has been the most ghastly awful summer I have ever lived through. . . . This week-end we had the fifteenth, sixteenth, seventeenth and eighteenth house guests since Memorial Day and the fifteenth and sixteenth are still here."

115. Stafford to Taylor, 5 September 1946. Vanderbilt.

116. Stafford to Mock, 6 September 1946. Dartmouth.

117. Stafford to Taylors, 9 September 1946. Vanderbilt.

118. Cf. Stafford's "A Country Love Story." Stafford also speaks of "the cold old house somehow enveloping her as if it were their common enemy, maliciously bent on bringing them to disaster."

119. Lowell to Ransom, n.d., but early February 1946. Kenyon.

120. Stafford to Taylor, 14 July 1946. Vanderbilt.

121. Lowell to Eberhart, 2 September 1946. Dartmouth.

122. "An Influx of Poets."

123. Cf. Eileen Simpson's description of the place in *Poets in Their Youth*, p. 146. "To get to his apartment," she recalled, after she and Berryman visited him there, "one had to duck behind a slaughtered sheep that blocked the street entrance."

PART II

CHAPTER 6

1. Stafford to Lowell, n.d., but early 1947. Houghton.

2. Berryman, "Randall Jarrell," in *Randall Jarrell, 1914–1965*, p. 15.

3. "For John Berryman, 1914–1972," in *CP*, p. 112.

4. Stafford to Mary Lee Frichtel, 19 November 1946. Colorado. "In my hysterical frenzy," she added, "I felt such hatred for him that I really wished the world would be rid of him and all his kind, all the Olympian Bostonians."

5. Stafford to Mary Lee Frichtel, 21 December 1946. Roberts, p. 254.

6. Taylor to Lowell, n.d., about 25 December 1946. "I am asking you both to take matters out of the hands of your lawyers for the time being and to agree to a postponement of the divorce for one year—till January 1, 1948. I ask that you agree not to communicate with each other during that interval, except through me." Houghton.

7. Lowell to Taylor, 27 December 1946. Vanderbilt.

8. Stafford answered Taylor on 31 December 1946. "Peter," she wrote, "by this plan he will only be free to reject me in his brutal fashion over a longer period of time than he has done already. Mind you, I would take him back now, and I would forgive him, because I love him." Vanderbilt.

9. Stafford to Taylor, n.d., about 11 January 1947. Vanderbilt.

10. *Partisan Review* 14, 2 (March 1947), 216. This was a verse review of Anne Finch's *Essay on Marriage: A Book of Verse.*

11. Allen Tate to Lowell, 25 October 1946. Houghton.

12. Karl Shapiro to Lowell, 15 November 1945. Houghton.

13. Randall Jarrell, "From the Kingdom of Necessity." *The Nation* 164 (11 January 1947), 75–77.

14. Jarrell to Lowell, August 1947. *Jarrell Letters,* p. 177.

15. John Berryman, "Lowell, Thomas & Co." *Partisan Review* 14, 2 (January–February 1947), 73–85. Reprinted in *Freedom of the Poet* as "Robert Lowell and Others," pp. 286 ff.

16. Howard Moss, "Ten Poets," *Kenyon Review* 9 (Spring 1947), 290–298.

17. Lowell to Louis Untermeyer, 20 February 1947. Indiana. Eighteen months earlier, for another anthology, he'd mentioned Jarrell, Shapiro, and Delmore "as much the best of the younger American poets." After the Ellery Street debacle Delmore slipped from his list.

18. Elizabeth Bishop. Notes for an unfinished essay, probably dating to the late 1970s. Vassar. Quoted in Brett C. Miller, *Elizabeth Bishop: Life and the Memory of It* (Berkeley: University of California Press, 1993), pp. 186–187. In a letter to Lowell written thirty years later, Bishop first of all remembered Lowell's "dishevelment, your lovely curly hair, and how we talked about a Picasso show then in N.Y., and we agreed about the Antibes pictures of fishing, etc.—and how much I liked you, after having been almost too scared to go. . . . You were also rather dirty, which I rather liked, too. And your stories about the cellar room you were living in and how the neighbors drank all night and when they got too rowdy one of them wd. say, 'Remember the boy,' meaning you." 16 January 1975. Houghton. Quoted in David Kalstone, *Becoming a Poet: Elizabeth Bishop with Marianne Moore and Robert Lowell* (New York: Farrar, Straus & Giroux, 1989), p. 110. There is also Lowell's note to the Berrymans written that April, thanking them for finding him his "new room in Mrs. Frank's second-best house." The place had "sunlight and, of course, a strange couple in the next room." Lowell to Berrymans, 25 April 1947. Minnesota.

19. Stafford's note to herself, February 1947. Hulbert, p. 227.

20. Stafford to Lowell, n.d., but late February 1947. Houghton.

21. "Her Dead Brother," in *The Mills of the Kavanaughs,* p. 104.

22. Lowell to Aunt Sarah Winslow, 21 April 1947. Houghton.

23. *Life* 22 (19 May 1947), 91–94.

24. Quoted in Hamilton, p. 125. The *Globe* called Lowell "MOST PROMISING POET IN 100 YEARS . . . MAY BE GREATER THAN JAMES AND AMY."

25. Stafford to Taylors, 24 April 1947. Vanderbilt.

26. Lowell, "Two Controversial Questions," 1965, *CP,* pp. 51–52.

27. Robert Lowell, "T. S. Eliot," in *New England and Further* (Summer 1977), *CP,* pp. 210–212.

28. Lowell to Gertrude Buckman, 8 July 1947. Quoted in Hamilton, p. 127.

29. Roethke to John Crowe Ransom, 28 July 1947. *Selected Letters of Theodore Roethke,* ed. Ralph J. Mills, Jr. (Seattle: University of Washington Press, 1968), p. 131. Hereafter *Roethke Letters.*

30. Roethke to Allan Seager, 29 July 1947. *Roethke Letters,* p. 131.

31. Robert Frost to Lowell, 17 July 1947. Houghton.

32. Lowell postcard to J. F. Powers and Bucklin Moon. Postmarked 3 August 1947. J. F. Powers.

33. Roethke to Kenneth Burke, 18 September 1947. *Roethke Letters,* p. 134.

34. Stanley Kunitz, "The Sense of a Life," *New York Times Book Review,* 16 October 1977, reprinted in Meyers, p. 231.

35. Lowell to J. F. Powers, 5 February 1948. J. F. Powers.

36. Lowell to Buckman, 2 September 1947. Quoted in Hamilton, p. 128.

37. Letter from J. F. Powers to author, 1992.

38. Karl Shapiro to Lowell, 29 July 1947. Houghton.
39. Lowell to Leonie Adams, 30 March 1948. University of Washington.
40. Lowell to Tate, 4 November 1947. Princeton.
41. Memo from Librarian to Personnel, dated 27 October 1947. Quoted in Hamilton, p. 129.
42. Buckman to Lowell, 22 September 1947. Houghton.
43. Buckman to Roberts, 1985. Quoted in Roberts, p. 281. Also, cf. Buckman's comment to Hamilton in 1980 that marriage with Lowell "would have been a crazy thing, really crazy. He wasn't husband material." Hamilton, p. 126.
44. Williams to Lowell, 25 September 1947. Houghton. Also, cf. Paul Mariani, *William Carlos Williams: A New World Naked* (New York: McGraw-Hill, 1981), for the Lowell story from Williams's perspective.
45. Lowell to Williams, n.d., but early October 1947. Yale.
46. Williams to Lowell, 12 October 1947. Houghton. "Don't tell me you are approaching the mood of Henry Adams!", Williams joked, honing in on Lowell's stylistic preoccupations.
47. Lowell to Gertrude Buckman, 1 October 1947. Hamilton, p. 130.
48. Lowell, "Ezra Pound," in *Notebook 1967–68* (New York: Farrar, Straus & Giroux, 1969), p. 71.
49. Lowell to Buckman, 1 October 1947. Hamilton, p. 130.
50. Lowell to J. F. Powers, 17 November 1947. J. F. Powers.
51. Lowell to Bishop, 20 November 1947. Vassar. A week later Williams wrote his editor, James Laughlin, that after reading the page proofs Lowell had "pronounced them the best long poem ever written by an American not excluding Eliot—which he may have added knowing my feelings about the Eliot (who, by the way, I hear, is coming to the U.S. more or less permanently this year, God help us!)." Williams to Laughlin, 28 November 1947. Hugh Witemeyer, ed., *William Carlos Williams and James Laughlin: Selected Letters* (New York: W. W. Norton & Co., 1989), pp. 143–144.
52. Lowell to Bishop, 20 November 1947. Vassar.
53. Lowell, "William Carlos Williams," *SP*, p. 179.
54. Lowell to Tate, 4 November 1947. Princeton.
55. Lowell to Bishop, 20 November 1947. Vassar.
56. Lowell to Powers, 1 December 1947. J. F. Powers.
57. Lowell to Bishop, n.d., but early December 1947. Vassar.
58. Lowell to Powers, 1 December 1947. J. F. Powers.
59. Stafford to Lowell, n.d., but October 1947. Houghton.
60. Stafford to Taylor, 17 December 1947. Vanderbilt.
61. George Santayana to Lawrence Smith Butler, 26 July 1947. *Letters of George Santayana,* ed., with introduction and commentary by Daniel Cory (New York: Charles Scribner's Sons, 1955), p. 366.
62. Santayana to John Hall Wheelock, 20 September 1947. Quoted in *John McCormick, George Santayana: A Biography* (New York: Knopf, 1987), p. 453.
63. Santayana to Lowell, 8 December 1947. Houghton.
64. Lowell to Santayana, 12 January 1948. Texas.
65. Santayana to Lowell, 28 January 1948. Houghton.
66. Lowell to Santayana, 2 February 1948. Texas.
67. Robert Fitzgerald. "Robert Lowell, 1917–1977," *Harvard Advocate* 113 (November 1979), 41.
68. Lowell to Bishop, early December 1947. Vassar.
69. "Falling Asleep over the Aeneid," *The Mills of the Kavanaughs,* pp. 101–103.
70. Carley Dawson to Joyce Grenfell, 18 February 1948. Oregon.
71. Lowell to Carley Dawson, 15 March 1948. Oregon.
72. Cf. letter from Lowell to Dawson, 22 March 1948. Oregon.
73. Dawson to Hamilton, 1980, in Hamilton, p. 132.
74. Lowell to Dawson, 24 March 1948. Oregon.

75. Lowell to Dawson, Good Friday, 26 March 1948. Oregon.
76. Lowell to Dawson, 29 March 1948. Oregon.
77. Lowell to Dawson, 31 March 1948. Oregon.
78. Dawson to Joyce Grenfell, 25 April 1948. Oregon.
79. Fitzgerald, "Robert Lowell, 1917–1977," *op. cit.,* 41.
80. Dawson to Grenfell, 25 April 1948. Oregon.
81. Dawson to Grenfell, 25 May 1948. Oregon.
82. From his parents' home in Boston, Lowell wrote Dawson on Sunday morning, 25 April 1948. Oregon.
83. Lowell to Dawson, 25 April 1948. Oregon.
84. Dawson to Grenfell, 14 May 1948. Oregon.
85. Lowell to Bishop, 9 June 1948. Vassar.
86. Stafford to Berryman, 17 May 1948. Minnesota.
87. Stafford to Lowell, n.d., but about 10 June 1948. Houghton.
88. Stafford to Taylor, 26 June 1948. Vanderbilt. "At last my divorce [from Jean Stafford] is over," Lowell wrote Bishop a week later. "Looking back, it seems strange that we could survive it, and now the conclusion is allaying and satisfying. While I was in New York, I saw Jean—all very affectionate and natural, thank God." But at the moment he felt "raw." Lowell to Bishop, 2 July 1948. Vassar.
89. Stafford to Lowell, n.d., but late June 1948. Houghton.
90. Lowell to Powers, 21 June 1948. J. F. Powers.
91. Dawson to Grenfell, 28 June 1948, from the Second Family House in New Lebanon, N.Y. Oregon.
92. Bishop to Lowell, 30 June 1948. Houghton. The female correspondent was Marcia Nardi, Williams's "Cress."
93. Lowell to Bishop, 2 July 1948. Vassar.
94. Bishop to Lowell, quoted in Millier's *Elizabeth Bishop: Life and the Memory of It,* p. 202.
95. Lowell to Dawson, 28 July 1948. Oregon. "A letter sent % Mrs. Ryan has been trailing you for more than a month, unless it's dead. Just as well, perhaps. . . . Worrying through it all again—from the beginning in wonder to the end in impasse—seems useless. It all seems to have been in the cards or stars; alas."
96. Dawson to Grenfell, 12 August 1948. Oregon.
97. Dawson to Grenfell, 21 August 1948. Oregon.
98. Dawson to Grenfell, 6 September 1948. Oregon.
99. Dawson to Grenfell, 21 August 1948. Oregon.
100. "Water," the opening poem in *For the Union Dead.* One wonders if this was another dead union Lowell was lamenting, as well as the loss of his "Old Flame," Jean Stafford, in the poem which follows.
101. Quoted in Hamilton, p. 135.
102. Lowell to Bishop, 16 August 1948. Vassar.
103. Parker to author, 1992.
104. Lowell to Bishop, 23 August 1948. Vassar. "I have acquired a phoney, spruce dissillusioned tone," he added, "but it's only Washington."
105. Lowell to Fitzgerald, 24 August 1948. Yale.
106. Lowell to Berryman, 30 August 1948. Minnesota. "Fitzgerald is good on the classics, and good (very straight Catholic, though) on religion. Terribly patient and earnest and somehow surprizingly subtle at times—and completely unselfish. I liked his Tate and Pound reviews—great saturation effort and fairness—a bit florid and pious." Go to Maine, he added, "if you can and stay as long as you can—I feel reborn."
107. Lowell to Charlotte Lowell, 24 August 1948. Houghton.
108. Robert Lowell, Sr., to Lowell, 26 August 1948. Houghton.
109. Charlotte Lowell to Lowell, 26 August 1948. Houghton.
110. Lowell to Berryman, 30 August 1948. Minnesota.

111. Lowell to Powers, "Saturday." Probably 4 September 1948. J. F. Powers.
112. Lowell to Santayana, 7—13 September 1948. Texas.

CHAPTER 7

1. Lowell to Bishop, 1 October 1948. Vassar.
2. Lowell to Santayana, 14 November 1948. Texas.
3. Lowell to Santayana, 15 July 1948. Texas.
4. Lowell to Bishop, 1 October 1948. Vassar.
5. Lowell to Robie Macauley, n.d., but October 1948. Texas.
6. Lowell to Robert W. Flint, 28 October 1948. R. W. Flint. Speaking of his poem "Mother Marie Therese," set in Canada in 1912, Lowell added that his Canada was actually a construct of Maine and the nineteenth-century historian Francis Parkman, since he'd never been to Canada. Parkman was "very good on the Jesuit martyrs," for, though he had "no sympathy" with them, "somehow through his honesty they come through as heroes— really come through."
7. Lowell to Allen Tate. 5 November 1948. Princeton.
8. Bishop to Carley Dawson, 10 November 1948. Oregon.
9. Lowell to Tate, "Friday" [12 November 1948]. Princeton.
10. Lowell to Bishop, 15 August 1957. Vassar. Bishop to Lowell, early September 1957. Houghton.
11. Williams to Lowell, 12 November 1948. Houghton.
12. Bishop to Carley Dawson, 1 December 1948. Oregon.
13. Bishop to Dawson. 26 November 1948. Oregon.
14. Bishop to Dawson, 1 December 1948. Oregon. "I didn't even have so very much to drink," she explained from her vantage, for "fortunately there wasn't much there."
15. Lowell to T. S. Eliot, 25 November 1948. Collection of Mrs. Valerie Eliot.
16. Lowell to William Carlos Williams, n.d., but about 24 November 1948. Yale.
17. Williams to Lowell, 27 November 1948. Houghton. On the 29th, Lowell replied to Williams by saying that though Eliot might be somehow maimed, the man was "not dull" and "not untrustworthy." In fact he felt he "could say anything to him, and be understood and sympathized with." There was, after all, "something wonderfully warm and human" about Eliot. Yale.
18. Lowell to Tate, n.d., but December 1948. Princeton.
19. Lowell to R. W. Flint, 5 May 1948. R. W. Flint. Bishop, he was convinced, was the genuine article. Except for Jarrell, her contemporaries all seemed "pretentious, faked, empty." Jarrell, he also admitted, had a better mind than him and "more contemporary interests," and was "more articulate and talented." On the other hand Jarrell was also "emotionally immature, puritanical, monstrous, odd," peculiarities which were also "part of his excellence."
20. Lowell to Leonie Adams, 29? November 1948. Washington.
21. Lowell to Williams, 29 November 1948. Yale.
22. Bishop to Lowell, 5 December 1948. Houghton.
23. Lowell to Santayana, 14 November 1948. Texas.
24. Lowell to Pound, 15 November 1948. Yale.
25. Lowell to Powers, 13 November 1948. J. F. Powers.
26. Lowell to Santayana, 14 November 1948. Texas.
27. Lowell to Bishop, 24 December 1948. Vassar.
28. Lowell to J. F. Powers, 15 January 1949. J. F. Powers. "I guess you're the only Catholic writer except for Flannery O'Connor. I haven't read her *Accent* story. It *is* a fairly early one, and so is she. 23 and only been writing about 3 years—I think she'll be hot in a few years." Cf. also Lowell to Caroline Gordon, n.d., but late December 1948 [Princeton]: "I

don't know how my soul is—pretty uncombed, I guess. But my spirits are fine. . . . There's a girl here named Flannery O'Connor, an admirer of yours, a Catholic and probably quite a good writer, who is looking for a teaching job."

29. Lowell to Santayana, 15 January 1949. Texas.
30. Stafford to Taylor, 22 December 1948. Vanderbilt.
31. Stafford to Lowell, 1 January 1949. Houghton.
32. Lowell to Santayana, 5 January 1949. Texas.
33. Lowell to Powers, 15 January 1949. J. F. Powers.
34. Lowell to R. W. Flint, 16 January 1949. R. W. Flint. Of *The Mills of the Kavanaughs,* he wrote that it now looked as if it would be "in 700 or 800 line sections—like the nun ["Mother Marie Therese"], but much more varied. I guess it'll take several years. I hope it will be hot and written as carefully as a sonnet or as my nun. What's the hurry? You learn things all the time. God, how wrong you can be when you start, but then there's always a temptation to forget when you were right, or on to something."
35. Lowell to Eliot, 18 January 1949. Valerie Eliot.
36. Lowell to Bishop, 24 January 1949. Vassar.
37. Lowell to Santayana, 14 November 1948. Texas.
38. The meeting of the board of directors was convened at Yaddo on Saturday, 26 February 1949. Lowell's comments are quoted at length in Hamilton, pp. 142 ff. The relevant papers themselves are at the Newberry Library in Chicago.
39. Lowell to Santayana, 15 January 1949. Texas.
40. Alfred Kazin, *New York Jew* (New York: Knopf, 1978), pp. 202–205. Reprinted in Meyers, pp. 250–251.
41. Malcolm Cowley to Louis Kronenberger, 8 March 1949. Newberry Library. Quoted in Hamilton, p. 148.
42. Lowell telegram to Tate, 1 March 1949, from the Earle Hotel, 103 Waverly Place. Princeton.
43. Tate to Hardwick, 3 March 1949. Houghton.
44. Robert Fitzgerald's journal quoted in Hamilton, pp. 149–150.
45. Fitzgerald to Tate and Gordon, 4 March 1949. Princeton. Hamilton, pp. 150–151.
46. Tate to Hardwick, 8 March 1949. Houghton.
47. Flannery O'Connor to "A," 16 December 1955. *The Habit of Being: Letters of Flannery O'Connor,* ed. Sally Fitzgerald. (New York: Random House, 1980), pp. 124–125.
48. O'Connor to "A," 14 May 1960. *Habit of Being,* p. 395.
49. Among the fifty-one Yaddo members who signed this letter were Eleanor Clark, Jean Stafford's old friend, Kappo Phelan, John Cheever, Alfred Kazin, Harvey Breit, Katherine Anne Porter, and Delmore Schwartz. Quoted in Hamilton, pp. 151–152.
50. Malcolm Cowley to Allen Tate, 27 March 1949. Newberry. Quoted in Hamilton, p. 151.
51. Quoted in the *New York Times* for 27 March 1949.
52. Lowell telegram to Tate, 29 March 1949. Princeton.
53. Tate to Hardwick, 30 March 1949. Houghton.
54. Tate to Hardwick, 31 March 1949. Houghton.
55. Tate to Malcolm Cowley, 4 April 1949. Newberry. Quoted in Hamilton, p. 155.
56. Tate to Hardwick, 4 April 1949. Houghton. Quoted in Hamilton, p. 156.
57. Allen Tate to Marcella Winslow, 20 April 1949. Houghton.
58. Peter Taylor interview with Hamilton, 1980, Hamilton, pp. 156–157.
59. Cf. Lowell's unpublished autobiography, and several of his draft manuscripts for poems written during the *Life Studies* period (1955–57). Houghton. Quoted in part in Hamilton, p. 157.
60. Cf. Kalstone, *Becoming a Poet: Elizabeth Bishop with Marianne Moore and Robert Lowell,* p. 148.
61. Peter Taylor to Wyatt Prunty. Related to the author, 1993.
62. Hamilton, p. 158.

63. Lowell to Williams, 10 April 1949. Yale.
64. Lowell to Berryman, 16 April 1949. Minnesota. He was still hoping to be out in time to spend a week at the Kenyon summer school with Tate. When Stafford learned what had happened to Lowell, she wrote her sister with a sigh of relief that Cal's breakdown proved that neither had been completely to blame for the failure of their marriage. Stafford to Mary Lee Frichtel, 12 April 1949. Colorado.
65. Charlotte Lowell to Peter Taylor, 16 April 1949. Vanderbilt.
66. Robert Giroux to Hamilton, 1979. Quoted in Hamilton, pp. 158–159.
67. Lowell to Taylor, "Low Sunday," 27 April 1949. Vanderbilt.
68. Stafford wrote Taylor on 9 May 1949 to say that Lowell had written her, insisting that their Catholic marriage was still valid. Vanderbilt.
69. Lowell to Taylor, 5 May 1949. Vanderbilt.
70. Parker to author, 1992.
71. Lowell to Jarrell, 21 May 1949. Berg.
72. "Mackie and I were terribly sorry to hear that you'd been sick," Jarrell wrote back, not quite knowing what to say and so keeping his distance. "As soon as you're better we want you to come for a long visit with us, as long as you want." He mentioned that Richard Wilbur was down for the Arts Forum, but not that Jean Stafford was also there. Cf. *Jarrell Letters,* p. 225.
73. Lowell to Leonie Adams, 18 June 1949. Washington.
74. Hardwick to Berryman, 22 June 1949. Minnesota.
75. Lowell to Hardwick, 6 July 1949. Houghton.
76. Lowell to Taylor, 7 July 1949. Vanderbilt.
77. Bishop to Lowell, n.d., but July 1949. Houghton.
78. Robert Lowell, Sr., to Lowell, 13 July 1949. Houghton.
79. Lowell to T.S. Eliot, 25 July 1949. Valerie Eliot.
80. Lowell to Taylor, 6 August 1949. Vanderbilt.
81. Parker to author, 1992.
82. Lowell to Taylor, 6 August 1949. Vanderbilt.
83. Lowell to Hardwick, 15 September 1949. Houghton.
84. Lowell to Taylor, unsent, n.d., but October 1949. Houghton.
85. Merrill Moore to Hardwick, 5 October 1949. Houghton.
86. Caroline Gordon to Hardwick, n.d., but October 1949. Houghton.
87. Tate to Lowell, 11 October 1949. Houghton.
88. Hardwick to Peter and Eleanor Taylor. 20 October 1949. Vanderbilt.
89. Lowell to his parents, 5 November 1949. Houghton.
90. Robert Lowell, Sr., to Lowell, 11 November 1949. Houghton.
91. Lowell to Peter Taylor, 21 November 1949. Vanderbilt.
92. Lowell to Charlotte Lowell, from 29 West 104th Street, 26 December 1949. Houghton.
93. Lowell to Tate, 29 December 1949. Princeton.
94. Lowell to Santayana, 22 December 1949. Texas.
95. Santayana to Lowell, 29 December 1949. Houghton.
96. Santayana to John Hall Wheelock, 30 December 1949. McCormick, *George Santayana,* p. 461.
97. Lowell to Santayana, 8 January 1950. Texas.
98. W. D. Snodgrass: "A Liberal Education: Mentors, Fomentors, Tormentors" in the *Southern Review* (Summer 1992).
99. Hardwick to Charlotte Lowell, 5 February 1950. Houghton.
100. Lowell to Charlotte Lowell, 10 March 1950. Houghton.
101. *Ibid.*
102. *Ibid.*
103. Hardwick to Charlotte Lowell, 5 February 1950. Houghton.
104. Lowell to Bishop, 10 March 1950. Vassar. "I've been back in my long poor poem—hours

and hours, have gotten some good new lines, but it's still a muddle getting it all together."

105. Lowell to Santayana, 8 January 1950. Texas.
106. Lowell to Bishop, 10 March 1950. Vassar.
107. Lowell to Tate, 15 March 1950. Princeton. The novel, published in 1955, was *The Simple Truth*.
108. Lowell to Taylor, 30 March 1950. Vanderbilt.
109. Lowell to Bishop, 10 March 1950. Vassar.
110. Lowell to Taylor, 30 March 1950. Vanderbilt.
111. Stafford to Lowell, n.d., but January 1950. Houghton.
112. Quoted in Roberts, p. 298.
113. Lowell to Taylor, 30 March 1950. Vanderbilt.
114. Lowell to Taylor, 29 July 1950. Vanderbilt.
115. Lowell to Bishop, 20 July 1950. Vassar.
116. Lowell to Bishop, 20 July 1950. Vassar.
117. Reported in Atlas, *Delmore Schwartz*, p. 290.
118. Lowell to Santayana, 8 January 1950. Texas.
119. When Lowell wrote Bishop in late August, the Pound issue was still on his mind. "Give my love to the Pounds," he wrote her in Washington, "I had many small brushes for his sake; though almost everyone seems to be on his side now." Lowell to Bishop, 20 August 1950. Vassar.
120. Lowell to Bishop, 20 August 1950. Vassar.
121. Randall Jarrell, "The Obscurity of the Poet," in *Poetry and the Age* (New York: Farrar, Straus & Giroux, 1953), pp. 10–11.
122. *Ibid.*, p. 13.
123. Lowell to Bishop, 18 September 1950. Vassar.
124. *Ibid.*
125. Lowell to Bishop, 20 August 1950. Vassar.
126. Charlotte and Robert Lowell, Sr., to Lowell, 26 August 1950. Houghton.
127. Lowells' telegram, 30 August 1950. Houghton.
128. Autobiographical fragment, 1955–1957. Houghton. Quoted in Hamilton, p. 169.
129. Autobiographical fragment, 1955–1957. Houghton.
130. Lowell to Bishop, from Beverly Farms. Vassar.
131. Lowell to Santayana, 18 September 1950. Texas.
132. Lowell to Pound, n.d., but about 24 September 1950. Yale.

CHAPTER 8

1. Lowell to Charlotte Lowell. Houghton.
2. Santayana to Lowell, 23 October 1950. Houghton.
3. Santayana to Dr. Luciano Sibille, 4 November 1950, *Letters of Santayana*, p. 392.
4. Santayana to Lowell, 23 October 1950. Houghton.
5. Elizabeth Hardwick to Robie and Ann Macauley, 12 November 1950.
6. Lowell to Bishop, 6 December 1950. Vassar.
7. Elizabeth Hardwick, "Living in Italy: Reflections on Bernard Berenson," in *A View of My Own* (New York: Farrar, Straus & Giroux, 1962), pp. 205–206.
8. Lowell to Santayana, 6 December 1950. Texas.
9. Lowell to Tate, 15 March 1954. Princeton.
10. Hardwick to John McCormick, 1985. McCormick, pp. 461–462.
11. Lowell to Bishop, 6 December 1950. Vassar.
12. Santayana to John Hall Wheelock, 30 January 1951. McCormick, p. 463.
13. Lowell to Bishop, 6 December 1950. Vassar.
14. "Beyond the Alps," *Life Studies*, pp. 3–4.

15. Lowell to Santayana, 6 December 1950. Texas.
16. Lowell to Bishop, 6 December 1950. Vassar.
17. Lowell to Santayana, 6 December 1950. Texas.
18. Lowell to Peter Taylor, 13 January 1951. Vanderbilt.
19. Lowell to Bishop, 22 January 1951. Vassar. "The Kenyon *Kavanaughs* is unchanged but my Harcourt Brace version is all ripped up and much better, though perhaps not essentially."
20. Lowell to Charlotte Lowell, 26 December 1950. Houghton.
21. Lowell to Taylor, 13 January 1951. Vanderbilt.
22. Lowell to Charlotte Lowell, 26 December 1950. Houghton.
23. Lowell to Harriet Winslow, 26 December 1950. Houghton.
24. Lowell to Taylor, 13 January 1951. Vanderbilt.
25. Lowell to Bishop, 22 January 1951. Vassar.
26. Lowell to Hardwick, 6 January 1951. Houghton.
27. Lowell to Hardwick, 5 January 1951. From Domaine de Fortis, Luynes, France. Houghton.
28. Frank Parker to author, 1992.
29. Lowell to Bishop, 22 January 1951. Vassar.
30. Lowell to Santayana, 1 February 1951. Texas.
31. Lowell to Taylor, 27 April 1951. Vanderbilt.
32. Lowell to Santayana, 1 February 1951. Texas.
33. Lowell to Bishop, 24 April 1951. Vassar.
34. Lowell to Santayana, 26 April 1951. Texas.
35. Santayana to Daniel M. Cory, 10 May 51. McCormick, p. 462.
36. Lowell to Charlotte Lowell, 13 June 1951. Houghton.
37. Lowell to Macauleys, 28 February 1952, from Amsterdam. "Your visit [the previous summer] was the best time we've had in Europe, I can still taste Chinon, and often dream of marching again in the Bastille Day parade carrying Bainville's Action Française history of France." Texas.
38. Lowell to Williams, 20 July 1951. Yale.
39. Williams to Lowell, n.d., but late July 1951. Houghton.
40. Lowell to Harriet Winslow, about 6 October 1951. Houghton.
41. Lowell to Charlotte Lowell, 18 October 1951. Houghton.
42. Lowell to Tate, 15 March 1954. Princeton.
43. Hardwick to Hamilton, Hamilton, p. 174.
44. Lowell to Hardwick, n.d., but about 15 September 1951. Houghton.
45. Lowell to Hardwick, 17 September 1951. Houghton.
46. Lowell to Jarrell, 6 October 1951. Berg.
47. Lowell to Hardwick, 17 September 1951. Houghton.
48. Lowell to Hardwick, n.d., about 16 September 1951. Houghton.
49. Lowell to Jarrell, 6 October 1951. Berg.
50. Lowell to Charlotte Lowell, n.d., but about 24 September 1951. Houghton.
51. *New York Times Book Review,* 7 October 1951, p. 7.
52. Lowell to Jarrell, 6 October 1951. Berg.
53. Jarrell to Lowell, n.d., but late October 1951. Houghton.
54. Lowell to Charlotte Lowell, 6 November 1951. Houghton.
55. Lowell to Bishop, 6 November 1951. Vassar.
56. *Ibid.*
57. Lowell to Macauleys, 28 February 1952. Texas.
58. Cf. *Life* 58 (19 February 1965), p. 55. "Do I feel left out in a Jewish age? Not at all. . . . My Jewish ancestors, oddly enough, were named Moses Mordecai and Mordecai Moses."
59. Lowell to Jarrell, 24 February 1952. Berg.
60. Hardwick to Macauleys. 22 February 1952. Texas.

61. Lowell to Jarrell, 24 February 1952. Berg.
62. Lowell to Bishop, 26 February 1952. Texas.
63. Lowell to Jarrell, 24 February 1952. Berg. "A View of Three Poets," *Partisan Review* 18 (November–December 1951), 691–700. While Jarrell called "Mother Marie Therese" the "best poem" Lowell had ever written, and "Falling Asleep Over the Aeneid" almost as good, he dismissed the title poem as nightmarish, a mere "anthology of favorite Lowell effects." In spite of which, Lowell was still "one of the best of living poets."
64. Lowell to Jarrell, 24 February 1952. Berg.
65. Harriet Winslow to Lowell, 25 January 1952. Houghton.
66. Lowell to Harriet Winslow, n.d., but about 24 February 1952. Houghton.
67. Lowell to Bishop, 26 February 1952. Vassar.
68. Lowell to Taylor, n.d., about 15 April 1952. Vanderbilt.
69. Lowell to Williams, n.d., but early March, 1952. Yale.
70. Lowell to Santayana, 10 March 1952. Texas.
71. Lowell to Bishop, 24 April 1952. Vassar.
72. Hardwick to Robie Macauley, 7 May 1952. Texas.
73. Lowell to Santayana, 10 March 1952. Texas.
74. Hardwick to Macauleys, 16 May 1952. Texas.
75. Postcard from Lowell to Tate from Vienna, 14 June 1952. Princeton.
76. Postcard from Lowell to Taylor, postmarked Vienna, n.d., but late June–early July 1952. Vanderbilt.
77. Lowell to Blair Clark, 15 September 1952. Blair Clark.
78. John McCormick, "Falling Asleep over Grillparzer: An Interview with Robert Lowell," *Poetry* 81 (January 1953), 269–279. Reprinted in Meyers, pp. 23–32.
79. "Words for Hart Crane," *Life Studies*, p. 55.
80. Hardwick to Macauleys, 24 August 1952. Texas.
81. Hardwick to Macauleys, 25 August 1952. Texas. The Macauleys had visited the Lowells that August in Salzburg and had witnessed Lowell's behavior, and now Hardwick asked them to keep the breakdown as quiet as possible.
82. Hardwick to Charlotte Lowell, 26 August 1952. Houghton.
83. "Beyond the Alps," *Life Studies*, p. 4.
84. Hardwick to Macauleys, 19 October 1952. Texas. Quoted in Hamilton, p. 194.
85. Lowell to Macauleys, 15 September 1952. Quoted in Hamilton, p. 194.
86. Lowell to Macauleys, 1 December 1952. Texas.
87. Hardwick to Macauleys, 19 October 1952. Texas.
88. In a letter to Lowell written in the spring of 1954, following a subsequent breakdown of Lowell's, Clark reminded Lowell of this conversation. Houghton.
89. Lowell to Blair Clark, 15 September 1952. Blair Clark.
90. "For George Santayana 1863–1952," *Life Studies*, pp. 51–52.
91. Lowell to Charlotte Lowell, 19 October 1952. Houghton.
92. Lowell to Tate, 5 November 1952. Princeton. When he wrote Ransom about teaching at the School of Letters in Bloomington, Indiana, Lowell suggested a course called *Couplet, Blank Verse and Lyric.* "It would be an unchronological survey of English poetry," he explained, "in which I'd use the fixed metrical patterns as a jumping-off point for various comparisons of craft and content, and to show what tricks and limitations each poet had to work with." Lowell to Ransom, 24 November 1952. Kenyon.
93. Lowell to Ransom, 24 November 1952. Kenyon.
94. Lowell to Tate, 5 November 1952. Princeton.
95. Lowell to Ransom, 24 November 1952. Kenyon.
96. Lowell to Tate, 28 November 1952. Princeton.
97. Lowell to Blair Clark, 3 December 1952. Blair Clark.
98. Lowell to Robie Macauley, 1 December 1952. Texas.
99. Lowell to Taylor, 7 December 1952. Vanderbilt.

100. Lowell to Harriet Winslow, 30 December 1952. Houghton.
101. "Beyond the Alps," *Life Studies,* p. 4.
102. "Skunk Hour," *Life Studies,* p. 90.

CHAPTER 9

1. Postcard of Faneuil Hall, Boston, from Lowell to J. F. Powers, 25 January 1953. J. F. Powers.
2. "Inauguration Day," *Life Studies,* p. 7.
3. Lowell to Charlotte Lowell, 3 March 1953. Houghton.
4. Lowell to Tate, 15 March 1953. Princeton.
5. Lowell to Charlotte Lowell, 3 March 1953. Houghton.
6. Lowell to Tate, 15 March 1953. Princeton.
7. Lowell to Taylor, 25 March 1953. Vanderbilt.
8. Lowell to Tate, 15 March 1953. Princeton.
9. Lowell to Tate, 15 April 1953. Princeton.
10. Lowell to Tate, 29 April 1953. Princeton.
11. Lowell to Robert Fitzgerald, 29 April 1953. Yale.
12. Lowell to Bishop, 14 June 1953. Vassar. That he did miss her, and that he feared he might already be losing her, is adumbrated in the dream Lowell shared with her: "Last night I had a dream. I was in France. Paris was again falling to the Germans, but it had become such a habit that one had to look closely to see that anyone really cared. I arrived in Paris (from the front, I think, but there wasn't much of one), went to a party, where I was surrounded by acquaintances. They became distant and shadowy when I approached them. Suddenly I saw you and gave you a tremendous hug. You moved to another table. I said: 'I know where there are a couple of good French restaurants.' You said: 'They're all French here.' You see. You must come back."
13. Lowell to Harriet Winslow, 29 April 1953. Houghton.
14. Lowell to Hardwick, 6 September 1953. Houghton.
15. Lowell to Hardwick, 10 September 1953. Houghton.
16. I have not been able to locate Lowell's letters to Flannery O'Connor, but in late August 1953 Flannery O'Connor wrote the Fitzgeralds that she had just "had a letter from Cal who said he was thirty-six years old and feeling very elderstatesmanish and peaceful to be in Iowa City again." Cf. *The Habit of Being,* p. 60.
17. Lowell to Harriet Winslow, 26 September 1953. Houghton.
18. Lowell to Tate, 29 April 1953. Princeton.
19. Lowell to Harriet Winslow, 29 April 1953. Houghton.
20. W. D. Snodgrass: "A Liberal Education: Mentors, Fomentors, Tormentors," *Southern Review* (Summer 1992), *passim.*
21. Philip Levine, "Mine Own John Berryman," *The Gettysburg Review,* 4.4 (Autumn 1991), 533–552.
22. In a letter dated 29 April 1953, Lowell told Fitzgerald that he'd yet to see *Homage to Mistress Bradstreet,* but that when he'd seen Berryman the previous January, he'd seemed "top of the world." He had the feeling, he added, that Berryman had "come to the surface, and that almost ten year stretch of burying himself and following his instincts" was now about "to pay off in a big way." Yale.
23. Letter from Philip Levine to author, 27 October 1992.
24. Lowell to Charlotte Lowell, 29 November 1953. Houghton. "Heaven must be a place we can smoke hundreds of cigarettes without cancer; I've already done it, but how long?" Lowell to Marcia Nardi, 4 September 1969. Collection of E. M. O'Neil.
25. Lowell to Bishop, 29 November 1953. Vassar. "I guess you've heard about Dylan Thomas's death. He died four days after a brain stroke which seems to have immediately

finished his mind. The details are rather gorgeously grim. He was two days incomunicado with some girl on [John Malcolm] Brinnen's staff in some New York hotel. Then his wife came, first cabling 'eternal hate,' and tried quite literally to kill *and* sleep with everyone in sight. Or so the rumors go in Chicago and Iowa City. It's a story that Thomas himself would have told better than anyone else." On December 2, he wrote Berryman that he'd been in Chicago the previous week and had "heard every kind of rumor about Thomas— as though his death were one of his stories!" Minnesota. Many of the details Lowell passed on to Bishop in fact had come from Berryman, who was with Thomas at St. Vincent's Hospital when he died. Cf. Mariani, *Dream Song.*

26. Lowell to Bishop, 24 April 1952. Vassar.
27. Lowell to Powers, 22 January 1954. J. F. Powers.
28. Lowell to Powers, 29 November 1953. J. F. Powers.
29. Lowell to Tate, 15 March 1954. Princeton.
30. Lowell to Bishop, 1 January 1954. Vassar.
31. Lowell to Bishop, 1 January 1954. Vassar. Since *Moby Dick* was for Lowell the best novel written in English, that was high praise indeed.
32. Hardwick to Blair and Holly Clark, 20 February 1954. Blair Clark.
33. Lowell to Hardwick, 17 February 1954, from the Pensione Tornabuoni Beacci in Florence. Houghton.
34. "Oh Europe!", he wrote J. F. Powers on March 15 from Cincinatti. "I arrived on a Sunday and left on the next. I have been in the outskirts of London, spent a night in Paris, a day and a half in Florence picking up Mother's trunks, and a night in Milan. There I saw the Last Supper and heard Elizabeth Schwarzkopf sing in Figaro at the Scala. Oh the riches of the world after the mid-west, after anywhere!" J. F. Powers.
35. "Two weeks ago, coming back on a boat [the *Cristoforo Colombo*] from Italy," Lowell wrote Williams on March 13, "I sat with a YMCA couple [in their sixties]. They didn't smoke. They didn't drink. They looked reproach at people who did smoke and drink. They were [Baptists and] anti-Jew, anti-Catholic." The talk circled around to religion. Lowell told them he was a bad Catholic; they spoke of the consolations of their own. "I think you have misunderstood," he explained to them. "I don't have any religion, if I did, I'd be Catholic." That ended the conversation. Yale.
36. Lowell to Blair Clark, 11 March 1954. Blair Clark.
37. Lowell to Harriet Winslow, 13 March 1954. Houghton.
38. Lowell to Williams, 13 March 1954. Yale.
39. *Ibid.*
40. Lowell to Tate, 15 March 1954. Princeton.
41. Lowell to J. F. Powers, 15 March 1954. J. F. Powers.
42. Lowell to Peter and Eleanor Taylor, 19 March 1954. Vanderbilt.
43. Flannery O'Connor to Sally Fitzgerald, 26 December 1954. *The Habit of Being*, p. 74.
44. Lowell to Pound, 20 March 1954. Yale.
45. Lowell to Blair Clark, 21 March 1954. Blair Clark.
46. Giovanna Madonia to Blair Clark, 19 March 1954. Hamilton, p. 213.
47. Lowell to Pound, 25 March 1954. Yale.
48. Lowell to Berryman, 25 March 1954. Minnesota.
49. Hardwick to Blair Clark, 27 March 1954. Hamilton, p. 208.
50. Pound Papers. Yale. Also quoted in Hamilton, pp. 211–212.
51. Cf. Mary Jarrell's commentary in *Jarrell's Letters*, pp. 394–395.
52. O'Connor to Sally and Robert Fitzgerald, 26 April 1954. *The Habit of Being*, p. 71.
53. Madonia to Lowell, 26 June 1954. Houghton.
54. Williams to Lowell, 15 March 1954. Houghton.
55. Williams to Lowell, 28 June 1954. Houghton.
56. Lowell to Harriet Winslow, 20 July 1954. Houghton.
57. Lowell to Aunt Sarah Cotting, 20 July 1954. Houghton.

58. Lowell to Clark, 6 August 1954. Blair Clark.

59. Hardwick to Blair Clark, 31 August 1954. Blair Clark.

60. Lowell to Taylor, 24 October 1954. Vanderbilt.

61. Lowell to Harriet Winslow, 4 October 1954. Houghton.

62. Lowell to Bishop, 14 November 1954. Vassar.

63. Lowell to Berryman, 6 October 1954. Minnesota. In a brilliant aperçu, he told Bishop that the Flaubertian prose he was using to write his more naked self was like knitting together "raw ends with fake velvet." Lowell to Bishop, 14 November 1954. Vassar.

64. Lowell to Harriet Winslow, 24 October 1954. Houghton.

65. Lowell to Bishop, 14 November 1954. Vassar.

66. Lowell to Harriet Winslow, 22 November 1954. Houghton.

67. Hardwick to Blair and Holly Clark, 29 November 1954. Blair Clark.

68. Hardwick to Taylor, 10 February 1955. Vanderbilt.

69. Lowell, "The Metamorphoses of Ovid," *Kenyon Review XVII* (Spring 1955), reprinted in *CP,* pp. 152–160.

70. Lowell to Ransom, 24 February 1955. Kenyon.

71. Lowell to Peter Taylor, 6 November 1955. Vanderbilt.

72. Lowell to Tate, 15 March 1954. Princeton.

73. Lowell to Bishop, 5 May 1955. Vassar.

74. Lowell to Bishop, 16 July 1955. Vassar.

75. Lowell to Bishop, 5 May 1955. Vassar.

76. Lowell to Taylor, 11 May 1955. Vanderbilt.

77. Hardwick to Harriet Winslow, 22 April 1955. Houghton.

78. Lowell to Pound, 17 April 1955. Yale.

79. Lowell to Bishop, 5 May 1955. Vassar.

80. Lowell to Taylor, 11 April 1955. Vanderbilt. History as amnesia and recall. "I want to invent and forget a lot," he added, "but at the same time have the historian's wonderful advantage."

81. Lowell to Blair Clark, 7 May 1955. Hamilton, p. 222.

82. Lowell to Bishop, 16 July–about 1 August 1955. Vassar. Lowell asked Bishop to forgive him this last image. It came, he said, "from bathing suits on the line, our washing-machine which became overloaded and stopped, looking at pictures of Pollaiuollo, and the heat—it is almost a hundred in the shade today." But it also came from an article on art and old age by Gottfried Benn which he'd read in the summer issue of *Partisan Review,* and which he mentioned in this letter. Berryman too read the Benn article and saw in the same image the extremities toward which any autobiographical writing—including his and Lowell's—tended. "And Gottfried Benn / said:—We are using our own skins for wallpaper and we cannot win." ("Dream Song 53")

83. Lowell to Bishop, 16 July–about 1 August 1955. Vassar.

84. Jarrell to Bishop, September 1956, in *Jarrell Letters,* p. 414.

85. Philip Booth, "Summers in Castine: Contact Prints, 1955–1965," *Salmagundi* 37 (Spring 1977), 37–53, reprinted in Meyers, pp. 196–213.

86. Lowell to Harriet Winslow, 1 November 1955. Houghton.

87. Lowell to Bishop, 6 November 1955. Vassar.

88. Lowell to Harriet Winslow, 1 November 1955. Houghton.

89. Lowell to Taylor, 6 November 1955. Vanderbilt.

90. Lowell to Bishop, 29 December 1955. Vassar.

91. Lowell to Dave McDowell, 15 November 1955. Columbia. "The [John] Thompsons have just left us, after a week-end visit. All through a long day's drive in the country and even through a furious and inattentive bridge game, we regurgitated the [Kenyon College] past, rewrote Peter's [Taylor] play for him, took Robie [Macauley] out of Intelligence, remarried Bill Clark, divorced Nerber, imagined what we would do if we sat in your chair at Random House."

92. Lowell to Taylor, 6 November 1955. Vanderbilt.
93. Lowell to Williams, 2 December 1955. Yale.
94. Lowell to Bishop, 29 December 1955. Vassar.

CHAPTER 10

1. Lowell to R. W. Flint, 7 August 1958. R. W. Flint.
2. Cf. "Dr. Williams," *Hudson Review* XIV (Winter 1961–62), 530–536; reprinted in *CP*, pp. 42–44.
3. *Ibid.*, 42.
4. Lowell to Harriet Winslow, 17 January 1956. Houghton.
5. Lowell to Harriet Winslow, n.d., but February 1956. Houghton.
6. Lowell to Harriet Winslow, 8 March 1956. Houghton.
7. Lowell to Caroline Gordon, 3 April 1956. Princeton.
8. Lowell to Harriet Winslow, 17 May 1956. Houghton.
9. Lowell to J. F. Powers, 16 May 1956. J. F. Powers.
10. Lowell to Caroline Gordon, 3 April 1956. Princeton. But see too Lowell's letter to Powers of May 16 on *The Malefactors,* a "dark" novel about Tate's conversion to Catholicism. "An important character [in the novel] is Dorothy Day, sublimated, canonized, the book dedicated to her, but made to perform a black mass and on the last page kissed on the mouth by Allen, or rather kissing Allen on the mouth, meaning peace. Dorothy [Day] saw the book in page proofs, blew up, and forced the removal of both the black mass and the dedication. . . . I guess I feel catty about Caroline because I wrote her what I took to be a shyly complimentary fan letter and got back a blast quoting praises from Jacques Maritain, who 'knows more about the *form* of the novel than anyone living,' but whose praise fell short of Caroline's own in which she claims to be the perfecter of Henry James and the heir of Jung."
11. Lowell to J. F. Powers, 16 May 1956. J. F. Powers.
12. Lowell to Bishop, 18 June 1956. Vassar.
13. Lowell to Taylor, 18 June 1956. Vanderbilt.
14. "Memories of West Street and Lepke," *Life Studies,* p. 85.
15. "Art and Evil," published for the first time in *CP*, pp. 129–144.
16. Lowell to Jarrell, 24 October 1957. Berg.
17. Lowell to Isabella Gardner, 19 September 1956. University of Washington.
18. Bishop quotes Moore's comments on the tea in a letter to Lowell of 4 September 1956. Houghton.
19. Lowell to Harriet Winslow, 17 September 1956. Houghton.
20. Lowell to Pound, 17 September 1956. Yale.
21. Lowell to Harriet Winslow, 17 September 1956. Houghton.
22. Lowell to William Carlos Williams, 5 September 1956. Yale.
23. Lowell to Harriet Winslow, 6 October 1956. Houghton.
24. Lowell to Harriet Winslow, 21 December 1956. Houghton.
25. Lowell to Bishop, 24 October 1956. Vassar.
26. Lowell to Pound, 24 October 1956. Yale.
27. Lowell to William Meredith, 19 December 1956. "The other night I was talking to Frost [about the Hungarian uprising] and he spoke of the horror in living in one of those countries where you had to die or dare to *not* die. Yet you could never know whether you were right or what it could come to." William Meredith.
28. Or like Roethke . . . or Churchill. Thus he wrote Bishop. 7 February 1957. Vassar.
29. Lowell to Harriet Winslow, 10 January 1957. Houghton.
30. Lowell to J. F. Powers, 6 February 1957. J. F. Powers.
31. Lowell to Tinkham Brooks, 22 January 1958. Yale.

32. Lowell to Bishop, 7 February 1957. Vassar.

33. Lowell to Bishop, 4 March 1957. Vassar.

34. Lowell to W. D. Snodgrass, 4? March 1957. Princeton.

35. Lowell to Harriet Winslow, 2 March 1957. Houghton.

36. Lowell to Berryman, 1 March 1957. Minnesota.

37. Lowell to Bishop, 7 February 1957. Vassar.

38. Lowell to Harriet Winslow, 10 April 1957. Houghton.

39. Lowell to J. F. Powers, 13 November 1957. J. F. Powers. The letters of Roethke which Lowell quotes from—with slight changes—are among the Lowell Papers at the Houghton.

40. Lowell to Hardwick, 29 March 1957. Houghton.

41. Lowell to Taylors, 17 April 1957. Vanderbilt. "I must have been a noisy and elated guest," he wrote, "and beg your forgiveness for many things. . . . I had the time of my life and treasure it all now in recollection, tranquillity and sobriety."

42. Lowell to Bishop, 29 April 1957. Vassar.

43. "The Art of Poetry: Robert Lowell," Interview with Frederick Seidel in *Paris Review 7* (Winter–Spring 1961); reprinted in *CP*, pp. 235–266.

44. "Dr. Williams," *CP*, pp. 41–42.

45. Draft of "Man and Wife," written May 1957. Houghton.

46. Lowell to Williams, 6 May 1957. Yale.

47. Lowell to Bishop, 29 April 1957. Vassar. "I must tell you," he wrote her, "that I've discovered a new poet, W. D. Snodgrass—he was once one of my Iowa students, and I merely thought him about the best. Now he turns out to be better than anyone except [Philip] Larkin." And Lowell on Larkin: "I have been rereading Philip Larkin lately and once more marvelling vainly at how he builds a poem, never deserting his structure, never overstepping or walling out his total feelings. I feel like an old outmoded battleship." Lowell to Richard Wilbur, 6 April 1960. Amherst.

48. Lowell to Taylor, 21 June 1957. Vanderbilt.

49. Lowell to Bishop, 3 July 1957. Vassar.

50. Lowell to Taylor, 21 June 1957. Vanderbilt.

51. Lowell to Bishop, 3 July 1957. Vassar.

52. Lowell to Robie Macauley, 27 July 1957. Texas.

53. Lowell to Williams, 24 June 1957. Yale.

54. Lowell to Bishop, 19 July 1957. Vassar.

55. Booth, "Summers in Castine," reprinted in Meyers, p. 200.

56. Lowell to Harriet Winslow, 26 July 1957. Houghton.

57. Lowell to Jarrell, 24 October 1957. Berg.

58. "The Two Weeks' Vacation," which recalls his visit to Bishop at Stonington and his rejection of Carley Dawson, placing that visit against the Castine visit in 1957.

59. Lowell to Bishop, 9 August 1957. Vassar.

60. Lowell read these words back to Bishop in his letter of 15 August 1957. Vassar.

61. Lowell to Bishop, 15 August 1957, Vassar.

62. Lowell to Bishop, 3 December 1957. Vassar.

63. "Robert Lowell in Conversation" [with A. Alvarez], *The Review* 8 (August 1963), 36–40, in Meyers, p. 81.

64. Lowell to Bishop, 15 August 1957. Vassar.

65. Lowell to Harriet Winslow, 8 October 1957. Houghton.

66. After Wilbur had written a critique of "Skunk Hour" as part of a symposium, Lowell wrote him that his analysis had brought out things in the poem he either hadn't known or had forgotten "or more probably sensed as shadows." The poem, he offered, was "about a sort of secular dark night of the soul, the only night most of us have ever run into; in the end I climb out with the skunks—the only joyful moment in the poem as one of my cousins said. Still, not quite out, they are skunks and a descent in the hierarchy of being, a

wish one cannot hold for long and must humanize. [George] Herbert in his *Affliction* says 'I wish I could be a tree.' He sees this as a wish to die, though not quite, for trees are somehow unfallen nature." Lowell to Wilbur, 8 January 1962. Amherst.

And to Berryman: "The 'sob in each blood-cell' is meant to have a haggard, romantic profilish exaggerated quality—true, but in the rhetoric of destitution, here the more matter of fact descriptive style gives out, won't do, and there's only the stagey for the despair. Then one leaves it for the skunk vision. Most people take the skunks as cheerful [but] they are horrible blind energy, at the same time . . . a wish and a fear of annihilation, i.e. dropping to a simpler form of life, and a hopeful wish for that simpler energy." 18 March 1962. Minnesota.

67. Lowell to Bishop, 11 September 1957. Vassar.
68. Lowell to Williams, 30 September 1957. Yale.
69. Lowell to Belle Gardner, 27 October 1957. University of Washington.
70. Lowell to Williams, 30 September 1957. Yale.
71. Lowell to Jarrell, 11 October 1957. Berg.
72. Lowell to Jarrell, 24 October 1957. Berg. The poems Lowell was speaking of had appeared in a new anthology, *The New Poets of England and America,* ed. by Donald Hall, Robert Pack, and Louis Simpson. In November 1951 Jarrell had written Lowell from Princeton, where he was then teaching, that he had "a boy at Colorado last summer who was good (an excellent Rilke translation) and most of his poems were excellent though unconscious imitations of you. You'd had him in a class. De Witt Snodgrass, poor ill-named one! When you influence people, when your poems influence theirs, that is—you really mow them down." Jarrell to Lowell, *Jarrell's Letters,* pp. 285–286.
73. Lowell to Bishop, 31 October 1957. Vassar.
74. Lowell to Jarrell, *Jarrell's Letters,* pp. 285–286.
75. Lowell to W. D. Snodgrass, n.d., but early November 1957. Princeton.
76. Lowell to Pound, 8 November 1957. Yale.
77. Lowell to Williams, 3 December 1957. Yale.
78. Lowell to Bishop, 3 December 1957. Vassar.
79. Tate to Lowell, 3 December 1957. Houghton. "They are," Tate added, "of course of great interest to me because I am one of your oldest friends. But they have no public or literary interest."
80. Williams to Lowell, 4 December 1957. Houghton. Ten months later, as he finished up *Life Studies,* Lowell would tell Williams that he liked "to think that often I have crossed the river into your world." Lowell to Williams, 26 September 1958. Yale.
81. Bishop to Lowell, 14 December 1957. Houghton.
82. Lowell to Harriet Winslow, 25 October 1957. Houghton.
83. Hardwick to Harriet Winslow, 22 November 1957. Houghton.
84. Dido Merwin, interview with Hamilton, Hamilton, pp. 238–239.

CHAPTER 11

1. Letter from Ann Adden to Lowell, 31 January 1958. Houghton.
2. Donald Junkins to author, 1992.
3. Early version of "Waking in the Blue," written about 14 December 1957. The original title of the poem was "To Ann Adden (Written during the first week of my voluntary stay at McLean's Mental Hospital)."
4. Hardwick to Harriet Winslow, 2 January 1958. Houghton.
5. Hardwick to Bishop, 20 January 1958. Vassar.
6. Hardwick to Harriet Winslow, 20 January 1958. Houghton.
7. Lowell to Williams, 22 January 1958. Yale.
8. Lowell to Pound, 29 January 1958. Yale. Lowell was not the only poet who in his manic

phase considered running for high political office. In a letter to J. F. Powers in the fall of 1960, he spoke of receiving "two rather sad notes from Ted [Roethke] who's in a sanitarium in Dublin, not as sick as he sometimes sounds but full of plans for a third political party with Stevenson, Mrs. Roosevelt and Archibald MacLeish." 17 October 1960.

9. Hardwick to Harriet Winslow, 2 February 1958. Houghton.
10. Lowell to Isabella Gardner from McLean's, 12 February 1958. University of Washington.
11. Hardwick to Blair and Holly Clark, 16 February 1958. Blair Clark.
12. Hardwick to Harriet Winslow, 15 February 1958. Houghton.
13. Hardwick to Harriet Winslow, 2 March 1958. Houghton.
14. Lowell to Bishop, 15 March 1958. Vassar.
15. Lowell to Taylor, 15 March 1958. Vanderbilt.
16. "Waking in the Blue," *Life Studies,* p. 82.
17. Lowell to Harriet Winslow, 15 March 1958. Houghton.
18. Lowell to Taylor, 15 March 1958. Vanderbilt.
19. Lowell to Roethke, n.d., but March 1958. Seattle.
20. Lowell to Roethke, 6 June 1958. "I feel great kinship with you. We are at times almost one another's shadows passing through the same jungle." Seattle.
21. Lowell to Harriet Winslow, 13 June 1958. Houghton.
22. "An embarrassing day comes to me of the day [sic] we visited the Adams' House and of the many times we got lost, I think ending up on a ten mile peninsula, a stone's throw from Boston, if there'd only been a bridge." Lowell to Pound in Rapallo, 18 March 1962. Yale.
23. Lowell to Bishop, 21 June 1958. Vassar.
24. Lowell to Harriet Winslow, n.d., but about 7 August 1958. Houghton.
25. Lowell to Bishop, 21 June 1958. Vassar.
26. Lowell to Harriet Winslow, 16 September 1958. Houghton.
27. Lowell to Bishop, 18 September 1958. Vassar.
28. Lowell to Taylor, 31 October 1958. "How frightful to die in your mid-fifties! So many people I know have. We too, perhaps. Eliot says he feels as foolish at seventy as he did at seventeen. I'd like to live long enough to say that." Vanderbilt. And in a letter to Bishop of 21 June 1958, Lowell spoke of seeing Eliot dancing "so dashingly" with his new bride "at a Charles River boatclub brawl that he was called 'Elbows Eliot.' " Vassar.
29. Lowell to Taylor, 31 October 1958, Vassar.
30. Lowell to Roethke, 18 September 1958. Seattle.
31. Anne Sexton, "Classroom at Boston University," *Harvard Advocate* 145 (November 1961), 13–14. Reprinted in Meyers, 178–180.
32. Anne Sexton to W. D. Snodgrass, 11 January 1959. Quoted in Diane Middlebrook's *Anne Sexton: A Biography* (Boston: Houghton Mifflin, 1991), p. 93.
33. Sexton to Snodgrass, 1 February 1959. Middlebrook, p. 93.
34. Sexton to Snodgrass, 9 June 1959, Middlebrook, pp. 93–94. "He taught me great," she told Snodgrass. "It was as easy as filling an empty vase."
35. Lowell to Bishop, 16 October 1958. Vassar.
36. Lowell to Caroline Gordon, n.d., but December 1958. University of Washington.
37. Lowell to Bishop, 16 October 1958. Vassar.
38. Lowell to Bishop, 12 December 1958. Vassar.
39. Lowell to J. F. Powers, 13 November 1958. J. F. Powers.
40. Lowell to Bishop, 19 November 1958. Vassar.
41. W. D. Snodgrass: "A Liberal Education: Mentors, Fomentors, Tormentors," *Southern Review* (Summer 1992), 147.
42. Lowell to Bishop, 19 November 1958. Vassar.
43. Williams to Lowell, 24 November 1958. Houghton.
44. Lowell to Williams, 29 November 1958. Yale.

45. Lowell to Bishop, 12 December 1958. Vassar.

46. Lowell to Jason Epstein at Random House, 19 December 1959. Columbia. "We too enjoyed our evening with you at Philip's [Rahv] and left once more nostalgic for New York and the unprovincial mind."

47. Hardwick, "Boston: A Lost Ideal," *Harper's* (December 1959). Reprinted in Hardwick, *A View of My Own,* pp. 145–159.

48. *The Journals of Sylvia Plath,* ed. Frances McCullough (New York: The Dial Press, 1982), p. 292.

49. *Plath Journals,* pp. 300–301.

50. Entry for 20 May 1959, *Plath Journals,* p. 306.

51. Lowell to Williams, 15 February 1959. Yale.

52. Lowell to Bishop, 7 April 1959. Vassar.

53. Lowell to Bishop, 9 February 1959. Vassar.

54. Lowell to Bishop, 5 March 1959. Vassar.

55. Lowell to Jarrell, 17 March 1959. Berg.

56. Lowell to Berryman, 15 March 1959. Minnesota.

57. Lowell to Bishop, 30 March 1959. Vassar. "Sometimes," he added, "I think we will all die fighting some terrible Fascist reform movement."

58. Lowell to Bishop, 7 April 1959. Vassar.

59. Lowell to Allen Ginsberg, 1 April 1959. Columbia.

60. Ginsberg to Lowell, 5 April 1959. Houghton.

61. Lowell to Ginsberg, 10 April 1959. Columbia. Sixteen months later he told Selden Rodman that American poetry seemed then "caught between beat mush and an academic veneer." Most of the Beats seemed "chaotic and artless" to him, while "the soberer ones" were "usually dull." Academic poets, on the other hand, were "very able, heavy and rather alike. I like Wilbur and Merwin, Adrienne Rich, and more than any Snodgrass. I also enjoy Ginsberg with a good many reservations and find him the best of his group. I like him less than Snodgrass and Philip Larkin. I find Starbuck a rather wrenched, memorable and small poet, and like another poet Ann[e] Sexton better." And while he thought *Song of Myself* "the longest good poem by an American," he did not want to make a cause of Whitman, who was no better, finally, "than Frost, or Eliot, or Crane, or even Stevens or Dickenson [sic]." It was not a matter of "one greatest poet, but handfuls almost of considerable ones." Besides, were "Whitman's beliefs worth more than Baudelaire's, or worth more for Americans?" In the long run, each writer was "sunk in the dust and mire of his own powers, likings, chances etc.," and "no line laid down by anyone" would do. Lowell to Selden Rodman, 14 August 1960. Selden Rodman.

62. Jacket of *Life Studies.*

63. Philip Larkin, "Collected Poems," *Manchester Guardian Weekly,* 21 May 1959, p. 10.

64. John Thompson, "Two Poets," *Kenyon Review* 21 (Summer 1959), 482–490.

65. Lowell to Tate, 22 October 1959. Princeton.

66. "Elegy in the Classroom," from *To Bedlam and Part Way Back* (Boston: Houghton Mifflin, 1960), p. 47.

67. Flannery O'Connor to Caroline Gordon, 10 May 1959. *The Habit of Being,* pp. 331–332.

68. Tate to Lowell, 8 May 1959. Princeton.

69. Allen Tate to Andrew Lytle, 25 May 1959. "Caroline is blocking the divorce. I waited to see whether she would give me any human reason, not merely the reason of the Church. Could she bring herself to say that she wanted us back again, instead of the theological line, I would have a very different view. But she is using the Church to 'save' me. All this has been complicated by a new maniacal outburst of Cal Lowell's. He has had another violent breakdown, at the pitch of which he telephoned Caroline several times and urged her to save me from a Boston divorcée [Isabella Gardner]. I like this woman, and will continue to

do so, but I could no more plan to marry her than I could fly, though I am frank to say I'd like to. The lady is a cousin of Cal's and an old friend whom he trusted. I am the object of his hostility. The Lowell vulgarity reached its height when he told C. [Caroline] that the lady wasn't very rich—that I could look around and do better." *The Lytle-Tate Letters,* p. 274.

70. Hardwick to Tate, 1 June 1959. Princeton.
71. Hardwick to Bishop, 24 June 1959. Vassar.
72. Lowell to Edmund Wilson, 11 May 1959. Yale.
73. Lowell to Bishop, 24 July 1959. Vassar.
74. Lowell to Tate, 22 October 1959. Princeton.
75. Lowell to Harriet Winslow, 9 August 1959. Houghton.
76. Lowell to William Meredith, 18 September 1959. William Meredith.
77. Lowell to Bishop, 11 April 1959. Vassar.
78. Donald Junkins to author, 1992.
79. Lowell to Berryman, 19 September 1959. Minnesota.
80. Lowell to Chard Powers Smith, 3 October 1959. Yale.
81. Lowell to Berryman, 19 September 1959. Minnesota.
82. Lowell to Bishop, 3 October 1959. Vassar.
83. Lowell to Harriet Winslow, 12 October 1959. Houghton.
84. Stanley Kunitz, "The Sense of a Life," *New York Times Book Review,* 16 October 1977. Reprinted in Meyers, pp. 230–235.
85. Lowell to Harriet Winslow, 8 January 1960. Houghton.
86. Lowell to Tate, 13 January 1960. Princeton.
87. Lowell to Harriet Winslow, 8 January 1960. Houghton.
88. Flannery O'Connor quoted Lowell's comments in a letter she wrote to the novelist John Hawkes on 2 June 1960. Lowell had sent the letter to O'Connor in late January 1960. She was sending Lowell's comments on, she said, because she thought they might help Hawkes with *The Lime Twig,* which he was writing at the time. *The Habit of Being,* p. 399.
89. Lowell to Jarrell, 30 January 1960. Berg. Nothing the Americans or English were writing in 1960 seemed to hold him, he confessed. "I have to bend and bend to enjoy new English and American poems, but easily become pious and uncritical reading Pasternak and Montale."
90. Lowell to Meredith, 3 March 1960. William Meredith.
91. "An Interview with Frederick Seidel," *Paris Review* XXV (Winter–Spring 1961), 57–95; reprinted in *CP,* pp. 235–266.
92. Lowell to Meredith, 3 March 1960. William Meredith.
93. Typescript of remarks at Houghton.
94. Lowell to Harriet Winslow, 26 April 1960. Houghton.
95. Donald Junkins to author, 1992.
96. Bishop to Lowell, 29 June 1960. Houghton.
97. Lowell to Bishop, 7 April 1959. Vassar.
98. Lowell to Taylor, 27 June 1960. Vanderbilt.

PART III

CHAPTER 12

1. Lowell to Taylor, 27 June 1960. Vanderbilt.
2. "On Translating Phèdre," *Racine/Phaedra: A Verse Translation by Robert Lowell* (New York: Farrar, Straus & Giroux, 1961), pp. 7–8. It may be of interest to note that Lowell dedicated this play, which is in part an exorcism of his mother's hold on him, to his surrogate mother, Harriet Winslow.

3. In late July Lowell wrote Edmund Wilson that he'd "finished a version of Racine's *Phèdre,* somehow not quite sounding in earnest when it gets into English heroic couplets, though something of the original's fierce air-tight reasoning remains." Lowell to Wilson, 28 July 1960. Yale. And to Cousin Harriet the following day: "It's all but impossible not to sound completely rhetorical and silly in [Racine's] language, in the shadow of his language slammed into English." 29 July 1960. Houghton.

4. Lowell to Taylor, 27 June 1960. Vanderbilt.

5. Lowell to Harriet Winslow, 1 July 1960. Houghton.

6. Lowell to Edmund Wilson, 28 July 1960. Yale.

7. Lowell to Harriet Winslow, 29 July 1960. Houghton.

8. Lowell to Harriet Winslow, 8 September 1960. Houghton.

9. Lowell to William Meredith, 30 March 1960. William Meredith.

10. Elizabeth Hardwick, "The Insulted and Injured: Books about Poverty," *Harper's,* collected in *A View of My Own,* p. 182.

11. Lowell to T. S. Eliot, 12 October 1960. Valerie Eliot.

12. Lowell to Peter Taylor, 12 October 1960. Vanderbilt.

13. Lowell to Adrienne Rich, 18 November 1960. Radcliffe.

14. Lowell to Harriet Winslow, 4 November 1960. Houghton.

15. Lowell to Adrienne Rich, 18 November 1960. Radcliffe. The Met tenors looked "like goons in the comic strip criminals," a bemused Lowell wrote Taylor in December. "I too sit in the dark unnoticed at the Met where there's no bad language. . . . No one speaks anything but German and Neapolitan. The directors say in heavy voices, "It's Lowell . . . no, Meredith, right?" Lowell to Taylor, 17 December 1960. Vanderbilt.

16. Meredith, interview with Hamilton, 1981. Hamilton, p. 283.

17. Lowell to Adrienne Rich, 18 November 1960, Radcliffe.

18. Lowell to Allen Tate, 18 November 1960. Princeton.

19. Lowell to Hardwick, 28 December 1960. Houghton.

20. Hardwick to Harriet Winslow, 10 January 1961. Houghton.

21. Lowell to Bishop, 15 February 1961. Vassar.

22. Hardwick to Harriet Winslow, 10 January 1961. Houghton.

23. Lowell to Bishop, 15 February 1961, Radcliffe.

24. Lowell to Eliot, 28 October 1960.

25. Lowell to Bishop, 15 February 1961. Vassar.

26. Lowell to Eliot, 28 October 1960. Valerie Eliot.

27. Lowell to Bishop, 15 February 1961. Vassar.

28. Blair Clark to Hamilton, 1980, in Hamilton, p. 285. Also interview with author, 1992.

29. William Meredith to Adrienne Rich and Philip Booth, 17 March 1961. William Meredith.

30. Hardwick to Allen Tate and Isabella Gardner, 18 April 1961. University of Washington.

31. Lowell to Bishop, 10 March 1962. Vassar.

32. Lowell to Allen Tate and Isabella Gardner, 22 May 1961. University of Washington.

33. Lowell to Hardwick, 16 June 1961. Houghton.

34. Hardwick to Lowell, 17 June 1961. Houghton.

35. Lowell to Bishop, 27 June 1961. Vassar.

36. *Imitations* (New York: Farrar, Straus & Giroux, 1961), p. 149.

37. Lowell to Powers, 17 October 1960. J. F. Powers.

38. Lowell to Harriet Winslow, 3 July 1961. Houghton.

39. Booth, "Summers in Castine," Meyers, p. 201.

40. Lowell to Harriet Winslow, 31 July 1961. Houghton.

41. Postcard from Lowell to Meredith, 7? August 1961. William Meredith.

42. Lowell to Bishop, 7 August 1961. Vassar.

43. Lowell to Bishop, 7 August 1961. Vassar.

44. *Ibid.*

45. Lowell to Taylor, 7 August 1961. Vanderbilt.

46. Lowell to Meredith, 8 September 1961. William Meredith.
47. Lowell to Adrienne Rich, 8 September 1961. Radcliffe.
48. Hardwick to Adrienne Rich, added to Lowell's letter of 8 September 1961. Radcliffe.
49. Lowell to Bishop, 3 October 1961. Vassar.
50. Lowell to Meredith, 20 October 1961. William Meredith.
51. Lowell to Mary McCarthy, 21 October 1961. Vassar.
52. Lowell to Jarrell, 7 November 1961. Berg. "I remember once, the last time at Greensboro [March 1959], I think, when you came into my room and began talking out of a blue sky about the ills of our culture, and Mary [Jarrell] said that I worried about personal matters while you were upset about the world. The world is very much under my skin and really seems like a murderous nightmare when one looks outward. I am sick of nations armed to the teeth. It can't be true we must raise a finger or a whisper!"
53. "Fall 1961," *For the Union Dead,* pp. 11–12.
54. Lowell to Jarrell, 7 November 1961. Berg.
55. Lowell to A. Alvarez, 7 November 1961. Quoted in Hamilton, pp. 292–293.
56. Lowell to Isabella Gardner, 10 October 1961. University of Washington. In early December, Lowell came down with chicken pox, so that he looked, he told Tate, rather like Sinclair Lewis "as described in reviews of [Mark] Schorer's biography." Lowell to Tate, 8 December 1961. Princeton.
57. Lowell to Bishop, 13 January 1962. Vassar.
58. Lowell to Taylor, n.d., but 13 January 1962. Vanderbilt.
59. *Ibid.*
60. Brad Gooch, *City Poet: The Life and Times of Frank O'Hara* (New York: Knopf, 1993), pp. 386–387.
61. Lowell to Richard Wilbur, 8 January 1962. Amherst. "I don't think you erred in staying at Wesleyan," Lowell added. "I think of John Ransom's blissful freedom from push, hurry and the wrong sort of ambition at Kenyon."
62. Lowell to Bishop, 10 March 1962. Vassar.
63. Lowell to Berryman, 18 March 1962. Minnesota. "I feel the time has come for some kind of Yeatsian somersault," he added, meaning that it was time to strip away the old style and replace it with the new. Rahv's sons in Lowell's dream of them were purely imaginary, since Rahv was childless.
64. Lowell to Bishop, 18 March 1962. Vassar.
65. Lowell to Bishop, 18 March 1962. Vassar.
66. Lowell to Alfred Kazin, 18 March 1962. Berg.
67. Lowell to Ezra and Dorothy Pound, 18 March 1962. Yale.
68. Lowell to Kazin, 18 March 1962. Berg.
69. Lowell to Ezra and Dorothy Pound, 18 March 1962. Yale.
70. Lowell to Bishop, 14 April 1962. Vassar. A new note enters here: the beginnings of what Lowell jokingly called his "Nineteenth-century decline." Puerto Rico had dissolved his angst and piles, "but the day after I got back I had diarrhea, an ear ache, a sore throat, then lumbago—all now gone."
71. Lowell to Edmund Wilson, 31 March 1962. Yale.
72. Lowell to Bishop, 14 April 1962. Vassar. "Also saw Jim Powers, and had a marvellous time," Lowell added, "talking ironic banter with him, just as though no time had passed. Wonderful moment, John [Berryman] in his exaggerated way and unbelievable accent, saying 'Why this man is the best *prose* writer in *America.* He is as good as *Checkov.* . . . Then Jim smoking, saying slowly, face unchanged, 'I don't know, I always thought Checkov wrote too much.' Jim, buried in St. Cloud all these years, is as confident as Randall, though all is irony. Now his novel [*Morte D'Urban*] is coming out. 11 years and should be a masterpiece."
73. This was the situation in the American university thirty years ago.
74. Lowell to Bishop, 14 April 1962. Vassar.

75. Lowell to Bishop, 15 May 1962. Vassar.

76. Lowell to Edmund Wilson, 31 May 1962. Yale.

77. Lowell to Bishop, 14 April 1962. Vassar.

78. Derek Walcott, interview with Edward Hirsch in *Paris Review,* Vol. 28, 101 (Winter, 1986), 225–227.

79. What follows is taken in large part from the diary notes Bishop kept during the Lowells' Brazilian stay. These handwritten notes are at Vassar. Also, cf. Hamilton's interview with Keith Botsford, in Hamilton, pp. 300–303.

80. Telegram dated 8:30 P.M., 10 September 1962. Vassar.

CHAPTER 13

1. Blair Clark to author, 1992.

2. Lowell to William Alfred, n.d., but September 1962. William Alfred.

3. Lowell to Bishop, 3 November 1962. Vassar.

4. Lowell to Berryman, 21 November 1962. Minnesota.

5. Lowell to Bishop, 24 December 1962. Vassar.

6. "Caligula," *For the Union Dead,* pp. 49–51.

7. Lowell to Bishop, 24 December 1962, Vassar.

8. *Ibid.*

9. Lowell to Keith Botsford, 25 January 1963. Yale.

10. Lowell to Harriet Winslow, 26 December 1962. Houghton.

11. Lowell to Harriet Winslow, 23 January 1963. Houghton.

12. *Ibid.*

13. Lowell to Keith Botsford, 25 January 1963. Yale.

14. Lowell to Bishop, 10 February 1963. Vassar.

15. Lowell, *New York Review of Books,* 29 August 1963. *CP,* pp. 8–11. "I suppose what I liked about Frost's poems when I read them thirty years ago was their description of the New England country, a world I knew mostly from summer and weekend dips into it. It was a boy's world, fresher, grainier, tougher, and freer than the city where I had to live." He was, Lowell noted, "our last poet who could honestly ignore the new techniques that were to shatter the crust."

16. "Dr. Williams," *CP,* p. 44.

17. Lowell to Bishop, 27 October 1963. Vassar.

18. "Sylvia Plath's *Ariel,*" *New York Review of Books* (12 May 1966), in *CP,* pp. 122–125.

19. Lowell to Bishop, 10 March 1963. Vassar.

20. Lowell to Bishop, 10 February 1963. Vassar.

21. Lowell to Bishop, 23 January 1963. Vassar.

22. Lowell to J. F. Powers, 28 May 1963. J. F. Powers.

23. Lowell to Bishop, 8 May 1963. Vassar.

24. Lowell to Marianne Moore, 10 June 1963. Rosenbach Library.

25. Lowell to Anne Sexton, 25 June 1963. Texas.

26. Lowell to Bishop, 5 July 1963. Vassar.

27. "Soft Wood," *For the Union Dead,* pp. 63–64.

28. Lowell to T. S. Eliot, 3 September 1963. Valerie Eliot.

29. Mary Jarrell, "The Group of Two," quoted in *Jarrell's Letters,* pp. 476–477.

30. Lowell to Mary McCarthy, 7 August 1963. Vassar.

31. Lowell to Hardwick, 24 July 1963. Houghton.

32. Lowell to Theodore Roethke, 10 July 1963. Washington.

33. Ms. draft of poem for Roethke. Houghton.

34. Lowell to Mary McCarthy, 7 August 1963. Vassar.

35. Lowell to Bishop, 8 May 1963. Vassar.

36. Lowell to Bishop, 12 August 1963. Vassar.
37. Prose draft among poetry mss. Houghton.
38. Lowell to Bishop, 11 September 1963. Vassar.
39. "The Severed Head," *For the Union Dead,* pp. 52–53.
40. Derek Walcott, "On Robert Lowell," *New York Review of Books,* 1 March 1984, p. 28.
41. Lowell to Bishop, 20 September 1963. Vassar.
42. Lowell to Mary McCarthy, 2 October 1963. Vassar.
43. Lowell to Bishop, 27 October 1963. Vassar.
44. "The New York Intellectual," *Notebook* (New York: Farrar, Straus & Giroux, 1969), p. 187.
45. "In the American Grain," *Notebook,* pp. 187–188.
46. Lowell to Bishop, 24 January 1964. Vassar.
47. Lowell to Adrienne Rich, 25 February 1964. Radcliffe.
48. William Meredith to Hamilton, Hamilton, pp. 306–307. "Cal is still here at home," Hardwick wrote Mary McCarthy on November 30, "and we have hopes that he will pull out of this excitement without any great upheaval." A trip to Chicago "with a number of fellow poets" had helped to bring this latest episode on, she thought, "and then the horrible assassination didn't help, of course." Hardwick to McCarthy. 30 November 1963. Vassar.
49. Lowell to T. S. Eliot, 4 March 1964. Valerie Eliot.
50. Read at the Library of Congress, 3 January 1964. Published in *Lincoln and the Gettysburg Address,* Commemorative Papers, ed. Allan Nevins (Urbana: University of Illinois Press, 1964). Reprinted in *CP,* pp. 165–166.
51. Hardwick to Tate, 9 January 1964. Princeton.
52. Lowell to Adrienne Rich, 25 February 1964. Radcliffe.
53. Lowell to Mary McCarthy, 20 February 1964. Vassar.
54. Interview with Richard Wilbur, 1993.
55. Lowell to Mary McCarthy, 20 February 1964. Radcliffe.
56. Lowell to Bishop, 24 January 1964. Vassar.
57. A. Alvarez, *Encounter* 24 (February 1965), 39–43. Reprinted in Meyers, pp. 99–108.
58. Lowell to Mary McCarthy, 20 February 1964. Vassar.
59. Lowell to Adrienne Rich, 25 February 1964. Radcliffe.
60. Lowell to T. S. Eliot, 4 March 1964. Valerie Eliot.
61. Lowell to Richard Wilbur, 10 March 1964. Amherst.
62. Lowell to Jarrell, 11 May 1964. Berg.
63. Lowell to William Meredith, 6 May 1964. William Meredith.
64. Lowell to Adrienne Rich, 3 June 1964. Radcliffe.
65. Lowell to Bishop, 8 May 1963. Vassar.
66. Lowell to Bishop, 15 June 1964. Vassar.
67. Lowell to Clark, 1 August 1964. Quoted in Hamilton, p. 313.
68. Lowell to Bishop, 10 August 1964. Vassar.
69. *Ibid.*
70. "Talk with Robert Lowell," *New York Times Book Review,* 4 October 1964, pp. 34–38. Reprinted in Meyers, pp. 84–90. And here is Lowell five years later on the fading erotics of New York:

> *Exhaust and airconditioning klir in the city. . . .*
> *The real motive for my trip is dentistry,*
> *a descending scale: long ago, I used to drive*
> *to New York to see a lover, next the analyst,*
> *an editor, then a lawyer . . . time's dwindling choice.*

"For Mary McCarthy 3," *History* (1973), p. 158.
71. Lowell to Bishop, 3 October 1964. Vassar.
72. Lowell to Bishop, 16 November 1964. Vassar.

73. Lowell to Bishop, 3 October 1964. Vassar.
74. *Ibid.*
75. Jonathan Miller, interview with Hamilton, 1980, in Hamilton, p. 314.
76. W. D. Snodgrass, "In Praise of Robert Lowell," *New York Review of Books* 3 (3 December 1964), pp. 8–10.
77. Randall Jarrell, "A Masterpiece," *New York Times,* 29 November 1964, sec. II, p. 3.
78. Lowell to Bishop, 16 November 1964. Vassar.
79. Lowell's response appeared in *The Village Voice* for 19 November 1964, p. 4.
80. Lowell to Bishop, 16 November 1964. Vassar.
81. Jonathan Miller to Hamilton, Hamilton, p. 314.
82. Stafford to Lowell, 6 May 1964. Houghton. In spite of the elevated language of Stafford's response to Lowell here, among her and Joe Liebling's friends she had taken to referring to her first husband as the Cassius Clay of literature.
83. "Cal is at work on something for me at Wesleyan," Stafford wrote Taylor in late May, "but that sounds very scary because there are intellectuals up there. Geographically it would be lovely, half way between Boston and New York, but I don't know how I'd attend to Edmund Wilson and Dick Wilbur." Stafford to Taylor, 26 May 1964. Vanderbilt.
84. Jean Stafford to Nancy Gibney, n.d. Quoted in Goodman, pp. 283–284.
85. Richard Wilbur in letter to author, 12 October 1992.

CHAPTER 14

1. Hardwick to Blair Clark, n.d., early January 1965. Blair Clark.
2. Lowell to Hardwick, 26 January 1965. Houghton.
3. Lowell to Hardwick, 9 February 1965. Houghton.
4. Hardwick to Lowell, n.d., but about 11 February 1965. Houghton.
5. Lowell to Bishop, 25 February 1965. Vassar.
6. Lowell to Charles Monteith, 26 February 1965. Copy at Houghton.
7. Lowell to Robert Giroux, 8 April 1965. Cf. "Homage to a Poet," *Harvard Advocate* 113 (November 1979), in Meyers, p. 259.
8. Lowell to Bishop, 25 February 1965. Vassar.
9. Lowell to Jarrell, 29 April 1965. Berg.
10. Lowell to Bishop, 15 June 1965. Vassar.
11. Lowell to Bishop, 25 February 1966. Vassar.
12. Blair Clark to Hamilton, 1980, in Hamilton, p. 320.
13. The first drafts of the letter, now at the Houghton, are dated May 30. Letter reprinted in *CP*, pp. 370–371.
14. Eric F. Goldman, *The Tragedy of Lyndon Johnson* (New York: Knopf, 1969), p. 429.
15. Lowell to President L. B. Johnson, reprinted in *CP*, p. 371.
16. Lowell to Bishop, 15 June 1965. Vassar.
17. Lowell to J. F. Powers, 6 October 1965. J. F. Powers. Powers's review of his friend Gordon Zahn's *In Solitary Witness: The Life and Death of Franz Jägerstätter,* appeared in the July issue of *Commentary,* 89–92. Jägerstätter was beheaded in Berlin on 9 August 1943.
18. "A Conversation with Robert Lowell," Ian Hamilton, *The Review* 26 (Summer 1971), 10–29. Reprinted in Meyers, p. 156.
19. *Ibid.*
20. Lowell to Bishop, 16 July 1965. Vassar.
21. Draft of "Waking Early Sunday Morning." Houghton.
22. "Waking Early Sunday Morning," *Near the Ocean* (New York: Farrar, Straus & Giroux, 1971), pp. 13–16.
23. Lowell to Bishop, 16 August 1965. Vassar.

24. Booth, "Summers in Castine," Meyers, pp. 211–212.

25. Lowell to Bishop, 16 August 1965. Vassar.

26. "The Opposite House," *Near the Ocean,* p. 22.

27. "Central Park," *Near the Ocean,* pp. 23–24.

28. Lowell to Eleanor Taylor, 6 October 1965. Vanderbilt.

29. *Jarrell's Letters,* p. 521.

30. Lowell to Bishop, 19 October 1965. Vassar.

31. *New York Review of Books,* 25 November 1965. Reprinted in *CP,* pp. 90–98.

32. "Randall Jarrell," *History* (New York: Fallar, Straus & Giroux, 1973), p. 135.

33. Alan Williamson, "Robert Lowell: A Reminiscence," *Harvard Advocate* 113 (November 1979), reprinted in Meyers, pp. 266–267.

34. Jacqueline Kennedy to Robert Lowell, 24 November 1965. Houghton.

35. Taylor to Tate, 7 December 1965. Princeton.

36. Tate to Taylor, 14 December 1965. Princeton.

37. W. H. Auden to George Monteith, 20 December 1965. Hamilton, p. 345.

38. Jacqueline Kennedy to Lowell, 30 December 1965. Houghton.

39. Lowell to Bishop, 25 February 1966. Vassar.

40. Robert Kennedy to Lowell, 18 February 1966. Houghton. The passage from Pushkin had been quoted by Edmund Wilson in his *The Bit Between My Teeth.*

41. Lowell to Robert Kennedy, 25 February 1966. RFK Papers. In Arthur M. Schlesinger, Jr., *Robert Kennedy and His Times* (Boston: Houghton Mifflin, 1978). Quoted in Hamilton, p. 377.

42. Snodgrass: "A Liberal Education: Mentors, Fomentors, Tormentors," *Southern Review* (Summer 1992), 128.

43. Lowell to William Meredith, 16 July 1966. William Meredith.

44. Lowell to Bishop, 16 July 1966. Vassar.

45. Lowell to Bishop, 15 September 1966. Vassar.

46. Lowell to Berryman, 5 November 1966. Minnesota.

47. Lowell to Philip Booth, 10 October 1966. Quoted in Hamilton, p. 351.

48. Williamson, *op. cit.,* in Meyers, pp. 269 ff.

49. Robert Seigel to author, 1993.

50. As good a teacher as Lowell was, Alan Williamson has written, Lowell's "taste had its rigidities. He was partial . . . to a kind of generic 1960s poem vaguely influenced by his own style in *Life Studies:* a freshly observed detail in every line, but a quiet, everyday, even slightly depressed, tone of voice. Poems influenced by his own high style, or any hermetic mode, left him deeply ambivalent ('good lines, but . . .'); he was also unsure how plain poetry could dare to be, in the interests of ascetic truthfulness ('underenergized'). The same conflicts expressed themselves in his judgments of his peers and predecessors: fascinated irresolution over Hart Crane; high praise for poets like [Alan] Dugan and Snodgrass; gingerliness toward Ginsburg, the Black Mountain School, [John] Ashbery (though he admired *Kaddish,* and had a late change of heart with Ashbery, over 'Self Portrait in a Convex Mirror')." Williamson, *op. cit.,* in Meyers, p. 270.

51. Robert Seigel to author, 1993.

52. Grey Gowrie to Hamilton, 1980, Hamilton, pp. 356–357.

53. William Alfred to author, 1991.

54. Frank Parker to author. Also, cf. Xandra Gowrie's recollections in Hamilton, p. 356.

55. Lowell to Bishop, 26 February 1967. Vassar.

56. Lowell to Bishop, 2 March 1967. Vassar.

57. Lowell to Bishop, 10 March 1967. Vassar.

58. Lowell to Bishop, 3 October 1966. Vassar.

59. John Gale, "Keeping the Lid on the World," *Observer* (London), 12 March 1967. Reprinted in Meyers, pp. 115–118.

60. *Prometheus Bound* (New York: Farrar, Straus & Giroux, 1967), p. 54.

61. "Author's Note," *Prometheus Bound,* p. v.
62. Lowell to Bishop, 14 June 1967. Vassar.
63. Lowell's Introduction, 17 May 1967, in *CP,* pp. 119–121.
64. Reported in the *New York Times* for 18 May 1967.
65. Lowell to Taylor, 4 June 1967. Vanderbilt.
66. Booth, "Summers in Castine," Meyers, p. 206.
67. Lowell to Adrienne Rich, n.d., but August 1967. Radcliffe.
68. Draft of "Afterthought" for *Notebook 1967–68.* Houghton.
69. Lowell to Mary McCarthy, 16 December 1967. Vassar.
70. *Notebook 1967–68,* p. 3.
71. Lowell to Adrienne Rich, n.d., but August 1967. Radcliffe.
72. Lowell to Eleanor Taylor, 7 October 1967. Vanderbilt.
73. Booth, "Summers in Castine," Meyers, pp. 209–210.
74. Lowell to Eleanor Taylor, 7 October 1967. Vanderbilt.
75. Lowell to Bishop, 9 October 1967. Vassar.
76. Lowell to Alfred Kazin, 18 March 1962. Berg.
77. Cf. Mailer's portrait of Lowell in *Armies of the Night* (New York: New American Library, 1968). Reprinted in Meyers, pp. 181–195.
78. "3. The March," *Notebook 1967–68,* p. 27.
79. Lowell was in Manchester, Massachusetts, visiting his Aunt Sarah when he first read Mailer's portrait of himself. It was from there that he wrote Lizzie his quip. In 1971, Lowell told Ian Hamilton that Mailer's picture of him wasn't "quite true. I am made more goy, New England, aristocratical and various things, a Quixote in the retinue of Sancho Panza," though he still thought it "the best, almost the only thing written about me as a living person. Later, I wrote [Mailer] I hoped we'd remain as good friends in life as we were in fiction." *The Review* 26 (Summer 1971), 10–29, reprinted in Meyers, p. 166.
80. Lowell to V. S. Naipaul, "Et in America Ego—The American Poet Robert Lowell Talks to the Novelist V. S. Naipaul," *The Listener* 82 (4 September 1969), reprinted in Meyers, p. 144.
81. Lowell to Mary McCarthy, 16 December 1967. Vassar.
82. "Che Guevara," *Notebook* 1967–68, p. 26.
83. "Caracas," *Notebook 1967–68,* p. 26.

CHAPTER 15

1. Lowell to Bishop, 12 January 1968. Vassar.
2. "Mexico 3," *Notebook 1967–68,* p. 59.
3. "Mexico 9," *Notebook 1967–68,* p. 62.
4. Lowell to Bishop, 12 January 1968. Vassar.
5. "My Death 1," *Notebook 1967–68,* p. 78.
6. Lowell to Bishop, 12 January 1968. Vassar.
7. Lowell to Mary McCarthy, 5 February 1968. Vassar.
8. Lowell quoted these sentences in his letter to Mary McCarthy of 5 February 1968. Vassar.
9. *Ibid.*
10. Richard Gilman interview with Lowell, "Life Offers No Neat Conclusions," *New York Times,* 5 May 1968. Reprinted in Meyers, pp. 119–123.
11. Lowell to Taylor, 16 March 1968. Vanderbilt.
12. Lowell to Mary McCarthy, 19 April 1968. Vassar.
13. Lowell to Taylor, 16 March 1968. Vanderbilt.
14. Lowell in *New York Times,* 28 March 1968.
15. Lowell to Richard Gilman, *New York Times,* 5 May 1968. The interview had taken place on Easter Sunday, April 14. Meyers, p. 122.

16. Lowell to Taylor, 16 March 1968. Vanderbilt.
17. Lowell to Hardwick, 22 March 1968. Houghton.
18. "April 8, 1968: 1. Two Walls," *Notebook 1967–68*, p. 87.
19. Lowell to Mary McCarthy, 19 April 1968. Vassar.
20. An acrimonious dispute between Lowell and Diana Trilling would continue over several issues of *Commentary,* beginning in the fall of '68 and going on into the spring of '69. Trilling had accused Lowell of being soft on student violence, and Lowell responded by dismissing Trilling's "rather majestic irony about my 'radical piety,' and my signing petitions, appearing at rallies," as if he'd acted "to draw applause from the young, get in fashion, or whatever." At least, he added, she would "not be indicted for activism. He wished he might be "a hundred percent pro-student," but a "photograph of students marching through Rome with banners showing a young Clarke-Gable-style Stalin and a very fat old Mao," had given him pause. "No cause," he added, "is pure enough to support these faces. We are fond of saying that our students have more generosity, idealism and freshness than any other group. Even granting this, still they are only us younger, and the violence that has betrayed our desires will also betray theirs if they trust to it."
21. Lowell to Adrienne Rich, 18 June 1968. Radcliffe.
22. "The Restoration," *Notebook 1967–68*, p. 110.
23. Lowell in Oregon, 26–28 May 1968. Cf. Jean Stein and George Plimpton, eds., *American Journey: The Times of Robert F. Kennedy* (New York: Harcourt Brace Jovanovich, 1970), quoted in Hamilton, p. 378.
24. Arthur M. Schlesinger, Jr., *Robert Kennedy and His Times,* quoting Lowell, pp. 910–911.
25. Andreas Teuber, special assistant for McCarthy's campaign, quoted in *American Journey;* Hamilton, pp. 380–381.
26. Blair Clark to Hamilton, 1979. Hamilton, p. 381. Also Clark to author, 1992.
27. Blair Clark to author, 1992.
28. "R.F.K.," *Notebook 1967–68*, p. 118.
29. Lowell to Donald Junkins, 21 September 1968. Donald Junkins.
30. Lowell to President Brewster of Yale, 30 May 1968. Houghton.
31. Lowell to Adrienne Rich, 18 June 1968. Radcliffe.
32. Lowell to Eberhart, 24 June 1968. Dartmouth.
33. Lowell to Harriet, 28 June 1968. Texas.
34. Lowell to Harriet, 13 July 1968. Texas.
35. Lowell to Harriet, 30 July 1968. Texas. Cf. also Lowell's comment to Taylor four months before about his daughter's "contrapuntal composition, so intricate she is unable to play it. What can be played sounds post-Schoenberg, but that may be due to her faulty command of what Allen [Tate] would call traditional skills." Lowell to Taylor, 16 March 1968. Vanderbilt.
36. "Summer: These Winds," *Notebook 1967–68*, p. 141.
37. Lowell to Adrienne Rich, 10 July 1968. Radcliffe.
38. "The Spock etc. Sentences," *Notebook 1967–68*, p. 132.
39. "For Michael Tate: August 1967–July 1968," *Notebook 1967–68*, p. 149.
40. Lowell to Tate, 14 July 1968. Princeton.
41. "The Races: 1. August," *Notebook 1967–68*, p. 136.
42. "Munich, 1938," *Notebook 1967–68*, p. 25. The poem is dated August 22, 1968. In a letter to Bishop five years earlier, Lowell wrote that he'd just "spent a week-end with the Ransoms at Kenyon. Before my reading John and I went to an exhibition of African masks." Lowell to Bishop, 8 May 1963. Vassar.
43. Lowell to Adrienne Rich, 23 August 1968. Radcliffe.
44. Lowell to Bishop, 21 February 1968. Vassar.
45. Lowell to Adrienne Rich, 23 August 1968, Radcliffe.
46. Lowell to Bishop, 5 September 1968. Vassar.
47. "The Races: 4. Fear in Chicago," *Notebook 1967–68*, p. 137. The poem is dated August 26, 1968.

48. Senator Ralph Yarborough to Lowell, 31 August 1968. Houghton.
49. "We Are Here to Preserve Disorder," *Notebook 1967–68,* p. 138.
50. "After the Convention," *Notebook 1967–68,* p. 138. Dated September 1, 1968.
51. Lowell to Bishop, 5 September 1968. Vassar.
52. Lowell to Philip Booth, 30 September 1968. Philip Booth.
53. Perhaps one of the best descriptions of what Lowell himself was after in his historical portraits was provided in a letter to Edmund Wilson praising him for his Civil War portraits in *Patriotic Gore.* "I am braced by your portraits," he'd written Wilson seven years before. "I see now, I think, that all your life you have been writing a sort of *Plutarch's Lives.* . . . One might use the phrase: moral aristocrats for them. By this, I mean some queer tense twist of principle, changed to virtue by having been lived through the undefinable multiplicity of experience. No two persons are alike, all are glaringly imperfect, still there are heroes. You can see I've just come from your [Oliver Wendell] Holmes, whose principles mean nothing to me literally, but whose life seems so shining and cantless. Pardon this sprawl, and let me salute you, dear old fellow questioning Calvinist, on your triumphant book." Lowell to Wilson, 31 March 1962. Yale.
54. Lowell to Berryman, 22 September 1968. Minnesota.
55. Lowell to Taylor, 5 November 1968. Vanderbilt.
56. "November 6," *Notebook 1967–68,* p. 140.
57. Lowell to Tate, 30 December 1968. Princeton.
58. Lowell to Hardwick, 9 January 1969. Houghton.
59. Cf. Lowell's poem, "Utopia for Racoons," with its surrealistic image of his "goiter expert" smiling "like a racoon," then two other racoons wearing "stethoscopes to count the pulse / of their geiger-counter and their thyroid scan" as they "sit sipping my radioactive iodine / from a small lead bottle with two metal straws." *Notebook 1967–68,* p. 82.
60. Lowell to Marcia Nardi, n.d., but probably late February 1969. Collection of E. M. O'Neil.
61. Lowell to Hardwick, 6 March 1969. Houghton.
62. Hardwick to Lowell, 9 March 1969. Houghton.
63. Lowell to Hardwick, 10 March 1969. Houghton.
64. Lowell to Anne Fremantle, 9 August 1968. Berg.
65. Israel 2, *History,* p. 30. At a dinner at Barbara and Jason Epstein's Manhattan apartment in late October 1967, Lowell questioned Edmund Wilson about the Bible, which Lowell was then teaching at Harvard. "His line," Wilson noted, "when he had talked about it on a previous occasion, had been 'Wasn't it just a lot of old Jewish folk tales?'; now, he would keep reiterating: 'Edmund, what do [you] think are the best things in the Bible?' Afterwards, he wrote a letter in which he apologized for having been 'loud and rude.' I guess the subject of this sacred book arouses the New Englander in him: he doesn't know what attitude to take to it—downgrading or enthusiastic." Edmund Wilson, *The Sixties,* ed. with an introduction by Lewis M. Dabney (New York: Farrar Straus Giroux, 1993), pp. 669–670.
66. Lowell to Hardwick, 31 March 1969. Houghton.
67. Lowell to Taylor, 16 March 1968. Vanderbilt.
68. Lowell to William Meredith at Bellagio, 14 April 1969. William Meredith.
69. *New York Times Book Review,* 15 June 1969, sec. VII, pp. 1, 27.
70. Robert Boyers, "On Robert Lowell," *Salmagundi,* no. 13 (Summer 1970), 36–44.
71. Lowell to William Meredith, 19 July 1969. William Meredith.
72. Lowell to Tate, 4 September 1969. Princeton.
73. Lowell to John Crowe Ransom, 6 September 1969. Kenyon.
74. Lowell to Alfred Kazin, 5 October 1969. Berg.
75. Lowell to Berryman, 9 September 1969. Minnesota.
76. "The Revolution," *Notebook,* pp. 220–221, revised as above in *History,* p. 155.
77. Lowell to Richard Tillinghast, n.d., but August 1969. Richard Tillinghast.
78. Lowell to Berryman, 25 September 1969. Minnesota.

79. Hamilton, p. 393.
80. Lowell to Bishop, 14 June 1967. Vassar.
81. "Robert Lowell in the Sixties," *Harvard Advocate* 113 (November 1979), in Meyers, pp. 262–263.
82. Lowell to James Dickey, n.d., but mid-October 1969. University of Washington.
83. Lowell to Bishop, 6 December 1969. Vassar.
84. Lowell to Bishop, 10 November 1969. Vassar.
85. Lowell to Meredith, 6 December 1969. William Meredith. In an earlier letter to Bishop, Lowell had mentioned that, like Bishop, who had begun teaching in her mid-fifties, Lizzie had also belatedly begun teaching (at age fifty). Lizzie's comment to him afterwards had been that, though the students weren't very good, she was. She'd given them "various non-fiction books such as Lévi-Strauss and *In the American Grain* and found them agape. Then they almost all wrote A papers, and she got quite enthused." Lowell to Bishop, 25 February 1966. Vassar.
86. Hardwick to Mary McCarthy, 9 February 1970. Vassar.
87. Lowell to William Meredith, 17 February 1970.
88. Lowell to Bishop, 20 February 1970. Vassar.
89. "For Elizabeth Bishop 4," *History,* p. 198.
90. Lowell to Bishop, 11 March 1970. Vassar.
91. Lowell to Bishop, 11 March 1970. Vassar.
92. Lowell to Tate, 19 March 1970. Princeton.
93. *Ibid.*
94. Esther Brooks, "Remembering Cal," *Robert Lowell: A Tribute,* ed. Rolando Anzilotti (Pisa: Nistri-Lischi, 1979). Reprinted in Meyers, pp. 281–287.

PART IV

CHAPTER 16

1. Lowell to Hardwick, 21 April 1970. Houghton.
2. Donald Davie to Lowell, 4 April 1970. Texas.
3. The letter from Chairman Philip Edwards at the University of Essex is dated 2 April 1970 and was sent to Lowell—c/o Lowell's old friend Huyck van Loeuven, 75(a) Vondelstraat, Amsterdam. Donald Davie had left Essex at the beginning of 1968. The note to Lizzie (undated, but late April) is on the verso of Edwards's letter. Texas.
4. Tate to Lowell, 30 March 1970. Texas.
5. Lowell to Tate, 25 April 1970. Princeton.
6. Lowell to Hardwick, 25 April 1970. Texas.
7. Lowell to Hardwick, 27 April 1970. Texas.
8. Hamilton, p. 398.
9. Lowell to J. F. Powers, 18 February 1973. J. F. Powers.
10. Lowell to William Alfred, 4 May 1970. William Alfred.
11. *Ibid.*
12. "America from Oxford," *Notebook,* p. 237.
13. Lowell to Hardwick, 17 May 1970. Texas.
14. Lowell to Harriet, 25 May 1970. Texas.
15. Lowell to Hardwick, 26 May 1970. Texas.
16. Lowell to Hardwick, 31 May 1970. Texas.
17. Lowell to Hardwick, 14 June 1970. Texas.
18. Lowell telegram to Hardwick, 20 June 1970. Texas.
19. Hardwick to Lowell, 26 June 1970. Texas. Hardwick had of course suspected the existence of another woman for some time now, but only the day before had she learned that

Blackwood was the other woman. "She hadn't seen Blackwood since New York, and then Blackwood had been very silent and withdrawn." Hardwick to McCarthy, 25 June 1970. Vassar.

20. "Caroline: 4. Marriage?", *The Dolphin* (New York: Farrar, Straus & Giroux, 1973), p. 26.
21. Lowell to Caroline Blackwood, n.d., but July 1970. Quoted in Hamilton, p. 400.
22. Hardwick, telephone conversation with Blair Clark, 29 July 1970. Quoted in Hamilton, p. 402.
23. Hardwick to Mary McCarthy, 2 August 1970. Vassar.
24. Hardwick to Mary McCarthy, 4 August 1970. Vassar.
25. Lowell to Hardwick, 6 August 1970. Texas.
26. Lowell to Hardwick, 9 August 1970. Texas. The image Lowell used here—the sign of the Covenant—was the same image he had closed "The Quaker Graveyard in Nantucket" with twenty-five years before: a residual sign, lasting long after the human actors themselves were gone.
27. Lowell to Blackwood, mid-August, 1970. Quoted in Hamilton, p. 402.
28. Lowell to Hardwick, 27 August 1970. Texas.
29. Lowell to Harriet, 27 August 1970. Texas.
30. Lowell to Bishop, 11 September 1970. Vassar.
31. Lowell to Bishop, n.d., but early October 1970. Vassar.
32. Lowell to Hardwick, 12 September 1970. Texas.
33. Dudley Young, "Life with Lord Lowell at Essex U.," *PN Review* 28 (1982), reprinted in Meyers, pp. 312–313.
34. Michael Waters to author, March 1991.
35. Lowell to Hardwick, 11 October 1970. Texas.
36. Lowell to Bishop, 7 November 1970. Vassar. Lowell to Hardwick, 16 November 1970. Texas.
37. Lowell to Hamilton, "A Conversation with Robert Lowell," *The Review* 26 (Summer 1971), reprinted in Meyers, p. 170.
38. William Alfred's letter [at Texas] is dated 15 October 1970. Lowell wrote Hardwick on the 18th. [Texas] On the 21st he wrote Alfred to say he'd written Hardwick. "Telling Elizabeth plainly and without ambiguity in a letter what I am going to do is hard. It's hard for me to be that certain even in my quietest thoughts. . . . Such an old and passionate love cannot be ended like slicing pie." Texas.
39. Lowell to Adrienne Rich, 21 October 1970. Radcliffe. "I imagine I'll get divorced," he added, "and all may be well, but the loss will never go." Lowell to Hardwick, 21 October 1970. Texas.
40. Hardwick to Blair Clark, 23 October 1970. Blair Clark.
41. Lowell to Taylor, 1 November 1970. Vanderbilt.
42. Lowell to Mary McCarthy, 2 November 1970. Vassar.
43. Lowell to Hardwick, 7 November 1970. Texas.
44. Lowell to Hardwick, 28 November 1970. Texas.
45. Lowell to Bishop, n.d., early December 1970. Vassar.
46. *The Dolphin*, p. 72.
47. Lowell cable quoted in Hamilton, p. 407.
48. "For John Berryman, 1914–1972," *New York Review of Books,* 30 (March 1972), in *CP,* p. 116.
49. Lowell to Berryman, 27 December 1970. Minnesota.
50. Lowell to Hardwick, 7 January 1971. Texas.
51. Lowell to Harriet, 14 March 1971. Texas.
52. Blair Clark to author, 1992.
53. Blair Clark to Lowell, 17 March 1971. Blair Clark.
54. Lowell to Hardwick, 20 March 1971. Texas.
55. Lowell to Hardwick, 29 March 1971. Texas.

56. Lowell to Adrienne Rich, 29 March 1971. Radcliffe.
57. *Ibid.*
58. Adrienne Rich to Lowell, 19 June 1971. Texas.
59. Writing to Taylor just after he received Rich's letter, Lowell spoke candidly about the downturn in his relationship with Rich. "I thought everything was too frenetic with them," he said, "but never guessed, tho Adrienne and I had lunches about once a month . . . She writes me odd unasked-for woman-libish advice. . . ." Lowell to Taylor, 24 June 1971. Vanderbilt.
60. Lowell to Tate, 29 March 1971. Princeton.
61. Tate to Lowell, 5 April 1971. Texas.
62. Lowell to Tate, 13 April 1971. Princeton.
63. Lowell to Taylor, 13 May 1971. Vanderbilt.
64. Lowell to Harriet, 4 May 1971. Texas.
65. Lowell to Harriet, 5 May 1971. Texas.
66. Lowell to Hardwick, 6 May 1971. Texas.
67. Lowell to Harriet, 23 June 1971. Texas.
68. Lowell to Taylor, 24 June 1971. Vanderbilt.
69. Lowell to Hardwick, n.d., but late February 1973. Texas.
70. I'm written dry," he told Lizzie, "after about four nonstop years. Or is it ten? Now nothing, except maybe translation." Lowell to Hardwick, 22 May 1971. Texas.
71. Lowell to Taylor, 13 May 1971. Vanderbilt.
72. Lowell to Clark, 15 May 1971. Blair Clark.
73. Lowell to Hardwick, 22 May 1971. Texas.
74. Lowell to Taylor, 24 June 1971. Vanderbilt.
75. "Life with Lord Lowell at Essex U.," in Meyers, p. 316.
76. Lowell to Harriet, 23 June 1971. Texas.
77. Lowell to Hardwick, 12 May 1971. Texas.
78. Lowell to Hardwick, 23 June 1971. Texas.
79. *Ibid.*
80. He thought the best part of the play Io's long speech and what followed immediately after. These he considered adding to his *Collected Poems* when the book was eventually published.
81. Lowell to Hardwick, 1 July 1971. Texas.
82. *Ibid.*
83. Jonathan Raban, in Hamilton, pp. 413–414.
84. Cf. Hamilton, "A Conversation with Robert Lowell," in Meyers, pp. 154–172.
85. Lowell to Harriet, 25 July 1971. Texas.
86. Lowell to Clark, 25 July 1971. Blair Clark.
87. Lowell to Hardwick, 3 August 1971. Texas.
88. Lowell to Hardwick, 18 August 1971. Texas.
89. Lowell to Philip Booth, 19 August 1971. Quoted in Hamilton, p. 415.
90. Lowell to William Alfred, n.d., but late August 1971. William Alfred.
91. Lowell to Hardwick, 24 September 1971. Texas.
92. Lowell to Hardwick, 1 October 1971. Texas.
93. Lowell to Harriet, 1 October 1971. Texas.
94. Lowell to Taylor, 9 October 1971. Vanderbilt.
95. "Robert Sheridan Lowell," *The Dolphin,* p. 61.
96. Lowell to William Alfred, 30 november 1971. William Alfred.
97. Lowell to Taylor, 9 December 1971. Vanderbilt.
98. Lowell to Frank Bidart, n.d., but about 1 December 1971. Houghton.
99. Lowell to Frank Bidart, 23 December 1971. Houghton.

CHAPTER 17

1. Frank Bidart to Hamilton, Hamilton, p. 421.
2. Lowell to Bishop, 6 February 1972. Vassar.
3. Lowell to Hardwick, 19 March 1972. Texas.
4. "For John Berryman," *Day by Day*, pp. 27–28.
5. Lowell to Hardwick, 5 February 1972. Texas.
6. "Ivana," *The Dolphin*, p. 64.
7. Lowell to Harriet, 22 February 1972. Texas.
8. Lowell to Hardwick, 4 March 1972. Texas.
9. Lowell to Harriet, 1 March 1972. Texas.
10. William Alfred to Lowell, 12 March 1972. Texas.
11. Lowell to William Alfred, 19 March 1972. William Alfred.
12. Bishop to Lowell, 21 March 1972. Houghton.
13. Lowell to Bishop, 28 March 1972. Vassar. The woman whose letters Williams had used in *Paterson* was Marcia Nardi, whom Lowell had met at a party in Cambridge in 1969, and with whom he corresponded sporadically. In 1947 Lowell had defended Williams's use of Nardi's letters to Bishop, even as he attempted to defend his use of Lizzie's letters now.
14. Lowell to Bishop, 4 April 1972. Vassar.
15. Lowell to Frank Bidart, 10 April 1972. Houghton.
16. Lowell to Stanley Kunitz, about 24 April 1972. "I tried the new version out on Peter Taylor, and he couldn't imagine any moral objection to *Dolphin.*" Quoted in Stanley Kunitz, "The Sense of a Life," *New York Times Book Review*, 16 October 1977, reprinted in Meyers, p. 233.
17. That September he could finally report to Alfred that *The Dolphin* was now muted and "written much better—both for art and kindness." Lowell to William Alfred, n.d., but about 12 September 1972. William Alfred.
18. Lowell to Harriet, 2 April 1972. Easter Sunday. Texas.
19. Lowell to Stanley Kunitz, 24 April 1972, *op. cit.*
20. Lowell to Bishop, 24 April 1972. Vassar.
21. Lowell to Hardwick, 6 May 1972. Texas.
22. Lowell to Hardwick, 9 March 1972. Texas.
23. Lowell to Harriet, 28 June 1972. Texas.
24. Lowell to Harriet, 2 August 1972. Texas.
25. Lowell to Taylor, 21 August 1972. Vanderbilt.
26. Lowell to William Alfred, n.d., but about 12 September 1972. William Alfred.
27. Lowell to Taylor, 21 August 1972. Vanderbilt.
28. "Last Night," *History*, p. 204.
29. Lowell to Harriet, 28 September 1972. Texas.
30. Lowell to William Alfred, 29 September 1972. William Alfred.
31. Lowell to Harriet, 3 November 1972. Texas.
32. Lowell to Blair Clark, n.d., but early November 1972. Blair Clark.
33. Lowell to Bishop, n.d., but early November 1972. Vassar. In a letter to the author dated 30 July 1993, Elizabeth Hardwick explained the terms of the divorce settlement more fully: "The Maine house and barn were left to me *alone* in Harriet Winslow's will, *which Cal saw and knew well.* In her will she stated that her decision was based on the belief that he was too unstable to take care of the property. Cal was wounded by this and I think that is why, when I sold one part, he was more or less pretending that I didn't have the right. I had a horrible time getting him to sign. On the other hand, I understood his feelings and the fact was that Cousin Harriet of course treasured Cal much more than me. And I always felt that even though I was the technical owner that it would have been ours, the three of

us, together. As it turned out, I am sad to say Miss Winslow was right, since Cal lived in England for seven years before he died and could not have maintained or occupied the place. But the Maine house and barn were in no way a part of the divorce settlement."

34. Lowell to William Alfred, n.d., but about 21 November 1972. William Alfred.
35. Lowell to Bishop, 10 September 1972. Vassar. Allen Tate had earlier offered to stand as godfather, but by the fall of 1972 he was too ill, bedridden with emphysema and hooked up to an oxygen tank.
36. Lowell to Frank Bidart, 1 December 1972. Houghton.
37. Lowell to Taylor, n.d., but late December 1972. Vanderbilt.
38. Lowell to Taylor, 18 March 1973. Vanderbilt.
39. Lowell to Hardwick, 10 January 1973. Texas.
40. Robert Lowell, "Digressions from Larkin's 20th-Century Verse," *Encounter* 40 (May 1973), 66–68.
41. Lowell to Bishop, n.d., but late January 1973. Vassar.
42. Lowell to Frank Bidart, n.d., late January 1973. Houghton.
43. Lowell to Frank Bidart, 9 September 1973. Houghton.
44. Lowell to Taylor, 17 February 1973. Vanderbilt.
45. Lowell to Bishop, 19 March 1973. Vassar.
46. *Ibid.*
47. Lowell to Frank Bidart, 22 March 1973. Houghton.
48. Lowell to Hardwick, 4 April 1973. Texas.
49. Lowell to Taylor, 27 May 1973. Vanderbilt.
50. Lowell to Harriet, 23 February 1973. Texas.
51. Quoted in Andrew Motion, *Philip Larkin: A Writer's Life* (London: Faber & Faber, 1993), p. 430.
52. Philip Larkin to Robert Conquest, 5 March 1966, in *Selected Letters of Philip Larkin: 1940–1985*, ed. Anthony Thwaite (London: Faber & Faber, 1992), p. 382. "Lord Hairy's Arsehole" is a neologism for *Lord Weary's Castle*. In general, Larkin appears to have dismissed Lowell as "simply barmy." Motion, p. 430.
53. Philip Larkin to Eva Larkin, 2 February 1973. Quoted in Motion, p. 430.
54. Lowell to Bishop, 30 April 1973. Vassar.
55. Lowell to Hardwick, 1 May 1973. Texas.
56. Lowell to Hardwick, 25 June 1973. Texas.
57. Lowell to Hardwick, 26 May 1973. Texas.
58. Lowell to Hardwick, 1 June 1973. Texas.
59. Lowell to Bishop, 3 May 1973. Vassar.
60. Lowell to Taylor, 1 June 1973. Vanderbilt.
61. William Pritchard, "Poetry Matters," *Hudson Review* 26 (Autumn 1973), 579–597.
62. "The Blank Now," *New Republic* 169 (7 July 1973), 24–26.
63. Lowell cable to Hardwick, 10 July 1973. Texas.
64. Lowell to Bishop, 12 July 1973. Vassar.
65. Lowell to Hardwick, 12 July 1973. Texas.
66. Lowell to Bishop, 12 July 1973. Vassar.
67. Bishop to Lowell, 22 July 1973. Houghton.
68. Adrienne Rich, "Carydid: A Column," *American Poetry Review* 2 (September–October 1973), 42–43.
69. Kathleen Spivack, "Robert Lowell: A Memoir," *Antioch Review* 43 (Spring 1983), 183–193; reprinted in Meyers, p. 356.
70. Hardwick to Bishop, 27 July 1973. Vassar.
71. Hardwick to Bishop, 18 October 1973. Vassar.
72. Lowell to Blair Clark, 31 July 1973. Blair Clark.
73. Lowell to William Alfred, 31 August 1973. William Alfred.
74. About 8 November 1973. Copy of remarks at Texas.

75. "Our Afterlife I," *Day by Day*, p. 21.
76. Lowell to Hardwick, 18 January 1974. Texas. Philip Rahv had died on December 23 in Cambridge. His last year had been wracked by illness and the breakdown of his short, unhappy fourth marriage. In early December he had telephoned Lizzie from Boston to ask her to spend New Year's Eve with him in New York. "I can't say I looked forward to it because there was plenty of harshness and bullying on the phone," Hardwick had written Mary McCarthy. Then a student had discovered Rahv's body in his apartment. Hardwick had flown up to Boston with Robert Silvers on Christmas Eve for the funeral, with burial afterwards at the Jewish Cemetery at Brandeis, the college where he'd taught since the 1950s. On the trip out to Logan Airport a student had told Hardwick that Bishop was lying in "a ghastly state" in her Boston Wharf studio, the result of alcohol and depression. Cf. Brightman, *Writing Dangerously: Mary McCarthy and Her World*, pp. 576–577.
77. Lowell to Hardwick, 18 January 1974. Texas.
78. Lowell to Frank Bidart, n.d., but mid-January 1974. Houghton.
79. Lowell to Bishop, n.d., but mid-January 1974. Vassar.
80. Lowell to William Alfred, 20 May 1974. William Alfred.
81. Lowell to Hardwick, 1 May 1974. Texas.
82. "Burial," *Day by Day*, p. 41.
83. Lowell to Taylor, 13 May 1974. Vanderbilt.
84. Lowell to Taylor, 3 June 1974. Vanderbilt.
85. Lowell to Taylor, 13 July 1974. Vanderbilt.
86. Lowell to Tate, 29 July 1974. Princeton. Tate in his sickness seemed intent on burning his bridges after him, lashing out angrily in his impotence with at least three of his sons: Berryman (irrevocably, even after Berryman sent him a card saying Tate had hurt him—to which Tate had merely written on the card that that had been his intention), Cal, and Taylor. "I am glad you saw Peter [Taylor]," Lowell wrote Tate now, "and made up before his stroke. . . . It seems so ahead of the calendar, twenty years earlier than one foresaw. I never stop thinking about him."
87. Lowell to Taylor, 13 July 1974. Vanderbilt.
88. "John Crowe Ransom: 1888–1974," *The New Review* (London) I, 5 (August 1974), 3–5; *CP*, pp. 20–28.
89. "Epilogue," *Day by Day*, p. 127.
90. Lowell to Hardwick, 16 August 1974. Texas.
91. A. Alvarex interviewing Lowell for the *New York Times*, 4 April 1976.
92. "George III," *Day by Day*, pp. 133–135. Cf. *Newsweek* for 4 July 1976. Lowell called this poem a "translation," a reading of Oscar Sherwin's *Uncorking Old Sherry: The Life and Times of Richard Brinsley Sheridan*.
93. Lowell to Taylor, 5 September 1974. Vanderbilt.
94. Lowell to Bishop, 6 October 1974. Vassar.
95. Lowell to Taylor, 9 October 1974. Vanderbilt.
96. "Our Afterlife II," in *Day by Day*, pp. 23–24.
97. Lowell to Hardwick, 13 October 1974. Texas.
98. Jean Stafford to Nancy Gibney, 16 June 1974. Quoted in Goodman, p. 311.
99. Stafford to Lowell, 23 September 1974. Houghton. She still saw Blair Clark and Jack Thompson from the old days, she added, and in general felt pretty well, though she wondered why she was known familiarly as "Jean" in the "admitting offices of New York Hospital and the Hospital for Special Surgery?"
100. Lowell to Bishop, 26 October 1974. Vassar.
101. Lowell to Frank Bidart, 14 December 1974. Houghton.
102. Lowell to Taylor, 12 December 1974. Vanderbilt.
103. Lowell to Hardwick, 13 December 1974. Texas.
104. Lowell to Bishop, 18 December 1974. Vassar.
105. Bishop to Lowell, 16 January 1975. Texas.

106. Letter dated 5 February 1975. Texas.
107. Caroline Blackwood to Hamilton, 1979, Hamilton, p. 444.
108. Robert Silvers to Hamilton, 1981, Hamilton, p. 446.
109. Robert Giroux to Hamilton, 1982, p. 445.
110. Lowell to Tate, 8 May 1975. Princeton.
111. Lowell to Taylor, 11 September 1975. Vanderbilt.
112. "Summer Between Terms: 1," *The Dolphin,* p. 28.
113. Lowell to Taylor, 1 July 1975. Vanderbilt.
114. Lowell to Tate, 22 July 1975. Princeton.
115. Lowell to Taylor, 1 July 1975. Vanderbilt.
116. Lowell to Frank Bidart, 7 August 1975. Houghton.
117. Lowell to Hardwick, 23 August 1975. Texas.
118. *Ibid.*
119. Lowell to Taylor, 11 September 1975. Vanderbilt.
120. Lowell to Hardwick, 11 September 1975. Texas.
121. Lowell to Taylor, 11 September 1975. Vanderbilt.
122. Lowell to Hardwick, 29 April 1976. Texas.
123. Caroline Blackwood to Hamilton, 1979, Hamilton, p. 448.
124. Jonathan Raban to Hamilton, 1979, Hamilton, p. 449.
125. Hamilton, p. 449.
126. Hardwick to Mary McCarthy, 30 December 1975. Vassar.
127. Caroline Blackwood to Hamilton, 1979, Hamilton, p. 449.
128. Seamus Heaney. "Gulliver in Lilliput: Remembering Robert Lowell," a speech delivered in 1987 at Harvard on the tenth anniversary of Lowell's death. Reprinted in *The Norton Book of Friendship,* ed. Eudora Welty and Ronald A. Sharp (New York: W. W. Norton & Co., 1991), pp. 546–548.
129. Hamilton, pp. 450–452.
130. "Visitors," *Day by Day,* pp. 110–111.

CHAPTER 18

1. Lowell to Frank Bidart, 15 February 1976. Houghton.
2. "Home," *Day by Day,* pp. 113–115.
3. "Dante 3. Buonconte," *History,* p. 57.
4. Lowell to Taylor, 4 March 1976. Vanderbilt.
5. "The Downlook," *Day by Day,* p. 125.
6. Lowell to Taylor, 4 March 1976. Vanderbilt.
7. Lowell to Blair Clark, 4 March 1976. Blair Clark.
8. Lowell to Bishop, 4 March 1976. Vassar.
9. Lowell to Blair Clark, 4 March 1976. Blair Clark.
10. Lowell interview with A. Alvarez, *New York Times,* 4 April 1976.
11. Lowell to Bishop, 15 April 1976. Vassar.
12. Lowell to Hardwick, 29 April 1976. Texas.
13. Page proofs for Lowell's *Selected Poems.* Frank Bidart's eagle eye had already caught some forty errors, he told Bishop. 15 April 1976. Vassar.
14. Lowell to Bishop, 15 April 1976. Vassar.
15. Lowell to Hardwick, 29 April 1976. Texas. The poem is "Off Central Park," *Day by Day,* p. 45.
16. Lowell to Bishop, n.d., but May 1976. Vassar.
17. Lowell's comments for a memorial for Benjamin Britten, January 1977. Texas.
18. "I remember Yvor [Winters] once startling me by saying he didn't know if he existed," he told Hardwick that June. "That was in my *Life Studies* day, and I couldn't believe it." Lowell to Hardwick, 8 June 1976. Texas.
19. Lowell to Marcia Nardi, 25 May 1976. Collection of E. M. O'Neil. As both Williams and

Lowell knew, the best of Nardi's poems deserved to be published on their own merits, apart from whatever role Nardi played as the female voice in *Paterson*.

20. Lowell to Hardwick, 8 June 1976. Texas.
21. Lowell to Taylor, 2 July 1976. Vanderbilt.
22. Lowell to Hardwick, 12 July 1976. Texas.
23. Lowell to William Meredith, 18 July 1976. William Meredith.
24. Hardwick to Lowell, 5 July 1976. Texas.
25. Lowell to Hardwick, 12 July 1976. Texas.
26. Lowell to Bishop, 4 September 1976. Vassar.
27. Lowell to Hardwick, 4 September 1976. Texas.
28. Lowell to Bishop, 4 September 1976. Vassar.
29. Lowell to William Meredith, 18 July 1976. William Meredith.
30. Lowell to Stafford, 4 September 1976. Colorado. Quoted in Hulbert, pp. 372–373.
31. Lowell to Taylor, 4 September 1976. Vanderbilt.
32. "Jean Stafford, a Letter," *Day by Day*, p. 29.
33. Lowell to Taylor, 4 September 1976. Vanderbilt.
34. Lowell to Bishop, n.d., but May 1976. Vassar.
35. Lowell to Taylor, 4 September 1976. Vanderbilt.
36. Lowell to Bishop, 4 September 1976. Vassar. "This morning when your *Mind Reader* came in the mail," Lowell had written Wilbur in June, "I felt I was visiting another country, not too distant from mine [in *Day by Day*] and with similar flashes—night and waking thoughts; age . . . nature and household description. What struck me as different and enviable is your pace. . . . You fix on it slowly and hesitantly—poking and puzzling. Your strict meters speak casually. All this is a good antidote to my narrower intensity. I think we both try for a fairly direct open language—open to experience, and open at times to splurges of rhetoric and intuition. Your style is perhaps a commentary or extension of Frost; or rather you draw on something earlier that he could use but is now almost unavailable to anyone but you—among other things an oblique use of autobiography, scenes peering into meditation." Lowell to Richard Wilbur, 8 June 1976. Amherst.
37. Lowell to Frank Bidart, 4 September 1976. Houghton.
38. "The Withdrawal," *Day by Day*, pp. 72–73.
39. Lowell to Taylor, 10 July 1976. Vanderbilt.
40. "I'm no use to him in these attacks," she told Hamilton in 1979. "They destroy me. I'm really better if I'm away if he has one. . . . It's like someone becoming an animal, or someone possessed by the devil. And that's what tears you apart. You think, I love this person, but I hate him. So where are you?" Quoted in Hamilton, p. 456.
41. Lowell to William Alfred, 30 October 1976. William Alfred.
42. "Runaway," *Day by Day*, p. 103.
43. Frank Bidart to Hamilton, 1981. Hamilton, p. 457.
44. Charlotte Goodman, 1984 interview with *New Yorker* writer Joseph Mitchell, who was in the room when Giroux visited. Goodman, p. 318. Also, cf. Hulbert, pp. 374–375.
45. Hardwick to Mary McCarthy, 15 June 1977. Vassar.
46. Lowell to Hardwick, 11 January 1977. Texas.
47. Lowell to William Alfred, 11 January 1977. William Alfred.
48. Thomas Lask, "Translation by Lowell," *New York Times Book Review*, 23 July 1978, p. 35.
49. Lowell to Hardwick, 11 January 1977. Texas.
50. Helen Vendler to Hamilton, 1980, Hamilton, p. 458.
51. "Phillips House Revisited," *Day by Day*, p. 87.
52. Lowell to Blackwood, 31 January 1977. Hamilton, p. 459.
53. Lowell to Blackwood, 28 February 1977. Quoted in part in Hamilton, p. 458.
54. Helen Vendler, "Lowell in the Classroom," *Harvard Advocate* 113 (November 1979), reprinted in Meyers, pp. 288–297.
55. "Ulysses and Circe," *Day by Day*, pp. 9–10.

56. Lowell to Blackwood, 2 March 1977. Quoted in Hamilton, p. 461.
57. Lowell to Blackwood, 18 March 1977. Quoted in Hamilton, p. 461.
58. Lowell to Blackwood, 14 April 1977. Quoted in Hamilton. p. 462.
59. "Last Walk?", *Day by Day,* pp. 13–14.
60. "The Downlook," *Day by Day,* p. 125.
61. Hardwick to Mary McCarthy, 15 June 1977. Vassar.
62. Blair Clark's "notes for a never-to-be-written 'memoir'," quoted in Hamilton, pp. 463–464.
63. Lowell to Blackwood, 19 April 1977. Quoted in Hamilton, p. 462.
64. Lowell to Blackwood, 22 April 1977. Quoted in Hamilton, p. 463.
65. Lowell to Blackwood, 3 May 1977. Quoted in Hamilton, p. 463.
66. Kathy Shorr to author, August 1993.
67. Blair Clark to Hamilton, 1980. Hamilton, pp. 464–465.
68. Esther Brooks, "Remembering Cal," reprinted in Meyers, p. 286.
69. Hardwick to Mary McCarthy, 15 June 1977. Vassar.
70. Note appended to Lowell's later poetry mss. Houghton.
71. In the winter of 1974 Lowell wrote Donald Junkins that he was forwarding his letter to Swan's Island and his Atlantic, Maine address, because the name seemed "so sheer and perfect, where water becomes heaven and allegory." Lowell to Junkins, 4 February 1974. Donald Junkins.
72. Lowell to Blackwood, n.d., late August 1977. Quoted in Hamilton, pp. 467–468.
73. Cf. "New England and Further" and "Epics," in *CP*, pp. 179–222.
74. Letter from William Styron to Hamilton, 1 July 1981. Hamilton, pp. 466–467.
75. Lowell to Blackwood, 17 July 1977. Quoted in Hamilton, p. 465.
76. Lowell to Blackwood, n.d., but late July 1977. Quoted in Hamilton, p. 467.
77. "Several months before he died," Bidart would recall, "[Cal] said to me with an air of resignation, despair, and pride: 'I don't know the value of what I've written, but I know that I changed the game.'" Frank Bidart, "Robert Lowell," *Harvard Advocate* 113 (November 1979), reprinted in Meyers, p. 276.
78. Hamilton, p. 467.
79. "Summer Tides," *New Review* 4, no. 43 (October 1977). Uncollected.
80. Helen Vendler to Hamilton, 1981, Hamilton, p. 468.
81. Blackwood to Hamilton, 1979. Hamilton, p. 472.
82. Seamus Heaney, "Robert Lowell," *New York Review of Books* 25 (9 February 1978), 37–38, expanded in *Agenda* 18 (1980). Reprinted in Meyers, p. 247.
83. Blair Clark to author, 1992.
84. Hardwick to author, 1992.
85. Hardwick to Mary McCarthy, 2 October 1977. Vassar.
86. William Alfred to author, 1992.
87. Derek Walcott, "On Robert Lowell," *New York Review of Books,* 1 March 1984, p. 25.
88. Bidart, "Robert Lowell," in Meyers, p. 276.
89. Hardwick to Bishop, 16 August 1978. Vassar. "I think about Cal a lot," Hardwick had written Mary McCarthy six months earlier, "and I more and more grieve for *him* to be gone, know that *he would like* to be stumbling about in his carpet slippers or Bucksport crepe-soles, smoking, drinking vodka, writing." Hardwick to Mary McCarthy, 4 February 1978. Vassar.
90. Elizabeth Bishop, "North Haven," *The Complete Poems (1927–1979)* (New York: Farrar, Straus & Giroux, 1983), pp. 188–189.

Index

Page numbers beginning with 464 refer to notes.